IRISH LITERATURE IN TRANSITION,
1980–2020

Irish Literature in Transition, 1980–2020 elucidates the central features of Irish literature during the twentieth century's long turn, covering its significant trends and formations, reassessing its major writers and texts, and providing path-making accounts of its emergent figures. Over the past forty years, life in the Republic of Ireland and Northern Ireland has been transformed by new material conditions in each polity and by ideological shifts in the way people understand themselves and their relation to the world. Amid these remarkable changes, culture on both sides of the border has emerged as a global phenomenon, one that both reflects and intervenes in rapidly changing contemporary conditions. This volume accounts for broad patterns of literary and cultural production in this period and demonstrates the value of contemporary Irish literature within Anglophone and European traditions and as a body of work that has kept its eye trained on the particularities of the island and its inhabitants.

ERIC FALCI is Professor of English at the University of California, Berkeley. He is the author of *Continuity and Change in Irish Poetry, 1966–2010* (2012) and *The Cambridge Introduction to British Poetry, 1945–2010* (2015), as well as a number of essays on twentieth- and twenty-first-century Irish and British poetry.

PAIGE REYNOLDS, Professor of English at the College of the Holy Cross, Worcester, MA, is the author of *Modernism, Drama, and the Audience for Irish Spectacle* (2007) and editor of *Modernist Afterlives in Irish Literature and Culture* (2016). She has published essays on modernism, drama, and contemporary Irish writing and performance, and is editor of the forthcoming collection *The New Irish Studies* for Cambridge University Press.

IRISH LITERATURE IN TRANSITION

General editors:
Claire Connolly, University College Cork
Marjorie Howes, Boston College

This six-volume series captures the dynamic energies transmitted over more than 300 years of the established literary landmarks that constitute Irish literary life. Ambitious in scope and depth, and accommodating new critical perspectives and approaches, Irish Literature in Transition captures the ongoing changes in the Irish literary canon. Each of the six volumes revises our understanding of established issues and texts and, simultaneously, introduces new questions, approaches, and authors. These volumes address periods of transition, but also periods of epochal upheaval and turning points of real significance. Each one of these books challenges in different ways the dominant approaches to a period of literature by shifting the focus from what happened to understanding how and why it happened. They elucidate the multifaceted interaction between the social and literary fields in the evolution of Irish literature until the present moment. As a whole, the Irish Literature in Transition series constitutes a new kind of literary history across centuries of intense cultural and literary creation. It offers a comprehensive analysis of the Irish literary experience, creating a new and dynamic version of literary history that highlights the significance of change as a lived, felt force.

Books in the Series

1. *Irish Literature in Transition, 1700–1780* edited by Moyra Haslett
2. *Irish Literature in Transition, 1780–1830* edited by Claire Connolly
3. *Irish Literature in Transition, 1830–1880* edited by Matthew Campbell
4. *Irish Literature in Transition, 1880–1940* edited by Marjorie Howes
5. *Irish Literature in Transition, 1940–1980* edited by Eve Patten
6. *Irish Literature in Transition, 1980–2020* edited by Eric Falci and Paige Reynolds

IRISH LITERATURE IN TRANSITION, 1980–2020

EDITED BY

ERIC FALCI

University of California, Berkeley

PAIGE REYNOLDS

College of the Holy Cross

CAMBRIDGE
UNIVERSITY PRESS

University Printing House, Cambridge CB2 8BS, United Kingdom

One Liberty Plaza, 20th Floor, New York, NY 10006, USA

477 Williamstown Road, Port Melbourne, VIC 3207, Australia

314–321, 3rd Floor, Plot 3, Splendor Forum, Jasola District Centre,
New Delhi – 110025, India

79 Anson Road, #06–04/06, Singapore 079906

Cambridge University Press is part of the University of Cambridge.

It furthers the University's mission by disseminating knowledge in the pursuit of education, learning, and research at the highest international levels of excellence.

www.cambridge.org
Information on this title: www.cambridge.org/9781108474047
DOI: 10.1017/9781108564373

© Cambridge University Press 2020

This publication is in copyright. Subject to statutory exception and to the provisions of relevant collective licensing agreements, no reproduction of any part may take place without the written permission of Cambridge University Press.

First published 2020

Printed in the United Kingdom by TJ International Ltd. Padstow Cornwall

A catalogue record for this publication is available from the British Library.

Library of Congress Cataloging-in-Publication Data
NAMES: Falci, Eric, editor. | Reynolds, Paige, editor.
TITLE: Irish literature in transition, 1980–2020 / Edited by Eric Falci, University of California, Berkeley ; Paige Reynolds, College of the Holy Cross.
DESCRIPTION: Cambridge, United Kingdom ; New York, NY : Cambridge University Press, 2020. | Series: Irish literature in transition; Volume 6 | Includes index.
IDENTIFIERS: LCCN 2019042497 (print) | LCCN 2019042498 (ebook) | ISBN 9781108474047 (hardback) | ISBN 9781108564373 (ebook)
SUBJECTS: LCSH: English literature – Irish authors – History and criticism. | English literature – 21st century – History and criticism | English literature – 20th century – History and criticism. | Irish literature – 21st century – History and criticism. | Irish literature – 20th century – History and criticism. | Literature and society – Ireland – History – 21st century. | Literature and society – Ireland – History – 20th century.
CLASSIFICATION: LCC PR8756 .I75 2020 (print) | LCC PR8756 (ebook) | DDC 820.9/9415–dc23
LC record available at https://lccn.loc.gov/2019042497
LC ebook record available at https://lccn.loc.gov/2019042498

ISBN 978-1-108-47404-7 Hardback

Cambridge University Press has no responsibility for the persistence or accuracy of URLs for external or third-party internet websites referred to in this publication and does not guarantee that any content on such websites is, or will remain, accurate or appropriate.

Contents

List of Contributors	*page* viii
Series Preface	xv
General Acknowledgements	xvii
Acknowledgements	xviii
Introduction *Eric Falci and Paige Reynolds*	1

PART I TIMES   25

1   The Contemporary Conditions of Irish Language Literature   27
     Ailbhe Ní Ghearbhuigh

2   The Cultures of Poetry in Contemporary Ireland   44
     David Lloyd

3   Troubles Literature and the End of the Troubles   65
     Julia C. Obert

4   Contemporary Irish Theatre and Media   81
     Paige Reynolds

5   Writing Childhood: Young Adult and Children's Literature   96
     Patricia Kennon

     Coda: Eavan Boland and Seamus Heaney   111
     Eric Falci

PART II SPACES   119

6   Habitations: Space, Place, Real Estate   121
     Adam Hanna

7	Crossings: Northern Irish Literature from Good Friday to Brexit *Stefanie Lehner*	136
8	Adaptations: Commemoration and Contemporary Irish Theatre *James Moran*	152
9	Relocations: Diaspora, Travel, Migrancy *Ellen McWilliams*	168
10	Arrivals: Inward Migration and Irish Literature *Anne Mulhall*	182
	Coda: Tom Murphy and Brian Friel *Patrick Lonergan*	201

PART III FORMS OF EXPERIENCE — 209

11	The Irish Realist Novel *Joe Cleary*	211
12	Faith, Secularism, and Sacred Institutions *Diarmaid Ferriter*	228
13	Writing the Tiger: Economics and Culture *Sarah Townsend*	246
14	Violence, Trauma, Recovery *Christopher Langlois*	263
15	Modes of Witnessing and Ireland's Institutional History *Emilie Pine, Susan Leavy, Mark Keane, Maeve Casserly, and Tom Lane*	278
	Coda: Edna O'Brien and Eimear McBride *Clair Wills*	295

PART IV PRACTICES, INSTITUTIONS, AND AUDIENCES — 305

16	Mediation and Translation in Irish Language Literature *Ríona Ní Fhrighil*	307
17	Irish Studies and Its Discontents *Ronan McDonald*	327

18	Historical Transitions in Ireland on Screen *Barry Monahan*	344
19	Irish Blockbusters and Literary Stars at the End of the Millennium *Stephen Watt*	360
20	Contemporary Literature and Public Value *Margaret Kelleher*	375
	Coda: *The Irish Times*, Tramp Press, and the Future Present *Paige Reynolds*	392

Index   401

Contributors

JOE CLEARY is Professor of English at Yale University. He is the author of *Literature, Partition and the Nation-State: Culture and Conflict in Ireland, Israel and Palestine* (Cambridge, 2002) and *Outrageous Fortune: Capital and Culture in Modern Ireland* (2007). He has edited *The Cambridge Companion to Irish Modernism* (Cambridge, 2014) and, with Claire Connolly, *The Cambridge Companion to Modern Irish Culture* (Cambridge, 2005) as well as special issues of *boundary 2*, *Éire-Ireland*, and *Modern Language Quarterly*.

ERIC FALCI is Professor of English at the University of California, Berkeley. He is the author of *Continuity and Change in Irish Poetry, 1966–2010* (2012) and *The Cambridge Introduction to British Poetry, 1945–2010* (2015), as well as a number of essays on twentieth- and twenty-first-century Irish and British poetry.

DIARMAID FERRITER is Professor of Modern Irish History at University College Dublin. His books include *The Transformation of Ireland 1900–2000* (2004), *Judging Dev: A Reassessment of the Life and Legacy of Eamon de Valera* (2007), *Occasions of Sin: Sex and Society in Modern Ireland* (2009), *Ambiguous Republic: Ireland in the 1970s* (2012), *A Nation and Not a Rabble: The Irish Revolution 1913–1923* (2015), and *On the Edge: Ireland's Offshore Islands, A Modern History* (2018). His latest book is *The Border: The Legacy of a Century of Anglo-Irish Politics* (2019). He is a regular broadcaster on RTÉ television and radio and a weekly columnist with *The Irish Times*.

ADAM HANNA is Lecturer in Irish Literature in the School of English and Digital Humanities at University College Cork, and the author of *Northern Irish Poetry and Domestic Space* (2015). He joined UCC as an IRC Government of Ireland Postdoctoral Fellow in 2015. Before this, he taught in the English departments of Trinity College Dublin, the

University of Bristol, and the University of Aberdeen. He has also trained and practised as a solicitor, an experience that informs his present research on law and literature. He is currently completing a study of the intersections between poetry and law in post-independence Ireland.

MARGARET KELLEHER is Professor and Chair of Anglo-Irish Literature and Drama at University College Dublin. She is UCD academic lead for the Museum of Literature Ireland (MoLI), a collaboration between UCD and the National Library of Ireland, open to the public at Newman House, St Stephen's Green from summer 2019. She is chair of the Irish Film Institute since 2014 and has developed a number of digital humanities projects, including the Digital Platform for Contemporary Irish Writing (www.contemporaryirishwriting.ie/). Her book *The Maamtrasna Murders: Language, Life and Death in Nineteenth-Century Ireland* was published in 2018.

PATRICIA KENNON is Lecturer in children's and young adult literature and culture in the School of Education, Maynooth University, Ireland. She is the president of the Irish Society for the Study of Children's Literature, a former editor in chief and features editor of *Inis: The Children's Books Magazine*, and a former president of iBbY Ireland, the Irish national section of IBBY (International Board on Books for Young People). Her research interests include young-adult science fiction, gender and sexualities in youth literature and popular culture, historical youth literature, and intercultural education.

CHRISTOPHER LANGLOIS teaches in the Department of English at Dawson College, Montreal, Canada. He is the author of *Samuel Beckett and the Terror of Literature* (2017), the editor of *Understanding Blanchot, Understanding Modernism* (2018), and is currently editing a volume of essays on Irish literature as world literature. Some of his previous work has also appeared in *Twentieth-Century Literature*, *College Literature*, *Mosaic*, *European Journal of English Studies*, *The Faulkner Journal*, *Samuel Beckett Today/Aujourd'hui*, and *ARIEL*.

STEFANIE LEHNER is Lecturer in Irish Literature and Culture at Queen's University, Belfast, and Fellow at the Senator George J. Mitchell Institute for Global Peace, Security and Justice. Her current research explores the role of the arts, specifically performance, in conflict transformation processes, with a focus on the Northern Irish context. She also researches on representations of trauma and memory in (Northern)

Irish drama, fiction, film, and photography. Stefanie is the author of *Subaltern Ethics in Contemporary Scottish and Irish Literature* (2011) and is editing a collection on *The Promise of Peace in Northern Ireland* (forthcoming). Her work has been published in *Contemporary Theatre Review*, *Irish Review*, *Irish Studies Review*, *Irish University Review*, and *Nordic Irish Studies*.

DAVID LLOYD, Distinguished Professor of English at the University of California, Riverside, works on Irish culture, settler colonialism, postcolonial and cultural theory, and visual art. His most recent books are *Beckett's Thing: Painting and Theatre* (2016) and *Under Representation: The Racial Regime of Aesthetics* (2018). *Arc & Sill: Poems 1979–2009* (2012) collected his new and selected poetry. *Bar Null* and *Furrow Archive* both appeared in 2019. A bilingual French/English edition of his play, *The Press/Le Placard*, was published by the Nouvelles Scènes series in 2018.

PATRICK LONERGAN is Professor of Drama and Theatre Studies at the National University of Ireland, Galway, and a member of the Royal Irish Academy. He has edited or written twelve books and anthologies about Irish drama and theatre, including *Theatre and Globalization* (winner of the 2008 Theatre Book Prize), *The Theatre and Films of Martin McDonagh* (2012), *Theatre and Social Media* (2015), and *Irish Drama and Theatre Since 1950* (2019). He is on the board of directors of the Galway International Arts Festival and the Galway Music Residency, an editorial associate of *Contemporary Theatre Review*, and co-editor of the *Critical Companions* series for Methuen Drama.

RONAN MCDONALD holds the Gerry Higgins Chair of Irish Studies at the University of Melbourne. He has research interests in Irish literature and the history of criticism. His books include *Tragedy and Irish Literature* (2002), *The Cambridge Introduction to Samuel Beckett* (2007), and *The Death of the Critic* (2008). Recent edited collections include *The Values of Literary Studies: Critical Institutions, Scholarly Agendas* (Cambridge, 2015) and *Flann O'Brien and Modernism* (2014).

ELLEN MCWILLIAMS is Senior Lecturer in English Literature at the University of Exeter and has published on Irish, Canadian, and American writing. She is the author of *Margaret Atwood and the Female Bildungsroman* (2009) and *Women and Exile in Contemporary Irish Fiction* (2013), and has received a number of awards for research, including an Arts and Humanities Research Council Fellowship and a Fulbright Scholar Award.

BARRY MONAHAN lectures on Film and Screen Media at University College Cork. His monograph *Ireland's Theatre on Film: Style, Stories and the National Stage on Screen* (2009) considers the relationship between the Abbey Theatre and cinema from 1930 to 1960. He has published on Irish cinema from theoretical and aesthetic perspectives in various collections including *Screening Irish America, Genre and Cinema: Ireland and Transnationalism*, and *Theorising the Visual: New Directions in Irish Cultural Studies*. He edited *Ireland and Cinema: Culture and Contexts* (2015), and his monograph *The Films of Lenny Abrahamson: A Filmmaking of Philosophy* was published in 2018.

JAMES MORAN is Professor of Modern English Literature and Drama at the University of Nottingham, UK. He is a recent recipient of both the Philip Leverhulme Prize and the British Academy mid-career fellowship, and he has presented a monthly book-review feature on BBC Radio Nottingham since 2010. His books include *Staging the Easter Rising* (2006), (as editor) *Four Irish Rebel Plays* (2007), *Irish Birmingham: A History* (2010), *The Theatre of Sean O'Casey* (2013), (as editor, with Neal Alexander) *Regional Modernisms*, and *The Theatre of D.H. Lawrence* (2015). He is currently editing a volume of Bernard Shaw's shorter plays.

ANNE MULHALL is Lecturer in the School of English, Drama and Film, University College Dublin, where she is also director of the UCD Centre for Gender, Feminisms and Sexualities (CGFS). She has published extensively in gender and queer studies, critical migration studies, and on contemporary Irish literature and culture.

RIÓNA NÍ FHRIGHIL teaches contemporary Irish-language literature at the National University of Ireland, Galway. She is the author of *Briathra, Béithe agus Banfhilí* (2008), a comparative study of the poetry of Eavan Boland and Nuala Ní Dhomhnaill. She has published extensively on contemporary poetry in Irish and has edited a number of essay collections, including *Filíocht Chomhaimseartha na Gaeilge* (2010). She is currently principal investigator of a large-scale research project titled 'Republic of Conscience: Human Rights and Modern Irish Poetry', funded by the Irish Research Council.

AILBHE NÍ GHEARBHUIGH lectures in Modern Irish at University College Cork. She holds a PhD in Irish Studies from NUI Galway. Her dissertation was awarded the Adele Dalsimer Prize at the American Conference for Irish Studies in 2013. She taught Irish at the City University of New York through the Fulbright programme. Research interests include the Gaelic Revival, international links with Irish culture, and contemporary writing. *The Coast Road*, a bilingual collection of poetry, was published in 2016.

JULIA C. OBERT is Associate Professor and Assistant Chair of English at the University of Wyoming. Her first book, *Postcolonial Overtures: The Politics of Sound in Contemporary Northern Irish Poetry* (Syracuse), was published in 2015. She has written widely on Irish literature, postcolonial literatures, and theoretical topics in publications ranging from *Irish Studies Review* to *Postmodern Culture* to *Interventions: International Journal of Postcolonial Studies*. Her current book project examines issues surrounding architecture and urban planning in a variety of postcolonial cities.

EMILIE PINE is Associate Professor of Modern Drama at University College Dublin. Emilie is editor of the *Irish University Review* (www.euppublishing.com/loi/iur) and director of the Irish Memory Studies Network (www.irishmemorystudies.com). She is principle investigator of the Irish Research Council New Horizons project 'Industrial Memories', a digital humanities re-reading of the Ryan Report on institutional child abuse (https://industrialmemories.ucd.ie). Emilie has published widely in the fields of Irish studies, performance studies, and memory studies, including *The Politics of Irish Memory: Performing Remembrance in Contemporary Irish Culture* (2011) and *The Memory Marketplace: Performance, Testimony and Witnessing in Contemporary Theatre* (2019). Her first collection of personal essays, *Notes to Self* (2018), was shortlisted for the Royal Irish Academy Michel Deon award, and has won the IACI Butler Literary Award, the An Post Irish Book Awards for Best Newcomer, and Book of the Year 2018.

PAIGE REYNOLDS, Professor of English at the College of the Holy Cross, Worcester, MA, is the author of *Modernism, Drama, and the Audience for Irish Spectacle* (Cambridge, 2007) and editor of *Modernist Afterlives in Irish Literature and Culture* (2016). Currently completing a monograph on contemporary Irish women's fiction, she has published essays on modernism, drama, and contemporary Irish writing and performance, and is editor of the forthcoming collection *The New Irish Studies* (Cambridge).

SARAH L. TOWNSEND is Assistant Professor of English at the University of New Mexico, where she specialises in modern and contemporary Irish fiction and drama. Her research on globalisation, immigration, and genre evolution in Irish and Anglophone literature has appeared in *New Literary History*, *Journal of Modern Literature*, *Journal of Commonwealth Literature*, and a number of edited collections. She is completing a monograph on the modern Irish Bildungsdrama and working on a new project about racial formation and the 'New Irish'.

STEPHEN WATT is Provost Professor of English and former Associate Dean of the School of Art, Architecture, and Design at Indiana University Bloomington. His most recent books include *Bernard Shaw's Fiction, Material Psychology and Affect: Shaw, Freud, Simmel* (2018), *'Something Dreadful and Grand': American Literature and the Irish-Jewish Unconscious* (2015), and *Beckett and Contemporary Irish Writing* (2009). He is currently working on a book on twenty-first-century political drama.

CLAIR WILLS is King Edward VII Professor of English Literature at the University of Cambridge. She has written widely on British and Irish poetry, and on the cultural history of twentieth-century Britain and Ireland. Her books include *Lovers and Strangers: An Immigrant History of Post-War Britain* (2017), shortlisted for the Orwell Prize, 2018; *The Best Are Leaving: Emigration and Post-War Irish Culture* (2015); *Easter 1916: The Siege of the GPO* (2009); and *That Neutral Island: A History of Ireland during the Second World War* (2007).

Series Preface

Irish Literature in Transition provides a new account of transitions between and across the centuries of Irish literature. Adopting varying frames and scales of reference, the series offers an original map of a territory too often navigated via the narrow channels of political history. Each of the six volumes revises our understanding of established issues and texts and, simultaneously, introduces new questions, approaches, and authors. Together, these books generate alternative genealogies across time and space and help readers to understand and interrogate the ways in which one period re-imagines and remakes another.

Discussions of Irish culture have long focused on the close relationship between literature and history. For all the power of such narratives, however, the field has yet to develop a sufficiently dynamic sense of that relationship. Literary transitions do not 'reflect' historical change in any simple or straightforward way. Rather, the complex two-way traffic between these realms involves multiple and uneven processes such as distortion, selection, repression, embrace, and critique. The temporal relationships involved in such traffic include simultaneity, time lag, and anticipation.

The six books in this series track patterns of transmission and transformation across Irish culture. More specifically, they ask: what kinds of transitions are registered and provoked by literature and culture? What are the levers and mechanisms of change? How helpful are our current concepts of literary movements, time periods, and national traditions? What is the status of the literary in our literary histories and how do we understand the relations among form, genre, and chronology?

We consider these questions from our own location in a time of scholarly transition. The sheer weight of archival material now available is transforming our sense of both the past and present of Irish literature, while prompting us to produce new kinds of critical narrative. Older literary histories of Ireland are coming under pressure from new modes of reading, such as those attuned to ecocritical issues, affect theory, queer genealogies, questions of scale, and diasporic and transnational geographies. As the concept of the 'survey' itself comes under scrutiny in classrooms and universities, these volumes show how authoritative interpretations can be innovative, challenging, and enabling for future readers and writers. Each volume intervenes in continuing critical conversations about culture rather than summarising the field or closing down debate. At the same time, the series charts the contours of literary history across the centuries in ways that highlight the significance of change as a lived, felt force.

Transition: the term means passage from one well-defined period to another; it also helps to track subtle interconnections, contingencies, or modulations; and it will provoke questions about the definition of change itself. In adopting that term, Irish Literature in Transition seeks to provide insight into the future of Irish Studies as it re-imagines the literary past and present.

CLAIRE CONNOLLY, *University College Cork*
MARJORIE HOWES, *Boston College*

General Acknowledgements

As General Editors of Irish Literature in Transition, we wish to record our thanks to everyone who helped bring this six-volume series to publication. Our fellow editors, Moyra Haslett, Matthew Campbell, Eve Patten, Eric Falci, and Paige Reynolds, have worked tirelessly on books that make significant new contributions to our understanding of Irish literature across time and space. We also record our thanks to the many contributors who helped shape the intellectual identity of this series with their thoughtful and innovative chapters. Dr Ray Ryan of Cambridge University Press prompted us to rise to the challenge of shaping a new narrative of Irish literature in transition. We thank him for that opportunity, and for all his insight and support along the way. Thanks also to Edgar Mendez of the Press for his help and hard work in seeing the books through to publication.

The support of the President's Strategic Fund of University College Cork and the Irish Studies Program at Boston College is gratefully acknowledged here.

CLAIRE CONNOLLY *(University College Cork)*
MARJORIE HOWES *(Boston College)*
General Editors

Acknowledgements

Thanks go first to our contributors, whose incisive thinking, diligent research, and good spirits made this collection a pleasure to edit. Thanks as well to the series editors of Irish Literature in Transition, Claire Connolly and Marjorie Howes. At Cambridge University Press, Ray Ryan offered vital support and encouragement, and Edgar Mendez provided timely, generous responses to our many queries. Thanks also to Síobhra Aiken, Leo Dunsker, and Jessica Laser who went above and beyond with their attentive and precise copy editing and proofreading; to Stephanie Scott for her bibliographic assistance; to Steve Cpiske who contributed his professional indexing skills as well as his unusually keen eye for editorial inconsistencies; and to Mary Morton, Sharon McCann, and Podhumai Anban for so assiduously seeing this book through the production process.

Editing a collection on contemporary Irish literature and culture from across the Atlantic means that financial and logistical support from many sides help to keep us abreast of literature and culture as it unfolds abroad. At the College of the Holy Cross, Peter Merrigan and the Edward Callahan Irish Studies Support Fund have underwritten readings and seminars offered by an array of writers studied in this collection, and support for relevant research and travel was provided by the Agnes Williams Mid-Career Fellowship, the Arthur J. O'Leary Faculty Recognition Award, and the Holy Cross Research and Publication Awards. We also thank the Folan Fund for Irish Studies and Dean Anthony Cascardi at the University of California, Berkeley, for providing financial support for this volume.

Gratitude, as well, to our many friends and colleagues, too many to name here, whose hospitality, conversation, revisions, rants, emails, and tweets have in various ways contributed to and thus helped to improve this volume.

Finally, a hearty and loving thanks to Mario and Asher Pereira, and to Amanda Post Whitehead.

Thank you to the following for permission to reproduce copyrighted material from the poems listed:

Acknowledgements

Gallery Press for excerpts from Ciaran Carson's 'The New Estate', from *The New Estate* (1976); Alan Gillis's 'Progress', from *Somebody, Somewhere* (2004); and Medbh McGuckian's 'Elegy for an Irish Speaker', from *Captain Lavender* (1995).

Wake Forest University Press for excerpts from Ciaran Carson's 'The New Estate', from *The New Estate* (1976); Michael Longley's 'Burren Prayer' and 'At Poll Salach. Easter Sunday, 1998', from *Collected Poems* (2007); and Medbh McGuckian's 'Elegy for an Irish Speaker', from *Captain Lavender* (1995).

The Random House Group Limited for excerpts from 'Burren Prayer' and 'At Poll Salach. Easter Sunday, 1998', from *Collected Poems* by Michael Longley, published by Jonathan Cape. Reprinted by permission of The Random House Group Limited. © 2006.

The Soho Agency for permission to reproduce in e-book format excerpts from 'Burren Prayer' and 'At Poll Salach. Easter Sunday, 1998', from *Collected Poems* by Michael Longley, published by Jonathan Cape.

Introduction

Eric Falci and Paige Reynolds

In the final decades of the twentieth century and into the first years of the twenty-first, both the Republic of Ireland and Northern Ireland experienced dizzying societal changes. At the beginning of the period at hand, in the early 1980s, conditions across the island seemed drearily familiar: the Irish economy was mired in recession, outward emigration was on the increase, social and political policy in the South continued to align with Catholic doctrine, sectarian conflict in Northern Ireland persisted, and the hard border between the Republic of Ireland and the North remained a fraught space of armed and ideological struggle. Yet halfway through these decades, on the cusp of a new millennium, the Irish economy was so strong that it had been anthropomorphised as the Celtic Tiger, inward immigration outpaced emigration, the longstanding moral authority of the Catholic Church had been destabilised, and the Good Friday Agreement indicated that the violence of the Troubles would diminish or even cease entirely.[1] By the end of the period covered by this book, the near present, the Irish Republic's economy had crashed and stutteringly restarted, Northern Ireland is no longer defined chiefly by sectarian violence, both countries are adapting to changing patterns of migration, and the majority of Ireland's electorate has supported several progressive social initiatives while remaining enthusiastic adherents to the European project, even as the open border between the Republic and the North is under threat within the intricate negotiations over the United Kingdom's departure from the European Union. Amid the remarkable social and political oscillations characterising these years, Irish culture on both sides of the border has emerged as a global phenomenon, one endeavouring to represent, as well as to intervene in, the rapidly changing contemporary conditions in which it is produced.[2]

It is little exaggeration to assert that these decades are rife with transitions so dramatic they seem themselves the stuff of fiction. Taking in tow the various complexities that are inherent to studying the contemporary, this final volume of *Irish Literature in Transition* aims to elucidate the central features of Irish literature during the long turn of the twentieth century, from 1980 to 2020, covering its significant trends and formations, re-assessing its major writers and texts, and providing path-making accounts of its emergent figures. The essays that follow identify broad patterns found across these decades, even as they consider what makes each stretch distinctive, placing, for example, the apparent insularity of the 1980s in contrast to the global turn of the early 2000s. Each historical era has its complexities, but approaching Irish literature of the vertiginous near-present through the long lens of 'transition' presents manifest challenges and opportunities. The contemporary moment is too near at hand; it has barely happened yet; we encounter it perpetually in mid-stream. From one angle, contemporary literature is all transition: seen from the inside, the overwhelming immediacy of the present can make locating any particular transitional node a difficult task since a vantage on a historical or cultural transition is obtained from some moment in that transition's future. A shift or pivot is apprehensible only when we can see with relative clarity the conditions both before and after, and can thus retrospectively recognise the point on which matters turned. Such a stance is not quite possible when looking at the literature (or any other cultural production) of our own historical moment.

So even as this volume marks broad transitions across recent decades, we acknowledge the impossibility of grasping completely the future meanings of those changes. As such, the date range of this volume – covering a period amidst that of its moment of publication – is meant as a somewhat cheeky admission of its necessary inadequacy or provisionality. By many measures, for instance, 1980 seems an odd starting point for the contemporary moment in Ireland. It does not feature a world-historical event, such as Ireland's accession to the European Economic Community in 1973, the Good Friday Agreement of 1998, the economic crash of 2008, or the election of the Republic's first openly gay Taoiseach in 2017. Nor does it have a particularly obvious literary-historical resonance. It may, in fact, be a year most notable in the public consciousness for Johnny Logan's victory in the Eurovision Song Contest. But, when actively fashioned into a meaningful, though perhaps interim, node, the year 1980 can powerfully demonstrate the critical and creative possibilities of retrospection amid the present, the value of locating certain literary and cultural transition points and claiming them as significant – even as they remain within our immediate purview, with their full implications still unfolding.

As an example of such fashioning, we might turn to Brian Friel's play *Translations*, which premiered at the Guildhall in Derry in 1980, and which inaugurated the influential work of Field Day and its search for a cultural 'fifth province' beyond political conflict.[3] Without positioning *Translations*, or Field Day for that matter, as the foremost literary-historical cause or origin point of the contemporary, we can use this occasion as one means to identify, unpack, and better understand certain significant transitions across these decades. Set in 1833, but premiering in the midst of the Troubles, *Translations* fictionalises the circumstances surrounding the Irish Ordnance Survey in its depiction of the historic colonial relation between Ireland and England. As such, it conveys the tendency of writers in Ireland to face the dilemmas of the present through the prism of the past. The play's attention to colonial legacies signalled the genesis of Field Day's influential postcolonial critique, while the subsequent production history of *Translations*, which has been staged across the globe, as well as Field Day's own international reach, might be regarded as an example of the 'worlding' of Irish culture. Pushed even further, this premiere might be read as predictive of a changing mood that would accept and even welcome peace and reconciliation: its premiere at the Guildhall, the symbol of unionist power in Derry, was seen as a moment of cultural unification, especially after the Protestant Lord Mayor launched the final standing ovation, and despite the nationalism underlying the play, a point that tended not to be pursued by early reviewers. In this light, *Translations* – both its textual substance and its unfurling context – becomes a means to understand the contours of the period, shedding proleptic light on the course of Irish literature and culture to come. But this case, as the essays on view skilfully demonstrate, is simply one of many sites – among them encounters, individuals, objects, texts, happenings, genres, media – that can be read in retrospect to illuminate the broader alterations in contemporary experience and the complex temporalities of those shifts. Such an approach signals, for us, the important role that the past plays for contemporary Irish writers and critics in understanding the present and imagining the future, as well as serving as a reminder that the transitions we emphasise here are adapting and adaptable to ever-changing conditions.

***

The past forty years have seen the overt manifestation of what scholars have labelled Ireland's belated modernity, a period in which social and cultural life in the Republic and – to a different degree and at a different pace – Northern

Ireland have been transformed by new material conditions in each polity, as well as by ideological shifts in the way people understand themselves and their relation to the world.[4] Perhaps the most dramatic changes of these years occurred within the political and social conditions of Northern Ireland. From the late 1960s until the verge of the twenty-first century, the North was wracked by the violence of the Troubles. Following the 1998 Good Friday Agreement, the country achieved peace and established a power-sharing government, although one that has been as notable for its long periods of suspension as for the substance of its governing. The ending of the Troubles brought about a slow and often tortuous process of coming to terms with the legacy of thirty years of strife, especially concerning the remembrance of the victims of the violence and the status of its perpetrators. As essays by Julia C. Obert and Stefanie Lehner show, Northern Irish writing gained especial prominence within the broader context of the Troubles, and writers have powerfully articulated the dynamics of the conflict and helped to shape its ongoing resolution.[5] A varied and rapidly changing media landscape has, even more influentially perhaps than the literary field, offered representations of the North during these years to audiences at home and abroad and demonstrated the profound influence of popular culture on understandings of contemporary Irish culture. During the Troubles, widely distributed commercial films, such as Neil Jordan's *The Crying Game* (1992) or Terry George's *Some Mother's Son* (1996), represented the North's political violence and strife as singular, an exceptional space characterised by sectarian violence and heroic protest. Such works continue to appear in the wake of the Troubles, as in the film *Hunger* (2008), directed by Steve McQueen, which graphically displays the bodily suffering undergone by the 1981 hunger strikers.

However, with the Good Friday Agreement two decades old and the large-scale violence seemingly relegated to the past, new ways of approaching and representing late-twentieth-century Northern Ireland have taken hold. This shift can be seen clearly in the comic television series *Derry Girls* (2017–), which follows the everyday exploits of snarky adolescents in the 1990s. The show does not shy away from the complexities of sectarian culture, political belief, and the intricacies of intergenerational family life within a highly divided culture. Yet it neither flattens the reality of Troubles-era Derry by reducing the city to a fixed backdrop for assorted teenage hijinks, nor requires that every feature of plot and characterisation depend on the conflict in Northern Ireland as the explanatory mechanism or determinative frame. In this series, available to international audiences through streaming services, the Troubles can be viewed from a distance, even from a wry angle, rather than with the adamant immediacy that characterised many depictions of the North in the 1980s and 1990s. Such fresh representations of the Troubles do not suggest, however, that the conflicts that fuelled those years are entirely resolved; this notion falls apart in light of the ongoing anxiety over Brexit and the future of the relationship between Ireland and Britain, as well as the overt re-emergence of sociopolitical divisions that were thought to have receded. In particular, the possibility of the return of a hard border between the Republic and the North, is – at the time of writing – a major topic within Irish political debates. In addition, the April 2019 murder of journalist Lyra McKee in Derry, which took place during a series of riots after police attempted to seize arms from dissident Republican groups in advance of parades commemorating the Easter Rising, has heightened tensions significantly even as the groups thought responsible have been roundly condemned.

The close attention paid to the Troubles during these decades does not mean that the North alone was the site of trauma. Long the arbiter of morality for Irish citizens, the Catholic Church in Ireland was exposed during these decades as systematically failing to protect its constituents and enabling the abuse of its most vulnerable subjects. In the 1990s, the disclosure of widespread child abuse and sexual assault by Catholic priests and within Magdalen Laundries, Industrial Schools, and Mother and Baby Homes fractured the bedrock of Catholicism and provoked an island-wide grappling with the past and its seeming sureties.[6] Sexual abuse, institutional as well as familial, has been a pervasive topic in recent Irish writing, and this subject has required writers to adapt their styles and modes of representation as they seek to understand and analyse such shattering maltreatment and cruelty. From the black humour of Patrick McCabe's *The Butcher Boy* (1992) and the heightened emotion of *The Magdalene Sisters* (2002) to the sardonic realism of Anne Enright's *The Gathering* (2007) and the Beckettian dialogue of THEATREclub's *We Don't Know What's Buried Here* (2018), writers, theatre practitioners, and film-makers have drawn from the spectrum of genres and styles to evoke and critique the horrifying cycles of violence and systemic abuse permitted and long concealed by so many institutions across Ireland.

In such ways, contemporary literature has demonstrated its capacity to intervene in history. For example, the 1984 death of 15-year-old Ann Lovett, as she gave birth to her stillborn son in a grotto, was memorably reconsidered several years later by Paula Meehan in 'The Statue of the Virgin at Granard Speaks' (1991). This poem, which asked readers to engage once more with the sufferings of this neglected teenager, was embraced by the Irish public as a necessary critique of church and state, and it went on to influence subsequent debates surrounding reproductive choice. Crucially, some of the most important texts to emerge in this period have been not works of literature but governmental reports, most notably the Ryan Report (2009) and the Ferns Report (2005), which documented the systemic abuse of children by priests and within Catholic institutions. Emilie Pine's essay in this collection urges the importance of closely and critically reading these disturbing reports via the methodologies of the digital humanities. By asking more of readers, Meehan's creative work and Pine's scholarly research are political in the best way: they do not operate as propaganda for an ideological position, but rather aim to represent and concretise the complexities of lived experience within systems that are unjust and oppressive to stir an aesthetic and intellectual response that might, however indirectly, buttress political action.

The revelations of shocking systemic failures and their devastating consequences have altered the ideological underpinnings of Irish society and have probably stoked the progressive nature of twenty-first-century Irish politics. Recent years have seen a remarkable rate of social change within a country long considered to be one of the most conservative and traditionally minded in Europe, a transformation perhaps most evident in matters of gender and sexuality. Over several decades, the Republic of Ireland has shown itself to be socially inclusive and forward thinking in many ways, a pattern initially symbolised by the election of Mary Robinson to the Irish Presidency in 1990. Yet in other instances, the country seemed to lag behind more liberalised attitudes towards gender equality and sexual freedom characterising much of the West during the late twentieth century; for example, contraception was only fully legalised in Ireland in 1993 and divorce in 1995. Today, however, Ireland finds itself at the fore of progressive initiatives on such matters, with two recent popular elections signalling the whiplash-inducing rate of cultural change. In the Republic, homosexuality was only decriminalised in 1993; yet in 2015, it became the first country to legalise same-sex marriage by popular vote, leading to the establishment of the Marriage Equality Act. A constitutional amendment banning abortion was passed in Ireland in 1983; yet in 2018, women were granted the right to legal abortion with the repeal of the eighth amendment of the Irish Constitution, again by popular vote. Notably, while the North decriminalised homosexuality in 1982 and introduced civil partnerships before Ireland, same-sex marriage remains legally unrecognised there, and legal abortion is currently prohibited. So once again, despite the increasing traffic – literal and imaginative – between north and south during these years, important social and cultural differences obtain.

In concert with these significant social transformations, one of the major features of Irish literature since the 1980s has been the increasing prominence of LGBTQ+ and women writers, which has brought an awareness of experiences once sequestered from view and expanded the compass of literary possibility. If these writers were, and sometimes continue to be, marginalised by the academy, reviewers, and the market, they have during the past forty years more openly and regularly obtained widespread critical and commercial success. Panti Bliss (Rory O'Neill), Mary Dorcey, Emma Donoghue, Frank McGuinness, Jamie O'Neill, Keith Ridgway, and Colm Tóibín are among those who have represented LGBTQ+ lives in diverse forms including historical fiction, drag performance, and newspaper editorials. The feminist turn also has had a massive impact on Irish literature and the study of it, leading to the inclusion of more women writers within the canons and institutions of contemporary literature. This attention to women writers has attracted new audiences to the work of those whose careers began in the mid-twentieth century, such as Jennifer Johnston, Eiléan Ní Chuilleanáin, and Máire Mhac an tSaoi, as well as to that of more recent figures, such as Marina Carr, Sinéad Morrissey, and Anna Burns. The massive impact of feminism, within and beyond the academy, has also engendered a systemic critique of the gendered ideologies of representational practices.[7] These shifts became apparent in the animated controversies that surrounded the marginalisation of female writers from the first three volumes of the landmark *Field Day Anthology of Irish Writing* (1991), which sparked critiques of the stubborn persistence of masculinist logics in the literary sphere, and spurred the publication of a further two volumes a decade on, *The Field Day Anthology of Irish Writing: Irish Women's Writing and Traditions* (2002). The dramatic alteration in attitudes towards gender and sexuality across these decades is one of this volume's major through-lines; it is apparent in nearly every essay that follows and given focused treatment in Clair Wills's coda on Edna O'Brien and Eimear McBride. Though LGBTQ+ and feminist writing, criticism, and activism are obviously characterised by substantial differences, considered together they demonstrate the massive significance of this shift – in terms of gender, sexuality, the politics of representation, and the textures of lived experience – during the contemporary moment in Ireland.

Another of the central historical dynamics that underlies the essays in this volume concerns the thoroughgoing conversion of the Republic's economic life at the end of the twentieth century. The sudden affluence brought by the Celtic Tiger inspired a burgeoning sense of national self-confidence, one that was buoyed by Ireland's changing status on the world stage. With the expansion of the European Union and economic policies sympathetic to foreign investment, Ireland moved in a relatively short time from being a relatively insular society and economy to one of the most globally connected countries in the world. Becoming an equal member of the European Economic Community with eight other European states in 1973, including the United Kingdom, had a transformative effect on Irish diplomacy, economic development, and politics, and the economic growth of the 1990s amplified and quickened changes already under way. With its friendly corporate tax rates, Ireland became a preferred destination for overseas investment and a favoured location for multinational corporations, especially in the technology sector, and open trade and the investment of foreign capital brought widespread employment to an historically underemployed population. That population grew to include many new migrants during a period of unprecedented growth of immigration in the late 1990s and early 2000s, a change that has exposed the limitations, and even the racialised contradictions, of the Republic's putatively progressive approach to globalisation.

As the problematic adjustment of the state to a new migrant population attests, this development has been neither even nor consistent. After the giddy stretch of Celtic Tiger exuberance, the Irish real-estate bubble burst in the wake of the twenty-first century's first global recession in 2008, leaving Irish banks massively overexposed, the Irish government scrambling to guarantee bankers' debts, the entire economy teetering, and a period of crushing austerity in the offing. The swift end of the real-estate and home-construction boom, which was driven by the speculative investments of property developers rather than the housing needs of communities, left behind swathes of ghost estates and a sea of mortgage debt. More generally, the gap between the rich and the poor has widened under Ireland's neoliberal regime and the economy's boom-and-bust cycle. The bust also triggered another wave of emigration, as immigrants who arrived at the height of the Celtic Tiger departed the country alongside young Irish people once again forced to look abroad for a livelihood. The end of the economic expansion, and the austerity measures that followed, severely dented the confidence that had characterised the preceding years, as did the 2010 decision to give over the regulation of the Republic's economy for three years to the Troika (the European Central Bank, the European Commission, and the International Monetary Fund) in exchange for a financial rescue package of €85 billion. In recent years, the

Irish economy has largely recovered from the losses of the early part of the decade. Today, the impending threat of Brexit means that Ireland has become a destination for corporations seeking a base in an English-speaking common law jurisdiction, a transition that suggests newly complicated economic conditions are on the horizon.

Irish writers have played an important role in documenting these conditions by focusing on the economic shocks and excesses of the past several decades. For instance, the real-estate boom of the Celtic Tiger led to a radical recalibration of the familiar Irish literary motif of the land. Donal Ryan has been the most adamant chronicler of the speculative frenzy that swept through rural Ireland during the real-estate boom, but other novels such as Enright's *The Forgotten Waltz* (2011), Claire Kilroy's *The Devil I Know* (2012), and Paul Murray's *The Mark and the Void* (2015), each appearing after the Tiger's end, also depict the arc of the boom and reflect upon what was left in its wake. A number of writers have focused more precisely on environmental and ecological concerns in the wake of unalloyed development, a topic that Adam Hanna addresses in his essay here. In their reconsideration of these years, writers have lodged trenchant critiques about the perils of Ireland's ready adoption of neoliberal policies and practices while attempting to envisage the future's possibilities and precarities. The rural perspective that has long been central to modern Irish writing has been re-mobilised in an age of environmental catastrophe, and it stretches the full range of Irish imaginative writing, from Michael Longley's ecocritical lyrics to Tim Robinson's compendious volumes on Connemara and the Aran Islands, late reflexes of the *dinnseanchas* tradition in a time of global ecological crisis.[8]

A more sustained source of self-confidence during this era has been provided by Ireland's continued authority in international letters. Throughout this period of dramatic transformation, Irish literature and culture have been on a remarkable global run.[9] Most clearly signalled by Seamus Heaney's 1995 Nobel Prize for Literature, the influence and stature of Irish writers have been vividly evident during these decades. Irish writers and artists have amassed significant cultural capital and international fame, have won a bevy of prestigious awards, and occupy prominent perches at the heart of the Anglophone literary and academic worlds. Those with well-established careers in Ireland, such as John Banville, John McGahern, and Eavan Boland, came to the surface of global consciousness in the 1990s and 2000 even as new generations of Irish writers found broad audiences, and outlets including the *Guardian* and *The New Yorker* have helped to single out younger talents like Claire-Louise Bennett and Sally

Rooney. Specific Irish cultural products – such as Frank McCourt's *Angela's Ashes* (1996) and Bill Whelan's *Riverdance* (1995) – have become blockbusters, and a handful of musical acts have found long-lasting global stardom, a dynamic traced by Stephen Watt in his analysis of Irish fame. Barry Monahan's essay provides a thick description of the wider field of Irish film and television in this period, a moment in which dramatists and film-makers have accrued shelves of BAFTA, Oscar, and Tony award statues.[10] Such popularity carries on, as seen in the celebrated film adaptations of Tóibín's *Brooklyn* (2009) and Emma Donoghue's *Room* (2010), each appearing in 2015, or in the continued celebrity of U2 or Celtic Woman, musical performers who profitably embrace the capacious 'brand' of Irishness.[11]

The pre-eminence of Irish work written in English in an increasingly global literary field, both its continuing cachet and its relation to Anglophone literatures, brings to the fore another aspect of the complex uncertainties of studying contemporary literature. The books and authors celebrated in their moment are not necessarily going to be those valued a half century hence. And it is inevitable – necessarily so – that some writer, performer, movement, genre, or style ignored or undervalued in the present will be rediscovered in the future: this is nearly a requirement of literary history, one grimly and gamely faced by any critic of contemporary culture. The difficulty of studying the contemporary is perhaps even more pronounced in this period because of the ever-greater commodification of literature: the lucrative awards that favour the few, the push for writers to brand themselves and their work, the need for publishers (many of which belong to huge multinational companies) to show a profit, and the subsequent promotion of those writers most likely to move product. It is sometimes quite difficult to separate the wheat of contemporary writing from the chaff of its marketing.[12]

Yet canny marketing and touristic appeals to Irish stereotypes alone have not ensured the global success of Irish literature. The capacity of Irish writers to represent contemporary conditions in notable works of art is key to their prominence. However, within those conditions' tense contingencies, that capacity has been tested at every turn. Some of the most highly esteemed contemporary Irish writers have come under significant critique for failing to transform their aesthetics – their thematic, generic, and stylistic propensities – so as to address more adequately the actualities of life in the twenty-first century.[13] To be sure, some of those most celebrated have remained most comfortable in relatively traditional forms: the realist novel with its tendency towards rural melancholia,[14] the first-person lyric seemingly unswayed by modernism,[15] or the realist drama set in cottage or pub.[16] A cache of essays threaded through this volume – by David Lloyd, Paige Reynolds, Patricia Kennon, Eric Falci, James Moran, Patrick Lonergan, Joe Cleary, and Sarah Townsend – take up different aspects of these complex genealogies, showing how writers have departed from or radically adapted traditional conventions, and how many continue to lean on given forms.

In addition to the contemporary re-gearing of traditional forms, one of the stories this volume tells is that of the growing importance and visibility of detective fiction, crime fiction, young adult novels, children's books, 'chick lit', and other kinds of genre fiction within considerations of Irish literature and within literary studies as a whole.[17] Another is about the role of translation, an issue at the heart of studies of contemporary global writing.[18] How best might a polyglot audience of readers gain access to Irish texts, and how might writers and publishers approach the complex relation between Irish-language originals and their translation into, most frequently, English? This is a familiar problem for Irish-language writers, one they have addressed with ingenuity over the past four decades. Although its readership remains small, Irish-language literature picked up significant momentum during this period, continuing a trend that began in the 1970s with the emergence of the *Innti* poets. Dual-language editions of Irish-language literature gained in popularity and several writers – most notably Nuala Ní Dhomhnaill – have found a broad audience in Irish as well as through English translation. Irish-language literature and culture have been bolstered by the continued prominence of RTÉ's Raidió na Gaeltachta and the emergence of TG4 in 1996, and the burgeoning of a lively online culture has enriched the production and presentation of Irish-language writing. In their essays, Ríona Ní Fhrighil and Ailbhe Ní Ghearbhuigh examine the textures and dynamics of Irish-language literature in this period and consider the role played by small presses, academic institutions, and arts organisations in sustaining this work.

A noteworthy feature of contemporary Ireland is the ongoing imaginative and practical support of literature. These decades evidence a demonstrable commitment to the arts by various organisations and institutions, from tourist boards and state agencies to universities and town councils, although Margaret Kelleher, in her essay here, suggests how this support might be made more effective and equitable. Writers have been bolstered by vibrant networks of institutions in Ireland and abroad, from Arts Council-funded programmes, such as Aosdána and the government-sponsored Culture Ireland, to important university centres throughout Northern Ireland and the Republic. An array of arts and literary festivals on view from Kilkenny to Ennis, Belfast to Galway, help sustain contemporary writing, as do summer schools orbiting particular writers. To draw the attention of audiences to contemporary performance practices, the Dublin Theatre Festival annually hosts indigenous and foreign drama, while the Dublin Fringe Festival stages new and often riskier productions. Annual festivals hosted in cities from Derry to Cloyne likewise provide a venue to showcase native and foreign film. A thriving network of periodicals supports literary writing – *The Yellow Nib*, *The Stinging Fly*, the *Honest Ulsterman*, *The Dublin Review*, *The Moth Magazine*, *gorse*, the *Dublin Review of Books*, and the longstanding *Poetry Ireland Review* among them. While London and New York remain the global centres of publishing, a handful of publishers in Ireland and abroad provide crucial support for Irish writers, such as Gallery Press, Salmon Poetry, Wake Forest University Press, Lilliput Press, The Stinging Fly, Cló Iar-Chonnacht, and Tramp Press, the latter the object of study, along with *The Irish Times*, in Paige Reynolds' coda. Across the whole of the period at hand, Irish culture has revealed itself to be a valuable commodity, both as a driving force of the domestic tourism industry and in the global flows of consumer culture, and Irish writers have become central producers within such flows.

As is evident in the cataloguing of these various transitions over the past four decades, a signal characteristic of contemporary Irish culture is retrospection. As sureties attenuated or were remoulded, nearly every aspect of the Irish past seemed to be called into question and subject to revision. This process occurred across social, cultural, and political life. The Republic of Ireland's 'Decade of Centenaries' commemorates those monumental events that led to Irish independence, from the introduction of the Third Home Rule Bill in 1912 to the establishment of the Irish Free State in 1922. In Northern Ireland, there have been analogous commemorations and re-examinations of this decisive period in the early twentieth century. A number of these, such as the 2016 events marking the centenary of the Battle of the Somme, are part of a distinct unionist historiography. Others, such as the ongoing commemoration and commodification of the sinking of the Titanic, have eclipsed the sectarian dynamics of cultural memory and political ideology and been embedded into the ongoing economic life of the North.[19] Such occasions and the conversations around them have served not only to mark the monumental political changes of the past century, but also to prompt large-scale reconsiderations of the not-so-distant past.

It has been a stunning period of historical reckoning, during which writers, scholars, and people on both sides of the border have had to re-assess their sense of the past and even to re-make their own memories of it.[20] Such re-alignments have profoundly affected cultural practices in Ireland. In the most visible example from recent years, the grassroots #WakingTheFeminists movement in Ireland, in tandem with the international #MeToo movement, drew considerable attention to the gender bias infecting Irish cultural institutions. Formed to protest the Abbey's male-dominated 1916 centenary programme, #WakingTheFeminists stimulated additional forms of feminist activism and engendered concrete practical changes at a number of cultural institutions. Within humanistic scholarship, new models of historiography have burgeoned to elucidate the experience of those typically overlooked. A number of essays published here, but especially those by Christopher Langlois and Diarmaid Ferriter, consider how contemporary literature and culture have approached, once again and from various angles, the Irish past, as well as how literature has served not only to reflect or display historical conditions but also to anticipate and even peremptorily critique periods of political and social transition.

In a moment of immediacy, acceleration, and instantaneity, it is intriguing – though perhaps not surprising – that Irish writers have favoured the recollective mode, as is made clear by the recent spate of historical novels by writers such as Mary Morrissy, Joseph O'Connor, Sebastian Barry, and Antonia Logue. These years have also seen more intimate accounts of the past recorded in well-received autobiographies, from Seamus Deane's autobiographical novel *Reading in the Dark* (1996) and Nuala O'Faolain's *Are You Somebody? The Accidental Memoir of a Dublin Woman* (1996) to Hugo Hamilton's *The Speckled People* (2003) and Sinéad Gleeson's *Constellations: Reflections from Life* (2019). In part a reflection of social media's mining and dissemination of highly personal experience via Facebook, Twitter, or blogs, the rising prominence of memoir and the personal essay in Ireland is one of those aspects of contemporary writing that invites inquiry and awaits further retrospection. Coming to terms with how digital culture has reshaped literary composition and reception is another of those open questions signalled by the future-oriented end date of our volume.

This close, critical attention to the past might help to shape more productive responses to the changing textures of the present and future. Since the mid-1990s, the Republic in particular has experienced rapid ethnic and racial diversification, which has introduced exciting new voices and traditions to what was once a fairly racially and ethnically homogeneous country, but has also triggered new forms of xenophobia and racism. Traveller communities have historically borne the brunt of such biases, but now a newly arrived immigrant community also faces bigotry within the textures of everyday life and the sphere of political institutions.[21] The progressive nature of elements of policy and practice in the Irish Republic related to gender and sexuality has not yet extended to its immigration and asylum policies, as is evident from the 2004 Citizenship Referendum. Likewise, the continuance of the system of Direct Provision for asylum-seekers, introduced in 1999, has been seen by many as a failure to preserve basic human rights. Again, the past might provide fresh ways of thinking about the future. How, for instance, might a revitalised understanding of Ireland's diasporic history abet more compassionate attitudes towards inward immigration and generate better practical support for an increasingly multi-ethnic populace?

An extensive history of migration has made for a massive Irish diaspora across the globe, one concentrated especially in the United States, the United Kingdom, Canada, and Australia. That the re-examined Irish past may bring news to the present is an implicit premise of recent works. Colum McCann's *This Side of Brightness* (1998) and *Transatlantic* (2013), for instance, consider the inheritances of Ireland's diasporic history and may engender more complex understandings of race in the contemporary moment, with these novels placing African American and Irish history in dialogue to illuminate crossings both literal and figurative. Ellen McWilliams examines how such works attend to the legacies and actualities of the Irish diaspora and its ongoing relation to the island of Ireland. Looking to the art generated amid large-scale inward migration in the 1990s and 2000s, Anne Mulhall explores the implications of a more racially and ethnically diverse Irish society, showing how different writers approach this experience and asking who can speak of the migrant experience.[22] Although migrant literature in Ireland is still nascent, multi-ethnic Irish society is a central topic in fiction such as Melatu Uche Okorie's *This Hostel Life* (2018), Oona Frawley's *Flight* (2014), and Roddy Doyle's *The Deportees* (2007), the poetry of Oritsegbemi Emmanuel Jakpa, the drama of Donal O'Kelly and Ursula Rani Sarma, and the applied theatre of Dublin's pan-African community.

Not only creative work, but also scholarship plays a vital role in representing and evaluating transitions in contemporary Irish culture. During these decades, as Irish literature became a lauded and marketable brand,

Irish Studies grew into a fully fledged academic field, as Ronan McDonald's essay in this volume shows. One important frame in this context, and a pedal point throughout this volume, is the centrality of postcolonial theories within accounts of Irish history and culture. The rise of Irish Studies programmes in the 1990s was shaped by the field of postcolonial theory inaugurated by Edward Said in *Orientalism* (1978) and catalysed by an understanding of modern Ireland as a distinctive, perhaps unique, part of the history of British colonialism. Some of the period's major critics either write from a postcolonial perspective or contest that perspective.[23] The centrality of 'Ireland' within such criticism – as an island, as a former colony, as a semi-colony, as partly a current colony, as a post-colony, and as an independent nation whose founding is premised upon its break from British imperialism – is such that it may seem difficult from such a perspective to conceive of the category of 'Irish literature' outside of the history of colonialism, decolonisation, and nation-making. That is, one of the issues many critics have faced, and which is a topic of many of the essays that follow, concerns the status of a category called 'Irish literature' outside or beyond a colonial dynamic, that is, as part of a larger global web rather than a Manichean binary that stretches the Irish sea.[24]

This seems to us a point worth elaborating: that in a critical moment focused on global rather than national literary traditions, Irish literature has long understood its status and value within a wider Anglophone and European literary tradition, even as it has kept its eye trained on the particularities of the island of Ireland. The delineation of place has been a key tendency of Irish literature, and this has not abated among contemporary writers. Just as earlier writers were attached to certain spaces and landscapes – Yeats and Sligo, Synge and the Aran Islands, Kavanagh and Monaghan – so have understandings of contemporary writers been filtered through their connection with and attention to specific places: Marie Jones and Belfast, Maeve Binchy and Dublin, Kevin Barry and Cork. However, reflecting the mobility and virtuality of contemporary life, the concept of the Irish writer has been in part untethered from the physical space of Ireland, with many of its most renowned figures currently writing from Britain, America, Canada, and Europe. More than simply a practical identifier of nationality, the space of Ireland is a conceptual framework that has been adjusted and reconceived in recent decades. If throughout much of the twentieth century the rural-urban or north-south dyads drove understandings of Irish cultural and social life, contemporary Ireland can no longer conform to such binaries (if it ever really could). Instead, multiple, overlapping geographies and peoples constitute Ireland in the late twentieth and early twenty-first centuries, as seen, for example, in the shifting importance of Ireland's borders (both internal and external) and in contested understandings of Irish identity. This fluidity, with its affordances and challenges, points to provocative questions for future writing and scholarship, ones that will shape how we think about Ireland and Irish literature well beyond 2020.

***

A word or two remains to be said about the structure and grain of this volume. As we have discussed, as aspects of Irish experience and identity have become increasingly open and porous in recent decades, contemporary Irish writing has taken a global turn while remaining keyed to local conditions and events. A similar dialectical logic informs the individual essays in this collection, which frequently bound across genres, national borders, and methodologies in their endeavours to accurately map the transformations depicted and interrogated in Irish literature. So as to undermine some of the traditional boundaries that have defined Irish literary and cultural studies, individual chapters deliberately weave together long-standing oppositions such as high and low genres, north and south counties, and male and female writers. The essays that follow take up and reconsider the matters that have characterised Irish literature and criticism in the past forty years, account for the historical and cultural transitions that define this era, and explore the artists who respond to and shape them. They do not, however, provide a neat synthesis. Nor do they follow from one another methodologically or analytically. Which is to say, these essays do not adhere to a single working model, they do not necessarily agree with one another, and the volume as a whole does not aspire to be a comprehensive literary history of the entire period or to cover every important author. Several essays survey a wide swathe of ground, moving through many texts in order to limn a full picture of an entire area. A handful focus on a few works to track a particular interpretive problem or to demonstrate a mode of reading and analysis. Several move well outside of what is typically thought of as 'literature' and 'literary criticism' in order to expand the ambit of what such criticism might be able to do. And some undertake several methods at once or fashion a hybrid approach to their objects of attention, themselves transitioning internally to catch the transitions that shape the period at hand. In all, they move along and beyond the usual discursive paths of Irish criticism, combining close reading and literary-historical analysis with turns to the techniques of the digital humanities, modes of scholarly activism or critical polemic, and

Introduction

attention to institutions in addition to authors and texts, as well as the occasional swerve into personal memory and commentary.

This volume is divided into four major sections – 'Times', 'Spaces', 'Forms of Experience', and 'Practices, Institutions, and Audiences' – although the overlap and crosstalk among the four is at least as important as their delineation. At the conclusion of each section, a short coda places two influential contemporary Irish figures or institutions in dialogue to showcase how writers and cultural practitioners of this period enact the transitions we have identified. We imagine each coda as a node or a relay rather than a summary gesture, and just as each essay speaks across the entire volume rather than remaining conceptually or thematically confined to its specific section, so does each coda aim to move laterally or anticipatorily even as it refocuses the essays that precede it. At a larger level, none of the four major headings can be thought about outside of the context of the other three, and each of the four terms ramifies differently at different moments, both within any given essay and as a term shadowing the other three sections. It is perhaps too much to say that one could entirely re-order this volume, moving essays willy-nilly from 'Space' to 'Time' or 'Time' to 'Forms of Experience', but the plasticity and permeability that characterise the section headings are vital for a set of essays that takes a critical perspective on what is so near to hand: any such textual scaffolding must needs stretch and bend in order to accommodate the shifting domains within them.

In this way, the volume's structure models, though loosely, the patterns and features of contemporary Irish literature and culture. Collectively, these essays confirm that these past four decades constitute a remarkable period of systemic change that has inflected nearly every aspect of life in Northern Ireland and the Republic of Ireland. The particular pressures of contemporary history – whether the Troubles and its aftermath in the North, the unspooling of the Catholic Church's authority, or the place of Ireland within a series of global economic and geopolitical networks – have transformed daily life on scales large and small. And yet, even as they account for these changes and their effects on contemporary culture, the essays also corroborate our reading of Irish literature as productively aware of and attendant to the past. Oftentimes, writers respond to present-day changes by maintaining the scaffolding of conventional genres and styles – the realist novel, the lyric poem, proscenium theatre, narrative film – while re-arranging and transforming these forms so that they might sufficiently address the actualities of contemporary life. A good deal of Irish literature still orbits around that familiar Joycean triad – 'nationality, language, religion' – but those terms have been re-oriented and re-imagined.[25] Even as the stuff of Irish history and the material of Irish myth remain a source repository for contemporary writers, such histories, myths, and linguistic traditions are most often employed as means to refract and unsettle the present rather than as modes of conservation and commemoration.

Amid the swift but by no means smooth transitions of the past four decades, contemporary writers have attempted to maintain a double focus, toggling between a wide-angled view that takes into account the massive forces shaping the global economy and planetary life and one that attends to the granularities of Irish culture amidst such precipitous forces. This dynamic has introduced new prospects for writers, scholars, and readers and has led to an exciting, and much-heralded, body of contemporary Irish writing across genres. As long-standing ideological norms and practical constraints lost their power to determine, and so limit, aesthetic possibilities and readerly tastes, writers have had more room in which to manoevre. As a result, authors who were not quite visible because of the narrowness of earlier literary protocols came to centre stage; artists could risk producing work that tackled a wider, more diverse range of experiences and topics; and audiences have welcomed increasingly capacious renderings of the complexities of contemporary life. Such changes also brought a sharper charge for writers: amid these rapidly shifting conditions, works of literature necessarily must absorb and represent those vertiginous changes, as well as consider their implications. As a number of essays show, the relatively favourable climate for writers in Ireland and the continuing popularity of Irish writing constitute a blessing and a curse: these conditions help to ensure an audience at home and abroad but also might congeal a set of expectations about what 'Irish literature' is meant to be about or look like. It remains to us, as readers and critics, as well as subjects, of the contemporary moment, to welcome and wrangle with the increasing diversity of creative work and scholarly analysis that has emerged, so as to be able to reckon with the transitions that might lie ahead.

Notes

1. We have not insisted on uniformity in nomenclature in this volume, especially as the matter of names and naming remains complex and fraught, and so contributors have been left to select the relevant terms describing topics under their consideration. For instance, here we refer to the 1998 all-party agreement that initiated devolution and the formation of a power-sharing government in

Northern Ireland as the Good Friday Agreement, although this same event may also be described as the Belfast Agreement.

2. On Irish society and culture in the late twentieth and twenty-first centuries, see Terence Brown, *Ireland: A Social and Cultural History, 1922–2002* (New York: Harper Perennial, 2004), pp. 315–429; Diarmaid Ferriter, *The Transformation of Ireland, 1900–2000* (London: Profile Books, 2004), pp. 623–759; R. F. Foster, *Luck and the Irish: A Brief History of Change from 1970* (Oxford: Oxford University Press, 2008); and Thomas Bartlett, ed., *The Cambridge History of Ireland, Volume 4: 1880 to the Present* (Cambridge: Cambridge University Press, 2018), pp. 407–638. On Northern Ireland, see David McKittrick and David McVea, *Making Sense of the Troubles: The Story of the Conflict in Northern Ireland* (Chicago: New Amsterdam Books, 2002); Jonathan Tonge, *Northern Ireland* (Cambridge: Polity Press, 2006); and Fearghal Cochrane, *Northern Ireland: The Reluctant Peace* (New Haven, CT, and London: Yale University Press, 2013).

3. The notion of the 'fifth province' in this context emerged in the pages of *The Crane Bag*, an important journal covering politics, culture, and the arts that was edited by Mark Patrick Hederman and Richard Kearney and appeared between 1977 and 1985. On Field Day, see Marilynn Richtarik, *Acting Between the Lines: The Field Day Company and Irish Cultural Politics, 1980–1984* (Oxford: Clarendon Press, 1994); and Aidan O'Malley, *Field Day and the Translation of Irish Identities: Performing Contradictions* (Basingstoke: Palgrave Macmillan, 2011).

4. For perspectives on Ireland, modernity, and globalisation, see Peadar Kirby, Luke Gibbons, and Michael Cronin, eds., *Reinventing Ireland: Culture, Society and the Global Economy* (London: Pluto Press, 2002); Eamon Maher and Eugene O'Brien, eds., *From Prosperity to Austerity: A Socio-Cultural Critique of the Celtic Tiger and Its Aftermath* (Manchester: Manchester University Press, 2014); and Michael O'Sullivan, *Ireland and the Global Question* (Cork, Ireland: Cork University Press, 2006).

5. On Northern Irish literature, see Edna Longley, *The Living Stream: Literature & Revisionism in Ireland* (Newcastle upon Tyne, England: Bloodaxe Books, 1994); Aaron Kelly, *Class and the City in Northern Irish Culture* (Basingstoke: Palgrave Macmillan, 2016); Richard Kirkland, *Identity Parades: Northern Irish Culture and Dissident Subjects* (Liverpool: Liverpool University Press, 2002) and *Literature and Culture in Northern Ireland Since 1965: Moments of Danger* (New York: Longman, 1996); Fiona Coleman Coffey, *Political Acts: Women in Northern Irish Theatre, 1921–2012* (Syracuse, NY: Syracuse University Press, 2016); Tom Herron and John Lynch, eds., *After Bloody Sunday: Representation, Ethics, Justice* (Cork, Ireland: Cork University Press, 2007); Tom Maguire, *Making Theatre in Northern Ireland: Through and Beyond the Troubles* (Exeter: University of Exeter Press, 2006); and Birte Heidemann, *Post-Agreement Northern Irish Literature: Lost in a Liminal Space?* (Basingstoke: Palgrave Macmillan, 2016).

6. See Tom Inglis, *Moral Monopoly: The Rise and Fall of the Catholic Church in Modern Ireland* (Dublin: University College Dublin, 1998); James M. Smith,

Ireland's Magdalen Laundries and the Nation's Architecture of Containment (Notre Dame, IN: University of Notre Dame Press, 2007); Marie Keenan, *Child Sexual Abuse & The Catholic Church: Gender, Power, and Organizational Culture* (Oxford: Oxford University Press, 2012); and Frances Finnegan, *Do Penance or Perish: Magdalen Asylums in Ireland* (New York: Oxford University Press, 2004).

7. On contemporary Irish literature, sexuality, and gender, see Heather Ingman and Clíona Ó Gallchoir, eds., *A History of Modern Irish Women's Literature* (Cambridge: Cambridge University Press, 2018), pp. 260–444; Susan Cahill, *Irish Literature in the Celtic Tiger Years, 1990–2008: Gender, Bodies, Memory* (London: Continuum, 2011); Claire Bracken, *Irish Feminist Futures* (New York: Routledge, 2016); Lisa Fitzpatrick, ed., *Performing Feminisms in Contemporary Ireland* (Dublin: Carysfort Press, 2013); Geraldine Meaney, *Gender, Ireland, and Cultural Change: Race, Sex, and Nation* (New York: Routledge, 2010); Elizabeth Butler Cullingford, *Ireland's Others: Gender and Ethnicity in Irish Literature and Popular Culture* (Notre Dame, IN: Notre Dame University Press, 2001); Patrick R. Mullen, *The Poor Bugger's Tool: Irish Modernism, Queer Labor, and Postcolonial History* (Oxford: Oxford University Press, 2016); Ellen McWilliams, *Women and Exile in Contemporary Irish Fiction* (Basingstoke: Palgrave Macmillan, 2013); Rebecca Pelan, *Two Irelands: Literary Feminisms North and South* (Syracuse, NY: Syracuse University Press, 2005); and Fintan Walsh, *Queer Performance and Contemporary Ireland: Dissent and Disorientation* (Basingstoke: Palgrave Macmillan, 2016). For a broader historical account, see Diarmaid Ferriter, *Occasions of Sin: Sex and Society in Modern Ireland* (London: Profile Books, 2009).

8. For ecocritical approaches to Irish literature, see Christine Cusick, ed., *Out of the Earth: Ecocritical Readings of Irish Texts* (Cork, Ireland: Cork University Press, 2010); Eóin Flannery, *Ireland and Ecocriticism: Literature, History, and Environmental Justice* (New York: Routledge, 2016); Kathryn Kirkpatrick and Borbála Faragó, eds., *Animals in Irish Literature and Culture* (Basingstoke: Palgrave Macmillan, 2015); and Sam Solnick, *Poetry and the Anthropocene: Ecology, Biology, and Technology in Contemporary British and Irish Poetry* (New York: Earthscan/Routledge, 2016).

9. For general surveys of Irish literature that focus on the past forty years, see Scott Brewster and Michael Parker, eds., *Irish Literature Since 1990: Diverse Voices* (Manchester: Manchester University Press, 2009); and Margaret Kelleher and Philip O'Leary, eds., *The Cambridge History of Irish Literature, Volume Two, 1890–2000* (Cambridge: Cambridge University Press, 2006), pp. 270–530 and 600–42. On various aspects of contemporary Irish literature, see Declan Kiberd, *After Ireland: Writing the Nation from Beckett to the Present* (Cambridge, MA: Harvard University Press, 2018); Paige Reynolds, ed., *Modernist Afterlives in Irish Literature and Culture* (London and New York: Anthem Press, 2016); Stephen Watt, *Beckett and Contemporary Irish Literature* (Cambridge: Cambridge University Press, 2009); Stefanie Lehner, *Subaltern*

Ethics in Contemporary Scottish and Irish Literature (Basingstoke: Palgrave Macmillan, 2011); Jennifer Keating-Miller, *Language, Identity, and Liberation in Contemporary Irish Literature* (Basingstoke: Palgrave Macmillan, 2009); and Michael Pierse, ed., *A History of Irish Working-Class Writing* (Cambridge: Cambridge University Press, 2017), pp. 303–96.

10. For studies of contemporary Irish media, see Christopher Morash, *A History of the Media in Ireland* (Cambridge: Cambridge University Press, 2012), pp. 166–230; Claire Lynch, *Cyber Ireland: Text, Image, Culture* (Basingstoke: Palgrave Macmillan, 2014); Barry Monahan, *Ireland and Cinema: Culture and Contexts* (Basingstoke: Palgrave Macmillan, 2015); Eóin Flannery and Michael Griffin, eds., *Ireland in Focus: Film, Photography, and Popular Culture* (Syracuse, NY: Syracuse University Press, 2009); and Michael Patrick Gillespie, *The Myth of an Irish Cinema: Approaching Irish-Themed Films* (Syracuse, NY: Syracuse University Press, 2008).

11. On Irish popular culture, see Diane Negra, ed., *The Irish in Us: Irishness, Performativity, and Popular Culture* (Durham, NC: Duke University Press, 2006); and Wanda Balzano, Anne Mulhall, and Moynagh Sullivan, eds., *Irish Postmodernisms and Popular Culture* (Basingstoke: Palgrave Macmillan, 2007).

12. For several perspectives on and theorisations of contemporary literature, see Theodore Martin, *Contemporary Drift: Genre, Historicism, and the Problem of the Present* (New York: Columbia University Press, 2017); Eric Hayot, *On Literary Worlds* (Oxford: Oxford University Press, 2012); Sarah Brouillette, *Literature and the Creative Economy* (Stanford, CA: Stanford University Press, 2014); and Sarah Brouillette, Mathias Nilges, and Emilio Sauri, eds., *Literature and the Global Contemporary* (Basingstoke: Palgrave Macmillan, 2017). On the question of the contemporary in the Irish context, see the 'Introduction' to Margaret Kelleher and Nicholas Wolf's special issue of *Éire-Ireland* on 'Ireland and the Contemporary', *Éire-Ireland*, 52.1&2 (2017), pp. 9–16.

13. On this line of critique, see Joe Cleary, '"Horseman, Pass By!": The Neoliberal World System and the Crisis in Irish Literature', *boundary 2*, 45.1 (2018), pp. 135–79, and *Outrageous Fortune: Capital and Culture in Modern Ireland* (Dublin: Field Day Publications, 2006).

14. On contemporary fiction, see George O'Brien, *The Irish Novel: 1960–2010* (Cork, Ireland: Cork University Press, 2012); Linden Peach, *The Contemporary Irish Novel: Critical Readings* (Basingstoke: Palgrave Macmillan, 2004); Liam Harte, *Reading the Contemporary Irish Novel, 1987–2007* (Malden, MA: Wiley-Blackwell, 2014); Derek Hand, *A History of the Irish Novel* (Cambridge: Cambridge University Press, 2011), pp. 254–92; and Marie Mianowski, *Post-Celtic Landscapes in Irish Fiction* (New York: Routledge, 2017).

15. On contemporary poetry, see Andrew Auge, *A Chastened Communion: Modern Irish Poetry and Catholicism* (Syracuse, NY: Syracuse University Press, 2013); Gail McConnell, *Northern Irish Poetry and Theology* (Basingstoke: Palgrave Macmillan, 2014); Lucy Collins, *Contemporary Irish*

Women Poets: Memory and Estrangement (Liverpool: Liverpool University Press, 2015); Julia C. Obert, *Postcolonial Overtures: The Politics of Sound in Contemporary Northern Irish Poetry* (Syracuse: Syracuse University Press, 2015); Eric Falci, *Continuity and Change in Irish Poetry, 1966–2010* (Cambridge: Cambridge University Press, 2012); Clair Wills, *Improprieties: Politics and Sexuality in Northern Irish Poetry* (Oxford: Clarendon Press, 1992); John Goodby, *Irish Poetry Since 1950* (Manchester: Manchester University Press, 2000); and Adam Hanna, *Northern Irish Poetry and Domestic Space* (Basingstoke: Palgrave Macmillan, 2015).

16. On contemporary drama, see Patrick Lonergan, *Theatre and Globalization: Irish Drama and the Celtic Tiger Era* (Basingstoke: Palgrave Macmillan, 2009); Dermot Bolger, ed., *Druids, Dudes, and Beauty Queens: The Changing Face of Irish Theatre* (Dublin: New Island, 2001); Anthony Roche, *Contemporary Irish Drama*, 2nd edn (Basingstoke: Palgrave Macmillan, 2009); Miriam Haughton and Mária Kurdi, eds., *Radical Contemporary Theatre Practices by Women in Ireland* (Dublin: Carysfort Press, 2015); Victor Merriman, *Because We Are Poor: Irish Theatre in the 1990s* (Dublin: Carysfort Press, 2011); Fintan Walsh, '*That Was Us*': *Contemporary Irish Theatre and Performance* (London: Oberon, 2013); and Eric Weitz, ed., *The Power of Laughter: Comedy and Contemporary Irish Theatre* (Dublin: Carysfort Press, 2004).

17. On genre fiction in contemporary Ireland, see Brian Cliff, *Irish Crime Fiction* (Basingstoke: Palgrave Macmillan, 2018); Elizabeth Mannion, ed., *The Contemporary Irish Detective Novel* (Basingstoke: Palgrave Macmillan, 2016); Jack Fennell, *Irish Science Fiction* (Liverpool: Liverpool University Press, 2014); Valerie Coughlan and Keith O'Sullivan, eds., *Irish Children's Literature and Culture: New Perspectives on Contemporary Writing* (New York: Routledge, 2010); and Aaron Kelly, *The Thriller and Northern Ireland Since 1969: Utterly Resigned Terror* (Aldershot: Ashgate, 2005).

18. On contemporary literature and the matter of translation, see Emily Apter, *The Translation Zone: A New Comparative Literature* (Princeton, NJ: Princeton University Press, 2006); and Rebecca Walkowitz, *Born Translated: The Contemporary Novel in an Age of World Literature* (New York: Columbia University Press, 2015). For an important overview of translation in the Irish context, see Michael Cronin, *Translating Ireland: Translation, Languages, Cultures* (Cork, Ireland: Cork University Press, 1996).

19. See William J. V. Neill, ed., *Relaunching Titanic: Memory and Marketing in the New Belfast* (New York: Routledge, 2014); and Bree T. Hocking, *The Great Reimagining: Public Art, Urban Space, and the Symbolic Landscapes of a 'New' Northern Ireland* (New York: Berghahn Books, 2015).

20. On contemporary Irish literature, culture, memory, and trauma, see Emilie Pine, *The Politics of Irish Memory: Performing Remembrance in Contemporary Irish Culture* (Basingstoke: Palgrave Macmillan, 2011); Oona Frawley, ed., *Memory Ireland*, 4 vols. (Syracuse, NY: Syracuse University Press, 2010–14); Kathleen Costello-Sullivan, *Trauma and*

Recovery in the Twenty-First-Century Irish Novel (Syracuse, NY: Syracuse University Press, 2018); and Graham Dawson, *Making Peace with the Past: Memories, Trauma, and the Irish Troubles* (Manchester: Manchester University Press, 2007).

21. See Jane Leslie Helleiner, *Irish Travellers: Racism and the Politics of Culture* (Toronto: University of Toronto Press, 2000); Micheál Ó hAodha, *'Insubordinate Irish': Travellers in the Text* (Manchester: Manchester University Press, 2011); and Bryan Fanning, *Racism and Social Change in Ireland*, 2nd edn (Manchester: Manchester University Press, 2012).

22. On issues surrounding Irish culture, race, ethnicity, and migration, see Charlotte McIvor, *Towards a New Interculturalism: Migration and Contemporary Irish Performance* (Basingstoke: Palgrave Macmillan, 2016); Sinéad Moynihan, *'Other People's Diasporas': Negotiating Race in Contemporary Irish and Irish-American Culture* (Syracuse, NY: Syracuse University Press, 2013); John Brannigan, *Race in Modern Irish Literature and Culture* (Edinburgh: Edinburgh University Press, 2009); Borbála Faragó and Moynagh Sullivan, eds., *Facing the Other: Interdisciplinary Studies on Race, Gender, and Social Justice in Ireland* (Newcastle: Cambridge Scholars Publishing, 2008); Amanda Tucker and Moira Casey, *Where Motley Is Worn: Transnational Irish Literatures* (Cork, Ireland: Cork University Press, 2014); Julieann Veronica Ulin, Heather Edwards, and Sean O'Brien, eds., *Race and Immigration in the New Ireland* (Notre Dame, IN: University of Notre Dame Press, 2013); Pilar Villar-Argáiz, ed., *Literary Visions of Multicultural Ireland: The Immigrant in Contemporary Irish Literature* (Manchester: Manchester University Press, 2014); and Pilar Villar-Argáiz, *Irishness on the Margins: Minority and Dissident Identities* (Basingstoke: Palgrave Macmillan, 2018).

23. Major studies in this vein include Seamus Deane, *Celtic Revivals: Essays in Modern Irish Literature, 1880–1980* (London and Boston: Faber and Faber, 1985) and *Strange Country: Modernity and Nationhood in Irish Writing Since 1790* (Oxford: Clarendon Press, 1997); Declan Kiberd, *Inventing Ireland: The Literature of the Modern Nation* (Cambridge, MA: Harvard University Press, 1996) and *Irish Classics* (Cambridge, MA: Harvard University Press, 2001); David Lloyd, *Anomalous States: Irish Writing and the Post-Colonial Moment* (Durham, NC: Duke University Press, 1993), *Ireland After History* (Cork, Ireland: Cork University Press, 1999), *Irish Times: Temporalities of Modernity* (Notre Dame, IN: Field Day/University of Notre Dame Press, 2008), and *Irish Culture and Colonial Modernity, 1800–2000: The Transformation of Oral Space* (Cambridge: Cambridge University Press, 2017); Luke Gibbons, *Transformations in Irish Culture* (Cork, Ireland: Cork University Press, 1996); Marjorie Howes, *Colonial Crossings: Figures in Irish Literary History* (Dublin: Field Day Publications, 2006); Stephen Howe, *Ireland and Empire: Colonial Legacies in Irish History and Culture* (Oxford and New York: Oxford University Press, 2000); and Edna Longley, *The Living Stream* and *Poetry in the Wars* (Newcastle upon Tyne: Bloodaxe Books, 1986).

24. For further consideration of these issues, see the forthcoming collection *The New Irish Studies: Twenty-First-Century Critical Revisions*, ed., Paige Reynolds (Cambridge University Press).
25. James Joyce, *A Portrait of the Artist as a Young Man*, ed., Seamus Deane (London: Penguin, 1992 [1916]), p. 220.

PART I

Times

CHAPTER 1

The Contemporary Conditions of Irish Language Literature

Ailbhe Ní Ghearbhuigh

The National Writers' Workshop was organised on an almost annual basis from 1976, hosting writer workshop weekends at University College Galway.[1] Funded by the Arts Council, the Workshop was seen as 'a radical new development' and every third year its focus would be on literature in Irish.[2] In 1985, director Seán Mac Mathúna chose to concentrate on Irish-language fiction, on the basis that prose writing lagged behind poetry in terms of vibrancy and visibility.[3] Indeed, by the mid-1980s, poetry in Irish seemed to be in relatively rude health, its practitioners building on the accomplishments of the *Innti* poetry journal, which had created a surge of energy on its launch in 1970 by students at University College Cork and which continued to appear sporadically until 1996. During the 1980s and 1990s, a number of poets central to *Innti* published individual collections, contributing to the swell of Irish-language poetry.

The state of prose writing in Irish, by contrast, was bemoaned by several commentators.[4] Bríona Nic Dhiarmada, however, was quick to point out that such complaints diminish the achievements of poetry in Irish.[5] There is an implied hierarchy of genre behind this argument, whereby if prose is, to quote Máirtín Ó Cadhain, 'tathán, coincréad, [agus] clocha saoirsinne an tsaoil' [the concrete base, the mason's cornerstone of life],[6] then poetry is, by comparison, not as robust nor as suited to the serious work of modern existence. Such binaries undermine the ambition of contemporary poetry in Irish and reveal a postcolonial anxiety to replicate the supremacy of the 'great English novel', as though Irish-language literature required legitimatising through 'prestigious' prose writing. Caoimhín Mac Giolla Léith summarises this tension between poetry and prose as follows: 'lyric poetry has been the flagship of twentieth-century Gaelic literature, the vehicle of its most celebrated successes, just as the struggle to establish a credible tradition of realist prose has been the source and the site of its most persistent anxieties'.[7]

This chapter provides a broad overview of literature in Irish from 1980 to 2020. Rather than focus on individual genres, it will treat six dominant developments in contemporary writing: literature drawing on the oral tradition, on ancient literature, and on historical sources, as well as 'taboo-breaking' literature, experimental literature, and writing informed by international literary trends. The infrastructure supporting Irish-language literature – criticism, publishers, awards, journals, organisations, schemes – will also be considered in order to survey the conditions in which this literature emerges.

From the Well: Oral Tradition as a Source

Nuala Ní Dhomhnaill, arguably the most revered of Irish-language writers, has created an astonishing *oeuvre* that simultaneously draws on folklore while ambitiously charting contemporary concerns, among them the postcolonial situation and the trauma of language loss. When awarding Ní Dhomhnaill the Zbigniew Herbert International Literary Award in 2018, Edward Hirsch, chairman of the panel of judges, stated: 'We have chosen a ground-breaking and courageous poet who is both local and international, a poet, who has helped to sustain and remake her language.'[8] Ní Dhomhnaill was Ireland Professor of Poetry from 2011 to 2014 and her work has been widely translated into English and other languages.[9] Robert Welch, writing on literature in Ireland since 1960, contends that Ní Dhomhnaill does not exploit the Gothic possibilities in Irish myth 'for gratuitous entertainment'; rather, in Welch's terms, she develops 'significant psychic and psychological formations that come out of Celtic tradition but which connect with contemporary anxieties concerning motherhood, nurturing, the responsibility we carry with regard to nature'.[10] Folkloric personages such as the goddess Mór, the Cailleach [The Hag], the Bean an Leasa [The Woman from the Otherworld], and the Murúcha [Merfolk] recur throughout her work, forming an intricate tableau onto which the poet projects modern-day anxieties. Ní Dhomhnaill is also innovative in terms of form: Bríona Nic Dhiarmada argues that, in collections such as *Feis* (1991) and *Cead Aighnis* (1998), Ní Dhomhnaill extends 'the lyric form to what can be best described as a form of contemporary epic'.[11]

Song, of course, is also a *sine qua non* of the oral tradition, influencing not only Ní Dhomhnaill, but also writers like Cathal Ó Searcaigh and Mícheál Ó Conghaile. Ní Dhomhnaill's love poems draw extensively on the folk-song tradition, producing poems that are 'forthright and unabashed in their explicit treatment of sexual encounters'.[12] Ó Searcaigh, meanwhile, exploits the tropes of traditional love songs in order to explore homoerotic longing, achieving in poems such as 'Ceann Dubh Dílis' ['Dear Dark-Haired Love'] subversive renderings of songs from the folk tradition. Mícheál Ó Conghaile, as Pádraig Ó Siadhail points out, has a similar objective, referencing 'Dónall Óg', a song about a girl abandoned by her male lover, and repackaging it 'as a lament by John Paul deserted by his same-sex lover'.[13]

Éilís Ní Dhuibhne also draws on the world of mythology and Irish folklore in her play, *Dún na mBan Trí Thine* [The Women's Fairy Fort is on Fire] (1998), whose heroine, Léiní, retreats from chaotic modern life to 'the Otherworld, that place of caprice and of sensual fulfilment where aging is suspended, to stage the crisis of [...] a wife and mother who is struggling to be an artist'.[14] In addition, Angela Bourke, perhaps prompted by her research in folklore, has written a number of short stories drawing on folk motifs that incorporate elements of magic realism as much as they comment on contemporary society.[15]

Retellings and Adaptations: Early Irish Literature

Early Irish literature, extant in manuscript form from earlier centuries, continues to provide raw material for contemporary writers. The conviction that these texts can renew and sustain modern literature motivated Leabhar Breac, a small publishing house based in Connemara, to publish mythological sagas in accessible Modern Irish. Among them are *Conaire Mór* (2017) and *Tuatha Dé Danann* (2018) by Diarmuid Johnson and *An Tromdhámh* (2018) by Feargal Ó Béarra. Leabhar Breac's founder, Darach Ó Scolaí, also produced his own version of *Táin Bó Cuailgne* (2017), that great Irish epic, insisting that it is neither a translation, nor a scholarly edition, but rather 'síneadh eile lenár dtraidisiún scéalaíochta, síneadh le hobair na scríobhaithe a bhreac an scéal i Leabhar na hUidhre agus i lámhscríbhinní eile le linn na Meánaoise' [a further extension of our storytelling tradition, an extension of the work of the scribes who wrote out the story in The Book of the Dun Cow and in other manuscripts during the Middle Ages].[16]

In *Táinrith* (2013), Biddy Jenkinson similarly expands the *Táin*, albeit in a 'female-centered, multi-layered and explicitly corrective retelling' of the epic.[17] A text that might be classified as prose poetry, it is a modern-day riff that addresses issues of matriarchy, authority, and heroism with a healthy measure of humour. Jenkinson's work is immersed in the Gaelic world and is wholly cognisant of 'the aristocratic learned tradition that stretches from the old Irish sagas to the bardic court poetry of early modern Ireland before the upheavals of the seventeenth century and the language shift from Irish to English that followed'.[18] Her work attempts to refute the notion that the past and present are irretrievably ruptured, instead presenting a world where history and the present are irrevocably intermeshed.[19] This approach is apparent in Jenkinson's remodelling of Mis, the wild mountainy woman who is mollified by the music of Dubh Ruis.[20] However, as Edyta Lehmann points out, 'the poet manages to avoid a simple denunciation of the patriarchal myth. Instead, she makes use of the multiplicity of voices inherent in the original text, exploiting the tension resulting from the confrontation of ideologies.'[21]

Another Old Irish tale provides the fabric for the poem 'Echtrae Chondlai' ['Conlae's Adventure'] by Aifric Mac Aodha, into which, in a poetic prologue, she weaves a comparison with James Joyce's short story 'Eveline'.[22] Mac Aodha, one of a younger generation of Irish-language poets,[23] also reworks Greek mythology in her work, notably in the poetic sequence 'Scéal Syrinx'.[24] The story of Deirdre and Naoise[25] has inspired many writers in English, among them Lady Gregory, Yeats, and Synge. In imagining Deirdre's first utterance, Doireann Ní Ghríofa's poem 'Céad Siolla Dheirdre' ['Deirdre: Her First Syllable'] resonates with an earlier poem by Máire Mhac an tSaoi, 'Labhrann Deirdre' ['Deirdre Speaks']. But whereas Mhac an tSaoi's Deirdre rationalises her choice to escape with Naoise, the subject of Ní Ghríofa's poem is a primal roar from the womb. Male poets have also taken licence to imagine the voices of female figures of mythology, as in Colm Breathnach's poetry collection *Scáthach* (1994), which uses the figures of Cúchulainn and the female warrior, Scáthach, to probe and problematise gender.[26] Worthy of note here, too, is Pádraig Ó Cíobháin, whose stylised, intertextual prose informs not only his retelling of Medieval Irish stories, *Dréachta Chrích Fódla* (2007), but also his recent novels.

Historical Sources

Historical literary fiction is a significant genre within contemporary prose writing in Irish.[27] While realist literature set in modern-day English-speaking cities in Ireland is sometimes called into question for its lack of believability,[28] historical fiction can circumvent this challenge by situating the events in the Gaelic-speaking Ireland of the past. Among the most critically acclaimed writers of historical fiction in Irish is Liam Mac Cóil. Many of his works include a transnational dimension, for example the multilayered *Fontenoy* (2005), which gives a fictional account by Captain Seán Ó Raghallaigh of the Battle of Fontenoy in Belgium in 1745 as told to a French scribe. Mac Cóil has also published two books of a trilogy set in early sixteenth-century Ireland and Europe, *An Litir* (2011) and *I dTír Strainséartha* (2014), which emphasise the close ties Gaelic Ireland had with the continent in the early modern period. Mac Cóil's publisher, Darach Ó Scolaí of Leabhar Breac, has also produced a historical novel set in Ireland and mainland Europe; the events in *An Cléireach* (2007) take place in the mid-seventeenth century against the backdrop of brutality that accompanied the Cromwellian invasion of Ireland.

An Fear Dána (1993) by Alan Titley centres on the life and poetry of the medieval poet Muireadhach Albanach Ó Dálaigh. The events are narrated by Ó Dálaigh himself – described by one critic as 'assertive, arrogant, lovable' – and the title connotes both 'a bold man' and 'a man of poetry'.[29] This remarkable postmodern novel is noted for its playful intertextuality, which ranges far beyond the thirteenth-century Ireland of Ó Dálaigh. In just a two-page sample, Bríona Nic Dhiarmada notes the many references to and jibes at poets from the Fianna cycle and syllabic poetry, to the eighteenth-century writer Aogán Ó Rathaille and the twentieth-century poet, Michael Davitt.[30] Although he lists his scholarly sources, Titley nonetheless insists that *An Fear Dána* is a fictionalised work. Structurally, it is a finely-wrought *oeuvre*: each of the seven chapters is divided into seven sections, the final section of each chapter being a poem. His later historical novel *An Bhean Feasa* (2014) is written entirely in verse and recounts, through the testimony of various voices, the life of an Irishwoman, Ann 'Goody' Glover, who was hanged as a witch in Boston in 1688.

Máire Mhac an tSaoi draws on the life and poetry of the 3rd Earl of Desmond, Gerald Fitzgerald (1335–98) in *Scéal Ghearóid Iarla* (2011), writing in elegiac and vivid prose. Mhac an tSaoi is, of course, primarily recognised for the excellence of her poetry, yet in an interview about *Scéal Ghearóid Iarla*, she maintains that she always wrote both poetry and prose, referring to her work in the civil service: 'tuilleamh mo bheatha ab ea an prós!' [prose was earning my living!] whereas poetry was her 'poll éalaithe' [means of escape].[31]

Contemporary Irish-language poetry, too, has delved into the past. Caitríona Ní Chléirchín has written a suite of poems inspired by the Flight of the Earls (1607), the most striking of them being 'Scaradh na gCompánach' [The Parting of the Ways], in which she dramatises the parting words of the Countess of Tyrone as she departs, forever, the shores of Ireland.[32] Biddy Jenkinson's long poem 'Gleann Maoiliúra' recounts the story of Róis Ní Thuathail who was married to Fiach Mac Aoidh Ó Broin, the Lord of Ranelagh, who was later executed by Elizabeth I.[33] Louis de Paor describes it as 'a love poem of considerable violence executed with a high degree of emotional and psychological conviction'.[34] It is worth noting that both Ní Chléirchín and Jenkinson imagine an aspect of Irish history from the perspective of women who witnessed significant events, thereby retroactively giving voice to female figures who left no written account of their own.

Society in Transition: Breaking Taboos

More broadly, a notable development over the period in question is the legitimisation of the female experience for literary treatment, particularly in the case of poetry. In the 1980s 'the strongest and most distinctive voices to be heard in Irish-language literature were arguably women poets [. . .] who were speaking in what was then a zeitgeist alive with feminist struggles'.[35] Among the poets who produced significant collections during this decade are Ní Dhomhnaill, Mhac an tSaoi, Jenkinson, Áine Ní Ghlinn, Deirdre Brennan, and Eithne Strong. This surge of women writing about subjects previously considered taboo – for instance, miscarriage, child abuse, and incest – reflects but one of the many transitions within Irish society since 1980. Brian Ó Conchubhair notes that '[a]ll that was once repressed and censored floods forth in abundance in the contemporary Irish novel', before specifying clerical celibacy, religious belief, child adoption scandals, homosexuality, drug smuggling, human bondage, devil worship, and sexual fantasy as among the once forbidden topics being explored by contemporary writers.[36]

Dramatists, too, tackled questions that Irish society had hitherto eschewed: Jenkinson's play 'Beannaithe' (2018), commissioned by the theatre company Guthanna Binne Síoraí, challenges the ban on women priests in the Catholic Church. 'Baoite' (2018) by Darach Mac an Iomaire, commissioned by the Abbey Theatre in partnership with An Taibhdhearc, examines the effects of fracking on a small fishing community and explores in vitro fertilisation and mental health issues. Liam Ó Muirthile's play *Fear an Tae* (1995), set in a psychiatric hospital, probes issues of addiction and alcoholism and portrays 'the internal conflict between intellect and instinct, logic and desire'.[37] His earlier work, *Tine Chnámh* (1984), a long dramatic poem, depicts the tensions between the lure of earthy debauchery, especially female sexual desire, and the gatekeepers of civic morality in dramatic voice. Similarly, Séamus Barra Ó Súilleabháin uses the figure of Dónall Dubh, a shadowy harbinger of death, as an alter ego to explore intoxication, drug (ab)use, and existential despair in *Beatha Dhónaill Dhuibh* (2016), his fine debut poetry collection.

Popular fiction also engages in taboo-busting, and one author in particular has attracted quite a large readership since his first novel, *Súil le Breith* (1983) [*Lovers* (1991)]. In this novel and in *Cíocras* (1991) [*Celibates* (1993)], Pádraig Standún explores clerical celibacy and extra-marital sex, a potentially delicate topic at the time, even more so given that the author is himself a Catholic priest. These works anticipated the furore that surrounded Bishop Eamonn Casey, who, it was revealed in 1992, had fathered a child with his secret lover, Annie Murphy. Similarly in touch with the *zeitgeist*, the novel *Cion Mná* [*A Woman's Love*] dealt with a lesbian love affair and was published in 1993, the same year that homosexuality was decriminalised in the Republic of Ireland. As the extent of clerical sexual abuse was uncovered in the 1990s and 2000s, Standún did not baulk at addressing it in his work: *Díbirt Dé* (2007) depicts the sheltering of a convicted paedophile priest in a rural parish. While Standún and other contemporary writers portray various societal transitions in Ireland, it should nonetheless be noted that contentious themes have previously been treated in Irish-language prose, such as sexual assault, rape, extra-marital pregnancy, and marital breakdown.[38]

Cathal Ó Searcaigh also confronts issues such as domestic violence, incest, rape, and infanticide, most notably in the poem 'Gort na gCnámh' ['The Field of Bones']. It is especially in terms of his homoerotic poetry that Ó Searcaigh can be considered 'taboo-breaking', as his work acknowledges the existence of alternate sexualities within the boundaries of the Gaeltacht. Frank Sewell observes that the poem 'Laoi Chumainn' ['Serenade'] marks 'the shift in Ó Searcaigh's poetry to even more heightened sensation and to frank representation of sexuality'[39] building on the aforementioned 'Ceann Dubh Dílis' ['Dear Dark-Haired Love']. Similarly, Mícheál Ó Conghaile's novel *Sna Fir* (1999), written in the realist mode, is 'as honest and as explicit a description of a young man's initiation and integration into gay community life as one is likely to find in any language'.[40]

Experimental Modes

To consider Ó Conghaile exclusively as a queer writer would not do justice to the range and versatility of his work. A proponent of both realist and anti-realist prose, his short fiction demonstrates his 'tremendous ability to weave together an accessible storyline and aspects of non-realism and surrealism to create a fictional world that is both engaging and menacing'.⁴¹ These achievements in the traditional and experimental modes are particularly notable in *An Fear a Phléasc* (1997), *An Fear Nach nDéanann Gáire* (2003), and *Diabhlaíocht Dé* (2015), the latter drawing especially on biblical motifs. Dara Ó Conaola's short fiction collections, *Mo Chathair Ghríobháin agus Scéalta Eile* (1981) and *Amuigh Liom Féin* (1988), are marked by their commitment to magic realism, as is the prose of Daithí Ó Muirí, such as in the Borgesian *Cogaí* (2002). The anthology of contemporary fiction *Gearrscéalta ár Linne* (2006) contains a number of stories in the surrealist vein, confirming the popularity of this mode in Irish writing. In his introduction, Brian Ó Conchubhair notes that many of the characters in contemporary short fiction are 'ar seachrán, go spioradálta, go fisiciúil, go meafarach agus go samhailteach' [spiritually, physically, metaphorically, and imaginarily adrift].⁴² While writing in a minority language may engender a certain sense of isolation from the mainstream, such isolation could also be understood as emancipatory: Máirín Nic Eoin posits that the experimentation in prose that characterises the 1980s and 1990s may indicate 'a freedom of expression' resulting from a sense of 'writing from the margin, independent of market forces'.⁴³

An early example of an experimental novel from the period in question is *Cuaifeach mo Londubh Buí* (1983) by Séamus Mac Annaidh, which is noteworthy not only for the author's precocity (he was 23 at the time of its publication), but also for swimming against the current of realism that was typical of Irish-language prose at the time. Titley describes it as 'a storm of a book linking prehistoric myth with lexicographical *séances* with student life with the Donegal Gaeltacht with rock bands with current politics in a thin wobbly interweaving narrative which went everywhere and nowhere and beyond'.⁴⁴ It was the first of a trilogy, which also includes *Mo Dhá Mhicí* (1986) and *Rubble na Mickies* (1990), and the most successful commercially and critically of the three novels. Another exemplar of the experimental novel is Liam Mac Cóil's metafictional *An Dochtúir Áthais* (1994), 'a dramatic exploration of Freudian theory, and in particular of the role of the narrative in personal identity'.⁴⁵ Colm Ó Ceallacháin's collection *I dTír Mhilis na mBeo* (2017) includes a modernist component that takes its cue from the French author George Perec's novel *La disparition* (1969). In Ó Ceallacháin's short lipogram, he undertook to only use words containing the letter 'i'.

There were a number of experimental voices in poetry, many of which were first published in the early days of the journal *Innti*. Noteworthy among them was Tomás Mac Síomóin, whose poetry was commended for its 'capacity for formal experiment that is unique in modern Irish', although his focus has shifted towards prose – both fiction and non-fiction – since the 1990s.[46] The poetry of Michael Davitt, the founding editor of *Innti*, is characterised by linguistic experimentation too, but it also extends boundaries in terms of form and subject matter. Given that these semantic ventures are based on the Irish language, it is difficult to render their originality in English. His work can 'surprise and sometimes shock readers by its appropriation into Irish of aspects of contemporary urban reality which had been previously considered the exclusive preserve of English'.[47] The range of Davitt's poetry is quite striking, commanding varying registers, from tender lyrics such as 'Chugat' ['To You'], to the unconcealed anger in 'Deora do Mheiriceá', to the existential angst in 'Paranóia'. The influence of the Beat poets, Bob Dylan, and e.e. cummings is particularly evident in his early work.

International Influences

Like Davitt, two other 'core' members of the *Innti* group, Liam Ó Muirthile and Gabriel Rosenstock, openly embrace international cultural influences. In a review of Rosenstock's first collection in *The Irish Times*, the poet Seán Ó Ríordáin remarked upon its sophisticated international and multilingual dimensions.[48] Rosenstock, more so than any of his contemporaries, rebuffs any notion of being pigeonholed as an 'Irish' writer, declaring: 'I am much more at home in Isaac Bashevis Singer's descriptions of Jewish Poland than I am in Ó Cadhain's Conamara. I'm not sure if I could ever live in the Gaeltacht, for instance, or be fully integrated in any Western society. I am nowhere happier, indeed, than in Kerala, India.'[49] His work is particularly informed by his fascination with Eastern culture and philosophies, specifically through his adaption of the haiku form to Irish and his prolific work as a translator. The sheer abundance of his output, however, runs the risk of overwhelming critics and publishers, who find it difficult to keep pace with the steady stream of diverse and multifarious projects.

Ó Muirthile's knowledge of French language and culture has prompted him to consider notions of identity throughout the French-speaking world. The novel *An Colm Bán* (2014) contains an appendix of poems (in Irish) written by an imagined poet of Senegal origin in the idiom of slam poetry. The novel is set in West Cork and Paris and is as much a tracing of ancestors as a tale of a *flâneur* in the French capital. Ó Muirthile's francophilia is also evident in his work as a translator, with a majestic translation of Rimbaud's *Le bateau ivre* appearing posthumously from Cois Life.[50]

A later *Innti* alumnus, Louis de Paor is another poet who looks outward, a perspective informed, no doubt, by the time he spent in Australia from 1987 to 1994.[51] In more recent work, he pays homage to American poets such as cummings and Galway Kinnell. Such references demonstrate not only de Paor's own receptivity to the work of others, but can also further illuminate the work of the poets he engages with. An example is 'Galway Kinnell sa Ghaillimh' ['Galway Kinnell in Galway'] which riffs on Kinnell's poem 'Saint Francis and the Sow'. Kinnell's phrase 'though sometimes it is necessary | to reteach a thing its loveliness' is repeated as a refrain throughout de Paor's poem, thereby adding to the depiction of the elder American poet as the benevolent Saint Francis.[52] In 'Luck', which takes place in a New York subway train, the speaker attempts to concentrate on reading a Langston Hughes poem in an effort to compose himself amid the unfolding racial drama around him. It is a brief meditation on the purpose of poetry in a brutal world that ends with a flawless translation to Irish of Hughes's poem. Notions of mediation in translation within an Irish-language context will be treated in a later chapter by Ríona Ní Fhrighil, but it is nonetheless important to note here that female poets also actively engage with international literature to enrich their own poetic projects, most notably through translation from European literature, as in the work of Máire Mhac an tSaoi and Nuala Ní Dhomhnaill.

Supporting Infrastructure

Beginning in the 1980s, scholars began to apply various critical theories to Irish-language literature, what Pádraig Ó Siadhail describes as the 'opening up of the field of critical studies in Irish'.[53] *Téacs agus Comhthéacs: gnéithe de chritic na Gaeilge* (1998), edited by Máire Ní Annracháin and Bríona Nic Dhiarmada, is a prime example of such engagement, albeit one aimed squarely at an academic audience. The poetry of Ní Dhomhnaill has received ample critical attention; aside from many individual articles and chapters, her work has been the focus of three monographs: *Tionscnamh Filíochta Nuala Ní Dhomhnaill* (1997) by Pádraig de Paor, *Téacs Baineann, Téacs Mná* (2005) by Bríona Nic Dhiarmada, and *Briathra, Béithe agus Banfhilí: Filíocht Eavan Boland agus Nuala Ní Dhomhnaill* (2008) by Ríona

Ní Fhrighil. Máirín Nic Eoin produced an astute study of cultural displacement in Irish literature, *Trén bhFearann Breac: An Díláithriú Cultúir agus Nualitríocht na Gaeilge* (2005), in which she emphatically argues for applying postcolonial theory to modern literature in Irish. The future of academic publishing is quite bleak, however, since the closure of An Clóchomhar (1954–2008), which published 101 titles in its research series 'Imleabhair Thaighde'.[54] Cló Iar-Chonnacht acquired the rights to the research series imprint, but a decrease in funding for academic publishing, as well as the cost and labour involved in producing monographs to a high standard, continue to be prohibitive factors.

The challenges faced by general Irish-language publishers are quite substantial given the small readership and poor distribution of books. Nevertheless, the 1980s saw the founding of new publishing houses in Dublin and in the Connemara Gaeltacht. Cló Iar-Chonnacht was originally established by the writer Mícheál Ó Conghaile to promote local writers from Connemara, though it now casts its net further afield.[55] Coiscéim, founded by Pádraig Ó Snodaigh in Dublin, initially placed a particular emphasis on poetry, but has since published every conceivable genre, somewhat indiscriminately: 1,350 books by the end of 2018. Several publishing houses were established in the 1990s, namely Leabhar Breac (1994), Cois Life (1995–2019), and Cló Mhaigh Eo (1995–2013), the latter of which developed the graphic novel in Irish, which has since become a staple of Irish-language publishing. Cois Life produced a wide range of books and audiobooks to a high standard for adult learners, academics, students, and children alike, totalling 155 titles by the end of 2019. However, it announced in July 2018 that it would be winding down, citing serious concerns about literacy levels and the marginalisation of literature in academic curricula. Other challenges include mounting administration, difficulty in sourcing skilled editors, the continued shrinking of an already small readership, and the dearth of reviews in newspapers.[56] While the monthly journals *Comhar* and *Feasta* feature reviews in each issue, Irish-language books receive little attention in national newspapers and only occasional coverage in broadcast media.

There are, however, a number of endeavours designed to address the challenge of ensuring the visibility of contemporary literature in Irish. 'Love Leabhar Gaeilge' is an initiative by Cumann na bhFoilsitheoirí [The Publishers' Association] to promote Irish-language books in bookshops and on social media. It was also the sponsor of the Irish-language Book of the Year Award at the An Post Irish Book Awards in 2018, the first year of the award. The significance of high-profile competitions should not be underestimated: Diarmuid Johnson's *Tuatha Dé Danann: Seilbh Inse Fódhla* was named Irish Language Book of the Year in 2018 and a second print run was announced at the end of 2018, due in no small part to the publicity arising from the An Post Award. While the annual literary competitions at Oireachtas na Samhna are among the most prestigious awards for a writer in Irish, these awards rarely make an impression on the Anglosphere.

The mission of Imram, an annual literary festival established in Dublin in 2004, is to bring contemporary Irish-language literature to audiences in the capital, often commissioning musicians or visual artists to enrich literary readings and increase the accessibility of the work. Since its inception, Liam Carson has been at the helm as festival director and curator, and it is largely to his credit that original writing in Irish, or the songs of Leonard Cohen and Bob Dylan translated to Irish, have attracted significant audiences. Some of its more successful shows have toured in Ireland and Paris.

An online archive of living Irish writers is another initiative to promote the visibility of Irish-language literature. 'Portráidí', a project instigated by Foras na Gaeilge in collaboration with the photographer Máire Uí Mhaicín, features portraits of 136 contemporary writers (including academics) on the website www.portraidi.ie, with more writers being added annually. This enterprise is now facilitated by Comhar, which published a selection of the portraits in book form.[57]

It is extremely difficult for any writer in Irish to earn a living from their creative output. Aosdána, an association of esteemed artists across various disciplines, provides a small *cnuas* or annual stipend to its 250 members. As of the beginning of 2019, only six members are known primarily for their writing in Irish.[58] The Arts Council supports Irish-language writers through the annual artists' bursaries scheme, although these are generally one-off awards. Most Irish-language writers work, or have worked, in other professions, as teachers, translators, civil servants, or in the media.

Conclusion

There are many writers who do not fit neatly or justifiably into the dominant trends outlined above, although their work merits critical attention. There are those with strong ties to a particular Gaeltacht, such as Joe Steve Ó Neachtain, Josie Ó Guairim (1956–2017), Proinsias Mac a' Bhaird, Dairena Ní Chinnéide, Simon Ó Faoláin, Ceaití Ní Bheildiúin, and Bríd Ní Mhóráin, the last of whose work is marked by a deep appreciation of the traditions and landscapes of Munster. There are female fiction writers, such as Éilis Ní Anluain and the crime novelist Anna Heussaff, and prose writers living abroad, Pádraig Ó Siadhail and Alex Hijmans, in Canada and Brazil respectively, and a plethora of bilingual poets including Michael Hartnett (1941–99), Celia de Fréine, Gréagóir Ó Dúill, Paddy Bushe, and the macaronic shape-shifting Gearóid Mac Lochlainn. Perhaps now more than ever, there is a great capacity for diversity in contemporary literature in Irish, confirming Nic Dhiarmada's musings on Irish-language writing into the new millennium: 'Irish-language texts can equally support reactionary ideas and progressive ideas, can be pre-modern, modern or postmodern, can be folk-tales or treatises on quantum physics, can be handbooks on IT, volumes of poetry or postmodern novels.'[59]

Given the turbulent conditions of publishing in Irish, the sheer variety of books being published in Irish today is laudable in itself, perhaps all the more so seeing as access to the printing press was denied to the Irish language until much later than in the case of other languages.[60] Volume does not equate to quality, of course, but it is remarkable that writers continue to choose Irish as their creative medium into the twenty-first century, each generation producing fine work across various genres, continuing a tradition that can be traced as far back as the sixth century. The case of contemporary Irish-language literature is comparable, perhaps, to the miraculous floating 'bothán' or 'hut' that Liam Ó Muirthile describes in his poem of the same name:

tráth a bheidh do bhothán	when your hut
ar luascadh san uisce	will rock in the water
ag teacht ar shnámhacht	finding a tricky
ghuagach idir a mheácan soladach	buoyancy between its solid weight
is an toirt aeir faoi á iompar	and the volume of air beneath that's
[...]	carrying it
neomat amháin gan bonn chun seasaimh	[...]
is neomat eile ag bairilleáil sa snámh	one minute with no footing at all
in aghaidh easa.	the next barrelling away
	against the waterfall.[61]

Notes

1. University College Galway has been known as National University of Ireland Galway since 1997.
2. G. D., 'Peter Bielenberg', *The Irish Times*, 26 March 2001, p. 17.

3. Laurence Cassidy, 'Brollach', in Seán Mac Mathúna, ed., *Ceardlann '85* (Dublin: Coiscéim, 1988), p. 1.
4. See Alan Titley, 'Clocha Saoirsinne agus Bláithíní an tSléibhe', *Comhar* 51.5 (1992), pp. 40, 42–52, 54–5; Gréagóir Ó Dúill, 'An Gearrscéal sa Ghaeilge', *Comhar* 53.4 (1994), p. 4.
5. See Bríona Nic Dhiarmada, 'Review of *An Fear Dána* and *Éagnairc*', *Fortnight*, 330 (Jul.–Aug., 1994), pp. 29–31; and 'Irish-Language Literature in the New Millennium', in Margaret Kelleher and Philip O'Leary, eds., *The Cambridge History of Irish Literature, Vol. II: 1890–2000* (Cambridge: Cambridge University Press, 2006), pp. 600–27.
6. Máirtín Ó Cadhain, *Páipéir Bhána agus Páipéir Bhreaca* (Dublin: An Clóchomhar, 1969), p. 37. Translation by Declan Kiberd in *The Irish Writer and the World* (Cambridge: Cambridge University Press, 2005), p. 108.
7. Caoimhín Mac Giolla Léith, 'Metaphor and Metamorphosis in the Poetry of Nuala Ní Dhomhnaill', *Éire-Ireland*, 35.1&2 (2000), pp. 150–72 (p. 160).
8. For further information on the award, see: www.fundacjaherberta.com/en/news/item/542-the-zbigniew-herbert-international-literary-award-2018 [accessed 13 December 2018].
9. Among them, French, German, Polish, Italian, Norwegian, Estonian, Turkish, and Japanese.
10. Robert Welch, *The Cold of May Day Monday: An Approach to Irish Literary History* (Oxford: Oxford University Press, 2014), p. 275.
11. Nic Dhiarmada, 'Irish-Language Literature in the New Millennium', p. 604.
12. Louis de Paor, 'Contemporary Poetry in Irish: 1940–2000', in Margaret Kelleher and Philip O'Leary, eds., *The Cambridge History of Irish Literature, Vol. II: 1890–2000* (Cambridge: Cambridge University Press, 2006), pp. 317–56 (p. 340).
13. Pádraig Ó Siadhail, 'Odd Man Out: Mícheál Ó Conghaile and Contemporary Irish Language Queer Prose', *The Canadian Journal of Irish Studies*, 36.1 (2010), pp. 143–61 (p. 150).
14. Anthony Roche, 'Staging the Liminal in Éilís Ní Dhuibhne's *Dún na mBan Trí Thine* (The Fort of the Fairy Women Is on Fire)', in Melissa Sihra, ed., *Women in Irish Drama: A Century of Authorship and Representation* (Basingstoke: Palgrave Macmillan, 2007), pp. 175–85 (p. 176).
15. See Angela Bourke, 'Iníon Rí an Oileáin Dhorcha', *Oghma*, 3 (1991), pp. 17–23; and ' Iníon Rí na Cathrach Deirge', in Eoghan Ó hAnluain, ed., *Leath na Spéire* (Dublin: An Clóchomhar, 1992), pp. 108–14.
16. Darach Ó Scolaí, *Táin Bó Cuailnge* (Inverin: Leabhar Breac, 2017), p. 7. English translations are the author's own unless otherwise indicated.
17. Caitlín Nic Íomhair, '*Mis* by Biddy Jenkinson', *The Stinging Fly*, 32.2 (2015–16), pp. 6–9 (p. 9).
18. Louis de Paor, ed., *Leabhar na hAthghabhála/Poems of Repossession* (Northumberland and Inverin: Bloodaxe Books and Cló Iar-Chonnacht, 2016), p. 417.

19. Máire de Búrca, 'Biddy Jenkinson', in Ríona Ní Fhrighil, ed., *Filíocht Chomhaimseartha na Gaeilge* (Dublin: Cois Life, 2010), pp. 167–80 (p. 173).
20. Biddy Jenkinson, *Mis* (Dublin: Coiscéim, 2002).
21. Edyta Lehmann, '"I Am a Clean Whirlwind from the Far Seas": Biddy Jenkinson's Conversation with the *Romance of Mis and Dubh Rois*', *New Hibernia Review/Iris Éireannach Nua*, 18.1 (2014), pp. 58–73 (pp. 72–3).
22. Aifric Mac Aodha, *Gabháil Syrinx* (Dingle: An Sagart, 2010), pp. 21–2. See also David Wheatley's translation in *Foreign News* (Oldcastle, Co. Meath: Gallery Press, 2017), pp. 88–9.
23. See for example, Peter Fallon and Aifric Mac Aodha, eds., *Calling Cards* (Oldcastle, Co. Meath: Gallery Press, 2018).
24. Mac Aodha, *Gabháil Syrinx*, pp. 12–14.
25. Also known as 'Longes mac nUislenn' or 'Oidheadh Chloinne Uisnigh'.
26. De Paor, 'Contemporary Poetry in Irish: 1940–2000', p. 349.
27. See Síle Ní Choincheannain, 'An tÚrscéal Stairiúil sa Ghaeilge 1993–2013' (unpublished doctoral thesis, Mary Immaculate College, Limerick, 2018).
28. For further discussion of this point, see Máirín Nic Eoin, *Trén bhFearann Breac* (Dublin: Cois Life, 2005), pp. 419–25; and Nic Dhiarmada, 'Review of *An Fear Dána* and *Éagnairc*', pp. 29–31.
29. James J. Blake, 'Present-Day Irish-Language Fiction', *New Hibernia Review/ Iris Éireannach Nua*, 5.3 (2001), pp. 128–41 (p. 132).
30. Nic Dhiarmada, 'Review of *An Fear Dána* and *Éagnairc*', p. 31.
31. Gaelchultúr, 'Interview with Máire Mhac an tSaoi', 18 January 2012: www.youtube.com/watch?reload=9&v=3-SjfIu1YI8&feature=youtu.be [accessed 14 December 2018].
32. See Caitríona Ní Chléirchín, *An Bhrídeach Sí* (Dublin: Coiscéim, 2014), pp. 25–9, p. 26. See Peter Fallon's translation of this poem in Fallon and Mac Aodha, eds., *Calling Cards*, pp. 44–5.
33. For a bilingual version of the poem, see de Paor, ed., *Leabhar na hAthghabhála/Poems of Repossession*, pp. 436–45.
34. De Paor, 'Contemporary Poetry in Irish: 1940–2000', p. 343.
35. Nic Dhiarmada, 'Irish-Language Literature in the New Millennium', p. 622.
36. Brian Ó Conchubhair, 'The Novel in Irish since 1950: From National Narrative to Counter-Narrative', *The Yearbook of English Studies: Irish Writing Since 1950*, 35 (2005), pp. 212–23 (p. 219).
37. Máirín Nic Eoin, 'Contemporary Prose and Drama in Irish: 1940–2000', in Margaret Kelleher and Philip O'Leary, eds., *The Cambridge History of Irish Literature, Vol. II: 1890–2000* (Cambridge: Cambridge University Press, 2006), pp. 270–316 (p. 305).
38. For discussion of novels such as *Cúrsaí Thomáis* (1927), *An Fánaí* (1927), *Cailín na Gruaige Duinne* (1932), and *Tonn Tuile* (1947), see Philip O'Leary, 'The Irish Renaissance, 1890–1940: Literature in Irish', in Margaret Kelleher and Philip O'Leary, eds., *The Cambridge History of Irish Literature Volume II: 1890–2000* (Cambridge: Cambridge University Press, 2006), pp. 226–69 (pp. 254–6).

39. Frank Sewell, *Modern Irish Poetry: A New Alhambra* (Oxford: Oxford University Press, 2000), p. 95.
40. Máirín Nic Eoin, 'Prose Writing in Irish Today', in Caoilfhionn Nic Pháidín and Seán Ó Cearnaigh, eds., *A New View of the Irish Language* (Dublin: Cois Life, 2008), pp. 131–9 (p. 134).
41. Ó Siadhail, 'Odd Man Out: Mícheál Ó Conghaile and Contemporary Irish Literature', p. 148.
42. Brian Ó Conchubhair, *Gearrscéalta ár Linne* (Inverin: Cló Iar-Chonnacht, 2006), p. 13.
43. Nic Eoin, 'Contemporary Prose and Drama in Irish: 1940–2000', p. 294.
44. Alan Titley, *Nailing Theses: Selected Essays* (Belfast: Lagan Press, 2011), p. 229.
45. Nic Eoin, 'Prose Writing in Irish Today', p. 134.
46. De Paor, *Leabhar na hAthghabhála/Poems of Repossession*, p. 216.
47. Louis de Paor, 'Disappearing Language: Translations from the Irish', *Poetry Ireland Review*, 51 (1996), pp. 61–8 (p. 66).
48. Seán Ó Ríordáin, 'File Nua', *The Irish Times*, 2 February 1974, p. 12.
49. Gabriel Rosenstock, 'How I Discovered Irish or How Irish Discovered Me', in Ciarán Mac Murchaidh, ed., *'Who Needs Irish?' Reflections on the Importance of the Irish Language Today* (Dublin: Veritas Publications, 2004), pp. 83–93 (p. 84).
50. The Rimbaud translation is part of a series of poetry collections by European poets translated to Irish, *File ar Fhile*, published by Cois Life in 2019. The series includes Antonella Anedda translated from Italian by Eiléan Ní Chuilleanáin, Antonio Machado translated from Spanish by Tomás Mac Síomóin, Andrée Chedid translated from French by Ailbhe Ní Ghearbhuigh, and Erich Fried translated from German by Gabriel Rosenstock.
51. De Paor was co-editor with Michael Davitt on issues 9–11 and editor of issues 12 and 13.
52. Galway Kinnell, *Three Books: Body Rags; Mortal Acts, Mortal Words; The Past* (Boston, MA and New York: Houghton Mifflin Company, 2002 [1980]), p. 81.
53. Ó Siadhail, 'Odd Man Out', p. 147.
54. A full list of titles is available at: www.cic.ie/images/uploads/common/pdf File_76200918177_7060.pdf [accessed 14 February 2019].
55. Pádraig Ó Siadhail, 'An Fear Aniar: An Interview with Mícheál Ó Conghaile', *The Canadian Journal of Irish Studies*, 31.2 (2005), pp. 54–9.
56. A statement from the company directors outlining the reasons for winding down is available at: www.coislife.ie/raiteas-o-cois-life/ [accessed 8 December 2018].
57. See Liam Mac Amhlaigh, ed., *Portráidí* (Dublin: Comhar Teo., 2016).
58. They are Nuala Ní Dhomhnaill, Mícheál Ó Conghaile, Criostóir Ó Floinn, Joe Steve Ó Neachtain, Cathal Ó Searcaigh, and Gabriel Rosenstock. Éilís Ní Dhuibhne and Paddy Bushe write in both English and Irish.

59. Nic Dhiarmada, 'Irish-Language Literature in the New Millennium', p. 627.
60. See Cathal Ó hÁinle, 'An tÚrscéal nár tháinig', *Promhadh Pinn* (Maynooth: An Sagart, 1978), pp. 74–98 (p. 98).
61. Liam Ó Muirthile, *An Fuíoll Feá – Rogha Dánta/Wood Cuttings – New and Selected Poems* (Dublin: Cois Life, 2013), pp. 164–7.

CHAPTER 2

The Cultures of Poetry in Contemporary Ireland
David Lloyd

One feature of Irish poetry and of the preponderance of the criticism it has spawned that makes it singular among contemporary Anglophone poetries is its resolutely anti-theoretical, not to say anti-intellectual, bias. Where rigorous and sometimes acrimonious debate and radical formal variation have invigorated post-war poetry and poetics in the United Kingdom, the United States, or the Caribbean, Irish poetry has for the most part remained sheltered from such challenges. Criticism, which ought to furnish theoretical stimulus and self-reflection, has tended to be at its most acrimonious the more it has advocated for a poetic conservatism whose time, one would have thought, is by now all too well outworn. This shell into which Irish poetry repeatedly withdraws in intellectual renunciation coincides with the niche that it has been assigned in the global market of Anglophone poetry. Irish poetry occupies a peculiar nook, long secured for it by the retailing of rural and decaying industrial backdrops and by their correlatives, the insistent formalism and programmatic adherence to the constancy of 'voice' that has dogged poetic production since Yeats, while tamely eschewing the rigorous violence that sustained his magisterial verse. Like deal dressers and hand-blown glass, Irish poetry offers a reliably commodified form of traditional craft, supplying a market segment within the larger global circuit of poetic production.

Those two components – formalism and the simulation of individual voice – have proven of greater importance and perdurability than the scene-painting: Irish poetry has for the most part survived the advent of Celtic Tiger neoliberalism and its post-industrial mode of production with little challenge to the established parameters. It continues to offer the Anglophone world serviceable exhibitions of poetic craft with sufficient formal prowess to maintain its market niche and furnish a digestible alternative to postmodern economic and cultural dislocation even where its thematic material embraces the Irish diasporic experience, no longer in Paris alone, but from Prague to San Francisco.[1] As with Irish theatre, Irish poetry offers a convenient bridge between the reassuring recourse to traditional forms and the frisson of novelty that access to international residence and performance offer. The 'mismatch' between the assurance of continuity that those forms symbolically communicate and the violent displacement that neoliberalism and its militarisation of the globe have occasioned is rarely engaged.[2] The 'fissure' between 'an innovative strain in Irish poetry open to international influences' and a 'liberal-conservative development of a self-consciously Hiberno-English poetic diction or prosody' is scarcely very evident here and Irish poetry seems to furnish a moderate and moderating alternative to poetry that seeks to work through in its matter as in its form both the spectacular and the 'slow violence' of global capitalist developments.[3]

This discrepancy is not new in Irish culture. In his 1934 book review 'Recent Irish Poetry', Samuel Beckett distinguished between a poetry of convention and a poetry of the actual, the latter having apprehended 'the new thing that has happened', that is, 'the breakdown of the object' or 'breakdown of the subject' and the 'rupture of the lines of communication'.[4] His remarks suggest at least one line of continuity between his modernist moment and our present. 'Conventional' poetry gives the impression that its materials have been processed to furnish a convenient metaphorical or anecdotal vehicle – a 'theme' – for the expression of a subject secure in its self-possession: contemporary Irish poetry offers all too many examples of the happy procedure of the poem that commences with a 'vividly realized' experience, draws from it some metaphoric thread, and winds up with a moral payload, validated by a nice turn of phrase, that brings metaphor and experience into graceful concord again, often enough 'clinched by final rhyme and a final perspective'.[5] As the Irish poet Trevor Joyce put it, 'this familiar marketable thing, the Irish poem, was invariably in the expressive mode: it took its theme from off the shelf, and told you, in lyric fashion, what the poet felt on the subject'.[6] The procedure of the 'well-made poem' is handily available for recycling and the world yields ample material for exploitation in this mode. That material is certainly more various now than the 'antiquarianism' that bothered Beckett: inane recourse to tribalist allegories to explain the Northern Irish Troubles, or suburbanite reflections on the transition from a past generation's rural customs into the land of breeze-block dance halls or IT have largely exhausted themselves in favour of a more cosmopolitan range of reference, if largely at the cost of any serious engagement with the legacy of colonialism in Ireland or its subsequent place in the emergence of neoliberal techniques of surveillance and counter-insurgency. Ironically, the new cosmopolitanism, with its celebration of global mobility and consumerism, all too often acts as the alibi for a retraction from the new things that have happened in our own time and which have, as it happens, all too much to do with the old things that we may be blithely assured we have left behind.

The subject and its relation to its object remain secure within the enclosure of the well-made poem. It is a peculiarity of Irish formalism that its commitment to craft or technical virtuosity within traditional modes, from sonnet to sestina, remains largely uninterrogated, even by explicit opposition to the various possibilities opened up by more innovative poetic work in English or other languages. The 'fascination with form' seems peculiarly unmotivated by any necessity in relation to the pressures that impinge on the language that is its material.[7] Likewise, critical appreciation tends towards the celebration of the 'vividly observed', the 'finely observant of the details', 'the balanced detailing, the accurate and yet indulgent eye', 'detailed descriptions', as if poetry were 'a literature of notations' whose material is the image rather than language.[8] Irredeemably social before it enters the particular artifice of the poem, language as the medium of the subject's subjection to heteronomy imposes constraints on the individual's expression that are far more determining, if more habitually disavowed, than the obvious constraints of traditional forms. All language use is 'under constraint'; the question is how the poet engages with a medium that is always in dialectical relation to the poem that, as artifice, marks its distinction from 'ordinary language' use. As Adorno put it:

> The paradox specific to the lyric work, a subjectivity that turns into objectivity, is tied to the priority of linguistic form in the lyric; it is that priority from which the primacy of language in general (even in prose forms) is derived. For language itself is something double. Through its configurations it assimilates itself completely into subjective impulses; one would almost think it had produced them. But at the same time language remains the medium of concepts, remains that which establishes an inescapable relationship to the universal and society. Hence the highest lyric works are those in which the subject, with no remaining trace of mere matter, sounds forth in language until language itself acquires a voice. The unselfconsciousness of the subject submitting itself to language as to something objective, and the immediacy and spontaneity of that subject's expression are one and the same: thus language mediates lyric poetry and society in their innermost core.[9]

Adorno's formulations are beautifully hedged: apparently subjective impulses are virtually products of the language, not spontaneous expressions of the autonomous subject; submission to the language proceeds in unself-consciousness – as he puts it just before this passage, the lyric 'is socially motivated behind the author's back'. If it is not merely to reproduce the social language unwittingly, poetry demands the utmost self-conscious vigilance.

For Adorno, the principal symptom of the heteronomy imposed by language as the medium of sociality and concepts was its instrumentality, its subjection to communicative ends. Sixty years after Adorno delivered these remarks, and in a location marked so deeply by the legacies of colonialism and counter-insurgency and absorbed by the depredations of neoliberal capitalism as Ireland, language perforce seems saturated with violence without having lost any of its instrumentality. The poet's motto might best be Maurice Scully's 'I made a song in a murderous | time. Listen to the sound of that.'[10] Not that this is by any means an unprecedented linguistic condition, though the casual brutality of daily speech might now make unselfconsciousness a peculiarly deluded state: the very spaces of domestication that seem to proffer shelter from violence are themselves shaped by the violent processes of civility. Civilisation is not 'the opposite of war', but each the other's intimate condition.[11] This is the peculiar dialectic of the civility of the well-made poem that seeks, through 'vivid observation', to save the object that it appropriates even as it affirms the stability of the subject whose perception apprehends it. It is a mode whose discretely didactic ends, as the pedagogical model at once for good poems and good subjects, demand repetition: the scene of wrought epiphany can only fulfil its function if it can be transferred to the reader. Its apparently chance occurrence is a form that must be capable of recurrence; it is thus an empty form that can be filled indifferently with any phenomenal content. Once the pattern is established, the object of perception ceases to matter: whether a hawk or a handsaw, its gleam in the subject's eye is what counts. What is repeated and affirmed is the subject–object relation and its reproducible auratic effect rather than its content. The object is thus annihilated for the sake of the subject.

Michael Longley is probably the master of this mode among current Irish poets, as well as having emerged as the widely acknowledged living master of Ireland's 'singing school'. He is capable of consummating the mode in a poem consisting of a single, crafted quatrain:

> While I was looking for Easter snow on the hills
> You showed me, like a concentration of violets
> Or a fragment from some future unimagined sky,
> A single spring gentian shivering at our feet.[12]

The poem is a condensed instance of impeccable craft: the gradual, whispering accumulation of alliterations on s- or sh-sounds that culminates in the final line, the careful delay of the climactic appearance of the gentian by the parenthetical similes, the canny transposition of the word 'unimagined' from qualifying the future to qualifying the sky that introduces a religiose, possibly apocalyptic note concordant with the Easter setting, and the ambiguity that transposition then prepares in the word 'shivering' – with cold, or for fear of being trodden, or for something a touch more portentous? Thematically, the scanning of the (presumably masculine) eye of the heights and horizon for a blanket phenomenon is countered by the close (detailed?) observation of the (presumably feminine) eye for the particular, ephemeral phenomenon, the irreproducible, unique, and entirely chance appearance of the flower. Except that nothing here is left to chance: the epiphany is thoroughly prescribed and anticipated insofar as the form of the poem itself requires it (and numerous instances of the same phenomenon can be identified in this and other volumes by the same poet). The object, shivering as it is, offers no resistance to its appropriation, is incapable of doing so by virtue of its very indifference for the accomplishment of the poem: any other object could take its place and satisfy the demands of the form. In this respect, the poem, appearing as it does to stand out in the name of the particular against the levelling of phenomena by their commodification, inadvertently reproduces the commodity form for which the exact quality of the object – its use or the satisfaction it may bring to the user – is a matter of indifference so long as it can be exchanged for any other object meeting those conditions. Repetition and exchangeability are the unwitting terms of the form, 'behind the author's back', as it were. The upshot of this contradiction is that language apparently imbued with signification becomes effectively phatic, emitting gestures that signal compulsively a content that matters only because the form requires its presence.

Ciaran Carson long ago sardonically abolished the routines of the well-made poem in the title poem of his first volume, *The New Estate* (1976), capturing precisely its relation to the fetishisation of the object and of the commodity form:

> Forget the corncrake's elegy. Rusty
> Iambics that escaped your discipline

> Of shorn lawns, it is sustained by nature.
> It does not grieve for you, nor for itself.
> You remember the rolled gold of cornfields,
> Their rustling of tinsel in the wind,
> A whole field quivering like blown silk?
>
> A shiver now runs through the laurel hedge,
> And washing flutters like the swaying lines
> Of a new verse. The high fidelity
> Music of the newly-wed obscures your
> Dedication to a life of loving
> Money. What could they be for, those marble
> Toilet fixtures, the silence of water-beds,
> That book of poems you bought yesterday?[13]

More importantly, however, it was Carson's signal achievement to break with what was by now the formal shell of the epiphanic lyric whose standard inner development is here inverted and parodied as an object of nostalgia, better forgotten. Between *The Irish for No* (1987) and *Opera Et Cetera* (1996), Carson developed the long, sinuous, mostly blank-verse line that proved capable of integrating the colloquial rhythms of bar-stool or barbershop conversation with a playful, associative, and often tongue-in-cheek intellectuality. Under the pressure of political violence and counter-insurgency, he forged a formal means to enact the attitude of ironic suspicion, visceral threat, and restless movement that are the conditions of mere survival as much as they are those of a new form of poetic critical address to a situation of state as well as paramilitary terror. His line proved capable of absorbing and rendering the vernacular traditions of urban folklore that have long found the means to negotiate the unstable interfaces of potentially violent encounters while enabling a citational practice that preserves an astonishing equilibrium between high intellectual parody and analytic precision. The mobility of the mode never congeals into the kinds of aesthetic condescension that is habitual in poems more convinced of their own civil superiority to the purveyors of violence but permits a peculiarly calibrated ethical work, at once ironic and empathetic:

> As usual, the clock in The Clock Bar was a good few minutes fast:
> A fiction no one really bothered to maintain, unlike the story
> The comrade on my left was telling, which no one knew for certain truth:
> *Back in 1922, a sergeant, I forget his name, was shot outside the National*
>   *Bank* . . . .
> Ah yes, what year was that they knocked it down? Yes, its memory's as fresh

As the inky smell of new pound notes – which interferes with the beer-and-
   whiskey
Tang of now, like two dogs meeting in the revolutionary 69 of a long sniff,
Or cattle jostling shit-stained flanks in the Pound. For *pound*, as some wag
Interrupted, was an offshoot of the Falls, from the Irish, *fál*, a hedge;
Hence, *any kind of enclosed thing*, its twigs and branches commemorated
By the soldiers' drab and olive camouflage, as they try to melt
Into a brick wall; red coats might be better, after all.[14]

Even so brief an extract from 'Hamlet', the long concluding poem of *Belfast Confetti* (1989), indicates the possibilities of Carson's formal innovations, as the 'enclosed thing' that is the poem opens up onto what seems a potentially endless movement of interruption and displacement that interweaves temporal frames, not only through citing the Belfast legend of the sergeant's ghost, which recalls *Hamlet* to mind in the midst of Belfast's 'troubled state', but also by invoking the 'redcoats' who in the nineteenth century oversaw the evictions by which the process of enclosure was enforced in Ireland. That violent process introduced a money economy, the circulation of the pound, at the expense of Ireland's subsistence agriculture and the people it supported. The Falls, indeed, was historically the product of the settlement of a displaced Catholic population on the western outskirts of the city. That Northern Ireland served as the laboratory for the modes of surveillance and urban counter-insurgency that have become ubiquitous phenomena of neoliberal regimes and their new forms of accumulation underscores the 'rhyme' between the redcoats and their camouflaged descendants.[15] Sometimes history rhymes not with hope but with the vicious replay of the violence of dispossession. Simile and resemblance function here not in the service of identity but as relays that open one 'scene' onto apparently disjunctive tracks that continually loop back with a new burden of historical matter. What appears, in other words, as loose association is seeded with precise and telling historical reference that, threading an oral narration with all its digressions and interruptions, effects a spatio-temporal account of political violence and its embeddedness in colonial histories: 'So we name the constellations, to put a shape | On what was there; so, the storyteller picks his way between the isolated stars.'[16] Allen Feldman has commented that the violence of the Troubles functioned like a language.[17] One could likewise see Carson's formal innovations as pursuing a language adequate to the everydayness of violence and to the vernacular modes of responding to and accommodating its constant imminence.

Between *The New Estate* and *Belfast Confetti*, Carson opened out the domesticated shelter *from* violence into the public spaces of the pubs and streets where violence is both staged and parsed. Carson's contemporary, Medbh McGuckian, is often cast as a poet of the 'rich inner world of feminine sensibility' and as an unusually obscure writer, drawing on private or hidden allusions and exploring the supposedly enclosed world of women's experience.[18] As several critics have recently confirmed, what appears private and hermetic is often woven from found language, now easily identified online.[19] Her construction of poems out of appropriated language has exacerbated the reservations felt by some critics as to whether the poems mean anything at all, a reservation that could be redeemed by the notion that these are instances of an *écriture féminine* and therefore absolved of needing to mean or that their meaning is subordinated to their musicality. The foundness of their language upset these somewhat patronising recuperations of her work and seems to have led to a sense of disappointment hard to distinguish from the accusation of deceit. Leontia Flynn's book-length leave-taking of her fellow poet is the type of such disappointment:

> The links and associative points to which her work connects seem potentially endless, part of the poem's refusal to 'represent' without suggesting an awareness of dozens of divergent, specific other representations of the same thing. Such connections could expand beneath or around the poems [...] to the point where the poem is more or less forgotten, if it is still relevant at all. These meanings then can now surely only fully be understood or *remembered* by the author herself. Moreover, none of this has anything to do with poetry, which has to generalise or 'represent' at least to the extent that it creates meanings for more than one person.[20]

This rather tight-lipped critical legislation of what poetry can be and how it can mean, of the relation of the poet's intention and consciousness to the verbal artefact of the poem, and of the latter's relation to the reader is, it must be said, severely impoverished and of doubtful value in reading McGuckian's work, let alone a wide range of post-Romantic poetry. Even William Empson faced the problem that, once set in motion, the movement of interpretation was 'potentially endless': the only limit that so attentive a critic could pose to reading was 'tact', an arbitrary closure of the reader's engagement in face of the uncontrollable dynamic that an active attention unleashes.[21] The demand for evident reference, for the anchoring of the poem in some kind of representation that can be 'generalised' for the sake of communication, goes hand in hand with the poem's closure in the well-regulated fulfilment of the subject's expressive intention, one that can be recalled and 'fully understood'. It is hard to see how this fading echo of British empiricism 'has anything to do with poetry' and its unsettling ways of meaning and unmeaning. Certainly, it is of little help in actually reading McGuckian.[22]

Flynn's sarcastic proclamation peculiarly extends several decades of efforts to domesticate McGuckian's work precisely by assuming its disconnection from the public world of communication and the political. But long before this, a more significant characteristic of McGuckian's work was identified by Clair Wills's pioneering study, *Improprieties*, that is, its capacity to weave together public and private experience in a way that dismantles the boundary that has long been supposed to separate the feminine domain of the home from the masculine public world, emphasising instead 'the interpenetration of these spheres on the social level' as a consequence of Ireland's colonial history.[23] Wills's brilliant reading of McGuckian preceded the latter's *Captain Lavender* (1995), the volume in which McGuckian's formal practices and material concerns seemed to come into their fullest articulation. Whatever may be said as to the extent to which the violence of the Troubles may have permeated McGuckian's earlier work – and it is often forgotten how the counter-insurgency tactic of 'normalisation' had the peculiar effect of domesticating terror, in the double sense of that term – *Captain Lavender* does not merely introduce the context of violence and political imprisonment as thematic material, but enacts its dissemination across the social and psychic fields. Indeed, without the publisher's blurb that comments on McGuckian's work as a teacher in the prisons, one might be hard put to grasp precisely how 'the war is in' these poems, as her epigraph from Picasso puts it. For it is not 'in' the poems as representational material, but dispersed rhizomatically across them, both within each individual lyric and across the book as a whole in a network of musical echoes and transformations. Across that network, imprisonment, colonial histories, and the politics of language and culture form nodes of connection that are also relays with what are usually taken to be other dimensions or spheres of experience: loss and grief, fatherhood and daughterhood, home-making and gardening or farming, religion and music. The procedure undoes the compartmentalisation of those domains of experience that was constitutive of colonial modernity, in Ireland as elsewhere. McGuckian's poetry is, as has often enough been noted, political not by its proclamations, provisional or otherwise, but by the movement of its language, that is, poetically.

This makes the knowledge that a poem like 'Elegy for an Irish Speaker' is composed extensively from phrases 'found' in writings by Osip Mandelstam of little final help in reading it.[24] Poems move off from their occasions, whether those occasions are the stimulus of another's words, read or overheard, or of sensory or social experiences. They do not remain at their apparent point of origin (which is likely to have been determined in any case by prior inputs) but disperse or disseminate from them. Even the given materials may be transformed in the process: it is not Mandelstam's Word that is 'born very slowly' in the poem's opening, but the date that will have marked an anniversary, the same day in the calendar but always differing from itself in its repetition:

> Numbered day,
> night only just beginning,
> be born very slowly, stay
> with me, impossible to name.[25]

Day cedes to night, the exact moment of either temporal states' becoming from the other proving 'impossible to name', as any phrase differs from itself as it moves though time or place. The date that appears to mark a definable, numbered series of returns – in this case, the reader assumes, the death of her father – instead marks the slippage of memory from its anchorages. In their inner difference, name and date shadow the displacement of the subject, at once self-identical and self-alienated, 'in words, made of words, others' words', as Beckett's Unnamable puts it.[26] Slippage of every kind is the principle of the poem, and not only the slippery misappropriation of another's words. In a possible echo of Sylvia Plath's 'Lady Lazarus', death itself is feminised as 'Miss Death' while the father appears successively as inseminator, embryo, and poetess:

> Are you waiting to be fertilized,
> dynamic death, by his dark company?
> To be warmed in your wretched
> overnight lodgings
> by his kind words and small talk
> and powerful movements?
> He breaks away from your womb
> to talk to me,
> he speaks so with my consciousness
> and not with words, he's in danger
> of becoming a poetess.[27]

The precise moment of change between states, which undermines both gender and biological identities, remains indeterminable, defying the differentiating functions of language itself.

The non-verbal play of non-identity – the domain of death itself – cannot be rendered in words, but here, as throughout McGuckian's work, is approximated by polysemy:

> Roaming root of multiple meanings,
> he shouts himself out
> in your narrow amphora,
> your tasteless, because immortal, wine.[28]

'Multiple meaning' arrives in diverse forms, ranging from the pun to the buried metaphor, from ambiguity to indeterminate reference. Hesitation constantly dogs the reader's progress through the poem: is 'tasteless' a gastronomic or an aesthetic term? Does 'he shouts himself out' imply the exhaustion of expression or the will to exit confinement? But reading is also directed onto various simultaneous tracks by resurrecting dead metaphors: 'the knitting together of your two spines | is another woman | reminding of a wife' shifts across at least three trajectories of the poem's layered matter – that of the biological, that of the materiality of the book, and that of the erotic – through which the dialectic of death and living-on plays out. These are not separable domains, any more than are the public and the private, but intersecting complexes that slip constantly between registers, fixed at one moment and unfixed at another. The amphora that contains – and seems to condense at once the funereal urn, the jar of wine, and the enclosure of the poem – is also the vessel that transports. The dialectic between the nomadic movement of dissemination and the settled, cultivating work of insemination courses constantly through *Captain Lavender* and constitutes another principle of the poetic work and of the reading it summons:

> Most foreign and cherished reader,
> I cannot live without
> your trans-sense language,
> the living furrow of your spoken words
> that plough up time.[29]

The movement of reading plays between a sense and the senses – the image that speaks to the eye is generally also a node for other tracks of meaning, so that the domination of the eye is undone by the displacement of meaning – as it also 'translates' the poem into the afterlife that is the fate of any work, its dislodgement from the time of its occasion into a future in which the author and the referent are equally absent.[30] Mandelstam's phrases both live their afterlife here and are 'trans-sensed', uprooted from their own soil and reseeded in a different field of associations.

Within the book itself, any moment of the figurative play of the poem is the 'second half | of a poetic simile lost somewhere'.[31] The reader constantly picks up the trail of some metaphoric complex elsewhere in the text as the process of reading any poem is replicated across the book as a whole. In 'The Albert Chain', the death of the father echoes and folds into the other deaths it is 'chained' to, that of the author and those that compose the historical legacy of colonial violence:

> Like a dead man
> attached to the soil that covers him,
> I have fallen where no judgement can touch me,
> its discoloured rubble has swallowed me up.
> For ever and ever, I go back into myself:
> I was born in little pieces, like specks of dust,
> only an eye that looks in all directions can see me.
> I am learning my country all over again,
> how every inch of soil has been paid for
> by the life of a man, the funerals of the poor.[32]

Return into the self, which might seem to promise the affirmation of identity, meets only a further dissemination, 'in all directions', that is also embedded in the history of the country and its people – dispersal, exile, migration having been the consequence of enclosure and settlement. What might quite rightly be read in one direction as a feminist poetic that critiques the fixation on gendered identity and gendered divisions of space folds over onto another that equally queers the political symbolism of the Republican prisoners in their '[s]tored statelessness' – 'men utterly outside themselves, with the taint of women'.[33] It is a poetic that responds to the conditions of a very modern epoch of political violence and counter-insurgency not by recourse to colonial stereotypes that oppose civility to atavistic tribalism, but with a practice whose 'trans-sense language' rebuffs all 'attempts to seal its meaning'.[34] It is a language acutely capable of absorbing the violent displacements of modernity and of imagining alternative languages of non-identity in which, indeed, one might 'hear two voices without either | disturbing the other – four harmonies | where there was only one'.[35]

Manifestly different as their poetic modes appear, and quite distinct in the demands they make on reading, what links Carson and McGuckian is the dialectic in their work between a form and the materials that determine it. Form, for each of them, is not an arbitrary or given container, but the specific shape poetic thinking takes in moving through the materials, linguistic, and historical at once, that it takes on. If those materials include the political violence of the Troubles that so spectacularly dissolved the boundaries between public and private experience, it is important to recall the degree to which the techniques and technologies of counter-insurgency that were developed in the laboratory of Northern Ireland have become part and parcel of the regime of neoliberal capital that has extended onto a global scale the violent policing and containment of the populations it has displaced and made disposable in the service of accumulation. One of the more baleful effects of the partition of the island has been the perception of 'separate development', culturally as well as economically and politically, that disjoins Northern Ireland and the Republic into distinct and non-communicating compartments.[36] That such distinct trajectories have left their mark on poetic practice and on conversations about poetry, despite continuous cross-border exchange, cannot be ignored. Critically, however, it remains important to identify what one might call the 'growth-points' of Irish poetry in relation to the formal engagement of poets with the 'new thing that has happened', in this case, the continuing subsumption of Ireland as a whole into that global capitalist sphere. This is not because it produces new thematic material for poetic anecdotes, but because the conditions of the present challenge the conception of the acting and perceiving subject that undergirds the well-made lyric just as powerfully as the 'breakdown of the subject' undid for Beckett the 'antiquarianism' of Irish poetry in the 1930s. The subject implicit in the well-made poem and its various formalist variants is a subject secure in its freedom and in the domain of private experience, communicable precisely because of the formal identity among individuals of which the poem is the model. The question that has to be confronted, as a question that is fundamentally and not casually addressed to poetry, is that of how to find forms adequate to the conditions of unfreedom that the neoliberal transformation of society in all its domains have produced.

It is this question that links the poetic procedures of Carson and McGuckian to poets working predominantly in the Republic, such as Trevor Joyce, Maurice Scully, and Catherine Walsh. Generally contained by terms like 'innovative' or 'experimental', their work might better be approached in terms of its pursuit of formal solutions that would allow poetry to address a moment when the anecdotal lyric that has been the typical Irish mode appears at best exhausted, at worst, irrelevant and inauthentic. Joyce, the most theoretically self-reflexive of Irish 'innovative poets', has articulated his fatigue with 'the standard bag of Irish tricks:

lyrics of description and expression dressed in the most transparent of formal attire' and linked it not only to the necessity to find new kinds of formal constraint, but also to find in those constraints a correlative to the social condition of language in which, as Adorno suggested, one is 'governed by forces and concerns in which one has had no hand, act, or part'.[37] Scully and Walsh are less committed to procedural writing or 'composition under constraint', but they share a disinterest in hand-me-down forms and a commitment to the construction of works that are in different ways resistant to easy consumption. Scully's work was for twenty-five years dedicated to the production of an eight-book work, *Things That Happen*, assembled from continuously interwoven poems in a variety of forms.[38] His emphasis is on the construction or assemblage of the book, not on the portable individual poem as an entity in itself. Walsh likewise constructs books out of an assemblage of diverse forms and of modes of language use, ranging from digressive prose 'essays' or memoirs to 'lyrics' composed largely out of apparently overheard speech.

Walsh's 2009 book, *Optic Verve: A Commentary*, opens with what appear on first glance to be little lyrics, mostly six to ten lines long, interspersed with brief phrases in Spanish on some of the left-hand pages. These turn out not to be what she elsewhere calls 'terribly intact box-like parameters [. . .] | [. . .] processed packaging of eagerness curiosity | quick commodification arrogance attempting dominance'[39] – a sequence that might suggest at once the lyric enclosure or the spatial enclosures inhabited by the contemporary subject – but little units of radically dismantled language:

> best why which can call given
> away so undo better for which remember
> thin with likely of which in all
> only where day call and forget change
> it as last could all that get
> many asked no one might be just can
> should be should what in all out of
> neither with a glad either welcome to
> known day all can who will or see
> without no wonder[40]

This poem, if such it is, presents as a lyric and, indeed, gestures towards the standard materials of the genre: memory and change, day met with gladness and wonder, call and questioning. It even invokes the buried performative forms of the marriage ceremony that bring about a change of state of man and woman into husband and wife – 'for better or worse', 'through thick and thin', 'given away' – but such faint echoes here signal little more than the formulaic sedimentations in even the most deconstructed language. Not only are reference, representation, and meaning evacuated from it, but predication of any kind is avoided. What remain are uncertain grammatical fragments and even those are subject to multiple possible recombinations that might gesture towards a sense that is almost immediately withdrawn again. One can continue to grasp for ways to reconstruct some kind of continuous sense across the lines and phrase-fragments, concluding, perhaps, with an affirmation of illumination, volition, and wonder reminiscent of the epiphanic lyric: the last lines of the citation above could, for example, be rendered as 'welcome to known day: all can who will or [will] see with [out no] wonder!'. But all such efforts are frustrated and the text remains a shuttling assemblage of part phrases deprived of predicates, for the most part even of nouns and verbs.

And yet this and the corresponding texts retain a haunting subliminal charge. A thin utterance seems to struggle to articulate, to piece together an ethical and ontological response to the world between the gaps and silences: another effort to reconstruct a determinate sense from the lines cited above might yield 'One might be just. Can | should be. Should what? In all ... Out of | neither ... With a glad ... '. In its refusal of any subject–object relations, any attempt at dominance, the little bursts of language seem to mime the unclosed speech-gestures of a being scanning the world and its possibilities, but constantly stopping short, suspending, in what one is tempted to call stutterance. Deconstructing the language of propositions about the world, the text could be taken as the discourse of what Walsh later calls 'this rattled subjectivity' in a poem also about stuttering, repetition, and recomposition.[41] And yet, for all its fragility, for all the feeling that it is 'governed by forces and concerns in which one has had no hand, act, or part', the text is resistant: it is resistant to appropriation by the reader, to the desire to offer a portable, paraphrasable meaning, as it is resistant to the instrumentalisation and commodification of language and experience: this lyric renders no luminous sentiment for the market in epiphanies.

As such, it is a minimal instance of the resistance that *Optic Verve*, which is made up in part of satiric prose and counter-history, poses to the neoliberal 'Celtic Tiger' boom of the moment in which it was written. The little text just cited may invoke only to refuse the 'given name', the 'proper name', but a text only a little further on addresses explicitly the issue of naming as if in a commentary on the Irish-language tradition of *dinnseanchas*, or place name poetry, that Carson and McGuckian also ironically invoke and which is a staple of the Irish lyric standard. But gentrification, demolition, and speculative development have put paid to the affective relation between the name and what it designates. Writing of the demolition of Dublin's working-class Fatima Mansions in one of the many prose texts that intersperse the lineated pages, Walsh asks:

> What will they call it? How can it not be Fatima, right there by Maryland? If there were no Luas [light-rail] line nearing completion (or bankruptcy) would anyone with access to power have given a damn?
>
> Whose place was it? To say what is its name is not tantamount to saying I don't know what it is. Naming is not a speculative art and not necessary, as many seem to assume, to actual comprehension. Understanding. Naming makes communicative interaction a lot less tedious and time consuming. A coded shorthand of the specific, necessary component of the everyday dialectic of our lives.
>
> Whose place was it? To say what its name is is saying I don't know whose it is. There's a girl somewhere, in London or Birmingham, Madrid or Barcelona, who says what its name is every time she tells her story. She says its name in her head, to hear the vowel sounds echo right; aloud they must be adapted for the pertaining local influence, to be understood, superficially.[42]

Two versions of naming contradict one another here, in this passage that might itself be a reading of the lyric just quoted: the name that designates, abbreviates, facilitates communication; and the name that resonates as sensuous material, reverberates with affective associations, echoes in the body and the ear, its enunciation bearing local inflection and intonation, accent and accident, in different languages. If the former lends itself to instrumental purposes – mapping, planning, surveying, and surveillance – and can be torn from place, the latter's resonances persist beyond its scheduled erasure, as a ghost that haunts the demolished site or, indeed, the dead body of the vagrant on the doorstep of the block that had been his life-long home.[43]

Walsh's work in its multiple modes reminds us that what reads as formal innovation is equally the means to imagine or recuperate 'structures of feeling' and forms of living that resist the unfreedom of universal commodification, producing a medium that itself defies easy subsumption: as in other 'semi-colonial' locations, there may be less contradiction between the most radical of modernist experiment and the non-modern practices in which the residual becomes emergent by virtue of its persistence than there is with the so-called traditional forms that actually accommodate the ongoing levelling of difference.[44] Innovative poetics spills over into the utopian projection of past possibilities as potentials that live on in the present, in the body as in the memory. *Optic Verve* culminates in diary entries that pose the surviving practices, language, and forms of sociality that persist in an unevenly and recently modernised culture like Ireland's:

> Baking to go, making dough. One hundred years ago the same. The one I know without having to look it up. My hands, after years away from this particular activity, take off in a rhythmical series of sequential movements each designed to fulfill a certain function necessary to the act of breadmaking. My head wanders through layers of thought while processing sudden vivid visuals that pop up in time, it seems, with my hands. It's soothing, restful, satisfying. Tasty. I learned this process from two or three, assistant to my grandmother, in the new store, the room that opened off the back of the ancient dairy.[45]

Bread-making and butter-churning are 'functional processes' with an aesthetic subordinated to those functions, and also practices in which memory is embedded.[46] This is not merely a domestic memory: as Leopoldina Fortunati has taught us, the 'feminine' scene of reproduction is no less integrated with capitalist modes of production than what the Marxist tradition has seen as productive, proletarian labour.[47] The domestic, precisely as a site of cultural reproduction, has also been a principal target of colonial modernisation, along with indigenous languages, replaced by 'that of commerce and international trade'.[48] This is, as Walsh remarks, 'not new colonialism', but 'very old, traditional, unchanged',[49] and at once global and profoundly intimate in its reach. Walsh's writing, which often works through the historical transformation of such spaces by technology and shifting modes of reproduction, is peculiarly alert to their juncture with capitalist and colonial modernisation. While much of her work is composed with an ear to the alienation and isolation of the suburban domestic space, it does not register it solely as a domain of unfreedom or of closure, but as a locus of survival in every sense. Sites of memory, they are also sites of possibility that challenge the relegation of older practices to obsolescence, 'outmoded by commercialization':[50]

> These matters are not just still within living memory or oral testament here in Ireland as in so many parts of the world, they are a crucial determining factor in how people choose to interact socially, what they aspire to attain, how they use language and how they view language.[51]

The radically mixed-genre work of *Optic Verve* styles itself neither as poetry, nor memoir, nor 'impositional narrative', but as 'A Commentary', thus knitting together the old medieval practice of annotation and glossing with the contemporary practices of critical reading.[52] Challenging 'authorship authority absolutism', it also challenges the prejudice that the innovative or experimental is necessarily bad cosmopolitanism, deracinated, abstracted from history.[53] As the work shows, and as Ireland's own history constantly testifies, it is possible to innovate, or renovate, to the fullest extent while still engaging with the potentials that are embedded in the cultural practices that live on in defiance of domination. This is what we would mean by alternative modernities or what Trevor Joyce nicely dubbed 'alternate planes of cleavage'. Any Irish poetry adequate to our moment is obliged to take on, if not to emulate, the example of such historically attentive, formally alert alternatives to poetic business as usual.

Notes

1. J. C. C. Mays has been critically alert to Irish poetry's paradoxical relation to commodity culture for several decades now. See 'Flourishing and Foul: Six Poets, Ideology and the Irish Building Industry', *Irish Review*, 8.1 (1990), pp. 6–11; and 'The Third Walker', *Irish University Review*, 46.1 (2016), pp. 48–62.
2. 'Mismatch' is Mays's term for a comparable contradiction between form and occasion ('The Third Walker', p. 60).
3. Matthew Campbell, cited in Fran Brearton, '"The Nothing Could Be Simpler Line": Form in Contemporary Irish Poetry', in Fran Brearton and Alan Gillis, eds., *The Oxford Handbook of Modern Irish Poetry* (Oxford: Oxford University Press, 2013), pp. 629–47 (p. 630). The term 'slow violence' is Rob Nixon's: see *Slow Violence and the Environmentalism of the Poor* (Cambridge, MA: Harvard University Press, 2013).
4. Samuel Beckett, 'Recent Irish Poetry', in Ruby Cohn, ed., *Disjecta: Miscellaneous Writings and a Dramatic Fragment* (New York: Grove Press, 1984), pp. 70–6 (p. 70).
5. Edna Longley, '"Altering the Past": Northern Irish Poetry and Modern Canons', in *Irish Writing Since 1950, The Yearbook of English Studies*, 35 (2005), pp. 1–17 (p. 5).
6. Trevor Joyce, 'The Point of Innovation in Poetry', cited in 'Irish Terrain: Alternative Planes of Cleavage', in Romana Huk, ed., *Assembling Alternatives: Reading Postmodern Poetries Transnationally* (Middletown, CT: Wesleyan University Press, 2003), pp. 156–68 (p. 157).
7. Brearton, 'The Nothing Could Be Simpler Line', p. 631.

8. The cited phrases come at random from a handful of pages in Justin Quinn, *The Cambridge Introduction to Modern Irish Poetry, 1800–2000* (Cambridge: Cambridge University Press, 2008), pp. 204–9. But such terms of critical commendation could be replicated in almost any work on Irish poetry and are the stock-in-trade of the poetry workshop. 'A literature of notations' is Beckett's phrase, from *Proust and Three Dialogues with Georges Duthuit* (London: John Calder, 1976), p. 76.
9. Theodor W. Adorno, 'On Lyric Poetry and Society', in Rolf Tiedemann, ed., *Notes to Literature*, trans. Shierry Weber Nicholsen (New York: Columbia University Press, 1991), vol. I, pp. 37–54 (p. 43).
10. Maurice Scully, *Livelihood* (Bray, Ireland: Wild Honey Press, 2004), p. 270.
11. Michael Longley, *Collected Poems* (London: Jonathan Cape, 2006), p. 253. The citation, unattributable in the poem, appears to come from Ursula LeGuin, *The Left Hand of Darkness*, where its meaning is considerably more unstable, possibly ironic.
12. Longley, *Collected Poems*, p. 253.
13. Ciaran Carson, *The New Estate* (Winston-Salem, NC: Wake Forest University Press, 1976), p. 41
14. Ciaran Carson, *Belfast Confetti* (Winston-Salem, NC: Wake Forest University Press, 1989), p. 105.
15. On both the economic and the counter-insurgency developments for which Ireland served as laboratory, see David Lloyd, *Irish Culture and Colonial Modernity, 1800–2000: The Transformation of Oral Space* (Cambridge: Cambridge University Press, 2011). Carson's story of the sergeant's ghost finds correspondences in Allen Feldman's ethnographic *Formations of Violence: The Narrative of the Body and Political Terror in Northern Ireland* (Chicago: University of Chicago Press, 1989), pp. 65–8.
16. Carson, *Belfast Confetti*, p. 107. On the formal and thematic characteristics of Carson's Belfast poetry, see Eric Falci, *Continuity and Change in Irish Poetry, 1966–2010* (Cambridge: Cambridge University Press, 2012), pp. 120–51; and Julia C. Obert, *Postcolonial Overtures: The Politics of Sound in Northern Irish Poetry* (Syracuse, NY: Syracuse University Press, 2015), pp. 22–76.
17. See Feldman, *Formations of Violence*, p. 1.
18. I deliberately draw the cited phrase from the fine if brief British Council web-page note on McGuckian by Eve Patten, which is one place where the baffled reader is first likely to turn for an introduction to the poet's work: https://literature.britishcouncil.org/writer/medbh-mcguckian [accessed 28 March 2019].
19. Shane Alcobia-Murphy, *Sympathetic Ink: Intertextual Relations in Northern Irish Poetry* (Liverpool: Liverpool University Press, 2006) is the most exhaustive account of McGuckian's borrowings: see especially pp. 43–91. The unsettlement that this practice and its extent in McGuckian's work has caused is somewhat odd in the Irish context, where practices of unoriginal writing, from fake translation to transcription and parody, have an honourable lineage

from James Clarence Mangan through James Joyce and, more figuratively, Samuel Beckett.
20. Leontia Flynn, *Reading Medbh McGuckian* (Sallins, Ireland: Irish Academic Press, 2014), p. 173.
21. William Empson, *Seven Types of Ambiguity* (New York: New Directions, 1966), pp. 244–7.
22. For a thorough-going alternative to this kind of reductive and censorious reading of McGuckian, see Maureen E. Ruprecht Fadem, *Medbh McGuckian: Iterations of Silence and the Borders of Articulacy* (Lanham, MD: Rowman & Littlefield, 2019).
23. Clair Wills, *Improprieties: Politics and Sexuality in Northern Irish Poetry* (Oxford: Oxford University Press, 1993), pp. 47–77 (p. 67). Wills's overall argument is a brilliant demonstration of the 'colonial consequences' that have determined a different historical trajectory of social experience in Ireland and represents an exemplary case for the intellectual necessity of postcolonial arguments about Irish culture.
24. On McGuckian's use of Mandelstam in this poem, see Alcobia-Murphy, *Sympathetic Ink*, pp. 236–7.
25. Medbh McGuckian, *Captain Lavender* (Winston-Salem, NC: Wake Forest University Press, 1995), p. 42. For the borrowing from Mandelstam, see Flynn, *Reading Medbh McGuckian*, p. 155.
26. Samuel Beckett, *Molloy, Malone Dies, The Unnamable* (London: Calder and Boyars, 1973), p. 390. On the differentiating return of the name and the date, and on the 'departure' of poem from 'occasion', see Jacques Derrida, 'Shibboleth: For Paul Celan', in Thomas Dutoit and Outi Pasanen, eds., *Sovereignties in Question: The Poetics of Paul Celan* (New York: Fordham University Press, 2005), pp. 1–64.
27. McGuckian, *Captain Lavender*, p. 42.
28. Ibid.
29. Ibid., p. 43.
30. Walter Benjamin, 'The Task of the Translator', in Marcus Bullock and Michael W. Jennings, eds., *Selected Writings, Volume I: 1913–1926* (Cambridge, MA: Harvard University Press, 1996), pp. 253–63 (p. 254).
31. McGuckian, *Captain Lavender*, p. 43.
32. Ibid., p. 68.
33. Ibid., p. 53.
34. Ibid., p. 34.
35. Ibid., p. 39.
36. On the two states' separate development, cultural as well as economic and political, see Joe Cleary, *Literature, Partition and the Nation State: Culture and Conflict in Ireland, Israel and Palestine* (Cambridge: Cambridge University Press, 2002), p. 77.
37. Trevor Joyce, 'The Phantom Quarry: Translating a Renaissance Painting into Modern Poetry', *Enclave Review* 8 (2013), pp. 5–8 (p. 6): http://enclavereview.org/the-phantom-quarry-translating-a-renaissance-painting-into-modern-poetry/

[accessed 28 March 2019]. Joyce gives in this essay a meticulous account of his poetic procedure, based on a transformation for spreadsheet composition of the traditional sestina. See also his 'Poetry, Form and Meaning', in *Cork Caucus: On Art, Possibility & Democracy* (Cork, Ireland: National Sculpture Factory and Frankfurt am Main: Revolver – Archiv für aktuelle Kunst, 2006), pp. 371–8. The latter essay elaborates the procedures through which he constructed 'The Peacock's Tale'. The difficulty of locating these low-circulation publications is an index of the inhospitability of such writing to easy commodification and a perhaps unwished-for sign of their success in that regard.

38. On Scully's writing, see – among an increasing number of essays – Kit Fryatt, 'The Poetics of Elegy in Maurice Scully's Humming'; and Romana Huk, '"Out Past/Self-Dramatization": Maurice Scully's *Several Dances*', both in *Irish University Review*, 46.1 (2016), pp. 89–104 and 105–18. A volume of essays on Scully, edited by Kenneth Keating, is forthcoming from Shearsman Press.
39. Catherine Walsh, *Optic Verve* (Exeter: Shearsman Books, 2009), p. 39.
40. Walsh, *Optic Verve*, p. 17.
41. Ibid., p. 62.
42. Ibid., pp. 23–4.
43. See Claire Bracken's beautiful commentary on the final paragraph of this prose segment that narrates the death of a homeless young man in 'Nomadic Ethics: Gender and Class in Catherine Walsh's *City West*', in *Irish University Review*, 46.1 (2016), pp. 75–88 (pp. 75–6). Bracken's essay insightfully elaborates the connections between Walsh's work and the Celtic Tiger.
44. On the 'residual' and the 'emergent', see Raymond Williams, *Marxism and Literature* (Oxford: Oxford University Press, 1977), pp. 121–7; I have commented on the need to see the residual in colonial spaces as a means to the emergent and resistant in *Ireland after History* (Cork, Ireland: Cork University Press, 1999), p. 78. The term 'semicolonial' is borrowed from the Peruvian poet César Vallejo, who thus described his nation. On Vallejo's use of the term 'semicolonial', see Adam Sharman, *Tradition and Modernity in Spanish American Literature: From Darío to Carpentier* (Basingstoke: Palgrave Macmillan, 2006), pp. 67–107 (p. 90).
45. Walsh, *Optic Verve*, p. 119.
46. Ibid., p. 120.
47. Leopoldina Fortunati, *The Arcane of Reproduction: Housework, Prostitution, Labor and Capital*, Jim Fleming, ed., trans. Hilary Creek (Brooklyn, NY: Autonomedia, 1995).
48. Walsh, *Optic Verve*, p. 123.
49. Ibid.
50. Ibid., p. 120.
51. Ibid., p. 124.
52. Ibid., p. 54.
53. Ibid.; spacing original.

CHAPTER 3

Troubles Literature and the End of the Troubles
Julia C. Obert

The early 1980s were a low point in the history of the Troubles: violence was at fever pitch; Margaret Thatcher's government was responding to Republican agitation with particularly brutal tactics; and one by one, political prisoners on hunger strike were dying in Long Kesh. However, this was also the moment at which the beginnings of a political solution to the conflict were first glimpsed. As the decade progressed, and as Sinn Féin began contesting elections, peace negotiations commenced in Northern Ireland. These negotiations, however, were abortive, as paramilitary groups on both sides responded to the ongoing talks by intensifying their campaigns, hoping to prevent political 'concessions'. Consequently, the late 1980s saw renewed physical insecurity in Northern Ireland, as well as disillusionment with the seemingly false promise of political conciliation. After a new round of negotiations in the early 1990s, both Loyalist and Republican paramilitaries declared ceasefires in 1994. Although the détente was broken in 1996 when the IRA bombed both the Canary Wharf area of London and Manchester city centre, the ceasefire was re-instated and talks resumed, and those talks eventually led to the Belfast Agreement of 1998.

Northern Irish literature of the period necessarily reflects both the conflict's relentless violence and the feeling of political whiplash that came with the country's tentative steps towards peace. Working across several genres, including novels, poetry, drama, and non-fictional prose, this chapter examines the ways in which writers represented the strife of the Troubles and the gradual gains of the peace process between 1980 and 1998. It considers various modes of Troubles literature, ranging from the historical displacements of Brian Friel's *Translations* – first published and staged at the Guildhall in Derry/Londonderry in 1980 – and Seamus Deane's *Reading in the Dark* (1996), to the realism of Ciaran Carson's *The Irish for No* (1987) and *Belfast Confetti* (1989), the staging of women's lives during the Troubles in Anne Devlin's *Ourselves Alone* (1985), the phantasmagorias of Paul Muldoon's poetry and the metaphorisations of war and violence in

Medbh McGuckian's verse, and the Belfast panoramas of Glenn Patterson's *Fat Lad* (1992) and Robert McLiam Wilson's *Eureka Street* (1996). However, while this chapter ranges across an eighteen-year period, it also reaches back centuries and forward to today and beyond – a long view of Northern Irish life on which the literature insists. Contemporary Northern writers contextualise the conflict (which was often framed in the popular press as 'inexplicable' brutality) by illuminating the country's colonial past; they narrate the structures of trauma by demonstrating the capacity of history to invade the present; they stage the looping cadences of traditional music and tale-telling as palliative correctives to the vicious linearity of the conflict; and they project possible resolutions to the exhausted (il)logic of sectarian strife. Time, in other words, is porous in this work: late twentieth-century Northern Irish literature is both populated by roving ghosts and prophetically open to the future.

Brian Friel's play *Translations*, the inaugural production of the Field Day Theatre Company, was written and premiered in 1980. The play was first performed on September 23rd of that year at the Guildhall in Derry/Londonderry: a highly charged location given the building's status as a symbol of state power and a frequent target of IRA bombings. Given Field Day's desire to establish a so-called 'fifth province', an imaginary and imaginative space outside the paralysing oppositions of Northern Irish politics, the fact that the production was largely seen as a bipartisan cultural event was hugely significant – the play heralded, albeit briefly, art's potential reconciliatory role in the North. However, the play's capacity to bring Protestant and Catholic communities together relied in part on its refracted take on the Troubles – its gazing askance at contemporary politics rather than tackling them head-on.

Translations dramatises the Ordnance Survey of Ireland, undertaken by the Royal Engineers between 1824 and 1846 and led by Major Thomas Colby. While the Ordnance Survey – the first ever mapping of an entire country on such a detailed scale – re-drew land boundaries for the purpose of resolving inequities in local taxation, its effort to standardise place names often had the effect of Anglicising Gaelic precedents and obscuring cultural memory. While the play explicitly tackles this historical moment, it also gestures tacitly towards the Troubles in a number of ways. For instance, Friel repeatedly mobilises the language of tribalism in relation to the theme of home and belonging – a move that interrogates the rhetoric of the Troubles. In *Translations*' final scene, Jimmy Jack asks Maire, 'do you know the Greek word *endogamein*? It means to marry within the tribe. And the word *exogamein* means to marry outside the tribe. And you don't cross those borders casually – both sides get very angry.'¹ The question of 'crossing borders' in intimate relationships, as Maire and her British lover Yolland attempt to do, was an inflammatory one during the Troubles, when the personal and the political were inextricably linked. Indeed, the Provos (Provisional IRA) were known, in the conflict's early years, to tar and feather young Catholic women who dared to enter into relationships with members of the largely Protestant Royal Ulster Constabulary (RUC) or British security forces. Seamus Heaney's poem 'Punishment', from his 1975 collection *North*, caused controversy several years before the publication of *Translations* for its speaker's concession that he is both 'outrage[d]' by and somehow accepting of this 'tribal, intimate revenge',² and Friel invokes this intertext so that the play's nineteenth-century landscape is shadowed by this contemporary scene. Moreover, *Translations* suggests that 'a civilization can be imprisoned in a linguistic contour which no longer matches the landscape of ... fact', and argues that 'we must never cease renewing [our] images; because once we do, we fossilise'.³ Although Friel's stated subject here is Ireland's history of language loss, these lines apply equally (if implicitly) to the contemporary North: essentialising genuflections to things 'authentically' British or Irish are, Friel implies, 'fossilising' barriers to a shared future.

In addition to the play's historical displacements heightening audience receptivity, they also countered conceptions in the popular press (particularly in England) of Troubles-era Northern Ireland as a 'naturally' brutal place wracked by irrational enmities. In other words, Friel contextualises the contemporary conflict by writing about colonial conquest; he connects territorial displacement, political oppression, and the suppression of native language and culture in centuries gone by to present-day violence, explaining without excusing that violence. When the Royal Engineers alter place names in the play – Lis na Muc becomes Swinefort; Poll na gCaorach becomes Sheepsrock – these changes are literally disorienting for locals; as the new map is being drawn, Owen asks Hugh, 'Will you be able to find your way?'.⁴ David Lloyd calls the cartographers' strategy a 'primary deterritorialization': a fundamental distancing of people from place, and from the sense of cultural continuity rooted *in* place.⁵ Friel's invocation of this 'deterritorialization' situates the Troubles in their historical context; the play does not justify violent Republicanism, but it does write back to conceptions of Irish Catholics as unaccountably primitive or savage by illuminating the grievances of a colonised people.

Similarly, Seamus Deane's semi-autobiographical 1996 novel *Reading in the Dark* speaks to the Troubles by outlining the protracted consequences of Partition (1921). Set in Derry and spanning the years 1945 to 1971, the novel draws a direct line from the establishment of the border between Northern Ireland and the Irish Republic to contemporary civil conflict. As Joe Cleary explains of Partition, 'in regions where the peoples concerned are geographically intermingled, the attempt to manufacture ethnically homogeneous states, or states with secure ethnic majorities, cannot be accomplished without extraordinary communal violence. This violence does not end with the act of partition: violence is not incidental to but constitutive of the new state arrangements thus produced.'[6] Put otherwise, the Troubles cannot be explained away as random acts of Republican 'terrorism'; without even broaching the conflict itself (the book concludes before Bloody Sunday in 1972), Deane implies that violence is 'constitutive' of the nascent nation-state. At one point in the novel, the narrator's mother provides a laundry list of the conditions faced by Northern Ireland's Catholic minority: 'Injustice. The police themselves. Dirty politics. [...] [Catholics] unemployed, gerrymandered, beaten up by every policeman who took the notion, gaoled by magistrates and judges who were so vicious that it was they who should be gaoled.'[7]

Moreover, by tracking the genesis of the Troubles, the novel performs its own acts of truth and reconciliation. *Reading in the Dark* was published in 1996, while the country was in the often-painful throes of its peace process, and it argues that animosity can only be assuaged by fully examining old wounds rather than by treating the conflict as a kind of *ex nihilo* anomaly. The weight of the past never dissipates in the novel; indeed, the book often collapses history into the present in invasive 'flash images' in order to reveal the workings of colonial trauma. In one telling scene, the narrator's mother asks him to 'let the past be the past', and the narrator responds, 'it wasn't the past and she knew it'.[8] Northern Ireland is a country 'possessed', Deane suggests, and its spectral histories must be remembered, repeated, and gradually worked through. That said, the book also highlights the possibility of cross-community empathy, indicating that the conflict, while rooted in the systematic oppression of Catholics, is also a cycle of mutual victimisation. The narrator's father, for example, sympathises with a man whose son, an English soldier, was shot on his doorstep in the lead-up to the Troubles, despite the father having himself been victimised by the British army: 'Poor man. [...] I feel for him. Even though his son was one of those. It's a strange world.'[9] Much as the book narrates a grim period in Northern Irish life, then, it also offers surprising glimmers of hope.

Unlike Friel and Deane, who route their analyses of the conflict through other historical moments, Ciaran Carson confronts the Troubles head-on in his collections *The Irish for No* (1987) and *Belfast Confetti* (1989). However, Carson's poetry is akin to Deane's prose in its insistent efforts to register the conflict's structures of trauma. In Carson's work, violence constantly unmakes and defamiliarises the cityscape: in fact, Carson refers to Belfast as a 'demolition city',[10] as its spaces are again and again 'sucked back into nothingness by the rewind button'.[11] Belfast's landmarks, Carson indicates, are all potentially temporary; the Grand Central Hotel, for instance, a favourite paramilitary target, is reduced to rubble, rebuilt, and bombed out again; and one minute Gass' Bicycle Shop is there, the next it's gone, 'a fresh breeze sweep[ing] through the gap'.[12] In fact, Carson argues that '[only t]he city ... [can be] a map of the city' during the Troubles, as maps simply can't keep pace with Belfast's newly minted roadblocks and freshly shorn blitz sites.[13]

The chronology of the conflict's violence also intersects in Carson's work with 'trauma time', a subject's repeated possession and re-possession by an unincorporable traumatic event. As Cathy Caruth explains, 'the impact of the traumatic event lies precisely in its belatedness, in its refusal to be simply located, in its insistent appearance outside the boundaries of any single place or time'. Traumatic events, she continues, 'assume their force precisely in their temporal delay'; '[T]he fundamental dislocation implied by all traumatic experience [...] is both testimony to the event and to the impossibility of its direct access.'[14] Carson's 'Ambition' echoes Caruth in describing such 'dislocations': 'For if time is a road, | It's fraught with ramps and dog-legs, switchbacks and spaghetti [...] | And bits of the landscape | Keep recurring.'[15] The theme of trauma is nowhere more apparent in Carson's work than in his poem 'Asylum', in which the past encroaches menacingly on the present for the narrator's Uncle John. Having suffered through a litany of paramilitary attacks, Uncle John is hypervigilant; he is discomfited by the 'yelps of children' and the sounds of cars backfiring, and he has developed a number of anxious tics (his 'jigging and clicking' the door latch; his pronounced stutter).[16] Moreover, the poem itself exhibits signs of trauma, as it neurotically repeats its central tropes: the backfiring car, for example, recurs compulsively throughout.[17] Carson explicitly highlights these compulsions, explaining both the psyche's and the poem's spontaneous returns to originary ruptures by saying, 'you can tell that this was all some time ago, although it does repeat itself'.[18]

However, Carson's poetry also proposes the cadences of traditional tunes and tale-telling as salves of sorts for violence. These are the rhythms of everyday life in Belfast – looping, recursive tempi – and they work, at least to some degree, against the conflict's forward march. Carson's *Last Night's Fun* (1996), a prose volume about Traditional Irish music, describes the genre as fundamentally nonlinear: during a Trad session, the same songs are repeated over and over with an eye (or an ear) to previous renditions, but different players also offer their own variations on the tunes' themes. This means that the participants' 'present time, imbued with yesterday, comes out with bent dimensions', but also that 'the music [is] always renewable in the light of the now'.[19] Put otherwise, traditional music bears at once towards the past and towards the future – it 'recalls' prior renditions, but it is also infinitely variable – and Carson tries to capture this curious temporality in his poetry. Carson also draws on the meandering lines of oral storytelling and Belfast 'bar-talk' in his work.[20] His signature 'long line' is indebted to the rhythms of the eight-bar reel and is shaped by the articulated playing common to traditional tunes and the accented tones of the dramatic tale-teller rather than by regular poetic metre.[21] This source material is evident in both theme and form in a poem such as 'Dresden', from *The Irish for No*. 'Dresden' is incredibly digressive and is full of distinctive verbal tics; the phrase 'or rather' is repeated over and over again. These patterns are initiated by the poem's elliptical opening lines: 'Horse Boyle was called Horse Boyle because of his brother Mule; | Though why Mule was called Mule is anybody's guess. I stayed there once, | Or rather, I nearly stayed there once. But that's another story.'[22] As this passage suggests, the poem manages stories within stories within stories, all with the lively tenor of the consummate yarn-spinner. Ultimately, Carson's poetry suggests that the conflict's death drive is not the only temporality that shapes lives in the North – his wandering lines move against the bluntness of violence and invite other times into the present moment. Poems like 'Dresden' range from past to present to future by way of the tale-teller's fluid, free-associative logic; like the traditional tune, they become 'family tree[s] ... way[s] of negotiating lost time' – not antidotes to 'trauma time', exactly, but pleasurable mnemonic repetitions that counter the repetition compulsions to be found elsewhere in Carson's work.[23]

Like Carson's poetry, Anne Devlin's play *Ourselves Alone* (first produced in 1985 and published in 1986) approaches the conflict with an unflinchingly realistic eye. However, Devlin responds to the marginalisation of women's lives in a time of masculinist violence in the North, and to the exclusion of those lives from local culture, by allowing her female characters to take centre stage. Devlin's play is set primarily in Andersonstown, a working-class Catholic community in West Belfast with strong

Republican leanings. *Ourselves Alone* counteracts, as C. L. Innes phrases it, the 'etherealisation' of women in the Irish nationalist tradition – typified by the Cathleen Ní Houlihan myth that asks men to sacrifice themselves for the 'motherland' while negating the material realities of actual women's lives – by amplifying that community's female voices.[24]

Donna, for example, is a case study in dormant selfhood, having agreed to tend home and hearth while her husband Liam languishes in Long Kesh. This enforced domesticity, however, is gradually revealed to be a social disease that writes its symptoms across Donna's body: she begins suffering from both panic attacks and prolonged episodes of depression, and she eventually concedes, 'I think I may have lost the capacity for happiness.'[25] Josie, on the other hand, is a passionate nationalist who devotes herself to the Republican cause, but she is largely confined to acting as a courier or concealing men on the run beneath her floorboards, 'smiling at soldiers' while male militants carry out the Provos' 'important' tasks.[26] Over the course of the play, she too realises that the political has poisoned the personal in Northern Ireland – she notes that when patriotism eclipses love, love is reduced to 'possess[ion]' – and she ultimately articulates a desire to 'stop for a while, look around me, plant a garden, listen for other sounds; the breathing of a child somewhere outside Andersonstown'.[27] Finally, Frieda is an aspiring singer-songwriter who wants to write songs that tell her story rather than performing 'Republican classic[s]' in which 'the women are doormats'.[28] Her refusal to take Republican politics seriously is initially framed by other characters as flighty and selfish, but eventually her rejection of chaste Irish female domesticity is revealed to be a radical act of self-care. The end of the play finds Frieda packing to leave Belfast with the intention of 'leaving the tribes behind. Both of them!': a decision suggesting that one must abandon the North to pursue self-actualisation, that one can only be 'oneself alone'.[29] This grim conclusion is an apt enough response to the claustrophobic violence of mid-1980s Belfast, though as we will see, over the course of the ensuing decade, other writers will find ways to choose both personhood and place as the possibility of peace begins to dawn in Northern Ireland.

Medbh McGuckian also offers a feminist take on the Troubles, though her poetry responds much more obliquely to war than does Devlin's play. McGuckian's work tends to proceed by the logic of metaphor, with violence inflecting the poetry in texture more than in theme. Her collections often stage the conflict's capacity to infiltrate even the most intimate of places – including, centrally, her home in Belfast, but even more importantly, the crevices of language and thus the 'homes' that are her poems. This is why McGuckian's writing evidences a tension between the desire to be hermetic and private and the inability to remain so.[30] 'The Soil-Map', for instance, from 1982's *The Flower Master*, is a kind of apostrophe, a direct address from the narrator to her house. The Catholic McGuckian had recently moved to a primarily Protestant area of Belfast's sectarian patchwork, a 'transitional' neighbourhood that was becoming too derelict for Protestants and that was therefore aspirational for relatively impoverished but upwardly mobile Catholics. The poem's references to the 'soil-map', a resource survey that measures the quality of the soil in various areas, and its labelling of the area as 'Hymenstown', suggestive of a barrier that is penetrable only through either desire or violence, indicate the history of the North's segregated spaces.[31] Areas of rich, fertile soil on the island were long assigned to Protestant settlers, while Catholics were left only barely arable land; in the early 1980s, McGuckian therefore feels her encroaching on Protestant territory as an 'auspicious | And dangerous' transgression, a domestic invasion.[32] The narrator's address to the home carries in some ways the intimacy of a blazon, as she describes in detail both its best features (its 'splendid fenestration' and 'slender purlins') and its flaws (its 'discolouring' and the 'saddling derangement of [its] roof'), but it is also, despite itself, necessarily a political statement.[33] As Adam Hanna explains it, '[t]he representations of the private space in "The Soil-Map", a poem that engages so much with public [politico-religious] narratives, is indicative of the intimate depth at which these narratives are felt'.[34] In other words, a Northern Irish poem about place, even one that purports to retreat from the world into interior spaces, will inevitably be 'invaded' by the weight of historical disputes and contemporary sectarian strife.

'The Sofa', from the same collection, explicitly stages the inability of the poem to be hermetically sealed, heedless of authorial intent. Its poet-speaker longs to narrate only private, intimate moments – 'his large, gentle stares, | How his soft shirt is the inside of pleasure | To me' – but the external world intrudes incessantly, demanding her writerly attentions (what, a friend asks, of '[t]he sun', '[t]he impudence of flowers', of 'nature, greenery, insects'?).[35] She feels this intrusion as 'the wear on my threshold' and describes her reluctance to engage with that which lies beyond her four walls: 'Somewhere | A curtain rising wonders where I am.'[36] Thus, like the house in 'The Soil-Map', here the poem itself – a more personal dwelling-place for McGuckian than any physical structure – is vulnerable to the pull of the public sphere, suggesting that perhaps all language must bear the weight of political discourse in the face of violence. This tension can be felt in many of McGuckian's poems, and indeed in much Northern Irish literature of the period. As Anne Devlin's character McDermot frankly puts it, 'there are no personal reasons any more. Everything is political',[37] and, similarly, as Seamus Deane explains, 'a political system, especially when it's a rancid one, as in Northern Ireland, has an effect on personal relationships – in fact, it spreads right through the whole society'.[38] McGuckian's work might metaphorise this 'spread', but her collections also concede that it can never be fully contained.

Unlike McGuckian's more domestic aesthetic, Paul Muldoon's wide-ranging phantasmagorias constantly allow the personal and the political, the poetic and the prosaic, and the local and the global to collide. Many of Muldoon's poems from the period are explicitly transtemporal; like Devlin, Muldoon satirises historical tropes that contribute to contemporary political myth-making and that freeze Northerners in antagonistic roles. 'Aisling', from Muldoon's 1983 collection *Quoof*, would appear, given its title, to be a Republican ballad of sorts: an aisling is a medieval form that was borrowed by eighteenth-century Irish Jacobites to foretell the 'rightful' restoration of the House of Stuart to its rule over the Gaelic world and that has been redeployed in service of nationalist politics ever since. The traditional aisling typically features the spectre of Mother Ireland appearing to a sleeping speaker in the guise of a beautiful young woman, who arrives to predict the revival of Irish fortunes and to ask the country's men to sacrifice themselves in the name of that revival. Muldoon's poem borrows several lines outright from an anonymous 1790s aisling called 'The Colleen Rue' (a transliteration of *cailín ruadh*, a red-haired girl): waking in a snow bank to a vision of Erin, its speaker asks, seemingly awestruck, 'was she Aurora, or the goddess Flora, | Artemidora, or Venus bright?'.[39] However, the speaker adds, as a brusque postscript to his address, 'or Anorexia, who left | a lemon stain on my flannel sheet?'.[40] By casting Erin as 'Anorexia', an ignoble hunger-striker and a sexual conquest circulating not nationalistic fervour but an STD, Muldoon deflates, even defames, the myth of Mother Ireland.

This refusal to romanticise Republicanism is redoubled in *Quoof*'s 'Gathering Mushrooms', in which Muldoon borrows from a traditional song of the same name the image of a 'fair maid' – yet another embodiment of Erin – gathering mushrooms. The song invests her with the full weight of sentimental nationalism: she is chaste and 'modest', but also powerfully erotic, passionately 'pressing' her 'parting breast' to the speaker's own. However, in Muldoon's hands, the maid's mushrooms are pharmacological rather than pastoral; as the poem's speaker confesses, 'We were thinking only of psilocybin.'⁴¹ Rather than stirring the speaker's patriotic ardour, Erin rather more crudely 'blow[s his] mind' – a move that undoes 'the Irish sexist myth of the nationalist siren' and thereby desacralises contemporary Republican imagery.⁴² When the poem concludes in a seemingly Republican voice, replete with images of prisoner internments and dirty protests – '*lie down with us now and wrap | yourself in the soiled grey blanket of Irish rain | that will, one day, bleach itself white. | Lie down with us and wait*' – that voice is channelled through 'the head of a horse', its sanctimonious sentiments proving no more than vivid hallucinations, the fruits of a bad trip.⁴³ Muldoon therefore approaches both Irish history and the contemporary conflict with tongue firmly in cheek, critiquing the opportunistic repackaging of the former as fodder for the latter.

In addition to being transtemporal, Muldoon's poetics are also insistently 'translocal': a term that Jahan Ramazani uses to describe poetry that links local affinities and global solidarities. 'Translocal' poetry, Ramazani explains, involves imaginative travel that enables close relationships between 'discrepant topographies'.⁴⁴ Muldoon's work performs precisely this sort of travel: it refuses to respect borders, framing the North's warring identity groups as unnecessarily insular and claustrophobic and instead forging cross-cultural sympathies and solidarities. 'The More a Man Has the More a Man Wants', a long poem also collected in *Quoof*, features one of Muldoon's most common imagined solidarities: that of Ireland and indigenous America. The poem superimposes Native America on Northern Ireland, loosely transposing Paul Radin's version of the Winnebago Trickster cycle to Muldoon's native Ulster. Its two main characters, the paramilitary Gallogly and the visiting Apache Mangas Jones, are cast as doppelgangers of a kind, perhaps flip sides of the slippery Trickster. Muldoon does acknowledge the thorny complexities of his strategic trans-Atlanticism; Mangas Jones arrives in Belfast to 'trac[e] the family tree | of an Ulsterman who had some hand | in the massacre at Wounded Knee', a move that highlights the historical complicity of the Irish in violence against American Indians.⁴⁵ However, as the poem progresses, Muldoon also charts the potential (if complex) sympathies between the two communities.

Muldoon's reference to Gallogly as a 'hot-foot from a woodcut | by Derricke', for example, yokes the stereotype of Native Americans as physical beings, rough and hardy but morally and intellectually wanting, to similar imperial pronouncements about the Irish.⁴⁶ The 'hot-foot' reference evokes the likes of cartoonist A. P. Adams' 'Hurry Up Hot-Foot' panels, which depicted a caricature of a 'Plains Indian' winning various athletic events by assaulting or cheating his competitors, and the mention of Derricke conjures his *The Image of Irelande*, a long poem with accompanying woodcuts (first published in 1581 and recirculated by Sir Walter Scott in the early nineteenth century) that mounted a defence of colonial conquest by portraying the Irish as 'wantone' and 'wilde' and casting their warrior woodkern as 'barbarous' and underhanded in combat.[47] Muldoon's final stanza goes so far as to project Jones's voice from Gallogly's body, making audible the poem's implied (post)colonial intimacies. Although its characters' allegiances to 'the tribe' never waver – Jones continues his quest for vengeance; Gallogly dies an ardent Republican, having perpetrated violence across the Irish countryside – the poem *itself* charts newly imagined communities by way of this strategic ventriloquy, communities not in 'race-consciousness' but in common cause.[48] In the face of the Troubles' calcified self/other dichotomies, this move de-essentialises belonging and offers a path to palliation if not to reconciliation for those exhausted by the conflict in the North.

Like the other authors mentioned here, Glenn Patterson and Robert McLiam Wilson represent Troubles-era time as porous in their sweeping Belfast panoramas. However, these writers, working as Northern Ireland approached the abortive 1994 ceasefire and then, finally, the hard-won 1998 Belfast Agreement, move beyond others' efforts to historicise the conflict; they mobilise past and present for the sake of the future, pointing forward towards possible peace. Patterson's *Fat Lad* (1992), for instance, allows its protagonist, Drew, to wander imaginatively through Belfast's long history: he researches the construction of Belfast's castle and early walled town and even learns about the area's pre-colonial occupants, with their 'megalithic tombs and the ancient, eponymous sandbank ford'.[49] This revisiting of Belfast's previous incarnations is transformative for Drew, as it allows him to excavate 'a different city altogether' than the '*this was where* and the *over there* of twenty years of violence' that drove him away from Belfast as a young man,[50] and thus also to glimpse a future for his city beyond that violence. Kay, Drew's lover and the owner of an architecture and design firm, is an especially suggestive character in this regard: she rushes around the city, 'pounding up the street in that way she had, determined, as always, to leave her mark'.[51] This is not the 'mark' of an empire-builder, although Patterson's rhetoric recalls historical occupations and forcible re-writings of place; rather, it is the aspiration of someone filled to the brim with the city's history – a history that begins long before the advent of the Troubles in 1968 – and inspired by foregoing efforts to capture its *genius loci*. Indeed, Kay celebrates not those who built Belfast's elaborate landmarks, magisterial buildings like Stormont and City Hall that assert colonial authority over local space, but those who first reclaimed the town from the Lagan, turning the riverbed and making land out of 'sleech'. She is inspired by men 'who had looked at mudflats and seen shipping channels, had looked at water and seen land. Belfast as a city was a triumph over mud and water', and locals 'had to build the land before they could work it [...] [fashioning] solidity from the morass, leaving an indelible imprint on the unpromising slobland'.[52] These sentiments indicate that Kay's investment in Belfast's built future involves looking back to the city's beginnings – and not simply its colonial beginnings, but also its much earlier roots as a strategic site for fording the Lagan. Ultimately, Kay's desire for a better future for Belfast reflects on the operations of the novel at large: Patterson's preoccupation with the 'triumphs' of Belfast's past also projects something of the potentially resonant future hidden in the city's rubbled midst.

McLiam Wilson's *Eureka Street* (1996) similarly imagines its way towards possible futures for the North, and it also telescopes time in service of this imagining. In the midst of the country's peace negotiations, McLiam Wilson tries to locate shared structures of feeling in a still-bloodied Belfast, suggesting cross-community affect as a possible source of post-Agreement reconciliation. In particular, the eleventh chapter, which describes a bombing in Belfast's Fountain Street, breaks from the standard pace of the novel's plot and from the lives of the book's protagonists, slowing time to a crawl in order to dwell, as McLiam Wilson explains it, on 'the weight of a human life lost'.[53] This 'weight', moreover, is a shared weight: the bodies turned to meat by the chapter's violence cannot be co-opted by any oversimplified sectarian narrative. In fact, the deaths in the Fountain Street bombing, which McLiam Wilson renders in excruciating detail, combat the conflict's discursive exhaustion by revealing the city, beneath its political divides, to be a 'conglomerate of bodies. A Belfastful of spines, kidneys, hearts, livers and lungs [...] [A] frail cityful of organs.'[54] Put otherwise, the condition of living in Belfast is one of shared vulnerability; in a gesture of conciliation, McLiam Wilson sketches the city's collective emotional terrain.

Seventeen people 'stop existing' during the Fountain Street bombing, and a further eleven are seriously injured. None of the dead or maimed are identified as Protestant or Catholic; rather, they are framed as human beings with human stories, stories indiscriminately foreshortened by political violence. From Rosemary Daye, a young woman fresh from a thrilling date with her new boyfriend Sean, to Martin O'Hare, 34, who 'had been to school', 'had read *Great Expectations* and had wanted to be an astronomer', 'had been in love with people and people had been in love with him', and who holds the door to the fatal sandwich shop for Rosemary;[55] from Angie Best, the owner of the sandwich shop, who, when she was 22, had 'passed her driving test and experienced an ecstasy and sense of freedom so extraordinary that no subsequent experience ever matched its intensity',[56] to Kevin McCafferty, who 'sang in a band whose name changed every gig' and who is working a double shift preparing sandwiches while dreaming of one day appearing on television[57] – all of these men and women, boys and girls, 'd[o] that trick the dead do' of moving '[f]rom living human to corpse – the fastest transition in the world'.[58] Additionally, in an almost unbearable genuflection to the conflict's brutality, McLiam Wilson notes that these victims – who 'all had stories [...] [that] shouldn't have been short stories' and rich 'networks of friendship and intimacy and relation that tied them to those they loved and who loved them, those they knew and who knew them'[59] – are indistinguishable in death. Whether Protestant or Catholic, whether political or apolitical, they become 'pounds of unidentified tissue', 'beef-like approximation[s] of the human form'.[60] And as McLiam Wilson observes in concluding the chapter, 'the pages that follow are light with their loss. The text is less dense, the city is smaller.'[61] In other words, *Eureka Street* indicates that, at root, Belfast is populated by a host of fragile bodies, and that this common human condition ought to propel the city, and the country as a whole, towards peacebuilding.

Like the work of many Troubles-era authors, *Eureka Street* is motivated, above all, by a genuine love of place. McLiam Wilson allows his protagonist, Jake, to ventriloquise this love in a final, incredibly intimate, almost ecstatic expression of homecoming: 'Tender is a small word for what I feel for this town. [...] Belfast – only a jumble of streets and a few big bumps in the ground, only a whisper of God.'[62] This tenderness is palpable in much of the literature of the period, whether that literature critiques the conflict's claustrophobic demands or attempts to envisage a future beyond those demands. Further, as against the seeming paralysis of the Troubles – the sense that war has overwhelmed all other Northern Irish narratives, fixing the country in place and rendering it both ahistorical and futureless – writers of the 1980s and 1990s try to loosen the hold of violence's overwhelming 'presentness'. The contemporary conflict is the culmination, these writers argue, of a long history of injustice, and only by undertaking the radically restorative move of sharing stories from both sides of that history can Northern Ireland finally broach the possibility of peace.

Notes

1. Brian Friel, *Translations* (London: Faber and Faber, 1981), p. 90.
2. Seamus Heaney, *North* (London: Faber and Faber, 1975), pp. 42, 44. For a particularly critical response to *North*, see Ciaran Carson, 'Escaped from the Massacre?', *Honest Ulsterman*, 50 (Winter 1975), pp. 183–6.
3. Friel, *Translations*, pp. 52, 88.
4. Ibid., p. 51.
5. David Lloyd, *Anomalous States: Irish Writing and the Post-Colonial Moment* (Durham, NC: Duke University Press, 1993), p. 16.
6. Joe Cleary, *Literature, Partition and the Nation State: Culture and Conflict in Ireland, Israel and Palestine* (Cambridge: Cambridge University Press, 2002), p. 11.
7. Seamus Deane, *Reading in the Dark* (New York: Vintage International, 1998), p. 213.
8. Deane, *Reading in the Dark*, p. 42.
9. Ibid., p. 245.
10. Ciaran Carson, *Belfast Confetti* (Winston-Salem, NC: Wake Forest University Press, 1989), p. 54.
11. Carson, *Belfast Confetti*, p. 58.
12. Ibid., pp. 57–8.
13. Ibid., p. 69.
14. Cathy Caruth, 'Trauma and Experience: Introduction', in Cathy Caruth, ed., *Trauma: Explorations in Memory* (Baltimore, MD: Johns Hopkins University Press), pp. 3–12 (p. 9).
15. Carson, *Belfast Confetti*, pp. 27–8.
16. Ciaran Carson, *The Irish for No* (Oldcastle, Co. Meath: Gallery Press, 1987), pp. 54–8.
17. Ibid., pp. 54–7.
18. Ibid., p. 56.
19. Ciaran Carson, *Last Night's Fun: In and Out of Time with Irish Music* (New York: North Point, 1986), p. 90; 'For All I Know: Ciaran Carson in Conversation with Elmer Kennedy-Andrews', in Elmer Kennedy-Andrews, ed., *Ciaran Carson: Critical Essays* (Dublin: Four Courts Press, 2009), pp. 13–27 (p. 15).
20. Ciaran Carson, 'Interview with John Brown', in John Brown, ed., *In the Chair: Interviews with Poets from the North of Ireland* (Cliffs of Moher, Ireland: Salmon Poetry, 2002), pp. 141–52 (p. 145).
21. Neil Corcoran, 'One Step Forward, Two Steps Back', in Neil Corcoran, eds., *The Chosen Ground: Essays on the Contemporary Poetry of Northern Ireland* (Bridgend, Wales: Seren Books, 1992), pp. 213–33 (p. 217).
22. Carson, *The Irish for No*, p. 11.
23. Carson, *Last Night's Fun*, p. 90.
24. C. L. Innes, *Cultural Nationalism and the Feminine* (London: Institute for Commonwealth Studies, 1992), p. 22.

25. Anne Devlin, *Ourselves Alone, with The Long March and A Woman Calling* (London: Faber and Faber, 1986), p. 89.
26. Devlin, *Ourselves Alone*, p. 31.
27. Ibid., pp. 73, 77.
28. Ibid., p. 13.
29. Ibid., p. 80.
30. Eric Falci, *Continuity and Change in Irish Poetry, 1966–2010* (Cambridge: Cambridge University Press, 2012), p. 86.
31. Medbh McGuckian, *The Flower Master and Other Poems* (Oldcastle, Co. Meath: Gallery Press, 1993), p. 37.
32. McGuckian, *The Flower Master*, p. 36.
33. Ibid.
34. Adam Hanna, *Northern Irish Poetry and Domestic Space* (Basingstoke: Palgrave Macmillan, 2015), p. 122.
35. McGuckian, *The Flower Master*, p. 25.
36. Ibid.
37. Devlin, *Ourselves Alone*, p. 61.
38. Andrew Ross, 'Irish Secrets and Lies: An Interview with Seamus Deane, Author of *Reading in the Dark*', *Salon.com*, 11 April 1997: www.salon.com/1997/04/11/deane/ [accessed 28 March 2019].
39. Paul Muldoon, *Quoof* (London: Faber and Faber, 1983), p. 39.
40. Ibid.
41. Ibid., p. 7.
42. Jonathan Hufstader, *Tongue of Water, Teeth of Stones: Northern Irish Poetry and Social Violence* (Lexington, KY: University Press of Kentucky, 1999), p. 161.
43. Muldoon, *Quoof*, pp. 8–9.
44. Jahan Ramazani, *A Transnational Poetics* (Chicago and London: University of Chicago Press, 2009), p. 58.
45. Paul Muldoon, *Poems 1968–1998* (New York: Farrar, Straus and Giroux, 2001), p. 134.
46. Ibid., p. 146.
47. The full text of *The Image of Irelande* is available at: www.docs.is.ed.ac.uk/docs/lib-archive/bgallery/Gallery/researchcoll/ireland.html [accessed 28 March 2019].
48. Daniel Corkery, *Synge and Anglo-Irish Literature* (Cork, Ireland: Cork University Press, 1931), p. 212.
49. Glenn Patterson, *Fat Lad* (Belfast: Blackstaff Press, 2012), p. 227.
50. Ibid., p. 224.
51. Ibid., p. 302.
52. Ibid., p. 225.
53. Sylvie Mikowski, 'Irish History Is a Brilliant Joke', *Source*, 7.1 (1999), pp. 83–6 (p. 83).
54. Robert McLiam Wilson, *Eureka Street: A Novel of Ireland Like No Other* (New York: Arcade Publishing, 1996), p. 396.

55. Ibid., pp. 222–3.
56. Ibid., p. 231.
57. Ibid., p. 223.
58. Ibid., p. 231.
59. Ibid.
60. Ibid., pp. 229, 223.
61. Ibid., p. 231.
62. Ibid., p. 396.

CHAPTER 4

Contemporary Irish Theatre and Media
Paige Reynolds

Contemporary Irish dramatists have incorporated tactics drawn from mass media and technology within their formal, affective, and presentational logics – even as they have maintained a commitment to artful language. Across the past four decades, this allegiance to the text has surfaced in the robust redeployment of time-honoured literary works, modes, and subjects, as seen in Lucy Caldwell's adaptation of Chekhov's *Three Sisters* (2016), Marina Carr's invocation of classical tropes in *Portia Coughlan* (1996), Martin McDonagh's radical take on the peasant play in *The Lonesome West* (1997), or Frank McGuinness's reworking of 'the big house' motif in *The Hanging Gardens* (2013).[1] In realist or naturalist plays such as these, media might appear in the text as symbols or plot devices, or in the dramaturgy as props or design elements. Alongside such plays sit important new works that overtly deploy innovations and insights derived from technologies of the moment. A significant amount of recent Irish theatre has moved away from the traditional proscenium stage and towards site-specific and immersive theatre that deftly employs multimedia technologies to convey meaning. Such productions might suggest that the authority of the text has declined; yet they often rely on source texts for inspiration, as well as on archival research, interviews, and other resources for content and design elements. For all of the innovative multimodal varieties of performance and stage craft now on view, there remains in contemporary Irish drama a powerful commitment to the value of the word and the live body in performance. A productive and provocative tension between word and image, manifest in the deployment of media and media devices, is central to drama and performance in contemporary Ireland.

Critics have bemoaned that many contemporary Irish novels, imaginative as they are, seem to take place in a vacuum closed off to technologies that shape everyday life.[2] In the late twentieth century, this claim was borne out not only in fiction, but also on the Irish stage. In the opening scene of

Brian Friel's *Dancing at Lughnasa* (1990), the character Michael speaks directly to the audience and announces that he vividly recalls the summer of 1936 from his childhood for two reasons: it was the summer his Uncle Jack returned home to rural Ballybeg from Uganda, and it marked the arrival of the family's 'first wireless set'.[3] Michael notes that the radio's arrival prompted a change in his mother and her four adult sisters: he 'had witnessed Marconi's voodoo derange those kind, sensible women and transform them into shrieking strangers'.[4] This play captures the repressive climate of mid-twentieth-century Ireland, revealing how the women in Michael's family long for some means of expression beyond those deemed appropriate by stifling cultural norms. That release comes, in part, from the radio. Roughly a third of the way into the play, the 'raucous sound' of music from a céilí band pours from the radio and elicits from his aunt Maggie 'a look of defiance, of aggression; a crude mask of happiness'.[5] Prompted by the music, this ludic energy soon spreads to his mother and her other sisters, who join together in a wheeling dance. When the music stops, as the radio overheats, the women are jolted back into real life, gasping for breath and slightly embarrassed. Later in the play, music from the radio prompts Michael's mother Chris and his estranged father Gerry to dance together, and to reconcile, if only temporarily. The radio triggers these moments of pleasurable release, but they inevitably culminate in a return to familiar patterns of repression and retreat. Towards the end of the play, Gerry dances with one of the sisters to the tune of Cole Porter's 'Anything Goes', only to have Chris shut off the radio – ostensibly to save the battery. But this gesture conveys an inability to embrace the logic of 'Anything Goes' pouring from the wireless. Though it centres on a technology new to this family, *Dancing at Lughnasa* conveys a familiar cynicism about the liberatory promise of mass media. In this play, the technology of the radio offers its listeners release from constraints, but these evaporate when the machine fails – when the radio overheats, or threatens to run out of batteries, or is deliberately shut off by a member of the household.

Additionally, the conceit of the memory play that governs *Dancing at Lughnasa* serves to imitate and complicate the radio's disembodied mediation. As Friel notes in a stage direction early in Act I, the adult narrator Michael, who stands downstage left and addresses the audience, is doubled by 'the (imaginary) boy Michael' on stage with whom characters interact.[6] Throughout the play, Michael ventriloquises the boy's lines of dialogue; the characters in the 1936 diegesis interact only with the imaginary boy and never look at or directly address the adult narrator. From a distance,

Michael speaks 'for' his boyhood self, and 'to' the empty stage space. The disembodied voice of the empty stage space serves as the uncanny double of the family radio. The music emanating from the radio symbolises a freedom that cannot be realised, and Michael's voice floating in the air, the inchoate substitute for the absent child at the centre of the scene, suggests that memory is ephemeral and insecure.

As Patrick Lonergan has demonstrated, in the 1990s, Irish drama took advantage of media to promote itself globally, to advocate for Ireland as a progressive and technologically savvy country, one able to embrace the economic promise of the contemporary moment.[7] But in many plays from this same decade, the technologies on stage or referenced in the text were often recognisable and commonplace. Wireless radios, telephones, films, television – these were vehicles as familiar to audiences as the realism of the plays themselves. For instance, Conor McPherson's *The Weir* (1997) depicts an evening of talk among locals in a rural pub that houses 'an old television' mounted in the corner and a 'small radio' behind the bar.[8] These devices are part of the *mise-en-scène*, but deliberately marginalised – the play keeps storytelling at centre stage, literally. Nonetheless, in the narrative, a telephone plays a pivotal role. The lone female character, a newcomer named Valerie, tells the men in the pub the story of her young daughter's accidental death by drowning. She explains that one recent morning, her home telephone rang, and when she picked it up, her daughter Niamh was on the line, asking to be fetched home: 'The line was very faint. It was like a crossed line. There were voices, but I couldn't hear what they were saying. And then I heard Niamh. She said, "Mammy?" And I . . . just said, you know, "Yes".'[9] The men attribute this ghostly experience to a dream or to shock, or to a wrong number, but Valerie remains adamant that her daughter telephoned her. Here, the mundane telephone is imbued with supernatural power. It connects living and dead, present and past, reality and dream. But in its excess, the telephone troubles Valerie's marriage and leads others to doubt her sanity – most distressingly, it cannot revivify her daughter. Just like Friel's radio, McPherson's telephone makes a promise it cannot keep. Yet amid the various tales of human suffering shared that night in the pub, Valerie's story of the telephone is received with sympathy and understanding by the men.

Like Friel's play, *The Weir* contains an uncanny double of its dominant form of media technology.[10] The story of Niamh's ghostly phone call is presaged by Jack's 'old' and 'good little story' describing an evening roughly a century before when Maura Nealon and her mother Bridie heard a mysterious and unaccountable knocking at the door.[11] Jack relates that 'only years later [] Maura heard from one of the older people in the area that the house had been built on what they called a fairy road'.[12] After clarifying that it 'wasn't a road', but what his pub mate Jim calls 'like a row of things', Jack elaborates:

> Yeah, like a ... From the fort up in Brendan's top field there, then the old well, and the abbey further down, and into the cove where the little pebbly beach is, there. And the ... legend would be that the little fairies would come down that way to bathe, you see. And Maura Nealon's house was built on what you'd call ... that ... road.[13]

Valerie, the newcomer who now lives in Maura Nealon's house, replies by articulating the reason for the mysterious knocking: 'And they wanted to come through.'[14] Jack's tale foretells aspects of Valerie's subsequent monologue: a mother–daughter dyad, the presence of water, a desire to communicate across incommensurable worlds. Both the telephone line and the fairy road's 'row of things' – the Irish Otherworld's ley lines – are 'crossed lines', vehicles for failed mediations that stand in opposition to the sympathetic interchanges among those speaking bodies in the pub.

As the Celtic Tiger roared, and as international computer, communication, and digital media companies set up shop across Ireland and Northern Ireland, Irish drama continued to convey a deep ambivalence about such technologies. In Enda Walsh's *The Walworth Farce* (2006), a father and his two sons re-enact each day a fictitious narrative of the events leading to their exodus from Ireland to a council flat on Walworth Road in London. Dinny, the father, has scripted a performance in which his sons Blake and Sean play the roles of various family members in a saga that recapitulates the murderous farce in which Dinny's siblings and in-laws are killed so that he might receive the inheritance from his recently deceased parents. One day, Hayley, a young woman from the local Tesco, follows Sean home to the flat and stumbles into this perverse production. Chaos ensues, and the play ends with both Dinny and Blake murdered, Hayley having escaped, and Sean left in the flat to recapitulate the performance, with its shocking new ending, in future days.

The Walworth Farce is filled with themes familiar from Irish theatre – murderous siblings, excessive drinking, family wakes, rural poverty, and emigration. But it self-consciously interrogates repetition, both formally and thematically, not least through its meta-theatricality. The traumatic story of these murders is retold and re-enacted each day, offering, as Dinny hopes, a comfort. And yet even as trauma theory suggests that recapitulated narrative can help victims to heal and move forward, the play suggests otherwise. These characters are too terrified to escape their familiar stories. Their entrapment is signalled by the media objects in the play, as when a tape recorder warbles timeworn Irish tunes such as 'A Nation Once Again' or 'An Irish Lullaby' to signal scene and tone changes during the performance. Here, as in Beckett's one-act *Krapp's Last Tape* (1958), the tape recorder serves both as prop and symbol. Similar to the radio in Friel and the telephone in McPherson, the tape recorder's disembodied voices represent a loss – in this instance, the loss of family and homeland. It is a device that also conveys the inherently repetitive nature of memory and experience, as well as highlighting the warped nostalgia that ensnares the characters. Television likewise plays a symbolic role in this family drama. Dinny is deeply attached to *The Waltons*, citing this 1970s American television series as an exemplar of family that can provide solace. Thanks to global syndication, episodes of this domestic drama regularly and predictably materialise on television sets, just as their family narrative invariably re-appears each day in the flat. Even the play's final image draws attention to the problems of media images in repetition. The play closes with Sean dressed in Hayley's coat, having painted his face with his father's brown shoe polish. Sean will now, in perpetuity, create a 'new story' from the day's events in which Hayley, a young black woman, will be a character. Sean might appear to be seeking verisimilitude, but his performance of blackface, drawn from racist American popular culture, is deeply unsettling. It suggests that he is trapped in an endless cycle of violence crafted not just by his father's narrative, but also by a society that similarly, on a larger scale, twists the truth to oppress and harm vulnerable subjects. Sean is a victim of these systemic abuses, but his appearance in blackface suggests that he will uncritically recapitulate those logics.

The media devices in *The Walworth Farce* thus carry a new symbolic weight that underscores the crucial importance not of words, but of images. When Blake and Sean attempt to reconstruct their childhood exodus from Ireland, Blake laments:

> Dad all talk of Ireland, Sean. Everything's Ireland. His voice is stuck in Cork so it's impossible to forget what Cork is. (*A pause.*) This story we play is everything. (*A pause.*) Once upon a time my head was full of pictures of Granny's coffin and Mr and Mrs Cotter and Paddy and Vera and Bouncer the dog and all those busy pictures in our last day. (*Smiling.*) 'Cause you'd say Dad's words and they'd give you pictures, wouldn't they, Sean? And so many pictures in your head ... Sure you wouldn't want for the outside world even if was a good world! You could be happy. (*A pause.*) But all them

pictures have stopped. I say his words and all I can see is the word. A lot of words piled on top of other words. There's no sense to my day 'cause the sense isn't important anymore. No pictures. No dreams. Words only.[15]

Here, Blake captures one problem of relying strictly on narrative. Without the documentary authority of pictorial or aural evidence, or even without the imaginative history of personal memory, words can warp the truth, bend the story, offer individuals 'alternative facts' that trap and cripple them. So while this play recapitulates the familiar suspicion of media technologies found throughout Irish drama, it also timidly and somewhat contradictorily suggests that in those technologies might rest a means of salvation from disabling, and even deathly, histories.

This point is buoyed up in the play by Hayley's cell phone, which sings out 'the Crazy Frog version of Destiny's Child's "I'm a Survivor"'.[16] This ring tone aligns Hayley with these African American pop singers via her race, feminine appeal, and strength of character; even as it threatens to expose her attempt to escape the flat and its horrors, the ring ultimately foreshadows her safe escape. So while ambivalent, because the chiming cell phone could help or hurt her, this new technology offers its British subject some hope for the future. This same ambivalence about media technology characterises Walsh's more recent work in the theatre, which has moved away from the naturalism of *The Walworth Farce* and become aggressively multimodal. *Arlington* (2016), for instance, fuses dance, visual art, live performance, and audio recordings to critique authoritarianism through its depiction of a technocratic dystopia under constant surveillance.

As critics have noted, references to film and television suffuse the plays of dramatists including Walsh, Martin McDonagh, and Mark O'Rowe – each of whom has gone on to further success as a screenwriter and/or director.[17] But as Clare Wallace observes, a similar engagement with media is not evident in the work of women playwrights during the same period.[18] However, some of the most innovative uses of multimedia in Irish theatre in recent years have been imagined by female theatre practitioners and playwrights. Founded in 2009 by Louise Lowe and Owen Boss, ANU Productions has produced a remarkable body of work based on subject interviews and historical research.[19] Working from this material, the company devises site-specific, immersive performances based frequently, though not exclusively, on recovering neglected experiences of the working classes, LGBTQ communities, sex workers, and other minoritised subjects. In these performances, multimedia devices serve as dramaturgical tools to evoke mood, as well as symbols to convey meaning. Examples include the cell phone cameras implicating spectators in the drug deals staged in *The*

Boys of Foley Street (2012), the static-filled television screens suggesting a suddenly abandoned North Side flat in *Other Rooms* (2016), or the refrains of a 1980s Eurythmics song in *The Sin Eaters* (2017) that re-stimulate the cultural anxieties provoked by the cases of Ann Lovett and the Kerry Babies.

The work of ANU Productions suggests a faith in documentation, in the notion that media forms might salvage, record, archive, and communicate the testimony of unjustly neglected individuals. These productions, like many scripted dramas of the past decades, are deeply concerned with Irish national history, and in particular with the pernicious repetition of oppressive cultural patterns. Amid their fantastically innovative uses of multimedia devices, ANU nevertheless insists on primacy of the body, and on the value of unmediated exchange among human beings in shared time and space. The rhythmic movements in the choreography of a play such as *Laundry* (2011) might convey the suffering of an individual character or they may allude to the recurring trauma endured by women more generally. This embodied repetition, performed by an actor before live audiences, re-infuses the oft-repeated story of these institutions – captured in documentaries such as *Sex in a Cold Climate* (1998) or films such as *The Magdalene Sisters* (2002) – with the harsh, intimate reality of physical suffering endured by these individual women. The sensory stimulation at all levels, mediated and performed, in this live performance works to re-imbue these stories with a poignancy that may have been dulled for those desensitised by media attention given to the Laundries. In doing so, this production – in keeping with other contemporary Irish theatre – relies greatly on written and oral testimony, and foregrounds performance, even as it offers measured optimism about the role technology might play in Ireland and the world.

Such optimism is complicated in the Belfast-born playwright Stacey Gregg's first full-length play, *Perve* (2011), which focuses on the tensions between word and image in the age of the Internet, a source of particular fascination for Gregg. This play eschews any faith in the constructive function of evidence and testimony that informs ANU's documentary theatre. In *Perve*, the protagonist Gethin deliberately generates a false rumour that he is a paedophile. A 23-year-old aspiring film-maker, he intends to track the rumour's consequences in a documentary, in order to demonstrate his thesis that society unfairly rushes to judgement of those suspected of paedophilia. As he explains to his 16-year-old sister Sarah and his mother Lorraine, 'I'm just researching how everyone goes crazy at the "P" word.'[20] As this rumour circulates, his community begins to suspect he is an actual paedophile. Even so, Gethin remains unapologetically committed to his social experiment. Only at the end of the play, when he is interrogated by the police and his friend Nick reveals that he was a victim of childhood sexual abuse, does Gethin finally understand the consequences of his documentary project.

Perve is another in the large corpus of Irish literature considering childhood sexual abuse and its consequences, but one situated in the present day where characters are well informed about, and wary of, paedophiles. The play stages a distinctly modern Ireland in which, thanks to new media technologies and devices, easy access to pornography is a given, and the eroticisation of childhood a matter of fact. *Perve* is suffused with sexual material drawn from song lyrics and magazines and with analogies that reference familiar pornographic plot lines. Not even the play's Irish mothers – once the literary exemplars of a national and religious purity – are immune: when we first encounter Lorraine and her neighbour, they are sharing a story about techniques for improved oral sex, as Lorraine mimics holding a penis like a microphone. As Lorraine notes, 'everything's about sex now, isn't it'.[21]

On one level, the play suggests that in the contemporary moment sexual language has been deracinated of its meaning and power. Yet the intensity of the term 'perve', with its capacity to provoke what he deems hysteria, is precisely what Gethin recognises and seeks to explore in his film: a digital subject, he is fascinated less by the pornographic images he stores on his computer than by the power of old-fashioned words. The candid references to erotic content and the casual use of sexual language throughout the play ironically highlight how difficult it is to have honest conversations about sex and sexuality even in, especially in, the digital age. For instance, after their kitchen banter about oral sex, Lorraine's friend haltingly expresses concern for Gethin's sister Sarah, who has been the victim of internet bullying. Later, we discover that Sarah is one of several girls whose face was attached digitally to nude photographs and circulated among their schoolmates. Lorraine normalises this behaviour, representing it merely as new-fangled bullying: 'They can do it on their phones and everything now. Sarah wasn't the only one. She said hers wasn't as bad as some of the others. It was obviously fake.'[22] Even amid the euphemisms and stalling and silences that characterise this discussion, they are able to discuss generatively a sensitive topic and to obtain mutual understanding. It matters that they are neighbours, that they have a shared friendship, that they are roughly the same age, that they are women – but perhaps it matters more that their unmediated, face-to-face interaction enables a difficult conversation characterised by humour and a sense of solidarity. Like many of her fellow contemporary Irish playwrights, Gregg evinces a real nostalgia for speaking bodies in shared time and space – not a huge surprise for a theatre practitioner.

In contrast, schooled by the Internet, which aggregates content and relies heavily on visual images, Gethin fails to comprehend the figurative, slippery nature of language. Embedded in isolating technologies, he is not attuned to the importance of linguistic nuance or to the communicative powers of gesture and tone. When taken in by the police, Gethin asserts, repeatedly, that he is not a 'perve', and he regards himself as beyond the social control of his community and the authorities. Part of his profound insensitivity and astonishing naiveté stems from his confidence in the documentary possibilities of language and image: he has recorded each step of his 'concept' on his computer desktop. Gethin's cluelessness suggests that, for him, mediation has ceased to serve as a channel of communication, one that helps to foster accuracy and truth-telling, and instead has become the negation, or inverse, of its intended purpose. Even when the authority reveals that it has examined the contents of his computer and found nude self-portraits and pornography in his files, he confidently retorts that 'everyone' downloads porn from the Internet.[23] As he tells the officer, 'come on, it's not the nineties'.[24]

Perve draws attention to what is lost when we rely on the Internet and other forms of media to convey what only bodies – and nuanced readings of the languages produced by those bodies – can communicate. In the only scene with a character alone on stage, Layla tells the authority that a topless photograph of her circulated through her school, leading her to withdraw from classes and, the play insinuates, to attempt suicide. The authority, who appears on stage in other scenes, is here an imagined interlocutor, which simultaneously heightens the Foucauldian nature of surveillance in the play and renders those in the stalls the intended audience for her story. Her monologue and her fidgety gestures showcase the 'mortifying, humiliating' consequences of online bullying that she attributes to Gethin.[25] Throughout this play, women's bodies speak – both online and in person. However, a character like Gethin, while fluent in media, is losing his ability to read and respond interpersonally and with sensitivity to others. Throughout the play, he fails to distinguish between his 'concept' (the term he uses to describe the rumour and film) and the real people deeply affected by the manifestation of that 'concept'.

In the play's final scene, Nick considers revenge against Gethin: he has deleted all of the computer evidence that Gethin had promised the authority as proof of his innocence. This is partially retribution for Gethin circulating Layla's nude photo, but it is also an attempt to elicit an apology from Gethin, who remains impervious to the suffering around him. Finally, when Nick shares that he was abused by Gethin's uncle when they were children, Gethin begins to sob and finally admits, 'I didn't think. I didn't think about you.'[26] His epiphany is slow and singular – unlike the fast pace of the play and the overlapping lines of dialogue that otherwise characterise this scene. Nick's revelation, spoken in shared time and space, prompts a meaningful apology from Gethin and a reconciliation between the two men. Yet the final scene direction that signals the end of their intense discussion, which unfolds in a tableau entirely devoid of screens and cell phones, reads, 'neither look at the other. End'.[27] The play's conclusion suggestively underscores the alienation that subsumes life in the digital age.

An allegiance to animate, speaking bodies in our highly mediated contemporary moment is evident not only in a play like *Perve*, but also in the pervasive employment of the monologue on the Irish stage. The past four decades are rife with 'one-handers', including Donal O'Kelly's *Catalpa* (1995), Mark O'Rowe's *Howie the Rookie* (1999), Pat Kinevane's *Forgotten* (2006), Colm Tóibín's *The Testament of Mary* (2011), and Raymond Scannell's *Deep* (2013), while Elaine Murphy's *Little Gem* (2008) is a 'three-hander' woven from monologues offered by three different female characters. Recent stage adaptations of Irish literary texts have similarly offered a single character speaking, as in Olwen Fouéré's *riverrun* (2014), a performance from Joyce's *Finnegans Wake*, or Annie Ryan's stage adaptation of Eimear McBride's *A Girl Is a Half-Formed Thing* (2016). These productions, which demand sustained attention to one speaking body on stage, insist on the enduring power of live performance, even when these performances are supplemented by canny stage devices. The rise of site-specific and immersive theatre during these years, including that produced by Brokentalkers, Corcadorca, THEATREclub, and THISISPOPBABY, has drawn audiences into the mix, intermingling spectators with productions that require their bodies, and even their spoken words, to collectively create contemporary Irish theatre.[28]

The collaborative Dead Centre is one of many theatre companies currently exploring the mutual relationship among text, bodies, and media, as evident in productions such as *Lippy* (2013) and *Chekhov's First Play* (2015). Written and directed by Bush Moukarzel and Ben Kidd,

Hamnet (2017) tethers the revered poetry of Shakespeare to clever images that underscore the play's focus on death, absence, and regret. In this play, the eleven-year-old son of William Shakespeare seeks to understand his absentee father, whose commitment to his work overrides his relationship with his young son. Throughout, a video simulation of father or son alternates and interacts with the live actors on stage. In a role originated by Ollie West, Hamnet at first appears alone on stage, delivering his monologue clad in the garb of a contemporary tween, wearing a hoodie and Converse sneakers, carrying a backpack. He opens the play by speaking to a video image of himself projected onto the back wall of the stage. When his father William takes the stage, the elder Shakespeare is at first a ghostly video projection, not an embodied performer. A medium is used here to accentuate the ineffable distance of the father from his son. More generally, the play's intermingling of stage performance and video calls into question any neat separation between living and dead, present and past – as well as unsettling the long-standing binary privileging the 'real' live over the 'artificial' mediatised event.[29]

The sophisticated stage devices of this play draw attention to the dynamic relationship between dramatic text and contemporary performance. When Hamnet asks his father if he prefers his fictional creation Hamlet to his actual son, Shakespeare replies by listing his protagonist's admirable characteristics, asserting, 'it's easy to know so much about a fictional character, because they're alive for such a long time'.[30] In contrast, as Shakespeare tells his son, children are more difficult to know because 'they're here one minute, then gone the next'.[31] The short lifespan of human beings is linked to the fast-paced contemporary moment: individuals and experiences are evanescent, but the printed word endures. Later, to secure his father's attention, Hamnet appears on stage costumed as Hamlet, reading the character's dialogue, much to Shakespeare's consternation. Here, language fails to bridge distance, a failure appearing again towards the end of the play when father and son briefly reconcile to perform together a line dance as they sing Johnny Cash's 'A Boy Named Sue.' As they sing, Hamnet's voice 'breaks, but in a strange, disturbing way, like a machine running out of power'.[32] Like the music on Friel's static-plagued radio, Hamnet's voice falters and fades away, and as in the ghostly telephone call shared over a faint, broken line between Valerie and Niamh in *The Weir*, the desired connection between parent and dead child is exposed as friable. Human frailty rests at the core of this production, which repeatedly calls into question the relationship between transient body and durable text. The stage devices and performance choices undermine assumed divisions between man and machine, an issue rife in popular anxieties about the rise of artificial intelligence as well as in the critical precepts of post-humanism. What, this play repeatedly asks, endures? Its final moment does not provide a soothing answer. *Hamnet* concludes as it began, with the video camera turned to the audience in the stalls: the live feed on the back screen of the stage at first shows the audience in its seats, but then the spectators 'suddenly disappear' and the 'seats are empty'.[33]

The power of *Hamnet* stems from its invocation of Shakespeare's poetry, the riveting performance of its young lead actor, and a canny manipulation of video images to convey the themes of the play. As such, it undermines any neat transition from the selective, and often cynical, engagement of media technologies found in a dramatic text to some satisfying rapprochement between words and media found in performance. In Irish theatre across the past four decades, the relationship on display between text, performance, and media is mutable, and even paradoxical. In 2013, Pan Pan Theatre, founded by Gavin Quinn and Aedín Cosgrove, produced an innovative staging of Samuel Beckett's radio play *Embers* (1959) that foregrounded the dynamic relationship between sound and image, in part through the overt display of media devices in the set design. As a radio play, *Embers* was intended to be heard rather than seen, its characters utterly disembodied and reduced to voices. The play, another of Beckett's ruminations on age and memory, opens with a monologue spoken by Henry, as he reviews his past during a walk by the sea, and then shifts to a conversation between Henry and his wife Ada.

In the Pan Pan production, the stage was dominated by an enormous sculpted skull made from plywood, designed by Andrew Clancy, and surrounded by many small speakers suspended from the stage ceiling. During the performance, Henry and Ada delivered much of their dialogue from within the skull, speaking over the sound of rushing waves. The theatre was filled with their voices emanating from the enormous skull, and with the recurring crash of the waves. Even as audience members were awash in these natural sounds, the suspended speakers insistently drew attention to their artifice; the age-old themes of loss and memory were captured in language and disbursed by innovative technologies. The production held on to *Ember*'s provenance as a radio play, but its innovative staging pointed to the possibilities rendered by multimodal live performance. The live performance of Beckett's rich dialogue insisted on the text, the sculptured skull insisted on the body, and the speakers insisted on the necessarily mediated nature of memory. Strikingly, this juxtaposition confused one reviewer of the play, who asserted that this tension 'made no sense at all'.³⁴ As she wrote, 'listening to a radio play in a theater is different from listening to one on the radio at home while you go about your business. It's easy to let words paint pictures if what's in front of you is mundane. But if, as here, the images are both beautiful and in conflict with the text, there's trouble.'³⁵

But at the core of contemporary Irish theatre is exactly that 'trouble' stemming from the conflict between images and text, bodies and machines, live performance and mass media. Various media technologies sit amid important works in contemporary Irish theatre, both as symbol and stage device, deliberately stoking conflict between word and image, seeking explicitly to draw attention to what that conflict might tell us about contemporary conditions. Cultural critics have long lamented the threat posed by mass media to high culture, and while it remains true that media can be distracting and undermine a willingness to labour over complex texts, it can also supplement, complement, and enrich language and performance. Studies of Irish theatre have taken a long time to turn their attention from page to stage, from text to performance and design, but that might be the register of a very good problem to have. In a national theatrical tradition filled with plays scripted by Sheridan, Boucicault, Shaw, Synge, Gregory, Beckett, and Deevy, to name only a very few, it is impossible to deny the enduring power of dramatic language in Irish plays to rivet audiences. But productions across the past decades are interrogating how media might work in concert with language, and with the bodies delivering that language in live performances, to enrich theatre's capacity for representation in our increasingly mediated, visual age and to engage audiences now enthralled by those technologies.

Notes

1. For relevant studies, see Lilian Chambers and Eamonn Jordan, eds., *The Theatre of Martin McDonagh: A World of Savage Studies* (Dublin: Carysfort Press, 2006); Cathy Leeney and Anna McMullan, eds., *The Theatre of Marina Carr: Before Rules Was Made* (Dublin: Carysfort Press, 2003); Eamonn Jordan, *The Feast of Famine: The Plays of Frank McGuinness* (Bern, Switzerland: Peter Lang, 1997); and Helen Lojek, *Contexts for Frank McGuinness's Drama* (Washington, DC: Catholic University of America Press, 2004).
2. This position was famously articulated in Alison Flood, 'Julian Gough Slams Fellow Irish Novelists as "Priestly Caste" Cut Off from the Culture', *The Guardian*, 11 February 2010: www.theguardian.com/books/2010/feb/11/julian-gough-irish-novlists-priestly-caste [accessed 16 February 2019].

3. Brian Friel, *Dancing at Lughnasa* (London and Boston: Faber and Faber, 1990), p. 1.
4. Ibid., p. 2.
5. Ibid., p. 21.
6. Ibid., p. 7.
7. See Patrick Lonergan, *Theatre and Globalization: Irish Drama in the Celtic Tiger Era* (Basingstoke: Palgrave Macmillan, 2009).
8. Conor McPherson, *The Weir* in *The Weir and Other Plays* (New York: Theatre Communications Group, 1999), pp. 1–72 (p. 7).
9. Ibid., p. 56.
10. Thanks to Eric Falci for identifying the 'uncanny doubles' of media forms in *Lughnasa* and *The Weir*.
11. McPherson, *The Weir*, p. 30.
12. Ibid., pp. 32–3.
13. Ibid., p. 33.
14. Ibid.
15. Enda Walsh, *The Walworth Farce and the New Electric Ballroom* (New York: Theatre Communications Group, 2009), p. 22.
16. Ibid., p. 66.
17. See Eamonn Jordan, *From Leenane to LA: The Theatre and Cinema of Martin McDonagh* (Dublin: Irish Academic Press, 2014); Patrick Lonergan, *The Theatre and Films of Martin McDonagh* (London: Methuen, 2012); Sarah Keating and Emma Creedon, eds., *Sullied Magnificence: The Theatre of Mark O'Rowe* (Dublin: Carysfort Press, 2018); Mary Caulfield and Ian Walsh, eds., *The Theatre of Enda Walsh* (Dublin: Carysfort Press, 2019).
18. Clare Wallace, 'Irish Drama since the 1990s: Disruptions', in Christopher Morash and Nicholas, eds., *The Oxford Handbook of Modern Irish Theatre* (Oxford: Oxford University Press, 2016), pp. 529–44 (p. 543, n. 55). See this same collection for invaluable essays on contemporary Irish theatre more generally.
19. See Miriam Haughton, 'From Laundries to Labour Camps: Staging Ireland's "Rule of Silence" in ANU Productions' *Laundry*', *Modern Drama*, 57.1 (Spring 2014), pp. 65–93; Emilie Pine, 'The Modernist Impulse in Irish Theatre: ANU Productions and the Monto', in Paige Reynolds, ed., *Modernist Afterlives in Irish Literature and Culture* (London: Anthem Press, 2016), pp. 163–74; and Brian Singleton, *ANU Productions and the Monto Cycle* (Basingstoke: Palgrave Macmillan, 2016).
20. Stacey Gregg, *Perve* (Dublin: Abbey Theatre, 2011), p. 12.
21. Ibid., p. 24.
22. Ibid., p. 23.
23. Ibid., p. 48.
24. Ibid., p. 49.
25. Ibid., p. 43.
26. Ibid., p. 78.
27. Ibid., p. 79.

28. See Sara Brady and Fintan Walsh, eds., *Crossroads: Performance Studies and Irish Culture* (Basingstoke: Palgrave Macmillan, 2009); Eamonn Jordan, *Dissident Dramaturgies: Contemporary Irish Theatre* (Dublin: Irish Academic Press, 2009); Bernadette Sweeney, *Performing the Body in Irish Theatre* (Basingstoke: Palgrave Macmillan, 2008); and Fintan Walsh, ed., *'That Was Us': Contemporary Theatre and Performance* (London: Oberon Books, 2013).
29. See Philip Auslander, *Liveness: Performance in a Mediatized Culture* (New York; Routledge, 2008 [1999]).
30. Dead Centre, *Hamnet* (London: Oberon Books, 2017), p. 33.
31. Ibid., p. 34.
32. Ibid., p. 39.
33. Ibid., p. 45.
34. Laura Collins-Hughes, 'Alone in a Skull, Talking to Himself', *The New York Times*, 18 September 2014: www.nytimes.com/2014/09/19/theater/becketts-embers-at-the-brooklyn-academy-of-music.html [accessed 16 February 2019].
35. Ibid.

CHAPTER 5

Writing Childhood: Young Adult and Children's Literature

Patricia Kennon

Since the 1980s, Ireland has undergone a series of social, political, legal, and economic transformations as it moved 'into, as well as away from, the Celtic Tiger phenomenon and, as a consequence, notions of Irish identity and nationality have been in constant flux'.[1] The concept of childhood and the status of children in Irish society have been central to many of these transitions. Indeed, 'the story of contemporary Irish society [...] is a narrative with the child as its central trope'.[2] Alongside the Irish government's ratification of the *United Nations Convention on the Rights of the Child* in 1989, the appointment of a Minister for Children and Youth Affairs in 2005, and the 2012 'Children's Referendum' (an Amendment to the Irish Constitution dedicated exclusively to children's rights), there has also been a growing awareness of the importance of children's literature and cultural experiences. For example, The Ark: A Cultural Centre for Children opened in 1995, Baboró (an annual arts festival dedicated to children and families) was launched in 1997, and author Siobhán Parkinson was appointed as the first Laureate na nÓg (Ireland's children's laureate) in 2010.

'Conflated with citizenry in the embryonic Irish republic',[3] childhood has long been utilised in constructions and regimes of Irishness, 'from the infantilization of the colonized subject under imperialism through to the imperatives of a model of heritage tourism that fetishized anti-modernity and was deeply invested in promoting the Irish people as quaintly charming and childlike'.[4] In his 1943 national radio address, Taoiseach Eamon de Valera famously consolidated the association of youth with an idealised Ireland filled with 'the romping of sturdy children, the contest of athletic youths and the laughter of happy maidens'.[5] Seven decades later, Fintan O'Toole noted youth's still-central importance in envisaging Ireland. Proposing that 'the novel of growing up, from James Joyce's *A Portrait of the Artist as a Young Man* (1916) to John McGahern's *The Dark* (1965) and Edna O'Brien's *The Country Girls* (1960), is the quintessential Irish form', he emphasised the opportunities that childhood and young characters afford authors regarding 'the most basic plot of all – the move from innocence to experience [...] the old reliable to which Irish writers return. But precisely because it is so old, it forces them to continually reshape it'.[6]

Concepts and meanings of childhood are interpolated and mediated within a plethora of adult desires, nostalgia, ambivalence, hopes, anxieties, institutions, educational agendas, and national interests. Simultaneously fluid and regulated, wild and a key site of socialisation and acculturation, childhood is 'a discursive conflict zone upon which cultural, political and economic engagements are waged'.[7] While some Irish writers of adult literature, such as Roddy Doyle, John Banville, and Cecilia Ahern, have been willing to 'cross over' and write for younger readers, children's literature has traditionally tended to be regarded as less 'literary' and less culturally valuable than adult literature. However, 'if we want to understand the way in which a culture envisions itself, we might look no further than the stories adults tell and retell to their children'.[8] Simultaneously constructed and surveilled, yet overlooked by adult agendas and interests, youth literature contains the potential for radical transformations. It therefore provides 'a curious and paradoxical cultural space [...] in which writers, illustrators, printers, and publishers have piloted ideas, experimented with voices, formats and media, played with conventions, and contested thinking about cultural norms (including those surrounding childhood) and how societies should be organised'.[9]

A further 'tangle of complexities' is involved when navigating the 'strange, complex, and fascinating place' of Irish children's literature.[10] While a preoccupation with national identity has been a central theme of Irish children's literature, English-language publishing in Ireland for children has been and continues to be a 'transcultural phenomenon'.[11] The Children's Books Ireland awards system (the leading children's literature awards in Ireland) accepts nominations for authors who are Irish citizens as well as those resident in Ireland but who are neither Irish by birth and/or who are not published in Ireland. I have applied this inclusive paradigm and therefore have approached Irish youth literature as including texts published in Ireland or internationally by writers and illustrators born and living on the island of Ireland, literature by children's authors of other nationalities now living in Ireland who are published by Irish publishers, and Irish authors of the diaspora whose work is published either in Ireland or elsewhere. I submit that the adoption of this capacious understanding of Irish youth literature is particularly appropriate and important in light of the field's transitions over the last four decades and the increasingly diverse nature of twenty-first-century Ireland and Irish society.

An Irish tradition of writing for children by authors such as Jonathan Swift, Maria Edgeworth, L. T. Meade, Padraic Colum, and Meta Mayne Reid has existed for over three centuries. Two prolific twentieth-century Irish authors whose work was effectively synonymous with 'Irish children's literature' were Patricia Lynch and Eilís Dillon. Acclaimed for her rich evocation of place and blending the otherworldly with Irish rural life, Lynch's fiction helped 'establish a new literature for Irish children, rooted in the situations in which they lived'.[12] Mostly set in Ireland's small struggling island communities, Dillon's novels present a 'fascinating particularity of her Irish setting, coupled with the universality of her insights into human nature and society'.[13] Lynch, Dillon, and contemporaneous Irish authors for children such as Joan Lingard were overwhelmingly published by international publishers since English-language publishing for children in Ireland was virtually non-existent until the 1980s. Owing to Ireland's geographical insularity and position between two behemoth publishing industries, Irish children's authors writing in English who wished to aspire beyond their local limited market were obliged to move to and adapt to British and American publishing systems and expectations. This all-too-often resulted in Irish children's writers producing and perpetuating 'stage-Irish' stereotypical scenes involving 'pigs in the kitchen [. . .] clamps of turf and heaps of muck, [. . .] illiteracy, bad whiskey and general "devilment"'.[14]

This previous readerly and authorly reliance on foreign markets 'changed utterly' at the turn of the twenty-first century, which witnessed a remarkable upsurge of indigenous children's publishing. Echoing Ireland's economic expansion and cultural re-invention, Irish institutional and infrastructural conditions evolved to enable the production of Irish children's literature in the Republic of Ireland on a significant scale. While the increase in quantity of publications over this relatively short span of time was impressive, its deeper ideological significance concerned issues of national representation and new opportunities for self-expression which helped to manifest Ireland's 'new-found confidence' during the 1990s.[15] For the first time, 'domestically produced children's literature' was able to explore 'Irishness on its own terms without having to cater for an external audience.'[16] In 1980, the state-funded Arts Council opened up its literature policy to children's Anglophone fiction and the subsequent subsidising of the production of Irish children's literature in English enabled the founding of independent presses such as The Children's Press, O'Brien Press,

Poolbeg, and Wolfhound Press. Less than a decade later, children's books was one of the most successful sectors of overall Irish publishing[17] and this 'Irish publishing revolution' was hailed as signalling 'Ireland's coming of age and maturing self-confidence [...] Can anything be more important for so small a country – and one still so young?'.[18]

A new interest in Irish children's literature intensified, supported by professional publications and the setting up of prizes and organisations such as the Children's Literature Association of Ireland in 1987, which produced *Children's Books in Ireland* (later renamed *Inis: The Children's Books Ireland Magazine*). A significant moment for Irish children's publishing occurred in 1996 when Ireland was the focal theme of the Frankfurt Book Fair and several publications for both national and international audiences were produced for this event, including *The Big Guide to Irish Children's Books*, which contained a foreword written by President Mary Robinson. Accompanying the increasing attention paid to youth literature in libraries and schools, the founding of The Irish Society for the Study of Children's Literature in 2002 marked the formalising of the Irish children's literature scholarly community. Since the late 1990s, children's literature studies in Ireland has been embedded as a core part of Irish teacher education and increasingly incorporated into university English departments, while two MA programmes in children's literature have been established and an increasing number of doctoral and postdoctoral students study this area in Irish institutions.

Two genres have been particularly strong in Irish children's literature since the 1980s: mythology and historical fiction. The dominance of these genres is not surprising given the concern of Irish writing and culture with links between past and present and the opportunities they afford for self-exploration. This focus on Irish history and the associated production and mediation of collective memory becomes further intensified when brought together with childhood and adult desires to harness youth's symbolic power and future-bound potential. In 1997, Cormac MacRaois, estimated that there were at least thirty books dedicated to the retelling of Irish legends and myths for children in Irish bookshops.[19] Lavishly illustrated collections such as Niamh Sharkey's *Irish Legends for the Very Young* (1996) and Malachy Doyle's *Tales from Old Ireland* (2000) re-presented these traditional stories for modern Irish children, the Irish diaspora, and the international tourist market. Prompted by commercial motivations and heritage agendas, these works were 'part of the wider Celticism operating within the capitalist global economy of the modern society they critique'.[20]

A wave of Irish fantasy fiction for children also emerged, including Cormac MacRaois's Giltspur trilogy (1988–91), animal stories such as Tom McCaughrean's *Fox* series (1983–99), Pat O'Shea's *The Hounds of the Morrigan* (1985), and Michael Scott's *Secrets of the Immortal Nicholas Flame* series (2007–12). English-born author Kate Thompson is regarded as one of the most distinguished Irish writers of the fantastic for young people. Having resided in Ireland since the early 1980s, Thompson's work is immersed in Irish music traditions, the Irish landscape, and Irish traditional storytelling. As I have argued elsewhere, Thompson's 'distinctive mixture of the realistic and the fantastic enables her to elegantly explore the impact of memory, heritage, cultural belonging and hopes for the future'.[21] Irish children's writers, such as Darren Shan, Sarah Rees Brennan, Dave Rudden, Peadar O'Guilin, F. E. Higgins, and Derek Landy, have also been drawn to dark fantasy and horror's opportunities for exploring transgression and challenging notions of childhood innocence. The popularity of horror in Irish youth writing since the turn of the millennium speaks to the Gothic's 'characteristically uncertain and unsettling approach to youth', which reflects 'Ireland's coming of age as an independent state'.[22]

Historical fiction holds special potency for Irish children's literature as it is both 'the area in which Irish children's need for a literature of their own is most acute' and the 'area in which Irish children's authors have been most sure-footed in their writing and in which Irish children have been best served by their writers'.[23] Changes in Irish educational curricula in the 1990s encouraged teachers to seek out historical fiction and the period saw a profusion of Irish-produced historical writing for children predominantly set in the Irish past and concerned with the place and/or absence of the child in these Irish historical landscapes. These included Gerald Whelan's works exploring the Irish struggle for independence in the early twentieth century, Michael Mullen's novels set in pivotal moments across Irish history, Joan O'Neill's *Daisy Chain War* series (1990–2004), set in the Irish 'emergency' during the Second World War, and Sam McBratney's *The Chieftain's Daughter* (1994), based during the Irish transition from paganism to Christianity. Marita Conlon-McKenna's *Children of the Famine* trilogy (1990–6), set during that cataclysmic period in the 1840s, was the major phenomenon of 1990s Irish children's publishing. Marking 'a new approach to the writing of historical fiction' for children, it has been hailed as 'a prime example of how skilfully the specific can be shown – and perceived – to be of universal relevance, enabling a transfer beyond the Irish context'.[24] John Boyne's *The Boy in the Striped Pyjamas* (2006) and its global critical and commercial success also helped raise the profile of Irish children's historical writing.

In her survey of Irish historical fiction in 1997, Celia Keenan observed that approximately a quarter of contemporary Irish children's books comprised historical narratives, and this genre continues to be a significant force in twenty-first-century Irish writing for young people. Emphasising historical fiction's particular importance in colonial and postcolonial cultures, Keenan concludes that the 'enormous growth in historical fiction for children in Ireland' reflected 'a new confidence in Irish society'.[25] This confidence was demonstrated through Irish children's literature's readiness to recognise and explore Ireland's past and its complex history of conflict, suffering, and violence: 'at a time when official historians and history teachers fought shy of emotional treatments of such contentious topics as the Famine or the Easter Rising, children's literature helped to rehearse the move beyond revisionist nervousness by frank confrontations with the issues raised'.[26] While the realities of conservative library and school markets imposed limitations on Irish writing for young people, Irish children's literature possessed an intriguing potential to explore territory that contemporary Irish adult literature was reluctant to acknowledge. Drawing upon the Irish youth publishing sector's financial and cultural momentum during this period, Irish children's authors could increasingly negotiate the paradoxical nature of this surveilled yet overlooked imaginative space and venture into more radical investigations of Irishness and Irish identity.

For example, Mark O'Sullivan's 1994 novel, *Melody for Nora*, was one of the first Irish novels for children or for adults to address the Irish Civil War. It unsentimentally considers cycles of violence and the impact that this traumatic time had and continues to have on Irish society. In this sense, Irish children's literature became 'pioneering in an Irish cultural context and engages with issues glossed over by "adult" or mainstream texts'.[27] Like *Melody for Nora*, Siobhán Parkinson's *Amelia* (1993) and its sequel, *No Peace for Amelia* (1994), were published during a politically charged period of peace initiatives in Northern Ireland. Focalised through the unconventional perspective of a young Quaker female protagonist and her family's egalitarian, pacifist world view, these novels draw upon debates in Irish society about Irish women's history, class, violence, religion, nationalism, and feminism. Elizabeth O'Hara's *The Hiring Fair* trilogy (1993–6) attends to a similarly neglected history of late-nineteenth-century young Irish working women. Buoyed up by Irish society's expansive mood during the 1980s and 1990s, these writers' works offer an interpretation of Irish history 'that deflates the triumphantly nationalist, and social and religiously conservative attitudes that publicly predominated in earlier years'.[28]

However, the boom in indigenous Irish children's publishing was not to last. In the mid-1990s seven Irish publishing houses regularly produced books for young people; yet by 2002, only the O'Brien Press consistently continued to publish a substantial children's list. Others had ceased to exist or significantly reduced their output. Paradoxically, two UK publishing conglomerates were simultaneously establishing children's divisions in Ireland in response to the strength of the Irish market and the availability of promising Irish children's authors. Ironically, 'in many ways, Irish children's publishing' had 'become a victim of its own success', with the Arts Council deciding to withdraw funding from Irish children's publishers due to their commercial success.[29] This dramatic reversal has many causes: a 'phase of identity-fatigue' due to the quantity of books produced during these decades; the uneven quality of the literature produced; inconsistent concern for editorial and production standards; British publishers pursuing marketable Irish authors with more lucrative contracts and the opportunity for international sales; a lack of mandatory school-library provision; and 'a culture of kindness in Irish reviewing [which] did not help to raise critical standards'.[30] Inconsistent quality and production standards and the pressures of managing dominant publishing industries in neighbouring countries are not unusual issues in emergent postcolonial children's literature, and an overly constructive reviewing culture has often been critiqued in the children's and young-adult literary communities in many countries. However, the decline of Irish youth publishing seems remarkable in its speed and scale.

Thankfully, though, recent Irish publishing for young people is in a healthier state. For example, the imprint Little Island was successfully launched in 2010 with the aim of fostering new Irish writing for young people and issuing translations of international children's literature. Yet, the significant challenge for Irish publishers to attract and retain promising and established Irish children's writers and illustrators remains. The desire of Irish children's authors to reach wider audiences and attain more financial security and success than the small domestic market can offer is understandable. However, moving to international – predominantly British and North American – publishers overwhelmingly results in a cultural elision of the Irish-specific content of Irish authors who have first been published in Ireland. Upon studying the novels of three representative children's writers – Maeve Friel, Marie-Louise Fitzpatrick, and

Eoin Colfer – after they were adopted by British publishers, Celia Keenan concluded that their work underwent a 'qualitative change'.[31] After Colfer (author of the popular *Artemis Fowl* series, which incorporates figures from Irish folklore and begins within an explicitly Irish landscape) joined a British publisher in 2001, 'almost all culturally specific references' in his subsequent fiction were either 'eliminated or rendered parodic' and the local and national 'ceded to the global'.[32] The erasure of Hiberno-Irish and of Irish myth and history give Colfer's books a highly successful globalised feel, but one which no longer engages with the richness of Irish identity politics or literary heritage. The loss of a distinctive sense of place and the pervasion of globalised, anonymous non-places was part of a wider transformation in the early 2000s as the country's economic success was hailed and promoted as a 'showpiece of globalisation'.[33] This pattern of identifiably Irish references being diluted and reconfigured into a more homogeneous, 'universal' style and setting for a more universal reader is common to both the adult and children's publishing world, and it 'is probably an insoluble problem in an overwhelmingly Anglophone country sandwiched between two Anglophone world centres of publishing'.[34]

Irish-language children's authors had and still have few opportunities to be published outside the country. Youth literature in Irish has been predominantly required to act in a language-teaching role and the embedded primary- and secondary-school market as well as the recent growth of *Gaelscoileanna* (Irish-language-medium schools) since the 1990s underpins the market for Irish-language youth literature. An evolution of Irish-language children's publishing began in the late 1970s when *An Gúm* – the Irish publications branch of the Department of Education and the main Irish-language publishing house – reviewed its standards in order to produce books that would evoke pleasure and enjoyment as well as support children's Irish-language reading skills. Encouraged by *An Gúm*'s review and a clear policy of direct state intervention, new authors began to produce literature in Irish for children and various independent Irish-language publishers for children emerged at the cusp of the twentieth century, including Cló Mhaigh Eo in 1995, Futa Fata in 1997, and An tSnáthaid Mhór in 2005.

The production of picture books in Ireland has been difficult in light of the constraints imposed by a small market and the costs of creating original artwork. Another factor inhibiting the 'relatively new' publishing of these 'indigenous' texts may be that 'the Irish, though highly literate verbally, do not have a great tradition of visual literacy'.[35] While English-language Irish picture book makers, such as Niamh Sharkey, Chris Haughton,

P. J. Lynch, Oliver Jeffers, and Martin Waddell, have been internationally acclaimed for their visual narratives, twenty-first-century Irish-language publishing for young people has demonstrated a particular capacity for visual storytelling. The first graphic novel for young people published in Ireland, *An Sclabhaí* [*The Slave*] (based on the early life of Saint Patrick) was produced in the Irish language by Cló Mhaigh Eo in 2002, and the subsequent series of graphic-novel retellings of Irish myths and legendary figures has attracted a diverse audience of child native speakers, older additional language learners, and international comics readers. Irish-language publishers have incorporated multimedia and audio CDs into picture books as a result of strong demand from the growing Irish-medium preschool and primary sectors. The creation of co-production imprints such as Walker Éireann has also helped meet the needs of indigenous readers and additional language learners, and navigate the challenges of a small-scale domestic market and minority-language publishing.

A 1988 Irish-language picture book, Marie-Louise Fitzpatrick's *An Chanáil* [*The Canal*], was one of the first Irish works of children's literature to recognise Ireland's increasing multiculturalism. Set along the changing urban and rural environment of the Grand Canal in Dublin, it realistically depicts diverse socio-economic conditions and cultures, including an image of an Indian woman in a sari and her child walking home. During the last three decades, Ireland rapidly moved from a nation formerly renowned for its emigrant outflow to one facing for the first time a multiplicity of incoming groups, including refugees, asylum-seekers, job-seekers, and returning Irish migrants. Although the Irish government pledged its commitment to cultural plurality and a respect for the 'new Irish', this transformation has been complex and uneasy. Irish youth literature has all too often assumed a default norm of whiteness and has been slow to acknowledge and challenge issues of racism and white privilege. As Victoria Flanagan states: 'Whiteness largely functions as an invisible category of identity, as it is by remaining invisible that it instantiates itself as normative.' This is particularly prevalent in postcolonial countries such as Australia and Ireland that now have diverse multicultural populations and Flanagan argues that 'the cultural hegemony of Whiteness [...] can only be displaced if the privilege attached to this particular identity is revealed and dismantled'.[36]

Contemporary novels addressing racial diversity include Siobhán Parkinson's *The Love Bean* (2002) and Vincent O'Donnell's *Out of the Flames* (2002), which explicitly examine negative media discourse around multiracial immigration and the relatively new phenomenon of African asylum-seekers in Ireland. These novels, however, are still presented from a white perspective. John Quinn's *Duck and Swan* (1993) was the first Irish children's novel to feature a black Irish character, and Mark O'Sullivan's *White Lies* (1997) and Patrick Devaney's *Tribal Scars* (2004) are two of the few Irish youth novels to feature an Irish biracial protagonist. Cliona Ó Gallchoir has emphasised the significance of these three novels, as they are 'not primarily concerned with the "Irish" response (sympathetic or otherwise) to "outsiders"; instead, they offer a more profound reflection on the processes of racialization that emerged in the Celtic Tiger period amidst Ireland's increasing racial diversity'.[37] Disappointingly, apart from the Bridges series of four picture books published in 2011 by O'Brien Press with the agenda of promoting multicultural education for Irish readers aged six years onwards, there has been almost no further Irish children's literature that has substantially addressed issues of race, plurality, or migrant communities within contemporary Irish settings.

Irish youth literature has also been reluctant to address other realities, such as abortion, sexuality, teen pregnancy, child abuse, homelessness, and divorce. However, from the late 1980s, fiction arose in which 'the first fictional intimations of the "new" Ireland were to be clearly perceptible' and which challenged traditional notions of what constituted taboo topics in texts for young people.[38] For example, Siobhán Parkinson's *Breaking the Wishbone* (1991) explored homelessness, Marita Conlon-McKenna's *No Goodbye* (1994) addressed divorce and step-families, and Michael Scott's *Judith* trilogy (1991–7) considered class frictions and prejudice around the Irish Traveller community. Tom Lennon's *When Love Comes to Town* (1993) was the first Irish youth novel to involve a gay character. Published by O'Brien Press in the same year that homosexuality was decriminalised in Ireland, the novel originally appeared in the publisher's adult list but now appears on their children's list. The book's publication history and reclassification optimistically suggest 'significant changes in cultural attitudes towards homosexuality in Ireland' and that 'it is now easier for publishers to place what may once have seemed controversial novels onto their children's lists'.[39] Meg Grehan's *The Space Between* (2017), Claire Hennessy's *Like Other Girls* (2018), Sarah Maria Griffin's *Other Words For Smoke* (2019), Deirdre Sullivan's *Perfectly Preventable Deaths* (2019), and Moïra Fowley-Doyle's *All the Bad Apples* (2019) feature LGBT characters. Since the legalisation of same-sex marriage in 2015, there has been a welcome increase of Irish novels representing queer characters.

During the last decade, the Irish young adult (YA) market has rapidly become one of the most buoyant fields in Irish youth literature and Irish literature generally. While Irish novels for teenagers can be traced back to the 1990s – Margrit Cruikshank's *Circling the Triangle* (1991) is regarded as the first Irish novel for adolescents – Ireland's relatively recent YA 'scene' (fostered by consistent new releases and an enthusiastic Irish YA reader and author community) is 'burgeoning, emboldened by political conviction and boosted by inventive retail'.[40] Eason, the leading Irish bookstore, introduced a YA category in 2011 and Dept 51 (a distinctive hybrid area that combines YA literature with forms of popular culture) was established in 2014. Dept 51 began featuring events in 2015 with DeptCon, an annual YA convention featuring a prestigious programme of Irish and international authors such as Juno Dawson, Patrick Ness, and Sarah J. Maas. YA fiction also attracts adult readers. Nielsen Bookscan studies during the last five years have revealed that a significant majority of YA fiction is consumed by readers over the age of 25. The YA Book Club, a Dublin-based reading group of YA fans from across the publishing industry, demonstrates the crossover appeal of YA fiction beyond the teenage demographic. Many critics have identified the allure of YA literature for 'those forced to occupy childhood well into their thirties' due to 'the preoccupation of the form with periods of transition, uncertainty, and identity formation'.[41]

The number and success of Irish YA women writers such as Louise O'Neill, Deirdre Sullivan, Sheena Wilkinson, Sarah Crossan, Sarah Maria Griffin, and Moira Fowley-Doyle is thus particularly significant. Observing how 'teenage girlhood tends to be associated with crisis and trauma, unexpected pregnancies and abuse' in twentieth-century Irish fiction, Susan Cahill commends the recent proliferation of Irish texts for young people that 'share a taking seriously of the teenage girl's consciousness and a celebration of the energies of the bold girl as a force for change'.[42] Contrasting the emphasis on masculine developmental modes in the Irish literary tradition and the way that Irish boyhood 'now constitutes a well-established literary genre of its own' with the constraints, rarity, and obscurity of novels exploring Irish female experience, Jane Elizabeth Dougherty has argued that 'childhood' in an Irish context 'has become a male genre'.[43] Novels such as Éilís Ní Dhuibhne's *The Dancers Dancing* (1999) and Eimear McBride's *A Girl Is a Half-Formed Thing* (2013) powerfully addressed 'the ways in which Irish literature refuses to see or hear the teenage girl'.[44] Instigated by the Kerry Babies and Ann Lovett tragedies that rocked Ireland in 1984, Siobhán Dowd's YA novel, *A Swift Pure Cry* (2006), re-invented the traditional 'problem novel' about teenage pregnancy and created a poetic examination of Irish society's hypocrisy and religious obsession. The elision of Irish girlhood has been increasingly challenged by recent feminist and women's rights movements around the representation of women in Irish theatre and Irish women's reproductive rights. Topping bestselling lists and winning literary awards, Irish women's YA fiction echoes the increased visibility, publication, and media attention of wider Irish women's writing.

A particular concern of Irish YA women's writing relates to discourses around the adolescent female body as a 'site of contradictory cultural expectations' which occupies 'a space between childhood and womanhood, between innocence and experience, between purity and fertility'.[45] Irish women's YA fiction that addresses the complexities and vulnerabilities of girlhood includes Kim Hood's engagement with mental health issues in *Plain Jane* (2016), Claire Hennessy's treatment of peer pressure and eating disorders in *Nothing Tastes as Good* (2016), Deirdre Sullivan's exploration of a teenage girl's experience of abuse and recovery in *Needlework* (2016), and her compelling collection of feminist retellings of fairy tales, *Tangleweed and Brine* (2017). Winner of the inaugural *The Bookseller* YA Book Prize in 2015, the 2015 *Children's Books Ireland* Eilís Dillon Award for debut literature, and Newcomer of the Year at *The Bord Gáis Energy* Irish Book Awards 2014, Louise O'Neill has been 'the most successful YA breakthrough in Ireland' and her work uncompromisingly traces 'the reduction of the teenage girl to commodity' in Irish society.[46] Spanning a range of genres, O'Neill's three YA novels to date interrogate female embodiment, misogyny, patriarchal power, and adolescent female agency. *Only Ever Yours* (2014) is based in a dystopian world where young women are bred for the pleasure of men, while *The Surface Breaks* (2018) is a feminist retelling of 'The Little Mermaid'. Her best-selling novel, *Asking for It* (2015), was inspired by the real-life 2013 case of 'Slane Girl': a photograph of a teenage girl performing oral sex on a young man at a concert in Slane Castle went viral on social media, resulting in the widespread excoriation of the girl, with no consequences for the young men involved. O'Neill's feminist activism and fiction have instigated important national conversations about issues of slut-shaming, rape culture, toxic masculinity, revenge porn, and the importance of education around consent and the ethical uses of social media in today's Ireland.

As Ireland transitioned into the twenty-first century, Robert Dunbar remarked that 'there are, in truth, many Irelands' in this new millennium and hoped that Irish youth literature would come 'to reflect and respect these pluralities'.[47] While Irish young adult fiction is in its own state of 'childhood', the progressive work of the increasing host of Irish YA authors presents the exciting potential of modern Irish writing for young people to challenge hegemonic norms, explore diverse perspectives, and re-imagine representations of youth experience.

Notes

1. Claire Bracken and Emma Radley, 'Introduction', in Claire Bracken and Emma Radley, eds., *Viewpoints: Theoretical Perspectives on Irish Visual Texts* (Cork, Ireland: Cork University Press, 2013), pp. 1–10 (p. 3).
2. Maria Luddy and James M. Smith, 'Introduction', in Maria Luddy and James M. Smith, eds., *Children, Childhood and Irish Society, 1500 to the Present* (Dublin: Four Courts Press, 2014), pp. 15–28 (p. 15).
3. Mary Shine Thompson, 'Republicanism and Childhood in Twentieth-Century Ireland', *The Republic: A Journal of Contemporary and Historical Debate*, 3 (2003), pp. 90–112 (p. 94).
4. Ruth Barton, 'Loss of Innocents: The Irish Child and Cinema', in *Children, Childhood and Irish Society, 1500 to the Present*, pp. 378–88 (p. 379).
5. Éamon De Valera, 'On Language & the Irish Nation', in Maurice Moynihan, ed., *Speeches and Statements by Eamon De Valera: 1917–73* (Dublin: Gill and Macmillan, 1980), pp. 466–8 (p. 466).
6. Fintan O'Toole, 'Why Irish Writers Don't Grow Out of Adolescence', *The Irish Times*, 6 November 2010, p. 8.
7. Lisa Farley and Julie C. Garlen, 'The Child in Question: Childhood Texts, Cultures, and Curricula', *Curriculum Inquiry*, 46.3 (2016), pp. 221–9 (p. 221).
8. Joseph Zornado, *Inventing the Child: Culture, Ideology, and the Study of Childhood* (New York: Routledge, 2006), p. 3.
9. Kimberley Reynolds, *Radical Children's Literature: Future Visions and Aesthetic Transformations in Juvenile Fiction* (Basingstoke: Palgrave Macmillan, 2007), p. 3.
10. Robert Dunbar, 'Rarely Pure and Never Simple: The World of Irish Children's Literature', *The Lion and the Unicorn*, 21.3 (1997), pp. 309–21 (p. 309).
11. Emer O'Sullivan, 'German and Irish Children's Literature: A Comparative Perspective', in Susan Tebbutt and Joachim Fischer, eds., *Intercultural Connections within German and Irish Children's Literature* (Trier, Germany: Wissenschaftlicher Verlag Trier, 2008), pp. 25–45 (p. 32).
12. Nancy Watson, 'A Revealing and Exciting Experience: Three of Patricia Lynch's Children's Novels', *The Lion and the Unicorn*, 21.3 (1997), pp. 341–6 (p. 345).
13. Rahn, Suzanne, 'Inishrone Is Our Island: Rediscovering the Irish Novels of Eilís Dillon', *The Lion and the Unicorn*, 21.3 (1997), pp. 347–68 (pp. 365–6).
14. Kenneth Reddin, 'Children's Books in Ireland', *Irish Library Bulletin*, 7 (1946), p. 74.
15. Declan Kiberd, *Inventing Ireland: The Literature of the Modern Nation* (London: Vintage, 1995), p. 651.

16. Emer O'Sullivan, 'A Sense of Place? The Irishness of Irish Children's Literature in Translation', in Mary Shine Thompson, ed., *Young Irelands: Studies in Children's Literature* (Dublin: Four Courts Press, 2011), pp. 137–53 (p. 137).
17. See Francis Fishwick, *The Book Market in the Republic of Ireland* (Dublin: Irish Books Marketing Group, 1987).
18. Jeremy Addis, 'Children's Publishing in Ireland', in Valerie Coghlan and Celia Keenan, eds., *The Big Guide to Irish Children's Books* (Dublin: The Irish Children's Book Trust, 1996), pp. 14–19 (p. 19).
19. Cormac MacRaois, 'Old Tales for New People', *The Lion and the Unicorn*, 21.3 (1997), pp. 330–40 (p. 330).
20. Ciara Ní Bhroin, 'Mythologizing Ireland', in Valerie Coghlan and Keith O'Sullivan, eds., *Irish Children's Literature and Culture: New Perspectives on Contemporary Writing* (London: Routledge, 2011), pp. 7–27 (p. 24).
21. Patricia Kennon, 'Contemplating Otherness in Speculative Fiction', in *Irish Children's Literature and Culture*, pp. 145–56 (p. 149).
22. Anne Markey, 'Coming of Age and National Character at Home and Abroad', in Ciara Ní Bhroin and Patricia Kennon, eds., *What Do We Tell the Children? Critical Essays on Children's Literature* (Newcastle upon Tyne: Cambridge Scholars Publishing, 2012), pp. 112–30 (p. 130).
23. Siobhán Parkinson, 'A View from the Other Island: Children's Books in Ireland', *The Horn Book Magazine*, 77.2 (2001), pp. 173–8 (p. 175).
24. Emer O'Sullivan, 'Irish Children's Books in Translation', in Valerie Coghlan and Celia Keenan, eds., *The Big Guide 2: Irish Children's Books* (Dublin: Children's Books Ireland, 2000), pp. 128–34 (p. 130).
25. Celia Keenan, 'Reflecting a New Confidence: Irish Historical Fiction for Children', *The Lion and the Unicorn* 21.3 (1997), pp. 369–78 (p. 369).
26. Declan Kiberd, 'Literature, Childhood and Ireland', in Clare Bradford and Valerie Coghlan, eds., *Expectations and Experiences: Children, Childhood and Children's Literature* (Lichfield: Pied Piper Publishing, 2007), pp. 13–26 (p. 23).
27. Pádraic Whyte, *Irish Childhoods: Children's Fiction and Irish History* (Newcastle upon Tyne: Cambridge Scholars Publishing, 2011), p. 27.
28. Valerie Coghlan, 'Questions of Identity and Otherness in Irish Writing for Young People', *Neohelicon*, 36.1 (2009), pp. 91–102 (p. 97).
29. Shirley Kelly, 'Children's Publishing Is Not Viable', *Books Ireland*, 299 (2007), pp. 278–9 (p. 278).
30. Emer O'Sullivan, 'Insularity and Internationalism: Between Local Production and the Global Marketplace', in *Irish Children's Literature and Culture*, pp. 183–96 (p. 187).
31. Celia Keenan, 'Divisions in the World of Irish Publishing for Children: Re-Colonization or Globalization?', in Mary Shine Thompson and Valerie Coghlan, eds., *Divided Worlds: Studies in Children's Literature* (Dublin: Four Courts Press, 2007), pp. 196–208 (p. 197).

32. Keenan, 'Divisions in the World of Irish Publishing for Children', p. 202.
33. Nicola Jo-Anne Smith, *Showcasing Globalisation: The Political Economy of the Irish Republic* (Manchester: Manchester University Press, 2005), p. 3.
34. Valerie Coghlan and Siobhán Parkinson, 'Introduction', in Valerie Coghlan and Siobhán Parkinson, eds., *Irish Children's Writers and Illustrators, 1986–2006: A Selection of Essays* (Dublin: Church of Ireland College of Education Publications, 2007), pp. 9–17 (p. 12).
35. Valerie Coghlan, 'Picture Books', in *The Big Guide to Irish Children's Books*, pp. 29–39 (p. 31).
36. Victoria Flanagan, 'A Similarity or Difference? The Problem of Race in Australian Picture Books', *Bookbird*, 51.2 (2013), pp. 13–21 (p. 14).
37. Cliona Ó Gallchoir, 'Whiteness and the Racialization of Irish Identity in Celtic Tiger Children's Fiction', *Breac: A Digital Journal of Irish Studies*, 25 August 2016: http://breac.nd.edu/articles/preface-to-childrens-literature-changing-paradigms-and-critical-perspectives-in-ireland-and-beyond [accessed 29 March 2019].
38. Robert Dunbar, 'Ireland and Its Children's Literature', in Margaret Meek, ed., *Children's Literature and National Identity* (Stoke on Trent, England: Trentham Books, 2001), pp. 79–88 (p. 84).
39. Pádraic Whyte, 'Young Adult Fiction and Youth Culture', in *Irish Children's Literature and Culture*, pp. 71–83 (p. 73).
40. Caroline Carpenter, 'Young Adult Fiction', *The Bookseller*, April 2017, p. 33.
41. Mavis Reimer and Heather Snell, 'YA Narratives: Reading One's Age', *Jeunesse: Young People, Texts, Cultures*, 7.1 (2015), pp. 1–17 (p. 3).
42. Susan Cahill, 'Bold Girls: A Literary History of Wild Irish Girls', *The Irish Times*, 9 March 2018: www.irishtimes.com/culture/books/bold-girls-a-literary-history-of-wild-irish-girls-1.3421134 [accessed 9 March 2018].
43. Jane Elizabeth Dougherty, 'Nuala O'Faolain and the Unwritten Irish Girlhood', *New Hibernia Review/Iris Éireannach Nua*, 11.2 (2007), pp. 50–65 (pp. 50, 54).
44. Susan Cahill, 'A Girl Is a Half-Formed Thing?: Girlhood, Trauma, and Resistance in Post-Tiger Irish Literature', *Lit: Literature Interpretation Theory*, 28.2 (2017), pp. 153–71 (p. 161).
45. Sara K. Day, 'Docile Bodies, Dangerous Bodies: Sexual Awakening and Social Resistance in Young Adult Dystopian Novels', in Sara K. Day, Miranda A. Green-Barteet, and Amy L. Montz, eds., *Female Rebellion in Young Adult Dystopian Fiction* (Farnham, England: Ashgate, 2014), pp. 75–92 (p. 75).
46. Cahill, 'A Girl Is a Half-Formed Thing?', p. 161.
47. Dunbar, 'Ireland and Its Children's Literature', p. 85.

Coda: Eavan Boland and Seamus Heaney
Eric Falci

Both Eavan Boland and Seamus Heaney are poets of the backward glance. Considering some of the broader dynamics explored in this volume, it is perhaps not surprising that the work of two of the most notable poets of the past fifty years is steeped in the past. Throughout their large and influential bodies of poetry and prose, both privilege recollection. Many of their most well-known poems are either based directly on memory work or attempt to imagine the more distant past to explore and critique the structures of the past that shape the present (in both cases this often occurs via a meditation on objects or discrete individuals). Heaney's programme of poetry as a form of historical excavation was announced in the opening poem of *Death of a Naturalist* (1966): 'The squat pen rests. | I'll dig with it.'[1] Even as his poetry shifted in tone and focus over a dozen major volumes – from a fascination with, as he puts it in 'At Toomebridge', the 'slime and silver of the fattened eel' to a poetry of 'negative ions in the open air' – he remained a writer nearly always bound to the past and to the galvanisation of memory to generate poetry.[2] From volume to volume, his poems settle in the past – most frequently in moments from his own past, but often in the deeper past, whether the Irish past (as in, say, 'Requiem for the Croppies' or the poems in *Station Island* [1984] launched off of his translations in *Sweeney Astray* [1983]) or further afield, as in the 'bog poems' that think back to Iron Age Northern Europe or in 'Mycenae Lookout' with its evocation of ancient Greece. A centripetally minded poet, Heaney generally aims to find the convergences between levels, between personal memory and the literary or historical analogue into which such memory has been twined.

Boland's memory work is different: while there are many poems that recollect a moment from her own past, the poems that take a broader view of history – primarily, though not exclusively, the history of Ireland – are catalysed by a recognition of the unbridgeable distance between the past and the present, and by an understanding that the past that Boland most wants to approach – the history of women's lives in a thoroughly patriarchal culture – cannot be reached. In Boland's imagination, then, the past is both refused – 'I won't go back to it', as the opening line of 'Mise Éire' has it – and reconstructed as an absence.[3] So, if Heaney's recollective poet is most like a digger, then Boland's is most often figured as an exile. This is perhaps the central leitmotif in her work, one made clear by the titles of the volumes *Outside History* (1990), *The Lost Land* (1998), and *A Woman Without a Country* (2014). Such a stance is elaborated in 'In Our Own Country', the title sequence of *Domestic Violence* (2007), which begins with a potentially positive sentiment about the future – 'they are making a new Ireland | at the end of our road' – but ends by re-iterating one of Boland's typical gestures:

> We walk home. What we know is this
> (and this is all we know): we are now
> and we will always be from now on –
> for all I know we have always been –
>
> exiles in our own country.[4]

The sureness and self-possession of the language – 'we walk home', 'our own country' – is undermined by the exilic chasm at its core. While Heaney's recollective imagination is premised upon the possibility of connectivity between the past and present and between the personal past and cultural history, then Boland's operates via a contradictory mechanism, one that is propelled by the desire to understand a past that it simultaneously understands to be inaccessible.

In both cases, this reliance on the past to spur the making of poems is the basis of a broader aesthetic conservatism. For the most part, Heaney and Boland rely on the traditional storehouse of lyric forms and strategies, and both can be seen as exemplars of the general conservatism underlying certain large sectors of Irish literature, as other essays in this volume suggest. And, to be sure, it is easy to locate strains of nostalgia in each of their oeuvres, inevitable for two poets frequently nudged into writing by thinking about some dimension of the past. At the same time, they attempt to shape poems not only as a means to evaluate the past but also to imagine how local and large-scale change happens. Which is to say, there are important moments in which they not only access the past – fixed and lost though it might be – and place it within the context of the present (if only within the 'present' of the poem's lyric utterance), but also in which they aim to consider the past as itself a mechanism of transition. In such instances, poetic structure models the mutability and uncertainty that accompanies every attempt to reckon with the past within the context of the present and with an eye towards the future.

For Boland, such work occurs within her sequences. Apart from the early 'Three Songs for a Legend', the first poem in her *New Collected Poems* (2005) that consists of multiple parts is 'Suburban Woman', the final poem in *The War Horse* (1975). From that point forward, lyric sequences appear regularly in her volumes. For the most part, each sequence elaborates and refracts the volume's central matters: 'Suburban Woman', for example, is riven by the conflicts between creative and domestic work that structure Boland's broader feminism, is dominated by images of war and predation, and comes to a temporary respite at the end of the final section, in which the thus far absent 'I' of the poem joins forces with the third-person 'she' who has been the protagonist: 'Defeated we survive, we two, housed || together in my compromise, my craft – | who are of one another the first draft.'[5] Several sequences speak to one another across volumes, such as 'Domestic Interior', a set of poems to and about the poet's relationship with her young daughter, and 'Marriage'. And the more substantial sequences contain poems that are given their own titles, even as they are numbered within the sequence. Such poems are doubly marked: both as independent texts and as part of a larger series. This gesture complicates our understanding of the sequence as a sequence, and, in so doing, allows Boland to use the sequence form as a mechanism for rethinking aspects of change, progression, and transition. Because, as I will show, many of the sequences are not clearly sequential: they suggest alternate modes of temporality.

It is this aspect of her sequences that are most inscrutable and potentially most generative. They operate quite differently than, say, Muldoon's long poems in numbered sections or Heaney's 'Station Island', in which the numbered sections are pegged to a deliberate arc of progression and journey. To put it perhaps too bluntly: Boland's sequences rarely display a simple sequential logic. Each poem tends to have an internal logic and can easily stand on its own, which complicates the attempt to understand the modes of relation at work between poems. Of course, there is often a broad thematic connection announced by the title, as in 'Marriage' or 'Colony', but there is typically not a clear progression from the first section to the last, as poems tend to move between disparate material that does not cohere into a narrative. At the same time, via paratextual devices, such as titles, subtitles ('a sequence'), and section numbers, Boland insists upon a reading that is at some level successive even if it feels forced. It is certainly not the case that individual poems are inscrutable: Boland's poetry is quite accessible and the basic cache of themes and concerns that most frequently occupy her have remained consistent over her long career. Rather, it is that her sequences constellate distinct poems that are eminently typical of Boland's style, but the act of yoking the poems together into a sequence estranges the poems from themselves and changes our own methods of readerly response.

In 'Writing in a Time of Violence', from *In a Time of Violence* (1994), for example, the first three poems look back to two earlier 'times of violence' in Irish history: the mid-nineteenth century Great Famine and the late eighteenth-century activities of the Peep o' Day Boys. The fourth poem takes place in St Louis and recollects Civil War-era America via a 'plastic figure' of 'a woman in a dress' that the poet sees in 'the Museum'.[6] The fifth 'recreate[s] Easter in Dublin' and the beginning of the 1916 Rising via the figures in Dublin's 'Dolls Museum'.[7] The penultimate poem, 'Inscriptions', swerves away from the pattern of historical recreation via scenes and objects, and instead takes place in a 'holiday room[]' in which the poet notices an inscription – 'Peter | was the name on the cot' – which leads into a meditation about this unknown boy's fate and culminates in a broader reverie on the inaccessibility of the long dead and their simultaneous spectral presence in the traces and inscriptions left behind, as well as those erased by 'the name-eating elements – the salt wind, the rain' that feed on headstones.[8] The final, eponymous poem returns to Boland's own 'last year in College' as she writes an essay on 'The Art of Rhetoric', and proceeds as an imagined address to and lesson for her earlier self about the slipperiness of language and of rhetoric 'where language is concealed'.[9] A sequence that had largely been about the second part of its title shifts its weight to take up the problems of the first word, 'writing'. The discrepancy between land and map that is the topic of the sequence's opening poem, 'That the Science of Cartography Is Limited', is re-inflected in the final poem and in turn re-inflects the various problematic forms of textuality and aesthetic mediation that appear in the preceding sections: the portrait being painted across the Irish Sea from the fires being set by the Peep o' Day Boys of part two, the imagined epistle of part three ('*March 1 1847. By the First Post*'), the figurines in parts four and five, and the inscription in part six.[10] Although each poem seems secure in its own representational stance and untroubled as it moves among historical moments and modes of artistic and textual media, the final section anatomises this by turning inward, away from historical reconstruction and towards the manoeuvres of memory. The sequence's final lines wind down a sentence that has been accreting over three stanzas and culminates in a brief, poignant warning, as the various words brought into view – '*Irish Ireland ours*', '*hate* and *territory* and the like' – are said to 'wait | and are waiting under | beautiful speech. To strike'.[11] The unnecessary break at the end – there's no grammatical reason why 'to strike' shouldn't be a part of the previous sentence – offers in miniature an instance of the double logic according to which this sequence unfolds: its signal about the dangers of words beneath the beauty of speech is replicated at the larger level, in the way in which the scrim of progression – in this case a sequence of seven numbered poems – covers a much more tenuous constellation of texts.

There are, to my mind, two broader implications to this mode in Boland's work. First, it concretises the contradictory impulse at the heart of her historical imagination. The pervasive sense of loss that underpins much of her poetry – both a lost history and a lost country – is coupled with the need to continually re-approach that void. In reading the sequences, we are again and again asked to locate an order or a logic that is elusive or that does not actually exist. The second implication is that the sequences, with their occulted modes of succession, present – implicitly and often against the grain of the individual poems – a more complex model of historical thinking than many critics have attributed to her, whether her articulations of a feminist philosophy or her accounts of Irish history. The straightforward certainties of individual poems are disturbed by their placement within a sequence that is itself partly alienated from its own inexorable forward motion.

In Heaney's case, we must look to one of his least-considered volumes (if such a thing could be said of a poet who has been the subject of 'so much, too much' attention from critics) to find the most intriguing examples of his attempt to render change and transition within lyric form.[12] *The Haw Lantern* (1987) is often overlooked or under-read, conceived as a somewhat slight volume compared with the momentous volumes that come before and after. *Station Island* (1984) is rightly understood to be a watershed volume, one in which Heaney works himself out of the channels that had defined his earlier work and makes a turn to something new, as the ghost of James Joyce tells him to do in the title poem's final section. Heaney's poetry would remain haunted by ghosts and revenants, but *Station Island* clearly marks a transition from one sort of poetry, and one approach to poetry, to another. In such a narrative of artistic progress (itself too simplified), *Seeing Things* (1991) is the moment when the gains promised in *Station Island* are realised. The title sequence manages to be both Heaneyesque in its four-square solidity (consisting as it does of four sections of twelve poems each, each poem containing twelve lines distributed over four tercets) and an unexpected extended meditation on the fleeting, the quick-changing, the marvellous, and the momentary – a long distance from the encumbered, dutiful, guilt-shook, earth-tethered poet from previous volumes.

In this admittedly too-neat scheme, *The Haw Lantern* is a bit of an outlier. Of course, it contains many poems that are typically Heaneyesque in their turn to the past or their evocation of rural life and traditional culture. But it also features a new key for Heaney, one that we might call, after the opening line of 'From the Canton of Expectation', the optative register. That poem, one of four analogously titled poems in the volume – along with 'From the Frontier of Writing', 'From the Republic of Conscience', and 'From the Land of the Unspoken' – begins with a parabolic scene-setting:

> We lived deep in a land of optative moods,
> under high, banked clouds of resignation.[13]

The past tense, which typically would be steeped in memories of the actual, is here pinned to what he calls in a poem from his final volume 'an elsewhere world'.[14] What occurs in the unmarked series of parable poems threaded through *The Haw Lantern* – the four poems mentioned above, 'Parable Island', 'The Mud Vision', and 'The Disappearing Island' – is the fashioning of a lyric register that can gesture towards futurity and that can open a space between an irrevocable past and its entailed present, what he describes in 'Hailstones' as 'the melt of the real thing | smarting into its absence'.[15] At one level, this is an effect of Heaney's consolidation of what he gleaned from Eastern European poets, such as Osip Mandelstam, Joseph Brodsky, and Czesław Miłosz. But this new register's internal dynamics are not fully explained by that inheritance. Stitched into the past-present weave of his poetry is now another thread: the imagined, or wished for, space of 'as if'. It is clearly apparent in the four 'From' poems, whose prepositional monikers cut sharply against Heaney's deeply held preference for nominative titles. The very few examples of non-nominative titles in his volumes before *The Haw Lantern* either show nominative force through a gerund ('Digging', 'Blackberry-Picking', 'Westering', 'Remembering Malibu', 'Unwinding', and 'Drifting Off') or begin with a preposition to indicate a certain location or addressee ('At a Potato Digging', 'For the Commander of the "Eliza"', 'In Small Townlands', 'In Gallarus Oratory', 'At Ardboe Point', 'Away From It All', 'In the Beech', 'In the Chestnut Tree', 'On the Road'). There are also a few titles that take the form of past tense or imperative verb phrases ('Twice Shy', 'Gone',

'Alerted', 'Come to the Bower', 'Whatever You Say, Say Nothing'). But the four 'From' parables in *The Haw Lantern* are up to something new: they indicate not simply the diegetic space or the space of writing, but a double zone that toggles ceaselessly between indicative and optative moods.

This is an imaginative space as much as a grammatical one, and it takes different shapes in the volume. 'The Spoonbait', for instance, presents a familiar Heaney sub-genre, the poem of the ramified object. The titular lure becomes instantly reflexive, the means by which the poet catches and tosses forward a symbolic narrative that reaches back into childhood. However, the poem opens with a new move, announcing its own imaginative effort: 'So a new similitude is given us | And we say:'.[16] The typical backward look is prefaced by a forwardly projecting speech act, as though Heaney means to open a new discursive channel in the poem's rhetorical unfolding. The memory work that beds his lyric ground is productively torqued by this optative register, which not only indicates that work's basis in verbal invention rather than simple recollection, but also provides an imaginative dimension by which Heaney's backward glances might be turned futureward by being somewhat detached from the actualities of the past but still answerable to them.

'The Mud Vision' is perhaps the culmination of this mode in *The Haw Lantern*, and, while space prevents a full reading of this poem, it is worth pointing out that Heaney is able not only to confect a world that both is and is not recognisable as Ireland but also that the vision itself occupies only a small part of the poem, a five-line passage that occurs fourteen lines into a 59-line poem:

> And then in the foggy midlands it appeared,
> Our mud vision, as if a rose window of mud
> Had invented itself out of the glittery damp,
> A gossamer wheel, concentric with its own hub
> Of nebulous dirt, sullied yet lucent.[17]

The rest of the poem is about what leads up to the vision and what comes after, how the people respond to its arrival and departure, what occurs in its aftermath, how it changed things and did not. Heaney gears the parable mode so that it might become a mechanism to 'to credit marvels' within an art of the actual.[18] In addition, this parable mode – and the optative register that I have linked to it – becomes a means to figure process and transition within a poetics adamantly trained on the past. Boland's use of the ambiguously sequential sequence serves to embed alternate temporalities and trajectories into what can seem to be an overly simple vision of historical motion and of the present's relation to the past. Analogously, the parabolic and optative dimensions that Heaney fashions in *The Haw Lantern* allow him to adjust the inwards and downwards and backwards looks that predominate throughout his work – all 'mud visions' of a sort – by bending them a bit towards the future, or at least towards a new set of thoughts about how change might happen. While remaining within the ambit of their established techniques, each conservative in its own way, both Boland and Heaney open their formal procedures, moderately but meaningfully, in order to register not only the present's entailment of the past or history's inexorable impingement on the future, but also the future's productively uncertain relation to the present world.

Notes

1. Seamus Heaney, *Poems 1965–1975* (New York: Farrar, Straus and Giroux, 1980), p. 4.
2. Seamus Heaney, *Electric Light* (New York: Farrar, Straus and Giroux, 2001), p. 3.
3. Eavan Boland, *An Origin Like Water: Collected Poems, 1967–1987* (New York: W. W. Norton & Co, 1997), p. 156.
4. Eavan Boland, *Domestic Violence* (New York: W. W. Norton & Co, 2007), pp. 27, 28.
5. Boland, *An Origin Like Water*, p. 88.
6. Eavan Boland, *In a Time of Violence* (New York: W. W. Norton & Co, 1994), p. 12.
7. Ibid., p. 14.
8. Ibid., pp. 16, 17.
9. Ibid., p. 18.
10. Ibid., p. 11.
11. Ibid., p. 19.
12. Seamus Heaney, *Field Work* (New York: Farrar, Straus and Giroux, 1979), p. 27.
13. Seamus Heaney, *The Haw Lantern* (New York: Farrar, Straus and Giroux, 1987), p. 46.
14. Seamus Heaney, *Human Chain* (New York: Farrar, Straus and Giroux, 2010), p. 44.
15. Heaney, *The Haw Lantern*, p. 14.
16. Ibid., p. 21.
17. Ibid., p. 48.
18. Seamus Heaney, *Seeing Things* (New York: Farrar, Straus and Giroux, 1991), p. 52.

PART II
Spaces

CHAPTER 6

Habitations: Space, Place, Real Estate
Adam Hanna

When the sun rose over Ireland on the first morning of the twenty-first century, it did so over a landscape that was in the midst of a vast transformation. Millions of tons of new bricks, concrete, and tarmac had recently become part of that landscape, and millions more would soon be added to it as huge numbers of new houses were built all over the island. An extraordinary result of this building boom was that, by 2006, over a quarter of all the housing in the Republic had been constructed in the ten preceding years.[1] As heavy machinery, high-visibility jackets, and arc lamps became familiar sights across the country, the tremors from this building work were felt in Irish writing. Perhaps ironically, for a time of such frenetic construction, the chief anxiety that is heard in Irish literature is for what, ecologically, materially and socially, might be swept away in this time of such dramatic change.

Eavan Boland's ominously named volume *Domestic Violence* (2007) casts a wary eye over the changes going on around her home in south Dublin. In the eponymous sequence, she first surveys the heavy equipment that is reshaping the country, then grimly observes that:

> They have been working here in all weathers
> tearing away the road to our village –
> bridge, path, river, all
> lost under an onslaught of steel.[2]

Boland and many other writers, including Seamus Heaney, Tim Robinson, Paula Meehan, and Michael Longley, drew attention to what was being lost in the steely 'onslaught' of property development that accompanied the boom years that began in the mid-1990s and came to an abrupt end in 2008. In later years, other writers notably charted the changed disposition of Irish space after this onslaught was ended, or perhaps paused, by the economic crash. William Wall's *Ghost Estate* (2011), Donal Ryan's *The Spinning Heart* (2012), and Mike McCormack's *Solar Bones* (2016) all tell the post-boom stories of different built spaces and, in doing so, register significant changes to life in Ireland. Across the border in Northern Ireland, related but different forces were at play during the same years. Writers including Medbh McGuckian, Leontia Flynn, and Glenn Patterson sought to reconcile old ideas of sectarian territory with a newly dominant vision of land as an asset which might be hoarded, bought, sold or rented out, and – sometimes ruinously – speculated over.

Land changed a great deal in the Irish popular imagination during the human lifespan that elapsed between the establishment of self-government in Ireland in the early 1920s and the turn of the twenty-first century. In the early years of the Free State, the nationalist writer Daniel Corkery famously accorded centrality to 'the Land' (capitalised in his 1931 work *Synge and Anglo-Irish Literature*), characterising it as one of the 'three great forces' – the other two were religious consciousness and Irish nationalism – that defined and made distinct a national identity.[3] By 'the Land', however, he was not primarily thinking of the qualities or properties of the soil itself; he meant, rather, the view of the world that arose from the engagement of the mass of the Irish population in agricultural work. At the time Corkery was writing, around half of the Irish workforce made their living through agriculture. By the turn of the twenty-first century, however, this number was down to 7%.[4] With this changing use of land, the meaning of 'the Land' in Ireland changed too.

What displaced the understanding of land that was known to Corkery and his generation was one of land as a nexus of cash values: an asset whose suitability as a site for housing, and therefore whose profitability, was its most important feature. On farms, the quality of the soil of a piece of land and its suitability for either arable or pastoral farming became less significant; its proximity to an urban centre, the possibility of its being rezoned as a residential space, and the quantity of its 'road frontage' (a feature which made it suitable for sale for development as housing) became much more so. In this changed view of land, its worth could not be assayed so much by its look and feel as by its position and classification on the planner's map. This more disembodied approach to land had wide-ranging consequences: in short, by the turn of the twenty-first century, the chief way of imagining land in Ireland had moved decisively from soils to sales.

Ireland's literature from the turn of the millennium registers these tectonic shifts in multiple ways. As the use and worth of a piece of land became something that could most readily be measured in the immaterial figures of a digitally stored bank balance, the corollary to this was a sense of ghostliness which, in literature, came to frequently imbue the built landscape itself. This changed view is hinted at in the faintly dissociative and voyeuristic title of Vona Groarke's volume of poetry, *Other People's Houses* (1999). This volume was published at the midpoint of what Ruth McManus identified as a 'decade-long housing mania [that] began in the mid-1990s and infected the whole country'.[5] During these years, a certain sense of unreality pervaded dealings in land as, according to the economist David McWilliams, the economic laws of gravity themselves came under question: 'both the supply of homes and the price of homes', McWilliams notes, 'rocketed to unsustainable levels'.[6] Groarke's *Other People's Houses* is imbued with the atmosphere of this heady and unsettling phenomenon and, as such, represents something new in Irish poetry. The novelty of her volume does not lie in its suburban focus: Dublin's northside suburbs had, after all, been depicted in the work of Paula Meehan, and its southside ones in the work of Eavan Boland. What made Groarke's collection distinctive was how unmoored it was from the traditional place-based tropes of Irish poetry. In a decade when hundreds of similar housing estates proliferated across the landscape, Groarke's work evinced a disconcerting tendency to imagine land not as a place, but as a space.

This shift from the affective to the geometric is everywhere in *Other People's Houses*, a volume in which houses are frequently imagined as mechanical and material entities. This tendency lends a somewhat deracinated and unreal air to the spaces Groarke depicts. The poems show a consciousness of the materials and methods of construction of these houses – there are angles and slopes, hinges and lintels – but there is an understatement and restraint in her language that somehow subdues the specificity of what she writes about. It is as if her houses, like the one in the poem 'House-bound', quoted below, are in danger of folding back down into their own plans:

> The blind holds it in check. As you let it down
> it tightens its grip on an evening otherwise unstirred.
> What you see is a calculated hour which he is likely
> to tie up in a darkened, half-dark upstairs room.[7]

While the nouns are dispassionately architectural, the verbs and adjectives are chilling: 'holds', 'tightens its grip', and 'tie up' conspire uneasily with 'calculated', 'darkened', and 'half-dark'. There are echoes here of Eavan Boland's downbeat boom-years collection *Domestic Violence*. In the work of both Groarke and Boland, the changing dispositions of land are inextricable from a knowledge of the presence of acquisitiveness and violence. These ugly emotions, both poets hint, arise from the conservative structures and hierarchies that a view of land as real estate propagates. The house itself, the solid thing that hulks in Groarke's poem, seems disturbingly non-specific, a commodity in a placeless anywhere.

Groarke's collection was written at a time when the idea of the ownership of land moved from indicating security to possibly signifying its opposite. It was published at the advent of what McWilliams has called 'Trackerville'. This was his term for:

> [a] vast swathe of thousands of starter homes that were financed by tracker mortgages [i.e., mortgages that followed the base rate of the European Central Bank], built at the height of the boom, existing in the precarious twilight world between huge loans that can only go up in cost and depleted take-home incomes that can only decline further still as taxes rise and unemployment encroaches.[8]

In other words, Groarke's volume was published at a time in Irish life when the ownership of land, in the form of a home, did not equate to the security and stability it once did. At the turn of the millennium, the certainties that had once been represented by the acquisition of property were coming into question. In Irish literature, houses changed as thousands of owners of the inflated debts that home-ownership brought found themselves, in the title of Groarke's poem, 'House-bound'.

Shoddy building practices during these years created more tangible risks than those caused by shaky financial models, as building scandals such as the one sparked by the use of pyrite (an unstable, low-cost fill) in the construction of tens of thousands of Irish houses came to public awareness. This recognition of the grimly literal shaky foundations of Irish prosperity is addressed in literature: at one point in Donal Ryan's post-boom novel *The Spinning Heart* (2012), a character observes: 'there were seven years there where you could build houses out of cardboard and masking tape and they'd be sold off of the plans. People queued all night to buy boxes of houses all crammed together like kennels.'[9] While more lurid stories of kidnap and murder make a vivid thread through this novel, the everyday post-boom conditions are its backdrop, and the story takes place amid daily insecurity and deprivation. Written in a series of first-person narratives, *The Spinning Heart* counts the human costs of the multiple lies and betrayals that went into the property bubble. During the course of the novel, readers do not only see unscrupulous property developers preying on the greed or desperation of buyers, they also see construction workers cheated out of social security payments by underhanded employment practices, and mortgage brokers convincing the novel's various protagonists that they can afford homes that, it transpires, they cannot. The problems with the houses themselves, and the societal problems that are depicted, are shown by Ryan to be linked. The building of poor-quality houses and the unethical treatment of people are, to Ryan, part of a continuum.

The macroeconomic tremors that led to a fall in house prices and a rise in unemployment are experienced as full-scale earthquakes in the lives of Ryan's vulnerable characters. A character in *The Spinning Heart* who, earlier, had been successfully panicked by an estate agent into buying an overpriced house, reflects: 'There are forty-four houses in this estate. I live in number twenty-three. There's an old lady living in number forty. There's no one living in any of the other houses, just the ghosts of people who never existed.'[10] The idea of the 'ghost estate' became a cliché in the years after the 2008 economic crash, but the nature of this new Irish ghostliness is significant. It was distinct from that of, say, the Californian ghost towns that arose amid the exuberance of gold-seeking before emptying out. The California ghost towns served as habitations at one time and, at least temporarily, became arenas in which human lives and dreams were played out. The same cannot be said for the Irish ghost estates, which came, in literature, to represent lives that were only ever notional.

Spectral children, those symbols of a thwarted future, feature prominently in literature that focuses on Irish ghost estates. In 'Ghost Estates', a 2011 poem by Joseph Woods, these gleaming, empty houses are inhabited by 'a chimera of silent children in the back | garden'.[11] Similarly, William Wall's poem 'Ghost Estate', published in the same year, contains 'unborn children' who 'play invisible games | of hide & seek' in uninhabited rooms.[12] These uninhabited houses, in which the shadows of non-existent children dart around, are the visible, tangible markers of a stillborn future. In Ireland, chillingly, the link between houses – for so long the sign of human inhabitation on a landscape – and human presence had been cut. Rather than representing life with all its drama, variety, and complexity, therefore, whole estates of uninhabited houses became instead the mere sign of the invisible, incompetent, hand of the market at work. Whereas the ghosts that had haunted the Irish landscape in the past – those of the famine dead, say, or of millions of departed emigrants – were those of real people, the ghosts that haunted the Ireland of the ghost estates were, perhaps uniquely, the ghosts of people who had never been there. The new ghosts that haunted Irish literature are those from a future that, for all the recklessness with which it was gambled on, remained unborn.

A similar sense of emptiness and unreality with regard to built space haunts Mike McCormack's novel *Solar Bones* (2016). Empty spaces are important to the typography as well as the themes of this novel: throughout the single unbroken sentence that forms the narrative, the blank spaces of indents and line breaks are deployed on the novel's pages in place of punctuation. McCormack's abandonment of the sentence as an ordering, subordinating unit has thematic parallels in the novel: his protagonist, an engineer called Conway, frequently dwells on spaces that are cleared out and reconfigured. At one point Conway meditates on:

> mapping and surveying so that the grid of reason and progress could be laid across the earth, gathering its wildness into towns and villages by way of bridges and roads and water schemes and power lines[13]

The novel's engineer-narrator is not imagining land here as the scene of historical depredations, nor as the object of distant longing, nor even as an asset whose soil or placement might promise financial or agricultural increase. This is land as envisaged in the planner's and the architect's disembodied dream. One of the key elements of the novel is a school which was poorly constructed, and which Conway is now under pressure to sign off on. As in the novels that Donal Ryan wrote in the aftermath of Ireland's property bubble, shoddy building work and defective values are brought into stark alignment. *Solar Bones* is a testament to what rezoning, building, and selling might do, but it is also a wry and angry exposition of the way that even the best-laid schemes, plans, and structures can decay and fail.

The falling away of the illusions of the boom, however, brings consolation in the form of a new clarity of vision. In *Solar Bones*, the bones of post-2008 Irish society come into view on the page with the eerie precision of the bones of a patient in an x-ray. In a reverie, the narrator sees how:

> the ghost house beneath the paint and fittings asserts itself, flickering like an X-ray with that neurological twitch and spasm which is imbedded in the concrete, in the vertical and horizontal run of all its plumbing and wiring, those systems which make the house a living thing with all its walls and the floors pulsing with oil and water and electricity [...] this web of utilities a tiny part of that greater circum-terrestrial grid of services which draws the world into community[14]

This exact metaphor, in which a house is re-imagined as a living organism that is dependent on a vast, continuous network for its maintenance, is the one that the Marxist theorist Henri Lefebvre used in *The Production of Space* (1974). In this work, Lefebvre sought to undermine what he considered the bourgeois notion of the house as a self-contained entity (as propounded by writers like Gaston Bachelard). Instead, Lefebvre's work focused on how the house's illusory containment gave way, under the lightest pressure of thought, to something more complex and interdependent: it was a place 'permeated from every direction by streams of energy which run in and out of it by every imaginable route: water, gas, electricity, telephone lines, radio and television signals'.[15] The corollary of McCormack's re-imagining of inhabited space, and of narrative, as single unbroken continuums is a critical rethinking of the individualistic society that was promoted by the property boom.

If, in the Republic, the traditional agricultural qualities of areas of land were overlooked in favour of their potential as building sites, in Northern Ireland related but differently inflected conditions were at work. Northern Irish authors recorded the development of weirdly placeless spaces that were primarily oriented towards the smooth operation of international consumerism. The fact that these spaces lie over the tops of traditional sectarian boundary lines increases the sense of disjunction, as the new and anodyne encroaches on old but still-sensitive spatial divisions. The slogan of post-ceasefire literature from Belfast might as well be Baudelaire's famous cry when considering the reconstructed Paris of the mid-nineteenth century: 'the shape of a town | Changes more quickly, alas, than the heart of a mortal'.[16] A phase of Northern Ireland's history had come to an end; no one was quite sure what had begun.

Leontia Flynn's poem 'Belfast' presents a place that, though a world away from the tense and watchful site of conflict that the city centre had once been, nevertheless echoes with undertones of a new kind of violence: 'Belfast is finished and Belfast is under construction. | What was mixed grills and whiskeys (cultureless, graceless, leisureless) | is now concerts and walking tours (Friendly! Dynamic! Various!).'[17] This poem's tone seems to mock by emulation the border-crossing capitalism that is its subject, splicing the spirit of Bashō with references to McDonald's and Louis MacNeice. The Japanese poet's haiku on longing for Kyoto while he was in Kyoto is very similar to Flynn's poem's opening formulation. Like Bashō's poem, Flynn's expresses the feeling of being in a place and yearning for the impossible return of its earlier incarnation. Her response to the rapid changes that occurred to Belfast's urban landscape illustrates the observation of the literary critic Jeremy Hooker that the poetry of place 'cannot be understood outside a context of loss'.[18] The question in relation to place that

Belfast literature raises is, what does it mean to mourn a past city, when the past of that city was such a painful one? The Belfast that has replaced the former one is, to many authors who live there, a pan-national, atemporal jumble of the kind Jean-François Lyotard imagined.

In *The Postmodern Condition* (published in English in 1984), Lyotard observed that 'eclecticism is the degree zero of contemporary general culture: one listens to reggae, watches a western, eats McDonald's food for lunch and local cuisine for dinner'.[19] Flynn's poem, however, is not just constructed from the flotsam of the contemporary: it also incorporates fragments of Belfast's literary history. The words 'harsh attempts at buyable beauty' come from a poem called 'Belfast' by Louis MacNeice, and indeed the poem seems to follow the documentary-realist form that MacNeice brought to the unsparing poems that he set in the city.[20] Flynn's Belfast has been rebuilt, or at least recladded, and the physical traces of its tragic past have been concealed beneath a glossy carapace. However, while the superficial form of the city has changed, both its literary and its other histories lie just beneath the surface.

For Medbh McGuckian, long the most recondite of Northern Irish poets, the shock of the new seemed to inspire a new mode of writing. In her 2015 collection, *Blaris Moor*, the closing poem 'Who Is Your City?' displays a very different tonality not only from her earlier books, but from the earlier poems in the same collection, as she takes an unexpectedly clear-eyed look at the city around her:

> Gone is the edginess of the city, cleansed
> of conflict, argument, debate, protest, ructions,
> and ribaldry, notwithstanding the spy cameras,
> the pop-up shops, the flash mobs of drink-
> fuelled petrolheads, the new Purple Flag award.[21]

This least characteristic of McGuckian's poems contains some odd furniture, among it the Purple Flag (an award scheme that enables city centres to advertise their safety and suitability as venues for nights out). This flag might well be the emblem of the new, commerce-friendly Belfast: its semiotics are antithetical to those of the national and paramilitary flags that adorn lamp posts in the city's working-class areas.[22] The listing of this flag as a feature of the new city alongside 'spy cameras' and 'flash mobs' suggests, like Flynn's poem about Belfast, that the new, post-ceasefire Belfast is subject to certain new instruments of coercion and control.

The same ambivalent consciousness of rapid spatial change that can be intuited from the poetry of McGuckian and Flynn is also central to Glenn Patterson's 2012 novel, *The Mill for Grinding Old People Young*. Patterson's is a historical fiction with evident contemporary resonances, set as it is in a late-eighteenth-century Belfast that is growing into a commercial hub with the development of its shipbuilding and linen manufacturing industries. This preoccupation with the consequences of rapid change for a city is signalled from the book's first epigraph: 'To the old, the new world of Belfast around them is generally too great for their grasp or comprehension.'[23] The fact that this epigraph is a quote from a history of Belfast that was published in 1880 does not blunt its contemporary relevance. Writing that focuses on Belfast from the first decade or so of the twenty-first century, both in poetry and prose, displays a distinct awareness that it is attempting to capture a rapidly moving target. In these years, the Belfast that appears in literature is a place of uneasily observed change. However, the mushrooming retail spaces, houses, flats, and roads that remade the Irish landscape, north and south, were not just examined for their homogenising effects: these changes were treated by many authors as irreparable destruction.

If one way to think about Irish land is economically, a second, increasingly significant way is to think about it ecologically. The words 'ecology' and 'economy' have a common etymology: 'eco' has its origin in the Greek word *oikos*, meaning house. 'Economics' has its roots in the idea of household management; it expresses an understanding of the house as a nodal point in supplies and flows of goods and services. 'Ecology', on the other hand, grows from a very different understanding of the *oikos*. It stems from an understanding of the *oikos* as a habitat, and it indicates the significance and necessity of the maintenance of habitable space. This ecological understanding of the *oikos* further carries ideas of an environment that might be dwelt in and that might, even, be eventually rendered uninhabitable. Despite their similar etymologies, there is a sense in Irish writing since 1980 that ecological ways of considering land might be a counterbalancing force to destructively simplistic ones that are primarily economic.

During the boom years, ecologically focused writers feared the long-term consequences of the increasing marketability of Irish land as an asset. The noted ecological writer Tim Robinson observed with unease the shift in values that held that land was increasingly thought of in terms of the sum of money it could command during the Celtic Tiger years: 'the selling off of Connemara is immensely profitable to landowners and developers, and as a result planning regulations are flagrantly subverted, with the connivance of clientele-dependent politicians. It corrupts our eyes, we see every field as a potential house site, flaunting a price tag instead of its ragged hawthorn tree.'[24] One might say that a focus not on money but on this ragged hawthorn tree, its roots, branches, and leaves, its origins and biology, its historic, mythical, and religious significances, would be a classic subject of one of Robinson's characteristic up-close, micro-fine investigations into the overlooked workings and mysteries of the physical world. With its insistent focus on the nature and qualities of the material realm, Robinson's work over the decades since the 1980s has come to constitute a powerful, if implicit, critique of the dominant economic value systems that have been applied to Irish land.

Centring his view of the world on the nominal peripheries of Aran and Connemara, Robinson's obsessive scrutiny of the land might at times bring the previously unknown to light. What are more important, however, are the occluded spaces that his close scrutiny reveals to be unknowable.[25] This is demonstrated in his chapter 'Who Owns the Land?', in which economic questions of title and saleability shrink into insignificance in comparison with much broader perspectives. In a piece in which he attempts to chart the idea of ownership of land in Connemara through various historical and mythological frames, Robinson concludes that any legalistic conception of ownership might represent a vain hope: 'if we know in our hearts that mountains and oceans have their day then our proprietorial attitude to patches of land appears in perspective, as a littleness'.[26] Essentially, Robinson's approach to land is one that involves the radical re-drawing of perspectives. To him, prevalent, primarily economic, approaches make possible a culture of casual depletion and destruction. Representing the land with nuance, detail, and a knowledge of the mystery that inheres in its deep silences results in writing with a distinctly countercultural cast. Land, when its value is assessed not in monetary terms, but for its ecological diversity and historical associations, might be recognised for its full value and preciousness.

Seamus Heaney, like Robinson, became aware that the changing place of land in the Irish imagination both resulted from and signalled a wider shift in Irish culture. Knowledge of this shift starts coming to the fore in the work he published during the Celtic Tiger years. At one point in his 2001 collection, *Electric Light*, Heaney has an imagined Co. Wicklow farmer reflect ruefully that 'Outsiders own | The country nowadays [...] | Small farmers here are priced out of the market'.[27]

In the same collection, this knowledge of the commercialisation of land is countered by a rather Robinsonian memory:

> On an old recording Patrick Kavanagh states
> That there's health and worth in any talk about
> The properties of land. Sandy, glarry,
> Mossy, heavy, cold, the actual soil
> Almost doesn't matter; the main thing is
> An inner restitution, a purchase come by
> By pacing it in words[28]

Heaney's 'purchase' is different from the purchases that were reported in newspaper property supplements at the time. The context for these lines is made explicit in *Stepping Stones* (2008), a series of interviews Heaney conducted with the poet Dennis O'Driscoll. In one interview, Heaney says that he suspects that the sacred dimension to Irish land was wearing thin, and was being replaced with something else: 'that old sense of tillage and season and foliage has disappeared. Once trees and hedges and ditches and thatch get stripped, you're in a very different world. You're deserting the ground for the grid.'[29] In these words, Heaney reflects the thoughts of Mike McCormack's imagined engineer in *Solar Bones*, whose daydreams are haunted by the 'wildness' that is subsumed under 'the grid of reason and progress'. However, if Irish literature in the early twenty-first century became a space in which writers could reflect on the threats to wild places, it was also one in which the necessity of these wild places could be passionately asserted.[30]

This tendency is a marked aspect of the work of the poet Paula Meehan. In 'Death of a Field', she pits the wonderful variety and diversity of nature against the homogeneity and blandness that is imposed when land is viewed through the flattening lens of the cash nexus. The poem is a stark lament for what is lost when economic values are prioritised over ecological ones:

> The field itself is lost the morning it becomes a site
> When the Notice goes up: Fingal County Council – 44 houses
>
> The memory of the field is lost with the loss of its herbs
>
> Though the woodpigeons in the willow
> And the finches in what's left of the hawthorn hedge
> And the wagtail in the elder
> Sing on their hungry summer song
>
> The magpies sound like flying castanets[31]

If nature represents music, beauty, vibrancy, and diversity, its loss (the words 'loss' and 'lost' echo dolefully through the opening lines of the poem) and its destruction offer merely death and sameness. Meehan's response to the changing uses of land in Ireland, as with so many of her peers, involves restorative linguistic specificity: this field is not just home to 'birds', but to woodpigeons, finches, wagtails, and magpies. This richness of the poem's vocabulary is her way of recognising and communicating the full, threatened, value of the natural world.

In the last fifty years, Michael Longley has been one of Ireland's most trenchant voices for the preservation of land as an ecological resource. To choose one example among many, 'Burren Prayer' (*The Weather in Japan*, 2000) represents a landscape that is embroidered with flowers and, in doing so, suggests that the natural world is worthy of the same care and detailed attention as human work:

> Gentian and lady's bedstraw embroider her frock.
> Her pockets are full of sloes and juniper berries.
>
> [...]
>
> Sea lavender and Irish eyebright at Poll Salach,
> On Back Head saxifrage and mountain-everlasting.
>
> Our Lady of the Fertile Rocks, protect the Burren.
> *Protect the Burren, Our Lady of the Fertile Rocks.*[32]

The poem's imagery of embroidery is enhanced by its form: the italicised chiasmus with which it ends replicates the knotting and linking of a garland. In an earlier poem, Longley had commemorated the killing of a shop owner with a similar list of Burren flowers, creating a sort of verbal wreath to lay at the site of the death of a victim of the Troubles.[33] The sense of loss communicated by 'Burren Prayer', however, is subtly magnified by the way it touches on other periods of devastation in Irish history. The way Longley presents the landscape as a vision of a woman, combined with his reference to 'Irish eyebright', raises the ghost of the early eighteenth-century Irish-language poet Aogán Ó Rathaille, whose best-known poem is a Marian-*aisling* vision of a feminised Irish landscape as the piercing-eyed '*gile na gile*': 'brightness of brightness'.[34] In this way, Longley taps into the energies of a writer whose work registers a wild despair at the changes Ireland was undergoing at a previous time of great upheaval. Longley's drawing on the long history of Irish poetry suggests that no sense of crisis exists in isolation: present-day fears of calamity are heightened and given resonance from the way they stir memories of crises and calamities further back. Though the ecological damage being inflicted on the Irish landscape has concomitants all over the world, Irish writers' responses are distinct because they are writing out of a distinct literary tradition – one in which the modes of mourning and protest are both prominent.

Modern Irish authors have imagined land in many different dispositions: as geology, the result of over a billion years of deposits and fusions that gave rise to the present island; as territory, to be guarded and defended; as an ecological resource and guardian of biodiversity; affectively, as a home. They have imagined land in all these ways at once. However, certain new elements have been added to these understandings in recent years: heavy mortgages and precarious employment mean that ownership of land does not necessarily signify prestige and security as it once did. The return of mass emigration after the economic crash means that a historic sense of disjunction between the concept of 'Ireland' and the location of the Irish people was felt with renewed force after 2008.[35] Finally, the depredations of, in Longley's words, 'contaminated lakes, fish-kills, ruthless overgrazing, "bungalow blight", chemical overkill, building on flood plains, oil spills, inappropriately sited motorways' have all made their mark on Irish literature.[36] Representations of space and place in Irish literature are, ultimately, as much a lens through which less tangible changes can be seen as they are records of changes to the physical world.

Notes

1. Ruth McManus, 'Celtic Tiger Housing', in F. H. A. Aalen, Kevin Whelan, and Matthew Stout, eds., *The Atlas of the Irish Rural Landscape* (Cork, Ireland: Cork University Press, 2011), pp. 156–65 (p. 156).
2. Eavan Boland, *Domestic Violence* (Manchester: Carcanet, 2007), p. 20.
3. Daniel Corkery, *Synge and Anglo-Irish Literature: A Study* (Cork: Cork University Press, 1931), p. 19.
4. Andy Bielenberg and Raymond Ryan, *An Economic History of Ireland Since Independence* (London: Routledge, 2013), p. 69.
5. McManus, 'Celtic Tiger Housing', p. 156.
6. David McWilliams, *The Good Room: Why We Ended Up in A Debtors' Prison – And How We Can Break Free* (Dublin: Penguin, 2012), p. 9.
7. Vona Groarke, *Other People's Houses* (Oldcastle, Co. Meath: Gallery Books, 1999), p. 21.
8. McWilliams, *The Good Room*, p. 7.
9. Donal Ryan, *The Spinning Heart* (Dublin: Lilliput Press, 2012), p. 26.
10. Ibid., p. 42.

11. Joseph Woods, 'Ghost Estates', *New Hibernia Review/Iris Éireannach Nua*, 15.3 (Autumn 2011), p. 55.
12. William Wall, *Ghost Estate* (Cliffs of Moher, Ireland: Salmon Poetry, 2011), p. 16.
13. Mike McCormack, *Solar Bones* (Dublin: Tramp Press, 2016), p. 92.
14. Ibid., p. 129.
15. Henri Lefebvre, *The Production of Space*, trans. Donald Nicholson-Smith (Oxford: Blackwell, 1998), p. 93.
16. Charles Baudelaire, 'Le Cygne', available at *Fleurs du Mal:* https://fleursdumal.org/poem/220 [accessed 30 January 2019].
17. Leontia Flynn, *Drives* (London: Jonathan Cape, 2008), p. 2.
18. Jeremy Hooker, *The Poetry of Place: Essays and Reviews 1971–1980* (Manchester: Carcanet, 1982), p. 181.
19. Jean-François Lyotard, *The Postmodern Condition: A Report on Knowledge* (Minneapolis, MN: University of Minnesota Press, 1984), p. 76.
20. For example, see Louis MacNeice, 'Belfast', in E. R. Dodds, ed., *Collected Poems* (London: Faber and Faber, 1966), p. 17.
21. Medbh McGuckian, *Blaris Moor* (Oldcastle, Co. Meath: Gallery Press, 2015), p. 82.
22. The Purple Flag award website states that the award recognises that 'a town's night-time economy offers clean and safe environments, great bars and clubs, a variety of arts and cultural attractions and excellent transport links': www.100ways.org.uk/purple-flag.html [accessed 30 January 2019].
23. Glenn Patterson, *The Mill for Grinding Old People Young* (London: Faber and Faber, 2012).
24. Quoted in Eóin Flannery, 'Essayist of Place: Postcolonialism and Ecology in the Work of Tim Robinson', in Derek Gladwin and Christina Cusick, eds., *Unfolding Irish Landscapes: Tim Robinson, Culture and Environment* (Manchester: Manchester University Press, 2016), pp. 218–36 (p. 232).
25. This is the subject of an essay by Kelly Sullivan: see 'Not Knowing as Aesthetic Imperative in Tim Robinson's *Stones of Aran*', in Derek Gladwin and Christina Cusick, eds., *Unfolding Irish Landscapes: Tim Robinson, Culture and Environment*, pp. 103–18.
26. Tim Robinson, *Connemara: Last Pool of Darkness* (Dublin: Penguin, 2008), p. 313.
27. Seamus Heaney, *Electric Light* (London: Faber and Faber, 2001), pp. 35–6.
28. Ibid., p. 14.
29. Dennis O'Driscoll, *Stepping Stones: Interviews with Seamus Heaney* (London: Faber and Faber, 2008), p. 24.
30. McCormack, *Solar Bones*, p. 92.
31. Paula Meehan, *Painting Rain* (Manchester: Carcanet, 2009), pp. 13–14 (p. 13).
32. Michael Longley, *Collected Poems* (London: Jonathan Cape, 2006), p. 249.
33. Michael Longley, *Gorse Fires* (London: Jonathan Cape, 1991), p. 49.

34. Aogán Ó Rathaille, 'Gile na Gile', quoted in Robert Welch, *The Cold of May Day Monday: An Approach to Irish Literary History* (Oxford: Oxford University Press, 2014), p. 52.
35. This argument, though about an earlier era, is part of Fintan O'Toole's *The Lie of the Land: Irish Identities* (London: Verso, 1997).
36. Michael Longley, *One Wide Expanse* (Dublin: University College Dublin Press, 2015), p. 56.

CHAPTER 7

Crossings: Northern Irish Literature from Good Friday to Brexit

Stefanie Lehner

Historically, culturally, and politically, Northern Irish literature has always been a nodal point for multiple crossings. First articulated in 1987, Edna Longley pointedly captured these literary crosscurrents with the *Denkbild* [thought image] of an open-ended 'cultural corridor', which is set against those political projects wishing to close it off, namely nationalism and unionism. Instead of fitting into these monolithic binary paradigms, for Longley, Northern Irish literature 'overspills borders and manifests a web of affiliation that stretches beyond any heartland – to the rest of Ireland, Britain, Europe'.[1] This is reflected in the critical category of Northern Irish literature itself, which – depending on where it is taught or sold – straddles and thereby questions the categories of English, Irish, and British literature. Coined during the peak of the North's political conflict, Longley's notion of a cultural corridor resonates in the post-conflict and Brexit eras: negatively, perhaps with the prospect of a hard border returning to isolate Northern Ireland from the Republic or an Irish Sea border isolating it from Great Britain; positively, in that Northern Ireland's receptivity to Europeanness (evinced in the region's majority vote to remain in the EU) mirrors similar sentiments along the 'Celtic fringe' in the Republic and Scotland.

The 1998 Belfast or Good Friday Agreement can be said to both affirm and trouble the open-endedness of Longley's conception in a number of ways. In its endeavour to end the three-and-a-half-decades of war and violence, euphemistically known as 'The Troubles', the Agreement aimed to set up a nationalist and unionist power-sharing government in Northern Ireland as a basis for lasting peace. Yet, the consociational model that underpins the new devolved assembly naturalises rather than transcends the divisions of the two dominant ideological blocs. This threatens to occlude a vast range of other relations, positions, and concerns that constitute the 'web of affiliation' that Longley envisages. On the question of whether Northern Ireland should remain in the United Kingdom or become part of a united Ireland, the Agreement suggested an openness to both possibilities by stating that there would be no change without the consent of the majority. As a multiparty agreement that also entails an international agreement between the British and Irish governments, its strands establish both North–South and East–West institutions, thereby affirming Northern Ireland as 'a zone where Ireland and Britain permeate one another'.[2]

The affirmation of British–Irish relations is, however, as much a matter of politics as it is of economics, intending, at the time, to re-integrate Northern Ireland into the neo-liberal global dispensation by extending the free market principles of the British 'Third Way' westwards and the (at the time still roaring) Celtic Tiger northwards.[3] Northern Irish poetry early on interrogated the progressivist logic of this new economic corridor, which suggested redevelopment and regeneration through multinational investment as the way forward for a society deemed 'backwards'. Sinéad Morrissey's 'In Belfast' (2002), for instance, visualises the market-driven ideology that has taken on a life of its own, devoid of actual people: 'The inhaling shop-fronts exhale the length | and breadth of Royal Avenue, pause, | inhale again. The city is making money | on a weather-mangled Tuesday.'[4] In turn, Leontia Flynn's 'Belfast' (2008) captures the way in which the new attempts to replace the old: 'Belfast is finished and Belfast is under construction. | What was mixed grills and whiskeys (cultureless, graceless, leisureless) | is now concerts and walking tours (Friendly! Dynamic! Various!).'[5] What such 'progress' can never achieve is cleverly foregrounded in Alan Gillis' eponymous poem:

> They say that for years Belfast was backwards
> and it's great now to see some progress.
> So I guess we can look forward to taking boxes
> from the earth. I guess that ambulances
> will leave the dying back amidst the rubble
> to be explosively healed.[6]

By reversing the arrow of time, Gillis foregrounds the ethical absences of such a teleological narrative of historical 'progress'. Resonant of Walter Benjamin's famous description of the 'Angel of History' who 'would like to stay, awaken the dead, and make whole what has been smashed' while he is 'irresistibly' blown backwards into the future,[7] the speaker contemplates the impossibility of resurrecting 'those who have died or been injured' during the Troubles.[8] In doing so, the poem questions the temporal logic underpinning the 1998 Agreement, which suggests that 'we can best honour them through a fresh start'.[9]

The fascination with novelty and new beginnings that is suggested in the Agreement's 'fresh start' is registered in Morrissey's 'Tourism' (2002), which sets the desire for 'new symbols, | a new national flag' against the way in which the Troubles' past has been cordoned off and commodified for tourists, pretending 'as though it's all over and safe behind bus glass | like a staked African wasp'.[10] Yet, as suggested by these examples, post-Agreement literature remains acutely aware that the 'staked' past can still sting and that the peace process may have created a rather different and more narrow corridor than that envisaged by Longley: one that, in its complicity with a ready-made futurity of global consumerism and neoliberal economics, resembles more a one-way street, as insinuated by the strategic street sign for the Agreement's 'Yes' campaign, reading 'Vote Yes. It's the way ahead'.[11]

Brexit reconfigures the fluid and complex dynamics that characterise the North as a corridor. This occurs on multiple levels and in several directions, but the major question concerns the placement of the UK-EU border: whether it is drawn in the Irish Sea or on the island of Ireland (as per the 'backstop' in Prime Minister Theresa May's defeated 2019 plan), the North-South and East-West dimensions of the 1998 Agreement will be ruptured. The implications extend to affiliations and identity articulations, which are safeguarded in the Agreement's recognition that national identity and citizenship are not a matter of binary choice but rather fluid and multiple.[12] For Irish nationalists, a 'hard' border will be understood to re-impose partition and re-invoke the troubled past, but an Irish Sea border will, in turn, alienate Ulster unionists. The unsettling of these dynamics extends to Scotland where nationalists there will question any special status granted or imposed on Northern Ireland in relation to the EU. In this regard, the demand for sovereignty implied in the Leave campaign's 'Take back control' slogan is exposed as out of place and out of time: the intertwined relations of Northern Ireland and Scotland mean that both within and between the two regions Brexit is less about self-determination and more about recognising the fragile bonds that constitute the Union. Arguably, this almost existential predicament has been overshadowed by security-related concerns over the types of opportunities and fears that a border will precipitate for loyalists and republicans in Northern Ireland and the very real threats that lie therein to the peace process as it has developed over the past two decades. Ironically, these fears are seemingly not shared by Northern Irish 'Leave' voters: the 2018 'Future of England

Study' reveals that 87% of such voters 'see the collapse of the peace process as an acceptable price for Brexit'.[13]

The uncertain and ambiguous position of Northern Ireland within Brexit is addressed in David Wheatley's poem 'Flags and Emblems' (2018), in which a 'man in a post office' questions whether a 'Northern Irish fiver' is 'part of us' (presumably the United Kingdom) or 'Southern Ireland'.[14] Both Northern Irish and Scottish banks have traditionally printed their own money, which is not classified as 'legal tender' in the rest of the UK and, as a result, often not recognised. As 'the postmaster' concludes, it is from 'somewhere anyway | in need of a cloot | to wipe itself down'. Wheatley's poem here uses the story of a malfunctioning sewage tanker in Crossgar, 'randomly | spraying clabbery glar', as what he describes as an 'over-obvious analogy for the resurgent English nationalism about to descend like a pall (of slurry) over Britain and Northern Ireland'. This image of English cross-contamination is juxtaposed with an emphasis on the specifics of Northern Irish locality ('gable-ends kerbstones'; 'flags on | the lampposts') and the use of several Scots vernacular forms in a poem that was itself first conceived when crossing from Belfast to Scotland. Thus, despite its deliberations on fixity – 'things mean | themselves and nothing | besides' – the poem enacts, and, in its own way, celebrates the inherent ambiguity and openness of Northern Ireland.

Even as the Brexit debate significantly complicates matters, post-Agreement literature remains committed to Northern Ireland as a place of interchange that enables various crossings. However, rather than accepting the 'post' as a temporal marker that designates a distinct break with what came before, these texts raise awareness of what remains to be worked through and addressed: these unresolved issues, silences, and absences connote a period of troubled, stalled transition, suggesting a sense of suspension that seems reflected in Northern Ireland's repeatedly suspended devolved assembly.[15] Indeed, suspension has remained one of the key critical categories for reading contemporary Northern Irish literature. Richard Kirkland's *Literature and Culture in Northern Ireland since 1965: Moments of Danger* (1996) proposed the Gramscian concept of the 'interregnum' to analyse Northern Ireland's 'crisis', which inspired John Brannigan's 2006 analysis of literary refractions of 'the paradoxical state of suspension which characterizes the interregnum'.[16] These studies have paved the way for more recent discussions of suspension as an aesthetic category, most notably in Birte Heidemann's *Post-Agreement Northern Irish Literature: Lost in a Liminal Space?* (2016), but also evident in Maureen E. Ruprecht Fadem's *The Literature of Northern Ireland:*

Spectral Borderlands (2015) as well as Declan Long's *Ghost-Haunted Land: Contemporary Art and Post-Troubles Northern Ireland* (2017). But while critics have suggested that this ongoing state of liminal suspension is a 'disabling condition', this chapter seeks to recover the recalcitrant dynamics of literary liminality as a crosscurrent to the homogenising and teleological thrust of the progress narratives underpinning both the Agreement and Brexit.[17] This emphasis on the active energies suggested by the motif of crosscurrents allows for a revision of the more passive concepts of the cultural corridor and suspension and foregrounds the potential of contemporary Northern Irish literature to establish new affiliations and reconciliatory discussions, and to undertake a dialogue between the temporal coordinates of a haunting past and a precarious 'fresh' future.

Commemorative Corridors: Traversing Temporalities

The unfinished business of the past haunts the Northern Irish peace process, which is reflected and refracted in post-Agreement literature. Public commemoration has been dominated by what Graham Dawson calls 'defensive remembering', 'where selective, discrepant and antagonistic narratives of the past clash and compete'.[18] There are still very few inclusive public memorials – most of which occur in the form of, or within, texts: most notably, the ambitious *Lost Lives* project, which tells the stories of all those that died as a result of the Troubles.[19] If Gillis' 'Progress', alongside other recent Northern Irish poetry, suggests alternative forms of commemoration, prose fiction has offered a more expansive space for what Dawson calls 'reparative remembering', which includes 'opening emotionally to the disavowed past, connecting and integrating traumatic histories, and engaging with the memory world of the other'.[20] Such a remembering shows the capacity to reconcile the proleptic and retrospective tendencies that, Neal Alexander suggests, characterise pre- and post-Agreement Northern Irish fiction, in order to open up a commemorative corridor between the past and future that disrupts the progressivist teleology of the peace process as well as one-sided forms of defensive commemoration.[21]

Glenn Patterson's fictional oeuvre offers an indicative example of this notion of a commemorative corridor. Despite their differences, his novels seem equally concerned to exhume what he himself terms 'alternative histories' of his native city, Belfast, which have been subsumed by the dominant narrative of the Troubles.[22] This interrogation of the past opens fresh perspectives on the unfolding future of the peace process. For instance, Patterson's *The International* (1999), is narrated retrospectively by Danny Hamilton, who revisits one day of his life in 1967 pre-Troubles Belfast as a barman at the eponymous hotel. Danny's narration encircles and thereby foregrounds the 'absence' of Peter Ward in his story, an International barman who was murdered by the UVF (Ulster Volunteer Force) in June 1966 as one of the first victims of the conflict and whom Danny replaced: 'I wish it was not so, but guns do that, create holes which no amount of words can fill.'[23] Aware of the irrevocability of his death, Danny re-inscribes his absent presence by noting his personal connection with him: 'Peter Ward was eighteen when he died. I turned eighteen a fortnight after he was buried, a fortnight after I started work in the hotel.'[24] In aligning and thereby integrating their stories, Danny's recollection works as an act of 'reparative remembering' that connects the events of the violent past with an anticipation of a non-violent future. The end of the novel suggests this through the 1994 announcement of the loyalist ceasefire by Gusty Spence, who was convicted of the murder of Ward. As he listens to Spence expressing 'the abject and true remorse of the Loyalist terror groups on whose behalf he was speaking', Danny's thoughts return to Ward, thereby connecting killer and victim, past and present, in a reconciliatory anticipation of the future: 'I believed him.'[25]

Despite its progressivist trajectory, moving from the pre-Troubles to the post-Agreement periods, Patterson's *Number 5* (2003) builds a socio-cultural and commemorative corridor by telling the stories of five successive occupants of a terraced house in the suburbs of Belfast from the 1950s to the millennium. The characters are representative of a diverse range of Northern Ireland's population and their move to this new location enables them to establish new affiliations that challenge established paradigms. For instance, the Chinese teenager Tan forms a friendship with the son of his Protestant neighbours, whose nickname is Tit, and together they insert themselves as 'T'n'T' into the walls of their neighbourhood, thereby subverting the codes of paramilitary sectarianism. While every new family is eager to make a fresh start in the house by redecorating it, traces of the previous occupants stand as powerful reminders of the haunting presence of the past in the present. The irrevocable temporality of such memorial traces, which disrupt the linear progression of the novel, is embodied in the figure of Ivy Moore. This neighbour, as her name suggests, twines traces of the past with future changes: most notably through the act of remembering the occluded story of the first occupant, Stella, whose daughter suddenly returns at the close of the novel.[26] In a comparable manner, Patterson unsettles the chronological delineation of Belfast's Peace Process in *That Which Was* (2004), a novel in which the amnesiac character Larry approaches a Presbyterian minister, Ken Avery, with the vague recollection of having committed murder during the Troubles. As Avery resolves to uncover the truth behind Larry's conviction of his guilt, Larry confides: 'I believe that memories come back to haunt you, even when someone has tried to erase them.'[27]

The thriller was the predominant mode for representing the Troubles,[28] and a notable number of peace process fictions have employed elements of the form, which has proven especially able to register the temporal and spatial crossings underpinning the Agreement, while contesting the notion that it could draw 'a line under the past'. As Patterson notes, in 2004 alone, three other novels came out that used the thriller genre to explore the unresolved business of the past in the post-Agreement present.[29] Eoin McNamee's *The Ultras* confronts the controversial issue of the collusion between the security forces and paramilitaries, and David Park's *Swallowing the Sun* explores the impact that psychological and physical violence in the past have on its main character, Martin Waring, whose daughter dies after taking Ecstasy. Sean O'Reilly's *The Swing of Things* questions to what extent it is possible to leave a paramilitary past and prison sentence behind by following Noel Boyle to Dublin, where he tries to change by enrolling at university.

In these novels, the haunting past takes on an ethical force which conjures up questions about responsibility, guilt, and justice. However, in keeping with the mystery element of the thriller, they also highlight the difficulty of conclusive truths and clear-cut morals, specifically regarding the roles of victim and villain. For instance, Stuart Neville's *The Twelve* (2010) actively foregrounds the problematic ethics of a broad conception of victimhood that can be seen to absolve those directly responsible for violence.[30] The ex-paramilitary prisoner Gerry Fagan reflects in this novel that 'the politicians on the outside had bartered for his freedom, along with hundreds more men and women. They called people like him political prisoners. Not murderers or thieves, not extortionists or blackmailers. Not criminals of any kind, just victims of circumstance'.[31] The ethical force of these thrillers resides in the reparative remembrance they can afford by emphatically connecting with the memory world of the other: whether these stories are told by innocent victims, guilty perpetrators, or those in positions in between, they intimate 'the sense of a collective responsibility to narrate, listen and respond to the stories of the dead'.[32] The reconciliatory potential that such a sharing of stories can have on individuals and societies has been emphasised by storytelling initiatives and also in several recent plays, perhaps most forcefully by

Owen McCafferty's *Quietly* (2012), which importantly revises the genre by staging a suspenseful encounter between a perpetrator and a victim.

If the thriller has been notably transformed in post-Agreement literature, the past five years have also witnessed the embrace of magical realist elements, specifically in short stories by Northern Irish women writers. Like the crime thriller, the magical realist mode seems apt to register the traumatic excesses of the recent violent past, which occur in these stories in the form of supernatural, surreal, or fantastical elements or characters.[33] For instance, Annie, the first-person narrator of Bernie McGill's 'No Angel' (2013), is haunted by the ghost of her recently deceased father who tries to forestall her putative 'love-across-the-barricades' relationship, as he and his deceased wife have not been able to get over the sectarian murder of Annie's younger brother, James. Although Annie's relationship fails, the end of the story allows for a reconciliation between the past, present, and future when Annie recognises that her ghost-father found her mother and brother, who join her as spectral audience members to watch a performance, and he accepts her request to let her go into her own self-determined future: '"I won't be told who to love by you," I said.'[34] In the Northern Irish literary imagination, this freedom of romantic choice, specifically in the form of a mixed marriage, has long functioned as a trope for a wider social reconciliation.[35] The challenges of such cross-community relationships are suggested in Roisín O'Donnell's 'Ebenezer's Memories' or Jan Carson's 'Children's Children' (both 2016), the latter of which envisages the allegorical coming together of the last inhabitants of an island's split northern and southern sides as 'a brave new direction'.[36] In contrast to this proleptic vista, many of these magical realist stories confine the repressed past to a contained space, such as the cupboard under the stairs in O'Donnell's 'Ebenezer's Memories', or the boxroom of Carson's 'Contemporary Uses for a Belfast Box Room' (2016).

Spatial Corridors: Border Crossings

A number of recent post-Agreement fictions explore physical journeys as a means to effect internal crossings; these journeys confront their protagonists with unresolved issues of the past. This is already apparent in Patterson's rarely discussed thriller, *The Third Party* (2007), which is narrated retrospectively by an unnamed Northern Irish businessman who works for a plastics company. The novel focuses on the last day of his trip to Hiroshima where he meets a fellow countryman and writer, known only as 'Ike', who attends the conference 'Writing Out of Conflict 2004'. The double connotations of this conference title (which parallels the double meaning of the novel's title) draw attention to the ways in which both men, in their different ways, trade on Northern Ireland's post-conflict politics: while Ike has written himself out by having exploited other people's pain and stories to write about the Troubles, the narrator-businessman has exploited the 'messy peace' by making a dodgy deal with an (ex)paramilitary 'Brigadier' to dispose of his company's dangerously defective 'U-bag prototype', a self-sealing bag to replace cling film, thereby causing hurt, misery, and physical deformations to babies in Sardinia, where the faulty product was resold.[37]

This novel takes the action outside of Northern Ireland, which is important because Hiroshima provides a foil to Belfast's dealings with past tragedy that emphasises the need to confront one's guilty conscience. In his three visits to the A-Bomb museum, the narrator notices that 'it was impossible to pass through any part of the museum without your conscience or compassion snagging on something'.[38] The last part of the novel depicts the titular 'third party', that is, the party after the after-party, a space of alcohol-fuelled stylistic surrealism, but it also introduces a third party to the Northern pair: the Japanese couple, Tadao and Mami. These two locals, whom the Irish reading audience would largely encounter as foreigners,[39] forge a surreal cultural corridor between Japan and Northern Ireland that forces the narrator to cross several boundaries at the close of the novel. First, Tadao confronts him with what has been previously left silenced in the story, thereby exposing his repressed responsibility and guilt. Secondly, Mami seems to trigger the narrator's uncertain suicide, whereby, crossing from the realm of living to the putative dead, he feels rescued by the eagle he imagined seeing that morning: 'I saw it all, and all at once, as though the talons were carrying me not on, or up, but beyond, to where time ceased to have meaning.'[40] This alterative perspective accepts the need and necessity to 'tell ... the whole story' as truthfully as possible.[41]

The motif of the journey as a means for possible restoration, renewal, and redemption from residual responsibilities emerges as an important trope in David Park's more recent work. In *The Truth Commissioner* (2008), James Fenton, a retired officer of the Royal Ulster Constabulary, envisages going 'away somewhere [to] come back whole and fresh, ready to move on'.[42] Fenton is haunted by his guilty conscience for recruiting Connor Walshe, a teenage petty criminal, as an informer. Walshe disappears, and to atone Fenton journeys to a Romanian orphanage. Yet, rather than providing him with the opportunity for a 'fresh start', his passage confronts him with the painful truth about his failed parental responsibility towards Connor. This topic is also the focus of Park's latest novel, *Travelling in a Strange Land* (2018), which follows Tom, a professional photographer and father of three, on his snow-covered journey from Belfast to Sunderland to bring back his son Luke for Christmas. Like Fenton, Tom is haunted by the absent presence of a dead figure: his first-born son, Daniel, whose substance abuse and penchant for stealing from his family caused his father to throw him out. Daniel disappeared for a time before his father found him dead in a shabby bare room. At his graveside, Tom feels 'in a no man's land between what should have been the future and the past that was and I don't know to which I belong'.[43] However, the close of the novel suggests a release from his traumatic entrapment in this temporal suspension when he visits the Angel of the North shortly before arriving at Luke's: noticing how the Angel's wings 'somehow point to the future', Tom says 'a secret prayer, because I've finally found the words'.[44]

These literal journeys also bring to light transitions in identity that characterise the peace process period. Park's exploration of the complexities of fatherhood signals a shift in the articulation and agency of masculine identity: from one associated with violence, silent authority, and control to one underpinned by the ethos of non-violence, uncertainty, sympathy, and concern for the other.[45] His concern with parenthood is also examined in *The Light of Amsterdam* (2012), which tells the stories of three different sets of protagonists who travel on the same flight from Belfast to Amsterdam for a long weekend. While they do not all meet, they are connected by their comparably strained, fractured relationships with their family travel companions. Through the fresh experiences and perspectives that Amsterdam offers, all the characters, in their different ways, experience a redemptive reconnection with their estranged family members, which is based both on unconditional love for one's children as well as respect for one's significant other and his/her story.[46]

These novels insinuate that this connection and sympathy with the other is not only enabled through the outside perspective afforded by a location outside Northern Ireland but also specifically through storytelling, the process of which is foregrounded in Lucy Caldwell's *All the Beggars Riding* (2013). In her attempt to come to terms with her deceased parents' clandestine love life across the Irish Sea that produced herself and her brother, the narrator, Lara Moorhouse, comes to realise the generative power of writing:

> Writing my story, I think, in many ways saved my life. It certainly changed everything: the course of bitterness and recrimination and despair that I fear I was set upon. It let me forgive my mother, and let go of my father. [. . .] It taught me that writing isn't self-expression, vomiting self-pity onto the page. It's the taking and shaping of things, carefully, again and again, until they make a sort of sense that not only you but others can understand, and maybe benefit from.[47]

In emphasising the way in which storytelling creates a corridor not only between an isolated self and other (or, indeed, as Lara mentioned, 'other selves')[48] but also among a wider audience, these reflections can be seen to gesture to the reconciliatory potentials of storytelling within the context of the Northern Irish peace process, emphasised, for instance, by the recent legacy-related Stormont House Agreement proposals, which include an Oral History Archive.[49] In Caldwell's novel, Lara's writing enables her to cross not only imaginatively to her own past and her parents' worlds but also, literally, to Belfast, where her father lived with his other, official family, and to connect there with her half-brother, 'and in a small way, help him too to let the past go'.[50]

These border crossings often work to confront the protagonists with repressed, half-forgotten memories of the Troubles. For instance, in Deirdre Madden's *Time Present Time Past* (2013), old photographs trigger for the middle-aged protagonist Fintan involuntary memories of 'his childhood in the North, where his granny had a little orchard'.[51] The novel is set during the final year of the Celtic Tiger's boom and Fintan seeks to stop its storm of progress by turning, like Benjamin's Angel of History, to the past. When he and his sister cross the Irish border to revisit the old family farm at the close of the novel, they are able to reconcile the past with the present, making them aware of 'how completely over [the past] is: you can't really get at it again'. To which Fintan replies: 'And it can't get at you either', emphasising the safety and security that distance from the past can bring.[52] Accepting the pastness of the past opens the present to the future – and this is what this novel does through its strong omniscient narrator who predicts not only the Republic's imminent economic crash but also the future of Fintan's family.

Such a temporal resolution is, however, problematic and problematised in texts set in the border regions, which were often the sites of intense conflict during the Troubles and which continue to be haunted by the unfinished business of a raw and recent past. This transgressive gothic mode reverberates in the notably different imaginations of the two McCabes (no relation) of Clones, County Monaghan: Eugene and

Patrick.[53] But it is also evident in the work of the playwright Abbie Spallen, most of whose plays are set in small, conservative Northern border towns. *Lally the Scut* (2015) offers an appropriately grotesque allegorical examination of post-Agreement peace politics through the efforts of its eponymous protagonist, who desperately seeks to rescue her son, who has fallen down a hole in a bog. Appealing for help, Lally is confronted by the self-serving opportunism of those in charge, and the intricacies of post-conflict politics, which bring endless hurdles for the rescue operation. The initial problem is that the location of the hole is in a field straddling the border, where it is 'impossible to tell [. . .] if it's in the North or the South'.[54] When the dig finally starts it is, in turn, halted as Republican politicians fear that the digging might unearth a 'Corpse of the disappeared'.[55] If the border bog contains the imminent danger of the traumatic return of the violent past, however, it also contains hope for a fresh future through the rescue of the child.

The liminality of the border is enshrined through the right to cultural hybridity in the Agreement, which, as I have described, is placed under a new kind of pressure under the shadow of Brexit. The 'Brexit Short' by another Northern Irish playwright, Stacey Gregg, 'Your Ma's a Hard Brexit' (2017), which was commissioned by *The Guardian*, registers the generational ambivalences felt by the Protestant community about Brexit. The unnamed protagonist, filmed on a school run with a young boy, recalls teasing her father about the benefits of getting an Irish passport and told him that even Ian Paisley Junior, a leading Unionist MP and Leave campaigner, urged his constituents to apply for one.[56] Yet despite the prospect of 'a united Ireland', as a middle-aged Protestant working-class woman from an interface area, she is keenly aware of the detrimental effects of past and present divisions through the border and peace walls (a topic explored in more detail in Gregg's 2015 play, *Shibboleth*). At play's end, she suggests that the child embrace the possibilities of Northern Ireland's institutionalised 'cultural corridor': 'At the end of the day, if you've your head screwed on, get your Irish passport: you're European and your [sic] British. Go after the work. And sure, that's the best the young ones can hope for, isn't it?'.[57] As the camera zooms out on the child, Gregg's short, like Spallen's play, seems to suggest that the limited hope for the future lies in the next generation.

With the prospect of Brexit, the future is certainly uncertain (pending a second referendum or a no-deal at the time of writing). Yet, as Siobhán Campbell emphasises in her poem 'Why Islanders Don't Kiss Hello' (2017), despite feelings of betrayal and anxieties (which, in the poem, concern the cultural traditions of kissing hello), it is important to honour the Agreement's embrace of a risky common future: 'we've learned because we must, | being from the island of largesse, | to give that peck of venture in a shared future'.[58] Indeed, Brexit could transmogrify the future of the Northern corridor in radically new ways. If Brexit affirms the significance of the Agreement's dedication to keep the North's cultural corridor open, it reminds us, at the same time, 'that the political architecture of the archipelago is radically open-ended'.[59] As Fintan O'Toole suggested in 2016, the new divisions created by Brexit might thus in turn facilitate a radical rethinking of the renewed affiliations and possibilities it created: 'To think, that is, about a new union – of Scotland, Ireland and Northern Ireland: SCINI.' This, O'Toole suggests, could also offer 'the only long-term solution to Northern Ireland's problem of double identity – the "British" part of that identity has always been much more Scottish than English'.[60] It will be interesting to see if the next generation of post-post-Agreement authors will respond to these new affiliations and (re)awaken the long tradition of Irish-Scottish cross-currents for future use in the wake of Brexit.[61]

Notes

1. Edna Longley, *The Living Stream: Literature & Revisionism in Ireland* (Newcastle upon Tyne: Bloodaxe Books, 1994), p. 194. Longley's concept of the 'cultural corridor' was first articulated in her article 'Opening up: A New Pluralism', *Fortnight*, 256 (1987), pp. 24–5.
2. Longley, *The Living Stream*, p. 195.
3. See Aaron Kelly, 'Geopolitical Eclipse: Culture and the Peace Process in Northern Ireland', *Third Text*, 19.5 (2005), pp. 545–53 (p. 548).
4. Sinéad Morrissey, *Between Here and There* (Manchester: Carcanet, 2002), p. 13.
5. Leontia Flynn, *Drives* (London: Jonathan Cape, 2008), p. 2.
6. Alan Gillis, *Somebody, Somewhere* (Oldcastle, Co. Meath: Gallery Press, 2004), p. 55.
7. Walter Benjamin, *Illuminations*, trans. Harry Zohn (London: Pimlico, 1999), p. 249.
8. *The Agreement: Agreement Reached in the Multi-Party Negotiations* [Good Friday Agreement], 10 April 1998, 'Declaration of Support', paragraph 2: https://assets.publishing.service.gov.uk/government/uploads/system/uploads/attachment/data/file/136652/agreement.pdf [accessed 13 August 2019].
9. Ibid.
10. Morrissey, *Between Here and There*, p. 14.

11. The 'YES' Campaign, *The 'YES' Campaign Flyer* (1998): http://cain.ulst.ac.uk/issues/politics/docs/yes220598a.pdf [accessed 18 August 2018].
12. See *The Agreement*, 'Constitutional Issues', paragraph 1.
13. Centre on Constitutional Change, 'Press Release', 8 October 2018: www.centreonconstitutionalchange.ac.uk/news/press-release-may's-'precious-union'-has-little-support-brexit-britain [accessed 13 January 2018].
14. David Wheatley, 'Poetry in the age of Brexit', *The Irish Times*, 23 June 2018: www.irishtimes.com/culture/books/poetry-in-the-age-of-brexit-1.3536218 [accessed 10 January 2019]. Subsequent quotations from this poem are taken from this same webpage.
15. The Northern Irish Assembly has been suspended five times since 1998 and at the time of writing (November 2019) has been in suspension since January 2017.
16. John Brannigan, 'Northern Irish Fiction: Provisionals and Pataphysicians', in James F. English, ed., *A Concise Companion to Contemporary British Fiction* (Oxford: Blackwell, 2006), pp. 141–63 (p. 146).
17. Birte Heidemann, *Post-Agreement Northern Irish Literature: Lost in a Liminal Space?* (Basingstoke: Palgrave Macmillan, 2016), p. 8.
18. Graham Dawson, *Making Peace with the Past? Memory, Trauma and the Irish Troubles* (Manchester: Manchester University Press, 2007), p. 76.
19. David McKittrick, Seamus Kelters, Brian Feeney, and Chris Thornton, *Lost Lives: The Stories of the Men, Women and Children Who Died as a Result of the Northern Ireland Troubles* (Edinburgh: Mainstream, 2001).
20. Dawson, *Making Peace with the Past*, p. 77.
21. Neal Alexander, 'Remembering to Forget: Northern Irish Fiction after the Troubles', in Scott Brewster and Michael Parker, eds., *Irish Literature Since 1990: Diverse Voices* (Manchester and New York: Manchester University Press, 2010), pp. 272–83 (p. 274).
22. Declan Burke, 'Review and Interview: The Rest Just Follows', *Irish Examiner*, 16 March 2014: www.irishexaminer.com/lifestyle/artsfilmtv/books/the-rest-just-follows-261920.html [accessed 8 August 2018].
23. Glenn Patterson, *The International* (London: Anchor, 1999), p. 318.
24. Ibid., p. 92.
25. Ibid., p. 318.
26. See Heidemann's reading of Ivy as a human 'trace' in *Post-Agreement Northern Irish Literature*, p. 74.
27. Glenn Patterson, *That Which Was* (London: Hamish Hamilton, 2004), p. 49.
28. See Aaron Kelly, *The Thriller and Northern Ireland Since 1969: Utterly Resigned Terror* (Hampshire, England: Ashgate, 2005), p. 1.
29. Patrick Hicks, 'An Interview with Glenn Patterson', *New Hibernia Review/Iris Éireannach Nua*, 12.2 (Summer 2008), pp. 106–19 (p. 107).
30. The legal definition of a 'victim' is inclusivist in effect. See 'The Victims and Survivors (Northern Ireland) Order 2006': www.legislation.gov.uk/nisi/2006/2953/contents [accessed 8 February 2019]. It has been criticised by some politicians and civil society groups as eliding bystanders, 'innocent' victims

and perpetrators – see, for instance, the submission by the South-East Fermanagh Foundation to the Northern Ireland Office's recent consultation on dealing with the past: https://seff.org.uk/wp-content/uploads/2018/10/SEFF-Consultation-Response.pdf [accessed on 2 January 2019].
31. Stuart Neville, *The Twelve* (London: Harvill Secker, 2009), p. 7.
32. Alexander, 'Remembering to Forget', p. 280.
33. See Dawn Miranda Sherratt-Bado, '"Things We'd Rather Forget": Trauma, the Troubles, and Magical Realism in Post-Agreement Northern Irish Women's Short Stories', *Open Library of Humanities*, 4.2 (2018), 1–30: https://doi.org/10.16995/olh.247 [accessed 29 March 2019].
34. Bernie McGill, 'No Angel', *Sleepwalkers* (Belfast: Whittrick Press, 2013), pp. 39–48.
35. See Joe Cleary, *Literature, Partition and the Nation State* (Cambridge: Cambridge University Press, 2002), pp. 97–141; and Stefanie Lehner, 'Reconciliation and the Politics of Friendship in Post-Troubles Literature', in Paige Reynolds, ed., *The New Irish Studies* (Cambridge: Cambridge University Press, forthcoming).
36. Roisín O'Donnell, 'Ebenezer's Memories', *Wild Quiet* (Dublin: New Island Books, 2016), pp. 1–21; Jan Carson, 'Children's Children', *Children's Children* (Dublin: Liberties Press, 2016), pp. 184–90 (p. 185).
37. Glenn Patterson, *The Third Party* (Belfast: Blackstaff Press, 2007), pp. 159–60.
38. Patterson, *The Third Party*, p. 50.
39. This argument takes into consideration that the novel is published by Blackstaff Press, which is a local press.
40. Patterson, *The Third Party*, p. 168.
41. Ibid.
42. David Park, *The Truth Commissioner* (London: Bloomsbury, 2008), p. 128.
43. David Park, *Travelling in a Strange Land* (London: Bloomsbury, 2018), p. 149.
44. Ibid., p. 164.
45. See Fidelma Farley, 'In the Name of the Family: Masculinity and Fatherhood in Contemporary Northern Irish Films', *Irish Studies Review*, 9.2 (2001), pp. 203–13 (p. 203). See also Stefanie Lehner, 'Post-Conflict Masculinities: Filiative Reconciliation in *Five Minutes of Heaven* and David Park's *The Truth Commissioner*', in C. Magennis and R. Mullen, eds., *Irish Masculinities: Critical Reflections on Literature and Culture* (Dublin: Irish Academic Press, 2011), pp. 65–76.
46. See Caroline Magennis, '"My Narrative Falters, as It Must": Rethinking Memory in Recent Northern Irish Fiction', in Chris Andrews and Matt McGuire, eds., *Post-Conflict Literature: Human Rights, Peace, Justice* (London: Routledge, 2016), pp. 31–42.
47. Lucy Caldwell, *All the Beggars Riding* (London: Faber and Faber, 2013), p. 238.
48. Ibid., p. 8.
49. Northern Ireland Office, 'Consultation Paper: Addressing the Legacy of Northern Ireland's Past', May 2018: https://assets.publishing.service.gov.uk/government/uploads/system/uploads/attachment_data/file/709091/Consultat

ion_Paper_Addressing_the_Legacy_of_Northern_Irelands_Past.pdf [accessed 8 February 2019].
50. Caldwell, *All the Beggars Riding*, p. 238.
51. Deirdre Madden, *Time Present and Time Past* (London: Faber and Faber, 2013), pp. 115–16.
52. Ibid., p. 222.
53. While many of Patrick McCabe's novels are set in a fictionalised border region, it is specifically *Breakfast on Pluto* (1998) that deals with the Troubles, as do many of the stories in Eugene McCabe's *Heaven Lies About Us* (2005), which were written over the past thirty years.
54. Abbie Spallen, *Lally the Scut* (London: Faber and Faber, 2015), p. 49.
55. Ibid., p. 84.
56. Stacey Gregg, 'Your Ma's a Hard Brexit', *The Guardian*, 19 June 2017: www.theguardian.com/stage/2017/jun/19/your-mas-a-hard-brexit-a-new-play-by-stacey-gregg-brexit-shorts [accessed 29 March 2019].
57. Ibid.
58. Siobhán Campbell, *Heat Signature* (Bridgend, Wales: Seren, 2017), p. 51.
59. Fintan O'Toole, 'Three-State Union May Be Answer to Brexit', *The Irish Times*, 26 July 2016: www.irishtimes.com/opinion/fintan-o-toole-three-state-union-may-be-answer-to-brexit-1.2734041 [accessed 20 September 2018].
60. Ibid.
61. For a detailed discussion of Irish-Scottish cross-currents, see Stefanie Lehner, 'Devolutionary States: Crosscurrents in Contemporary Irish and Scottish Fiction', in Liam Harte, ed., *The Oxford Handbook of Modern Irish Fiction* (Oxford: Oxford University Press, forthcoming).

CHAPTER 8

Adaptations: Commemoration and Contemporary Irish Theatre

James Moran

During the build-up to the centenary of the Easter Rising in 2016, the Irish media reported upon, and helped to generate, a number of controversies about the planned commemorations. For example, in the wake of the Queen of England's visit to Ireland in 2011 – the first such by a British monarch in a century – commentators debated whether a member of the British royal family should be present at the General Post Office, which served as the headquarters of the Rising, for the official Irish state event on Easter Sunday. Others argued about how to involve the grandchildren and relatives of the dead rebels, and disputed how to treat the revisionist opinions of figures such as the former Taoiseach John Bruton. Some criticised the launch of the government's commemorative programme at the GPO in November 2014, when the minute-and-a half-long video that was made especially for that launch – a breezily corporate piece called 'Ireland Inspires' – featured the international rugby player Brian O'Driscoll scoring a try and other uplifting images of modern Ireland, but lacked any mention of the actual Easter Rising or any of its participants.

As Ireland prepared for its 'Decade of Centenaries', Sean O'Casey's play about the 1916 Rising *The Plough and the Stars* repeatedly found itself at the heart of such controversies. For example, Senator David Norris made a significant intervention in the long-running saga about the proposed relocation of Ireland's national theatre (the Abbey Theatre) when in 2009 he argued that the entire playhouse should be moved into the GPO by the centenary, an idea that gained traction within the government for a time. Norris wrote in *The Irish Times*: 'For me now the gloves are off. The idea is in play. Picture it! 2016 O'Connell Street. Easter Week – the Abbey Theatre re-opening in the GPO with a revival of Sean O'Casey's great Dublin trilogy including *The Plough and the Stars*.'[1]

In a separate brouhaha, in January 2014, *The Irish Times* made a Freedom-of-Information request to find out what had been said by a three-person panel that had been assessing the recent productions of the Abbey. The newspaper published unflattering extracts from those verdicts, accompanied by negative front-page comment. The assessors examined the Abbey's 2012 revival of *The Plough and the Stars*, and one declared: 'The acting was generally below a level I would have expected ... Bluster replaced truthful emotion and the production seemed totally dislocated from the imperatives of its period [...] A long and wasted night.'[2] The Abbey director Fiach Mac Conghail justifiably labelled the leaking of these reports as 'cruel'.

Then, most famously, at the end of October 2015, the Abbey Theatre published details of the programme that would mark the centenary of the Easter Rising. In this commemorative year, the Abbey had included ten plays on the bill, but only one of them was written by a woman, and seven would be directed by men.[3] The one female-authored piece was Ali White's play, *Me, Mollser*, effectively a single-hander inspired both by O'Casey and by Tim Crouch's recent dramas retelling Shakespeare's stories from the viewpoint of one particular character (*I, Peaseblossom* of 2006 and *I, Malvolio* of 2010). *Me, Mollser* therefore narrates the story of O'Casey's *The Plough and the Stars* from the perspective of the consumptive child Mollser, in a production that the Abbey toured to Irish schools. The fact that this show appeared to be happening well away from the main Abbey stage – although it did appear there on Easter Monday 2016 – gave the impression that women had been exiled from the national theatre at this important moment in the nation's history. Some complained that the author, Ali White, did not even appear to have been invited to the season launch.[4] There followed an intense debate about the role of women in the arts in Ireland, about the leadership of the two best-funded Irish theatres in Ireland (Dublin's Abbey and Gate), and about the place of women in Ireland more broadly.[5]

Such controversies reveal how the Irish theatre provides a touchstone for debates about Irish society, and they also illustrate that O'Casey's *The Plough and the Stars* has often provided the terrain on which public discussions have taken place. Indeed, hints of O'Casey's legacy can be found even in performances that make no direct reference to him. For example, when the well-known broadcaster Pat Kenny presented his final episode of *The Late Late Show* in 2009, the comedian Pat Shortt joined Kenny on the special edition of the show and performed a parodic poem called 'Nineteen and Sixteen'. Shortt declared:

Back came the British officer, he says, 'in the name of her royal majesty I insist
  you must surrender.'
'I like the queen, I like the queen', says Pádraig Pearse, who we think might have
  been a bender.
Then in came a Monto jezebel, she was selling her affection.
She says, 'Ah, for two and six, I could do some tricks, that'll give you boys an
  insurrection.'
Then in through the gates swanned W. B. Yeats, he said, 'It is my duty,
  to tell you all things have utterly changed, it's a terrible fecking beauty.'
Then in came a fireman with a big hose, a little tramp came in behind him.
A man named Lee came selling tea, said Pádraig Pearse, 'Just ignore him.'
Then a circus clown jumped up and down, which I know you'll find surprising.
To see a circus clown jump up and down, in the middle of a fecking rising.[6]

Here Shortt was operating in the tradition established by O'Casey, of mocking the best-known leader of the rebellion, Patrick Pearse, and connecting the Rising with prostitution, subversive expressions of sexuality, and slapstick comedy. As with O'Casey's play, Shortt's version of 1916 includes an accretion of colourful comic detail and sidelines the political cause for which the rebels were actually fighting.

A similarly subversive take on the Rising was given in 2015 by the Limerick comedians, The Rubberbandits. Their television show, *The Rubberbandits Guide to 1916*, was first broadcast on New Year's Eve 2015 and was based on the premise that the president of Ireland asks the Rubberbandits (Mr Chrome and Blindboy Boatclub) to present an official history programme about the Easter Rising. The Rubberbandits then decide to consult James Joyce about this:

JAMES JOYCE: Okay okay, we'll teach you about Irish history if you get a big
  tattoo of Éamon De Valera on your back.
MR CHROME: Oh man, I don't even like David Valera's music [...]
JAMES JOYCE: They'll never understand that the revolution was a working-class
  revolution. All you hear in the history books is the poet, the painter, the
  teacher, the lawyer, no working-class men. That's a post-de-Valera narrative
  that's been sorted.
BLINDBOY BOATCLUB: So imagine, right, you're planning this giant rave,
  right, you're going to have the best warehouse, gonna have all your
  favourite drugs, gonna have security, loads of *beoirs* [women], lots of
  favourite tapes of music, Judge Jules, the lot [...] But then, the drugs
  don't come through, all the girls don't come through, the security doesn't
  come through. Nothing comes through. There's just a load of lads in
  a warehouse.
MR CHROME: Man that sounds awful.
BLINDBOY BOATCLUB: That was the Rising.[7]

Here again, the Rising is deflated, associated with a kind of out-of-control intoxication. Where O'Casey set part of his play in a pub, the Rubberbandits' updated reference describes music, drugs, and a rave. Once more, for comic purposes, the Rising is connected with sexuality, just as O'Casey connected the participants of the Rising with the prostitute Rosie Redmond; and both O'Casey and the Rubberbandits seek to place a working-class narrative at the heart of the historical events. As with O'Casey and Pat Shortt, the comic riff here contains problematic ideas about gender, tending to overlook the important female contribution to the Rising itself, and instead reducing certain women to erotic objects. Furthermore, just as O'Casey's play had kept the Abbey profitable during the late 1920s, so did *The Rubberbandits Guide to 1916* prove to be extremely popular: the television show was rebroadcast at midnight on Easter Monday 2016 on RTÉ 2, in the midst of the televised anniversary commemorations, and it quickly became the second most-viewed programme on the online RTÉ player (only bested by the reverent 'Centenary' commemorative concert that was broadcast from the Bord Gais Theatre), revealing the Irish appetite for subversive renderings of national history. Thus, in a country that has continued to contest the meaning of the 1916 Rising, Irish drama has continued to play a significant part in provoking revised thinking about the event.

Since its original performance, O'Casey's *Plough* has proved to be a remarkably persistent fixture in the Irish cultural debate. As we have noted, although O'Casey's play first appeared onstage in 1926, the work has continued to resonate in recent debates. This chapter will therefore focus on four key Abbey Theatre productions of the script: the Garry Hynes version of 1991, Ben Barnes's production of 2002, Wayne Jordan's staging in 2010, and Sean Holmes's interpretation of 2016. I will examine the onstage realisation of the text, showing how these four versions of O'Casey's work show Irish theatre-makers navigating a set of contemporary concerns, from historical revisionism, through the Celtic Tiger boom, to the economic crash, and into the era when various kinds of institutional abuse have been revealed. Shifts in performance style also reveal changes in thinking about theatrical form in Ireland and help illuminate the role of the Irish national theatre during a period when other nearby national theatres have come to operate in profoundly different ways.

When O'Casey's *Plough* first appeared at the Abbey Theatre, the piece quickly achieved fame after causing a riot, as those associated with the dead men of 1916 entered the venue to protest that O'Casey's depiction of the Easter Rising looked unfair. The play remained consistently popular during the ensuing years, being revived by the Abbey for more than 100 performances in each decade from the 1930s to the 1970s.[8] Alan Brien feared that O'Casey was in danger of being 'relegated to the attic as an antique' at the start of the 1960s, but this prediction never came true, as the violence of the Troubles made O'Casey's play appear freshly pertinent.[9] In 1966, shortly after the rebuilt Abbey Theatre opened its doors, the company performed *The Plough* for seven weeks, and in 1976 the Abbey staged a lavish golden-jubilee production of the play directed by the theatre's artistic director Tomás Mac Anna. He perceived that *The Plough* might speak to the contemporary situation in the North and gave Ulster accents to the Dublin Protestant characters, which quickly became the theatrical norm despite well-reasoned objections from figures including Seamus Deane.[10] There followed major revivals by the British National Theatre in 1977 and the Abbey in 1984.

Then, in 1991, the Abbey staged a new version of *The Plough* that Desmond Rushe, the drama critic for the *Irish Independent*, acclaimed as 'the most revolutionary and controversial presentation ever seen of the theatre's most performed masterpiece'.[11] This production was directed by a 38-year-old female director from the West of Ireland, Garry Hynes. Hynes had recently become artistic director of the theatre, and chose to begin her tenure with a version of O'Casey's play that did away with much of what Abbey audiences had come to expect. Spectators saw no comfortingly familiar Georgian tenements, no jolly music-hall turns. Instead, Hynes presented a stark, monochrome set; female actors with shaved heads; and, in the wheezing and jerking character of Mollser, a particularly disturbing vision of illness and impoverishment.

One of the best-known moments of the play comes in Act Two, when the words of Patrick Pearse are delivered offstage while the characters of the play listen from a bar. O'Casey's original script specifies that *'through the window is silhouetted the figure of a tall man who is speaking to the crowd'*.[12] This figure, although nameless in the play, delivers quotations that were drawn verbatim from three separate parts of the 1922 volume of Pearse's writings.[13] In real life, Pearse had only delivered one of these sections of writing verbally, on 1 August 1915 at the grave of O'Donovan Rossa in Dublin's Glasnevin Cemetery, in front of thousands of uniformed nationalists and members of the Irish Citizen

Army. Pearse wrote the other two pieces as newspaper articles rather than speeches.[14] But O'Casey included in his play these decontextualised extracts, which were among the most bloodthirsty comments that Pearse ever set down. For instance, the first time that the orator in O'Casey's play speaks, the figure speaks the following lines from 'The Coming Revolution':

> It is a glorious thing to see arms in the hands of Irishmen. We must accustom ourselves to the thought of arms, we must accustom ourselves to the sight of arms, we must accustom ourselves to the use of arms .... Bloodshed is a cleansing and sanctifying thing, and the nation that regards it as the final horror has lost its manhood .... There are many things more horrible than bloodshed, and slavery is one of them!'[15]

O'Casey himself felt deeply uneasy about recycling Pearse's words so selectively, and their inclusion did indeed anger spectators when the drama first appeared onstage in 1926.[16] As we shall see, this moment retained its potential to continue arousing audience hostility six and a half decades after its premiere.

When the Abbey produced Hynes's version of the play in 1991, the Troubles in the North were well into their second decade, and had resulted in more than 3,000 deaths.[17] Accordingly, in that same year, the seventy-fifth anniversary of the Rising was celebrated mutedly with a low-budget ceremony at the GPO. After all, during the previous two decades revisionist historians had promoted the idea that the Rising, although often remembered as a brave battle against the oppression which underpinned the British empire, had actually served to undermine the work of constitutional nationalists who wanted to liberate Ireland, with the rebels promoting a lamentable set of ideas about bloodshed and slaughter.[18] At the Abbey, then, Hynes opted to abandon O'Casey's stage directions at this point of the play in order to provoke a Brechtian moment of alienation. In Hynes's version of *The Plough*, the Pearse figure rose from a seated position among the audience members. Audience members could see themselves and the orator reflected back in an enormous onstage mirror, potentially asking spectators to contemplate how they might be implicated in the ideas being outlined. How might those who felt a sense of pride in 1916 feel when confronted with Hynes's frank depictions of violence, sexuality, and death? After all, Hynes included a brutally unambiguous moment when the nationalist Jack Clitheroe was shown to be responsible for his wife's miscarriage.

Of course, this bold style attracted criticism. The playwright Hugh Leonard, for example, only watched the first half of the show but then wrote to the newspapers asserting Hynes had neglected the 'fun and passion' of the play.[19] However, the production also won many admirers, became a box-office hit, and is generally remembered as a critical milestone in twentieth-century Irish drama. Hynes's work offers compelling evidence for Christopher Murray's thesis that Irish drama holds the 'Mirror Up to Nation'.[20]

By the time of the next staging of *The Plough* at the Abbey Theatre, the 1998 Good Friday Agreement had been secured, and Irish society had been transformed by the Celtic Tiger economic phenomenon. Although Ireland had been one of the poorest European countries when it joined the Common Market in 1973, from 1994 national output grew by 8.6% per year, and Irish GDP overtook that of the United Kingdom by 1996.[21] Books appeared with titles such as *The Celtic Tiger: Ireland's Continuing Economic Miracle* and *The End of Irish History?*.[22] In this climate, the Abbey staged a 2002 version of *The Plough*, directed by the theatre's artistic director Ben Barnes. This was a visually and aurally opulent version of O'Casey's play, including features such as impressive sound recordings of traditional Irish music that underscored the action as well as projected flames that enveloped the stage at the conclusion. Barnes installed a new sound system for the production and removed the front rows of seats from the main house, replacing them with tenement flotsam and jetsam. Of course, O'Casey had written his original play in a rage about the appalling poverty of Dublin's tenements, and so there was a certain irony in the Abbey Theatre spending a great deal of money on creating the illusion of poverty onstage. Even during those boom years, the city surrounding the Abbey was evidently affected by chronic inequality, with drug addiction and homelessness remaining particular blights. In this context, the luscious optics and exquisitely delivered sound effects sat uneasily with O'Casey's play text, as noted in *The Irish Times* by Fintan O'Toole, who had acted as literary adviser to Hynes eleven years earlier, and who commented, 'the play demands the texture of real poverty: hunger, disease, dirt. Here, everyone looks well-fed and well-dressed. Even the dwindling spectre of the consumptive Mollser (Laura Murphy) looks far healthier than most supermodels.'[23] When the show travelled to London, *The Guardian* reviewer, Michael Billington, felt similarly bewildered by the fact that Bessie Burgess 'is supposedly "hardened by toil and a little coarsened by drink," [but] is inexplicably played by the beautiful Catherine Byrne'.[24] In a telling critique, Patrick Lonergan argued that the production actually had less to do with addressing the problems of contemporary Ireland, and more to do with aligning the theatre with a neoliberal economic agenda: 'The use in *The Plough and the Stars* of a range of authenticating markers allowed the production to be branded as Irish, a status that made it recognizable to audiences throughout the world, facilitating international touring and enhancing access to the theatre for tourist visitors to Ireland.'[25]

However, Barnes did recognise the expressionism of O'Casey's play. Since the 1920s, the Abbey has struggled to reconcile the apparently realist O'Casey of the Dublin trilogy (which includes *The Plough*) with the later, more experimental work he produced from *The Silver Tassie* onwards. By contrast, Barnes (like Garry Hynes) realised that O'Casey's early plays do not necessarily present a photographically accurate vision of Dublin, and so Barnes incorporated a series of non-realistic and abstract effects. Barnes opted to produce the famous pub scene of *The Plough* with the Pearsean orator not appearing on a human scale, but as a giant silhouette in the bar window, literally overshadowing the far smaller actors below, with a strident voice pre-recorded by actor Mark Lambert and then amplified in playback. O'Casey's script is scarcely generous to Pearse in any event, but in this version of the play, the giant image of the orator had an effect similar to that of fascist architecture, reminding spectators of the everyday individual's smallness and powerlessness.

The Abbey revived Barnes's version of *The Plough* in 2003, and brought it to London in 2005 as part of the theatre's centenary programme. Despite the lavishness of the production, however, in the early 2000s the Abbey was, like O'Casey's Boyle family, living beyond its means. Barnes's production of *The Plough* has since been eclipsed by this legacy: he left the artistic directorship of the Abbey Theatre in 2005, with the theatre almost €4 million in debt, which required a three-year bailout of €26 million from the government.[26] The Abbey, in this regard, offered a premonition of what was about to happen to the entire country. In 2008, there occurred a nation-wide financial crash resulting in:

> one of the most dramatic and largest reversals in economic fortune ever experienced by an industrial country. Real GDP would fall by 3 per cent in 2008 and by an unprecedented 7 per cent in 2009. Unemployment would triple to almost 14 per cent end-2010 and net emigration – thought to have been banished – would restart on a very sizable scale. The Irish banking system would undergo a near collapse, necessitating a bailout, first via a comprehensive government guarantee in 2008, and later, by way of massive capital injections to be paid for by tax payers.[27]

The next production of *The Plough* at the Abbey therefore opened in more straitened circumstances in 2010 (and was revived for a UK and Irish tour in 2012). This version was directed by the young Dublin-born director Wayne Jordan, and, in its first iteration, it contained a standout performance from Denise Gough as Nora. But now O'Casey's play looked very different from the slick and glossy version of 2003. At the start of Jordan's interpretation, the audience was confronted with a stage of broken and rusted metal girders: the set looked like a half-abandoned construction site, a reminder of the many aspirations that had disappeared with the recent property collapse. The rest of the ghost-estate-style scenery was provided by crumpled and faded curtains, on which were printed images of the poverty-stricken Dublin tenements as well as the ruined headquarters of the Easter Rising. If the audience had missed the contemporary resonances, the theatre's artistic director Fiach Mac Conghail made sure to underscore the point, writing in the playhouse's brochure that O'Casey's work 'allows Irish theatre artists to comment on society', and the production appeared as part of the same season that saw the celebrity economist David McWilliams diagnosing the country's flaws in a one-man show.[28] Jordan's direction of *The Plough* thus formed part of a wider attempt to show that the national theatre stage might remain an appropriate platform from which to address widespread public anxieties.

When the orator appeared in Act Two of *The Plough* in 2010, Jordan changed the stage directions so that the actor strode onto the stage itself, where the bar doubled as the speaker's platform. The orator's stance – drawing back his coat to reveal his gun – literalised the words being spoken and gave a vivid reminder of the bloodshed involved in the Irish revolution. And in Jordan's version, as this orator spoke, a massive Irish tricolour hung over his head in a faded and tattered condition. Whatever Pearse's hopes for a free Ireland, the flag indicated that such dreams might result in disappointment: Jordan potentially encouraged the audience to consider what exactly Ireland had done with the freedom gained through the revolutionary period. After all, shortly after this production opened, *The Irish Times* famously posed the Yeatsian (and ultimately Wordsworthian) question 'Was it for this?' and pondered 'whether this is what the men of 1916 died for: a bailout from the German chancellor with a few shillings of sympathy from the British chancellor on the side.'[29]

Hot on the heels of Wayne Jordan's version of O'Casey's play, the Abbey Theatre staged another new version of *The Plough* during the 2016 centenary of the Easter Rising. This time the production was directed by Sean Holmes, the artistic director of the Lyric Theatre, Hammersmith. The production again toured, in Ireland and the US, and in 2018 appeared at London's Lyric and Dublin's Gaiety theatres. The Abbey therefore designed the set to be readily re-assembled in an array of different venues, self-consciously drawing attention to the provisional nature of the setting. A scaffolding tower dominated the stage, giving the impression that most of the action was taking place around the bottom of a tower block, with the scaffolding collapsing onto its side for the final act, in what was perhaps an echo of the 2001 destruction of the World Trade Center in New York.

During the build-up to this production, Ireland had been wracked by a series of reports about abuse in church and state-run institutions. In 2005, the Ferns Report revealed 100 allegations of abuse of children by an assortment of priests during the previous four decades. The Ryan Report of 2009 showed that rape and sexual abuse were 'endemic' in industrial schools attended by 30,000 children between the 1930s and 1990s. Similar horrors emerged from the Dublin Archdiocese Report in November 2009 and the Cloyne Report of 2011. In 2014, allegations arose about the Bon Secours Mother and Baby Home at Tuam, a maternity 'home' for single mothers and their children. The institution had been in operation between the 1920s and 1960s, and it was now reported that up to 800 children had been buried in a mass grave on the site. The Easter Rising may have been launched with the 1916 Proclamation's professed aim of 'cherishing all the children of the nation equally', but the independent Irish state that the rebellion had helped usher into existence had manifestly failed in its basic duty of care for some of its most vulnerable citizens.

In this context, the Abbey Theatre's 2016 production of *The Plough* made Mollser central to the drama, a character who '*is about fifteen, but looks to be only about ten, for the ravages of consumption have shrivelled her up*'.[30] This child speaks only fourteen sentences in O'Casey's original play text and is usually seen onstage for a very small proportion of the play. But in Sean Holmes's version, there was only a very brief interlude when either the actor playing Mollser, or the coffin containing her remains and adorned with her clothing, was *not* present on the stage. Mollser began the entire drama by standing alone, dressed in red trainers and a red Manchester United shirt, singing the national anthem. During the run, many spectators stood and joined in with the anthem at this point. But the singing ended with an explosion of coughing from Mollser, who appeared to retch blood from her mouth into her handkerchief.

The actor playing Mollser then stayed onstage for the entire first half of the play, remaining visible during the second-act barroom scene during which the Pearsean orator appears. Usually Mollser is absent at the time when Pearse's words are spoken: O'Casey's original script does not situate her in this part of the play. But in the Abbey's 2016 version she remained observable throughout that scene, playing a computer game, seated on the sofa bed upon which Jack and Nora had recently been intimate. The Pearse-style orator then intruded into this domestic space, as well as into the part of the stage demarcated as the bar, but this time his words and image were shown on a television screen rather than delivered directly by an actor. Here then, the theatre illustrated something of Guy Debord's idea of representation replacing authentic social life: as Debord puts it, 'spectators are linked only by a one-way relationship to the very center that maintains their isolation from each other [...] The spectacle corresponds to the historical moment at which the commodity completes its colonisation of social life.'[31] In Holmes's production, the consumptive Mollser was dying, yet she had been abandoned alone to her computer games, with human contact for the child reduced to the flickering image of the television screen. Meanwhile, also visible in the pub was Mrs Gogan, who had brought her baby into the bar, started a fight, and then left without the infant, provoking panic among the men who were left with it. In O'Casey's script, the barman declares, 'take it up, man, an' run out afther her with it, before she's gone too far. You're not goin' to leave th' bloody thing here, are you?'.[32] But Sean Holmes's production of the play reminded spectators of the other 'bloody' child who had been abandoned, Mrs Gogan's older child Mollser, who was left at home after having spewed blood over herself at the start of the performance. And these two 'bloody' children offered an ironic counterpoint to the television orator, who claimed, in the words of Patrick Pearse, that 'bloodshed is a cleansing and sanctifying thing'.

Of course, these different versions of *The Plough* have scarcely been happening in a vacuum, and audiences as well as reviewers have been able to compare the Abbey's versions with productions of O'Casey's work that have been staged at different playhouses by other high-profile directors. In 1991, for example, the Abbey's production of the play was onstage during the same year as a production by Sam Mendes at London's Old Vic Theatre. In summer 2010, audiences in Dublin were able to compare Wayne Jordan's Abbey production with a touring production of Garry Hynes's Druid version of O'Casey's *The Silver Tassie*, which arrived at the Gaiety Theatre in Dublin for five nights at the same time as the Abbey show. And in 2016, while the Abbey produced Sean Holmes's version of *The Plough*, at the other end of O'Connell Street the Gate Theatre staged Mark O'Rowe's version of O'Casey's *Juno and the Paycock*. Later that year the National Theatre in London staged another version of *The Plough*, directed by Howard Davies and Jeremy Herrin. Some spectators may even have recognised that certain aspects of the Abbey's 2016 production – including the video-screen version of the orator and the English soldiers dressed in modern military uniform – echoed Stephen Rea's 2000 version of the play at Dublin's Gaiety.

Furthermore, by 2016 it was possible to compare O'Casey's drama at the Abbey with theatrical ideas about O'Casey that were being staged away from formal playhouse venues. During the Dublin Theatre Festival in 2016, one tale of the Easter Rising was given by CoisCéim Dance Theatre in collaboration with the experimental company ANU, at a building on the site where O'Casey was born (84–6 Dorset Street). This show, *These Rooms*, allowed audiences in small groups to move through a range of different rooms (and between the settings of 1966 and 1916) in order to explore a fractured storyline that included dance, survivor testimony, and archival film. Also in 2016, the Dublin Theatre Festival included a four-and-a-half-hour immersive play about the Troubles by THEATREclub, *It's Not Over*, that included a range of music, dramatic tableaux, and a fragmented set of lines and ideas from O'Casey's *The Plough*. Subsequently, the Abbey Theatre co-produced a site-specific work with ANU at the 2018 Dublin Theatre Festival. This work, *The Lost O'Casey*, took inspiration from O'Casey's relatively unknown script *Nanny's Night Out*, but did so very loosely, leading audience members through north inner-city Dublin in order to point to contemporary problems of alcoholism and homelessness.

The Abbey Theatre's versions of O'Casey, performed from 1991 to 2016, remained consistently reverent about reproducing the spoken words (if not the stage directions) of O'Casey's script. But by 2016 a theatrical philosophy could be discerned in Dublin that had been primarily associated with German theatre, which sees the literary text as ripe for multiple adaptations. For example, when Thomas Ostermeier directed *Richard III* in 2016, he observed that, 'it has become possible to tell the play's full narrative even without all the business of the battle that makes up the play's final 20 or so pages'.[33] ANU and THEATREclub therefore worked on O'Casey in the way that theatre directors in mainland Europe had grown accustomed to, making increasingly creative decisions derived from the playwright's original concepts but departing significantly from his original text.

Thus, although the Abbey maintains its status as national theatre, it has recently been moving beyond a fixed Irish literary canon, towards European theatre styles, and into unfamiliar theatre spaces. This strategy is fraught with the risk of making Irish artists feel less included and less nurtured by the organisation, but it is clearly driven by developments elsewhere.[34] In the past few years, the national theatres of Wales (established 2009) and Scotland (established 2006) have been operating without a permanent playhouse space of their own, instead touring to different venues and site-specific locations, and the National Theatre in London has embarked on an extensive programme of broadcasting its shows to cinemas (from 2009), as well as staging site-specific work in collaboration with Shunt (2004) and Punchdrunk (2013–14).[35] All of this activity potentially made a national theatre that was primarily staging literary drama in one capital-city playhouse look somewhat conservative and old-fashioned. Accordingly, in July 2016, Neil Murray and Graham McLaren, respectively the executive producer and associate director of National Theatre Scotland, were appointed as the new co-directors of the Abbey, and each indicated a willingness to change conceptions of the Irish national theatre. Earlier artistic directors of the Abbey such as Mac Anna, Hynes, and Barnes felt compelled to direct their own versions of *The Plough*, but the new co-directors pointedly responded to questioning about whether they would produce that particular play by declaring, 'probably not on the stage of the Abbey, for a while. A small moratorium. No new productions planned.'[36] McLaren stated that O'Casey's well-known work had 'simply been done too often'.[37] Instead, as McLaren declared, 'when we were going up for the job and we were asking what were the things we could do? And we said: It's Ireland, we should do a show in pubs [. . .] The important thing is that it's out there in tiny village pubs where your mum and dad go and say: "I saw that in my boozer and they did it here first. They did it for us. That's our national theatre".'[38] Hence a new set of theatrical ideas has repositioned the Abbey, with these co-directors launching a season that celebrated the best work of the independent sector in 2017 and drawing it closer to the ideas that motivated companies such as ANU and National Theatre Scotland. Of course, this strategy is fraught with risk, and raises difficult questions about the status of the theatre building itself, about the Abbey's role in nurturing Irish creative talent, and about the playhouse's relationship with canonical Irish texts.

If the directors of the Abbey Theatre have long taken pride in staging innovative versions of Act Two of *The Plough* by bringing the Irish pub onto the playhouse stage, a kind of reversal now appears to have taken place. By working with creatives from ANU, the Abbey has moved the audience into real-life locations that have not conventionally been the working environment of the actor and the dramaturg. O'Casey's drama has been a regular fixture on the national theatre stage since the 1920s, and it has consistently helped citizens to understand their changing society during the past three decades. If his work is now adapted for new immersive and site-specific modes of performance, and if the Abbey can maintain its fine tradition of fostering Irish talent, O'Casey's writing has the potential to help the theatre demonstrate its continuing relevance during ongoing national debates. After all, as the recent referendums to legalise same-sex marriage (2015) and abortion (2018) have shown, vital public argument in Ireland is occurring in a wide range of real and virtual spaces, and some of the key shifts in Irish politics can be discerned, as in 1916 itself, when campaigners arrive at the GPO, at Dublin Castle, and on the streets of the capital.

Notes

1. David Norris, 'Iconic Marriage of Yeats and Pearse in Abbey GPO', *The Irish Times*, 15 October 2009: www.irishtimes.com/opinion/iconic-marriage-of-yeats-and-pearse-in-abbey-gpo-1.757513 [accessed 9 February 2019].
2. Fintan O'Toole, 'Abbey Confidential: Outside Experts Unimpressed by our National Theatre', *The Irish Times*, 18 January 2014: www.irishtimes.com/culture/abbey-confidential-outside-experts-unimpressed-by-our-national-theatre-1.1658923 [accessed 9 February 2019].
3. By contrast, elsewhere in October 2015 the Royal Court theatre in London announced its sixtieth anniversary programme, in which eight of the thirteen plays (over 60%) were by female playwrights, and three of the five plays authored by men had female directors. See 'Sixty Years New: The Royal Court Theatre Announces its 60th Year of Work, January 2016 to October 2016', 12 October 2015: https://royalcourttheatre.com/60-years-new-the-royal-court-theatre-announces-its-3/ [accessed 9 February 2019].
4. Chris McCormack, '"Them's the Breaks": Gender Imbalance and Irish Theatre', *Exeunt Magazine*, 4 November 2015: http://exeuntmagazine.com/features/thems-the-breaks-feminism-and-irish-theatre/ [accessed 9 February 2019].
5. Fiach Mac Conghail, the artistic director of the Abbey, was widely criticised for his initially dismissive response to the 'Waking the Feminists' campaign, although he subsequently apologised for this. By the end of 2016, he had stepped down from his post after twelve years, as had Michael Colgan, the artistic director of the Gate for thirty-three years. Disturbing allegations subsequently emerged in the Irish press about Colgan's apparent bullying and sexism.
6. Pat Shortt, 'Nineteen and Sixteen', *The Late Late Show*, RTÉ 1, 29 May 2009, 9.30pm.
7. *The Rubberbandits Guide to 1916*, RTÉ 2, 31 December 2015, 11pm.

8. I am grateful to Mairead Delaney for her assistance navigating the Abbey Theatre Archives.
9. Alan Brien, 'O'Casey for Today', *Sunday Telegraph*, 7 October 1962, p. 10.
10. Deane argued that O'Casey offered an entirely false distinction between political engagement and domestic contentment, and so 'it would be wrong, especially in present conditions, to take him as our paradigm of a dramatist who made political preoccupation central to his work'. Seamus Deane, 'Irish Politics and O'Casey's Theatre', *Threshold*, 24 (1973), pp. 5–16 (pp. 11–12).
11. Desmond Rushe, 'A Mould Breaking Debut of Courage', *Irish Independent*, 8 May 1991, located in the Abbey Theatre Archives, Box 64 [reviews of *The Plough* 1991].
12. Sean O'Casey, *The Complete Plays of Sean O'Casey*, 5 vols. (London: Macmillan, 1984), I, p. 193.
13. *Collected Works of Padraic H. Pearse: Political Writings and Speeches* (Dublin: Maunsel, 1922), pp. 133–8, 89–100, 213–18.
14. Padraic Pearse, 'The Coming Revolution', *An Claidheamh Soluis*, 8 November 1913, p. 6; and [Padraic Pearse], 'Peace and the Gael', *The Spark*, December 1915, pp. 1–2.
15. O'Casey, *The Complete Plays*, I, pp. 193–4.
16. James Moran, *The Theatre of O'Casey* (London: Bloomsbury, 2013), pp. 55–6.
17. Malcolm Sutton, *An Index of Deaths from the Conflict in Ireland*: http://cain.ulst.ac.uk/sutton/ [accessed 9 February 2019].
18. See Francis Shaw, 'The Canon of Irish History – A Challenge', *Studies*, 242 (1972), pp. 117–53.
19. Hugh Leonard, 'Not While I'm Eating', *Sunday Independent*, 19 May 1991, p. 3L; Garry Hynes, '"The Plough" at the Abbey', *The Irish Times*, 23 May 1991, p. 11.
20. Christopher Murray, *Twentieth-Century Irish Drama: Mirror Up to Nation* (Manchester: Manchester University Press, 1997).
21. See Dermot McAleese, 'The Celtic Tiger: Origins and Prospects', *Policy Options Politiques* (2000), 46–50 (pp. 46–7).
22. Paul Sweeney, *The Celtic Tiger: Ireland's Continuing Economic Miracle* (Dublin: Oak Tree, 1999); and Colin Coulter and Steve Coleman, eds., *The End of Irish History? Critical Approaches to the Celtic Tiger* (Manchester: Manchester University Press, 2003).
23. Fintan O'Toole, 'Review: A Bit Too Well-Fed for this Rare Fare', *The Irish Times*, 23 November 2002: www.irishtimes.com/culture/review-a-bit-too-well-fed-for-this-rare-fare-1.1127502 [accessed 9 February 2019].
24. Michael Billington, 'The Plough and the Stars', *The Guardian*, 21 January 2005: www.theguardian.com/stage/2005/jan/21/theatre1 [accessed 9 February 2019].
25. Patrick Lonergan, *Theatre and Globalization: Irish Drama in the Celtic Tiger Era* (Basingstoke: Palgrave Macmillan, 2009), p. 71.

26. Michael Quinn, 'Fiach Mac Conghail: "I'm More Interested in Long-Term Achievement than Short-Term Goals"', *The Stage*, 22 September 2016: www.thestage.co.uk/features/interviews/2016/fiach-mac-conghail-im-more-interested-in-long-term-achievement-than-short-term-goals/ [accessed 9 February 2019].
27. Donal Donovan and Antoin E. Murphy, *The Fall of the Celtic Tiger* (Oxford: Oxford University Press, 2013), p. 2.
28. Fiach Mac Conghail, *April–September 2010 Abbey Theatre Programme* (Dublin: Abbey Theatre, 2010), p. 5.
29. 'Was It For This?', *The Irish Times*, 18 November 2010: www.irishtimes.com/opinion/was-it-for-this-1.678424 [accessed 9 February 2019].
30. Casey, *The Complete Plays*, I, p. 190.
31. Guy Debord, *The Society of the Spectacle*, trans. Donald Nicholson Smith (New York: Zone, 1995), pp. 22, 29.
32. Casey, *The Complete Plays*, I, pp. 206–7.
33. Thomas Ostermeier, 'Embodying Dark Desires', *Richard III, Schaubühne Berlin, Lyric Theatre Programme* (Edinburgh: Edinburgh International Festival, 2016), p. 22.
34. For instance, in January 2019, 300 Irish artists wrote a letter complaining of the reduced opportunities and pay being offered by the Abbey. See Deirdre Falvey, 'Abbey Theatre Uproar', *The Irish Times*, 7 January 2019: www.irishtimes.com/culture/stage/abbey-theatre-uproar-300-actors-and-directors-complain-to-minister-1.3750135 [accessed 9 February 2019].
35. National Theatre Scotland did establish a permanent headquarters at Rockvilla in north Glasgow in 2017, even as it continued to commit to being a 'theatre without walls'.
36. Graham McLaren quoted by Michael Smith, 'McLaren and Murray, Fresh New Faces in Control of the Abbey', *Village Voice*, 24 May 2017: https://villagemagazine.ie/index.php/2017/05/mclaren-and-murray-fresh-new-faces-in-control-of-the-abbey/ [accessed 9 February 2019].
37. Graham McLaren quoted by Joseph Farrell, 'SRB at the Theatre: In Dublin', *Scottish Review of Books*, 2 June 2018: www.scottishreviewofbooks.org/2018/06/srb-at-the-theatre-in-dublin/ [accessed 9 February 2019].
38. Graham McLaren quoted by Michael McDermott, 'First Act: Neil Murray and Graham McLaren Directors Abbey Theatre', *Totally Dublin*, 3 April 2017: www.totallydublin.ie/more/first-act-neil-murray-graham-mclaren-directors-abbey-theatre/ [accessed 9 February 2019].

CHAPTER 9

Relocations: Diaspora, Travel, Migrancy
Ellen McWilliams

Stephen Dedalus's insistence in *A Portrait of the Artist as a Young Man* (1916) that 'the shortest way to Tara was *via* Holyhead' is James Joyce's most dramatic reminder that Irish literature is dominated by stories of departure and return, of journeys, real or imaginary, by which the Irish writer comes to claim a place in the world and all the better negotiate a relationship with home.[1] The work of the Irish Literary Revival of the late nineteenth and early twentieth centuries and the avant-garde experiments of Irish modernism were determined by the siren call of different places; W. B. Yeats moved between London, Dublin, and Sligo, while the mapping of a newly vivid relationship between Ireland and Europe is at the heart of the work of Joyce and Samuel Beckett. This pattern is one that is repeated with new resonances in the later decades of the twentieth century and into the new millennium. During this period of Irish literary history, a fresh understanding of Ireland's relationship with its diaspora emerged along with a body of work that sought to engage with the realities of emigration in the 1980s and the emergence of new narratives of Irish migration during the Celtic Tiger years of the 1990s and beyond. The result was the rise of a new kind of Irish writing about migration and return, journeying, and exploration, and an accompanying public and academic discourse that sought to illuminate more fully the story of the Irish abroad.

This essay is especially interested in how Irish writing from 1980 to the present responds to the differently inflected stories of migration and diaspora. Long a figure of anxiety, the Irish emigrant – from the nineteenth-century famine victim to the migrant of the economically depressed Ireland of the 1950s – haunts the work of more recent Irish writers as the story of Irish emigration is recovered and re-animated in literary culture. The narrative of the Irish abroad is also foregrounded in the fashioning of a new idea of the Irish literary canon, one that expands outwards beyond the limits of the nation to engage with writers of the diaspora. At the same time, for some writers, the possibilities of creative escape through reaching for horizons beyond more familiar and dominant Irish landscapes offer a means of transcending the limits of a narrative dominated by Ireland's colonial history and the Irish Troubles, north and south of the border.

For Fintan O'Toole, 'emigration and exile, the journeys to and from home, are the very heartbeat of Irish culture. To imagine Ireland is to imagine a journey'.[2] And, yet, for all the importance of this symbol of the 'journey', the history of Irish emigration has only fully emerged as a significant preoccupation among literary critics in recent decades. History and the social sciences have led the way in the development of the fields of Irish migration and Irish diaspora studies, but over the course of the last twenty years, literary studies has begun to keep pace.[3]

Migration and the Irish Diaspora in the 1980s and 1990s

In *The Lie of the Land: Irish Identities* (1997), O'Toole collates a series of dramatic statistics about the social impact of emigration in Ireland in the twentieth century:

> Emigration has been the single biggest fact in the 75-year history of the Irish State. Only half those born in Ireland in the early 1930s, for instance, were still living there thirty years later. The rate of emigration dropped rapidly in the 1960s, but picked up again in the late 1970s and early 1980s, so that the 1996 census showed that nearly 20 per cent of those born in 1970 were by then living in some other country.[4]

If the most dominant narratives of Irish emigration focused on the history of Irish exile in Britain and the United States, Jim Mac Laughlin notes that the 1980s and 1990s were marked by a government response that at its core seemed to suggest that increasingly 'Irish emigrants were moving to benign taxfields and fields of opportunity in Europe.'[5] The equation of emigration and 'opportunity' found particularly contentious expression in Minister for Foreign Affairs Brian Lenihan's insistence on the necessity of emigration as a safety valve for the Irish economy and his now infamous exasperated pronouncement in 1987: 'We can't all live on a small island.'[6]

In 1993, reflecting on the centrality of migration as a centripetal force in Irish cultural life, Joseph O'Connor concluded:

> Emigration is as Irish as Cathleen Ní Houlihan's harp, yet it is only since the sixties and the generation of Edna O'Brien that Irish writers have written about the subject at first hand. [. . .] It has been taken as read that Exile is an

important theme in Irish writing, like The Big House or The Catholic Church. But if it is, it's an inconsistent and entirely intermittent preoccupation.[7]

A previous generation of writers had already begun to address this lacuna by articulating the Irish writer's experience of exile at mid-century. Edna O'Brien's *The Country Girls* trilogy, the first instalment of which appeared in 1960, served as a landmark study of the lives of young Irish women in the west of Ireland, Dublin, and London, and it is part *Bildungsroman*, part dissection of the insular conservatism of post-independence Ireland. O'Brien would go on to spend most of her life outside of Ireland and her memoirs *Mother Ireland* (1976) and *Country Girl* (2012) offer vivid accounts of the complexities of a relationship with a home place that, most certainly in the early chapters of her creative life, was openly hostile to her writing. John McGahern's *The Leavetaking* (1974) reflects upon the impossibility of staying in Ireland for the Irish artist and looks back to his own experience of being forced to leave the country in the 1960s after the publication of his novel *The Dark* (1965), which was banned for its candid depiction of young adult sexuality. Furthermore, McGahern's short stories and his early unpublished novel *The End or The Beginning of Love*, written between 1957 and 1961, return time and again to the experience of Irish navvies in Britain, in part a refraction of his own time as a labourer on London building sites in the 1950s.

O'Brien, McGahern, and other writers of their generation continued this excavation of post-independence Ireland into the 1980s and 1990s, while these decades also saw the emergence of a new generation of writers less interested in remembering the past and more concerned with confronting the present-time experience of emigration. The 1980s exodus led to a new kind of writing about leaving home brought about in part by the scale of emigration in these years. Joe Cleary records that 'by 1987 emigration in the Republic had risen to rates estimated at approximately 30,000 to 40,000 people per annum, something not witnessed since the bleak decade of the 1950s'.[8] The most determined response to these developments came in the form of Dermot Bolger's *Ireland in Exile: Irish Writers Abroad* (1993), which set out to engage directly with the lived experiences that lay behind these extraordinary statistics. Bolger's poetry collection *Internal Exiles* (1986) took up this theme, but his novel *The Journey Home* (1990) gives powerful voice to a new generation and their experience of emigration. Set in Dublin, the novel examines the different forms that exile takes and is interested in 'internal migration' patterns from rural Ireland to

Dublin as well as the more familiar narrative of migration to Britain and the United States.⁹ Exile also serves as a metaphor for the estrangement between generations, as the main character Hano's father is bound by memory to his 'homeland' of Co. Kerry, while Hano struggles with the realities of contemporary Dublin. His father's displacement from rural Kerry to suburban Dublin is imagined as a culture shock akin to arriving in a new country: 'They planted trees in the image of their lost homeland, put down potato beds, built timber hen-houses. [...] When the radio announcer gave the results of the provincial Gaelic matches the backs would straighten, neighbours reverting to county allegiances as they slagged each other.'¹⁰ The apparent inevitability of emigration is a key concern of the novel, and it draws a direct comparison between past and present: 'He remembered the farewells in Murtagh's, no longer cardboard suitcases and cattle boats, but green cards and holiday visas. [...] As the airport posters proclaimed, they were the young Europeans, fodder now not just for factory floors but for engineering and computer posts.'¹¹

Like Bolger, Joseph O'Connor responded directly to the emigration crisis of the 1980s in his early novel *Cowboys and Indians* and short-story collection *True Believers* (both 1991). In the story, 'Last of the Mohicans', a character denounces 1980s Ireland as a 'glorified tax haven for rich tourists and popstars. A cultural backwater that time forgot. He said no one who ever did anything stayed in Ireland'.¹² A coming-of-age story set in the 1980s, *Cowboys and Indians* charts Eddie Virago's picaresque adventures in London. He meets Marion Mangan, a young woman from a small town in Donegal and the traumatic secret at the heart of the novel – Marion's flight to London for an abortion – gradually reveals itself. In a lighter vein of the novel, O'Connor satirises the place of the Irish in London yuppie culture as Eddie contemplates what it might mean to become a NIPPIL (New Irish Professional Person in London).

Emma Donoghue's early work also features an awareness of how emigration shaped Irish life in these decades. In *Hood* (1995), the material realities of emigration are reflected in the minutiae of the text: 'Across the road was a tacky religious goods shop and an advice centre, its window featuring pamphlets called *Think Before You Emigrate* and *Coping with London*.'¹³ Her short story 'Going Back', collected in Bolger's *Ireland in Exile*, is Donoghue's most direct intervention in confronting Ireland's homophobia, as the main character describes herself as feeling 'more of an exile for twenty years in Ireland than I ever have in the twelve I've been out of it'.¹⁴

In the same period, London Irish playwright Martin McDonagh emerged as an important figure determined to write back to his Irish origins in particularly vivid ways. McDonagh's plays set in the West of Ireland revisit the dramatic territory of the writers of the Irish Literary Revival with new purpose. For example, *The Cripple of Inishmaan* (1997) is set against the backdrop of the filming of Robert Flaherty's *Man of Aran* (1934), a sentimental exploration of life on the Aran Islands, but gives the islanders free voice in their right of reply to Flaherty's vision. In one scene a young woman vents her ire at having been sidelined in the making of the film and denounces Flaherty's project in no uncertain terms: 'I think I might go pegging eggs at the film tomorrow. The *Man of Aran* me arsehole. "The Lass of Aran" they could have had, and the *pretty* lass of Aran. Not some oul shite about thick fellas fecking fishing.'[15] McDonagh has more recently gone on to carve out a place for himself on the international scene as director of films such as *In Bruges* (2008) and *Three Billboards Outside Ebbing, Missouri* (2017), but his early work as a playwright constitutes a highly self-conscious and charged letter home from the diaspora.

The 1980s and 1990s were especially important decades for capturing the testimonies of the Irish in Britain and, most particularly, Irish women in Britain, who as late as 1995 remained, in the words of one historian, the 'great unknown' of Irish emigrant history.[16] In the same period, two important voices emerged across the water in the work of Maude Casey and Moy McCrory, both of whom addressed what McCrory characterises as the silence of second-generation Irish people in Britain.[17] Set in the Irish community in Liverpool, McCrory's collection *The Water's Edge* (1985) explores the tensions and fractures between generations. A poignant story in the collection, entitled 'Prize Giving', captures one such moment of estrangement: 'Sometimes he could not understand how Siobhan was their daughter. Her ways were so very different. She was so English, a foreigner to her parents. To her, Mayo was just a postmark on a card from cousins she did not know very well.'[18] Maude Casey's *Over the Water* (1987) is also concerned with such alienation as the teenage girl at the centre of the novel feels set apart by her parents' Irishness.

The experiences of Irish women migrants in this period command attention, not least because of the ways in which Irish women's lives and bodies were policed at home. Siobhán Kilfeather offers a striking summing-up of the circumscription of Irish women's lives at this time:

In the 1980s and 1990s public debates over issues to do with privacy, reproductive rights and alternative sexualities were centred on a series of scandals in which print and broadcast media personalised the issues through sensationalised exemplary cases: the death in childbirth of 15-year-old Ann Lovett and her baby in 1984; the trial of Joanne Hayes for the murder of the Kerry babies in 1984; the decision of rape survivor Lavinia Kerwick to renounce anonymity and speak on a radio programme in 1990.[19]

Such public surveillance and regulation of Irish women's reproductive rights are addressed in a number of works concerned with what Ann Rossiter, in her anthology of testimonies of Irish women who were left no choice but to travel to England for an abortion during these decades, calls 'The Hidden Diaspora'.[20] Evelyn Conlon's collection *My Head Is Opening* (1987) offers glimpses of Irish women's lives under the same conditions. In Conlon's short story 'Transition', a young woman becomes pregnant unexpectedly and escapes a doomed affair by leaving for England, a journey characterised by the juxtaposition of freedom and peril: 'She was now responsible, twenty-three, and learned. She had become a silent citizen, a fool. No. No, not that. A silenced citizen, away, with a destroyed life and name. A freed person – there was nothing left to lose.'[21] William Trevor's novel *Felicia's Journey* (1994) tells of a similar journey to England as the eponymous heroine leaves home when she discovers she is pregnant in order to follow the father of her baby to Birmingham. She is abandoned by her homeland, another 'silent citizen', and left vulnerable and isolated in the unfamiliar territory of urban-industrial Birmingham.

For Irish poets, the navigation of the journey between homeland and hostland has taken on a new purchase. Eavan Boland, whose work is so concerned with recovering lost histories and creating a space for the Irish woman poet, also turned her eye to the elided history of the Irish migrant. Her poem 'The Emigrant Irish' (1987) honours the story of Irish emigration and a diaspora too long ignored: 'Like oil lamps we put them out the back, || of our houses, of our minds.'[22] The same poem was one of the inspirations for President Mary Robinson's 1995 address to the Houses of the Oireachtas, 'Cherishing the Irish Diaspora', in which she called for a renewal of 'our love and remembrance on this island for those who leave it behind'.[23] At times Boland directly addresses her own childhood experience of leaving Ireland for England, as in 'An Irish Childhood in England, 1951'. Yet her work travels across time and history – often fusing classical with Celtic mythology – and tracks her own movement as a poet and academic between Ireland, Britain, and America. This might be interpreted as a necessary vigilance about predetermined roles for the Irish woman poet on home soil, and as such exemplifies what Boland identifies as the ever-present need to evade the powerful 'imagery and emblem of the national muse'.[24]

Emigrant Hauntings and the Rise and Fall of Celtic Tiger Ireland

If Irish writing about journeying out into the world was marked by a concern with engaging with emigration as it played out in real time in the 1980s and early 1990s, then the unprecedented prosperity of the Celtic Tiger years in the 1990s and 2000s, and the rise of immigration and return migration, led to a new kind of literary meditation on the past. In her study of Celtic Tiger literature, Susan Cahill argues that Anne Enright belongs to a new category of writer whose primary concern is to 'explore and question the dominant narratives that served to support the Irish state, particularly in relation to questions of genealogies and generations (maternal and otherwise), occluded histories, and the material bodies that are affected by such repressions'.[25]

One such 'occluded' history is the story of the emigrant, as the Irish writer began to offer a new kind of account of the history of Irish migration, a history that for Piaras Mac Éinrí had been for too long characterised by 'palpable public silence',[26] and that for Fintan O'Toole (writing about the Irish in Britain) had been suppressed by a kind of cultural 'amnesia and evasion'.[27] For O'Toole this coming to consciousness served as a particularly important counterpoint to the rise of anti-immigrant rhetoric in Celtic Tiger Ireland – as Ireland moved from being a country historically defined by emigration to an immigrant destination, it also became one characterised by what O'Toole diagnosed as an 'increasing tendency to see "Irish" and "immigrant" as opposed categories of humanity'.[28] Sinéad Moynihan has explored the tectonic shifts that came about in this period and the way in which '(re)imagining Irish diasporic experience in the United States in various ways – particularly as it relates to Irish interactions with African Americans – became absolutely central to representations of multicultural Ireland during the Celtic Tiger years'.[29]

Different strands of Irish writing during the Celtic Tiger years as well as after the economic crash of 2008, which saw a return to outward migration, continued to engage with overlooked narratives of the Irish diaspora. During this time, Irish writers in Britain negotiated between past and present experiences of migration with a new kind of vividness. In the poem 'To Those Who Have Inherited a Country' from his 2008 collection, *Slipping Letters Beneath the Sea*, Birmingham-Irish poet Joe Horgan offers an especially resonant reply to the economic success of Celtic Tiger Ireland from the point of view of the Irish in Britain: 'If we'd known | we'd have stayed. | We could have lingered | outside your electronic gates, | built your crowded motorways, | instead of theirs.'[30] This turn to history is taken up and expanded in Kit de Waal's most recent novel, *The Trick to Time* (2018), which is set, in part, among the Birmingham-Irish community in the 1970s. In recent years the story of the London Irish has been explored in the documentary films *Men of Arlington* (2011) and *Breaking Ground: The Story of the London Irish Women's Centre* (2013), and in studies such as Tony Murray's *London Irish Fictions: Narrative, Diaspora and Identity* and Clair Wills's history *The Best Are Leaving: Emigration and Post-War Irish Culture* (2015), while Liam Harte's anthology *The Literature of the Irish in Britain: Autobiography and Memoir* (2009) is an ambitious compendium of life writing that reaches from 1725 to 2001.

As the diaspora continued to write home via different media, on home territory these years were marked by a concern with stories of return and recovery as well as departure. In an interview Anne Enright described the process of addressing missing histories in the story of Ireland: 'We are bringing them all back home: it is not just recent emigrants who are returning to Ireland, but the dead, the lost, the long-ago disappeared.'[31] Enright's work from the 1990s to 2000s is deeply concerned with different kinds of departure and return, from the return home from London to Dublin in *The Wig My Father Wore* (1996) to the story of mistaken and reclaimed identity in *What Are You Like?* (2000). However, the most extended meditation on how Irish emigrants have been written out of the national tale appears in *The Gathering* (2007) via Veronica Hegarty's journey from Dublin to Brighton to repatriate the body of her dead brother, a traumatised figure who is all but abandoned by his family.

Other writers offered a more familiar story of the returnee during these years, in a reworking of a familiar figure in Irish literary culture: the emigrant who is drawn back to Ireland by personal crisis, family duty, or curiosity about the place they left behind.[32] In Kate O'Riordan's *The Memory Stones* (2003), the main character is called home to Ireland from Paris to her daughter, a recovering drug addict, when she gets a call from a concerned neighbour. On her arrival back in Ireland she has to negotiate between her concern for her troubled daughter and her granddaughter and the freedom and autonomy of her life in France. This contemporary returnee narrative is held up against memories of stories told by her uncle of the Irish in England:

> They'd talk and talk about going back, what they were going to do, who they were going to see. For weeks they'd be out of their heads from excitement and whiskey. Buying presents for brothers and sisters, half of John Lewis for their mothers. And then they'd get to Paddington to catch the boat train, wave their mates good-bye, slip into the nearest pub, get slaughtered and take the bus back to their lodgings to spend the next two weeks in a drunken stupor.[33]

Edna O'Brien's *The Light of Evening* (2006) explores a more sympathetic and conciliatory relationship between returnee and homeland through an epistolary exchange between the woman writer and her mother that revisits O'Brien's early work and attempts to establish new lines of communication between the Irish woman emigrant and her homeland.

Transatlantic Affinities

The narrative of Irish emigration to the United States remains the most pervasive and since the 1980s a number of novelists have contributed to the consolidation of this mythology. Colum McCann's *This Side of Brightness* (1998) is set in New York in the early decades of the twentieth century and focuses, in part, on immigrants labouring on the New York subway system – the lives of Irish, Italian, and African American workers from the south intersect and intertwine across three generations. McCann's *TransAtlantic* (2013) is a more explicit literary engagement with Atlantic crossings by public figures, from Frederick Douglass to Senator George Mitchell. Joseph O'Connor's *Star of the Sea* (2002) is one of the best-known and most celebrated navigations of the 'Irish Atlantic' in recent decades.[34] But perhaps the most striking navigation of this terrain remains Colm Tóibín's *Brooklyn* (2009); published just after the economic crash of 2008, it was especially attuned to the cultural implications of return migration to Ireland during the economic prosperity of the Celtic Tiger years, despite being set largely in 1950s America.[35]

While the work of Irish-born writers shows a particular interest in recovering and re-purposing migrant narratives, the literature of the Irish diaspora has also gained new currency in the last forty years. In this, Irish-American writing has been especially significant and the publication of Charles Fanning's *The Irish Voice in America: 250 Years of Irish-American Fiction* in the early 1990s was a landmark moment in Irish-American literary studies. The book follows a timeline from the eighteenth century to the twentieth-century and the work of writers such as Edward McSorley and James T. Farrell.[36] In the same decade the writing of a number of Irish-American women writers came to prominence. While the recovery of the work of *New Yorker* writer Maeve Brennan, who was born in Ireland but spent most of her adult life in the US, represents one version of this history, writers such as Elizabeth Cullinan, Mary Gordon, and Alice McDermott began to give voice to a rapidly changing Irish-American culture in the decades after the Second World War.

If for the Irish-American writer there is a rich tradition to draw upon and resist in turn, the Irish writer in Canada tells a rather different story. In Brian Moore's *The Luck of Ginger Coffey* (1960), the hapless eponymous emigrant arrives in Canada and suffers a series of disappointments as his new life fails to launch. As part of the emergence of Irish-Canadian literature, women writers have been especially important in charting new kinds of transatlantic encounters. While Margaret Atwood's *Alias Grace* (1996) is perhaps the best-known contemporary novel about the Irish in Canada in the nineteenth century, the fiction of Irish-Canadian writer Jane Urquhart offers an extended meditation on Irish-Canadian history, from her early novel *Away* (1993), a story of flight from Ireland during the famine years, to *The Night Stages* (2015), a historical novel set in Ireland in the 1950s. The distant and recent history of the Irish in New Zealand and Australia has also begun to emerge in contemporary fiction, as in Coral Atkinson's *The Love Apple* (2005), Evelyn Conlon's famine novel *Not the Same Sky* (2013), and E. M. Reapy's post-crash novel *Red Dirt* (2016).

Relocating the Contemporary Irish Writer

The history of Irish migration and diasporic relations remain dominant critical frameworks for thinking about the relationship between the Irish writer and other spaces and places. At the same time, foreign settings and locations can themselves serve as a means of breaking new imaginative ground beyond the more familiar paradigms of the Irish literary tradition. In the case of the Northern Irish poet, this is partially informed by the challenge of engaging with the political violence and conflict on home ground and the importance of movement and perspective in bearing witness to the Troubles. For Seamus Heaney, this challenge was accompanied by the dilemma of seeing his work co-opted as British and by the need to move through 'the identity gears'.[37] *Wintering Out* (1972) and *North* (1975) set a precedent for this interest in movement and identity as he locates the 'bog poems' at the heart of *North* in Iron-Age Danish

Jutland, distant in both time and place from Troubles-era Ulster. London, like Derry and Dublin, emerges as an important writing location in Heaney's expansive geography, as suggested in the title poem of *District and Circle* (2006), an extended meditation on political violence set against the backdrop of the London underground.

In the essay 'The Irish Poet and Britain', Heaney ponders the particular dilemma of the Northern Irish poet and the inheritances of place:

> And these things accumulated even more problematically in the mid-1960s, when I had started to publish poems and began to be included in anthologies with titles like *Young Commonwealth Poets* and *Young British Poets*. Probably I could have gone on living and hesitating to speak had I gone on living in Northern Ireland and had the question of British versus Irish loyalties not mutated into the deadly complications of our more or less civil war. [. . .] By 1983, my family and I had been resident for eleven years in the Irish Republic, although I should emphasize that when we moved, it was not in order to flee the violence but in order that I might take advantage of an offer of a house in Wicklow that was a kind of writer's retreat; anyhow, there we were, and in order to make a new coherence between where we were living and who and what I was, I had taken out an Irish passport.[38]

Other Northern Irish poets explore a different kind of fluidity and multiplicity of identity that destabilises some of the more familiar co-ordinates of Irish literary culture; in one strand of their work, these poets transcend the story of the nation as one defined by colonial and postcolonial conflict and divine creative possibilities for seemingly remote places. Such poetic nomadism serves a special purpose for poets whose work is so often read through the fixed lens of the politics of the Northern Irish Troubles – they find imaginative refuge in places and historical moments that untether their work from the more predictable critical paradigms that dominate discussions of Northern Irish writing. Examples include Paul Muldoon's American poems and investigations of Native American history in volumes such as *New Weather* (1973) and *Meeting the British* (1987), Derek Mahon's epistolary poems from his time in New York City in *The Hudson Letter* (1995), and Sinéad Morrissey's sequence of poems about Japan in *Between Here and There* (2001). The close identification of writers Justin Quinn with Prague and Julian Gough with Berlin is a reminder that the European metropolis is as much home to the Irish writer in the twenty-first century as its Hibernian equivalent.

A related strain in contemporary Irish fiction concerned with mobility and travel shows a greater preoccupation with journeys than origins or destinations. For instance, Anne Enright's *The Pleasure of Eliza Lynch*

(2002) is a transnational historical adventure that takes in Paris, Paraguay, and Argentina while in Enright's *The Green Road* (2015) the global scattering of the family is presented as an inevitable fact of Irish life. Joseph O'Neill's *Netherland* (2008) is, in part, concerned with the stories of migration that comprise the history and cultural fabric of the United States, but it is also a contemporary novel in which the most significant geography is configured via Google Maps. Paula McGrath's *Generation* (2015) explores intertwined histories across time and moves between different cultures as a means of locating the story of Irish migration within a larger global framework. What these writers share is an interest in releasing the Irish experience of movement, travel, and journeying from the more immediately familiar narrative of loss and gain that so often accompanies writing about emigration and diaspora. The Irish writer's journey out into the world is, then, one that takes in the real histories and lived experiences of emigrant generations and the Irish diaspora as well as the possibilities of adventuring into new territory in the interests of pushing against the limits of the national imagination.

Notes

1. James Joyce, Seamus Deane, ed., *A Portrait of the Artist as a Young Man* (London: Penguin, 1992), p. 273.
2. Fintan O'Toole, *The Ex-Isle of Erin: Images of a Global Ireland* (Dublin: New Island, 1997), p. 157.
3. See, for example, Patrick Ward, *Exile, Emigration, and Irish Writing* (Dublin: Irish Academic Press, 2003); Liam Harte, *The Literature of the Irish in Britain: Autobiography and Memoir: 1725–2001* (Basingstoke: Palgrave Macmillan, 2009); Sinéad Moynihan, *'Other People's Diasporas': Negotiating Race in Contemporary Irish and Irish-American Culture* (Syracuse, NY: Syracuse University Press, 2013); Ellen McWilliams, *Women and Exile in Contemporary Irish Fiction* (Basingstoke: Palgrave Macmillan, 2013); Tony Murray, *London Irish Fictions: Narrative, Diaspora and Identity* (Liverpool: Liverpool University Press, 2014); Moira Casey and Amanda Tucker, eds., *Where Motley is Worn: Transnational Irish Literatures* (Cork, Ireland: Cork University Press, 2014); Enda Delaney and Ciaran O'Neill, eds., 'Beyond the Nation: Transnational Ireland', special issue of *Éire-Ireland*, 51.1–2 (2016); Sinéad Wall, *Irish Diasporic Narratives in Argentina: A Reconsideration of Home, Identity and Belonging* (Oxford: Peter Lang, 2017); and Ailbhe McDaid, *The Poetics of Migration in Contemporary Irish Poetry* (Basingstoke: Palgrave Macmillan, 2017).
4. Fintan O'Toole, *The Lie of the Land: Irish Identities* (London: Verso, 1997), p. xiv.

5. Jim MacLaughlin, 'Introduction', in Jim Mac Laughlin, ed., *Location and Dislocation in Contemporary Irish Society* (Cork, Ireland: Cork University Press, 1997), pp. 1–36 (p. 3).
6. Brian Lambkin and Patrick Fitzgerald, *Migration in Irish History, 1607–2007* (Basingstoke: Palgrave Macmillan, 2008), p. 246.
7. Dermot Bolger, 'Introduction', in Dermot Bolger, ed., *Ireland in Exile: Irish Writers Abroad* (Dublin: New Island, 1993), pp. 11–18 (p. 16).
8. Joe Cleary, '"Misplaced Ideas"?: Colonialism, Location, and Dislocation in Irish Studies', in Clare Carroll and Patricia King, eds., *Ireland and Postcolonial Theory* (Cork, Ireland: Cork University Press, 2003), pp. 16–45 (p. 18).
9. Lambkin and Fitzgerald, *Migration*, p. 210.
10. Dermot Bolger, *The Journey Home* (London: Penguin, 1991), pp. 6–7.
11. Ibid., p. 47.
12. Joseph O'Connor, 'Last of the Mohicans', in *True Believers* (London: Flamingo, 1992), pp. 3–13 (p. 7).
13. Emma Donoghue, *Hood* (London: Penguin, 1996), p. 189.
14. Emma Donoghue, 'Going Back', in Bolger, ed., *Ireland in Exile: Irish Writers Abroad*, pp. 157–70 (p. 160).
15. Martin McDonagh, *The Cripple of Inishmaan* (London: Methuen, 1997), p. 51.
16. Donald Harman Akenson, *The Irish Diaspora: A Primer* (Belfast: Institute of Irish Studies 1993), pp. 157–8.
17. Moy McCrory, '"This Time and Now": Identity and Belonging in the Irish Diaspora: The Irish in Britain and Second-Generational Silence', in Christine Berberich, Neil Campbell, and Robert Hudson, eds., *Land and Identity: Theory, Memory, and Practice* (Amsterdam: Rodopi, 2012), pp. 165–90.
18. Moy McCrory, 'Prize Giving', in *The Water's Edge and Other Stories* (London: Sheba, 1985), pp. 128–39 (p. 136).
19. Siobhán Kilfeather, 'Irish Feminism', in Joe Cleary and Claire Connolly, eds., *The Cambridge Companion to Modern Irish Culture* (Cambridge: Cambridge University Press, 2005), pp. 96–116 (p. 111).
20. See Ann Rossiter, *Ireland's Hidden Diaspora: The 'Abortion Trail' and the Making of a London-Irish Underground, 1980–2000* (London: Iasc, 2009).
21. Evelyn Conlon, 'Transition', in *My Head Is Opening* (Dublin: Attic Press, 1987), pp. 43–56 (p. 56).
22. Eavan Boland, *Collected Poems* (Manchester: Carcanet, 1995), p. 129.
23. Mary Robinson, 'Cherishing the Irish Diaspora: An Address to the Houses of the Oireachtas' (1995). See McWilliams, *Women and Exile in Contemporary Irish Fiction*, p. 1.
24. Eavan Boland, *Object Lessons: The Life of the Woman and Poet in Our Time* (Manchester: Carcanet, 1995), p. 137.
25. Susan Cahill, *Irish Literature in the Celtic Tiger Years 1990–2008: Gender, Bodies, Memory* (London: Continuum, 2011), p. 19.

26. Piaras Mac Éinrí, 'Introduction', in Andy Bielenberg, ed., *The Irish Diaspora* (Harlow, England: Pearson, 2000), pp. 1–15 (p. 3).
27. Fintan O'Toole, 'Forgotten Irish in UK Deserve Recognition', *The Irish Times*, 19 September 2000: www.irishtimes.com/opinion/forgotten-irish-in-uk-deserve-recognition-1.1104433 [accessed 13 August 2019].
28. Ibid.
29. Sinéad Moynihan, *'Other People's Diasporas'*, p. 3.
30. Joseph Horgan, *Slipping Letters Beneath the Sea* (Tralee, Ireland: Doghouse Books, 2008), p. 52.
31. Anne Enright, 'Review of The Story of Chicago May by Julia O'Faolain', *The Times*, 1 January 2006: www.thetimes.co.uk/article/the-story-of-chicago-may-by-nuala-ofaolain-2m9vg7p256j [accessed 29 March 2019].
32. Sinéad Moynihan, *Ireland, Migration and Return Migration: The "Returned Yank" in the Cultural Imagination, 1952 to present* (Liverpool: Liverpool University Press, 2019).
33. Kate O'Riordan, *The Memory Stones* (London: Simon & Schuster, 2003), p. 177.
34. Sinéad Moynihan, 'Ships in Motion: Crossing the Black and Green Atlantics in Joseph O'Connor's *Star of the Sea*', *Symbiosis: A Journal of Anglo-American Literary Relations*, 12. 1 (2008), pp. 41–58.
35. For a detailed analysis of the novel's engagement with discourses of Celtic Tiger and Post-Celtic Tiger Ireland, see Sinéad Moynihan, '"We are where we are": Colm Tóibín's *Brooklyn*, Mythologies of Return and the Post-Celtic Tiger Moment', in Leslie Eckel and Clare Frances Elliott, eds., *The Edinburgh Companion to Atlantic Literary Studies* (Edinburgh: Edinburgh University Press, 2016), pp. 88–102.
36. Other studies of Irish-American writing include Marion R. Casey and J. J. Lee, eds., *Making the Irish American: History and Heritage of the Irish in the United States* (New York: New York University Press, 2006); Christopher Dowd, *The Construction of Irish Identity in American Literature* (London: Routledge, 2010); Sally Barr Ebest, *The Banshees: A Literary History of Irish American Women Writers* (Syracuse: Syracuse University Press, 2013); and Tara Stubbs, *American Literature and Irish Culture, 1910–1955: The Politics of Enchantment* (Manchester: Manchester University Press, 2013).
37. Seamus Heaney, 'Through-Other Places, Through-Other Times: The Irish Poet and Britain', in *Finders Keepers: Selected Prose 1971–2001* (New York: Farrar, Straus and Giroux, 2003), pp. 396–415 (p. 401).
38. Heaney, *Finders Keepers*, p. 401.

CHAPTER 10

Arrivals: Inward Migration and Irish Literature
Anne Mulhall

> Two types of borders divide the global world. The first and most obvious type is the national border, which separates different nation-states. The second and less obvious type is a racialized class border, which separates two different experiences of mobility in the world of national borders. [...] On the one hand, we have a world where 'third-world-looking' transnational working-class and underclass citizens live, and are made to feel that national borders are exceptionally important and difficult to cross. [...] On the other hand, we have a world experienced as open, in which people move smoothly across national borders, experiencing the world as almost borderless. This is the experience enjoyed by the largely White upper classes, who are made to feel truly at home in the world.
> – Ghassan Hage, *Is Racism an Environmental Threat?*[1]

Introduction: Whiteness and the Literary Representation of 'Multicultural' Ireland

An increase in the number of people migrating to Ireland in the 1990s spurred a parallel interest in literary representations of a new multicultural Ireland. Until very recently, such representations have been authored by white Irish writers such as Roddy Doyle, Chris Binchy, Mary O'Donnell, Oona Frawley, Colm Tóibín, Donal Ryan, and Keith Ridgway. While this dynamic has also predominated in theatre and performance, there were earlier breakthroughs in those fields by migrant playwrights and production companies that attenuated the hegemony of a white Irish vantage point. Critics such as Charlotte McIvor and Jason King have done extensive work mapping this field.[2] Critical work has also been carried out in relation to prose fiction and poetry by mostly white Irish authors (and white critics from the global North) that addresses 'multicultural Ireland'.[3] In this chapter, I will instead focus on fiction and poetry produced in the last decade by migrant writers of colour in Ireland, such as Ifedinma

Dimbo, Melatu Uche Okorie, Ebun Joseph Akpoveta, and Oritsegbemi Emmanuel Jakpa, as well as a younger generation of writers including Felicia Olusanya, Dagogo Hart, Chiamaka Enyi-Amadi, and Denise Chaila. The perspective afforded in this work is not simply an add-on to the already existing body of literary work about 'multicultural Ireland'. Rather, it is, among other things, a corrective to the centring of the dominant white 'native' point of view on the 'migrant other'. In the last decade, and particularly in the last few years, migrant writers of colour are breaking through into the literary and cultural mainstream with work that centres migrant of colour consciousness and, particularly in the case of young emerging artists, that experiments with form, genre, and medium in ways that circumvent established literary norms and circuits of exchange.

The categorisation of people as 'migrants' and of writers as 'migrant writers', particularly by those of us who do not carry the burden of such designations ourselves, can be racialising, dehumanising, and ghettoising. The category 'migrant writer' threatens a confinement that the writer may find difficult to escape, a segregated silo adjacent to the literary mainstream. Özgecan Kesici, a poet who grew up in Turkey and is now living in Ireland, emphasises the importance for writers not to be curtailed within 'that migrant frame' and of 'allowing spaces for migrants to be represented beyond their migrant identity'.[4] As Fatima El-Tayeb notes, that migrant frame is racialised: 'persons born in a European nation, of parents born and raised there as well, are thus routinely identified as "third generation migrants," manifesting their position outside the community of citizens'.[5] This racialisation of migrancy, legible in the differential attribution of '"hereditary" migrant status' according to race and the global apartheid line, is operative in Ireland as elsewhere in Europe.[6] As Elena Moreo points out, contemporary migration regimes 'as well as media, political and everyday discourses, tend to construct some migrants as *more migrants* than others (who may alternatively be called ex-pats, international professionals or not considered migrants at all) based on legal status, ethnicity, language, religion, occupational status and class'.[7] She further notes the consequences of being represented as the 'other', the 'arrival', or the 'outsider', citing Frantz Fanon's description of 'the feeling of being composed by others "out of a thousand details, anecdotes, stories" in which the voices of the racialized never resonate' and which corrode the person's agency and trust in their own experience.[8]

What Kensika Monshengwo describes in an interview with Ronit Lentin as the 'colonial charity model' that pervades the migrant advocacy non-profit sector in Ireland has also – inevitably perhaps – inflected the literary representation of 'migrants' and the framing of contemporary migration in the Irish context.[9] The Trócaire/Poetry Ireland annual poetry competition is an interesting illustration of this dynamic, situated as it is at the intersection between the Irish global development sector and the Irish literary establishment. The competition, started in 2013, 'uses the arts to raise awareness of the leading global justice issues of our time'.[10] The 2016 theme was 'Forced to Flee: This Is Our Exodus', inviting poetic responses to the forced migration of people from Syria and the Middle East. In the published poet category, all three winning poems were written by women poets who have migrated from Scotland and England, and between Zambia, Zimbabwe, and Ireland. However, the difference that whiteness and the racialised divide between the global North and global South makes is clear in the distance between the point of view articulated by the speaker and that of the subjects/objects of the poems. All three poems are lyrics that call upon exoticising pastoral tropes of rural non-modern simplicity, references to ancient ritual, and analogies between the human subjects of the poem and the natural world that intend, perhaps, to emphasise the naturalness of migration but instead, if only by way of unintentional irony, contribute to the dehumanisation of people forced to move (for instance, the migration of Monarch butterflies is used as an extended metaphor for the migrant trail through Mexico, concluding with the line 'a storm of wings that fills the ears like rain').[11] These fetishising representations elide the political and economic power structures that undergird the genocidal injustices of our contemporary global migration regime. Instead, the winning poems are intended to elicit the pity of the reader who is presumed to be on the other, charmed side of that regime. Such literary representations of migration can entail an additional dispossession of those at the sharp end of global migration regimes who are fashioned into mediated objects of identificatory pity.

Interculturalism in Irish Fiction and the Elision of Race: Two Case Studies

For Dale Tracy, 'to imagine ourselves in the place of another is always still to imagine that other from our own viewpoint, not theirs'.[12] This simple but essential observation is useful when thinking about the treatment of inmigration in Irish literature and literary criticism – bodies of work that have been dominated by white Irish authors (and white critics from the global North). One recurring trope in prose fiction about 'multicultural' Ireland has been the romance plot, with interracial relationships figuring the resolution of cross-race conflict and the hopes for harmonious and easy integration. As Jason King notes of Roddy Doyle's stories in *The Deportees* (2007), 'the repeated resolution of cultural conflict through romantic fulfilment symbolises Irish acceptance of immigrants whose presence constitutes no underlying threat to the nation's normative self-image', and such resolutions are 'achieved through the elision rather than accommodation of cultural difference'.[13] Doyle's short story 'I Understand' (first serialised in *Metro Eireann* in 2003–4) uses the interracial romance plot between a white Irish and a black Nigerian protagonist to resolve cultural differences, race and class hierarchies, and the realities of the migration regime, while also attempting to address the realities of systemic racism in contemporary Ireland. The first-person narrator, Tom, who is seeking asylum, also works two jobs, necessarily in the 'grey' labour market, as the Republic's ban on people seeking asylum working was only partially lifted under legal duress in 2018. This situation of state-enforced legal and economic precarity leaves Tom vulnerable to multiple forms of exploitation. Tom meets Ailbhe; they have sex and spend some time together, and the story ends with him calling at her flat and Ailbhe inviting him in. The budding romance across the race/class/status divide obviates Tom's isolation and vulnerability so that even the gangsters who had tried to violently coerce him into working for them fade into the background. As Maureen Reddy notes, 'I Understand' marks a significant departure by centring the perspective of a black African migrant rather than viewing 'multicultural Ireland' solely from the standpoint of white Irish protagonists. However, as Reddy also observes, 'Doyle's own positionality – white, Irish, settled, male, economically secure – cannot be ignored: he is the one ventriloquizing blackness, so to speak. In "I Understand", an African speaks for himself but only through the good offices of a white Irishman. From that perspective, the Other remains silent.'[14] I would add that Ailbhe, though not the focalising protagonist, is recruited as a kind of white saviour figure, even asking soon after they meet (though comically, helping to extricate Tom from the unwanted attentions of another woman), 'do you need rescuing?'[15] It is through his relationship with the white Irish love interest that Tom is indeed 'saved'.

A more recently published work (though written a decade before its publication), Oona Frawley's novel *Flight* (2014) is another acclaimed exploration of contemporary migration and border regimes in the Irish context. Frawley uses a third-person omniscient narrator who switches between the four protagonists, all of whom have different experiences of transnational mobility: Elizabeth, her parents Clare and Tom, and

Sandrine, who works as Clare and Tom's carer. Clare and Tom left Ireland in the 1960s in pursuit of Tom's ambitions in the spice trade. From New York City they travel to Vietnam and become embedded in white expat culture amidst the post-war dereliction of Hanoi and the mostly destitute Vietnamese people. Their daughter Elizabeth is compelled to travel with them; miserable in Vietnam, she returns to the United States as soon as she can for college. She moves back to Ireland, and on the slow slide to old age, her parents return too. Their lives intersect with Sandrine's, a woman who comes to Ireland from Zimbabwe on a student visa, leaving her husband and young son behind her. Unbeknownst to her husband, Sandrine is pregnant and hopes that an Irish-born child will enable her and her family to obtain residency in the Republic. Arriving in Ireland in the shadow of the 2004 Citizenship Referendum, however, Sandrine, as a pregnant black African woman, is the target subject of the hostile white gaze of the 'natives' and the nation state. She finds work as a carer for Tom and Clare, and Sandrine and Elizabeth slowly get to know each other. The novel makes clear the vast disparity between the different characters' relation to the border regime and to global mobility. For Clare, Tom, and Elizabeth, no matter what dislocations they may experience, the world is traversed with ease because of their whiteness and their Irish citizenship. The borders that open for Elizabeth are shut to Sandrine or crossed at risk and with severe restrictions.

While there is no idealisation of 'multicultural Ireland' in Frawley's novel, there is as Liam Lannigan has noted a certain 'utopian impulse in the narrative trajectory'.[16] For Lannigan, this is manifested in Sandrine's 'self-actualization and assertion, enabled by an emergent transnational solidarity'.[17] That is, Sandrine's agency is regained through her friendship with Elizabeth. For most of the narrative, Sandrine is almost entirely isolated. She has no friends and little contact with anyone in her immediate environment apart from her employers. In Ireland, Sandrine is at once hyper-visible as 'the migrant other' and yet utterly invisible as a person in her own right: 'here in Ireland, it does not seem possible for her to just be, and for her own voice to be heard'; 'Here, she has no story.'[18] While the narrator delivers these reflections, the narrative at the same time denies Sandrine any connection to other Africans or the diasporic community. 'Sandrine stares at other Africans when she sees them', we are told. 'They do not speak. They exchange glances on the bus, on shopping queues, on the road.'[19] This does not ring true, but it is perhaps a solution to the difficulties of representing a community of colour consciousness as a white majority culture author. The result is the erasure of that community and the re-centring of whiteness. This re-centring is evident in the treatment of Sandrine's deportation. While the injustice of the border regime is made clear, the full violence of deportation is played down, with the narrator even reporting the kindness of the immigration officers as they inform Sandrine that she will be forcibly removed from the country. The concluding focus on Sandrine and Elizabeth's enduring friendship after she has been returned to Zimbabwe brings a hopeful closure despite the violence of the state's migration regime, but again this hopefulness is dependent on interracial harmony at the personal level rather than political struggle and structural change.

Whiteness Decentred: Recent Fiction by Migrant Writers of Colour

These two 'case studies' are included not to specifically critique Doyle's and Frawley's important contribution to the Irish canon of the literature of migration but are presented as two relatively complex examples of a pervasive tendency in that canon. The pervasiveness of the intercultural paradigm across the spheres of policy, advocacy, arts funding, and literary representation in Ireland has the result (whether intentional or not) of centring the white perspectives that have dominated accounts of migration since the 1990s and, moreover, of delegitimating resistance against racist regimes as a reasonable option in achieving justice in favour of depoliticised culturalist models of 'diversity'. While the intercultural trope of the interracial romance plot is used in Cauvery Madhavan's *Paddy Indian* (2001) and in Bisi Adigun's and Doyle's adaptation of *The Playboy of the Western World* (2007), the trope is less common in recent fiction by migrant writers of colour in Ireland. Instead, the most interesting work describes forms of intercultural negotiation and exchange to which white Irish people are largely peripheral or merely a hindrance. For instance, in recent works of fiction by Ifedinma Dimbo, Ebun Joseph Akpoveta, and Melatu Uche Okorie, three Nigerian writers living in Ireland, the female protagonists are most often women from Nigeria or occasionally other African countries whose primary friendships and relationships are with other black African women and men. Akpoveta, Dimbo, and Okorie all challenge traditional oppressive gender roles in their novels and call into question 'a celebratory and conciliatory Irish multicultural self-image in their representations of female migrant protagonists who must constantly struggle to gain an equal place within their own families and Irish society at large'.[20]

In Dimbo's novel *She Was Foolish?* (2012), Gift leaves Nigeria for the United Kingdom with her children to escape her abusive husband Osahon.

Ifeoma, her best friend from Lagos University (who was born and grew up in England), advises Gift to go to Ireland – a place Gift has never heard of – as Gift is pregnant and Ifeoma has heard that it is possible to be granted residency if your child is born in Ireland (the 2004 Citizenship Referendum looms large in Dimbo's novel).[21] The novel ends with a romantic resolution that figures hope for the future but rather than this hinging on the presence of a white person, Gift falls in love with Obinna, an African-American man with Igbo roots. Ebun Joseph Akpoveta's novel *Trapped: Prison Without Walls* (2013) tells the story of Ola Peters, a Nigerian woman who moves to Dublin to pursue a Master's degree and is joined by her husband Deji, a violent abuser. The novel explores the pressure on Ola to remain silent about the abuse she suffers, as well as the lack of support available to her as a migrant of colour and a Nigerian woman in Ireland. Akpoveta critiques the systemic failure of the state and its institutions to intervene in cases of gender-based violence in minority ethnic communities and contexts. This failure means that the equality and protections that the state may afford to white settled Irish citizen women are not as readily available to many other women. The lack of access to resources is compounded by institutionally embedded racist assumptions about particular communities and nationalities. As Akpoveta notes, such access coupled with respect for difference is the real litmus test for 'diversity' in Ireland. As she states in an interview with Asier Altuna-García de Salazar:

> what we have in Ireland is closer to assimilation than integration where to be is to be like. [...] Integration does not manifest itself just in organizing events to share food, music and dance of different cultures. It is in their shared access to resources, in being treated fairly, equally and with respect.[22]

Akpoveta (like Dimbo) concludes her novel on a note of hope, with a hopeful future signposted by Ola's relationship with Ray, not a white saviour but a Nigerian man. While both Dimbo's and Akpoveta's novels employ the romance plot to signal hope and new beginnings, this trope is not used as an allegory for interracial, intercultural harmony, but instead centres relationships between black African people rather than presenting whiteness as the antidote to systemic racism, misogyny, and the obstacles that their women protagonists face and overcome.

Melatu Uche Okorie's debut short story, 'Gathering Thoughts', won the *Metro Eireann* writers' award in 2009. In 2018, her collection of short stories, *This Hostel Life*, was published by Skein Press to immediate acclaim. Okorie came to Ireland to seek asylum and spent eight and a half years in the Direct Provision system, a hostel style of accommodation where international protection applicants stay while they await a decision on their case, which most often takes many years in Ireland's dysfunctional asylum process.[23] She prefaces her stories in *This Hostel Life* with this context, and the book finishes with a short essay by legal scholar Liam Thornton describing the conditions, legal and material, of people seeking protection in Ireland. Okorie, then, explicitly frames her short stories within the political context of the contemporary migration, asylum, and deportation regime. This regime is focalised through the daily lives of her characters in what she calls her 'asylum cycle'. 'This Hostel Life' is the latest published story in the cycle. It is set in a Direct Provision centre where the residents are queuing for the weekly distribution of basic provisions. Okorie emphasises people's resilience while exposing through the narrator's perspective and the characters' dialogue how institutional abuse works at a micro level through power dynamics, enforced dependency, and the manipulation of interpersonal relationships. The narrator Beverlée explains the routines in the centre, where access to food, toiletries, medicine, and other essentials is granted according to a strict and arbitrary schedule set by the centre's management:

> In my last hostel, dey give you provision any day, but it's gonna be one month since you collect last. So if you get toilet paper today, it's gonna be one month before you get another. Dat is why me I happy when dey give me every week for here, but now, me I don feel happy again. Dis direct provision business is all the same, you see, because even if you collect provision for every week or you collect for every month, it is still somebody dat is give you the provision. Nothing is better than when you decide something for yourself.[24]

This apartheid logic of the border regime appears at the micro level of the interpersonal, spelled out in the petty cruelties of the manager's actions at the end of the narrative. When Beverlée's friend Ngozo objects to the manager giving honey to one resident and withholding it from Ngozo, the manager responds by closing the store room and so leaving the waiting residents without their provisions for the week, punishing everyone for Ngozo's transgression against the 'master' and isolating Ngozo from her resentful co-residents.

The dialogue and narrative voice also manifest a wry comic grasp of the absurdity of the situation and a keen ear for the witty, sometimes harsh give and take of the women's conversation. Okorie's representation of the multicultural community created by people in Direct Provision resonates with the analysis of Vukašin Nedeljković, an artist-activist who created the website *Asylum Archive* and who is himself a survivor of Ireland's Direct Provision system. While powerfully condemning the system and its destruction of years of human life and potential, Nedeljković also emphasises the strength and resourcefulness of people kept in this state of exception: 'Direct Provision Centres cannot be perceived only as the sites of incarceration, social exclusion or extreme poverty.' They are also, he continues, 'sites where different nationalities and ethnic groups exist(ed) and persist(ed) in spite of the confinement created by the State'.[25] 'This Hostel Life' presents the 'multilingual, multiethnic and multiracial' community created in Direct Provision, focalised through the first-person narrator, Beverlée, whose voice Okorie created to capture this multicultural reality.[26] Okorie describes Beverlée's language as a feat of communicative ingenuity by a woman with little French and less English, 'made up of the Englishes that are being spoken around her: the West African Broken English, Standard English, the American English that she picks up from watching television', filtered through her Congolese inflections.[27]

The setting for Okorie's short story 'Under the Awning' is a writers' workshop, where the main protagonist takes her turn reading her work – a 'story within the story' – to the group. The figure of the 'white saviour' and the metaphor of intercultural harmony are deconstructed through the character of Dermot, a friend of the mother in the workshop story. Dermot 'had worked with a lot of charities in Africa' and talks excitedly about his plans to start a project 'helping migrant children and teenagers to integrate through football and dance' while grooming the young protagonist, eventually offering her 100 euros to have sex with him.[28] Once the narrator has finished reading her story, the class critique confirms the pervasive racism that the narrative described. She is told that her story is too 'bleak and negative', and that the main character is 'paranoid' and does not adequately explain why she 'feels such self-loathing and self-hatred'.[29] So, the writer changes the story. She resolves the discomfort of her white peers by interpreting the racist aggression she had described as the product of her own over-thinking:

> *Your classmates who asked their friends to mind their bags were actually not doing anything wrong: the bus driver who dropped you two stops away from your bus stop could have done so be due to road works; the man in the supermarket who asked your mother for a BJ is just sick; and the children who called out 'Blackie' at you whenever they saw you passing could just be what they were, children.*[30]

Border Regimes: Race, Migration, and the Literary System

It is not possible to speak of migration in the contemporary world without speaking of the border, and borders in their various manifestations feature heavily in contemporary writing by migrant writers of colour about migration in Ireland. The border is not confined to the border of the state or the mobilities that borders impede or facilitate, the lives they enable to flourish and those they are intended to let die. National literatures can also be places where the border appears. For poet and academic Sandeep Parmar, the English lyric poem operates through a form of racialised border politics. 'To my mind', she says, 'it is impossible to consider the lyric without fully interrogating its inherent premise of universality, its coded whiteness'.[31] The same can be said of the Irish lyric; it encodes assumptions about shared 'experience, language and tradition' and 'national idealisations of the state and its culture'.[32]

Oritsegbemi Emmanuel Jakpa addresses poetic and global border regimes in his poem 'Harmattan', which invokes one of Seamus Heaney's best-known lyrics, 'Digging', in articulating the realities of violence and displacement in the post-colony and at the border. In 'Harmattan', the noise of the digger's spade outside the speaker's window signals our intrusion into the memories of the digging man and his time in Kirikiri Prison, where he was 'useless as free papers in a printing press'.[33] The poem makes connections between cheap life in the post-colony and colonisation, between the colonial appropriation of rights to oil in the Niger Delta and the post-independence history of bloody conflict, sanctioned murder of activists, environmental destruction, and the violent displacement of the population, in the name of corporate and government power and profit: 'So the periodic spade strikes, each stroke | the rasped desolation and anger of the soul. | Tribulations of a black-gold age.'[34] By the close of the poem, the digger has become the digger of the oil company that the speaker blocks with his body: 'Before the harmattan and the digger | unmoving I sit'.[35] The processes and consequences of racial capitalism are manifest in the global border regime, a global system of biopolitical classification based on racism and wealth. Jakpa's description recalls exactly Hage's diagnosis of the global control of movement:

> In our airtight dragnet, roadblocks everywhere,
> Borders tight as steel ziplocks
> checkmate every hope.
> Yet many people of lesser talent
> slip out, unabated, with ease.[36]

'Harmattan' implicates Ireland as part of the world system that Jakpa describes and uses the deliberate invocation of Heaney's lyric to reconstruct other lives and genealogies than those that define the traditional Irish lyric. While Jakpa works primarily in poetry for the page, Dagogo Hart is part of a new generation of migrant poets of colour in Ireland whose work spans performance and spoken-word genres. His poem 'Badagry' addresses the genealogical connection between the colonisation of Africa and the Atlantic slave trade, and the conditions of the post-colony and contemporary migration from the continent. Badagry is a coastal town in Hart's home place of Lagos, Nigeria, and his poem recalls its history as a slave port, 'the place of no return', from the sixteenth to the nineteenth centuries: 'things haven't changed in a thousand years | Badagry. | The place of no return.'[37] Hart connects contemporary globalisation to the forced migration of African people as slaves to fuel the world capitalist system, and he connects his own migration to those of his ancestors, a lineage of forced leavings. People may now 'leave of their own accord', but the conditions of their movement are marked by the necropolitical divide between colonised and coloniser that still structures global relations.

The border often manifests as the inaccessibility of spaces and opportunities to which access is taken for granted by the privileged subject. In 'This Country That Is Yours', Nita Mishra places the carefree mobility of the poem's addressee against the stuckedness of the speaker in short, staccato lines that contain and convey her paralysis and anger: 'Like streams in the monsoons | hurtling down | the pebbly surface | unrestrained || Leaving fear far behind | trusting your strength, your instinct | you and your bike | disappear beyond the mist to | the other side || The other side | unreachable | For me.'[38] For many migrant writers, the established Irish literary institutions have operated as another kind of border control. As Okorie notes, it is difficult for writers lacking in mainstream cultural capital to negotiate the literary system, especially in relation to publishing. In addition, material difficulties in terms of 'day to day survival' preclude the kind of 'dedication and hard work' that writing for publication takes.[39] Dimbo also emphasises the racialised nature of Irish literary norms, including circulation and reception; when she published her novel Dimbo 'was told by a reputable bookseller that nobody is interested in what a Nigerian has to say'.[40] For the writers who were part of WWINI (Women Writers in the New Ireland) Network, the 'canon' of Irish literature was also a technology of exclusion. As Olutoyin Pamela Akinjobi notes, 'there appear to be ethnic boundaries in Irish literature, which set conditions as to who can be included in it, and who cannot'.[41] Akpoveta describes the barriers she came up against from publishers, mainstream bookshops, and media outlets when trying to publish her novel. The migrant person of colour has to become an entrepreneur of the self in order to 'negotiate racial stratification' in the literary and publishing milieu.[42] As Sara Martín-Ruiz further points out in an essay on Dimbo's and Okorie's fiction, self-publishing has been supplemented by publishing in 'small, often immigrant-focused media' that have not generally provided a platform to mainstream notice.[43]

However, these obstacles are being short-circuited by a younger generation of migrant writers of colour in Ireland who are producing some of the most interesting and innovative work in poetry and performance poetry. The spoken-word scene in Ireland has not depended on established routes of publication and circulation and has developed independently of literary and funding institutions. Writers and performers often work with others in collaboration and collectives, disseminating their work via video and other digital media as well as reaching large audiences through live performance.

Performance Poetry, Digital Cultures, and the New Generation

The surge in popularity of performance poetry in Ireland during the early 2000s (and particularly during the recession), coupled with the proliferation of online forms of production and circulation, has enabled poets to produce their work independently of the funding, publication, and circulation structures of established Irish literary institutions. Writing in *The Stinging Fly* in 2016, Dave Lordan describes the proliferation of performance poetry and a 'multimedia revolution' in the mediums and dissemination of poetry. He asserts that this situation 'seems to have been made for the political or, if you wish, public poet'.[44] He draws a connection between these developments – most importantly, their autonomy from established institutions – and the political turn in Irish writing since the 2008 crash, with many poets performing at marches and demonstrations and contributing work to political campaigns such as the campaign to Repeal the 8th, which succeeded in changing Ireland's restrictive abortion laws.

Writers of migrant, minority ethnic, LGBTQI, and working-class backgrounds have been central in driving these transformations. Often more interested in being accessible to a large and diverse audience than in publication in literary magazines, a generation of poets of colour and of migrant background who are now coming into their own often work in spoken word and other forms of live performance (though many also publish page-based poetry), circulate their work in video formats (whether

DIY or in more elaborately produced versions), and work in collaborations and collectives with other artists. Some of the most influential spoken-word poets in the Irish scene over the last decade have been writers of colour, such as Abby Oliveira, a spoken-word poet from Glasgow based in Northern Ireland, as well as Raven and Clara Rose Thornton, both poets of colour who came to Dublin from the United States. Projects such as Fried Plantain Collective, established by spoken-word poet Osaro Azams, and the Word Up Collective (which includes well-known spoken-word artists Felicia Olusanya [FeliSpeaks] and Sasha Terfous) have fostered artists working at the crossroads between poetry, hip-hop, spoken-word, and other musical and performance genres, and have brought them large audiences through performances and curated events at (for instance) the Dublin Fringe Festival and Lingo, the hugely successful Dublin-based spoken-word festival that ran from 2015 to 2017.

Writing about the development of spoken-word and performance poetry in the United States, Susan B. A. Somers-Willett notes that these genres have become closely associated with marginalised identities. Somers-Willett notes that slam poetry's 'emphasis on diversity, inclusion, and democracy have resulted in a "pluralism" among its poets' and that in the US, as Tyler Hoffman observes, spoken-word poetry became associated with 'powerful social movements that reframed – and validated – cultural identities of minorities'.[45] These observations hold true in the Irish context where the centrality of a performative personal 'I', a progressive political position, and an emphasis on identity and narrative are also features across the genres of performance poetry.

How do these emerging migrant writers of colour, no longer objects in someone else's imagining of multicultural Ireland, engage with issues of identity, belonging, race, racism, and migration in a contemporary Ireland viewed as part of the world system rather than an isolated island nation? In and through performance poetry, migrant and minority ethnic writers 'claim, negotiate, and sometimes refigure marginalized identities'.[46] The performance/poem itself constitutes an act of exploring, asserting, and reconfiguring identity against the backdrop of a majority white settled society that takes whiteness and an imagined homogeneous Irishness as the grounds of belonging. 'And he asked me | 'No, where are you *really* from?' begins 'Where am I from?', a poem by young Portadown poet Anesu Khanya Mtowa.[47] In 'Duel Citizenship', Denise Chaila repeats the line, 'Where are you from, originally?' with varying inflections until the line becomes self-parodying. 'Belonging', she argues, must be taken, not given, when your belonging is a point of public contestation: 'I have spent my whole life learning that I must make myself take my belonging | It will not just be handed to you.'[48] Her art is one powerful way of asserting ownership of her own experience and claiming the dual citizenship that is her due, despite some thinking her 'beyond the pale'.[49]

Younger feminist women writers are challenging traditions, practices, silences, and erasures across social, political, aesthetic, and literary contexts. Chiamaka Enyi-Amadi's video-poem 'I Will Not Be Shamed' is an unapologetically political poem that seeks to raise awareness about female genital mutilation (FGM) in Ireland. Enyi-Amadi's introduction situates FGM as a European as well as Asian and African practice that is on the increase in Ireland, despite its status as a criminal act. The poem mimics the form of prayer, using the refrain as well as Christian and Islamic symbolism to enact a powerful refusal of shame in the name of culture or religion:

> In rebuilding this temple
> I will not be shamed.
>
> Let me in to the tabernacle
> I will not be shamed.
>
> I have washed my sheets
> cleaned my linen of all past sins.
> I will not be shamed.[50]

Felicia Olusanya, also known as spoken-word artist FeliSpeaks, is also explicit about the political role of her poetry. Many of her poems and performances centre the lives of women and girls who are not the privileged subjects of a dominant feminism and who struggle to break free of the external and internal bonds of patriarchal structures. 'What About Us' and the longer spoken-word performance *Lady Na Master & the Synaptic Room* (performed in Smock Alley Theatre in Dublin on 16 June 2018) foreground the violence and shame women and girls are subjected to, particularly women of colour, and the necessity of resistance and reclamation. Both pieces speak explicitly within the context of feminist activism in Ireland and elsewhere, resisting ideologies that leave some traumas unspoken and many women and girls invisible and excluded from the bonds of feminist solidarity. 'Who will march for us?' the speaker of 'What About Us' asks, 'for girls who are fattened, bred and fed for men whose appetites fill like basket water, | Devoured but never enough.'[51] Both texts implicitly refuse the hegemonic norm of womanhood whereby the migrant or minority ethnic woman is always an add-on and insist that the lives of women and girls pushed to the margins, and issues often seen as too difficult to address, must also be part of the struggle of all women in solidarity. Olusanya has said she wants her work to 'shake the table of the diaspora' in Ireland, by articulating experiences that are masked by silence and taboo.[52] The need to break through such silences is also articulated by Enyi-Amadi: '*We speak too silently of women who are broken. | We talk in whispers of girls | whose bodies are in need | of repair.*'[53] Olusanya's 'For Our Mothers' expresses this desire to break free of the narratives and norms 'about womanhood, and what is expected of a woman' that are passed down transgenerationally between women within a patriarchal order:

> Nne, I can't do this any longer.
> I cannot fold my arms and rest,
> Watching lonely wives wrap their head ties so large,
> Filling it with confiscated feelings,
> Hoping truths get knotted and bound on Sunday mornings,
> Covering up tired dark eyes with white powder and red lipstick,
>
> [. . .] Our mothers are dancing on thanksgiving Sundays
> With bitter stories in their mouths
> Too afraid to spit it out
> Their knees darkened by the weight of prayer[54]

Conclusion

The connection between immigration, politics, and cultural expression, between migrant justice and the arts, has been apparent in Ireland since the 1990s. It is apparent in the use of the arts within migrant justice campaigns, as with Young, Paperless and Powerful, the youth group of Justice for the Undocumented, who have used spoken-word poetry to articulate their right to legal and social inclusion in the state. Literary writing by people of migrant backgrounds has often been published in NGO (non-governmental organisation) reports or in publications sponsored by NGOs, as in the 2017 Immigrant Council of Ireland's *My Language, My Words* project, or in anthologies such as *Embers of Words* (2012), edited by Theophilus Ejorh and part-sponsored by the New Communities Partnership. These interconnections have also been apparent in the community arts sector, where at times the approach of cultural institutions to 'migrant communities', taking its lead from state-led integration strategies and interculturalist rhetoric, has tended to erase people of migrant and ethnic minority background as writers and cultural producers in their own right.

The last two years have seen significant shifts in this situation. Following the release of data that demonstrated the almost total absence of writers of colour in major Irish literary magazines (*Poetry Ireland Review* and *The Stinging Fly*), Poetry Ireland published their 2018 Inclusion and Diversity Strategy, which stated, refreshingly enough, that 'we do not believe this mission to be altruistic; we know that it is necessary for the health and relevance of Irish poetry'.[55] Create, the National Development Agency for Collaborative Arts, has begun to redress the racialised dynamics of the white artist/minority community dyad in significant ways, by, for instance, awarding an Arts & Activism bursary to Vukašin Nedeljković in 2017 and a research and development mentoring award to musician and writer Farah Elle, and by launching in the same year a series of residencies for artists from 'culturally diverse backgrounds'.[56]

However, it would be a mistake to place too much weight on established institutions when considering the inevitable transformation of the literary and cultural landscape in Ireland by a new generation of writers and cultural producers, many of whom have created their own platforms and collaborations without institutional support. Even initiatives in more traditional forms of publishing such as Skein Press (publishers of Melatu Uche Okorie) or the 2019 anthology *Writing Home: The 'New Irish' Poets*, co-edited by Chiamaka Enyi-Amadi and Pat Boran for Dedalus Press, are the result of these creative, collaborative, often resolutely autonomous, and grassroots energies. It seems that the literary establishment in Ireland may be learning to listen to the way emergent migrant writers of colour in Ireland are writing rather than waiting for them to write the way we are used to reading.

Notes

1. Ghassan Hage, *Is Racism an Environmental Threat?* (Cambridge: Polity Press, 2017), Kindle edn, loc. 605.
2. In particular, see Charlotte McIvor, *Migration and Performance in Contemporary Ireland: Towards a New Interculturalism* (Basingstoke: Palgrave Macmillan, 2016); and Charlotte McIvor and Matthew Spangler, eds., *Staging Intercultural Ireland: New Plays and Practitioner Perspectives* (Cork, Ireland: Cork University Press, 2014).
3. See Pilar Villar-Argáiz, ed., *Literary Visions of Multicultural Ireland: The Immigrant in Contemporary Irish Literature* (Manchester: Manchester University Press, 2014).

4. Anne O'Connor, Andrea Ciribuco, and Anita Naughton, *Language and Migration in Ireland* (Dublin: Immigrant Council of Ireland, 2017), p. 51.
5. Fatima El-Tayeb, '"The Birth of a European Public": Migration, Postnationality, and Race in the Uniting of Europe', *American Quarterly*, 60.3 (September 2008), pp. 649–70 (p. 652).
6. Ibid.
7. Elena Moreo and Carla de Tono, 'Theorizing Migrant-Led Activism', in Ronit Lentin and Elena Moreo, eds., *Migrant Activism and Integration from Below* (Basingstoke: Palgrave Macmillan, 2012), pp. 21–41 (p. 30).
8. Elena Moreo, 'On Visibility and Invisibility: Migrant Practices between Regimes of Representation and Self-Determination', in *Migrant Activism and Integration from Below*, pp. 72–94 (p. 77).
9. Ronit Lentin, 'There Is No Movement: A Brief History of Migrant-Led Activism in Ireland', in *Migrant Activism and Integration from Below*, pp. 42–78 (p. 48).
10. Trócaire Poetry Competition: www.trocaire.org/getinvolved/poetry-competition [accessed 5 March 2019].
11. Angela T. Carr, 'Mountain of Butterflies', *Forced to Flee: 'This Is Our Exodus'– Trócaire and Poetry Ireland Poetry Competition 2016* (Dublin: Trócaire and Poetry Ireland, 2016), p. 8: www.poetryireland.ie/content/files/2016_Trocaire.pdf [accessed 5 March 2019].
12. Dale Tracy, *With the Witnesses: Poetry, Compassion and Claimed Experience* (Montreal and Kingston, Canada: McGill-Queen's University Press, 2017), p. 5.
13. Jason King, 'Irish Multicultural Fiction: Metaphors of Miscegenation and Interracial Romance', in James P. Byrne, Padraig Kirwan, and Michael O'Sullivan, eds., *Affecting Irishness: Negotiating Cultural Identity Within and Beyond the Nation* (Oxford: Peter Lang, 2009), pp. 159–77 (p. 167). For an astute development of King's argument, see Amanda Tucker, 'Strangers in a Strange Land? The New Irish Multicultural Fiction', in *Literary Visions of Multicultural Ireland*, pp. 50–63.
14. Maureen Reddy, 'Reading and Writing Race in Ireland: Roddy Doyle and *Metro Eireann*', *Irish University Review*, 35.2 (Autumn/Winter 2005), pp. 374–88 (p. 386).
15. Roddy Doyle, *The Deportees and Other Stories* (London: Jonathan Cape, 2007), p. 233.
16. Liam Lanigan, 'Non-Nationalizing the Story of Ireland: Transnationalism and Narrative in Oona Frawley's *Flight*', *Irish University Review*, 47.2 (2017), pp. 234–50 (p. 248).
17. Ibid.
18. Oona Frawley, *Flight* (Dublin: Tramp Press, 2014), pp. 117, 118.
19. Ibid., p. 142.
20. Asier Altuna-García de Salazar, 'Multiculturalism and the Immigrant "Irish Woman" After the Celtic Tiger: Marginalisation, Gender-based Violence and

Family Dysfunction in Ebun Akpoveta's *Trapped: Prison Without Walls*', *Irish Studies Review*, 24.1 (2016), pp. 95–104 (p. 96).
21. The 2004 Citizenship Referendum removed the constitutional right to Irish citizenship for children born in Ireland to two 'non-national' parents. For a detailed critical analysis of the referendum and the lead up to it, see Eithne Luibhéid, *Pregnant on Arrival: Making the Illegal Immigrant* (Minneapolis, MN: University of Minnesota Press, 2013).
22. Asier Altuna-García de Salazar, '"Migrant Women Are Always Added": In Conversation with Ebun Joseph Akpoveta', *Estudios Irlandeses*, 12 (2017), pp. 158–66 (pp. 160, 161).
23. For information and testimony about the Direct Provision system, see Vukašin Nedeljković, *Asylum Archive* (Dublin: Create, 2018); and Ronit Lentin, 'Asylum Seekers, Ireland and the Return of the Repressed', *Irish Studies Review*, 24.1 (2016), pp. 21–34. For grassroots activist resistance to direct provision and deportation in Ireland, see MASI – Movement of Asylum Seekers in Ireland's Facebook page: https://m.facebook.com/MASI-Movement-of-Asylum-Seekers-in-Ireland-321969801334321 [accessed 5 March 2019].
24. Melatu Uche Okorie, *This Hostel Life* (Dublin: Skein Press, 2018), p. 3.
25. Vukašin Nedeljković, 'Direct Provision Centers as Manifestations of Resistance', *Transactions*, 2 (2017): http://transactionspublication.com/direct-provision-centers-as-manifestations-of-resistance/ [accessed 5 March 2019].
26. Ibid.
27. Sara Martín-Ruiz, 'Melatu Okorie: An Introduction to Her Work and a Conversation with the Author', *Lit: Literature Interpretation Theory*, 28.2 (2017), pp. 172–84 (p. 181).
28. Okorie, *This Hostel Life*, p. 33.
29. Ibid., pp. 37, 38, 39.
30. Ibid., p. 40; emphasis original.
31. Sandeep Parmar with Bhanu Kapil, 'Lyric Violence, the Nomadic Subject and the Fourth Space', *Poetry London*, 88 (Autumn 2017), pp. 29–32 (p. 29).
32. Ibid.
33. Oritsegbemi Emmanuel Jakpa, 'Harmattan', *African American Review*, 44.1-2 (Spring/Summer 2011), pp. 267–8 (p. 267).
34. Ibid., p. 268.
35. Ibid.
36. Ibid., p. 267.
37. Dagogo Hart, 'Badagry', *Boundless & Bare* podcast, Episode 3: Dagogo Hart, 10 May 2018: https://boundlessandbare.com/podcast/2018/5/10/ubp5ft5odlli3cqomgpbu3ei7nqi9q [accessed 5 March 2019].
38. Nita Mishra, 'This Country That Is Yours', *Baobab*, 4 (2018), p. 62.
39. Martín-Ruiz, 'Melatu Okorie', p. 177.

40. Sara Martín-Ruiz, '"The Way the Irish Asylum System Turns People into Un-human is My Problem": An Interview with Ifedinma Dimbo', *Estudios Irlandeses*, 10 (2015), 109–14 (p. 114).
41. Jody Allen Randolph, *Close to the Next Moment: Interviews from a Changing Ireland* (Manchester: Carcanet, 2010), p. 196.
42. Altuna-García de Salazar, 'Migrant Women Are Always Added', p. 165.
43. Sara Martín-Ruiz, 'Literature and Dissidence Under Direct Provision: Melatu Okorie and Ifedinma Dimbo', in Pilar Villar Argáiz, ed., *Irishness on the Margins: Minority and Dissident Identities* (Basingstoke: Palgrave Macmillan, 2018), pp. 263–83 (p. 265).
44. Dave Lordan, 'The Multimedia Revolution in Poetry', *The Stinging Fly*, 33.2 (Spring 2016), pp. 222–3 (p. 223).
45. Susan B.A. Somers-Willett, *The Cultural Politics of Slam Poetry: Race, Identity, and the Performance of Popular Verse in America* (Ann Arbor, MI: The University of Michigan Press, 2009), p. 6.
46. Somers-Willett, *The Cultural Politics of Slam Poetry*, p. 14.
47. Anesu Khanya Mtowa, 'Where Am I From?', *Baobab*, 4 (2018), p. 8.
48. Denise Chaila, 'Duel Citizenship', Soundcloud, 29 January 2019: https://soundcloud.com/user-556625270 [accessed 31 March 2019]. On the theme of identity and belonging, see also Sahar Ali, 'An Introduction', dir. by Victoria Curtis, YouTube, 4 May 2018: www.youtube.com/watch?v=95NN1Mt-GMs&t=1s [accessed 5 March 2019]; and Sasha Terfous, 'Identity', RTE2fm, Represent, YouTube, 25 April 2018: www.youtube.com/watch?v=mWP31aIg-6Q [accessed 5 March 2019].
49. Chaila, 'Duel Citizenship'.
50. Chiamaka Enyi-Amadi, 'I Will Not Be Shamed', text quoted by permission of the author. For the video-poem, see *The Unimaginable Things*, 7 February 2019: https://theunimaginablethings.wordpress.com/2019/02/07/i-will-not-be-shamed-fgm-awareness/ [accessed 5 March 2019].
51. FeliSpeaks, 'What About Us?', text quoted by permission of the author. For the video-poem, see Felispeaks, 'What About Us?', filmed by Caliburn TV, Word Up Collective, YouTube, 20 April 2017: www.youtube.com/watch?time_continue=126&v=QW6q6rMbfLg [accessed 5 March 2019].
52. FeliSpeaks, 'For Our Mothers', text quoted by permission of the author. For the video-poem, see Felispeaks, YouTube, 8 September 2017: www.youtube.com/watch?v=cRYxJSeZhYw [accessed 5 March 2019].
53. Enyi-Amadi, 'I Will Not Be Shamed'; emphasis original.
54. FeliSpeaks, 'For Our Mothers'.
55. Poetry Ireland/Éigse Éireann, *Inclusion & Diversity Strategy 2018*: www.poetryireland.ie/content/files/PoetryIreland_InclusionDiversity2018-20.pdf [accessed 12 March 2019].
56. Create: National Development Agency for Collaborative Arts, 'Arts and Cultural Diversity': www.create-ireland.ie/evaluations-and-case-studies/diversity [accessed 30 March 2019].

Coda: Tom Murphy and Brian Friel

Patrick Lonergan

At a public event in October 2001, the Irish playwright Declan Hughes was called upon to define the differences between Tom Murphy (1935–2018) and Brian Friel (1929–2015) – and, in particular, to speculate about why Friel's work had achieved international success while Murphy's remained generally unknown beyond Ireland. Hughes was quick to reply. 'Friel', he said, 'is like the Beatles': he writes plays that are loved by audience members whether they are aged nine or ninety. But Murphy is more like the Rolling Stones: 'catchy but with a raw, often dark edge. You can't really understand [Murphy's] plays until you've experienced the rage of adolescence, and the frustration of adulthood.'[1]

The audience listening to these remarks laughed, apparently finding the analogy instantly comprehensible. Hughes had nimbly encapsulated the received wisdom about both dramatists: that Friel is an accessible playwright whose works are sometimes bittersweet but for the most part uplifting – while Murphy places emotional demands upon his audiences but offers them rewarding (if intense) experiences in return. That distinction in turn explains the relative international stature of the two writers, Hughes implied.

My aim here is to demonstrate how that received wisdom is based on an incomplete understanding of Friel and Murphy – but also to concede that if writers, critics, and audiences have learned to think about the pair in the manner described above, that is because there are good reasons for them to have done so. In defence of Hughes's analogy, we might, for example, think about the approach each writer took to dramatising the impact of the Great Irish Famine of the late 1840s – which in Friel's case was his 1980 masterpiece *Translations* and in Murphy's 1968 Brechtian tragedy *Famine*.

Rather than directly addressing the Great Hunger, Friel sets the action of his play in the decade before that catastrophe. Part of the power of *Translations* comes from its audience's knowledge that the mostly peaceful setting of the 1830s is about to give way to a major disaster: one that will not be shown on stage. Friel demonstrates how that tragedy is driven not just by colonialism (the play's subject) but also by environmental collapse; indeed, the interplay of those forces is signalled by one character's identification of a 'sweet smell' in the air: in the world of the play, that odour comes from the burning canvas tents of English soldiers, but it is also an allusion to the potato blight that caused the Great Hunger.[2] *Translations* thus exemplifies how Friel's plays are often set in the moments before something irrevocable occurs – the emigration of a young man to America in *Philadelphia, Here I Come!* (1964), the death of a family patriarch in *Aristocrats* (1979), the last summer before a family is broken up in *Dancing at Lughnasa* (1990), or the final collapse of Gaelic Ireland in *Translations*.

Murphy, in contrast, has almost always written dramas set in the moments 'after tragedy' (to borrow the phrase that gave the title to his first collection of plays).[3] Where *Translations* ends with a death, *Famine* begins with one, opening with the funeral of the daughter of the protagonist, John Connor. 'How am I to overcome it?' John asks, devastated by his loss.[4] But before the play is over, John will be forced to overcome many worse challenges, ultimately determining that he has no choice but to murder the surviving members of his family, reasoning that a fast death is more merciful than leaving them to starvation. In almost all of Murphy's plays, his characters grapple with similarly appalling choices. The death of children is a persistent image, appearing not just in *Famine* but also in *The Sanctuary Lamp* (1975), *Bailegangaire* (1985), *The House* (2000), and *Alice Trilogy* (2005), among others. Such plays are both moving and inspiring in showing how their characters strive to rebuild themselves after the worst has happened – but Murphy will always demand that we gaze unblinkered at the despair that they must first overcome.

Yet, while allowing for the fact that Hughes's comment was intended as an incisive joke rather than a considered appraisal, it is important to resist the suggestion that Friel and Murphy are as different from each other as the above contrast might suggest. After all, the observation that prompted Hughes's comment – that Friel had achieved international success but that Murphy had not – overlooks the reality that, of the two, it was Murphy who first made an international breakthrough. That was when *A Whistle in the Dark* (1961), which had been rejected by the Abbey, was staged to great acclaim in London. Friel would have to wait until 1966 to match that success, as he did when *Philadelphia, Here I Come!* opened on Broadway.

And those first international successes demonstrate the limitations of the ideas that exist about the relationship between the two authors in many other ways. Murphy is often considered the more adventurous of the two playwrights, but *Whistle* is technically conservative, written in the form of a tragedy that (mostly) observes the Aristotelian unities and is presented in a (mostly) realistic style. *Philadelphia*, however, features what for the time was a markedly innovative approach to characterisation in Friel's decision to split his lead character Gar into public and private personae, each played by a different actor.

But before we judge *Philadelphia* to be the more innovative play, we might consider how each work reacted against existing traditions. *Whistle* was written from Murphy's determination to reject the dominance of the country kitchen as a setting within the Irish theatre, instead presenting the action in urban England.[5] Yet much of *Philadelphia* takes place in exactly the setting that Murphy was reacting against, and at the time of its Dublin premiere it was criticised for being too similar to the Abbey plays of the 1950s.[6] Towards the end of his career, however, Friel would often subvert and complicate the stage image of the kitchen, in such plays as *Dancing at Lughnasa* and *Wonderful Tennessee* (1993) – while Murphy would write his way back into that setting in *Bailegangaire*. In short, a tendency detectable in the writing of one dramatist can usually be found in the work of the other, even if they rarely mined the same seams simultaneously.

Something similar can be said of the tone of each writer's plays. In a 1967 lecture titled 'Theatre of Hope and Despair', Friel expressed his frustration with dramatists who present humanity as 'lost, groping, confused, anxious, [and] disillusioned'.[7] But if he seemed to reject the bleakness of writers such as Beckett, he did so partly because he was seeking to resist that predisposition in himself – one that can be detected subterraneanly throughout his writing.[8] Murphy's rage was often visible on the surface – as was apparent when he attacked the Catholic Church in *The Sanctuary Lamp* or the hypocrisies of small-town life in *The Wake* (1997). But Friel too could express rage, whether in the controlled fury of his treatment of Bloody Sunday in *The Freedom of the City* (1973), his dramatisation of the violent rejection of a gay visitor to an isolated community in *The Gentle Island* (1971), or his ferocious satire about a government scheme to turn the west of Ireland into a mass graveyard for Irish-Americans in *The Mundy Scheme* (1969).

And in both writers' *oeuvres*, the most negative treatment of what it means to be an artist appears not in Murphy's plays but in Friel's – that is, in *Give Me Your Answer, Do!* (1997), in which a failing writer seeks to persuade an American university to purchase his archive by admitting to having written two (unpublished) pornographic novels. Murphy too would see the act of writing as representing a kind of Faustian pact, but in his major exploration of that theme – *The Gigli Concert* (1983) – he showed that the artist can overcome mundane preoccupations to achieve moments of miraculous transformation, as happens when his primary character, the washed-up psychotherapist JPW King, acquires the ability to sing like the tenor Gigli.

A further similarity is how Friel and Murphy both displayed a persistent preoccupation with storytelling, whereby the act of delivering a narrative is presented metaphorically as an encapsulation of the entirety of a human life. For Friel, that theme was explored in his 1979 play *Faith Healer*, in which the eponymous healer, named Frank Hardy, speaks directly to the audience about the events that led to his death. Elements of his story are contradicted by two other monologues, one delivered by Frank's wife Grace and the other by his business manager Teddy. The resultant confusion – something that Friel would later describe as a 'necessary uncertainty' – becomes the precursor and precondition for the creation of the play's meaning.[9]

In *Bailegangaire*, Murphy takes the audience in the opposite direction, moving from confusion to revelation through his characterisation of Mommo – a senile old woman who repeats the same story night after night about a laughing competition that resulted in several deaths. On the day in which the play is set, Mommo's granddaughters Mary and Dolly finally cajole Mommo into completing her tale and, in doing so, they reveal the circumstances that brought about the death of Mommo's husband and of their own brother Tom.

Faith Healer and *Bailegangaire* place intense demands upon audiences' concentration, requiring them to listen carefully to complex stories that involve long periods of unbroken narration. But it is Murphy's play that ends with a moment of reconciliation, concluding with his characters lying in bed together and imagining the future of a baby who will soon be born to Dolly. In Friel's drama, the action concludes with Frank's death; and since the audience knows that Frank's only child died at birth and that Grace later committed suicide, they will realise that he has literally reached the end of his line. In a comparison of these two plays, it is Friel rather than Murphy who seems to want to paint it black.

Where the Beatles/Stones analogy might seem more appropriate, however, is in the importance of music and musicality for both writers. Friel and Murphy draw extensively on music – from opera to orchestral compositions to pop – using it both incidentally and as integrated elements of the action. Friel's tendency is to include music that is accessible and lively, as seen in the use of Chopin's scherzos and waltzes in *Aristocrats* or the popular melodies of Thomas Moore and Cole Porter in *The Home Place* (2005) and *Dancing at Lughnasa* respectively. One of his late plays, *Performances* (2003), even places the composer Leoš Janáček onstage, having him appear alongside a string quartet who perform his *Intimate Letters* in its entirety. And one of Friel's most famous scenes is the wordless dance of the Mundy sisters in *Lughnasa*, performed to the beat of a traditional Irish melody called 'the Masons Apron'.

Murphy's choices are more wide-ranging. They include the use of a delicate Schubert nocturne that both begins and ends *Bailegangaire* (underscoring the play's treatment of the theme of repetition) and the integration of Berlioz's *Symphonie Fantastique* into *The Morning After Optimism* (1971), the impact of which is to emphasise the dreamlike quality of that play. *The Wake* features a long scene in which members of a family perform 'party pieces', each of which subtly reveals character and advances the plot, drawing on traditional Irish airs, minstrelsy, and popular standards. And perhaps most importantly, in *The Gigli Concert* Murphy integrates opera throughout, notably in a technically mesmerising scene in which one of his characters narrates a version of Gigli's life story in careful synchronicity with a recording of Toselli's *Serenade*. In Friel and Murphy's use of music, we therefore find differences of approach in an area of shared interest.

So perhaps it should be suggested that many of the supposed differences between Friel and Murphy arise because more is known about the former than the latter. Friel, for example, is sometimes referred to as the 'Irish Chekhov', but Murphy was also influenced by that writer, as evident in his 2004 adaptation of *The Cherry Orchard* – a play that also influenced *The House*. Both men directed their own plays: Friel did so unhappily (with the premieres of *Molly Sweeney* in 1994 and *Give Me Your Answer, Do!* three years later), but Murphy staged successful revivals of *Bailegangaire* in 2001, *Alice Trilogy* in 2006, and *The Sanctuary Lamp* in 2008. Friel has rightly been praised for the impact that his Field Day Theatre company had when it toured rural Ireland – often activating latent meanings in his plays, as for instance when his *Making History* (1988) travelled to towns associated with its hero Hugh O'Neill.[10] But during the same period (the early 1980s), Tom Murphy was working closely with Galway's Druid Theatre, which took some of his plays on what that company jokingly termed URTs (unusual rural tours). That included taking *Conversations on a Homecoming* (1985) on a tour of Irish prisons, a setting that must have enhanced that play's exploration of the themes of freedom and escape.[11]

Put simply, Friel is often praised for doing things that Murphy did too, but without the same level of notice.

Ultimately, it might be best to see Friel and Murphy as operating not in opposition or competition, but rather symbiotically. *Philadelphia, Here I Come!* might not have succeeded internationally if *A Whistle in the Dark* had not first shown that an audience for Irish plays existed; and Murphy might not have been willing to risk creating Mommo if Friel had not first created Frank Hardy. Friel dedicated much of his career to exploring the roots and legacies of the Northern Ireland Troubles, and much of the scholarship on his work has sought to present him in that context. But Murphy carried out a similarly forensic investigation of the Irish Republic, especially in his treatment of religion and social class. Both writers explored the themes of emigration, alcoholism, and father–son relationships; both offered new ways to think about Ireland's history; and separately they revolutionised Irish stagecraft – often by working with the same directors, actors, and designers. What is essential, therefore, is to understand how the career of one writer only fully makes sense when placed in dialogue with that of the other – and how the Irish theatre was deeply enriched by the presence of both.

Notes

1. These remarks were made at a playwrights' panel that was held as part of the Abbey's 'Tom Murphy: A Celebration' event in October 2001, which I attended. The event was also documented in Brian Lavery, 'Irish Theatre's Best Kept Secret', *The New York Times*, 7 November 2001, p. E2, from which the material in quotation marks is taken.
2. Brian Friel, *Plays 1* (London: Faber and Faber, 1996), p. 441.
3. Thomas Murphy, *After Tragedy: Three Irish Plays* (London: Methuen, 1988).
4. Tom Murphy, *Plays 1* (London: Methuen, 1992), p. 7.
5. Murphy's first play *On the Outside*, co-authored with Noel O'Donoghue and staged in 1959, was written according to one criterion: 'One thing is fucking sure, it's not going to be set in a kitchen' (remarks often attributed to Murphy but actually made by O'Donoghue). See Thomas Kilroy, 'A Generation of Playwrights', *Irish University Review*, 22.1 (1992), pp. 135–41 (p. 139).
6. 'One wondered', wrote one critic, 'why [everything] hadn't all been said years ago, and at the Abbey, which is [. . .] its proper place?'. See 'K' [Seamus Kelly], 'Brian Friel's Sadly Comic Story', *The Irish Times*, 29 September 1964, p. 6.
7. Brian Friel, *Essays, Diaries, Interviews: 1964–1999* (London: Faber and Faber, 1999), p. 33.
8. The actor Catherine Byrne, who worked extensively with Friel during the 1990s, told Tony Coult that 'there's a bleak side to Brian's plays but he doesn't

always like that highlighted', demonstrating her belief that positive and negative forces exist in dynamic tension in his work. See Tony Coult, *About Friel – the Playwright and the Work* (London: Faber and Faber, 2003), p. 57.
9. Brian Friel, *Give Me Your Answer, Do!* (Oldcastle, Co. Meath: Gallery Press, 1997), p. 80.
10. See Aidan O'Malley, *Field Day and the Translation of Irish Identities* (Basingstoke: Palgrave Macmillan, 2011), pp. 1–32.
11. See Shelley Troupe, 'When Druid Went to Jail: Returned Migrants, Irish Prisoners, and Tom Murphy's *Conversations on a Homecoming*', *Irish Studies Review*, 22.2 (2014), pp. 224–37.

PART III

Forms of Experience

CHAPTER 11

The Irish Realist Novel

Joe Cleary

I

Irish realist fiction's most notable feature over the last half century is its thematic obsessiveness and consistent inconsistency. The Irish novel has developed significantly in that period and its most prominent realist versions are characterised by sometimes considerable ambitions of form, searching social critique, memorable characterisation, and lyrical writing. The difficulty has been to integrate these, something that few novelists have managed strongly to achieve more than once or twice in a career. The resulting unevenness can appear to represent a welcome open-endedness that makes Irish realism seem experimental or unpredictable. However, the handicaps are a certain repetitiveness of subject matter half-concealed by jagged improvisations and the diminution of the kind of socio-literary authority that accrues to writers only when they have demonstrated a steady mastery of vision and form over a considerable period.

Like other narrative modes, realism is defined not only by its intrinsic properties but with reference to other dominant modes in the literary field. In the case of the nineteenth-century Irish novel, realism is defined against a considerable tradition of Anglo-Irish Gothic fiction; for the early- and mid-twentieth century period, in contrast to distinguished forms of high and late modernism. These other modes contain their own elements of verisimilitude: the fantastical element in Gothic is realised only when realist codes and conventions are established and then subverted; modernist avant-garde narratives deploy realist devices even when they self-consciously expose and undo them. Likewise, it would be difficult to imagine some pure realism entirely purged of elements from these other modes. In the late twentieth century and early twenty-first centuries, novelistic realism – in its classical, psychological, social, historical, and documentary modes – has to compete with other media such as cinema and television drama. This does not mean that literary realism is only a minor form in Irish culture. But it does mean that even though there has long been a considerable body of realist narrative it has rarely enjoyed the kind of primacy over other modes that it did in nineteenth- and twentieth-century British and French literary history or in certain periods of modern American, British, or Italian cinema. Realism, in short, describes a persistent but often taken-for-granted body of work in Irish writing that has recurrently been overshadowed, sometimes eclipsed, by other modes.

It will be useful to situate contemporary Irish realism from 1980 onwards in this larger context to measure continuity and change. Though the historical novels of the Banim brothers and the more ethnographic realism of William Carleton represent formative strands in the development of Irish realism, until the mid-twentieth century the Big House novel furnished the most accomplished versions of Irish realism. In its less fantastical forms at least, the Big House novel is essentially an inverted historical novel that tracks not the emergence of the middle class or the transition from one mode of production to another – that sense of dynamic historical movement and consciousness that Georg Lukács argues represents that genre's most vital contribution to classical realism generally – but the incremental fall of a rentier-aristocratic class.[1] If the study of social mores, character and group psychology, historical situatedness, thick description, and an acute grasp of the interconnections between these, are what we expect from realist narrative, then there are few other currents of Irish realist fiction that achieved a formal stability and artistry to match that of the Big House novel that ran from Somerville and Ross to Molly Keane. In works such as Somerville and Ross's *The Real Charlotte* (1894) or *The Big House of Inver* (1925), Elizabeth Bowen's *The Last September* (1929), or Molly Keane's *Two Days in Aragon* (1941), the struggles of the Irish Protestant landed elite to come to terms with its own disintegration are vividly dramatised. Well after that class had faded as a political force, the Big House novel has continued to thrive, sometimes in more postmodern metafictions as in John Banville's *Birchwood* (1973) but also in more realist versions as in Aidan Higgin's *Langrishe, Go Down* (1966), Jennifer Johnston's *The Captains and the Kings* (1972), or William Trevor's *The Story of Lucy Gault* (2002). Modern Irish realism, then, in one of its inceptions bears the stamp of a body of writers, mostly women and upper class, often unionist in sympathy, whose works regard the emergence of a modern Catholic Ireland with dismay or fastidious fatalism. This is a quasi-aristocratic, top-down-view realism much at odds with those Anglo-American cultural histories that associate realism with the rise of the middle class in its radical phase or with a democratising interest in lower social *milieux*.

A second iteration of Irish realism developed alongside that described above that depicted the professional Catholic middle and artisanal classes viewed only remotely, if at all, in the Big House genre. Here, key figures include George Moore, James Joyce, Daniel Corkery, Seán O'Faoláin, Kate O'Brien, Frank O'Connor, Mary Lavin, and Patrick Kavanagh. Written in an age when conceptions of the bourgeois revolution as a heroic event or of the middle class as a progressive, democratising force had already become outmoded in European fiction, and in a literary epoch when the artist was widely viewed as a bohemian spiritual enemy of bourgeois life or as a fearless exposer of its darkest iniquities, this strand of Irish realism actually coincided with the long middle-class revolution of the Land Wars and the War of Independence. Though many of the writers who cultivated this realism were participants in or sympathetic to the republican struggle, as writers they were tendentially antagonistic to middle-class mores. In some of the major realist works before the War of Independence (1918–21), as in Moore's *The Lake* (1905) or Joyce's *Dubliners* (1914) and *A Portrait of the Artist as a Young Man* (1916), the stress falls on the crippling constraints of lower-middle-class respectability and Catholic formation, and liberation is conceived not politically or communally but as a struggle against family and society for personal self-realisation, the latter conceived sexually and intellectually. In the *Threshold of Quiet* (1917) and more so in his critical work, *Synge and Anglo-Irish Literature* (1931), Corkery is the outlier here, calling for a realist fiction more empathetically attuned to the habits, faith, and aspirations of Ireland's newly empowered rural or urban Catholic middle class. But against a backdrop of post-1921 Catholic religious conservatism and crass state censorship writers felt besieged by religious and political establishments, and in O'Faoláin's writings in *The Bell* magazine (1940–54) realism was tasked to represent not Corkery's hidden Ireland but an Ireland cramped by hypocrisy and timorousness. Prescriptively hostile as it was to the more heroic or 'romantic' (to use a much-favoured bugbear) temper of Yeatsian Revivalism, the realism encouraged by *The Bell* was self-thwarted because it was constitutively antiheroic in disposition even as it simultaneously lamented post-independence Ireland's anti-heroic mediocrity and failure to live up to any higher version of itself.

In the latter half of the last century the Big House version of Irish realism still yielded occasional accomplishments but generally diminishing returns while the second mode continued to be elaborated. In John McGahern and

Edna O'Brien, the former mainly resident in an ingrown expatriation in rural Leitrim and with limited output, the latter a proximate expatriate in London and highly prolific, the post-*Bell* versions of realism found their two most influential contemporary contributors. Their *Bildungsromane*, *The Dark* (1965) and *The Country Girls* trilogy (*The Country Girls*, 1960; *The Lonely Girl*, 1962; *Girls in Their Married Bliss*, 1964), took the earlier Joycean version in new directions that were to be particularly formative for other late-twentieth-century practitioners. However, even at this juncture Irish society and realism found themselves again arguably out of step. Just as McGahern and O'Brien, both born in rural Ireland, were coming to national and international attention, Ireland became for the first time in its history a predominantly urban society, the Northern Irish Troubles resurrected questions of national struggle and imperialism thought closed since the Civil War, and second-wave feminism propelled women's issues and the woman writer into unprecedented prominence. Circumstances ought maybe to have been ripe for substantive new flowerings of Irish realism, though, as mentioned earlier, the results have been mixed. In what follows, I will consider three significant realist modes – the family novel, the *Bildungsroman*, and political fiction and the expatriate novel (this latter pair closely connected) – and their interconnections.

II

Irish writers have rarely attempted multi-tier social novels like George Eliot's *Middlemarch* (1871–2) or, after the mid-twentieth-century at least, multigenerational family sagas of the sort to be found in various forms from Thomas Mann's *Buddenbrooks* (1901) or John Galsworthy's *The Forsyte Saga* (1906–21) to Gabriel García Marquez's *One Hundred Years of Solitude* (1967) or Alex Haley's *Roots* (1976). Instead, they have favoured a single nuclear-family form that obviously offers a narrower social range and foreshortened historical time span reaching from parents to children. The form is intrinsically Oedipal and claustrophobic, the parental generation weighing on the younger one attempting to find its own identity and values. After two city-based novels published in the 1970s and a long interlude, John McGahern published *Amongst Women* (1990), one of the most influential works in modern Irish fiction. The central protagonist, Moran, a small farmer and ageing veteran of the War of Independence and Civil War, is a tormented domestic tyrant. After an adventurous youth as a guerilla leader, he remains afterwards outwardly religious and conformist but inwardly contemptuous of the clergy and professional classes generally.

All at odds with himself, Moran seeks to relieve his inner turmoil through scrupulous family rituals, but despite the care of his second wife, Rose, and his children's compliance, he erupts periodically in terrific violence, permanently alienating his eldest son Luke, who has emigrated to London, and terrorising his other children, though, as he ages, they learn to cope with his vicissitudes and to make decent lives for themselves in Dublin and London. Indeed, as Moran approaches his end, Rose and Moran's daughters tend to him with great solicitude and appear to find new purpose and resolve in this common cause. Though Moran's sudden assaults on those around him are graphically depicted, the narrative mellows when Moran realises his mortality and ends on a cathartic note, as if some turbulent force had been laid to rest, and with Moran's wife and children (Luke excepted) fortified by sustaining their connection to each other despite everything.

One way to read *Amongst Women* would be to suggest that part of its accomplishment is that it works the antinomies of the kind of realism advocated by *The Bell* up to perfect pitch without trying to resolve them, suspending them in elegant irresolution. Always antipathetic to heroic styles and militant values but chafing also at the mundane monotonies of post-historical time and middle-class respectability, this *Bell*-shaped realism often produced fictions that swung jarringly between these polarities, finding closure only in forced resolutions or running down in disenchantment. Part of *Amongst Women*'s genius is that it finds in Moran the means expressively to concentrate the stymied character of the very realist form that creates him. Having known the glamour of wartime leadership, Moran can never afterwards find fulfilment in small farming or cattle-jobbing, nor even much satisfaction in his children, who achieve the social mobility that eluded him. However, despite his daughters' urgings that he commemorate his youthful military past, Moran refuses any nostalgic view, sourly dismissing the entire War of Independence as 'a bad business' resulting only in '[s]ome of our own johnnies in the top jobs instead of a few Englishmen'.[2] Likewise, the novel deals empathetically with the younger Morans' attempts to appease their father and with the long grind of schoolwork and exams needed to take them away from Great Meadow. Nevertheless, the urban society towards which the children gravitate is depicted as featureless and the regularity with which the girls especially return to tend the dying Moran and to restore themselves in their old home indicates an emotional deficiency in the world they have entered.

The success of *Amongst Women* is accounted for in part at least by its fatalism, its disinterest in endorsing either the revolutionary past or the post-historical temporality of the Ireland in which Moran's children will live, and in its suggestion that in the face of human mortality all life is grass, the individual's confrontation with death the most meaningful reality. In his final novel, *That They May Face the Rising Sun* (2002), McGahern retained cardinal features of the realist novel and moved away from the tightly familial to a looser communal form but dispensed almost wholly with plot or any attendant sense of developmental time or eventfulness. That work's unhurried pace, its preference almost for still-life stasis over movement, showed McGahern again expert at putting the realist form to work against itself. Though *That They May Face the Rising Sun* appeared at the height of the Celtic Tiger boom, McGahern paid little heed in this final work to that new Ireland, and in many respects his work's languid temporality might be read as a rebuke to the brusque busyness that defined neoliberal Ireland.

When *Amongst Women* appeared in 1990 it vied with the very different family novel being developed by Roddy Doyle in his Barrytown trilogy, *The Commitments* (1987), *The Snapper* (1990), and *The Van* (1991). The contrast in styles is extreme. Where McGahern's fiction sought literary *gravitas* and depicted worlds where personal relations were damaged and conversation limited and strained, Doyle's style was jocular, vocal, and feisty, full of youthful zest, the narrative zippiness achieved by dispensing almost entirely with realism's conventional thick description. Furthermore, where McGahern's Ireland, before his final novel at least, was typically burdened by the unpredictable rage of a grim *pater familias*, Doyle's Barrytown offered an inverted comic world where parents, especially the affectionately drawn Jimmy Rabbitte Snr, struggle to keep up with a teeming family of unruly teenagers who dismiss adult pieties with heedless mockery. In this topsy-turvy anti-authoritarian atmosphere parents and children alike inhabit a mass-cultural universe where popular music, international football, and pubs are as palpable as religion and nationalism are in McGahern.

Though *The Snapper* and *The Van* move towards more serious themes, *The Commitments* represents Doyle's most remarkable break with earlier Irish realism. The novel tracks the efforts of Jimmy Rabbitte Jnr to assemble an American-style soul band in Dublin's northside. *The Commitments* comes to a climax when the band's most publicised gig is to be viewed by a visiting Wilson Pickett, the group now on the brink of its big breakthrough. However, in an anti-climactic climax, Pickett fails to appear and the Commitments collapses ignominiously as clashing egos and internal sexual rivalries ruinously explode. Precedents for Doyle's style might be sought in Sean O'Casey's *Dublin Trilogy* or in Brendan Behan's *Borstal Boy* (1958), works that had also pitted ebulliently irreverent working-class dialect and wit against pieties of faith and nation. However, in those earlier works the comic plots are counterpointed by grimmer narratives dealing with ongoing republican struggles (O'Casey had been a member of the Irish Republican Brotherhood and the Irish Citizens Army before writing his Abbey plays, Behan had served a prison sentence for his part in an IRA bombing mission), whereas in *The Commitments* politics are irrelevant and 'revolution' has been subsumed into mass culture just as religious or African-American 'soul' has become mass-market soul music. For Jimmy, soul is the antithesis of 'bourgeois' music and expresses 'the rhythm o' the people'.[3] Trying to instil a sense of mission into his band, Jimmy urges them to think of Northside Dubliners as oppressed African-Americans, or 'the niggers of Europe', and declares that they will carry soul's message – 'REVOLUTION!' – to their audience.[4] 'Bringing The People's Music To The People' becomes the band's mission slogan, but it is clear that neither Jimmy nor the band nor the Dublin audience take this commitment seriously; it is simply good show business, the jargon of revolution become marketing jargon.[5] Despite their evident differences, then, what *Amongst Women* and *The Commitments* share is the suggestion that Ireland was finally laying its revolutionary promissory time to rest and making truce with more commonplace end-of-history temporalities. In McGahern's and Doyle's fictions, the days of revolution and big breakthroughs are over; as that sense of open-ended future vanishes, the characters must learn to inhabit the mundane present world and its temporalities differently.

The Barrytown Trilogy has a postmodern weightlessness that makes it seem more 'contemporary' than *Amongst Women*, but the latter work has had the greater impact on subsequent Irish fiction. Colm Tóibín, Deirdre Madden, Anne Enright, Claire Keegan, Belinda McKeon, Mary Costello, and Donal Ryan have all written family novels (or in Keegan's case a novella) that are also national allegories; several have paid tribute to McGahern's influence. These writers have brought new content to the inherited form – AIDS, the Northern Irish conflict, sexual abuse and suicide, adoption, the rise and fall of the Celtic Tiger – but few have meaningfully stretched it. However, one substantive reconfiguration is Anne Enright's *The Green Road* (2015). Here, Enright moves her fictional imagination out of its customary Dublin southside and into the west while also internationalising the inherited structures of the family novel by including extended overseas narratives set in New York and Africa. She has also significantly re-tilted the form's gender axis by replacing the irascible McGahernesque patriarch with a petulant matriarch who, Lear-like, hungers for her alienated children's care but cannot herself emotionally nurture them.

The shift from father to mother as central figure in *The Green Road* indicates a wider softening of patriarchal authority in Irish society, though not necessarily of any unilaterally progressive sort, while the overseas scattering of the Madigan sons conveys how Celtic Tiger Ireland remains tethered to the traumas of its long past even as it navigates the globalising world of the neoliberal present. Dan, an ex-priest who has lost his vocation and had gay relationships while living through the harrowing era of AIDS-devastated New York, and Emmett, an idealistic but emotionally stunted Third World relief worker, represent liberal-secular versions of the once-famed Irish Catholic missionary and revolutionary anti-imperialist movements. Both men, however, are personally adrift and thus suggest that the transmission of Catholic-nationalist idealisms into new post-transcendent humanist vehicles is somehow lacking, evidence more of a hunger for vocation than vocation attained. Hannah, a disappointed actress and alcoholic, and Constance, the only Madigan child who has remained in County Clare, a prosperous but overweight mother, are each named after militant Irish republican heroines but their shortcomings too are evident. Hannah's failed acting career indicates that she, like her brothers, is seeking some higher role or self to inhabit but cannot find it. Constance, as her name suggests, has qualities of endurance that bring a kind of muddling-through contentment that makes the best of Celtic Tiger affluence. In her, Enright comes closest to elaborating the spirit of Moran's coping daughters in McGahern's *Amongst Women* and to endorsing the values of steady-as-it-goes adjustment expressed in that novel.[6]

The Green Road is indicative of the ways in which contemporary Irish realism finds itself tethered to inherited national narratives and novelistic forms even as it appears to find both increasingly constrictive. Doyle's broad comedy or Enright's offbeat, quirky ironies dispense with the solemnities of McGahern's prose, and their works, like those of the other novelists mentioned earlier, move readers into lifeworlds more fully modernised and globalised than McGahern's. None of this changes the fact, dictated by the exigencies of the form, that the worldview offered here remains fundamentally constant: the old Catholic nationalist or revolutionary republican Ireland has been negated by late capitalist consumerism, but while the post-historical perpetual present offering to replace these may be less violent it by definition fails to provide strong purpose or direction.

The receding Catholic nationalist world commands no intellectual allegiance, the new world emerging in its place no strong emotional attachment. Critics have generally tended to stress that these novels are at odds with their society and perhaps they at least keep alive some hunger or hope for wanted alternative. But it might also be argued that in their mostly modest refurbishments of old conventions the Irish realists have been content to practise in literary terms a gradualist pragmatism not wholly different from that of contemporary Irish society at large in other respects.

III

From a distance, the *Bildungsroman* or coming-of-age novel appears essentially a more compressed version of the family novel, the narrative of nuclear family relations telescoped into a chronicle of individual self-realisation. Nevertheless, the sheer persistence of the form across the twentieth-century and beyond – 'No Irish childhood goes unpublished' as the *Kirkus Review* joked –, the role of Wilde, Moore, and Joyce in the elaboration of the early modernist *Bildungsroman* or *Künstlerroman*, and the form's close relationship to the equally popular memoir, all attest to the abiding centrality of this genre to Irish writing.[7]

Contemporary scholarship seems broadly agreed that the modernist *Bildungsroman* represents a refusal of the classical realist version committed to ideals of individual maturation and social integration. The modernist rupture is usually ascribed to a larger shift from national-industrial to a more corporate globalised capitalism that makes it harder to coordinate the fates of individual and national development narratives.[8] Viewed thus, there is a tendency to see the arrested narratives of the early and high modernist *Bildungsromane*, where the protagonist fails to realise achieved selfhood or to find a useful career and social role, as deliberate gestures of ideological refusal, meaning an unwillingness to accept either bourgeois humanist models of individuation or the whiggish temporalities of capitalist-imperialist modernisation. Maybe. However, these readings tend to slide towards an assumption that the ideals of stable selfhood and social integration are always inherently conservative, as though social reconciliation of any available kind could only be damagingly conformist. This may concede more to the inherently crisis-prone tendencies and antisocial tempos of modern capitalism and to its preference for mobile, provisional identities and lifelong self-refashioning than critics might wish.[9]

One of the least-commented-upon features of *A Portrait of the Artist as a Young Man*, the foundational text for the modern Irish genre, is the manner in which the novel elaborates, then evacuates, that strange ubertemporality constitutive to religious ontologies: eternity. This accomplished, the novel then valorises its antithesis, profane time, the latter needing subsequently to be re-consecrated in the yet-to-be-achieved work of art. Section III of *Portrait*, its fulcrum-point, is devoted to Fr Arnall's fantastically elaborated attempt to convey to the Belvedere boys some sensual appreciation of what 'eternity' might sensibly feel like, something he can communicate only by stressing the visceral horrors of perpetual physical suffering and spiritual damnation – 'ever', 'never' rhythmically intoned – the bliss of eternal salvation being harder to communicate. It is only after he has surrendered to the contemplation of eternity and accepted its mesmeric allure that Stephen cathartically dispels this fascination in Section IV, and then experiences the raptures of the flesh and profane time in the famous bird-girl scene, this ecstatic vision leading directly into Section V where Stephen commits himself to exilic solitude, artistic vocation, and forging the belated consciousness of his race.

In the Irish Catholic *Bildungsromane* between *Portrait* and *The Country Girls* and *The Dark*, this mixture of attraction-repulsion to sacred time and profane time and an interest in art's attempt to mediate between the two persists. But in McGahern's and O'Brien's post-Second World War versions, generic turning points each, religion appears as always-already desacralised, the clerical life only a worldly profession suitable to the submissive or to the repressed individual fleeing sexuality. But now, in contrast to Joyce, the lives of the artist and intellectual are similarly disenchanted, becoming mere pathways to a modest social refinement rather than anything redemptive. McGahern's Young Mahoney works hard to get to university, then soon dismisses its attractions as only another seeking after fake authority. O'Brien's Cait Brady is bright and bookish but, led by Baba, abandons a Catholic education to find some more glamorous social life by means of affairs with more cultured men, these invariably ending badly. By the end of the *Country Girls* trilogy Cait, like her mother, has committed suicide. In these stymied protagonists, religious or artistic routes to anything higher than middle-class modernity may be unavailing but the available secular humanist educational or bohemian-hedonistic alternatives also represent dead ends.

Patrick McCabe's *The Butcher Boy* (1992), probably the most popular *Bildungsroman* in recent decades, is a remarkable Gothic-realist not-coming-of-age novel. Its most telling innovation is the narrative voice of Francie Brady, a voice now middle-aged and worn down by years of shock treatment in an asylum yet somehow remaining recalcitrantly resistant to rehabilitation and as lunatic as ever. Francie belongs to a dysfunctional underclass family for whom narratives of social mobility or personal improvement are never options. Consequently, the boy loses himself in all sorts of compensatory fantasy worlds taken from mass culture, but his incapacity for progress, personal or social, allows him a madcap zest – initially puckish, then vengeful – that wreaks havoc.

However, *The Butcher Boy*'s wonderfully manic vitality is not dissociable from its bleakness. Francie is a traumatised lunatic but the social worlds to which he belongs are as crazed. The small-town Catholic Ireland where Francie lives is animated by the spectre of the Cuban missile crisis, this prospective apocalypse summoning up collective hallucinations of redemptive apparitions of the Blessed Virgin. The middle-class Mrs Nugent, who represents the social mobility closed off to the Bradys, is tellingly the butcher boy's victim, her body mutilated and buried in a dunghill. Though Francie is molested by priests, he appears more at home in his imaginary conversations with the Blessed Virgin than in Mrs Nugent's well-scrubbed modernising Ireland. This may be part of Francie's determinedly regressive and stubbornly nostalgic perversity, but the Irish public's embrace of the novel was surely connected to *The Butcher Boy*'s capacity to channel some inner frisson of carnivalesque recalcitrance of similar kind. McCabe's version of De Valera's Ireland is not softened in sepia, but that world's sheer zaniness compels in ways Mrs Nu-Gent's gentrified suburban version does not.

One of the best-crafted *Bildungsromane* since *Portrait*, Seamus Deane's *Reading in the Dark* (1997) might be read as an antithesis to *The Butcher Boy*. Where *The Butcher Boy* exudes an antic energy, *Reading in the Dark* proceeds ruminatively, each short chapter a tight self-contained set piece, these arranged like album photographs to constitute not an integrated family narrative but a composite of partial exposures. Like Francie Brady, Deane's child narrator lives in a world where history, fable, fantasy, superstition, rumour, and the sacred bleed into each other. Unlike Francie, though, Deane's protagonist is a child sleuth who proceeds from innocence to experience partly through schooling and reading, more so through an Oedipally-obsessive determination to solve the mysteries that will explain parental suffering. However, intellect is conceived here as a dialectic of enlightenment whereby every successive epiphany that diminishes the inherited familial murk simultaneously augments the protagonist's alienation. In some respects, this traces a familiar working-class narrative arc whereby education allows the intelligent child a pathway to social advancement at the price of removing him or her from the warmth of natal working-class community. This process of costly knowledge is compounded by the novel's Oedipal dimension whereby the searcher's attempt to discover suffering's source reveals not the latter's primal origins but its fathomless depths, its cancerous pervasiveness. Like many working-class *Bildungsromane*, *Reading in the Dark* closes as the adolescent leaves behind school, family, and native city for university, though in this case the ending is intensified by its coincidence with the outbreak of the Troubles and the stroke that forever silences the boy's mother, consigning child and parent to a permanent mute complicity. Here, historical time is finally ruptured by a revolution of sorts, but the novel conveys little sense of liberation. Read allegorically, *Reading in the Dark* suggests that any progress that Ireland might make towards its enlightened modernity will be hard won, *claritas* requiring a determined self-knowledge indistinguishable from self-shattering devastation.

As might have been expected, the Good Friday Agreement and the Celtic Tiger brought with them a hectic crop of *Bildungsromane* and memoirs. Slow secularisation and sudden affluence in the South, the imperfect peace in the North, and the historical atrocities that neither wealth nor peace nor time could banish, proved fertile ground for trauma and survival memoirs, misery literature, and realist narratives of partial overcoming. Edna O'Brien's *In the Forest* (2002), a novel based on the real-life murder of Imelda Riney, her young son, Liam, and Father Joseph Walsh, by an abused and mentally disturbed homeless youth, Brendan O'Donnell, proved eerily similar in outline to the tragedy enacted in *The Butcher Boy*. In a decidedly non-realist form, Eimear McBride's *A Girl Is a Half-Formed Thing* (2013) braided similar themes of abuse, Irish Catholic piety, working-class abjection, and damaged adolescence. In recent decades the gay or lesbian coming-out narrative has been a significant development, several of the more interesting versions turning away from realist narratives of liberal humanist selfhood towards picaresque and contingent, permanently unsettled conceptions of selfhood. Jamie O'Neill's *At Swim, Two Boys* (2001), Keith Ridgway's *The Parts* (2003), Mícheál Ó Conghaile's *Sna Fir* (1999), and Barry McCrea's *The First Verse* (2008) all take pleasure in linguistic experiment and an easy allusiveness to earlier Irish writers, including Wilde, Joyce, and Flann O'Brien, that the grimmer mid-century realist *Bildungsromane* rarely countenanced.[10]

IV

The political novel is the form at which Irish realism has proved least capable. This type of novel is hard to accomplish at any time, but the Irish experience is impoverished. Here, the contemporary writer will find little strong precedent in the Big House tradition, the modernist classics, or any version of Counter-Revivalist realism. Naturally, there are lots of novels in a variety of modes that deal with political topics – the Troubles, the condition of women or the working classes, the historical novel, or the post-2008 fall of the Celtic Tiger. But if the political novel means something more than a political setting or topic, if it implies a capacity to make politics seem nutritive to personal and social life and an ability to give vibrant expression to the working out of the contradictions of collective socio-political destinies (whether of class or nation or gender, or these in combination), then it is hard to name strong and enduring Irish political novels. Nor, in an era when there are so few compelling grand narratives of political progress or plausible projects of social transformation, do conditions seem propitious for such fiction. But if the novel is to be anything more than just a receding entertainment in an ever-more visually mediatised and digitised age, then it would be fatuous to think that the weakness of the political novel is not damaging.

Against this, an intriguing development in recent decades has been a tendency for Irish writers to locate their most ambitious and accomplished political novels outside of Ireland. Stronger works of this kind include Aidan Higgins's *Balcony of Europe* (1972), Brian Moore's *Black Robe* (1985), Colm Tóibín's *The Story of the Night* (1996), Ronan Bennett's *The Catastrophist* (1997), Ronan Sheehan's *Foley's Asia* (1999), Anne Enright's *The Pleasures of Eliza Lynch* (2002), John Banville's *Shroud* (2002), Joseph O'Neill's *Netherland* (2008), and Sebastian Barry's *Days Without End* (2016). Not all of these fictions are realist; most display the merging of realist verisimilitude and modernist technique now familiar everywhere. Why the Irish political novel might fare better overseas begs questions. Sceptics might propose that this development signals a failure of confidence in any wider than local significance of Irish subject matter and a searching after the now enormous Anglophone global market. More sympathetic observers might say that the pile up of calcified forms in Ireland – the Troubles thriller in the North, the detective genre in the South – have so saturated the domestic field for political writing that Irish writers can find fresher scope for invention elsewhere.

Ronan Bennett's *The Catastrophist* suggests the possibilities involved. The novel's focalising consciousness is that of James Gillespie, a Northern Irish-born but English-educated writer who returns to the Belgian Congo to see if he can recuperate his relationship with his Italian lover, Inès Sabiani, a reporter for *L'Unità*, a left-wing newspaper founded by

Antonio Gramsci. Though they earlier had travelled to Ireland and Africa, Gillespie's and Inès's romance is now strained due to the couple's temperamental differences. Gillespie had been a Cambridge-trained historian before becoming a novelist and has long been soured against things Irish by his early Northern formation; he greatly values what he considers political objectivity and dispassion. Inès is the daughter of an Italian communist partisan during the Second World War and prizes the sense of political solidarity nurtured by this background. Whereas Gillespie's reflex tendency is to be sceptical of political struggles, Inès is an enthusiast and activist by instinct, someone drawn to charismatic figures and good causes.

Behind these different temperaments, one conceived as 'male' and emotionally dyspeptic, the other 'female' and socially giving, there is a larger drama: that between literary commitment and autonomy, a conflict played out here as that between engaged journalism and ironic postmodern fiction. In the Graham Greene-style form that is his vehicle, Bennett strives to brush the late imperial literary thriller's inherent value system against its grain and thus to challenge both British liberal responses to Anglo-American colonialism and Irish revisionist takes on Ireland. When Patrice Lumumba is murdered in a Belgian and CIA-sponsored plot, Gillespie and Inès grow further apart: she is frustrated by his want of political passion; he feels her zealous identification with the Congolese struggle overrides the cool analytical detachment essential to strong reporting. However, Inès fiercely repudiates that assertion: '"To write about injustice without anger", she shouted at my stiff back, "is another injustice."'[11] Gillespie retaliates: 'I feel confident I could make a stronger case for exactly the opposite proposition', and he utters this in a tone of 'the disdainful calm I knew incenses her'.[12] Neither the righteous anger provoked by a just cause as felt by Inès nor Gillespie's 'disdainful calm' is given a free pass in *The Catastrophist*; the couple's romantic struggles are developed as part of a larger interrogation of the normative structures of feeling encouraged by contemporary journalistic or literary fields more widely. In the wider context of self-serving US regime management in Africa and British coercion in Northern Ireland, Gillespie's preference for impartiality is not nearly so value-free as he likes to think it, and *The Catastrophist* can be read as Bennett's response to Irish revisionist historians and critics and as his attempt to develop an alternative form of novel to revisionist-leaning Irish fictions.

Colm Tóibín may now be the most accomplished contemporary Irish realist writer. *The Master* (2004), his fictive recreation of Henry James's later years, is his most ambitiously accomplished novel to date. Set largely in England, though offering retrospects of visits to America, Ireland, and Europe, the novel reflects the burgeoning internationalisation of Irish realism mentioned earlier and offers an extended reflection on the relationship between 'writing' and 'life' that is also a concern in *The Catastrophist*.

The Master opens with James's nervy excitement as he awaits the opening-night reception of *Guy Domville*, hoping that his play might break the solitude of a novelistic career and win the popular success that has eluded him. Nursing his anxiety by attending Oscar Wilde's *An Ideal Husband* as his own play is being performed nearby, James disdains what he considers the 'silliness' of Wilde's comedy acted out as if it were 'a higher manifestation of truth' and he is glad to avoid 'Wilde himself, loud and large and Irish as he was'.[13] Hurrying back to St James's Theatre to discover his own play hissed, James is crushed, this mortifying episode compelling him to withdraw again into the solitude he had hoped to leave. However, his retreat is redeemed because he will ultimately wrest from that isolation the triumphant novels of his later years. As *The Master* unfolds it becomes clear that James's life is a succession of such withdrawals. He has avoided the American Civil War in which his younger brothers fought, eluded the affections of Minny Temple and Constance Fenimore Woolson, and repressed his attraction to several men, including Oliver Wendell Homes and Paul Joukowsky. If Wilde represents the idea associated with European aestheticists and avant-gardes that the beautifully lived life might be the finest work of art or that art and life must be re-connected, in *The Master* James comes to embody the necessary, if regretful, separation of life and art.[14] Tóibín's James maintains a steely distance from extra-literary long-term commitments of all kinds, personal and political, the better to hone his professionalism and transmit something of his unspent passion into his art.

Some have read *The Master* as a critique of the American writer for his want of passion and daring, this making Tóibín's James like Bennett's Gillespie a 'cold fish'.[15] Because *The Master* is empathetically focalised for the reader from the perspective of 'Henry' (as the writer is termed throughout), this reading seems forced; in fact, Tóibín's prose style – lucid, spare, unshowy – and the hushed atmosphere of *The Master* seem silently to second the productive contemplative life that James has chosen. Indeed, *The Master* might be read as the reverse image of *The Catastrophist*. In Bennett's novel, Gillespie really is a cold fish and his professionalism results in an ironical postmodern fiction that is critically and commercially successful but damagingly divorced from human feeling or political engagement; in Tóibín's novel, Henry may be repressed, but he has a dignity and self-possession that earn him the respect of his peers and of readers.

The Master, in sum, is the masterwork of the most feted Irish 'gay writer' of the twenty-first century, but in stylistic terms it is a self-consciously sober-minded, unshowy work, as far from the camp or dandyism of Wilde or even Bowen as one could imagine and as distant from any retro-kitschy version of Irishness as Irish writing has managed. In that novel, we may conclude, Irish writing finds a new if slightly leaden triumph that conveys in the Henry James figure a subdued celebration of professionalism, of the non-political, non-passionate working life. The time when Irish writers like Wilde or Moore, Yeats, Joyce, or Bowen liked to cut aristocratic or bohemian mandarin figures has passed. So too has the manic-depressive mid-twentieth-century period when the writer typically appeared as a drunken *poète maudit* like Patrick Kavanagh, Flann O'Brien, or Brendan Behan, or as unbowed republican renegades like Francis Stuart, Peadar O'Donnell, or Máirtín Ó Cadhain. Ever since Beckett, and confirmed most recently in the remarkable careers of Seamus Heaney, Tóibín, and Anne Enright, heroic styles have been decommissioned and the most internationally celebrated Irish writers have mostly been consummately professional, another way in which Irish writing marks its distance from the past and reflects back to the contemporary nation's readers a now-preferred image of their country. The passing of the writer as a figure posed as permanently outside or against society is not greatly to be regretted, but for the new professionalism there is also a price to pay.

Notes

1. See Georg Lukács, *The Historical Novel*, trans. Hannah and Stanley Mitchell (Boston: Beacon Press, 1963).
2. John McGahern, *Amongst Women* (London: Faber and Faber, 1990), p. 5.
3. Roddy Doyle, *The Barrytown Trilogy* (New York: Vintage, 1998), p. 38.
4. Ibid., pp. 13, 37.
5. Ibid., p. 73.
6. For an extended reading, see Emer Nolan, *Five Irish Women: The Second Republic, 1960–2016* (Manchester: Manchester University Press, 2019), pp. 187-92.
7. Cited in Marshall Lewis Johnson, '"The Uncreated Voice of the Nation": James Joyce and the Twentieth Century Irish Bildungsroman' (unpublished doctoral thesis, University of Southern Illinois Carbondale IL, 2016), pp. 3–4.
8. See Gregory Castle, *Reading the Modernist Bildungsroman* (Gainesville, FL: University of Florida Press, 2006); and Jed Esty, *Unseasonable Youth:*

Modernism, Colonialism, and the Fiction of Development (Oxford: Oxford University Press, 2012).
9. See Sarah Brouillette, *Literature and the Creative Economy* (Stanford, CA: Stanford University Press, 2014).
10. See Michael G. Cronin, *Impure Thoughts: Sexuality, Catholicism and Literature in Twentieth-Century Writing* (Manchester: Manchester University Press, 2012), and '"Our Nameless Desires": The Erotics of Time and Space in Contemporary Irish Lesbian and Gay Fiction', in Liam Harte, ed., *The Oxford Handbook of Modern Irish Fiction* (Oxford: Oxford University Press, forthcoming).
11. Ronan Bennett, *The Catastrophist* (London: Review Press, 1988), pp. 46–7.
12. Ibid., p. 47.
13. Colm Tóibín, *The Master* (New York: Scribner, 2004), p. 15.
14. See Peter Bürger, *Theory of the Avant-Garde*, trans. Michael Shaw (Minneapolis, MN: University of Minnesota Press, 1984).
15. Mendelsohn, Daniel, 'The Passion of Henry James', *The New York Times*, 20 June 2004: www.nytimes.com/2004/06/20/books/the-passion-of-henry-james.html [accessed 15 February 2019].

CHAPTER 12

Faith, Secularism, and Sacred Institutions
Diarmaid Ferriter

In the past four decades the Irish relationship with religious attitudes and practices has been transformed due to the combined effects of a Catholic Church discredited and shamed by physical and sexual abuse scandals and the increasing pervasiveness of a global secularism with its strong emphasis on the rights of the individual and the shortcomings of organised and controlled faith. This shift from what was historically regarded as an insular Catholic state for a Catholic people to a socially liberal and more pluralist Republic produced strong impulses to expose and critically question traditional attitudes, social and cultural taboos, and clandestine behaviour in forums as diverse as state-initiated reports, novels, memoirs, and site-specific theatre performances.

At the start of the period covered by this volume, the September 1979 visit of Pope John Paul II to Ireland had generated fervour, occasional hysteria, and national giddiness. For all the enthusiasm about the 1979 visit, however, the decline in religion's status in Ireland had actually prompted the invitation to the Pope. One summation of the visit suggested that 'if ready cheers meant real faith Pope John Paul would have no reason for concern about the young Catholics of Ireland'.[1] But the cheers did not denote a deep faith, and the visit did not reverse trends already in motion, such as birth rates moving towards the European average or the legalisation of contraceptives. Tom Garvin has suggested that 'the papal visit may actually have had the effect of destabilising an already fragile public-belief system'.[2]

While in Ireland, Pope John Paul II stressed the need to resist 'alien' influences such as materialism, secularism, and permissiveness, but an acute contemporary observer noted that:

> while the Pope expects his influence will have a socially radicalising effect on the Irish church, it is by no means certain that this is what will happen. The implicitly triumphalist nature of much of the festivities inevitably fosters

the reactionary elements in the Irish church, the concentration on Mariology, which is implicitly antipathetic to women's rights, and the assaults on materialism, also contribute to a strengthening of the conservative elements in Irish Catholicism.[3]

The decade after the Pope's visit witnessed the flexing of muscles by those conservatives. Irish women's rights had been addressed in different ways in the 1970s, reflected in European directives on equality, the payment of an allowance to unmarried mothers, the introduction of family planning legislation, and the establishment of rape crisis centres. But there was something of a backlash in the 1980s, which one of Ireland's best-known feminists, Nell McCafferty, referred to as a 'pig ignorant slurry of women hating'.[4] Referenda on abortion (1983) and divorce (1986) were bordered by toxic debate, intimidation, and coarseness, so much so that they earned the label the 'politics of denial and cultural defence'.[5] But such conservative crusades could not be sustained. By the time of the visit of Pope Francis in 2018, the Catholic Church in Ireland had endured three decades of revelations about its dark underbelly and, combined with trends starting in the 1960s, including economic modernisation, increased personal liberties, and feminism, its dominance was challenged and its credibility on many issues eroded, even before the full extent of child abuse and institutional scandals was made apparent.

During the late twentieth and early twenty-first centuries, numerous inquiries into child abuse in Catholic-run institutions ensured that Ireland's hidden histories received unrelenting exposure. Investigations resulted in the Ferns Report (2005) in relation to the abuse of children in a Wexford diocese, the Ryan Report (2009) into historic child abuse in institutions run by religious orders and funded by the state, and the Murphy Report (2009), which followed an investigation into the handling of abuse allegations in the Dublin diocese by church and state authorities from 1975 until 2004. Collectively, these reports vindicated many abused children and revealed much about how power was used and abused for decades. In providing such an overwhelming body of evidence about an 'obsessive concern with secrecy and the avoidance of scandal' and 'little or no concern for the welfare of the abused child', these reports provided a corrective to the atmosphere of secrecy and shame that had surrounded these experiences for so many years.[6] The Murphy Report also made it clear that the extent of the sexual assaults on children could not be explained by maintaining that the country was too poor and ignorant;

there were calculated cover-ups by the church and a deliberate abdication of state responsibility.

The abuse scandals were just one indication of a Catholic Church in crisis; other relevant factors included the decline in religious vocations and mass attendance. Ordinations declined by 66% from 1990 to 1998, and by that year the number of priests who died or left the priesthood was five times that of new priests joining the fold.[7] In addition, an opinion poll in April 2005 revealed average weekly mass attendance was 44% among Irish adults; this compared with national figures of 78% in 1992 and 65% in 1997.[8] One estimate in 2011 put the weekly mass attendance rate in Dublin at 14%.[9] It was also clear that a *laissez faire* approach to Catholicism was now firmly and irreversibly established: three quarters of Irish adults agreed in 2005 that the Catholic Church should allow women priests, support IVF treatment for couples, and relax its views on sex before marriage, divorce, and having a child outside marriage. An even higher proportion (83%) did not accept the church's view on the use of artificial contraception.[10] Clearly, many Irish adults had decided to be Catholics on their own terms.

Ireland was the first country in the world to legalise gay marriage as a result of a referendum in 2015, and in May 2018 a referendum to remove the Eighth Amendment to the Irish Constitution, inserted as a result of the 1983 referendum to ensure courts and legislators could not allow legalised abortion in Ireland, was carried by the same margin (2:1) that had led to its insertion. The themes relevant to these transformations over the last four decades include the status of women, the vindication of individual rights, the exposure of the consequences of excessive Catholic power, the potency of personal testimony, and increased secularisation and wealth.[11]

Irish artists responded to these debates in a variety of ways, but they had, long before the era of the exposure of Church scandals, been meditating on these subjects and engaging with their hidden histories. Satire and defiance in the 1970s were common means to reject the pieties and suffocations of the older generation, or what has frequently been referred to (and derided) as 'De Valera's Ireland', a reference to the dominant conservative politician of twentieth-century Ireland, Eamon de Valera, who served as Taoiseach from 1932 to 1948, 1951 to 1954, and 1957 to 1959, and President of Ireland from 1959 to 1973. In his 1978 poem 'Making Love outside Áras an Uachtaráin' [the residence of the president], Paul Durcan imagines De Valera as an old, cranky killjoy who catches the lovers 'in his green, green grass':

> I see him now in the heat-haze of the day
> Blindly stalking us down;
> And, levelling an ancient rifle, he says 'Stop
> Making love outside Áras an Uachtaráin'.¹²

As Declan Kiberd characterised it, in the 1980s, 'as young Ireland went into a ferocious reaction against the older pieties, it seemed that no aspects of national tradition would be left unscathed'.¹³ At the beginning of the decade, for instance, Bernard MacLaverty's novel *Lamb* (1980) presented a Christian Brother so infuriated by the abuse of children that he drowns a child in order to save him from an unjust system of child neglect backed by the state. The 1980s was also a decade when certain tragedies became very public, including the case of Ann Lovett, the fifteen-year-old schoolgirl who died shortly after giving birth alone in a grotto in Granard, County Longford. In 'The Statue of the Virgin at Granard Speaks', Paula Meehan offered a powerful indictment of a culture that reeked of double standards and decades of targeting 'fallen women' as if they had become pregnant on their own. It is the statue of the Virgin Mary that speaks in Meehan's renowned poem:

> On a night like this I remember the child
> who came with fifteen summers to her name,
> and she lay down alone at my feet
> without midwife or doctor or friend to hold her hand
> and she pushed her secret out into the night,
> far from the town tucked up in little scandals,
> bargains struck, words broken, prayers, promises,
> and though she cried out to me in extremis
> I did not move,
> I didn't lift a finger to help her,
> I didn't intercede with heaven,
> nor whisper the charmed word in God's ear.¹⁴

The silence about the Lovett case locally was not mirrored nationally, where women on radio shared stories of concealed pregnancies, broke taboos encouraging shame and silence, and shattered the myths of Irish chasteness. The Lovett case remained a reference point for those who sought to depict the dangers of secrets and Catholic moralism. In 2018, the year Lovett would have been 50 had she lived, her former boyfriend gave a newspaper interview in which he broke a long silence about the traumatic incident, announcing 'at the beginning I was silent out of fear and then it was out of respect'.¹⁵ He recalled that a Catholic bishop had told him he had to swear a vow of silence, sealed by the kissing of the bishop's ring, a claim the bishop denied.[16]

Those silences were a major part of the Catholic Church's mechanisms of control. Female poets had increasingly challenged these secrecies as they responded to socio-sexual issues and 'the 1980s saw an explosion in the publication of women's poetry, with over 35 poets beginning book publication in that decade'.[17] Many were seen as giving vital expression to elements of the female psyche that had long been repressed. Eavan Boland deconstructed the myth of female purity with defiance in her poem 'Mise Éire' (1987): 'I won't go back to it – | my nation displaced | into old dactyls, | oaths made | by the animal tallows | of the candle.'[18] The women who appeared to Boland like visions included those 'who fled the hot breath of the god pursuing, | who ran from the split hoof and the thick lips | and fell and grieved and healed into myth'.[19] Three years later, Boland wrote from the perspective of women 'Outside History': 'out of myth into history I move to be | part of that ordeal | whose darkness is | only now reaching me from those fields'.[20]

Non-fiction, especially in the form of memoirs, also challenged these silences when it dwelt on themes of exclusion, religiosity, and compromised childhoods. When Paddy Doyle published his memoir of childhood, *The God Squad* (1988), he received a sceptical reaction to his story of, among other things, the violence of the nuns of the St Michaels' Industrial School in Cappoquin in Waterford. He recalled: 'I used to hear people refer to me as "one of the children from the orphanage", which was the phrase locals used to soften the brutal reality of the industrial school in their midst.'[21] Abuse simply had to be got used to, according to Mannix Flynn, author of *Nothing to Say* (1983) and a resident of Letterfrack Industrial School in Connemara: 'Everything that I owned was being taken away from me piece by piece and was being replaced by something. That something I couldn't figure out, so I could not fight it or protect myself against it. I felt there was nothing I could do about it except get used to it.'[22] The violence was in turn mirrored by the boys. The tenderness of Flynn's initial sexual encounter with another boy in the laundry room gave way to fear as he is sexually abused by an older boy. Such instances of abuse also threatened to breed further and future injustices. Bernadette Fahey, a resident at Goldenbridge in Dublin, not only recalled the ritual public humiliation of punishment, but also her shock at how she too became capable of cruelty.[23] For Dermot Healy, in *The Bend for Home* (1996), 'when you stepped into Brother Felim's class with the roll-call book he brought you in behind his desk and felt your mickey as you called out the names'.²⁴ The same year saw the publication of *Angela's Ashes*, the best-selling memoir of Irish childhood of this era, and its author Frank McCourt was caustic about 'the way the Church slammed doors in my face'; his mother queued near the Redemptorist Church on Henry Street in Limerick with 'a small crowd of people outside the door of the priest's house [. . .] waiting to beg for any food left over from the priest's dinner'.²⁵

Memoirs and novels highlight the gulf between the rhetoric of aspiration that characterised expressions of Ireland's supposed advantages as an unsullied, predominantly Catholic rural idyll with the bedrock of the institution of the family, and the reality of a society, and indeed many families, that hopelessly failed to give credence to such rhetoric. Dermot Bolger's excoriating novel *The Journey Home* (1990) singled out priests, teachers, politicians, class discrimination, and the tolerance of institutional sexual abuse. Bolger seemed to be trying to jolt readers into an awareness of hidden abuses, though he was also accused of exaggerating depictions of official misconduct.²⁶ In the novel, Pascal's experience of sexuality is perverse because 'nobody ever let me be who I am [. . .] gentleness was a luxury for the likes of me'.²⁷ The same year saw the publication of John McGahern's *Amongst Women*, which was partly about delineating the dark forces in Irish family life. In his work, 'the suffocating sense of the entrapped individual' is central as church and state created a new, but not a free, southern Ireland from the 1920s onward.²⁸ McGahern's work shed light on many themes, including the family as an institution: he meditates on parenting, religion, education, health and welfare, institutionalisation, violence, physical and sexual abuse, and class and the significance of the environment in which a child is reared.

It is clear from McGahern's fiction, non-fiction, and interviews that he was particularly interested in the extent of the Catholic Church's power, but his overall assessment of religion is nuanced and qualified. There is no doubt he took serious swipes at the suffocating abuse of power by the church, as seen in the description he provided of some priests who 'looked and acted as if they came from a line of swaggering, confident men who dominated field and market and whose only culture was cunning, money and brute force. Though they could be violently generous and sentimental at times, in their hearts they despised their own people.'²⁹ McGahern was also preoccupied with the Church's obsession with sexual morality to the detriment of spirituality.

But there was more to the power and pervasiveness of Catholicism than this; in McGahern's words, 'people drew solace from its authoritarian certainties' but were also pragmatic: 'most ordinary people went about their sensible pagan lives as they had done for centuries'.³⁰ In McGahern's final novel, *That They May Face the Rising Sun* (2003), Jamsie and Ruttledge talk of going to mass 'to see all the other hypocrites', a phrase that also appears in his 1993 essay, 'The Church and Its Spire'.³¹ McGahern described his memories of the Redemptorist missionaries who came every few years to his parish like a band of strolling players who thundered hell and damnation for an entire week. As he saw it, they were simply brought in to purify through terror, but in his experience 'they were never taken seriously, though who can vouch for the effect they might have had on the sensitive or disturbed. [. . .] Some of the local priests were a match for these roaring boys, and while they were feared and accepted, I don't think they were liked by the people, though they'd have a small court of pious flunkies.'³²

Fear and acceptance, however, were on the wane as a more secular ethos took root in the 1990s. The same year as McGahern's *Amongst Women* was published, Roddy Doyle's *The Snapper* appeared just when it seemed Ireland was on the cusp of more optimism and less piety. In this novel, conventional roles are somewhat upended as Jimmy Rabbitte and his family go their own way in the face of one of the great taboos in Catholic Ireland: a daughter's pregnancy outside of marriage. For Derek Hand, this novel is also about how communities operate 'in a vacuum: the state and the traditional moral and social structures of the church have no leverage'.³³ The version of shame represented in *The Snapper* is not a consequence of traditional Catholic guilt; Doyle explained that he intentionally constructed Sharon's predicament around 'this yawning big hole of embarrassment', but that it is primarily secular, another indication of the marginalisation of the Catholic Church in Doyle's Ireland.³⁴

This theme was explored in a very different way in Colm Tóibín's novel *The Heather Blazing* (1992). For the judge Eamonn, there is the challenge of interpreting the 1937 Irish Constitution in 'a world in which opposite values lived so close to each other', as a pregnant school girl challenges the Catholic school managers' insistence on expelling her.³⁵ The crux of the issue as articulated by Eamonn is 'the right of an ethos to prevail over the right of an individual'.³⁶ As he ponders such dilemmas, 'the idea of God seemed more clearly absurd to him than ever before; the idea of a being whose mind put order on the Universe [. . .] What was a family? The Constitution did not define a family, and at the time it was written in 1937 the term was perfectly understood; a man, his wife and their children.' He goes on to ask, 'could not a girl and her child be a family?'³⁷

Abortion also continued to cause controversy. The ambiguity of the wording of the church-backed 1983 'pro-life' amendment, which gave equal rights to the life of the mother and the unborn, caused endless dilemmas and an English solution to an Irish problem, as over 150,000 women travelled abroad for abortions in the three decades after the amendment's introduction. In 2000, journalist Medb Ruane concluded that in relation to Irish women and abortion, 'theological and legal arguments supplant the personal testimony of women'.[38] However, the increasing power and visibility of individual stories associated with the Irish abortion question challenged that supplanting. In 1992, a fourteen-year-old suicidal rape victim was prevented from leaving the state to have an abortion, a decision later overturned by the Supreme Court. In the words of Supreme Court Justice Niall McCarthy, referring to the 1983 constitutional amendment, 'the failure by the legislature to enact the appropriate legislation is no longer unfortunate, it is inexcusable. What are pregnant women to do? What are the parents of a pregnant girl under age to do? What are the medical profession to do?'[39] These were also questions pondered by poet Paula Donlon in 'The State Acknowledges the Right to Life of the Unborn': 'We are driven to carry | images that will not be aborted.' Donlon echoes Catholic liturgy and the sacrament of communion to underline her defiance and rejection of the Catholic Church's subjugation of women: 'She is saying; | *This is my body* | Listen.'[40]

During the 1990s, much creative work explored the implications of increased secularism and the extent to which one of the darker stains on modern Ireland's copybook had been physical and sexual abuse. In Patrick McCabe's *The Butcher Boy* (1992), for example, the victim of abuse turns predator, attacking the priest who abused him. Some saw McCabe's novel as a response to the clash between the sacred and the secular with its continuous glorification of American pop culture, capitalism, and television rivalling the Catholic Church's authority. Martin McDonagh's depiction of priests reveals the declining status of clerics. Father Welsh, a 35-year-old priest, is referred to in the first two plays of McDonagh's Leenane Trilogy and finally appears in the third play, *The Lonesome West* (1997). The opening scene makes clear that Father Welsh has no control over the community. When the priest instructs Coleman not to swear on the day of his father's funeral, Coleman responds, 'I'll be swearing if I want to be swearing.'[41] The drunken Father Welsh sees himself as 'a terrible priest', to which Coleman replies, 'you don't go abusing poor gasurs, so, sure, doesn't that give you a head start over half the priests in Ireland?'.[42] But as Father

Welsh says, 'nobody ever listens to my advice. Nobody ever listens to me at all.'⁴³ He departs with a suicidal walk into the water at Leenane.

But what did increasing secularism mean in practice? Was it the 'process by which religious institutions, actions and consciousness lose their social significance', with an ensuing abandonment of church membership and church attendance?⁴⁴ Or simply an effect of the increasing 'privatisation' of religion?⁴⁵ These various interpretations of secularisation were in some ways applicable to Ireland, but there was no clear-cut break with religion, which underlines why much Irish writing demonstrates in detail 'how the old Ireland haunts the new'.⁴⁶ This was evident in part by the continued prevalence during these years of various popular devotional practices. Even following the decade of revelations in the 1990s, as Terence Brown notes, the fact that 'about a million people turned out to pay their respects to the relics of Saint Thérèse of Lisieux, when they were toured through the country in the summer of 2001 bespeaks vibrant popular piety'.⁴⁷ Or as Tom Garvin characterised it in 2007, 'many people who ignore the Church's instructions and who rarely go to church see themselves as perfectly good Catholics and see no contradiction in their point of view. This is an almost "Protestant" stance that would have been quite impossible forty years ago, but now is probably mainstream.'⁴⁸ This was part of a wider process of a breakdown in deference, to the point where Catholic bishops could be 'swiftly seen to be isolated by public opinion' – what sociologist John Fulton describes as a 'form of pro-religious anti-clericalism' among the Catholic community.⁴⁹ In Roddy Doyle's *Paddy Clarke Ha Ha Ha* (1993), the representation of Catholicism is ironical and satirical and religion provides little solace as Paddy listens to his parents fight: 'all I could do was listen and wish. I didn't pray; there were no prayers for this. The Our Father didn't fit, or the Hail Mary.'⁵⁰

Politicians also gradually came to reject, in the words of Barry Desmond, a Minister for Health in the 1980s, the idea that 'the common good' was the same as 'the Catholic good'.⁵¹ But others wondered somewhat mournfully about the vacuum generated as a result. In 2003, former Taoiseach Garret FitzGerald wrote about the decline of the influence of religion in the Republic and the 'inadequacy of any alternative lay or civic ethic, especially in the face of the double hazard of the siren call of individualist liberalism on the one hand and the off-putting face of fundamentalist Catholicism on the other'.⁵²

While countenancing this new era, there was a continued focus by writers on what Roy Foster characterised as the 'coming to terms with cultural memory'.⁵³ This was again particularly notable in the artistic reaction to child abuse scandals and institutionalisation, underpinned by a strong sense of a 'duty to remember' and a 'duty to tell'.[54] This was apparent in relation to the Magdalen Laundries, institutions run by congregations of nuns, that incarcerated those deemed to be 'fallen women' and where 26.5% of the 10,000 inmates between 1922 and 1996 ended up after referral by the state.[55] Many of the women who were sent to the Laundries – not just by the state, but also by families or priests – were judged harshly due to the environment and values of the time. The attitudes towards them, underlined frequently in contemporary documents cited by the McAleese Report (the report of the interdepartmental committee to establish the facts of state involvement with the Magdalen Laundries, published in 2013), generated descriptions of the women as 'sub-normal', 'delinquent', 'inmates', and 'mentally deficient', and it was clear that they were seen as 'incarcerated', another word regularly used.[56]

There were a number of reasons the women entered the Magdalen Laundries and a host of power alliances and socio-moral attitudes that facilitated their entry. Patricia Burke Brogan's play *Eclipsed* (1994) dramatises the strategies of five penitent women to resist and survive as well as their desires to escape, targeting in particular the Church's collusion with the state and sexual double standards. From Burke Brogan's perspective, the nuns were also imprisoned. But, crucially, in an approach that was to be replicated by others, the play calls on the audience to acknowledge societal collusion as Rosa, a young adoptee looking for her mother in the laundry, reads from the entry ledger: 'Signed in by her parents ... Signed in by her employer.' As another character states starkly, 'nobody wants any of us'.[57]

Peter Mullan's film *The Magdalene Sisters* (2002), set in a convent on the outskirts of Dublin in the mid-1960s, challenges the Irish family as a 'responsible agent in the betrayal and mistreatment of the women'.[58] A rape victim's father and a priest decide her fate as the men convene behind closed doors, re-victimising her, while another inmate, Crispina, addresses her priest attacker Father Fitzroy by repeating twenty-five times, 'you are not a man of God'.[59] For her troubles, she is sent to an asylum. The film also, however, offers a cartoon villain depiction of nuns as avaricious and sadistic and with no internal feelings.

In 2011, a site-specific performance, *Laundry,* directed by Louise Lowe for ANU Productions, took place in the convent building attached to the former laundry in Gloucester Street, Dublin, and gave voice to hundreds of names, with each audience member asked to remember four names; the performance disrupted the 'rule of silence' with the staging of testimonies and recovered histories. Its interactivity counteracted the women's historic invisibility and presented the daily routine of their lives, including the 'poisonous smell of carbolic soap'. Audience members were also challenged directly: 'People said they didn't know what was going on. Would you have done anything?'[60]

Following the collapse of the Irish economy beginning in late 2008, people did not embrace religion for solace; strikingly, in the best novel on the effect of the crash on different communities, Donal Ryan's *The Spinning Heart* (2012), religion plays little part in the lives of the characters. God is mentioned usually defiantly or angrily; acceptance of God's will, the bearing of crosses, or abject deference to priests are all rejected emphatically. Bridie, who loses her son in a tragic accident, is paid a visit by the priest Father Cotter:

> I never found peace. I told John Cotter to go way and fuck off for himself one time. There aren't too many have actually said that to a priest in spite of all the auld bile you hear people spouting these days. He got an awful shock; he'd been sitting there, in my house, talking gently the way he does, with those lovely words that most people would let rub gently against their wounded hearts, but I could only feel the anger building and building inside me until I knocked my tea off of the arm of my chair on purpose, I slapped it clean across the good room, and he jumped and looked at me and he must have seen the devil looking back at him because his face dropped and he hopped up from his chair and I told him where to go and where to shove his Scriptures.[61]

Another character, Rory, had been taught by Father Cotter in school, where he used to tell the students that if faced with a moral dilemma they should ask themselves only one question: 'What would Jesus have done?' Rory muses on that question in light of his current adult predicament:

> How would I know what Jesus would have done? That fella was a mass of contradictions as far as I can see. One minute he says to turn the other cheek, the next minute he's having a big strop and kicking over lads' market stalls. He says blessed are the meek and he goes around shouting and roaring the odds to everyone. He rises from the dead and then shags off a few weeks later and leaves his buddies in the shit.[62]

By the first part of the twenty-first century, then, deference to the Catholic Church had undoubtedly been relegated on the political priority list. In 2011, Taoiseach Enda Kenny excoriated the Vatican for its alleged lack of co-operation with Irish inquiries into child abuse, while the Irish embassy at the Vatican was closed down, supposedly on the grounds of cost. Kenny also declared, in contrast to some of his predecessors, that he was a Taoiseach who happened to be Catholic rather than a Catholic Taoiseach.[63]

But the advance of secularism can be exaggerated. The Catholic newspaper *Alive* declared, in the context of the referendum to appeal the eighth amendment in May 2018, 'we're at war [. . .] the secularists, in general, know they are at war, who the enemy is, and that it must be first restricted and then destroyed', and Catholics, it chided, were 'complacent, unaware they are in a war, unclear what they stand for'.[64] This, however, was overly simplistic; many of the 'secularists' supposedly at war identified themselves as Catholics in the 2016 census, 78% of the population of the Republic of Ireland. While on paper, 'the victory of the liberal left in the Irish culture war has been extraordinary and near total', Ireland in the early twenty-first century is still 'a pretty Catholic country', with just 9.8% indicating that they had 'no religion'.[65]

Despite this, a cultural adherence to Catholicism endures in Ireland. Many younger people, while not mass-goers, marry in churches and baptise their children. Over 90% of the primary schools in the country remain under the patronage of the Catholic Church, and as a result many non-Catholic students are still being educated in Catholic schools, with little indication in sight of an end to such dominance. Many 'lapsed' or 'cultural Catholics' appear content with this state of affairs, which brings to mind the assertion of playwright Brian Friel decades previously, in 1970: 'I suppose I'm a sort of practising lapsed Catholic [. . .] and I don't see any great contradiction in this either.'[66]

Alongside this, however, a more secular younger generation had rejected historic pieties, while some of the older generation had witnessed things that made them increasingly sceptical about Church absolutes (which was also reflected in the vote in May 2018 to repeal the Eighth Amendment; the two-thirds majority was a product of cross-generational support). Yet many immersed in a Catholic Ireland for most of their lives still clung to the certainty and sense of belonging with which that religion provided them. The tension between the two impulses is captured in Bernard MacLaverty's masterful 2017 novel *Midwinter Break*, which focuses on the retired couple Gerry and Stella Gilmore. For Stella, 'her church was her everything', but Gerry is scornful:

> Gerry had said once to her in the middle of an argument that he didn't believe in souls but if, just perchance, they did exist hers would be like a razor. She had been made that way by the Catholic Church, he said.

> Inflexible, narrow, capable of doing terrible damage by her adherence to rules and systems. But she totally objected. She told him that if she was a good person at all it had come from her religion. If she had any sense of justness and fairness, any concept of equality, then it had come from the Church. [...] No room in it for snobbery or hatred of any kind. Except, Gerry would always say, for 'the treatment of your own fair sex'.[67]

Although the Catholic Church had long retreated from the policy realm, its rituals were still of enough relevance for Catholicism to remain central to popular culture in the Irish Republic. As playwright and journalist Colin Murphy characterised it in the aftermath of the 2018 abortion referendum:

> I don't see a people fleeing from the Church, or being bullied into submission and secularism by the high-priests of liberalism. I see a people trying to reconcile a traditional, community-based identity with the weakening of one of the main institutional pillars of that identity and the imperative to acknowledge the wrongs and abuses that were done in its name.[68]

Those 'wrongs', however, continued to loom large in Irish fiction. John Boyne's epic *The Heart's Invisible Furies* (2017) appeared two years after the Irish electorate approved marriage equality. This novel tracks the life of its gay protagonist Cyril Avery across the twentieth century, as he struggles with the biases and injustices directed towards him in Catholic Ireland. The 2015 marriage equality referendum campaign underlined, among other things, the potency and relevance of personal testimony in changing attitudes and minds about what constitutes, not just marriage, but human happiness, diversity, and the family unit. What marked the referendum campaign as different from previous ones was the space afforded to individual stories, including testimony from gay men and women, young and old, and their siblings, friends, parents, and grandparents.

This stands in stark contrast to the way in which individuals profoundly affected by decisions in referendum votes in the past were too often invisible or regarded as abstractions during the campaigns. Marriage redefinition was not seen by most as threatening or negative, but rather as profoundly affirmative and perhaps necessary to atone for historic prejudice. In *The Heart's Invisible Furies*, Cyril Avery experiences the full extent of a homophobic Ireland at various points throughout the twentieth century, and from the outset of the novel the church is placed firmly in the dock for its perceived rank hypocrisy, its cruel strangleholds, and its delusional depictions of supposed Irish purity in contrast to British paganism and permissiveness. Cyril was born out of wedlock to a sixteen-year-old girl, Catherine Goggin, who is cast out from her rural Irish community by the parish priest:

> Long before we discovered that he had fathered two children by two different women, one in Drimoleague and one in Clonakilty, Father James Monroe stood on the altar of the Church of Our Lady, Star of the Sea, in the parish of Goleen, West Cork, and denounced my mother as a whore.[69]

After physically assaulting her, the priest tells her, 'there's houses in London that have been built for the likes of you and beds there where you can throw yourself on your back and spread your legs for all and sundry to satisfy your wanton ways'.[70] By the end of the novel, Cyril has survived to witness 'The new Ireland' and so can say, 'sure everyone can get married now'.[71] Now aged 86, even his mother Catherine is getting married ('My mother and he had met on Tinder').[72] Nonetheless, she vividly remembers the terror of seventy years previous:

> 'He was wrong, wasn't he?'
> 'Who?' I asked.
> 'Father Monroe. He said I'd never have a wedding day. He said that no man would ever want me. But here that day is. He was wrong.'
> 'Of course he was wrong', I told her. 'They were all wrong. They were wrong about everything.'[73]

Notes

1. *The Visit of His Holiness Pope John Paul II, 1979 Ireland* (Dublin: A.C.W Art Publishers, 1979), p. 24.
2. Tom Garvin, *Preventing the Future: Why Was Ireland So Poor For So Long?* (Dublin: Gill & Macmillan, 2004), p. 208.
3. Vincent Browne, 'A Pilgrim of Peace', *Magill*, 30 October 1979: https://magill.ie/archive/pilgrim-peace [accessed 9 February 2019].
4. Nell McCafferty, *The Best of Nell: A Selection of Writing Over Fourteen Years* (Dublin: Attic Press, 1984), p. 58.
5. See Tom Garvin, 'The Politics of Denial and of Cultural Defence: The Referenda of 1983 and 1986 in Context', *The Irish Review*, 3 (1988), pp. 1–7.
6. Minister of Justice and Equality, *Report of the Commission of Investigation into Catholic Archdiocese of Dublin* [The Murphy Report], 29 November 2009, pp. 9,

10: www.justice.ie/en/JELR/DACOI Part 1.pdf/Files/DACOI Part 1.pdf [accessed 12 February 2019].
7. See Diarmaid Ferriter, 'Twenty-First-Century Ireland', in Richard Bourke and Ian McBride, eds., *The Princeton History of Modern Ireland* (Princeton, NJ: Princeton University Press, 2016), pp. 168–89 (p. 177).
8. 'New Pope Shouldn't Ignore New Realities', *Sunday Tribune*, 24 April 2005, p. N14; and James S. Donnelly, 'A Church in Crisis: The Irish Catholic Church Today', *History Ireland*, 8.3 (Autumn 2000), pp. 12–27 (p. 16).
9. See 'Irish Census (2016)', *Faith Survey*: https://faithsurvey.co.uk/irish-census.html [accessed on 9 February 2019].
10. Kevin Rafter, 'To Heaven and to Oblivion', *Sunday Tribune*, 24 April 2005, p. N7.
11. See Diarmaid Ferriter, *Occasions of Sin: Sex and Society in Modern Ireland* (London: Profile Books, 2009); Máiréad Enright and Fiona De Londras, *Repealing the 8th: Reforming Irish Abortion Law* (Bristol, UK: Policy Press, 2018); and Grainne Healy, Brian Sheehan, and Noel Whelan, *Ireland Says Yes: The Inside Story of How the Vote for Marriage Equality was Won* (Dublin: Merrion Press, 2015).
12. Paul Durcan, *A Snail in My Prime: New and Selected Poems* (London: Harvill, 1993), p. 41.
13. Declan Kiberd, *Inventing Ireland: The Literature of the Modern Nation* (London: Vintage, 1996), p. 609.
14. Paula Meehan, *The Man Who Was Marked by Winter* (Oldcastle, Co. Meath: Gallery Press, 1991), p. 42.
15. Rosita Boland, 'I Was Ann Lovett's Boyfriend', *The Irish Times*, 5 May 2018: www.irishtimes.com/life-and-style/people/i-was-ann-lovett-s-boyfriend-the-award-winning-article-1.3484311pp [accessed 9 February 2019].
16. Ibid.
17. Catriona Clutterback, 'Irish Women's Poetry and the Republic of Ireland: Formalism as Form', in Ray Ryan, ed., *Writing in the Irish Republic: Literature, Culture, Politics 1949–1999* (London: Macmillan, 2000), pp. 17–43 (p. 18).
18. Eavan Boland, *The Journey and Other Poems* (Manchester: Carcanet, 1987), pp. 10–11.
19. Ibid., pp. 27–8.
20. Eavan Boland, *Outside History* (Manchester: Carcanet, 1990), p. 45.
21. Paddy Doyle, *The God Squad* (Dublin: Corgi Books, 1988), p. 42.
22. Mannix Flynn, *Nothing to Say* (Dublin: Ward River Press, 1983), p. 63.
23. Bernadette Fahey, *Freedom of Angels: Surviving Goldenbridge Orphanage* (Dublin: O'Brien Press, 1999), p. 122.
24. Dermot Healy, *The Bend for Home* (London: Harvill, 1996), p. 102.
25. Frank McCourt, *Angela's Ashes: A Memoir of a Childhood* (London: Scribner, 1996), pp. 332, 250.

26. See Michael Pierse, 'Reconsidering Dermot Bolger's Grotesquery: Class and Sexuality in *The Journey Home*', *Irish University Review*, 40.2 (Autumn/Winter 2010), pp. 86–106.
27. Dermot Bolger, *The Journey Home* (Austin, TX: University of Texas Press, 2008 [1990]), p. 140.
28. Brian Liddy, 'State and Church: Darkness in the Fiction of John McGahern', *New Hibernia Review/Iris Éireannach Nua*, 3.2 (Summer 1999), pp. 106–21 (p. 106).
29. John McGahern, 'The Church and Its Spire', in Stanley Van Der Ziel, ed., *Love of the World: Essays* (London: Faber and Faber, 2009), pp. 133–48 (p. 139).
30. John McGahern, 'Whatever You Say Say Nothing', *The Irish Times*, 26 October 1999: www.irishtimes.com/culture/whatever-you-say-say-nothing-1.243040 [accessed 9 February 2019].
31. John McGahern, *That They May Face the Rising Sun* (London: Faber and Faber, 2002), p. 2; McGahern, 'The Church and Its Spire', p. 147.
32. McGahern, 'The Church and Its Spire', pp. 138–9.
33. Derek Hand, *A History of the Irish Novel* (Cambridge: Cambridge University Press, 2011), p. 266.
34. Caramine White, *Reading Roddy Doyle* (Syracuse, NY: Syracuse University Press, 2001), p. 151.
35. Colm Tóibín, *The Heather Blazing* (New York: Viking Books, 1992), p. 90.
36. Ibid.
37. Ibid., pp. 86, 91.
38. Mebh Ruane, 'Introduction', in Irish Family Planning Association, ed., *The Irish Journey: Women's Stories of Abortion* (Dublin: Irish Family Planning Association, 2000), pp. 6–11 (p. 6).
39. *Attorney General v. X* [1992], IESC 1; IR 1, p. 90.
40. Quoted in Lia Mills, '"I Won't Go Back to It": Irish Women Poets and the Iconic Feminine', *Feminist Review*, 50 (Summer 1995), pp. 69–88 (pp. 85, 86; emphasis original).
41. Martin McDonagh, *The Lonesome West* (London: Methuen Drama, 1997), p. 1.
42. Ibid., p. 7.
43. Ibid., p. 35.
44. Bryan Wilson, *Religion in Secular Society* (London: Watts, 1966), p. 14.
45. See Daithi O Corráin, 'Catholicism 1880–2015: Rise, Ascendancy and Retreat', in Tom Bartlett, ed., *The Cambridge History of Modern Ireland, Vol. IV: 1880 to the Present* (Cambridge: Cambridge University Press, 2018), pp. 726–64 (p. 755).
46. Quoted in Susan Cahill, *Irish Literature in the Celtic Tiger Years, 1990–2008* (London: Continuum, 2011), p. 175.
47. Terence Brown, *Ireland: A Social and Cultural History, 1922–2002* (London: Fontana Press, 2004), p. 371.
48. Tom Garvin, 'Turmoil in the Sea of Faith: The Secularization of Irish Social Culture, 1960-2007', in Thomas Hachey, ed., *Turning Points in*

Twentieth-Century Irish History (Dublin: Irish Academic Press, 2011), pp. 155–66 (p. 163).
49. Quoted in R. F. Foster, *Luck and the Irish: A Brief History of Change from 1970* (Oxford: Oxford University Press, 2007), p. 57.
50. Roddy Doyle, *Paddy Clarke Ha Ha Ha* (London: Secker and Warburg, 1993), p. 154.
51. Quoted in Ferriter, *Occasions of Sin*, p. 425.
52. Garret FitzGerald, *Reflections on the Irish State* (Dublin: Irish Academic Press, 2003), p. x.
53. Foster, *Luck and the Irish*, p. 63.
54. See James M. Smith, *Ireland's Magdalen Laundries and the Nation's Architecture of Containment* (South Bend, IN: Notre Dame University Press, 2007), p. 90.
55. Martin McAleese, 'Introduction', Department of Justice and Equality, *Report of the Inter-Departmental Committee to Establish the Facts of State Involvement with the Magdalen Laundries* [2013], pp. 1–11 (p. 1): www.justice.ie/en/JELR/ 2013Magdalen-Introduction by the Independent Chair (PDF - 82KB).pdf/ Files/2013Magdalen-Introduction by the Independent Chair (PDF - 82KB).pdf [accessed 14 February 2019].
56. See Department of Justice and Equality, *Report of the Inter-Departmental Committee to Establish the Facts of State Involvement with the Magdalen Laundries,* 2013: www.justice.ie/en/JELR/Pages/MagdalenRpt2013 [accessed 17 July 2018].
57. Quoted in Smith, *Ireland's Magdalen Laundries*, pp. 95, 98.
58. Ibid., p. 141.
59. Quoted in ibid., p. 148.
60. Miriam Haughton, 'From Laundries to Labour Camps: Staging Ireland's "Rule of Silence" in Anu Production's *Laundry*', *Modern Drama*, 57.1 (Spring 2014), pp. 65–93 (pp. 72, 77).
61. Donal Ryan, *The Spinning Heart* (Dublin and London: The Lilliput Press, 2012), p. 72.
62. Ibid., p. 112.
63. See Patrick Kiely with Dermot Keogh, 'Turning Corners: Ireland 2002-11', in T. W. Moody and F. X. Martin, eds., *The Course of Irish History* (Cork, Ireland: Mercier Press, 2011), pp. 358–98.
64. Quoted in Colin Murphy, 'A Matter of Faith: The Decline of Catholic Ireland', *Sunday Business Post*, 10 June 2018: www.businesspost.ie/magazine/ a-matter-of-faith-418348 [accessed 7 February 2019].
65. Ibid.
66. Paul Delaney, ed., *Brian Friel in Conversation* (Ann Arbor, MI: The University of Michigan Press, 2000), p. 81.
67. Bernard MacLaverty, *Midwinter Break* (London: Jonathan Cape, 2017), pp. 217–18.
68. Murphy, 'A Matter of Faith: The Decline of Catholic Ireland'.

69. John Boyne, *The Heart's Invisible Furies* (London: Hogarth, 2017), p. 5.
70. Ibid., p. 9.
71. Ibid., p. 579.
72. Ibid., p. 578.
73. Ibid., p. 578.

CHAPTER 13

Writing the Tiger: Economics and Culture
Sarah Townsend

At the midpoint of Anne Enright's 2011 novel *The Forgotten Waltz* nestles one of the most apt distillations of the Irish recessionary mindset: 'It is what it is – that's what I say. *It is what it is.*'[1] Pithy and pragmatic, the expression captures the resignation of narrator-protagonist Gina Moynihan, who has inherited her late mother's house in mid-2007 just as Ireland's real-estate bubble begins to collapse. Like many of her contemporaries saddled with properties that refuse to sell, Gina accepts her newfound state of financial burden as fitting penance for personal failings – in her case, infidelity and filial neglect – and it is no stretch to hear in her expression the moral self-reckoning of a newly chastened populace. After the hedonism of the 'Celtic Tiger' boom, the frugality of austerity; after the illusions of prosperity, the plain facts of economic stagnation. Gina styles herself as a hard-nosed realist among a sea of sentimental fools, yet the substance of her utterance undermines her forthright demeanour. 'It is what it is' is, in fact, an exceedingly common expression, and the act of self-attribution wedged between the two iterations only emphasises the speaker's lack of originality. Gina repeats an already repetitive phrase, creating a level of redundancy that borders on the absurd. Far from delivering cogent truth-bombs to self-deluding peers, Enright's protagonist regurgitates a cliché, possibly to audiences that exist only in her imagination.

The discrepancy between the insight Gina hopes to convey and the trite phrase she actually uses points to the novel's larger preoccupation with the illusory singularity of human experience and the painful discovery of its unshakeable banality. The plot syncopates the progression of an extramarital affair to the Celtic Tiger, the period of rapid economic growth in Ireland that began in the early 1990s and ended with the global financial crisis of 2008.[2] Through the sequencing of the timeline – the lovers meet in 2002 amid prosperity, become involved several years later at the peak of the boom, and leave their respective marriages right as the downturn begins – *The Forgotten Waltz* limns the bewildering inextricability of private life and economic milieu. Enright likens the intensities and susceptibilities of Gina's romance with Seán to those of financial risk. The initial rush of the lovers' dalliance, thrilling in large part because it promises to be both extraordinary and restrained, spills over into a familiar series of clichés: one last time, then one more, becoming emotionally invested, getting in over their heads, until finally, the day of reckoning. If the events of the affair and its fallout are predictable, so too is the script. Of the breakup with her husband, Gina comments only on wording: 'Much cliché [...] And not one word of it mattered. Not one stupid word. *You never. I always. The thing about you is.*'³ But life has a way of repeating itself for Gina, and a year or so later she is surprised to hear herself and Seán, with whom she is now living, arguing in nearly identical terms. '*You always. You never. The thing about you is.* It was', she concedes, 'in a spooky way, just like being married.'⁴

The push and pull of cliché that structures *The Forgotten Waltz* also appears in debates about the state of contemporary Irish literature. A common criticism levelled against Irish authors during and after the Celtic Tiger was their obsession with history. Rather than address the socio-economic landscape of the present, the argument went, writers were stuck in the past rehashing timeworn grievances and exhausted tropes. In a 2010 interview posted subsequently to his website, Julian Gough lambasted a sanctimonious literary establishment, retorting, 'reading award-winning Irish literary fiction, you wouldn't know television had been invented'.⁵ Fintan O'Toole, meanwhile, framed the issue in terms of quality: 'A sanitised, rustic landscape is still marketable and most competent writers can do it with their eyes closed', he noted in a 2001 *Irish Times* editorial. 'But the cost in twee cliche is too high for any serious writer.'⁶ As a number of commentators pointed out, these and other likeminded assessments rehearsed longstanding critical commonplaces all the while calling out literary cliché. Gough's outline of an antiquated literary establishment, for instance, finds precursors in early criticisms of the Abbey Theatre.⁷ Meanwhile, O'Toole's equating of 'serious writ[ing]' with 'a great Irish social novel' traces back to the nineteenth century, as Margaret Kelleher has shown.⁸ Moreover, feminist authors and scholars noted how many of Irish literature's detractors neglected to take into account the literary output of women writers, an omission so familiar that it has become a cliché in its own right.⁹ In a tongue-in-cheek response to Gough's comments, Éilís Ní Dhuibhne quipped, 'maybe that's what the fuss is about? Not enough men – famous men – have written fiction dealing with contemporary Ireland? Well then. But of course. Good fiction about contemporary Ireland does not exist. QED.'[10]

Throughout this debate in which opposing parties could agree on very little, the verdict on cliché was remarkably consistent: a pitfall to be avoided, whether at the level of style, argument, or methodology; an object of universal scorn. There is good reason for this aversion. Although the term cliché derives from nineteenth-century French printmaking and photographic technology, it has accrued the broader meaning of an oft-repeated and therefore unoriginal expression.[11] Bugbear for a range of linguistic sins, cliché serves as a 'scapegoat for all language's inevitable tendency toward repetition and calcification', as C. Namwali Serpell has argued.[12] But the generalised allergy to cliché has been re-inforced, Serpell continues, by the decades-long dominance of ideology critique (or symptomatic reading) within literary criticism, which sees it as 'a *sign* of unwitting artistic debasement, bourgeois collusion, and complicity with bad politics'.[13] Translated into Celtic Tiger terms, one might say the proliferation of literary cliché, especially in historical fiction, indexes the commodification of Irish identity through a newly prosperous culture industry. I see two problems with this proposition. First, it makes hasty assumptions about the parochialism of historical fiction, neglecting to consider how narratives set in the past can lend fresh critical insight into the conditions of a globalised present.[14] Second, it makes equally hasty assumptions about the liability of cliché, treating it as a failure of craft or politics without considering why writers might invoke it as a purposeful choice. If we correct for this latter assumption, however – that is, if we take cliché seriously as a constitutive formal element of the Irish boom and bust – a new pattern of Celtic Tiger literary production begins to emerge.

Cliché, in fact, flourishes in contemporary Irish literature not only in tropes of 'dead mammies and peeling potatoes and farms and bogs' but also in works focused specifically on the Celtic Tiger and the ensuing downturn.[15] In contrast to the oft-discussed clichés of historical fiction, those that appear in literature of the recession have received surprisingly little literary-critical attention.[16] Nevertheless, they perform an important function, re-inforcing narratives of bourgeois personhood amid a bewildering socioeconomic milieu. In *The Forgotten Waltz* and Tana French's *Broken Harbor* (2012), cliché takes the form of popular generic conventions developed in the mid-twentieth century.[17] The narrators summon formulaic clichés from romance and the police procedural in the hope of organising their precarious domestic, financial, and professional lives into recognisable narrative arcs that end in satisfaction and resolution. While cliché assuages disorienting shifts in middle-class experience by providing temporary narrative and affective ballast, it also enmeshes Enright's and French's novels in long-running battles over the value of genre fiction that have been re-ignited by recent transformations in the literary marketplace. By sustaining inadequate yet necessary patterns of post-Celtic Tiger labour and dwelling, cliché mediates what Lauren Berlant calls the 'impasse' of recession, an indeterminate period of crisis where 'one no longer knows what to do or how to live and yet, while unknowing, must adjust'.[18]

Narrative Convention and the Genres of Middle-Class Living

Among the many injuries inflicted by the end of the Celtic Tiger, the damage to the sense of bourgeois stability was especially acute. Social science researchers have documented a 'middle class squeeze' during the Irish recession, where the professional, managerial, and middle income classes suffered significantly higher relative increases in economic stress compared with other social and income classes.[19] *The Forgotten Waltz* and *Broken Harbor* register the newly felt precarity ushered in by the recession as a breakdown in narrative expectations: each novel opens by gesturing towards the genre in which the middle-class narrator's life ought to have unfolded. In *The Forgotten Waltz*, Gina's romance with Séan begins as a slow-motion film scene, paused at the instant before their eyes meet: 'my first sight of Séan (in this, the story I tell myself about Séan) takes place at the beginning of my first exhalation: his body; the figure he makes against the view, made hazy by the smoke of a long-delayed Marlboro Light. [...] He is about to turn around, but he does not know this yet.'[20] In *Broken Harbor*, detective Mick Kennedy introduces his murder investigation as a nearly perfect police procedural: 'this case [...] should have ended up in the textbooks as a shining example of how to get everything right. By every rule in the book, this should have been the dream case.'[21] Both preludes function as wistful counterfactuals, an admission implied in Gina's case by her hyper-metatextuality – 'I add in the late summer light and the view', she concedes – and marked grammatically in Mick's case by his use of the conditional tense.[22] What follows is less 'life as it is actually lived' than life recounted as a series of generic adjustments. Enright's and French's novels offer retrospective meditations on the shattering of middle-class illusion and the compromises people make in order to continue telling the story of their existence in a recognisable way.

The fact that the two narrators cleave to popular genres like romance and the police procedural is unsurprising given their historical role in consolidating middle-class identity. While the realist novel's connection to the rise of the bourgeoisie is well established in scholarship, middlebrow fiction (which does not consist exclusively of genre fiction but includes a significant amount of it, including both romance and crime fiction) has received comparatively little critical attention. The category of the middlebrow was long dismissed by scholars as hackneyed fare consumed by naïve, mostly female readers, but pioneering studies in the 1980s and 1990s by Nicola Bauman, Janice Radway, Alison Light, and Joan Shelley Rubin prompted a critical re-evaluation that is ongoing.[23] Although the parameters of middlebrow literature, like the parameters of the bourgeoisie, are malleable and contentiously debated, Beth Driscoll outlines a set of common features: 'The middlebrow is middle-class, reverential towards elite culture, entrepreneurial, mediated, feminized, emotional, recreational, and earnest.'[24] Marketed towards non-academic college-educated readers, though not consumed solely by them, middlebrow fiction has mediated vast transformations in middle-class domesticity and labour that have transpired over the past 100 years. Its perception as a type of escapism or personal therapy, a source of cultural capital, or a profitable sector in a flagging contemporary publishing industry tends to elicit vociferous responses, from enthusiasm to derision.[25] We might say that the category of the middlebrow serves as a litmus test for attitudes about the democratisation of culture. For instance, a December 2017 Arts Council England (ACE) report about declining sales in literary (or, highbrow) fiction, which coincided with the release in early 2018 of several reports about the growth in self-published ebooks and genre fiction, prompted some commentators to celebrate middlebrow fiction's triumph over traditional literary gatekeeping and others to lament the woeful deterioration of literary value.[26]

In *The Forgotten Waltz* and *Broken Harbor*, Gina's and Mick's investments in the generic conventions of romance fiction and the police procedural suggest the degree to which reading and other acts of narrative consumption are imbricated in bourgeois consciousness. Both genres have their origins in the mid-twentieth-century expansion of the middle class and the emergence of a corporatised consumer culture. The explosion of romance fiction, in particular, proceeded from post-war developments in market research, advertising, and mass distribution, which allowed North American and UK publishers to capitalise on middle-class women's patterns of domesticity and leisure consumption. As Janice Radway argues, the breakout success of imprints such as Harlequin (established in 1949) and Silhouette Books (established in 1980) is evidence not of 'some *greater* need for [generic] reassurance among [...] women' but, rather, of a calculated marketing strategy predicated, as one Harlequin executive put it, on 'deliver[ing] exactly what the customer expects'.[27] The conventions of romance have continued to structure the increasingly global commodification of middle-class women's desire. Since the 1980s, a succession of niche genres has adapted the love/marriage plot to the shifting conditions of the neoliberal economy. If the romcom, the chick flick, and chick lit have 'pigeonhole[ed] the perceived truths of women's experiences in a "lifestyle" culture', as Diane Negra claims, more recent variants like hen-lit and recessionista lit have draped female consumption in a thin veil of contrition and frugality all the while maintaining romance as an increasingly unconvincing narrative resolution to unemployment or economic hardship.[28] It is no accident that throughout *The Forgotten Waltz*, Gina draws on the familiarities of romance to offset the precarious financial and domestic conditions of the downturn, nor that she derives reassurance from it: the genre has been engineered for that very purpose.

The police procedural also arose as a distinctly bourgeois genre. Its institutional history mirrors that of romance novels: it was promoted by publishers hoping to anchor the market in middle-class male readers when paperback mystery sales declined at mid-century.[29] Like its precursor, the detective novel, the procedural developed from out of the anxieties of urbanisation. But whereas classic and hardboiled detective fiction and *film noir* featured the romantic individualism of armchair and private/semi-private investigators, the procedural focused on the bureaucratic work of professional police. In the United States, the genre arose amid a wave of police reform that applied the principles of management science and human relations in order to improve public perceptions of law enforcement, while in the UK it accompanied the cultural rehabilitation of middle-class masculinity.[30] The genre performs a double ideological function in these and other post-war and contemporary contexts: it offers stable depictions of routinised (predominantly male) professional work during a period when middle-class labour has shifted from entrepreneurship to white-collar and casualised forms of employment, and, moreover, it sutures the police profession to the production of domestic life and social consensus.[31] In *Broken Harbor*, the role of detective, which is always already informed by the narrative conventions of the police procedural, re-inforces Mick's flagging sense of bourgeois agency even as the novel's metatextuality intimates the genre's inadequacy in resolving the contradictions of late capitalist society.

Middlebrow literary genres, then, historically underwrite popular narratives about bourgeois normalcy, satisfaction, and success that emerge during the post-war period. And they resurface in post-Celtic Tiger novels like enfeebled would-be guarantors of middle-class futurity. It is the combination of their reassuring familiarity and grave insufficiency that accounts for the sheer proliferation of cliché within these works. Whereas all genre traffics by definition in a certain amount of cliché, the volume and intensity in Irish recessionary fiction is noteworthy. In *The Forgotten Waltz* and *Broken Harbor*, Enright's and French's narrators draw upon the genres of romance and the police procedural in the hope that they will furnish formal means for fulfilling middle-class expectations that no longer seem tenable. When those genres begin to falter, cliché goes into overdrive.

The Affordances of Cliché

Although the love affair in *The Forgotten Waltz* begins cinematically, Gina likens her affair to various artistic media. The novel's overarching conceit is musical: the chapters are titled after classic love songs, and while Enright refrains from printing the lyrics, they echo in the crevices of the narration, attesting to the innate flexibility of the love metaphor. If love is a fleeting addictive pleasure in Duke Ellington's 'Love is like a Cigarette', it is a slow dance in Leonard Cohen's 'Dance Me to the End of Love', a song that 'change[s] from major to minor' in Cole Porter's 'Ev'ry Time We Say Goodbye', a pricey gamble in 10cc's 'The Things we do for Love', and a distraction that 'don't pay my bills' in Barrett Strong's 'Money (That's What I Want)'.[32] Gina wills her affair to play out like one of these love songs (or a love story, or romantic movie), but the problem with these narratives is that they are built upon clichés so varied they cancel one another out. As Serpell argues, 'that there is a cliché for every situation suggests that each one is both self-evidently true and entirely controvertible'.[33] This redundancy does not prevent Gina from trying to make her life mirror art, but it does require persistent narrative adjustment. For instance, in describing an early rendezvous with Séan, she struggles to find the appropriate cliché to account for their silence:

> We didn't talk much.
> Silence made it that bit filthier, of course. And people do not speak, in a dream. [. . .] It was daylight . . . There wasn't much kissing. Maybe this is why it all seemed so clear – too clear – why so few words were said.
> But also, perhaps [. . .] there was too much to say, and all of it wrong.

Or maybe I am being romantic, here. I mean, who knows what Séan was thinking, at that stage. He did say – I think I remember him saying – 'Sssh.' And, actually, that first time in the Gresham was a bit hurried and mishandled. Séan afterwards a little agitated, almost brusque. But the second time. The second assignation. Was perfect.[34]

Having re-evaluated and revised the scene past the limits of what qualifies as romance, Gina establishes the *next* 'assignation' as perfect – and leaves it at that.

Despite the appearance of wistful sentimentality, Gina's use of cliché is both deliberate and calculated. It functions as a form of loss aversion: if Enright's narrator can convince herself that the affair with Séan was exceptional (not just good but *Hollywood* good), then it will have been worth the cost in damage to their respective families. The descriptions of the affair operate not as isolated utterances but as part of an ongoing, high-stakes process of rationalisation and memory formation where wording matters enormously. Thus, during the flirtation phase, Gina is not just aroused but 'trembl[ing]' with desire; once the affair begins, the couple do not merely sneak around but play 'the office game' and 'the game of hotel assignations and fabulous, illicit lust'.[35] Later, Gina reflects on how the refrain 'I love him' sustains her during the difficult period after their infidelity is made public: '*I love him*: dull, like a pain, when no one rang: thrilling and clarion in the arguments I had with my sister, *I love him!*'[36] The alchemy of cliché ensures that everything up to and including the narrative present (early 2009) continues to be 'worth it' because it must be made worth it. The price Gina and Séan pay for the affair is literal – the ending of their respective marriages saddles the couple with considerable debt – and ongoing insofar as they will remain financially immobile until the economy improves.

The collapse of the housing market changes the terms of the lovers' relationship. It is not that their investment in one another is suddenly monetised (it already was) but that they become newly aware of its monetisation. 'You think it is about sex', Gina remarks, 'and then you remember the money.'[37] The couple continue to split mortgages with each of their ex-spouses plus some or all of the costs associated with Gina's late mother's house, in which they are temporarily living; the situation will not change until the market recovers enough to sell one or more of the properties, probably at a loss. The clichés of romance become indispensable during this extended waiting period. They enliven sober economic realities and the routines of a now-familiar relationship by re-introducing (often clumsily) a bygone element of risk: the couple are not just indebted but 'living on stolen time'; they buy 'boxes of laundry tablets like Bonnie and Clyde'.[38] By doubling down on romance, Gina is also able to deny her mounting disappointment in a genre that concludes at the point of maximum happiness and that thus cannot accommodate the later stages of her relationship, like the banal horror of watching herself and Séan settle into a less appealing set of clichés: the younger woman, the controlling man, the jaded lovers. The clichéd conventions of romantic love furnish Gina with an affective means for sustaining what Berlant calls 'cruel optimism', that persistent attachment to the late capitalist fantasy of 'the good life' despite overwhelming evidence of its unattainability.[39] They enable Enright's narrator to continue telling her story in a recognisable genre; they ensure that she does not run out of breath, both literally and figuratively.

In *The Forgotten Waltz*, and in contemporary Irish literature more broadly, cliché functions as a form of patchwork (in Caroline Levine's capacious sense of form) for good-life genres that have fractured under the pressures and contradictions of the Irish recession. According to Levine, form is at once aesthetic and political; it is *'an arrangement of elements'* whose 'affordances' (or potential uses) organise aesthetic and sociopolitical experience.[40] In the case of recessionary fiction, cliché's aesthetic affordances – the ways it summons and sustains familiar genres – are inextricable from its affective and political potential to sustain faith in the attainability of bourgeois satisfaction. Although this sustenance is unquestionably political, it is not necessarily hegemonic. Just as it is a mistake to equate the conventionality of middlebrow genres with political naiveté or agnosticism, so too is it a mistake to discredit cliché's weak powers of affective and narrative maintenance, which may not inspire radical hope or outrage, yet which undoubtedly manifest more than acquiescence or despair.

The counterpart to the narrative conventions of middle-class romance are those of the bourgeois workplace. Whereas the former organises the domestic sphere through intense feeling, the latter anchors public life through professionalism, rationality, and restraint. While Enright's protagonist exhibits a penchant for romance throughout *The Forgotten Waltz*, she also has a successful career in IT, and the clichés of managerial competency creep into her narration whenever she begins to think about the financial crash: 'It is what it is'; 'It's fine. Everything is fine'; 'Nothing, as I am tired of saying, went wrong.'[41] Insofar as they are meant to steel Gina against the anonymous caprices of modern economic life and to establish authority over what would otherwise be uncontrollable chaos, these brusque expressions resemble those of Detective Mick Kennedy in

Broken Harbor. A divorcé living in a pricey city-centre apartment that does not particularly suit him, Mick staves off the disappointments of his failed marriage and sterile home life by throwing himself into work, and his narration teems with the clichéd aphorisms of the police procedural. French's detective fires off pithy nuggets of professional knowledge the same way he approaches a crime scene, 'at a swift, efficient pace'.[42] These aphorisms range from the procedural (the simplest solution is the right solution) to the behavioural (everyone lies; women talk; infidelity is human nature) to the downright corny ('Places are like people are like sharks: if they stop moving, they die.').[43] Mick even has a professional aphorism to justify his fondness for driving a Beemer: 'If you want to come out a success [. . .] you cannot go in smelling of failure.'[44] His torrent of clichés is partly pedagogical (he is mentoring a new rookie, Richie Curran) and partly a nod to the *film noir* voice-over, but it also suggests the degree to which Mick wields his professional identity to compensate for private vulnerabilities.

Mick's work life, like his personal life, is an extended exercise in contingency management. He understands the role of detective as a final bulwark against societal chaos, a voice that 'say[s], when no one else will, *There are rules here. There are limits. There are boundaries that don't move.*'[45] More than self-aggrandisement, this conception of his professional function grants Mick a crucial sense of agency that he has been chasing since childhood. Son of a depressive mother who drowned herself on a family holiday, Mick now serves as occasional caretaker for his adult sister Dina, whose mental illness he attributes to their mother's suicide. It is his aphoristic conviction in the direct relationship between action and consequence that allows Mick to succeed in his job and to manage his familial trauma. 'Believing in cause and effect isn't a luxury', he tells Richie. 'It's an essential, like calcium, or iron.'[46] But this faith proves a liability in the murder case that rests at the heart of French's novel. Mick and Richie are called to the Dublin outskirts to investigate the stabbing of a young couple, Pat and Jenny Spain, and their two children. Jenny is the sole survivor of the attack, which took place in the family's home, one of the few finished properties in an abandoned luxury housing development. *Broken Harbor* draws an analogy between the phenomenon of the Celtic Tiger ghost estate (those partially finished, often pre-purchased properties that developers abandoned when the housing market crashed) and the savagery of prosperity, and Mick follows suit: his initial hunch is that the Spains were running drugs to maintain their aspirational lifestyle. Mick reserves little sympathy for Pat and Jenny's generation, who had 'never been broke, never seen the country broke'.⁴⁷ Yet, as the investigation proceeds, he develops a compromising attachment to the Spains' determination to make life conform to their bidding.

As the detectives piece together Pat and Jenny's lives, they begin seeing the couple the way their peers do, as poster children for the Celtic Tiger: high school sweethearts, married in 2002, homeowners by 2006, doting parents, popular, beautiful, and by all accounts, madly in love. Even after the downturn when Pat loses his job, they maintain the appearance of success. Jenny, in particular, ascribes to the power of positive thinking, that staple of pop-psychology which traces its origins to the post-war religious self-help movement in the US and the rise of corporate culture. Her husband would find employment, she assumed, because '[t]hat's how it *works*. Everyone knows: if you don't have a job, it's because you're crap at what you do, or because you don't actually want one. End of story.'⁴⁸ During his interrogations of Jenny, Mick comes to recognise in her forced idealism a counterpart to his own insistence that 'what you get out of life is mostly what you planted'.⁴⁹ Both characters maintain optimism in the face of indiscriminate precarity by adhering to the neoliberal credo of personal responsibility, an injunction that sanctions the erasure of social protections by appealing to the moral-cultural virtues of free-market individualism. As Melinda Cooper argues, 'the imperative of *personal responsibility* slides ineluctably into that of *family responsibility* when it comes to managing the inevitable problems of economic dependence'.⁵⁰ Jenny's determination to '*make everything lovely for [Pat]*' is also a pledge to manage the family's economic woes in the private sphere of the home, and it inspires in Mick an admiration that compromises his professional objectivity: he fails to recognise her as the killer until the investigation has spiralled beyond his control.⁵¹ Invested as he is in the effort-reward continuum, Mick cannot imagine the depth or violent consequences of Jenny's grief at having seen her – their – worldview shattered.

The botching of the Spain case undermines Mick's long-cherished confidence not only in the value of his work as a detective, but also in the value of self-management and bureaucratic procedure as formal structures of professional life. Mick cannot reconcile the tidy logical and narrative resolutions demanded in the case report with the sheer contingency and lack of accountability he witnesses in post-Tiger society. While his clichéd aphorisms about the routines of investigative work and the inherent order of civil society temporarily allow Mick to continue narrating his life according to the fraying generic conventions of the police procedural, by the novel's end he announces his intention to leave the profession, telling his Superintendent, 'I think it's time for a change.'⁵² In this final exchange, French's narrator continues to participate in the ritualised procedures and conventions of the bourgeois workplace (the formal resignation, the euphemisms of professional politeness) even as he looks to flee the world of bureaucratised labour. His conflicted behaviour encapsulates the ambivalent metatextuality of a novel that deconstructs the very narrative of professional success that it re-inforces all the while, through its glowing reception and the ascendant trajectory of the author's meteoric career.

Genre, Gender, and the Literary Marketplace

Unlike French's narrator, Irish readers have had few misgivings about the conventionality of the police procedural, if book sales are any indication. Crime fiction has flourished during and especially after the Celtic Tiger. Scholars and authors have credited its popularity to the psychological desire for order following the vertiginous social upheavals of the past two decades.⁵³ Meanwhile, publishers and industry analysts hail its 'recession-proof' resilience, a designation also bestowed upon other varieties of genre fiction.⁵⁴ For all its market success, however, crime fiction's status within the literary world remains fraught. The contentiousness of its perceived merit can be gleaned especially vividly in the reception of French's novels. Consider two enthusiastic reviews of *Broken Harbor* in the *Irish Independent*, published a week apart. In the first, Myles McWeeney pronounces French 'the First Lady of Irish Crime'; in the second, Claire Coughlan predicts the author will soon be recognised 'not only as the queen of Irish crime fiction, but the queen of Irish fiction, full stop'. Coughlan's endorsement appears the more emphatic of the two insofar as she extends the scope of the author's proverbial dominion from crime fiction to all fiction, but promoting French to 'fiction, full stop' also requires substantial preemptive effort. Coughlan lists French's awards and accomplishments, details her 'international' readership, even assures crime-fiction sceptics that 'this is a good place' to start.⁵⁵ Genre writing *can* be excellent, the review would seem to suggest, but only when it looks a lot like literary fiction.

French makes no apologies for genre. In an interview published around the time of *Broken Harbor*'s release, she calls herself a 'mystery writer' and discusses the state of the crime-fiction market.⁵⁶ Nevertheless, those who read and write about her work continue wanting to promote it (implicitly or explicitly) to the ranks of literary fiction or, in the terms of a Goodreads.com reader, the 'cut-above-genre' shelf.[57] Enright, meanwhile, occupies an uncontested place within the echelon of literary fiction. Yet even there, the woman writer is made chronically aware of her supposed susceptibility to genre contamination. The reception of *The Forgotten Waltz* offers a case in point: a number of reviews commented on the protagonist's shallowness and unlikeability, yet the novel was generally well received. '*The Forgotten Waltz* is a book we read with enjoyment and admiration but not for the usual pleasures of language, suspense, sensibility and so forth', declares Francine Prose in *The New York Times*; instead, it is 'at times, like eavesdropping on a very long, crazily intimate cellphone conversation'.[58] That Prose's review should conclude by calling *The Forgotten Waltz* 'courageous' says something about Enright's stature: at this point in her career she presumably gets a pass, though not without being reminded that the shallow materialism and 'pop-psychology clichés' of the protagonist place her novel in dangerous proximity to chick lit.

When Enright voluntarily plays with the conventions of romance fiction within a literary novel, and when French publishes crime fiction that literary readers consume, they are unsettling the hierarchies of generic and gendered prestige that professional writers (especially women writers) must continually navigate. As the market in literary fiction shrinks, the balance between making a living and building a legacy as an author comes down increasingly to a question of genre. According to Mark McGurl, 'fiction in the Age of Amazon *is* genre fiction, a highly gendered and age-differentiated genre system' structured by 'tested models of market success' and 'an audience ready to be pleased again and again within the terms of an implicit contract'.[59] But the history of mass-market publishing reminds us that the contractual expectations and financial compensations of genre have governed middle-class literary writing and reading since at least mid-century. The cliché of fiction in the age of Amazon, or in the era of post-Celtic Tiger recession, is one that Harlequin's vice president for marketing knew back in 1980: that it pays financially – and costs professionally – to 'deliver exactly what the customer expects'.

Notes

1. Anne Enright, *The Forgotten Waltz* (New York: Norton, 2011), p. 147.
2. The moniker 'Celtic Tiger', source of many a subsequent feline pun, was coined in 1994 by the investment firm Morgan Stanley to describe Ireland's

resemblance to the booming 'Asian Tiger' economies of the post-war period. See Kevin Gardiner, 'The Irish Economy: a Celtic Tiger', *Morgan Stanley Euroletter*, 31 August 1994, pp. 9–21.
3. Enright, *The Forgotten Waltz*, p. 160.
4. Ibid., p. 201.
5. Alison Flood, 'Julian Gough Slams Fellow Irish Novelists as "Priestly Caste" Cut Off from the Culture', *The Guardian*, 11 February 2010: www.theguardian.com/books/2010/feb/11/julian-gough-irish-novlists-priestly-caste [accessed 19 August 2019].
6. Fintan O'Toole, 'Writing the Boom', *The Irish Times*, 25 January 2001: www.irishtimes.com/culture/writing-the-boom-1.273557 [accessed 27 July 2018].
7. For example, J. M. Synge worried that without sufficient challenges to its revivalism, the Abbey might become 'a purely fantastic unmodern ideal breezy springdayish Cuchulanoid National Theatre'. Quoted in Declan Kiberd, *Synge and the Irish Language* (London: Macmillan, 1979), p. 111.
8. O'Toole, 'Writing the Boom'; Margaret Kelleher, 'Wanted an Irish Novelist: The Critical Decline of the Nineteenth-Century Novel', in Jacqueline Belanger, ed., *The Irish Novel in the Nineteenth Century: Facts and Fictions* (Dublin: Four Courts Press, 2005), pp. 187–201.
9. Susan Cahill, *Irish Literature in the Celtic Tiger Years 1990–2008: Gender, Bodies, Memory* (London: Continuum, 2011), pp. 6–9, 13–15.
10. Éilís Ní Dhuibhne, 'Irish Literary Writers "Cut Off" from Current of Culture', *The Irish Times*, 11 March 2010: www.irishtimes.com/opinion/letters/irish-literary-writers-cut-off-from-current-of-culture-1.636167 [accessed 27 July 2018].
11. Catherine E. Clark, *Paris and the Cliché of History: The City and Photographs, 1860–1970* (Oxford: Oxford University Press, 2018), p. 9.
12. C. Namwali Serpell, 'A Heap of Cliché', in Elizabeth S. Anker and Rita Felski, eds., *Critique and Postcritique* (Durham, NC: Duke University Press, 2017), pp. 153–82 (p. 157).
13. Ibid.; emphasis original.
14. See Eve Patten, 'Contemporary Irish Fiction', in John Wilson Foster, ed., *The Cambridge Companion to the Irish Novel* (Cambridge: Cambridge University Press, 2006), pp. 259–67; and Elizabeth Cullingford, 'American Dreams: Emigration or Exile in Contemporary Irish Fiction?', *Éire-Ireland*, 49.3–4 (Fall/Winter 2014), pp. 60–94.
15. Declan Hughes, *Shiver* (London: Methuen, 2003), p. 43.
16. One exception is Patrick Lonergan's blog post about Claire Kilroy and the conventions of Celtic Tiger satire. See Patrick Lonergan, 'Claire Kilroy's The Devil I Know, Faust and Post-Celtic Tiger Literature', 21 June 2013: https://patricklonergan.wordpress.com/2013/06/21/claire-kilroys-_the-devil-i-know_-and-post-celtic-tiger-literature/ [accessed 8 August 2018].
17. French's novel was released in the UK, Irish, and US markets with different spellings (*Broken Harbour/Harbor*). For the sake of consistency, I cite the US edition and retain the US spelling throughout the essay, except in citations.

18. Lauren Berlant, *Cruel Optimism* (Durham, NC: Duke University Press, 2011), p. 200.
19. Christopher T. Whelan, Brian Nolan, and Bertrand Maître, 'Economic Stress and the Great Recession in Ireland: The Erosion of Social Class Advantage', *The Economic and Social Review*, 49.3 (Autumn 2018), pp. 259–86; Dorothy Watson, et al., 'Socio-Economic Variation in the Impact of the Irish Recession on the Experience of Economic Stress among Families', *The Economic and Social Review*, 47.4 (December 2016), pp. 477–98.
20. Enright, *The Forgotten Waltz*, p. 13.
21. Tana French, *Broken Harbor* (New York Penguin, 2012), p. 2.
22. Enright, *The Forgotten Waltz*, p. 9.
23. Nicola Bauman, *A Very Great Profession: The Woman's Novel 1914–39* (London: Virago, 1983); Janice Radway, *Reading the Romance: Women, Patriarchy, and Popular Literature* (Chapel Hill, NC: University of North Carolina Press, 1984); Alison Light, *Forever England: Femininity, Literature and Conservatism Between the Wars* (London: Routledge, 1991); and Joan Shelley Rubin, *The Making of Middlebrow Culture* (Chapel Hill, NC: University of North Carolina Press, 1992).
24. Beth Driscoll, 'The Middlebrow Family Resemblance: Features of the Historical and Contemporary Middlebrow', *Post45*, 2 July 2016: http://post45.research.yale.edu/2016/07/the-middlebrow-family-resemblance-features-of-the-historical-and-contemporary-middlebrow/ [accessed 22 October 2018]. See also Beth Driscoll, *The New Literary Middlebrow: Tastemakers and Reading in the Twenty-First Century* (Basingstoke: Palgrave Macmillan, 2014).
25. For a discussion of middlebrow fiction's therapeutic effects, see Timothy Aubry, *Reading as Therapy: What Contemporary Literature Does for Middle-Class Americans* (Iowa City, IA: University of Iowa Press, 2011). On the relationship between middlebrow fiction and cultural capital, see Janice Radway, *A Feeling for Books: The Book-of-the-Month Club, Literary Taste and Middle-Class Desire* (Chapel Hill, NC: University of North Carolina Press, 1997).
26. Examples of the former response include Adam Rowe, 'How Indie Genre Fiction Ebooks Are Thriving Online', *Forbes*, 13 January 2018: www.forbes.com/sites/adamrowe1/2018/01/13/how-indie-genre-fiction-ebooks-are-thriving-online/-4e7270cc11fa [accessed 25 October 2018]; Tim Lott, 'Why Should We Subsidise Writers Who Have Lost the Plot?', *The Guardian*, 1 January 2018: www.theguardian.com/commentisfree/2018/jan/01/subsidise-writers-lost-plot-literary-fiction-authors-readers-story [accessed 25 October 2018]; Sophie Hannah, 'It's No Mystery that Crime is the Biggest-Selling Genre in Books', *The Guardian*, 12 April 2018: www.theguardian.com/books/booksblog/2018/apr/12/mystery-crime-fiction-bestselling-book-genre-sophie-hannah [accessed 25 October 2018]; and Adam Rowe, 'Science Fiction and Fantasy Book Sales Have Doubled since 2010', *Forbes*, 19 June 2018: www.forbes.com/sites/adamrowe1/2018/06/19/science-fiction-and-fantasy-book-sales-have-doubled-sin

ce-2010/-60484df02edf [accessed 25 October 2018]. Meanwhile, *The Guardian*'s culture editor Claire Armistead responded to the ACE report by calling for increased funding for authors in ways that implicitly devalued genre fiction. Euphemistically lamenting the 'less adventurous' reading choices of her contemporaries, which she attributes to 'branding and familiarity' rather than aesthetic merit, Armistead goes on to claim that literary fiction 'has a measurable social value, increasing empathy levels in readers where more popular forms of genre fiction do not'. Claire Armistead, 'Literary Fiction is in Crisis. A New Chapter of Funding Authors Must Begin,' *The Guardian*, 15 December 2017: www.theguardian.com/commentisfree/2017/dec/15/literary-fiction-crisis-chapter-funding-authors-arts-council-england [accessed 25 October 2018].

27. Radway, *Reading the Romance*, p. 45; quoted in Radway, *Reading the Romance*, p. 43.
28. Diane Negra, *What a Girl Wants? Fantasizing the Reclamation of Self in Postfeminism* (London: Routledge, 2009), p. 8. For discussions of hen-lit and recessionista lit, see Marion McKeone, 'The Rise of Recession Lit', *The Irish Times*, 26 September 2009: www.irishtimes.com/life-and-style/the-rise-of-recession-lit-1.745825 [accessed 30 March 2019]; and Diane Negra and Yvonne Tasker, 'Neoliberal Frames and Genres of Inequality: Recession-era Chick Flicks and Male-centred Corporate Melodrama', *European Journal of Cultural Studies*, 16.3 (June 2013), pp. 344–61 (pp. 350–3).
29. Christopher P. Wilson, *Cop Knowledge: Police Power and Cultural Narrative in Twentieth-Century America* (Chicago and London: University of Chicago Press, 2000), p. 71.
30. Ibid., pp. 66–71; Gill Plain, 'Structures of Authority: Post-war Masculinity and the British Police', *Itinéraires: Littérature, Textes, Cultures*, 2014.3 (2015): https://journals.openedition.org/itineraires/2613 [accessed 30 March 2019].
31. See Andrew Hoberek, *The Twilight of the Middle Class: Post-World War II American Fiction and White-Collar Work* (Princeton, NJ: Princeton University Press, 2005), pp. 17–18.
32. Enright, *The Forgotten Waltz*, pp. 16, 122, 129, 230, and 167.
33. Serpell, 'A Heap of Cliché', p. 160.
34. Enright, *The Forgotten Waltz*, p. 73.
35. Ibid., pp. 60, 61.
36. Ibid., p. 157. For a reading of 'I love you' as a cliché made meaningless through repetition, see Serpell, 'A Heap of Cliché', pp. 168–9.
37. Ibid., p. 172.
38. Ibid., pp. 138, 176.
39. Berlant, *Cruel Optimism*, p. 2.
40. Caroline Levine, *Forms: Whole, Rhythm, Hierarchy, Network* (Princeton, NJ: Princeton University Press, 2015), pp. 3, 6; emphasis original.
41. Enright, *The Forgotten Waltz*, pp. 147, 232, and 179.
42. French, *Broken Harbor*, p. 14.
43. Ibid., pp. 11–12.

44. Ibid., p. 11.
45. Ibid., p. 85; emphasis original.
46. Ibid., p. 160.
47. Ibid., p. 51.
48. Ibid., p. 392.
49. Ibid., p. 159.
50. Melinda Cooper, *Family Values: Between Neoliberalism and the New Social Conservatism* (New York: Zone Books, 2017), p. 71; emphasis original.
51. French, *Broken Harbor*, p. 393; emphasis original.
52. Ibid., p. 447.
53. Elizabeth Mannion and Brian Cliff have cautioned that the tradition of Irish crime fiction is older as well as more thematically and contextually diverse than such an account allows. Elizabeth Mannion, 'A Path to Emerald Noir: The Rise of the Irish Detective Novel', in Elizabeth Mannion, ed., *The Contemporary Irish Detective Novel* (Basingstoke: Palgrave Macmillan, 2016), pp. 3–4; Brian Cliff, *Irish Crime Fiction* (Basingstoke: Palgrave Macmillan, 2018), pp. 3–10.
54. Motoko Rich, 'Recession Fuels Demand for Romance Novels', *The New York Times*, 7 April 2009: www.nytimes.com/2009/04/08/books/08roma.html [accessed 25 October 2018]; Declan Burke, 'Twists and Turns of a Recession-Proof Business', *The Irish Times*, 2 July 2011: www.irishtimes.com/culture/books/twists-and-turns-of-a-recession-proof-business-1.590188 [accessed 25 October 2018]; John Mullan, 'The Triumph of Fantasy Fiction', *The Guardian*, 3 April 2015: www.theguardian.com/books/2015/apr/03/george-rr-martin-game-of-thrones-and-the-triumph-of-fantasy-fiction [accessed 25 October 2018]; and Anita Singh, 'Crime Pays: Thrillers and Detective Novels Now Outsell All Other Fiction', *The Telegraph*, 11 April 2018: www.telegraph.co.uk/news/2018/04/11/crime-pays-thrillers-detective-novels-now-outsell-fiction/ [accessed 25 October 2018].
55. Myles McWeeney, 'Review: Thriller: Broken Harbour by Tana French', *Irish Independent*, 1 July 2012: www.independent.ie/entertainment/books/review-thriller-broken-harbour-by-tana-french-26870947.html [accessed 29 October 2018]; and Claire Coughlan, 'Review: Broken Harbour by Tana French', *Irish Independent*, 9 July 2012: www.independent.ie/entertainment/books/review-broken-harbour-by-tana-french-26873987.html [accessed 29 October 2018].
56. Alison Flood, 'Tana French: I'm Haunted by Ireland's Ghost Estates', *The Guardian*, 27 June 2012: www.theguardian.com/books/2012/jul/27/tana-french-interview [accessed 3 November 2018].
57. www.goodreads.com/review/list/4162791-claudia-putnam?shelf=cut-above-genre [accessed 3 November 2018].
58. Francine Prose, 'An Unrepentant Adulterer', *The New York Times*, 30 September 2011: www.nytimes.com/2011/10/02/books/review/the-forgotten-waltz-by-anne-enright-book-review.html [accessed 29 October 2018].
59. Mark McGurl, 'Everything and Less: Fiction in the Age of Amazon', *Modern Language Quarterly*, 77.3 (September 2016), pp. 447–71 (p. 460).

CHAPTER 14

Violence, Trauma, Recovery

Christopher Langlois

In a short article chronicling his reaction to the news of 31 August 1994 that the Provisional IRA had declared 'a complete cessation of military operations', Seamus Heaney recalls being torn between feelings of hopeful elation and indignant despair:

> I went outside to try to recollect myself and suddenly a blind seemed to rise somewhere at the back of my mind and the light came flooding in. I felt twenty-five years younger. I remembered what things had felt like in those early days of political ferment in the late sixties. How we all were brought beyond our highly-developed caution to believe that the effort to create new movement and language in the Northern context was a viable project.
>
> But as well as feeling freed up, I felt angry also. The quarter century we have lived through was a terrible black hole, and the inestimable suffering inflicted and endured by every party to the conflict has only brought the situation to a point that is politically less promising than things were in 1968.[1]

Heaney's ambivalent reaction was not atypical at the time, for reasons owing, on the one hand, to the hard-learned necessity of guarding oneself against overly optimistic evaluations of the chance for peace in a political climate steeped in twenty-five years of seemingly intractable sectarian conflict, and, on the other, to the diagnosis of the Irish Republic and Northern Irish economies at the end of the twentieth century and segueing into the twenty-first. It is a historically apt coincidence that 1994 witnessed the announcement of a tentative cessation to military operations, thereby paving the way for the Belfast Agreement of 1998, as well as the coinage of the phrase 'The Celtic Tiger' to describe an optimistic economic future of unrestrained prosperity and growth. The Celtic Tiger phase of economic ascendancy in the Irish Republic joined the 'Road to Belfast' phase of political reconciliation in the North as processes of transitional uncertainty, of cautious hope admixed with expectant disappointment, that dominated the cultural discourse of Ireland in the last decade of the twentieth century. The optimism invested in the real chance at reconciliation following the announcement of the ceasefire in the North was strengthened, in other words, by the prospect that the economic miracle of the Irish Republic would cross the border into the North as well. From Heaney's perspective, however, neither of these reciprocally enhancing prospects should have been advanced too confidently and therefore too aggressively without taking honest measure of just how deep and how wide the 'terrible black hole' of violence had been dug.

Heaney concludes his reflections on the 'cessation of violence' by seizing on the 'opportunity to open a space – and not just in the political arena but in the first level of each person's consciousness – a space where hope can grow'.[2] His insistence that the opportunity for opening this space can and must be actualised publicly (politically) but also privately (individually) is not a proposal for the faint of heart. Heaney's Janus-faced perspective, looking back at historical violences and forward to recovery, re-inscribes the poetics of self-division and self-scrutiny, never shying away from moral self-accusation, that had rendered his poetic voice so vital throughout the preceding twenty-five years of conflict. Heaney gives sufficient reason to suspect that in order to begin to endorse any authentic hope of recovery from the violences and counterviolences of the Troubles, indeed from the insecurities of living with the boom and bust of the Celtic Tiger, it is necessary to insist that while the space of history does not provide a place where the hope for recovery can organically grow beyond the toxic shadow of the past, it is nevertheless in history articulated as a worldly history of violence and trauma where the process of recovery must be (and is) tragically, ineluctably confined. Through the lens of Heaney's sober-eyed investment in opening spaces in history where hope can defiantly grow, this chapter reads Patrick McCabe's *Breakfast on Pluto* (1998) and Edna O'Brien's *The Little Red Chairs* (2015) as two novels conversant both with the punishments of history and with the need to nurture the prospects of hope in historical recovery.

McCabe's *Breakfast on Pluto* was published the year of the Belfast Agreement, but it was completed during the cautiously optimistic years after 1994. In his 'Prelude' to the American edition of the novel, McCabe takes stock of the novel's publication coincident with the Belfast Agreement to survey the violent historical origins of the 'dysfunctional double-bind of border-fever' that are responsible for 'mapping out the universe' into which Mr Patrick 'Pussy' Braden, the novel's narrator and protagonist, 'found himself tumbled': 'In 1745 a crofter was garoted. In

1848 a landlord dragged from his bed and put to the rope. Not long after that, twenty protestants burnt in a barn. Xmas 1881, a Catholic man disappeared and was found in a ditch, a crucifix hammered into his head.'[3] Set on the borderland of the fictional 'village of Tyreelin (pop. 1500) on the Southern side of the Irish border', 'approximately one mile from [. . .] a place that looks mysteriously like his but yet is a separate state', Pussy's story inherits a violent national history that has not yet revealed how its narrative cycle of violence and counterviolence will end.[4] And yet, McCabe uses the miraculous occasion of the Belfast Agreement as a platform for stepping outside of history and into the recently re-opened future, voicing his hope that with 'the war over, now perhaps we too can take – however tentatively – those first few steps which may end unease and see us there; home, belonging, and at peace'.[5] McCabe's interpretive intervention is far from inconsequential. Is this novel to be read as a Troubles or a post-Troubles novel? A novel of unredeemed, unhealed violence and trauma, or a novel of reconciliation and recovery? Are readers expected to privilege Pussy's 'personal revolution' or the political context leading up to and circumscribing the years of the Troubles that overshadows Pussy's narrative throughout?[6] As history would have it, such distinctions not only *cannot* be made cleanly, from an analytical perspective, but also *should not* be made too insistently, from an ethical perspective, given the intermingled, knotted realities of violence that had hitherto carried the tune of Ireland's savage, mournful historical rhythms up to this point in 1998.

McCabe opted for 1955 as the year of Pussy's birth, thereby ensuring that Pussy's formative years would overlap with the uneven political and economic developments in the Irish Republic and in the North. Pussy belongs to a generation born in the Irish Republic, as Declan Kiberd explains it, that 'had been enjoying a rare period of affluence when Northern Ireland erupted into violence; they feared that the spill-over of such disorder into the south could only threaten their new material well-being'.[7] *Breakfast on Pluto* is every bit a (pre-)Celtic Tiger novel as it is a (post-)Troubles novel, and these two horizons are not mutually exclusive for deciphering where in the 'dysfunctional double-bind of border-fever' the novel's centre of gravity is located. Pussy is thrown into the maelstrom of this tension between the ascending economic fortunes of the South, and the descending political misfortunes of the North. Equipped with a campy taste for consumerist pleasures and escapes, Pussy confronts the counter-taste for violence that overwhelmed the North, threatening, and perhaps succeeding, to overwhelm Pussy as well. Throughout the various antagonistic encounters between these two 'tastes', however, McCabe never loses sight of what is arguably the more illuminating perspective that *Breakfast on Pluto* articulates regarding how economic and political horizons interact within the novel and without. The more adept Pussy becomes at throwing herself into fantasies of consumerism and romantic bliss (and the securities promised by stereotypical ideals of feminine domesticity), the more vulnerable she is to suffering the violences from without as well as the unhealed-because-unhealable traumas from within.

Pussy's childhood is experienced as an exercise in turning away from the Irishness associated with a post-1916 Ireland and towards a cosmopolitan identity as a global player on the world stage of capitalist consumerism, newly enriched with the purchase power to buy its way out of the historicopolitical quagmire of colonisation, civil war, and sectarian conflict plaguing it right up until the end of the twentieth century. The price of Ireland's economic modernisation, uneven through and through, came at the expense of sacrificing any real hope of a collective recovery from the traumas of its historical memories of colonialism and sectarianism on the altar of a far tamer sort of recovery predicated on a neoliberal reconstruction of individuality. Ultimately, however, Pussy's headlong immersion in the pleasures of consumerism doubles as a self-defeating evasion of the mounting pressure of traumatic violences originating from the historico-political realities of Northern Ireland:

> How all that started was that 1966 was the jubilee commemoration of the 1916 rising and no matter where you went in Tyreelin, everyone was waving a tricoloured flag or singing an Irish ballad. [. . .] To tell you the truth, we didn't much care that much for the wars in the end. But Irwin – he was going clean mad over them! He had even taken to wearing his James Connolly rebel hat around the town and going off over the fields on his own to practice drilling. To keep him happy, we kept on saying the wars were great and then running off back to the hut to put on the Beatles and go absolutely mad as we clicked our fingers and jived in and out among the sheep and cows.[8]

This scene comes to terms with the tensions between fantasy and reality, playing and not-playing in the playground of history that the novel will continue to highlight, particularly as it concerns Pussy's decisions about where and how to flee the violences of the Troubles.

From Pussy's viewpoint on the political realities that insistently intrude into her narrative, there is very little difference between getting all dressed up for playing at 'international modelling', and donning, as does Pussy's childhood friend, Irwin, the requisite uniform for a commemoration of

1916, for an anti-internment march in Bogside, Derry in 1972 – 'that silly shirt with the great big fist bursting through a chain. "*Smash Internment Now!*"' – or for 'a *real* soldier to become, to take up arms and: "Fuck anyone who gets in the way!" He really was hilarious when he got started!'[9] Pussy's claim to being 'much too preoccupied with my own personal revolution to be bothered with anything so trivial' as 'the balloon in Northern Ireland having gone up in earnest', as Pussy so flippantly describes it, is not to be taken as evidence that this is a novel of historicopolitical evasion.[10] As Pussy is occasionally flush with cash, spending Saturdays in a 'Dublin marketplace' where 'my arms I filled with Max Factor, Johnson's Baby Oil, Blinkers eye-shadow, Oil of Olay, Silvikrin Alpine Herb shampoo, Eau de toilette, body moisturizers, body washes, cleansing milks', she becomes increasingly, albeit poorly, anaesthetised (and therefore more vulnerable) to the violent reality assaulting her immanently fractured psychological defences.[11]

Nowhere in the novel is the intersection between internalised fantasy and externalised violence more devastating than in Pussy's encounter with 'Silky String'. Now in London, where she has recently emigrated and is working as a prostitute, Pussy is dangerously susceptible to being wooed simply through the playing of a favourite pop song or the flashing before her eyes of a beautiful piece of silk, the fabric *par excellence* of luxurious consumerist consumption: 'I have to tell you – I was really beginning to like Silky. And when it was Vic Damone and "*Stay With Me*" that came over the airwaves just then – well! I must have jumped a little or shrieked perhaps, because he started laughing and said: "You like that, don't you?" as I dropped my eyes and replied: "Yes".'[12] The scene plays out traumatically, and thus not only violently, precisely through the weaponisation of what Pussy desires in what was, just a second ago, the context of sexual pleasure and the fantasy of falling metonymically in love with Silky. The silky string introduced into the sexual act proves not to be pleasurable, a fabric conducive to sexual enhancement due to its connotation of wealth, but a deeply unpleasurable 'ligature of some sort, soft but not so when about your Adam's apple it's drawn tight as it will go'.[13] Foreshadowing Pussy's inability to recover from her violent interrogation later in the novel under suspicion of perpetrating an IRA terrorist attack on a London pub – after which she writes to Terence, her therapist, that 'all I can say is, if you weren't whistling Dixie backwards on the far side of Pluto by the time they were finished with you, dearies, then you were made of strong stuff and no mistake – which, sorry to say, Miss Pussy wasn't!'[14] – the novel is focused here on Pussy's failure to convince 'that, like everything else, time began to pass and eventually my wounds healed'.[15] Violences such as this, whether an interrogation linked to the Troubles or a private, intimate experience of sexual assault, have a way of converging in *Breakfast on Pluto* as variations on the theme of a perpetual trauma.

Perched on the historical border of an avowed end of the Troubles and the acceleration of the Celtic Tiger ascendancy, McCabe's 1998 novel refuses to convert fantasies of recovery from violence into realities of recovery from violence, thus privileging the permanence of its protagonist's traumatised subjectivity. Readers of *Breakfast on Pluto* are saved from the illusory optimism that Neil Jordan affords viewers of his 2006 film adaptation of the novel. Whereas McCabe, in his novel, locks Pussy in a prison-house of fantasy right up until the concluding paragraph in which Pussy communicates her domestic, consumerist desire 'to be left alone' in London, 'flicking through my magazines', hoping one day 'to wake up in the hospital with my family all around me, exhausted after my ordeal maybe, but with a bloom like roses in my cheeks, as I stroke his soft and tender head, my little baby',[16] Jordan opts to portray Pussy's fantasy as a reality, and thus transitively portrays *Breakfast on Pluto* as a neoliberal fantasy of the individual's power to transcend historical, political, and economic catastrophe. Jordan, in other words, paints an ideologically corrupted picture of Pussy's meanderings through violence as nothing more than temporary obstacles to her inevitable recovery, a personal recovery that re-inforces the Celtic Tiger myth of an Ireland that had successfully conquered and moved on from its violent past. Here are two competing ideological viewpoints on contemporary Irish history, with McCabe's reflecting a cautious outlook from the threshold of the Belfast Agreement, and Jordan adopting a confident post-Troubles, Celtic Tiger view on an Irish future soon to be rattled by economic collapse.

Commenting on the excerpt taken from Roberto Bolaño's *By Night in Chile* that serves as one of two epigraphs for her novel *The Little Red Chairs*, 'an individual is no match for history', Edna O'Brien explains that Bolaño's words were, 'if you like, my guide, my mantra, in taking on this story of a woman who meets a man whom she thinks is a healer, who is not a healer, is a killer – but has both the aspect of healing and charm and if you like mesmerisation, and the other aspect of slaughter'.[17] Published in 2015, *The Little Red Chairs* appeared fifty-five years after O'Brien's monumental, controversial first novel, *The Country Girls*, and it concludes on an uncynical note of sympathy, not unfamiliar to readers of McCabe's *Breakfast on Pluto*, with the desire to be at home, safe from the violences of history and their repetitive, traumatic incursion into the present. Marking Bolaño's sobering words as the lodestar of the narrative about to unfold, readers of *The Little Red Chairs* are on notice that however psychologically complex, however courageous in her confrontation with the violent, patriarchal forces of Irish (and world) history, O'Brien's protagonist will not necessarily happily recover from the forthcoming violence and trauma.

O'Brien's vision of history is characteristically unforgiving of how that history is experienced by Irish women; but if *The Little Red Chairs* marks a departure from O'Brien's earlier writing, it is that Irish history, viewed from the perspective of this latest novel's female protagonist, is not fundamentally different from world history. A transnational, multicultural cast of supporting characters assists the protagonist, Fidelma, in understanding this. Whereas her 1994 novel *House of Splendid Isolation*, according to Michael Harris, represented for O'Brien a move away from 'the individual subject' and towards 'the national culture', interrogating 'contemporary Ireland by examining the national culture that shapes the individual subject', *The Little Red Chairs* signals a refreshing reversal of sorts, but without having disavowed, *pace* Harris, the postmodernist critique of national history previously performed.[18] Here the focus is not squarely on the national history of Ireland; rather, *The Little Red Chairs* begins to view history as a planetary history of violence visited upon individual subjects who are no match for its ubiquitous reach.

In O'Brien's compassionate hands, the characters deal with this worldly history of violence in fits and starts, in particular times and particular places, without the grandiose thinking that, individually, they can outmanoeuvre this history's toxic advance. O'Brien's decision to subject Fidelma to a grisly rape as punishment for her love affair with (and impregnation by) a charismatic stranger who takes up residence in her small rural Irish town, but who is later revealed as a fugitive from the massacre and siege of Sarajevo, 'Dr. Vlad', is a risky one. It hazards making this a novel of the unspeakability of trauma, of trauma's capacity to void language of its expressibility. It is a risk, as the novel goes on to expose, precisely because the trauma suffered by Fidelma is so tragically global in its variegated, all too frequent occurrence. *The Little Red Chairs* concerns not, or not only, the trauma of one; rather, it is a novel about the trauma, and thus also the shared vulnerability, of many, the unspeakable, untranslatable trauma that nevertheless binds a global community of women around the gendered specificity of experiencing sexualised violence.

The Little Red Chairs is driven by Fidelma's survival of a trauma that robs her of the power to locate the words that might narrate her trauma in service of her recovery:

The nurse is reeling off the next stage of her recovery, the rehabilitation process, learn to cope again and regain control of herself and her body. Staff are there for her, to give care and counselling. Words. Words. There is a place inside her that no care and no counsellor can reach. But she still smiles the grateful smile of the obligated [...].

'What will they want?' she asked the nurse.
'The oral evidence ... what happened to you out on the mountain.'
'I can't tell them that.'
'You must tell them ... you must ... for the law to do its duty.'
'I don't have the ... vocabulary.'
'Then you'll have to find the vocabulary.'
'They butchered me ... ' she said and gave a little insane laugh.[19]

Giving Fidelma the words 'I don't have the ... vocabulary' to articulate nothing more, but also nothing less than what, of her individuality and self, she has lost, provokes the question of what a sufficiently equipped vocabulary would look like and include. The ellipsis is key here, isolating and casting suspicion upon what the word 'vocabulary' would denote in this context: access to a secret store of words ready-made for voicing the expressive black hole of trauma. Responsibility for the post-traumatic impoverishment of expressivity does not, then, reside on the side of language, powerless as it constitutively is in the face of what calls insistently for expression. Here, the horizon of trauma that shrouds *The Little Red Chairs* gets threaded with the horizon of a post-Celtic Tiger Irishwoman who has been atomised as an individual. Stripped of the symbolic resources of community, of the confidence of a woman who had hitherto known only a sense of Irish belonging and middle-class security, Fidelma must take sole responsibility for providing testimony for what balks at the language of testimony. The responsibility for answering for trauma, then, is not first and foremost the responsibility of language, but of the individual acquiring a new knowledge of the self in the aftermath of her post-traumatic survival. This task cannot be completed alone, solely between the self and its vocabulary. Unfortunately for Fidelma, no outside assistance at this point in the novel aids in her reconstruction of self, symptomatic of the widespread communal alienation of the individual in the twenty-first century.

Through Fidelma, Vlad's former bodyguards, the 'Preventiva' who have lost 'everything, our fathers, our comrades, our lands ... then peace, lousy peace', exact revenge through the rape of Vlad's lover and then, after a panicked Fidelma shouts 'Don't kill it', the murder of Vlad's unborn child, for 'it is Vlad they want, it is him they have come to revenge themselves upon'.[20] Fidelma is not the immediately intended victim; she is Vlad's innocent, coincidental plenipotentiary, and not much more, but this does nothing to soften the force of the punishing assault that ensues (i.e. this barbaric act of intimate revenge, *pace* Heaney, is far from being only an Irish phenomenon); quite the contrary. Her participation in this act of revenge is vicarious only in the eyes of her assailants, before the one referred to as

> the Medico, furious at the time wasted, [...] takes the bar, holds it between her parted thighs and then rams it into her, slewing and tilting, then raking, as if raking earth. The pain is so violent that she cannot scream, only bleats of terror escape her and her screams are no more. The moaning of a dying animal, except she is not dying fast enough. Bound and held to that spot, she is calling on Jesus, on Christ, her hands pitifully outstretched, wantonly asking her killer to be her saviour. Half-lucid, half-crazed thoughts flit through her mind with each worsening thrust, and she remembers reading that at the very end, a dying person finds the courage to be brave, but no such courage befriends her. He is shouting for the torch to be held higher and for an instant, her sight is blanketed out by the glare and then it begins to happen, a slippage, as if all of her insides are being dislodged and from the two hooligans a shout of victory, as the blood comes churning out in fitful gushes. He withdraws the bar with the same savagery as he inserted it and flings it in disgust so that it hits then capsizes the second torch as both fall with a clang.[21]

This is O'Brien's vocabulary for what happened to Fidelma, and in its unflinching descriptiveness, it balks at the readerly expectation that the central event of traumatic violence in the narrative will be captured obliquely, or only through echoes in the subsequent representations of Fidelma's post-traumatic recovery. The vocabulary required for *the law to do its duty* is all too present in a novel composed through a narrative voice that weaves in and out of the mind of its protagonist, and thus it is a vocabulary (of wounded, wounding words) that is now Fidelma's most personal, most corrosive possession.

For O'Brien, what resists easy narrative capture is less the act of violence that precipitated Fidelma's trauma than her recovery:

> Coming back. Broken but not dead. The days, or was it weeks, in the hospital are a blur, being hefted on and off trolleys, hearing voices of doctors and nurses talking to one another, in muffled tones. What had they seen. What had they to do to her, to piece her back together. She would never

know. She only knew what happened on the mountain and she pushed it away each time, like pushing a heavy door.'²²

Ostracised from her community in Cloonoila after news spread of her marital infidelity and affair with a war criminal, Fidelma does what numerous Irish men and women (and what Patrick 'Pussy' Braden) had done before her (and will continue to do) – she moves to London.

After staying 'the first three nights in a B&B in Ebury Street, not far from Victoria Station', she remarks that 'I could have been any tourist, except that I wasn't, I had to find work.'²³ In recovery, Fidelma is not spared the reality many immigrants face immediately upon arrival: the need for employment. Fidelma's story, in other words, is not only that of a recovery from embodied trauma, but also of economic recovery after the bust of the Celtic Tiger. When she interviews for a job cleaning a bank after hours, Fidelma is isolated, stripped of virtually everything that had hitherto defined her knowledge of self. Fidelma hands the young man who interviews her for this menial position, Bluey, 'the two references she had brought, the one from Gerry her solicitor and the other from Father Eamonn. [. . .] Bluey read bits of it aloud, her breeding, her family descended from kings and queens, her convent education, her cultural yearnings, her love of literature, her French-themed boutique, which, alas, was lost during the financial crisis.'²⁴ Her prospects for employment post-2008 in the global metropolis of London differ from what a woman of her age, cultural background, and class might have expected. By landing this job, Bluey says encouragingly, she is being given the same opportunity that he gives to everyone, 'Latinos, Africans, Eastern Europeans, Angolans, West Indians, Chinese'.²⁵ Watching these colleagues 'as they dusted, trying to learn their techniques, some so brisk, some flicking the cloth, skidding and skiddering over the surfaces', Fidelma concludes that she has become, like them, one of the 'night people, one step away from ghosts, and strangers to each other. [. . .] Many had fled horror, countries they could never go back to, while still others yearned for home.'²⁶

The novel's global resonance is starkest in the aptly titled chapter 'The Centre', which narrates Fidelma accompanying one of her friendlier colleagues, Maria, to a building located on a 'cul de sac, under the flyover, with the constant thump-thump of traffic overhead'.²⁷ There is nothing glamorous about this place where Fidelma goes as one of many others who are 'there because they have nowhere else to go. Nobodies, mere numbers on paper or computer, the hunted, the haunted, the raped, the defeated, the mutilated, the banished, the flotsam of the world, unable to go home, wherever home is.'²⁸ For readers inclined to spot moments of inexpressibility in literatures of trauma, Fidelma's earlier assertion that she does not 'have the ... vocabulary' will begin to echo as the novel depicts, in this chapter, narratives of trauma from far away places that have gravitated to this place 'called the Centre', this place outside of midnight work where these 'nobodies' gather 'to share the stories of their fractured lives'.²⁹ Readers may be excused for asking, as they come upon this chapter, whether this will be the place where Fidelma will indeed 'find the vocabulary' that her nurse insisted was needed for the commencement of her recovery. Will it be through the words of others that Fidelma will succeed in bringing to memory (and thus beginning to mourn) what she lost of herself on that awful day in the 'large room with a clay floor that smell[ed] of animals and dried dung'?³⁰

Fidelma fades momentarily from the narrative spotlight in this chapter, and a history of violence is exposed in the lives of several supporting characters. Oghowen's story of her female circumcision, conveyed from Fidelma's perspective, diminishes Fidelma's sense of victimhood, but also provides her with a common language of gendered violation and violence. Oghowen includes in her narrative the detail that she was 'brought in and told to lie on the floor. It is a clay floor. I dig my fingers into the clay because I have nothing to hold onto.'³¹ It is this detail about the clay floor that Fidelma will repeat, almost verbatim, when she is alone with Maria and Varya, the coordinator of the Centre, and is asked to try to tell her own story again after her sense of having failed to do so truthfully in front of the other group members. Fidelma recalls what happened to her with a clarity of memory suggesting that it has not ceased happening in her mind: 'then the three brutes. Their smell, their sunglasses, one mended with Sellotape, the hut with the clay floor and nothing to hold onto, when it happened. When it happened.'³² Beginning with descriptions of the rain in Ireland and concluding with a quotation from an Emily Dickinson poem, Fidelma is perhaps right to be disappointed that in her first storytelling performance she lacked the appropriate vocabulary for convincingly communicating her pain, judging 'that it was not truthful, that it was too inconclusive, too lofty'.³³

Discovering in Oghowen a common language through their common experience of being violently prostrated, left helpless, and mutilated on a clay floor does little to stem Fidelma's self-accusatory judgement, iterated in her first (failed) telling of her story, that hers, unlike Oghowen's, is nevertheless a trauma for which she is partially responsible as retribution for her vicarious complicity, her innocent complicity, paradoxically, through her sexual affair with Vlad, in the genocidal crimes against Sarajevo: 'I feel that by having been with him I am an accomplice to those appalling things. I feel a guilt that is, if you like, counterfeit guilt and so I stand accused.'[34] There is a difficult truth lurking in Fidelma's self-accusation, one that has nothing whatsoever to do with the responsibility of a victim for her victimisation; rather, it has to do with the disproportionate vulnerability of female bodies to being imposed upon physically and over-coded socially. Victimised in a social context where 'girls are disposable', Oghowen retains a measure of innocence that Fidelma perceives she lacks because of her marital infidelity and her flagrant disregard, from a conservative, patriarchal perspective, for socially acceptable female behaviour.[35] To expect that Fidelma had not internalised fragments of this perspective is to grossly underestimate the degree to which any and all individuals are shaped by where they are from and by what and how their community thinks. Fidelma has left de Valera's Ireland geographically, but not necessarily psychologically, which is reflected in O'Brien's decision to devote the penultimate, but not the concluding, chapter to Fidelma's nostalgic desire to return home to Cloonoila after her time spent in London. This the novel cannot let her do, precisely because this is not an Irish novel in the same way that O'Brien's preceding novels so straightforwardly were. This is a novel that assigns its protagonist an identity as a woman like any other woman recovering from sexual violence, rather than an *Irish* woman recovering from an *Irish* violence.

When read juxtapositionally, the penultimate and concluding chapters put a maximum of pressure on the idea of recovery, and this in spite of the hopeful note the novel seeks to strike in its closing sentences. Between Ireland and the Centre, the place in the novel where 'the world comes in [...] every day', O'Brien opts for the latter to designate where Fidelma feels most at home, where she has the greatest hope for recovery, a fact that baffles Varya, who asks Fidelma, '*Why could I not go home, big house, four bedrooms, walled kitchen garden, a veranda, the lot*. I told her I could not go home until I could come home to myself.'[36] This is a destination that the novel gives no reason to assume will be conclusively reached. Nevertheless, it is a destination towards which the novel inexorably tends, with the all-important caveat that as a destination existing always in the future, it will be forever pinned just out of reach on the horizon of its approach. O'Brien, like Heaney, aspires to an Adornian sense of reconciliation predicated always tenuously on disharmony between what is and what is professed, dreamily, to be. Hers, like Heaney's, like McCabe's, is a conception of home that rhymes more half-truly with exile than it does with the 'permanence', the 'familiarity, the wood so quiet, the thin brown branches scrolling the air, a stillness, that hyphen between evening and night' that Fidelma remembers so romantically about being at home with her husband Jack in Ireland.[37]

In the concluding chapter, Fidelma joins the survivors of the Centre – 'Father. Mother. Brother. Sister. Shattered worlds. Lost embryos'[38] – in staging a Christmas performance of Shakespeare's *A Midsummer Night's Dream*, and 'for the finale, the word *Home* was to be sung and chanted in the thirty-five different languages of the performers. [. . .] *Home. Home. Home.* [. . .] You would not believe how many words there are for *home* and what savage music there can be wrung from it.'[39] With its closing emphasis on the 'savage music' of homes beyond Fidelma's home in Ireland, *The Little Red Chairs* reveals that it is not an optimistic novel; it is a hopeful novel, in a worldly sort of way. The distinction is subtle, yet crucial, and to understand why, we must make our way back to Heaney's 1994 reflections on how to seize the opportunity for hope after the suspension (and not yet, perhaps not ever, the cessation) of violence.

For Heaney, there are few words more misleading in the vocabulary of recovery than the word *hope*. If it is to hold good as a trusted watchword of recovery from historical violence, if this most fragile, most overused of words is allowed to circulate with a confidence that the historical facts on the ground do not truly support, then it risks operating as an alibi to bypass the ethical imperative of reconciliation and to speed us all too prematurely to amnesiac reconstruction. Conversely, hope is not, strictly speaking, it turns out, a historical category that must ask for permission from history to take flight. For Heaney, while in the throes of recovery from historical or personal trauma, and above all from the trauma that the Troubles caused for the participants in, as well as the bystanders to, its violence, it is necessary to understand hope as the act of assuming a historical standpoint *against* history, of learning, in the words of Maurice Blanchot in *The Writing of the Disaster*, how to stand 'outside history, but historically so'.[40] Heaney looks, in this part of 'Cessation 1994', outside of Ireland to the Czech dissident Vaclav Havel for instruction on how best to articulate hope. This is how Havel understands it, Heaney reminds his Irish readers, and it is an understanding that all (and not only the Irish) who are engaged in the difficult work of recovery from violence and trauma would be doing themselves a disservice to do without:

it seems to me that his definition has the kind of stoical clarity that should appeal to every realist in the north, Planter or Gael, Protestant or Catholic, optimist or pessimist.

Hope, according to Havel, is different from optimism. It is a state of the soul rather than a response to the evidence. [. . .] Its deepest roots are in the transcendental, beyond the horizon.[41]

The transcendental, in this sense, can and should be included in the vocabulary not of the religious or the metaphysical, but in the vocabulary of a worldly language of belonging that underwrites *The Little Red Chairs*. Fidelma's hope to sing the savage music of home rests precisely in the worldly 'Centre' of this novel, in the place where global strangers congregate around nothing so binding as their harmonious, disharmonious vocabulary of violence, trauma, and recovery.

Notes

1. Seamus Heaney, 'Cessation 1994', in *Finders Keepers* (London: Faber and Faber, 2002), p. 45.
2. Ibid., p. 47.
3. Patrick McCabe, *Breakfast on Pluto* (New York: HarperCollins, 1998), p. x.
4. Ibid., p. ix.
5. Ibid., p. xi.
6. Ibid., p. 22.
7. Declan Kiberd, *Inventing Ireland: The Literature of the Modern Nation* (London: Vintage, 1996), pp. 574–5.
8. McCabe, *Breakfast on Pluto*, p. 18.
9. Ibid., pp. 18, 38, 22.
10. Ibid., p. 22.
11. Ibid., pp. 35–6.
12. Ibid., p. 66.
13. Ibid., p. 69.
14. Ibid., pp. 143–4.
15. Ibid., p. 71.
16. Ibid., p. 199.
17. Edna O'Brien, quoted in Benedicte Page, 'Edna O'Brien: Interview', *The Bookseller*, 23 October 2015: www.thebookseller.com/profile/edna-obrien-interview-315176 [accessed 6 September 2018].
18. Michael Harris, 'Outside History: Edna O'Brien's *House of Splended Isolation*', *New Hibernia Review/Iris Éireannach Nua*, 10.1 (2006), pp. 111–22 (p. 114).
19. Edna O'Brien, *The Little Red Chairs* (New York: Little, Brown and Company, 2016), pp. 149–50.
20. O'Brien, *The Little Red Chairs*, p. 144.

21. Ibid., p. 146.
22. Ibid., p. 148.
23. Ibid., p. 166.
24. Ibid., p. 172.
25. Ibid.
26. Ibid., pp. 175, 176.
27. Ibid., p. 203.
28. Ibid.
29. Ibid.
30. Ibid., p. 143.
31. Ibid., p. 213.
32. Ibid., p. 217.
33. Ibid., p. 215.
34. Ibid.
35. Ibid., p. 213.
36. Ibid., pp. 293, 294; emphasis original.
37. Ibid., p. 289.
38. Ibid., p. 293.
39. Ibid., p. 297; emphasis original.
40. Maurice Blanchot, *The Writing of the Disaster*, trans. Ann Smock (Lincoln, NE: University of Nebraska Press, 1995), p. 40.
41. Heaney, 'Cessation 1994', p. 47.

CHAPTER 15

Modes of Witnessing and Ireland's Institutional History

Emilie Pine, Susan Leavy, Mark Keane, Maeve Casserly, and Tom Lane

> On behalf of the state and all its citizens, the government wishes to make a sincere and long overdue apology to the victims of childhood abuse for our collective failure to intervene, to detect their pain, to come to their rescue ... 'all children need love and security'. Too many of our children were denied this love, care and security. Abuse ruined their childhoods and has been an ever present part of their adult lives reminding them of a time when they were helpless. I want to say to them that we believe they were gravely wronged, and that we must do all we can now to overcome the lasting effects of their ordeals.
>
> Bertie Ahern, Irish Taoiseach, 1999[1]

For most of the twentieth century, Ireland had a system of residential institutions – known as Industrial Schools – for children.[2] These institutions were funded and overseen by the Irish State and run by the religious orders of the Catholic Church. Though the institutions were intended to provide children with vocational education for industrial employment and to respond to perceived problems of poverty and anti-social behaviour, in reality children were incarcerated in these residential institutions and physically, emotionally, and sexually abused. This happened for more than seven decades, to tens of thousands of children. And almost no one intervened; the institutions' walls kept people in and, arguably, enabled everyone else's oblivion. This chapter traces the recent transition from not-knowing to knowing and considers how contemporary narrative practices and technologies can facilitate understanding Ireland's difficult past, so as to help us tell different stories.

Apologising for the Past

In May 2009, then Taoiseach Bertie Ahern apologised to the survivors of institutional child abuse in Ireland, acknowledging 'collective failure' on behalf of the citizens of Ireland, and recognising the long-term damage of child abuse. Ahern's statement that he believed the victims' memories of abuse was a first necessary step in transforming attitudes towards survivors. Ahern's apology is not without fault – the binary of 'citizens' and 'victims' is noticeable, defining one community as 'we' and the other as 'them' – nevertheless it was a significant and overdue development in the trajectory of public and official recognition of survivors' rights. For decades survivors and their advocates had been working to have the abuse they suffered in institutions recognised. From fictionalised works such as *Nothing to Say* by Mannix Flynn (1983) and investigative books such as *Children of the Poor Clares* by Mavis Arnold and Heather Laskey (1985),[3] to harrowing individual memoirs of survivors such as *The God Squad: A Remarkable True Story* by Paddy Doyle (1988) and *You May Talk Now* by Mary Drennan (1994), there grew a body of work seeking to make the public realise the extent of the abuse of children in Industrial Schools.[4] The resistance to this in the 1980s can be gauged by the struggle Arnold and Laskey faced as they sought to publish their book on the orphanages run by the Poor Clare nuns – they submitted it to more than fifteen publishers before their manuscript was accepted, and even then it was only published with significant changes, specifically with the 'political' material taken out.

By the later 1990s, contemporary forms of mass media proved an effective means to share these stories with more sizeable audiences. Louis Lentin's pioneering television documentary, *Dear Daughter* (1996), was screened by RTÉ 2 in 1996.[5] *Dear Daughter* was based on the testimony of survivors of Goldenbridge Girls' Industrial School in west Dublin, primarily that of Christine Buckley, and it documented the emotional and physical abuse suffered by former child residents. There was significant media and public response, including a follow-up RTÉ *Prime Time Investigates* programme, and widespread radio coverage.[6] The impact of the media taking up these stories cannot be overestimated. Indeed, Ahern's apology was issued just hours before the broadcast of the final part of the three-part RTÉ series, *States of Fear* (directed by Mary Raftery, 1999). Whereas previous publications and programmes had concentrated on individual stories, *States of Fear* made larger claims, including that the Department of Education had been aware of the abuse within the system, for example, instances of 'starvation' and 'sadism', and that they did 'nothing' or, worse, covered up evidence of abuse.[7]

Ahern's expression of regret had real-world effects: following the apology, the government established the Commission of Investigation to

Inquire into Child Abuse (CICA, 2000–9) and the Residential Institutions Redress Board (established following the Redress Act, 2002).[8] The CICA proceedings had two parts: a committee of investigation, and a confidential committee. The confidential committee held private meetings to hear and record survivor testimony. The investigation, in contrast, convened adversarial proceedings, during which survivors were cross-examined. Unsurprisingly, survivors reported extreme stress and negative impacts after giving testimony to the committee of investigation. These effects were compounded by the process for participation in the Redress Board, which required survivors to sign a confidentiality agreement in order to receive financial compensation. The negative psychological effects of this, with some survivors claiming the process caused their recovery to regress,[9] means that the processes of truth commissions are not inherently positive – there is a significant cost to the survivor of witnessing.

On 20 May 2009, a decade after the apology, CICA published its official report (commonly known as the Ryan Report, after its author Judge Sean Ryan). The Ryan Report found conclusively that the Industrial Schools had constituted an emotionally, physically, and sexually abusive system in which thousands of children were seriously damaged.[10] Claims by the Catholic orders, and indeed the state, that the children, now adults, were lying about the abuse, were completely swept away as the report revealed the scale of the cruelty, violence, and exploitation of children; for the first time, and with the authority of the state, the report described in great detail the 'climate of fear' in the institutions and the 'systemic' nature of abuse.[11]

The publication of the Ryan Report demanded and provoked a rewriting of the past. The official state-led nine-year investigation, and the thorough detailing of the history of the institutions it investigated,[12] was the authoritative voice needed to re-inforce survivors' individual stories of abuse, and to demonstrate not only individual failures, but systemic abuse.[13] The Ryan Report is thus one of the most important publications in the history of the Irish state, but it is also one of the least read: the report runs to 2,600 pages, over a million words. Its thoroughness is its virtue, but it also makes for daunting reading. Its pages, filled with details of abuse, make the reader doubt the humanity of all those involved. But it is important that we know and understand this history. We cannot go back in time and intervene, but, through understanding what happened, we can pledge to ensure that it never happens again. Reading it seems the least we can do. So how do we make the transition from this difficult text to an engaging and accessible one?

What creative and technological tools are available to us as readers and scholars?

In What Forms Is This Story Available to Us?

Artistic and literary representations from memoir to theatre preceded the Ryan Report, creating the cultural context that led to Ahern's apology. In turn, the report's publication created not only a new context, but also a new wave of representations. After its publication, for instance, the Abbey Theatre directors met to discuss how best the National Theatre could respond to its significance; their decision was to commission a documentary play. Aideen Howard, then Literary Director of the Abbey, suggested that the documentary form would do justice to this history in a more direct way than a fictionalisation could.[14] Though the media coverage of *No Escape* was widespread, this theatre piece was a chance for audiences to access in more depth some of the detail and individual testimony of the report.

The Abbey astutely asked journalist Mary Raftery to create the play, as Raftery's work over the previous two decades, most significantly the series *States of Fear*, had pioneered and championed the case of survivors of abuse; she had an exhaustive knowledge of the institutional system, as well as an authoritative public identity and cultural capital as a campaigner. Although *No Escape* is a tiny slice of the vast data in the report – the play is just under ninety minutes long – Raftery worked with the National Theatre team, including Howard and director Róisín McBrinn, to make these excerpts feel representative of the whole history.

No Escape demonstrates the powerful role that creative artists can play in shaping narratives of abuse to educate and engage audiences. Raftery used a dramatic editing technique, imported from her experience in television production, combining information from different sections of the report into unified scenes, and alternating testimony between survivors, the religious congregations, and civil servants. Raftery also thematised the sections of the play so that, roughly speaking, the first scenes are concerned with physical abuse of boys and girls, the next section is concerned with sexual abuse, and the final sections are concerned with the institutional system and its legacy for survivors. In a review of the play, Catriona Crowe argued the dramatic format was 'a very successful way of dealing with a huge public issue that convulsed [. . .] and is still convulsing the country'.[15]

No Escape was staged by the Abbey in the Peacock Theatre as part of a programme called 'The Darkest Corner', a reference to then Taoiseach

Brian Cowen's depiction in his official apology of the abuse of children in institutions as Ireland's 'darkest corner'.[16] 'The Darkest Corner' series also included two earlier plays: *The Evidence I Shall Give* by Richard Johnson (first produced in 1961) and *James X* by Mannix Flynn (Farcry Productions, first produced in 2003), both attesting to the existence of prior representations – and knowledge – of this history of abuse.[17] Other new productions also emerged: in Galway, performance artist Dominic Thorpe mounted the durational work *Redress State* (2010). *Redress State* was set in a space with no natural light, and Thorpe was present inside the room during the entirety of the piece, sitting at a desk, writing on the walls, and pulling apart raw sheep's wool.[18] Words upon the walls – 'Why didn't you complain', 'Silence', 'Are you sure you remember' – were scrawled in large capitals. Participants entered the room (which was completely darkened, though, if requested, a torch could be used) and felt their way through the space, an embodiment of the 'darkness' of abuse. Thorpe's work required viewers to be more active as witnesses to make up for the past failures of bystanders who 'did not intervene'. The following year, Brokentalkers produced *The Blue Boy* (Dublin Theatre Festival, 2011), a dramatic merging of verbatim theatre, video, music, and dance, and a powerful mediation of the emotional shock caused by the report.[19] The staging of *No Escape* by the Abbey and the premiering of *The Blue Boy* at the Dublin Theatre Festival, alongside other shows exploring Ireland's institutional past, such as ANU Productions' *Laundry* (funded by Dublin City Council & Dublin Theatre Festival, 2011), profoundly illustrate not only the transition in attitudes to that past, but also the ethical turn of mainstream (and core-funded) Irish culture in the second decade of the twenty-first century.

Although these works take the message of the report and translate it for new audiences, those audiences were necessarily limited due to the nature of live performance. *No Escape* ran for two weeks in the Peacock Theatre. Plans for a national tour were not fulfilled.[20] The play was revived for a one-off staged reading in January 2014 at the Peacock,[21] and in 2015 it was translated into Portuguese and performed as a staged reading by the Cia Ludens company in São Paulo, Brazil (10 November 2015). *The Blue Boy* played for the Dublin Theatre Festival and has toured over the intervening years, predominantly to European dance festivals. *Redress State* was a one-off performance, running in May and June 2010. Though these works engage deeply with the subject matter of the Ryan Report, and constitute further reckonings with the facts, legacies, and stories of institutional abuse, the Ryan Report itself functions solely as a starting point. Just as vital, however, is our duty as readers to engage with the report itself, not simply as a carrier of information about what occurred, but itself as a complex narrative and discursive account of the interlinked systems of power, cruelty, and apathy that structured institutional care in Ireland for much of the twentieth century. The kind of reading this process of engagement requires is challenging, both emotionally and intellectually, but it can also offer us new ways of interpreting texts that may seem, on the surface, reader-unfriendly.

What Do We Do with the Report?

Helping to shape and share the content of the report with the public is not only the work of the state, the press, activists, and artists. Academics and academic institutions also bear this responsibility. Since 2010, I have taught *No Escape* alongside *Eclipsed* (1992), a play by Patricia Burke Brogan set in a Magdalen Laundry, as a way of illuminating this painful history to university students. Even today, many students in Ireland have no knowledge of this history as it is not currently taught at second level. Despite recent and regular revelations about clerical and institutional abuse in Ireland and across the globe, the legacy of silence persists.

The innovations of the digital humanities have an important role to play here – both by making the report more available and providing a forum in which to interrogate it. In 2015 I was awarded New Horizons funding from the Irish Research Council to create an Arts-STEM project, with Professor Mark Keane in University College Dublin's Computer Science Department, to respond to the continued silence and lack of knowledge around the Ryan Report. We started the *Industrial Memories* project with the mission to act as witnesses to this history and to increase access to, and understanding of, the report. With Dr Susan Leavy, project fellow, the first step for *Industrial Memories* was to digitise the report in order to transform it into a database. There were two strong reasons to undertake this task. First of all, though the report is available on the Internet (in either PDF or HTML formats), it was not searchable. Any reader looking for a particular reference or name, had to go through each chapter to find what they were looking for. Second, the structure of the report makes it hard to obtain certain vital information. The report is split into five volumes, with volumes one and two covering the history of the religious orders in charge of the institutions – the Christian Brothers, the Rosminians, the Sisters of Mercy, and the Sisters of Charity – and the histories of the institutions themselves. Volumes three, four, and five give contextual information, from the social and demographic profile of witnesses to the financial reports on the institutions and the historical background to out-of-home care of children in Ireland and the UK. While the latter three volumes thus give an overview of certain aspects of the system, the first two volumes are split into individual chapters on each order and each institution. If a child or a staff member were transferred between institutions, though the transfer is noted in two separate chapters, there is little sense of the movement across, or the impact of that movement on, the system as a whole. While the financial and contextual volumes give oversight of more than one institution at a time, the structure of the first two volumes of the report works to obscure a systemic analysis.

By digitising the report, the research team was able to treat it as a data corpus, rather than a linear narrative. This had two main advantages: it enabled us to understand better the story that this source was telling us (such as transfers between institutions), and also to tell potentially different stories.

The Digital Report

These digital innovations allowed for a transparency unavailable in the five-volume Ryan Report. In the report, all religious staff were anonymised with pseudonyms (even where the staff member had been convicted of abuse). By using Latinate names, such as Brother Bruno or Brother Dax, the commissioners linked the Irish orders to their origins in Rome, but this also effaced the fact that these were actually Irish religious staff (Bruno and Dax are, in reality, Sean Barry and Maurice Tobin, both convicted of multiple counts of child sexual abuse).[22] And yet, by retaining names – albeit disguised – for each staff member, the report makes it possible to identify individuals. Using named entity recognition,[23] Leavy created a 'People Directory',[24] which lists every named actor in the report, arranged in categories, including religious (by far the largest category), lay staff, state inspectors, and politicians. This renders the institutions not as parts of a nameless or faceless system, but as the identifiable manifestation of people's actions.

This familiar form of interrogative critical reading, applied now to a government document, also benefits from the creation and use of newly available technological tools. Digital tools change the scale at which we can 'read'. I say 'read' to signal, as Johanna Drucker has pointed out, that machines don't 'read'; rather the kinds of methodologies adopted by digital humanities computationally process textual information, according to a set of criteria set by humans.[25] This process has come to be known as 'distant reading', a term popularised by Franco Moretti and adopted by digital humanities scholars to describe the use of digital tools to read at scale – distantly – so that patterns can be identified in large corpora, beyond what could be achieved by a single (or even team of) human reader.[26] Though this form of analysis enables pattern analysis across large and complex texts,[27] it risks losing meaning by separating text from context. The potentiality of digital tools then needs to be balanced with close contextual analysis – so that it may be better to think of 'middle-reading' as a useful term for digital humanities.

As an example of this combined methodology (close + distant reading), Leavy created a text classification model that could identify descriptions of, and testimony about, abuse using by-hand identification of paragraphs about abuse, which then formed the basis for machine learning.[28] This was a necessary, if toxic, task, involving Leavy identifying descriptions of terrible physical, emotional, and sexual abuse, which she then used to generate an automatic classifier. The text classifier then analysed the entirety of the report, and fed back 1,173 entries that matched the contours of an 'abuse event'. One striking feature of these results was that not all of the entries described obvious abuse events; perhaps they included descriptions of waiting for, or expectations of, punishment. There is much work still to be done in this area, but this analysis indicates that language – how we talk about what has happened to us, or by us – carries markers of the underlying sentiment attached to events such as abuse. Even in discussions of non-abuse events, the language used signals an individual's feelings as being associated with abuse.

Digital tools can help readers to navigate texts and thus to generate alternative narratives. Taking the pre-existing narrative of the Ryan Report, the Industrial Memories team attempted to identify a particularly pernicious literal form of 'transition' that enabled this abuse, otherwise not available through a straightforward reading of the text. The synergy of digital humanities is thus nowhere more powerfully demonstrated than in Mark Keane's analysis of transfers of staff within the system. One of the recurring patterns in the system, evident from reading the report, was the transfer of alleged abusers from one institution to another. This pattern is noted by the report's 'Executive Summary': 'When confronted with evidence of sexual abuse, the response of the religious authorities was to transfer the offender to another location where, in many instances, he was free to abuse again.'[29] Yet to access information about transfers, readers have to search the institutional chapters; the report gives no analysis of how transfers happened. Keane identified eighty alleged abusers who had been transferred within the institutional system. Keane then generated a network of transfers using Gephi,[30] visually illustrating the pathways of each of the abusers, and then used association rule analysis to uncover patterns within the network.[31] The graph has immediate visual impact, illustrating how abusers moved within the system between different institutions. Each institution is represented by a circle; the larger the circle, the higher the frequency of transfers in and out of the institution. The circles are grouped together to represent the different religious orders. The largest institutional circles belong to the Christian Brothers, and the largest circle is represented by Artane boys school. This was the largest institution and thus the frequency of transfers involving Artane is partly to be expected. The school's size is a contributing factor in another way, however, in that the number of boys incarcerated there led to a harsh regime in order to keep total control over them; sexual abuse was one dimension of this. Additionally, the proximity of the Brother's bedroom, off the main boys' dormitory, created ideal conditions for taking boys out of their beds to abuse them.[32]

The smallest circles on the graph illustrate the individual abusers; each of these small circles is connected by lines to the institutions where that individual worked. On the right of the graph, large circles represent alternative options to transferring an individual to another residential institution: Dismissal, Order House, and Day School. In rare cases, particularly for repeat abusers, a 'dispensation' was granted for that Brother to leave the order, resulting in their dismissal. Alternatives to dismissal included being sent to an Order House, where the individual would have no contact with children, or being sent to a day school, which was seen as safer given that the children did not sleep on the premises.[33] In terms of patterns, the research team can show that the Rosminian order were more likely than the Christian Brothers to move abusers to an Order House, while the Sisters of Mercy dismissed lay staff abusers but transferred the religious sister to a day school. What is perhaps most striking about this graph are the criss-crossing lines. These lines indicate *multiple* transfers. As Keane argues, the repeated transfer of abusers suggests a lack of memory within the system – once the staff member is transferred, their abusive past is conveniently forgotten. The reading methods developed within the *Industrial Memories* project thus allow for a mode of interpretively, analytically 'remembering' what the system itself was designed to forget: the actual paths and histories of abusers as they moved from node to node. I would add that the motivation for transfer may be the avoidance of scandal, but the *result* of the transfers is to spread abuse across the whole of the system. Children were not only unprotected by this policy, but were in fact more likely to be victimised as a result of it.

Our own highly mediated contemporary moment provides valuable new tools for the interrogation of abuse, but it is also important to maintain personal contact with survivors/victims and to hear directly stories of their lived experience. Network analysis is a useful tool to apply to large data corpora, giving a picture of the connections and patterns between objects and people. Yet in conversations with survivors and victim support groups, I learned survivors were unhappy with the report's failure to identify the institutions as socially embedded because by representing those institutions as isolated, the report retrospectively condoned people's failure to intervene. Since these were institutions, they were isolating environments to live in, akin to prisons. But unlike prisons these institutions were not sealed off – many lay staff worked there, children often attended mainstream national schools, and children were highly visible as they walked through towns and laboured in the fields. Thus, Susan Leavy and I wanted to demonstrate the social embeddedness of the institutions. We identified key actors (from politicians and government staff to religious managers to parents) and Leavy used word embedding[34] to then identify and link every act of communication between these actors.[35] As can be seen on the Industrial Memories website, the dynamic communication graphs illustrate how actively people communicated about the institutions – such as parents communicating with politicians and institutional managers about their children. We can also see on these graphs the direction of communication. So, for example, though fathers wrote to the Department of Education, the Gardai, the Minister for Agriculture, the President of Ireland, and so on, not one of these figures, or their offices, ever replied.[36]

Active Listening

Digital tools can help us to understand the large-scale and system-wide features of Irish institutional history. In turning towards digital methodologies, however, the research team did not want to lose connection to the individual voices and their stories. Taking my lead from Mary Raftery, I determined to exploit digital media to increase both access to and intimacy with those stories. Using my academic background in theatre, and drawing on recent moves in

Irish theatre towards site-specific performance, I dreamed up a plan for an experiential audio walking tour of one of the institutions. This tour would concentrate on small moments from the report and encourage an audience to transition from passive reception to active engagement. Working with public historian Maeve Casserly and composer Tom Lane, the research team created *Echoes from the Past*, a digital application (free to download) that operates as a location-triggered walking tour of Goldenbridge School in West Dublin.[37] We chose Goldenbridge because it was easily accessible by public transport, and because we wanted to focus on a girls' school since so much of the media attention has been on boys.[38] The script is based verbatim on the report, foregrounding testimony from survivors (recorded by actors). Through headphones (or through their handheld device), the listener hears testimony describing children's experiences: forced and brutal haircuts, having to scrabble for food scraps, being deprived of education, and being beaten for minor infractions of the rules. It does not make for easy consumption, but it underscores the ethical importance of listening and not switching off. As Paul Ricoeur writes: 'some witnesses [...] never encounter an audience capable of listening to them or hearing what they have to say'.[39] In Ricoeur's formulation, forgotten or hidden histories are not due to the failure of the original witness to speak. It is not, as some critics suggest, that trauma has prevented the original witness from articulating the events of their lives. Rather, forgetting is the fault of the audience for not listening, a failure of listenership. Re-animating listening, then, has a political function in asking the listener to act, in turn, as a witness.

How does this witnessing happen? One of the factors in creating the tour was the issue of the changing cityscape – many of the buildings, including the dormitories, have been demolished since the school closed in 1983. In many ways, then, the tour's audience walks a landscape of absence. At first this worried us in the research group, but it has proven crucial – the disjuncture between what the audience hears, and what they see, creates a reflective space for the listener to think about continuities and discontinuities between the past and present. This act of reflection mirrors the process of narrative reframing undertaken by the *Industrial Memories* project overall. The app makes explicit the social world of the institutions (then and now), adopting techniques of site-specific drama to move beyond interpretation, and to exploit the ability to take the text both in and out of context as the listener engages with the original text while generating an entirely new, autonomous narrative.

Conclusions

With the *Echoes from the Past* app, we created a new script, a new documentary-based literary narrative. This was a creative outcome from a process of deep literary-critical and digital analysis of the report; it is forged out of fragments of the report that, while tiny in relation to the whole, nevertheless represent the sense of the whole. The app, while digital, is thus an example of a form of close reading perhaps more aligned with traditional modes of reading in the humanities, foregrounding affect and individual experience, in place of identifying patterns of event occurrence. This is not to prioritise one form of reading over another, but to gesture towards the possibilities of a methodology that includes both.

In chapter 4, 'The Gates', the tour's script includes testimony from a woman who was put into Goldenbridge as a young child and left alone. She says, 'and this is what I find so hard to tell you, there was never anyone there for you'.[40] This is heart-breaking testimony which tells us so much about the isolation of the abused child. In his account of first-hand witnessing, J. D. Peters argues that 'you can be marked for life by being the witness of an event'.[41] The testimony in the report reveals that children were marked not only by their own experiences of abuse, but also by witnessing other children being abused. Abuse is a kind of contagion. Yet, the risk Peters identifies is so much less for us, the second- or third-hand witnesses, which brings to mind Marianne Hirsch's provocative question: 'How can we allow the knowledge of past atrocity to touch us without paralyzing us?'[42] As academics of literature, we tend not to read and analyse government reports. Their scope, their voice, and their sheer size make them unwieldy as texts. Yet as humanities scholars we are equipped with the skills necessary to ask vital questions about this history as it is related by these kinds of texts. We need to expand our generic inclusiveness and as readers, with our reading potentially enhanced with digital tools, take up the responsibility of witnessing in the twenty-first century for as many audiences – embodied and mediated, collective and individual, national and international – as possible.

Notes

1. See 'Government Responses', *Caranua*, 2017: http://caranua.ie/useful-resources/government-responses/ [accessed 17 February 2019].

2. For a history of the schools, see Mary Raftery and Eoin O'Sullivan, *Suffer the Little Children: The Inside Story of Ireland's Industrial Schools* (Dublin: New Island, 1999). Also see Sarah-Anne Buckley, *The Cruelty Man: Child Welfare, the NSPCC and the State in Ireland 1899–1956* (Manchester: Manchester University Press, 2017).
3. Doyle continues to comment on the emerging story and treatment of abuse on his website 'The God Squad' at www.paddydoyle.com, while Mannix Flynn has written for the stage (including *James X*, a stage play which addresses industrial and reform schools, produced at the Project Arts Centre, Dublin in 2002) and has also produced art installations which reflect on the issue of abuse in Irish society.
4. Parallel to this strand, we can also see the emergence in the same period of works that addressed the Christian Brothers' cruelty to children in day schools, e.g. *Our Boys*, directed by Cathal Black (1981), and the abuse of women in the Magdalen Laundries, e.g. *Eclipsed* by Patricia Burke Brogan (1992). Both Black and Brogan encountered significant obstacles to making these stories public – Black's film was made for RTÉ television but not screened until 1991, and Brogan's play could not get a production in Ireland and so was first produced at the Edinburgh Fringe Festival, where it created a sensation, leading to the Channel 4 documentary *Sex in a Cold Climate* (Channel 4, 1998).
5. *Dear Daughter* – about the survivor Christine Buckley – was narrated by Bosco Hogan and directed by Louis Lentin (Crescendo Concepts for RTÉ, 22 February 1996). See Mary Drennan, *You May Talk Now* (Cork: OnStream Publications, 1994).
6. One of the outcomes of Lentin's documentary was the emergence of Christine Buckley as a leading activist for the rights of survivors. Buckley, along with Carmel McDonnell Byrne (also a Goldenbridge survivor), campaigned for the recognition, in particular, of the educational needs of this community, and established in 1999 the Aislinn Centre for Education and Support. The Centre has recently been renamed, in memory of its co-founder, as the Christine Buckley Centre, see: www.aislinn.org/our-achievements [accessed 17 February 2019].
7. *States of Fear*, prod. Mary Raftery (RTÉ, 1999), episode 1. The Ryan Report was not the first report to identify abusive conditions within the system. Previous reports had been commissioned and ignored. See reports by Cussen (1936), Kennedy (1970), Tuairim (1966), and the Task Force on Childcare (1980) for examples of evidence of prior knowledge of the failings of the system.
8. See www.childabusecommission.ie/ and www.rirb.ie/ for the official websites of both the Commission and the Redress Board. Financial compensation to date (Annual Report, 2017) has been €180,705,335.29, with an average of c. €12,000 to each survivor (there have been 15,367 claims). In 2017, a report revealed that the religious orders had contributed only 13% of the funds paid to survivors and owed the state significant monies and property it had promised. See Noel Baker, 'Religious Orders Gave Just 13% to Cost of Abuse Redress

Scheme', *Irish Examiner*, 10 March 2017: www.irishexaminer.com/ireland/re
ligious-orders-gave-just-13-to-cost-of-abuse-redress-scheme-444865.html
[accessed 17 February 2019].

9. Based on personal conversations between the author and survivors. See also Sharon Commins, 'Survivors of Abuse Must Be Allowed to Speak Freely', *The Irish Times*, 18 March 2010: www.irishtimes.com/opinion/s urvivors-of-abuse-must-be-allowed-speak-freely-1.639465 [accessed 17 February 2019].

10. The Ryan Report has been followed by a number of other, more focused reports, which had very similar findings, e.g. the Murphy Report (2009) and the Ferns Report (2005). The McAleese Report, a much less detailed (and less useful) report, was published in 2013 on the history of the Magdalen Laundries in Ireland. At the time of writing, there is an ongoing inquiry into the history of Mother and Child Institutions (known as Mother and Baby Homes, but these were not 'homes' and children were often kept for years in these institutions, beyond babyhood). See also the publication of the Report of the Historical Institutional Abuse Inquiry in Northern Ireland (2017) and the Royal Commission into Institutional Responses to Child Sexual Abuse (Australia) (2017) for evidence that the abusive culture of such institutions was not unique to the Irish Free State/ Republic of Ireland.

11. 'Executive Summary', *The Report of the Commission to Inquire into Child Abuse* (Ryan Report), 20 May 2009, p. 20: www.childabusecommission.ie/ rpt/ExecSummary.php [accessed 17 February 2019]. See, for example, the editorial in the *Irish Times* a week after the report's publication, noting 'that public opinion has finally woken up to the scale and depth of this scandal'; 'Reflections on the Ryan Report', *The Irish Times*, 30 May 2009: www .irishtimes.com/opinion/reflections-on-the-ryan-report-1.773776 [accessed 17 February 2019]. Also notable is the statement by the One in Four support group for survivors of abuse, which reported a 'huge surge in new client numbers in the three months since the Ryan Report', press release, 15 September 2009.

12. The Ryan Report does not include details of all the Industrial School institutions in Ireland, but instead concentrates on those institutions about which most survivors made allegations.

13. For an analysis of the need to move away from the view of abuse as the result of 'a few bad apples', see Marie Keenan, *Child Sexual Abuse and the Catholic Church: Gender, Power, and Organizational Culture* (Oxford: Oxford University Press, 2011).

14. Listen to Howard discuss the emergence of *No Escape* as part of 'Ways of Representing the Past: Documentary Theatre in Ireland and Brazil', Irish Memory Studies Network: http://irishmemorystudies.com/index.php/past-events/documentary-theatre-2/ [accessed 17 February 2019].

15. Catriona Crowe reviewing *No Escape*, alongside Padraig Ó Morain, on *Arena with Sean Rocks*, RTÉ Radio One, 15 April 2010: www.rte.ie/radio1/

arena/programmes/2010/0415/352096-arena-thursday-15th-april-2010/ [accessed 10 May 2016].

16. For the full apology, see Ine Kerr, 'Shining a Light into the State's Darkest Corner', *Irish Independent*, 12 June 2009: www.independent.ie /irish-news/shining-a-light-into-the-states-darkest-corner-26543104.html [accessed 2 February 2019].

17. Indeed, Johnson's play is cited in the Ryan Report as evidence of public awareness of the problem of institutional abuse. For a discussion of the series, see Emilie Pine, 'The Abuse of History/A History of Abuse', in Christopher Collins and Mary P. Caulfield, eds., *Ireland, Memory and Performing the Historical Imagination* (Basingstoke: Palgrave Macmillan, 2014), pp. 207–22. For another, less direct theatrical response to the report, see Thomas Kilroy, *Christ Deliver Us!* (Oldcastle, Co. Meath: Gallery Press, 2010).

18. For images of the installation and performance, see: http://showerofkunst .com/sok/2010/07/26/images-from-redress-state-questions-imagined/ [accessed 17 February 2019].

19. For a discussion of *The Blue Boy*, see Emilie Pine, 'Theatre-as-Memory and as Witness: Active Spectatorship in *The Walworth Farce, The Blue Boy* and *Laundry*', in *Breac: A Digital Journal of Irish Studies*, 10 July 2014: https:// breac.nd.edu/articles/theatre-as-memory-and-as-witness-active-spectatorship-in-the-walworth-farce-the-blue-boy-and-laundry/ [accessed 1 April 2019].

20. A production was hoped for the UK, given that many institutional survivors settled in the UK as emigrants, but finances were not available.

21. This reading was part of the Abbey's 'Theatre of Memory' conference, January 2014.

22. See 'Victim Mutilated Himself After Sexual Abuse', *The Irish Times*, 26 February 1999: www.irishtimes.com/news/victim-mutilated-himself-after-sexual-abuse-1.156863; and 'Some of Those Convicted in Abuse Cases', *Irish Independent*, 25 November 2009: www.independent.ie/opinion/analysis/some-of-those-convicted-in-abuse-cases-26585419.html [both accessed 17 February 2019].

23. See Christopher D. Manning, Mihai Surdeanu, John Bauer, Jenny Finkel, Steven J. Bethard, and David McClosky, 'The Stanford Core NLP Natural Language Processing Toolkit', *Proceedings of the 52nd Annual Meeting of the Association for Computational Linguistics: System Demonstrations* (2014), pp. 55–60.

24. The People Directory is available at: https://industrialmemories.ucd.ie/ryan-report/report/actors [all webpages from this site accessed 1 April 2019].

25. See Johanna Drucker, 'What Distant Reading Isn't', *PMLA*, 132.3 (2017), pp. 628–35.

26. See Franco Moretti, *Distant Reading* (London: Verso, 2013).

27. The corpus does not have to be large to represent a complex corpus that is suitable for digital analysis – see, for example, Tanya Clement's illuminating work on Gertrude Stein, '"A thing not beginning and not ending": Using

Digital Tools to Distant-Read Gertrude Stein's *The Making of Americans*', *Literary and Linguistic Computing*, 23.3 (2008), pp. 361–81.
28. See Leo Breiman, 'Random Forests', *Machine Learning*, 45.1 (2001), pp. 5–32.
29. 'Executive Summary', *Commission to Inquire into Child Abuse*, Conclusion 22: www.childabusecommission.ie/rpt/ExecSummary.php [accessed 17 February 2019].
30. See Mathieu Bastian, Sebastien Heymann, and Mathieu Jacomy, 'Gephi: An Open Source Software for Exploring and Manipulating Networks', *Proceedings of the Third International Conference on Weblogs and Social Media*, 8 (2009), pp. 361–2.
31. The Transfer Graph is available at: https://industrialmemories.ucd.ie/project/the-transfer-graph
32. See for instance, testimony about this practice in *Commission to Inquire into Child Abuse*, vol. 1, chap. 7, para. 163: https://industrialmemories.ucd.ie/ryan-report/report/1-7-163). Searching for 'out of bed' as a key term in the Industrial Memories database produces 31 results, illustrating the recurrence of the practice of taking children out of bed and either sexually or physically abusing them (most frequently in relation to boys, but also in two girls schools). This testimony is given in relation to Artane, Letterfrack, Tralee, Daingean, Marlborough House, Upton, Ferryhouse, Greenmount, Goldenbridge (girls school), Dundalk, and Kilkenny (girls school). Search at: https://industrialmemories.ucd.ie/ryan-report/
33. See *Commission to Inquire into Child Abuse*, vol. 1, chap. 6, para. 85: https://industrialmemories.ucd.ie/ryan-report/report/1-6-85
34. See Tomas Mikolov, et al., 'Distributed Representations of Words and Phrases and their Compositionality', *Advances in Neural Information Processing Systems*, 26 (2013), pp. 3111–19.
35. It should be noted that the report is obviously a partial and selective source – Leavy identified every act of communication noted in the report; this serves, however, as only a sample of the full scale of social communication about and awareness of the institutions.
36. See: https://industrialmemories.ucd.ie/networks/communications/#Father. Again, it should be stressed that this finding is based on the Ryan Report and not the full records of those departments. While those records remain sealed and confidential, the report is the only source we have to go on.
37. *Echoes from the Past* is a free downloadable app for Mac and Android devices. Users follow a GPS-location-triggered 15-point tour of the Goldenbridge area of west Dublin. In order to increase access to this resource, users can also listen to the audio online. See: https://industrialmemories.ucd.ie/project/echoes-from-the-past
38. See Emilie Pine, 'Commemorating Abuse: Gender Politics and Making Space' for a discussion of how Irish institutional history has been gendered, so that public memory concentrates on Industrial Schools for boys, while girls are remembered in relation to Magdalen Laundries and Mother and Child

Institutions. Audio recording and transcript available at: www.ucd.ie/scholarcast/scholarcast34.html [accessed 17 February 2019].

39. Paul Ricoeur, *Memory, History, Forgetting*, trans. Kathleen Blamey and David Pellauer (Chicago: University of Chicago Press, 2004), p. 166.
40. Access this testimony at: https://industrialmemories.ucd.ie/project/echoes-from-the-past and click on chapter 4.
41. John Durham Peters, 'Witnessing', in *Media, Culture & Society*, 23 (2001), pp. 707–23 (p. 14).
42. Marianne Hirsch, 'Connective Histories in Vulnerable Times', *PMLA*, 129.3 (2014), pp. 330–48 (p. 334).

Coda: Edna O'Brien and Eimear McBride
Clair Wills

Published fifty years apart, Edna O'Brien's *Country Girls Trilogy* (1960, 1962, and 1964) and Eimear McBride's dyad of novels *A Girl Is a Half-Formed Thing* (2013) and *The Lesser Bohemians* (2016) both proved to be publishing sensations. While O'Brien and McBride both anatomise women's experience at crucial junctures in the twentieth and twenty-first centuries, their critical fates were different. O'Brien's work was banned in the 1960s for its reputedly salacious content. In contrast, Eimear McBride's sexually explicit 2013 novel took years to find a publisher, but was immediately embraced by critics and celebrated as an exemplar of contemporary Irish writing.

One simple way of understanding this contrast is as a sign of progressive cultural change – in a society that has largely rejected the teachings of the Catholic Church with regard to the expression of female sexuality, and that has decisively rejected the cruelties and institutional abuses carried out in the Church's name, representations of female desire and of masculine violence and abuse of power are no longer considered threatening. Indeed, they have become a necessary part of a society's reckoning with its own past. In the context of recent Tiger and Post-Tiger legislative changes, brought about by grass-roots agitation and ensuing referenda on the decriminalisation of homosexuality (1993), divorce (1995), marriage equality (2015), and abortion (2018), and the series of searing reports into the abuse of children in institutions such as Industrial Schools, Magdalen Laundries, and Mother and Baby Homes, the role of Irish fiction which touches on these issues has changed. No longer working against the pull of a society unwilling to acknowledge its own investment in a corrupt and unequal sexual system, fiction that exposes sexual abuses of certain kinds now finds itself flowing with the cultural tide. On this account McBride's novels are engaged in a form of cultural witnessing shared with, for example, Anne Enright's exploration of the impact of sexual abuse on several generations of an Irish family in *The Gathering* (2007), Emma

Donoghue's anatomy of sexual violence and childhood in *Room* (2010) and *The Wonder* (2016), or Sally Rooney's account of violence and female masochism in *Normal People* (2018). The climate for contemporary Irish women's fiction has, from this perspective, caught up with the fiction itself.

There are intriguing parallels between the celebrated debuts of O'Brien and McBride. Both writers like to draw attention to the speed with which their first works were written, both were relatively unschooled in the art of fiction writing, and both describe a personal encounter with the work of James Joyce (in O'Brien's case a book picked up on a Dublin street; in McBride's, a reading of *Ulysses* on a London bus) that altered their sense of fictional possibility. And the two writers have drawn attention to their relationship to one another: McBride has written a preface to a re-issue of *The Country Girls* (2017), positioning herself as both inheritor and guide to the earlier work. In what follows I assess the different challenges that O'Brien and McBride pose to their contemporary moments.

Edna O'Brien made her name writing apparently spontaneous and unstudied fiction about the hopes, loves, and torments of young women in 1960s Ireland and London. Her first novel, *The Country Girls*, caused a sensation when it was published in 1960 for its portrayal of sexually liberated young girls who reject convent school life and rural mores in favour of the lure of city life, or at any rate a job in a Dublin grocer's and a shared room on the North Circular Road. In fact, the sex in the novel is minimal – the main character Caithleen (Cait) Brady does not even lose her virginity until halfway through the second volume of the trilogy, *Girl with Green Eyes* (published in the United States as *The Lonely Girl*). The popularity and infamy of the stories sprang not from the portrayal of sexual fulfilment but of hope and desire, all spoken in the winningly direct words of a couple of girls – one impossibly naïve, the other hilariously brazen – on the cusp of womanhood:

> 'But we want young men. Romance. Love and things,' I said despondently. I thought of standing under a streetlight in the rain with my hair falling crazily about, my lips poised for the miracle of a kiss. A kiss. Nothing more. My imagination did not go beyond that.[1]

True, her imagination stretches to being kissed by a much older married neighbour, the (naturally) French Mr Gentleman: 'Paris? I thought of girls and sin at once.'[2] The aura of artlessness in her early novels is so convincing that readers are continually tricked into imagining that the ironies are accidental, a by-product of O'Brien's immersion in her world, her natural poetic sensibility.

In a 1984 interview with Philip Roth, O'Brien described her writing self as subject to the commands of a subconscious force:

> This recollection, or whatever it is, invades me. It is not something that I can summon up, it simply comes and I am the servant of it. My hand does the work and I don't have to think; in fact, were I to think, it would stop the flow. It's like a dam in the brain that bursts.[3]

Her fiction, she suggested, was brought into being by dreams, chance, or 'the welter of emotion stimulated by a love affair'.[4] This is one way of reassuring us that what we get when we read O'Brien is the truth, or at least a conception of truth which conforms to the shape explored in mid-twentieth-century psychoanalysis, to which O'Brien was no stranger. She has described a harrowing experience of taking LSD with R. D. Laing, at a point when she was worried that 'the flow' had stopped.[5] From this perspective, writing is a product of sensibility rather than craft. It may take time and effort to nurture that sensibility, to feed the creative drive, but the writing itself is easy. It is work, and requires concentration. But it is also the opposite of work, in that thinking is inimical to it ('were I to think, it would stop the flow'). Thinking is the enemy of feeling, and feeling, on this account, is the true language of the novel. The emotions of love, hatred, desire, or despair are the real, and the task of the writer is to access those emotions.

All this is a deeply unfashionable way of talking about writing, and I draw attention to it here not to set O'Brien up for sophisticated censure, or to measure her against a fancy theoretical yardstick which rates textuality above the idea of creative genius. Instead, I suggest that O'Brien's belief in the truth value of her own femininity, accessed through dreams and love affairs, is the reason why her novels – though they angered members of her own local community and those who saw themselves as the country's moral arbiters – resonated so widely with women readers through the sixties and seventies. And it is also why they later fell out of favour, particularly with critics.

O'Brien's 1960s novels triumphantly perform the contradictions of a woman writing in a pre-feminist moment, at a time when women were still thought of as mysterious, including and perhaps especially to themselves. They are a romance version of Doris Lessing's *The Golden Notebook* (1962). After all, according to John Osborne (a friend with whom O'Brien stayed when her marriage was disintegrating), 'what distinguishes a woman is her lack of imaginative vitality. She will hardly ever do anything for its own sake. Her roots are so deep in sexuality that she is the natural enemy of the visionary, the idealist.'[6] The women in O'Brien's novels all do, indeed, have their roots deep in sexuality, are driven by a hopeless longing for love. Attention is all on the inner life. But O'Brien argues that sex is also the source of the visionary – the creative force which invades her, and against which she must not think. Indeed, for Irish Catholic readers of the 1960s there was an added frisson in that the emotional inner world, the sensations of female consciousness, was not only a new mental territory to explore: it was also a substitute for religious faith. 'I think love replaced religion for me in my sense of fervour,' she told Philip Roth. 'When I began to look for earthly love (i.e. sex), I felt that I was cutting myself off from God. By taking on the mantle of religion, sex assumed proportions that are rather far-fetched. It became the central thing in my life, the goal.'[7]

There is, then, a great deal at stake in O'Brien's explorations of desire. A kiss is not just a kiss. Cait Brady's freedom to imagine a kiss represents a rejection of one kind of inner life for another, the rejection of religion for the transcendence of individual desire. And it should not be thought surprising that the novels were burned and banned – they were accurately read as reflecting a new state of the nation, one in which the repressions of the church, and its many related institutions, would be challenged by a new religion.

As it turned out the new religion turned out to be money not love, and certainly not female sexuality. Eimear McBride's two novels were written during the Celtic Tiger boom, and the subsequent financial crash. They reprise O'Brien's female *Bildungsroman*, as the reader follows the growth and development of a girl in small-town Ireland, her social and sexual awakening, a spell in Dublin, and eventual emigration to London. But McBride's novels inhabit a far more violent landscape, and a very different stylistic terrain from O'Brien's earliest work. The radically fragmented speech that stutters across the pages in *Girl* is less 'interior monologue', as critics sometimes claim, than the central character's one-way conversation with her brother, written in a style that verges on the pre-verbal, or sub-verbal. McBride has said that the style of the novel was an attempt to represent experience 'at the moment before language becomes formatted thought'.[8] At certain points in the novel it becomes clear that the language is less spoken than 'incorporated'. Many unspeakable things happen – the wound inflicted on the girl's brother, abandonment by the father, physical abuse by the mother, rape by the uncle, and a series of willed, violent sexual encounters which dominate much of the latter half of the novel. These events and experiences cannot be spoken in any straightforward way, but are articulated as snatches of sound. (Listening is a central trope too in

McBride's second novel, *The Lesser Bohemians*.) The 'half-formed' girl may be hard of speech but she is not hard of hearing, as in this re-presentation of a conversation between her mother and grandfather attests:

> Come in here and say hello to your Grandfather. He's come all the way to see you, isn't that right? Just slip on that kettle as you come past. And can you get any sleep? Desperate at your time of life. Come you in and say hello to your brother. Oh god, look at the face on that.[9]

The play with overheard sound in the early parts of the novel echoes Stephen shutting and opening the flaps of his ears at the beginning of *A Portrait of the Artist as a Young Man*, but McBride's young woman will never develop into a character, or personality, capable of distancing herself from her formation in the manner of Stephen Dedalus. Her voice can never evolve. Her story has far more in common with the curtailed futures common in post-independence and mid-century Irish writing, such as the girl 'who had never really been born' in Beckett's *All That Fall* (1957).[10]

A Girl Is a Half-Formed Thing draws an explicit link between the girl's experience of rape and sexual abuse and the baleful influence of Catholicism on her, her family, and her community. The figure of Christ suffering on the cross is absorbed into the girl's imagination as a lesson in the pain of childhood: 'Stick it in him. I like it hurts so much. His mother is crying to see him. Lovely blood on thorns and scourging is the best thing though this picture doesn't show his back. Holes of wounds for stabbing in lances or nails.'[11] Later in the novel the girl appears to seek out sexual violence as a way of sharing in her brother's pain, or perhaps taking it on herself. 'I'll wash your face of sacrament. Let sin to sinner return.'[12] The girl's desire for sexual debasement is represented as an inevitable consequence of the violence within the family and the church.

McBride's exploration of abuse and shame can usefully be compared with O'Brien's work of the early 1970s, particularly *A Pagan Place* (1970), a novel that explicitly ties together religious piety, sexual violence, and the institutions of the church. The young girl at the centre of the story is abused by a priest, but instead of being protected by her family she is punished ('flayed') by them for being 'brazen'. The encounter with the priest and his 'grotesque' penis is described as both frightening and manipulative: 'He tried to part your knees, to prise them open, said it would be lonely for him, it would be unfriendly but you were petrified and you would not yield.'[13] But her beating by her father is described in detail as a violent rape. The girl in turn punishes her mother for failing to protect her by becoming a nun – in effect she swaps the institution of the family for the church, revealing their mutual interdependence: 'The thing you had to be was fervent and more fervent and most fervent.'[14] The entire narrative is spoken in the second person, making the girl's sexual shaming representative rather than, or as well as, unique.

Like McBride's 'Girl', O'Brien's protagonist is clearly not responsible for her own abuse, though she is unable to articulate her victimisation. Yet – unlike McBride – O'Brien's representations of abuse, sexual pleasure, and desire were in themselves read as 'shameless', and even 'brazen'. In effect readers and critics alike found it hard to separate O'Brien from her central female characters. She was castigated by conservatives for writing 'filth', and by feminist critics for her representations of 'passive' female characters, caught in abusive relationships.

In a review of *A Scandalous Woman* (1974), for example, the novelist Julia O'Faolain objected to the fact that O'Brien was still writing about the sexual fall in the 1970s: 'Despite feminist efforts on behalf of their kind, Miss O'Brien's sex-dazzled heroines continue to race like lemmings towards unhappiness.' In O'Brien's world, suggested O'Faolain, biology is destiny to such an extent that 'she nurtures her fiction on the compost of defeat'.[15] What O'Faolain objected to most strongly was the fact that, in her eyes, O'Brien was unable to put female experience into perspective – her characters fail to learn from, still less to control their own experience. In effect O'Faolain indicted O'Brien's characters because they fail to garner hope from the changing culture around them.

Forty years later, the failure of McBride's Girl (or Rooney's Marianne in *Normal People*) to gain insight and understanding into their own experience is read as an indictment of male violence rather than female masochism. So what has changed? One way of understanding this shift is to suggest that Irish culture is 'ready' now to look at its own history of violence and abuse, and we might plausibly argue that this is in part a consequence of the triumph of the feminist efforts O'Faolain extolled. Part of what is at stake here is the role of contemporary art and literary culture in articulating political critique. If sex was the new religion for O'Brien and at least for some of O'Brien's readers, now it is faith in the power of art, storytelling, and contemporary culture 'in itself' to expose the truths of Irish experience – precisely to 'put things into perspective', and allow us to make judgements. McBride's novels entered a cultural landscape which has been shaped by a number of campaigning documentary and cultural projects that have played a key role in the exposure of the abuse scandals, such as Mary Raftery's late-1990s TV documentary series *States of Fear* and Peter Mullan's 2003 film drama *The Magdalene Sisters*.

The Commissions of Inquiry that have begun to expose the full extent of Ireland's complex network of carceral institutions were set up in response to the work of activists and investigative print and broadcast journalists. Contemporary Irish political (and legal) debate has followed in the footsteps of culture.

This is testament the importance of the role of storytelling in the culture – but it also suggests that readers and reviewers may only be willing to credit stories of the violent abuse of women and girls when it appears that that violence is part of Ireland's past rather than Ireland's present. That is certainly the implication of Enda Kenny's 2013 statement on the Magdalenes, when he apologised to the unmarried mothers and other women who were incarcerated in church-state institutions, the last of which did not close until the 1990s:

> Today we live in a very different Ireland with a very different consciousness and awareness. We live in an Ireland where we have more compassion, empathy, insight and heart. We do, because at last we are learning those terrible lessons. We do, because at last we are giving up our secrets. We do, because in naming and addressing the wrong, as is happening here today, we are trying to make sure we quarantine such abject behaviour in our past and eradicate it from Ireland's present and Ireland's future.[16]

In this formulation violence against women belongs to the past; the present is superior to the past not only because we know more but also because we are willing to tell the truth about what we know. Leaving aside the decidedly open question about whether sexual violence and the exploitation of women can be said to have ended in this 'more compassionate' Ireland, Kenny's faith in historical progress must surely give us pause, and particularly his idea that the present offers a vantage point from which the past can be judged, and 'quarantined'. Given the role that contemporary fiction plays in what Kenny calls 'naming and addressing the wrongs' of Ireland's history of abuse and the incarceration of women and children, it is pertinent to ask what might be being lost through the very close involvement between fictional and political witnessing. Are contemporary novels in danger of cleaving to Irish culture's own sense of its progression into modernity?

Julia O'Faolain's irritation with the work of Edna O'Brien sprang from her sense that knowledge is never really clearly accessed by the characters in O'Brien's novels, and perhaps not even clearly by the reader. What she laments is O'Brien's lack of external perspective and judgement on women's experience, and her diagnosis is surely correct, if not her assessment of that diagnosis. Arguably, through her expressive rendering of disempowered girls in her early novels, O'Brien showed us what it was like to be caught inside the 'abject behaviour' that Kenny believes we can quarantine. Although McBride's Girl is also unable to see beyond her situation, the causes of her victimisation are not obscure to the reader, who is addressed as a member of a culture that knows sexual violence is to be condemned, that has a perspective on it. We cannot read the work of Edna O'Brien or Eimear McBride (or Enright, Rooney, Donoghue, and a host of other women poets, dramatists, story writers, and novelists) and maintain the fiction that the impact of violence and exploitation of women in Ireland either was or is unknown. What, then, does it mean to expose abuses that are already known? The real revelation is the shamelessness with which we have carried on despite the knowledge.

Notes

1. Edna O'Brien, *The Country Girls* (New York: Alfred A. Knopf, 1960), p. 184.
2. Ibid., p. 183.
3. Philip Roth, 'A Conversation with Edna O'Brien', *The New York Times Book Review*, 18 November 1984, pp. 38–40 (p. 38).
4. Roth, 'Conversation', p. 39.
5. See Edna O'Brien, *Country Girl: A Memoir* (New York: Little, Brown and Company, 2012), pp. 202–10.
6. John Osborne, *Daily Mail,* 14 November 1956, quoted by Francis Beckett and Tony Russell, *1956: The Year That Changed Britain* (London: Biteback Publishing, 2015), pp. 269–70.
7. Roth, 'Conversation', p. 40.
8. David Collard, 'Interview with Eimear McBride', *The White Review*, May 2014: www.thewhitereview.org/feature/interview-with-eimear-mcbride/ [accessed 17 February 2019].
9. Eimear McBride, *A Girl Is a Half-Formed Thing* (Norwich: Galley Beggar Press, 2013), p. 11.
10. Samuel Beckett, *All That Fall* (London: Faber and Faber, 1957), p. 37. See the essay by Clair Wills in Marjorie Howes, ed., *Irish Literature in Transition: 1880–1940* (Cambridge: Cambridge University Press, forthcoming).
11. McBride, *A Girl Is a Half-Formed Thing*, p. 20.
12. Ibid., p. 183.
13. Edna O'Brien, *A Pagan Place* (London: Faber and Faber, 2016 [1970]), p. 195.
14. Ibid., p. 203.

15. Julia O'Faolain, 'A Scandalous Woman', *The New York Times Book Review*, 22 September 1974, p. 3.
16. Enda Kenny, 'Statement of the Magdalene Laundries Report', *Kildare Street*, 19 February 2013: www.kildarestreet.com/debates/?id=2013–02-19a.387 [accessed 10 February 2019].

PART IV

Practices, Institutions, and Audiences

CHAPTER 16

Mediation and Translation in Irish Language Literature

Ríona Ní Fhrighil

In 2015 and 2016, more than sixty years after its publication in Irish, the appearance, in quick succession, of two English translations of Máirtín Ó Cadhain's masterpiece *Cré na Cille* (1949) brought contemporary Irish-language literature, its translation, and reception into sharp focus. The two divergent English translations of this particular novel prompt further questions about the practice and politics of translation, particularly between two national languages that coexist in an asymmetric relationship in a postcolonial context. More broadly, the history of *Cré na Cille* itself, from its checkered publication history in Irish to its multiple rebirths in translation, affords valuable insights into Irish-language production, publication, and mediation more generally. In what follows, key aspects of that record will serve as a stimulus for the discussion of the wider literary landscape to give a nuanced overview of pertinent issues and emerging trends in Irish-language literature, its translation and literary afterlives, publication, and mediation.

Dual-language Publishing in Ireland

Even though *Cré na Cille* was awarded an Oireachtas literary prize in 1947,[1] and even though An Gúm, the Department of Education's Irish-language publication office, had previously published two of Ó Cadhain's short-story collections,[2] it was reluctant to publish a novel as stylistically experimental and verbally ribald as this one. Instead, Sáirséal agus Dill, a newly established independent press, published the novel in 1949, without any financial assistance from the state, and *Cré na Cille* became a milestone text for literature and publishing in Irish. The first edition of 2,000 copies sold out in the first month, an unprecedented occurrence in Irish-language publishing at the time, and one that has remained unparalleled. It was this success that hastened the establishment in 1952 of Bord na Leabhar Gaeilge, a non-statutory State body, to give financial assistance to private Irish-language publishing houses.³ Our starting point – the 1980s – coincides, however, with the end of an era in Irish-language publishing. In 1981, Sáirséal agus Dill, the press that had played a pioneering role in the development of a modern literature in Irish, and that had also provided writers such as Ó Cadhain, Seán Ó Ríordáin, and Máire Mhac an tSaoi, to name but a few, with a much-needed alternative to the state's publishing house, announced its intention to wind down. The history of Sáirséal agus Dill and the personal sacrifices made by its founders, who were driven by a cultural and not a financial goal, is arguably a microcosm of Irish-language publishing more generally, the latter being dependent largely on part-time publishers who undertake editorial, marketing, and distribution work as well as apply for state funding in their spare time.⁴

At the same time, other developments were afoot in publishing in Ireland more generally. Breandán Ó Doibhlin, in reviewing the essay collection *The Pleasures of Gaelic Poetry* (1982), appeared optimistic about a *détente* between writers of both linguistic traditions:

> What is gratifying to report is the unaffected sympathy and seriousness with which these writers, most of whom have distinguished themselves in the English language, take unto themselves the Gaelic literary inheritance. This, I think, is in contrast to attitudes a generation ago, because I have a clear memory of my own pain and bafflement at the contempt which was common in Dublin literary circles when I first came to know them. What my Northern education had preserved me from was the other side of the coin, the priggish and bone-headed policies of official revivalism.⁵

Ó Doibhlin's appraisal was most likely also inspired by other recent publications that attested to increased creative interaction and translation activity: *Rogha an Fhile* (1975), edited by Eoghan Ó Tuairisc, contained a selection of Irish poems with translations by the poets themselves; *The Road to Brightcity* (1981) was a selection of short stories by Ó Cadhain translated by Ó Tuairisc; and *An Duanaire 1600–1900: Poems of the Dispossessed* (1981), a bilingual anthology, translated and edited by Seán Ó Tuama and Thomas Kinsella, was immediately recognised as a text of literary and historical import.⁶ In his preface to *The New Oxford Book of Irish Verse* (1986), Kinsella commented on the lack of Irish-language material in the preceding *Oxford Book of Irish Verse* (1958). Accordingly, the stated aim of this new anthology was 'to present an idea of these two bodies of poetry and of the relationships between them'.⁷ The Irish-language originals, however, did not accompany Kinsella's English translations. In this context, the Irish–English bilingual poetry anthologies *The*

Bright Wave/An Tonn Gheal (1986) and *An Crann faoi Bhláth/The Flowering Tree* (1991), were of particular significance, focusing, as they did, on contemporary Irish-language poetry and making that poetry visible in bilingual format.

This surge of translation activity was no doubt influenced by the Arts Council's policy initiative (1983–5) in relation to bilingual interaction between Irish and English. Along with publication grants, funding was also made available to translators. Goldsmith Press was encouraged by the Arts Council to publish the dual-language volume *Selected Poems: Tacar Dánta* (1984) by Máirtín Ó Direáin, translated by Tomás Mac Síomóin and Douglas Sealy.[8] Over the next decade, a number of other dual-language collections followed, published mainly by Gallery Press (1970–) and by Raven Arts Press (1977–92). Dermot Bolger, founder of Raven Arts Press, considered the publication of Irish–English anthologies an act of defiance: a bid to unbridle literary output in Irish from the establishment's agenda of language restoration.[9] It was as part of the press's European Translation Series that Michael Davitt's *Selected Poems: Rogha Dánta, 1968–1984* (1987) and Nuala Ní Dhomhnaill's *Selected Poems: Rogha Dánta* (1988) were published. Bilingual anthologies are now a matter of course; Gallery Press continues to introduce the work of established poets such as Ní Dhomhnaill to international readers of poetry, while the bilingual volume *Calling Cards* (2018) showcases the work of ten younger poets. Likewise, Arlen House has published a number of bilingual poetry volumes, most notably by Cathal Ó Searcaigh, Deirdre Brennan, and Celia de Fréine.

It is usual, however, for poets to publish in Irish first and to publish a bilingual collection in subsequent years, usually in collaboration with one or more poet-translators. The bilingual collection is often a selection of poems from one or more of the poet's Irish-language volumes, rather than an exact replica of any one of the original volumes. Gearóid Mac Lochlainn's bilingual collections, *Sruth Teangacha/Stream of Tongues* (2002), *Rakish Paddy Blues* (2004), and *Criss-Cross Mo Chara* (2011), are characterised by subversive compositional strategies that undermine clear delineations between original and translated texts. These multicoded texts involve the reader in the process of translation.

Dual-language anthologies were generally welcomed and a wider readership along with a greater recognition for Irish-language poets often presupposed.[10] Notwithstanding the merits of individual collections, however, these publications prompted questions about the practice and politics of translation in Ireland.[11] The extent to which the canon of writing in Irish might be (re)defined by prestigious bilingual anthologies such as *The Field Day Anthology of Irish Writing* (1991) and *An Crann faoi Bhláth/ The Flowering Tree*, for example, concerned Seán Ó Tuama. Given that the editors of the latter volume aimed to give an overview of the 'variety, quality and concerns of modern Irish language poems', Ó Tuama's surprise at the omission of at least an extract from Seán Ó Curraoin's book-length poem *Beairtle* (1985) was well-founded.[12] The eponymous hero's journey from his native Connemara to Dublin, Paris, Rome, and the Congo could be interpreted as a timely exploration of Irish–European identity and heritage. As the inaugural publication of Cló Iar-Chonnacht, a publishing house that will be discussed in more detail below, *Beairtle* was a volume of significance not least because of its playful deconstruction of romantic depictions of native Irish speakers, as well as its lightly veiled suspicion of uncomplicated cosmopolitanism which echoed the renowned text written by Ó Curraoin's uncle, namely *Cré na Cille*.[13]

Notes of caution sounded by Tomás Ó Floinn in his review of *The Bright Wave/An Tonn Gheal* related to the power differential between English and Irish and echoed concerns that were debated at the time and which continue to inform commentary on literary translation in Ireland.[14] A reluctance on the part of poets such as Biddy Jenkinson and Louis de Paor to endorse bilingual publishing in Ireland was informed by an acute awareness of the complexity of translation in a postcolonial context.[15] De Paor, concerned by the increasing marginalisation of Irish both as a living language and as a literary medium, published bilingually in Australia during the 1990s but chose not to do so in Ireland until 2005. Following the publication of his well-received poetry collection *Dialann Bóthair* (1992), Liam Ó Muirthile refrained from writing poetry in Irish for an extended period during the 1990s. This was partly due to the dismay he felt at the liberties taken by those translating poems from Irish to English.[16] His first bilingual collection, *An Fuíoll Feá – Rogha Dánta/Wood Cuttings – New and Selected Poems* (2013), was instigated by fellow-poet and translator, Gabriel Rosenstock. Ó Muirthile described this collaboration, which did not necessitate literal translations or glosses, as liberating and creatively inspiring.[17] As noted by Ní Ghearbhuigh in this volume, Ó Muirthile's multilingualism has informed his own creative writing and his literary translations.

Alert to similarities between the situation in Ireland and in other postcolonial contexts, Michael Cronin has repeatedly insisted on the importance of scholarly engagement with translation discourses, from a minority language perspective, and he has urged Irish-language scholars to develop a theory of translation.[18] Not surprisingly, it is the work of Ireland's most translated poet, Nuala Ní Dhomhnaill, that has gained most critical attention in this regard. Ní Dhomhnaill is an advocate of translation and has a self-confessed *laissez-faire* attitude to translations of her poems.[19] Given his exuberant approach to translation, it is not surprising perhaps that commentary has focused almost exclusively on Paul Muldoon's translational strategies.[20] It is unfortunate, however, that Ní Dhomhnaill's collaboration with other poet-translators, and in particular with Medbh McGuckian and Eiléan Ní Chuilleanáin in *The Water Horse: Poems in Irish* (1999), has been left virtually unexplored. The contrasting qualities of McGuckian's multicoded, feminist translations of Ní Dhomhnaill's poems and Ní Chuilleanáin's more understated but surefooted translations are illuminating refractions worthy of critical attention and sustained analysis.

The interconnectedness of translation and reception is most evident in Ní Dhomhnaill scholarship. Essentially, there exist two bodies of literary criticism: an extensive one in Irish which includes three monographs[21] and a plethora of essays and book chapters, based on Ní Dhomhnaill's Irish poems, and another smaller but substantial corpus of individual essays and book chapters written in English and largely reliant on the bilingual volumes. The most notable divergence between the two bodies of criticism is the importance attributed to Ní Dhomhnaill's re-imagining and intertextual use of folklore motifs and personages. This divergence may be explained by the fact that bilingual volumes do not contain the introductory folklore story that functions as a conceptual framework in her Irish-language collections. In addition, the highly structured grouping of poems, particularly evident in her latter two collections *Feis* (1990) and *Cead Aighnis* (1999), tends not to be reproduced in full, if at all, in bilingual volumes. Critical interpretations of Ní Dhomhnaill's 'mermaid sequence', for example, are heavily influenced by the context in which they are framed in bilingual sequences and in Irish respectively. Psychoanalytical interpretations appear to have been prompted by the title of the bilingual volume *The Fifty Minute Mermaid* (2007), ostensibly referring to the psychoanalyst's hour.[22] Postcolonial, psycholinguistic, and human rights-based interpretations reference the title of the original Irish collection, *Cead Aighnis*, an allusion to an anti-colonial eighteenth-century folk song, as well as examining the facets of the international folk motif that Ní Dhomhnaill has chosen to re-imagine in the extended sequence.[23] The structure of the Irish-language volume, with its inclusion of a number of translations to Irish from the poetry of Paul Celan and Ferida Duraković, among others, is an important prelude to the mermaid sequence which places it in a wider international context beyond the English–Irish dichotomy that often dominates critical interpretations.[24] This sequence of eight poems simply titled 'Aistriúcháin' [Translations] is not replicated in the bilingual volume. That is not to diminish the validity of interpretations based largely on bilingual collections, but rather to recognise the diversity of critical interpretations and thus the value of a bilingual approach within literary criticism itself.

The title of the most comprehensive dual-language poetry anthology to date, *Leabhar na hAthghabhála: Poems of Repossession* (2016), edited by de Paor, may well be understood as a conscious effort to develop the type of critical discourse and reflexive translation strategies that Cronin has so often proposed; a reclamation that will bring a minoritised language perspective to bear on both the politics and the practice of translation in Ireland in order that Irish-language poetry can be accessed and understood on its own terms. If the tone of the editor's introduction is very different from his earlier polemical essay, 'Disappearing Language: Translations from the Irish', de Paor's impulse is largely the same: to make the reader critically aware of the refractory nature of translation. The editor, in an unusual move, details how poet-translators were chosen and the general guidelines given to translators (which appear to encourage a form of subversive literalism rather than 'fluent' or less literal translation strategies), and also includes the poet-translators' reflections on the act of translation as well as notes on individual poems.[25] The collaboration between publishers Cló Iar-Chonnacht and Bloodaxe Books may be understood as a mark of both confidence in, and ambition for, the source material; the diminished circumstances of the Irish language in Ireland make the imperative of an international readership all the more urgent. The national and international critical attention that this publication attracted, including being chosen as the *Poetry Book Society's* recommended translation for Summer 2016, attests to the strategic importance of such collaborations.

Developments in Irish-language Publishing

Of course, the balance between encouraging translation activity and fostering new original literature is complicated and particularly delicate in the case of a minoritised language. Bilingual collaborations supported by English-language publishers in the 1980s were important, but so too was the establishment of new private publishers in Irish, such as Coiscéim (1980–) and Cló Iar-Chonnacht (1985–), and later Leabhar Breac (1994),

Cois Life (1995–2019), and LeabhairCOMHAR (2010–). At a time when government funding for publishing in Irish was deemed insufficient and at risk of being further reduced, the establishment of new publishing houses in the 1980s may have appeared, at least to some, as inauspicious.[26] Cló Iar-Chonnacht Founder Mícheál Ó Conghaile was to become the first full-time, private, Irish-language publisher and, in the initial stages, sought primarily to promote the literature of the Connemara Gaeltacht.[27] As indicated by its inaugural publication *Beairtle*, this new publishing house championed literary works that confronted contemporary issues, especially of a sexual nature, frankly and in utter contrast to the popular image of literature in Irish as being chaste and bucolic and almost exclusively for an academic audience.

Cló Iar-Chonnacht became the publisher for Pádraig Standún, an author of popular fiction whose audacious treatment of clerical celibacy in his first two novels *Súil le Breith* (1983) and *Cíocras* (1991), in particular, brought Irish-language literature to the attention of the public at large. Indeed, in a relatively short period of time, Poolbeg Press, publishers of well-known authors of popular fiction including Maeve Binchy and Patricia O'Scanlon, published Standún's first three novels *Súil le Breith*, *Cíocras*, and *Cion Mná* (1993) as *Lovers* (1991), *Celibates* (1993), and *A Woman's Love* (1994), respectively. The salacious cover of *Lovers*, as well as hyperbolic press coverage,[28] no doubt whetted the public's appetite; *Lovers* was the third most popular paperback bestseller on 21 September 1991 and ranked higher than Roddy Doyle's *The Snapper* (1990).[29] Standún's work has also benefitted from Cló Iar-Chonnacht's commitment to promote Irish-language literature abroad: *Súil le Breith* and *An tAinmhí* (1992) have each been translated into five other languages, while *Stigmata* (1994) is available in English and Polish.[30] A decade after its establishment, Bernard O'Donoghue described Cló Iar-Chonnacht as 'a historical phenomenon': a small press that was not seeking to replicate contemporary mainstream publishers.[31]

In his role as both publisher and as author in his own right, Mícheál Ó Conghaile has played a central part in the emergence of contemporary queer literature in Irish.[32] It was his publishing firm, Cló Iar-Chonnacht, that published Cathal Ó Searcaigh's poetry collection, *Na Buachaillí Bána* (1996), and his bilingual volume *Out in the Open* (1997). These were the earliest volumes by Ó Searcaigh in which homosexual love and desire were suggested visually on the book covers, and openly and explicitly celebrated in the poems themselves. The subversive nature of Ó Searcaigh's poetry, at once traditional yet open to a range of literary influences, including the homoerotic poetry of C. P. Cavafy, has prompted much critical commentary in both Irish and English.³³ Arguably, the most radical aspect of Ó Searcaigh's work is not its exploration of sexual desire and orientation *per se*, but rather his contention, creatively expressed, that neither the language itself, its literary tradition, nor the rural context in which it is predominantly rooted were ever as uniformly traditional or as puritanically conservative as is often imagined.

Ó Conghaile's prose writings are an important addition to the small but significant body of queer writing in Irish. His collection *An Fear a Phléasc* (1997) contains the short story 'Athair', a sensitively narrated coming-out story awarded the Hennessy Literary Award in 1997.³⁴ Ironically, the publication process itself involved an act of conformity for when Ó Conghaile submitted the short story to the *Sunday Tribune* in Irish, it was neither acknowledged nor accepted, but was published a year later when he resubmitted it in English. Although his short stories have been published in a number of European languages, a book-length selection of Ó Conghaile's short stories only became available in English in 2012, under the title *The Colours of Man*.³⁵ In his review of Ó Conghaile's third short-story collection, *An Fear Nach nDéanann Gáire* (2003), Seán Kearney predicted that certain stories included in the collection would shock Irish-language readers.³⁶ By then, however, readers in Irish were accustomed to Ó Conghaile's uninhibited exploration of male homosexuality as, for example, in his first novel, *Sna Fir* (1999), which had earned critical acclaim and was awarded an Oireachtas literary prize.³⁷ His first play, *Cúigear Chonamara* (2003), was ostensibly influenced by his work as translator into Irish of Martin McDonagh's plays *The Beauty Queen of Leenane* (1996) and *The Lonesome West* (1997).³⁸ Ó Conghaile's play is a dark kitchen drama that echoes the tragic comedic style and many of the themes in McDonagh's works. The protagonist of *Cúigear Chonamara* is not, however, a frustrated heterosexual, but rather a male cross-dresser who leads a double life in an isolated rural community. The play garnered three literary awards³⁹ and has been translated into English and Romanian under the titles *The Connemara Five* (2006) and *Cei Cinci din Conamara* (2008), respectively. This instance of multilayered dialogue across languages, via translation, serves to underscore the importance of broadening reflections on translations and transitions beyond the Irish–English dichotomy.

Fostering original work in Irish is, of course, the main priority for all Irish-language publishers. Nonetheless, Ó Conghaile considers translation to other languages important for the reception of Irish-language literature and acknowledges the valuable role of Literature Ireland.⁴⁰ Cló Iar-Chonnacht has played a leading role in promoting Irish-language literature through the medium of translation. The company has published a small number of English-language translations,⁴¹ but prefers to collaborate with English-language publishers who have alternative marketing opportunities and distribution networks.⁴² This strategy has been instrumental in introducing canonical texts in Irish to English-language readers, particularly in recent years. The poetry collection, *An Paróiste Míorúilteach/The Miraculous Parish*, for example, published in collaboration with O'Brien Press (2014), introduced a substantial part of Máire Mhac an tSaoi's poetic *oeuvre* to an English-language audience for the first time. It is a collection that unsettles and complicates the widely held belief that female poets such as Eavan Boland who came to the fore during the first wave of the feminist movement, had few, if any, relevant literary foremothers available to them. Cló Iar-Chonnacht's most ambitious translation project to date involves Ó Cadhain's canonical novel *Cré na Cille* and includes not just linguistic translation but also stage adaptation.⁴³

Translating *Cré na Cille*

As An Gúm appeared reluctant to publish *Cré na Cille*, so too translators appeared reluctant to translate the novel into English. Michael Cronin's appeal in 2001 for an English translation was finally answered with two translations, both published by Cló Iar-Chonnacht in collaboration with Yale University Press. Both translations were part of the Margellos World Republic of Letters series, which supports English-language translations of works of cultural and artistic significance. Alan Titley's translation *The Dirty Dust* appeared in 2015 while the other translation, *Graveyard Clay*, by Liam Mac Con Iomaire and Tim Robinson, was published in 2016. The absence for almost seventy years of a published English-language translation of a prose text regarded as an Irish classic deserves further consideration. The title of a review article in the *New Yorker*, 'The Irish novel that's so good people were scared to translate it', is suggestive if not fully illuminating.⁴⁴

Indeed, Ó Cadhain's publishers Sáirséal agus Dill were anxious to have the novel translated from early on. Ó Cadhain was initially receptive to the idea, but became increasingly incensed by what he perceived as a neglect of the Gaeltacht by official Ireland and, on principle, became reluctant to endorse an English translation. The fact that financial assistance for the publication of the proposed initial translation was arranged by the

Department of Foreign Affairs in 1959 and was to be funded by UNESCO and the Council of Europe is a clear indication of the novel's status. The publisher's numerous attempts to find a suitable translator with the time, as well as the linguistic ability, to translate the novel were in vain.[45]

Although undoubtedly a daunting task, Ó Cadhain's linguistic dexterity and aesthetic complexity in *Cré na Cille* did not prove insurmountable for translators such as Jan Erik Rekdal and Ole Munch-Petersen. Rekdal's Norwegian translation, *Kirkegardsjord*, was published in 1995 while Munch-Petersen's Danish translation, also entitled *Kirkegardsjord*, appeared in 2000. Joan Keefe had previously translated the text into English as part of her doctoral dissertation at the University of California, Berkeley, but her translation has not been published.[46] Therefore, linguistic competency and time constraints alone do not explain the delay in translating *Cré na Cille* into English. Mac Con Iomaire and Robinson allude to previous practical constraints associated with copyright issues as well as a strong sense of reverence or 'linguistic piety or cultural decorum' that may further explain the delay.[47] The latter concern was and is inextricably linked with the larger sociolinguistic and sociocultural context. Publishers and would-be translators were no doubt aware that *Cré na Cille* would have metonymic importance in a charged linguistic context where language politics were to the forefront.[48] The literary merit of *Cré na Cille* and, by extension, the literary merit of all contemporary prose writing in Irish would potentially stand or fall on the basis of a single translation. Furthermore, reticence to translate may also have been due, in part, to an awareness that Ó Cadhain's prose did not conform to readers' preconceptions of writing in Irish: the internecine competitiveness and jealousy among the characters as well as their innate racism were radically different from the portrayal of native Irish speakers in the Blasket Island autobiographies, which appeared to confirm official state ideology.

In his introduction to his translation, *The Dirty Dust*, Alan Titley observes that Ó Cadhain's mixture of traditionalism and experimentalism 'suited his own [Ó Cadhain's] genius'.[49] The same might be said of this manically playful translation. Titley is arguably the foremost prose writer in Irish in the period under discussion, and his short stories and novels are noted for their experimental forms and verbose, flamboyant style.[50] Not surprisingly, very much in the style of Muldoon, his translation does not bear the mark of dutiful reverence to the original but rather appears to relish its loquaciousness. *The Dirty Dust* replicates the ribald, effusive style and the anarchic humour, if not always the exact meaning, of the original. In his preface to *Graveyard Clay*, Liam Mac Con Iomaire refers disapprovingly to Titley's 'free-wheeling' approach.[51] Tellingly, in describing their respective approaches to translation, Titley uses the term 'equivalence' while Robinson employs the paradigm of faithfulness.[52] The meticulous discussion of individual phrases and consultation with particular scholars outlined in the translators' notes are indicative of Mac Con Iomaire's and Robinson's sense of responsibility to, and reverence for, Ó Cadhain's original text.[53] The latter translation is undoubtedly more linguistically and socioculturally accurate and is an invaluable bridging text for the reader who wishes to access the Irish-language original. The publication of two very different translations in the same series was indeed a *coup de maître* that frustrates claims of canonicity and authenticity.[54] It will no doubt prompt comparative analysis and commentary as part of a new branch of Ó Cadhain scholarship.[55]

The two English translations appeared in the run-up to and during the centenary commemoration of the 1916 Easter Rising. Art, its function in society, and its complicated role in nation-building processes, was under discussion and *Cré na Cille* was one of the 100 artworks included in a project that traced 'the modernisation of the state' through selected works.[56] The Anglophone translations also coincided with the twentieth anniversary celebrations of the Irish-language television station, TG4, which occurred with great fanfare in 2016. This concurrence, though not planned, is not altogether irrelevant. TG4 is often associated with a rebranding of the Irish language: marketing it as a modern medium engaged with, and adequate for, the contemporary period. The station's tagline 'súil eile' [another perspective] suggests its unique insight and current relevance. In short, the sociocultural context was favourable. The literary context was also conducive. *The Key/An Eochair* (2015), a bilingual publication of Ó Cadhain's short story (published in 1953), translated by Louis de Paor and Lochlainn Ó Tuairisg and published by Dalkey Archive Press, was very positively received.[57] In addition, as de Paor notes, Ó Cadhain's subversive innovation in *Cré na Cille* is very much in line with the tendency towards experimentalism apparent in contemporary Anglophone Irish writing.[58]

It is important, however, to recognise that English-language translations are only part of a larger multilingual project planned by Cló Iar-Chonnacht, including perhaps stage adaptations.[59] A further three translations of *Cré na Cille* were published in 2017: *Grabgeflüster* translated to German by Gabriele Haefs, *Onder de Zoden* translated to Dutch by Alex Hijmans, and *Hřbitovní hlína* translated to Czech by Radvan Markus. Remarkably, perhaps, a number of translations to date were directly from

Irish, not dependent on English as a bridge language: the Norwegian, Danish, Dutch, German, and Czech translations of *Cré na Cille* were undertaken by native speakers of those languages who translated directly from Irish.[60] The significance of these intercultural exchanges for Ó Cadhain scholarship, and their implications for canon formation in Irish Studies, is discernible from the German blog article titled 'Joyce und Beckett finden ihren verlorenen Drilling wieder' [Joyce and Beckett find their lost triplet again].[61] Of course, these literary affiliations had previously been identified and discussed, most notably perhaps by Robert Welsh and Declan Kiberd, but were, until recently, generally overlooked.[62] Czech scholar and translator Radvan Markus discusses *Cré na Cille* in a wider European context, relating it specifically to the carnivalesque as defined by Mikhail Bakhtin and to Jaroslav Hašek's novel *The Good Soldier Švejk and His Fortunes in the World War* (1921–3).[63]

Translating to Irish

If the question of translating from Irish is sometimes a vexed one, there appears to be a consensus on the importance, and indeed, the necessity of translating into Irish.[64] Children's literature, for example, is an area of strategic importance for the future of the Irish language, and there has been a notable increase of translation activity in this area. Titles from popular series in English such as *The Diary of a Wimpy Kid* by Jeff Kinney, *The Famous Five* by Enid Blyton, *The Hobbit* by J. R. R. Tolkien, *Horrid Henry* by Francesca Simon, and *Harry Potter* by J. K. Rowling, as well as classics such as *The Lion, the Witch and the Wardrobe* by C. S. Lewis, *Kidnapped* by Robert Louis Stevenson, and a number of Roald Dahl titles are now available to young readers in Irish. Publishers have also sought to promote other intercultural connections by providing Irish translations of texts from other European languages including translations of *Le Petit Prince* by Antoine de Saint-Exupéry and a number of titles from *Les Adventures de Tintin* by Hergé along with picture books from Catalan by J. C. Girbés.[65]

A desire to broaden the linguistic range of the Irish language as well as its intellectual, aesthetic, and literary repertoire is often expressed by both scholars and practitioners.[66] That this aspiration is matched by genuine commitment is evidenced by the number of translations of literary works into Irish since the early 1980s, many by established poets and creative writers in Irish who are themselves multilingual.[67] This development has been led to a great extent by Coiscéim; to date it has published in excess of 100 works of translation into

Irish from over twenty different languages. Source texts range from canonical literary texts including Homer's *Odyssey*,[68] Rabelais' *Gargantua*,[69] and Camus' *L'étranger*[70] to literary works by authors less known in Western Europe such as Estonian poet Kristiina Ehin,[71] 'father' of the Japanese short story, Ryūnosuke Akutagawa,[72] and Russian prose writer Viktor Pelevin.[73]

Coiscéim regularly publish trilingual poetry collections, including *An Góstfhear/Guǐ Nán/The Ghost Man* (2004), translations into Irish and English of Chinese poems by Zhang Ye, and *21 Dán/21 Poemes/21 Poemas* (2010) by Tomás Mac Síomóin, who translated his own Irish poems into Catalan and Spanish. Hans-Christian Oeser and Gabriel Rosenstock have collaborated to produce more than ten German/Irish/English collections. Rosenstock's translations of the poetry of Muhammad Iqbal, an Urdu and Persian poet,[74] and of Munir Niazi, an Urdu and Punjabi poet from Pakistan,[75] reflect his own interest in cultural diversity and specifically in non-Western perspectives. His commitment to the act of translation as a political act is evidenced by his translation of the poetry of, among others, Korean poet and activist, Ko Un,[76] as well as the anthology *Poems from Guantánamo: The Detainees Speak* (2007), under the title *Guantánamo* (2008).

Internal translation is a priority area for Leabhar Breac, who have produced Modern Irish versions of a number of classic texts from Old, Middle, and Early Modern Irish, including *An Ceithearnach Caolriabhach* (2002), *Táin Bó Cuailnge* (2017), *Tuath Dé Danann* (2018), and *An Tromdhámh* (2018). Publisher and author Darach Ó Scolaí believes that access to the richness of the long literary tradition in Irish is crucial for the cultivation of contemporary literature in the language. Although these modern versions have proven immensely popular with contemporary readers, funding agencies appear not to share this enthusiasm. Ó Scolaí's interpretation of the language ideology at play is insightful: English-language translations by writers such as Seamus Heaney, Thomas Kinsella, and Ciaran Carson are encouraged and endorsed, but the idea of translating these texts into modern Irish is deemed retrograde and at odds with the presentist branding attempts of the establishment that wishes to promote Irish as a thoroughly modern language.[77]

Conclusion: Publication and Circulation in a Global Context

Publishing in Irish is, of course, inextricably linked with and influenced by larger global contexts and trends. With the advent of what Michael Cronin has termed the virtual and the diasporic Gaeltacht – globally dispersed networks of Irish speakers – online sales are increasingly important.[78]

Digital publishing and marketing technologies have afforded new opportunities to publishers. Cois Life (1995–2019), whose key market was adult language learners, were early innovators and developed an online shop and made titles available in a range of formats, including audiobooks and e-books. By 2018, the company's final year, Cois Life had published fifty-two e-books, while Cló Iar-Chonnacht had produced in excess of 100. The emergence of Irish Studies programmes, particularly in North America, has boosted the sales of e-books aimed at language learners.[79] Gaelchultúr's online book club, ClubLeabhar.com, encourages readers in Ireland and abroad to read Irish-language books and provides a number of attractive online resources to support readers and to stimulate discussions.

Notwithstanding these developments, the main challenges facing Irish-language publishers have changed little since the era of Sáirséal agus Dill and, in a recent review of the current situation, Philip O'Leary has correctly observed 'that there has never been a time when Irish-language publishing was not in crisis'.[80] The core readership in Irish is a relatively small one, and levels of literacy in the language are a matter of concern. Sales figures are influenced, to a large extent, by school and university curricula. Individual titles rarely sell in excess of 1,000 and in recent years the average sale figures for individual titles have dropped substantially.[81] Marketing and distribution are ongoing challenges.

The very term 'literary afterlife', generally used in a positive sense to denote how a text 'lives on' in another medium or context, arouses a certain unease when used in the context of a language whose death has long been predicted, and whose very existence as a community language appears to hang in the balance. The implied longevity of literary texts is, in this instance, tempered by the sociolinguistic reality. That is not to discount the relevance of the concept, but rather to inflect it from a non-dominant language perspective. Literary 'afterlives' are often discussed from a diachronic perspective. However, the foregoing discussion underlines the importance of including synchronic perspectives, particularly when considering the literature of minoritised languages which rely heavily on timely outward translations for mediation and circulation, and on regular inward translations for increased vitality and sustenance. English-language translations undoubtedly play an influential role in the publication, circulation, and reception of Irish-language literature. The shortcomings of monolingual methodologies in Irish Studies become clear, however, when one considers the linguistic profile of Irish-language writers – all of whom are at least bilingual – along with the wider multilingual contexts in which Irish-language literature, like all other literatures, exists, interacts, and circulates in an increasingly interconnected world.

Notes

1. Oireachtas na Gaeilge is an annual festival of Irish-language culture. Its literary awards are prestigious, competitive events highly regarded by writers in Irish.
2. *Idir Shúgradh agus Dáiríre* (Dublin: Oifig an tSoláthair, 1939) and *An Braon Broghach* (Dublin: Oifig an tSoláthair, 1948).
3. Cian Ó hÉigeartaigh and Aoileann Nic Gearailt, *Sáirséal agus Dill 1947–1981: Scéal Foilsitheora* (Inverin, Ireland: Cló Iar-Chonnacht, 2014), pp. 41–8 (p. 47).
4. See Mícheál Ó Conghaile, 'Gnéithe d'fhoilsitheoireacht na Gaeilge inniu', *Comhar*, 71.4 (2011), pp. 6–10.
5. Breandán Ó Doibhlin, '*The Pleasures of Gaelic Poetry* by Seán Mac Réamoinn', *The Furrow*, 34.4 (1983), pp. 263–5 (p. 265).
6. See Paul Muldoon, 'The Victory of Kinsella', *The Irish Times*, 19 September 1981, p. 12.
7. Thomas Kinsella, 'Introduction', in Thomas Kinsella, ed., *The New Oxford Book of Irish Verse* (Oxford: Oxford University Press, 1986), pp. xxiii–xxx (p. xxvii).
8. Laurence Cassidy, 'The Arts Council/An Chomhairle Ealaíon: Translating the Success of Irish Literature: An Address on Public Policy on Literary Translation in Ireland', *Books Ireland*, 164 (1992), pp. 1–4 (pp. 2–3).
9. Dermot Bolger, ed., *The Bright Wave/An Tonn Gheal: Poetry in Irish Now* (Dublin: Raven Arts Press, 1986), pp. 9–11.
10. See, for example, reviews by Micheál Ó Ruairc, 'Poetry Now' (Review of *The Bright Wave [An Tonn Gheal]*), *Irish Literary Supplement*, 5.2 (1986), p. 28; Liam Prút, 'A Decade of Anthologies', *Poetry Ireland Review*, 39 (1993), pp. 28–43.
11. For the terms of this debate, see Barra Ó Séaghdha, 'The Tasks of the Translator', *The Irish Review*, 14 (1993), pp. 143–7; Seán Ó Cearnaigh, et al., 'Debate: Thoughts on Translation', *Poetry Ireland Review*, 39 (1993), pp. 61–71; Louis de Paor, 'Disappearing Language: Translations from the Irish', *Poetry Ireland Review*, p. 51 (1996), pp. 61–8.
12. Seán Ó Tuama, 'Coiscéim na hAoise seo – agus duanairí eile', *Comhar*, 51.5 (1992), pp. 68–74 (p. 73).
13. Gearóid Denvir, 'Oidhreacht Uí Chadhain', in *Litríocht agus Pobal* (Inverin, Ireland: Cló Iar-Chonnachta, 1997), pp. 119–40 (pp. 120–4); Lillis Ó Laoire, 'Seán Ó Curraoin agus Micheál Ó Cuaig', in Ríona Ní Fhrighil, ed., *Filíocht Chomhaimseartha na Gaeilge* (Dublin: Cois Life, 2010), pp. 205–31 (pp. 215–16).

14. Tomás Ó Floinn, 'Léirmheasanna' [Review of *The Bright Wave/An Tonn Gheal*], *Comhar*, 46.1 (1987), pp. 32–3.
15. See Biddy Jenkinson, 'A Letter to an Editor', *Irish University Review*, 21.1 (1991), pp. 27–34; de Paor, 'Disappearing Language', pp. 61–8.
16. Liam Ó Muirthile, 'Ag cur crúca in inspioráid', *An Aimsir Óg* (Dublin: Coiscéim, 1999), pp. 71–92 (pp. 89–90).
17. Liam Ó Muirthile, *An Fuíoll Feá – Rogha Dánta/Wood Cuttings – New and Selected Poems* (Dublin: Cois Life, 2013), pp. xxxix–xli.
18. Michael Cronin, 'Movie-Shows from Babel: Translation and the Irish Language', *Irish Review*, 14 (1993), pp. 56–64.
19. Kaarina Hollo, 'Acts of Translation: An Interview with Nuala Ní Dhomhnaill', *Edinburgh Review*, 99 (1998), pp. 99–107 (p. 107).
20. For largely positive assessments of Muldoon's translational strategies, see David Wheatley, 'The Aistriúchán Cloak: Paul Muldoon and the Irish Language', *New Hibernia Review/Iris Éireannach Nua*, 5.4 (1991), pp. 123–34; Eric Falci, 'Translation as Collaboration: Ní Dhomhnaill and Muldoon', in Fran Brearton and Alan A. Gillis, eds., *The Oxford Handbook of Modern Irish Poetry* (Oxford: Oxford University Press, 2012), pp. 328–40; and Maria Johnston, '"Other Modes of Being": Nuala Ní Dhomhnaill, Paul Muldoon and Translation', in Peter Robinson, ed., *The Oxford Handbook of Contemporary British and Irish Poetry* (Oxford: Oxford University Press, 2013), pp. 442–60. Less favourable assessments of Muldoon's dynamic approach include Barry Ó Séaghdha, 'The Task of the Translator', *The Irish Review*, 14 (1993), pp. 143–7; Kaarina Hollo, 'From the Irish: On *The Astrakhan Cloak*', *New Hibernia Review/Iris Éireannach Nua*, 3.2 (1999), pp. 129–41; and Justin Quinn, *The Cambridge Introduction to Modern Irish Poetry 1800–2000* (Cambridge: Cambridge University Press, 2008), pp. 99, 149–50.
21. See Pádraig de Paor, *Tionscnamh Filíochta Nuala Ní Dhomhnaill* (Dublin: An Clóchomhar, 1997); Bríona Nic Dhiarmada, *Téacs Baineann Téacs Mná: Gnéithe de fhilíocht Nuala Ní Dhomhnaill* (Dublin: An Clóchomhar, 2005); and Ríona Ní Fhrighil, *Briathra, Béithe agus Banfhilí: Filíocht Eavan Boland agus Nuala Ní Dhomhnaill* (Dublin: An Clóchomhar, 2008).
22. See Hiroko Ikeda, '"Towards our own 'Murúch": Reading Nuala Ní Dhomhnaill's "The Fifty Minute Mermaid"', *Journal of Irish Studies*, 25 (2010), pp. 36–47; and Cary Shea, 'Of Mermaids and Others: Remarkable Revelations in "The Fifty Minute Mermaid"', *Nordic Irish Studies*, 9 (2010), pp. 1–12.
23. For a range of interpretations, see Ríona Ní Fhrighil, '"The Mermaids on Land": The Exile of the Irish at Home and Abroad in the Poetry of Nuala Ní Dhomhnaill', in Rosa González, ed., *The Representation of Ireland/s. Images from Outside and From Within* (Barcelona: Universitat de Barcelona, 2003), pp. 145–55; Máirín Nic Eoin, *Trén bhFearann Breac: An Díláithriú Cultúir agus Nualitríocht na Gaeilge* (Dublin: Cois Life, 2005), pp. 284–320; and Tríona Ní Shíocháin, 'An táirseachúlacht bhuan agus múnlú na suibiachta i nuafhilíocht na Gaelainne', *Léann*, 4 (2016), pp. 63–84.

24. Ríona Ní Fhrighil, 'Of Mermaids and Changelings: Human Rights, Folklore and Contemporary Irish Language Poetry', *Estudios Irlandeses*, 12.2 (2017), pp. 107–21 (pp. 112–19).
25. See Louis de Paor, 'Nótaí na n-aistritheoirí/Translators' notes', in Louis de Paor, ed., *Leabhar na hAthghabhála: Poems of Repossession* (Northumberland and Inverin: Bloodaxe Books and Cló Iar-Chonnacht 2016), pp. 501–25.
26. See Tomás de Bhaldraithe, 'Cothú na litríochta', *The Irish Times*, 14 March 1985, p. 11; and Seán Mac Réamoinn, 'Lopsided Bilingualism', *The Irish Times*, 26 July 1985, p. 10.
27. Pádraig Ó Siadhail and Mícheál Ó Conghaile, 'An Fear Aniar: An Interview with Mícheál Ó Conghaile', *The Canadian Journal of Irish Studies*, 31.2 (2005), pp. 54–9 (p. 56).
28. Suggestive newspaper headlines included 'The Gaeltacht Answer to the "Thorn Birds" Out this Week' and 'Fathers and Lovers', a feature article by Kate Shanahan in *Irish Press*, 7 September 1991, pp. 16–17.
29. 'Bestsellers: Paperback Fiction', *The Irish Times*, 21 September 1991, p. 8.
30. *Súil le Breith* has been translated to English, Polish, Bulgarian, Albanian, and Slovenian. *An tAinmhí* has been translated to English, German, Romanian, Polish, and Bulgarian.
31. Bernard O'Donoghue, 'Reviewed Works: *The Anvy* by Pádraig Standún; *Exile* by Pádraic Ó Conaire, trans. by Gearailt Mac Eoin; *Out in the Open* by Cathal Ó Searcaigh, trans. by Frank Sewell; *Poems I Wish I'd Written: Translations from the Irish* by Gabriel Fitzmaurice', *Translation and Literature*, 7.2 (1998), pp. 260–3 (p. 260).
32. See Pádraig Ó Siadhail, 'Odd Man Out: Mícheál Ó Conghaile and Contemporary Irish language Queer Prose', *The Canadian Journal of Irish Studies*, 36.1 (2010), 143–61.
33. See Lillis Ó Laoire, 'Dearg Dobhogtha Cháin/The Indelible Mark of Cain: Sexual Dissidence in the Poetry of Cathal Ó Searcaigh', in Éibhear Walshe, ed., *Sex, Nation and Dissent in Irish Writing* (Cork, Ireland: Cork University Press, 1997), pp. 221–34; Frank Sewell, *Modern Irish Poetry: A New Alhambra* (Oxford: Oxford University Press, 2000), pp. 54–103; James Doan and Frank Sewell, eds., *On the Side of Light: the Poetry of Cathal Ó Searcaigh* (Galway, Ireland: Arlen House, 2002); and Pádraig de Paor, *Na Buachaillí Dána: Cathal Ó Searcaigh, Gabriel Rosenstock agus ról comhaimseartha an fhile sa Ghaeilge* (Dublin: An Clóchomhar, 2005), pp. 15–161.
34. For a perceptive analysis of this short story, see Sarah McKibben, '"Amach leis!" (Out with it!): Modernist Inheritances in Mícheál Ó Conghaile's "Athair" ("Father")', in Paige Reynolds, ed., *Modernist Afterlives in Irish Literature and Culture* (London: Anthem Press, 2016), pp. 75–90.
35. Brian Ó Conchubhair, 'Introduction', in *The Colours of Man*, by Mícheál Ó Conghaile (Inverin, Ireland: Cló Iar-Chonnacht, 2012), pp. 7–15 (pp. 7–8).
36. Seán Kearney, 'Oh Mercy! Is This the Future?', *Fortnight*, 421 (2004), p. 27.

37. See reviews by Antain Mac Lochlainn, 'Faoi chaibidil: Úrscéal Aoibhinn Aerach', *Comhar*, 59.12 (1999), pp. 29–30; and Pádraigín Riggs, 'Idir shúgradh agus dháiríre', *The Irish Review*, 27 (2001), pp. 189–193.
38. Published by Cló Iar-Chonnacht as *Banríon Álainn an Líonáin* (1999) and *Ualach an Uaignis* (2002), respectively.
39. It won the Stewart Parker/BBC Award, an Oireachtas Literary Award, and a Writers' Week/Listowel Award.
40. Ó Siadhail and Ó Conghaile, 'An Fear Aniar: An Interview with Micheál Ó Conghaile', p. 57. Literature Ireland was formerly known as The Irish Literature Exchange, and is funded by Culture Ireland and the Arts Council: www.literatureireland.com/ [accessed 9 August 2018].
41. See Cló Iar-Chonnacht's catalogue at: www.cic.ie/books/published-books/category/irish-literature-english-and-bilingual-works [accessed 8 August 2018].
42. Máirín Nic Eoin, '"Writers in Search of a Market": An Interview with Mícheál Ó Conghaile, Founder and Director of Cló Iar-Chonnacht', *Éire-Ireland*, 52.1&2 (2017), pp. 354–71 (p. 369).
43. Nic Eoin, 'Writers in Search of a Market', pp. 366–8.
44. William Brennan, 'The Irish Novel that's So Good People Were Scared to Translate it', *The New Yorker*, 17 March 2016: www.newyorker.com/books/page-turner/the-irish-novel-thats-so-good-people-were-scared-to-translate-it [accessed 30 March 2019].
45. Ó hÉigeartaigh and Nic Gearailt, *Sáirséal agus Dill 1947–1981*, pp. 181–7.
46. Joan O'Keefe, 'Churchyard Clay: A Translation of Cré na Cille by Máirtín Ó Cadhain with Introduction and Notes' (unpublished doctoral thesis, University of California, Berkeley, 1984).
47. Liam Mac Con Iomaire, 'Introductory Note', in *Graveyard Clay = Cré na Cille: A Narrative in Ten Interludes*, trans. Liam Mac Con Iomaire and Tim Robinson (New Haven, CT: Yale University Press, 2016), pp. vii–xxxiii (p. xxii).
48. Hugh Rowland, 'An choimhlint idé-eolaíochta idir Misneach agus an LFM le linn chomóradh 50 bliain an Éirí Amach', *ComharTaighde*, 2 (2016), pp. 2–15. For English-language summary see: https://comhartaighde.ie/eagrain/2/rowland/en/ [accessed 8 August 2018].
49. Alan Titley, 'Translator's Introduction', in *The Dirty Dust* (New Haven, CT: Yale University Press, 2016), pp. vii–xvi (p. vii).
50. See James J. Blake, 'Present-day Irish Language Fiction', *New Hibernia Review/Iris Éireannach Nua*, 5.3 (2001), pp. 128–41 (pp. 128–33); and Máirtín Coilféir, *Titley* (Dublin: LeabhairCOMHAR, 2018).
51. Mac Con Iomaire, 'Introductory Note', p. xxi.
52. Titley, 'Translator's Introduction', p. xiv; Tim Robinson, 'On Translating Cré na Cille', in *Graveyard Clay*, pp. xxxv–xxxviii (p. xxxv).
53. Ibid., pp. xxxv–xxxvi.
54. Máirín Nic Eoin, 'Graveyard Clay/Cré na Cille Review: New Lease of Life for the Irish Classic', *The Irish Times*, 9 April 2016, p. C10: www.irishtimes.com/culture/books/graveyard-clay-cré-na-cille-review-new-lease-of-life-for-irish-classic-1.2603435 [accessed 26 August 2019].

55. See Margaret Kelleher, 'From Clay to Dust: Cré na Cille in English', *Breac*, 23 February 2016: https://breac.nd.edu/articles/from-clay-to-dust-cre-na-cille-in-english/ [accessed 9 August 2018].
56. Catherine Marshall and Eibhear Walshe, 'Introduction', in Fintan O'Toole, ed., *Modern Ireland in 100 Artworks* (Dublin: Royal Irish Academy, 2016), pp. ix–xv (p. ix).
57. Eileen Battersby, 'The Key/An Eochair, by Máirtín Ó Cadhain: Frenetic Satire with Linguistic Flair', *The Irish Times*, 18 April 2015, p. B13: www.irishtimes.com/culture/books/the-key-an-eochair-by-máirt%C3%ADn-ó-cadhain-frenetic-satire-with-linguistic-flair-1.2179593 [accessed 26 August 2019].
58. Louis de Paor, 'Traidisiún an Aistriúcháin', in *Ag Caint leis an Simné?: Dúshlán an Traidisiúin agus Nualitríocht na Gaeilge* (Spiddal, Ireland: Cló Iar-Chonnacht, 2018), pp. 178–208 (p. 206).
59. Nic Eoin, 'Writers in Search of a Market', p. 367.
60. It is worth noting that *Cúirt an Mheán Oíche* [The Midnight Court] by Brian Merriman was translated directly from Irish to Japanese by members of the Kyoto Society for Research of the Irish Language and Literature in Japan and published in 2015.
61. Andrea Diener, 'Joyce und Beckett finden ihren verlorenen Drilling wieder', *Frankfurter Allgemeine*, 19 October 2016: http://blogs.faz.net/buchmesse/2016/10/19/joyce-und-beckett-finden-ihren-verlorenen-drilling-wieder-1099/ [accessed 9 August 2018].
62. See Robert Welch, *Changing States: Transformations in Modern Irish Writing* (London: Routledge, 1993); Declan Kiberd, *Irish Classics* (London: Granta, 2000), pp. 574–89.
63. See Radvan Markus, 'Jest radno slyšeti: halasný svět *Hřbitovní hlíny*', afterward to Máirtín Ó Cadhain, *Hřbitovní hlína*, trans. Radvan Markus (Prague, Czech Republic: Argo, 2017), pp. 336–54. See also Radvan Markus, 'The Carnivalesque against Entropy: Máirtín Ó Cadhain's *Cré na Cille*', *Litteraria Pragensia*, 28.55 (2018), pp. 56–69.
64. See Ó Cearnaigh, et al., 'Debate: Thoughts on Translation', pp. 61–71.
65. For a comprehensive account, see Órla Ní Chuilleanáin, *Tíortha na hÓige: Litríocht Ghaeilge na nÓg agus Ceisteanna an Aistriúcháin* (Dublin: LeabharCOMHAR, 2014).
66. See Breandán Ó Doibhlin, 'Obair an Aistritheora', *Aistí Cultúir agus Critice III* (Dublin: Coiscéim, 2009), pp. 211–24; and Gabriel Rosenstock, 'The Translation Impulse', *Éire-Ireland*, 35.1&2 (Spring 2000), pp. 20–6.
67. See Anne Markey, '*Valparaiso*: Translation and Irish Poetry', *Translation Studies*, 4.3 (2011), pp. 325–41 (pp. 335–9).
68. Translated by Pádraig de Brún as *An Odaisé* (Dublin: Coiscéim, 1990).
69. Translated by Breandán Ó Doibhlin as *Gargantua* (Dublin: Coiscéim, 2004).
70. Translated by Diarmuid Ó Gráinne as *An Strainséara* (Dublin: Coiscéim, 2012).

71. Coiscéim has published two trilingual collections of Ehin's poetry: *Põletades Pimedust/An Dorchadas á Dhó/Burning the Darkness* (2009), trans. Ilmar Lehtpere and Gabriel Rosenstock, and *Lume Lõplik Minek/Imeacht Deireanach an tSneachta/Imeachd Dheireannach an t-Sneachda* (2013), translated into Irish and Scots Gaelic by Roddy Gorman. Aogán Ó Muircheartaigh translated a collection of Ehin's poems, essays, and short stories into Irish under the title *Péarlaí Corraigh* (Dublin: Coiscéim, 2018).
72. Seán Ó Dúrois translated the short-story collection *Rashōmon* (1915) into Irish under the title *Rashoomon* (Dublin: Coiscéim, 1995).
73. Pelevin's debut novel *Omon Ra* (1992) was translated into Irish by Mark Ó Fionnáin under the title *Amón-Rá* (Dublin: Coiscéim, 2012).
74. A selection of poetry and prose was translated by Rosenstock and published under the title *Iqbal: dréachtaí próis agus filíochta* (Dublin: Coiscéim, 2009).
75. Munir Niazi, *Gaotha ar Fán*. trans. Gabriel Rosenstock (Dublin: Coiscéim, 2006).
76. Ko Un, *Scairt Feithide: Rogha Dánta*, trans. Gabriel Rosenstock (Dingle, Ireland: An Sagart, 2012).
77. Lee Vahey, 'ColúnLee: Agallamh eisiach le Darach Ó Scolaí, foilsitheoir', *RTÉ*, 12 January 2019: www.rte.ie/gaeilge/2019/0108/1021990-colunlee-agallamh-eisiach-le-darach-o-scolai-foilsitheoir/?fbclid=IwAR3_ddUilL5uP9TyCrILSA9fS1TbYq6XMbd1dV6b68lIvII5NEkplQoilWs/ [accessed 13 February 2019].
78. Michael Cronin, *An Ghaeilge san Aois Nua* (Dublin: Cois Life, 2005), pp. 47–9.
79. Nic Eoin, 'Writers in Search of a Market', p. 357.
80. Brian Ó Conchubhair, Máirín Nic Eoin, Mícheál Ó Conghaile, and Philip O'Leary, 'Is Irish-Language Publishing at a Crossroads?', *New Hibernia Review/Iris Éireannach Nua*, 22.2 (2018), pp. 54–66 (p. 56).
81. Nic Eoin, 'Writers in Search of a Market', p. 356.

CHAPTER 17

Irish Studies and Its Discontents
Ronan McDonald

Institutions and Cultural Capital

'Irish Studies' in an academic context does not just mean the study of Ireland *tout court*. The term usually refers to a particular institutional configuration emerging from the humanities, interdisciplinary in aim, that developed in the final two decades of the twentieth century. The period since 1980 has, then, seen the waxing of Irish Studies in this sense. This period, one of intense social change in Ireland, has also witnessed manifold scholarly and intellectual breakthroughs, a weighty library of historiography, and a fluorescence of cultural criticism that has greatly enriched our understanding of Ireland and the Irish story. Yet despite its scholarly and intellectual achievements, there are besetting contradictions and conflicts in Irish Studies. Its emphases and cleavages have often been determined by institutional factors, by existing fields and disciplinary divides, which are themselves part of transnational academic trends and developments.

Irish Studies has a national focus, but an inextricably international institutional ecology. Its emphases and theoretical fashions are almost always imported. Furthermore, it needs to negotiate conflicting images of Ireland among its stakeholders. Irish Studies specialists scrutinise, with all requisite critical scepticism, nostalgic or sentimental ideas of Irish identity, to which the wider culture, including the philanthropists who fund it, are often quite attracted. Ireland enjoys huge academic resources and attention relative to his size because, first, of its diaspora and second because of its benign reputation internationally. Ireland was sufficiently of the West not to be threatening and not of it to be exotic and alluring. The Irish in Britain and America had certainly suffered persecution and oppression. But as the 1980s ceded to the 1990s, Irishness, and by extension Irish Studies, enjoyed a revamped reputation and glimmered with cultural allure, especially as economic success finally arrived in Ireland. Possessing an Anglophone culture, with a huge diasporic presence in the major cultural powers in the world, Ireland enjoyed visibility out of proportion to its population. Official Ireland responded to this self-conscious international image too, marketing its heritage as a land of writers, funding literary festivals and commemorations of authors, many of whom had been shunned and censored during their lifetimes. Irish radicals, however, might have reflected on the connection between the huge attention to Ireland and Irishness with capitalist image-making or, more troublingly, with the whiteness and the assimilability of the Irish compared with dumped and disregarded ethnicities around the globe. Irish Studies flourished in the universities of America and Britain, whereas Congolese studies or Puerto-Rican studies did not. In that respect at least, though the story of Ireland often seems ill-fated, the story of Irish Studies seems blessed, ideally positioned to thrive in the world's academic and cultural networks.

Irish Studies in 1980 was greatly helped by its earlier winners in the global literary marketplace.[1] The huge international success of figures such as Edgeworth, Wilde, Yeats, Joyce, and Beckett meant that Irish Studies could utilise the existing circuitries of literary studies. From the middle decades of the twentieth century, leading American literary scholars, such as Richard Ellmann and Hugh Kenner, were promoting the great Irish modernists from nodal points of academic power. To their names one could add T. R. Henn and Norman Jeffares in Britain. Irish literature had an international prestige and network of scholarship that multidisciplinary Irish Studies could readily deploy. Here is one reason why literary studies looks so large within the Irish Studies matrix. Even if metropolitan critics could often downplay or overlook the Irishness of Joyce or Beckett, their presence in the first rank of Western literature was assured. The synergy between Irish Studies and literary studies is attested by the scholarly 'greening' of the major modernists from the 1990s as a slew of scholarship emerged that firmly located first Joyce and then (and to a lesser extent) Beckett in their formative Irish context.[2]

Irish Studies is inseparable from this wider international academic environment. There were Irish Studies initiatives in Ireland certainly, such as the Institute of Irish Studies at Queens University Belfast established by the Welsh geographer Estyn Evans in 1965, and master's degrees in Irish Literature at University College Dublin and Trinity College. Yet Christina Hunt Mahony is surely right in crediting American universities, specifically those with Irish connections, with nurturing multidisciplinary Irish Studies.[3] The Boston College Irish Studies programme was formed in 1978, Glucksman Ireland House was established in New York University in

1991, and the Donald and Marilyn Keough Irish Studies programme was established at the University of Notre Dame in 1993. These three have been the most prominent US centres of Irish Studies since 1980 and significant drivers for its institutional development, though other initiatives and programmes are scattered around the country. In Britain, the environment was a little different, not least because the universities were less reliant on philanthropy. But, like in North America, Irish Studies tended to cleave to cities historically associated with Irish migration: the Institute of Irish Studies in Liverpool established in 1988; the Irish Studies Centre in St Mary's University Twickenham in 1991; and the more sociological Irish Studies Centre in North London Metropolitan University (then the Polytechnic of North London) in 1986.

The pre-1980 infrastructure included professional bodies, with associated journals and regular conferences. The American Conference for Irish Studies (ACIS) was established in 1960 (as the American Committee for Irish Studies); 1962 saw the establishment of the Irish American Cultural Institute, which has published the journal *Éire-Ireland* since its foundation in 1966. The British Association of Irish Studies (BAIS), established in 1985, was founded in different cultural and institutional circumstances, inflamed by the ongoing Troubles, but also, as Shaun Richards points out, heady with the radical politics and dissident ethos avowed by the Birmingham University Centre for Cultural Studies.[4] The *Irish Studies Review*, founded in 1992 at Bath Spa University, became affiliated with BAIS and is a major organ of interdisciplinary Irish Studies in the UK. If BAIS has its roots in cultural studies, the Conference of Irish Historians in Britain, founded by Roy Foster and Marianne Elliot in 1976, brought together historians with an Irish interest. Foster held the Carroll Chair of Irish History at Hertford College, Oxford between 1991 and 2016, which, together with the visiting Parnell Fellowship at Cambridge established in 1992, afforded Irish Studies the imprimatur of England's most famous universities. With the poet-critics Tom Paulin and Bernard O'Donoghue also based there, and the leading Yeats scholar John Kelly, Oxford was, during this period, one of the nodes in the international Irish Studies network. The raised profile of Irish historiography within the British academic and journalistic establishment was salutary, and figures like Foster worked hard against ingrained ignorance of Irish matters in the British education system. As the century neared its end, the Celtic Tiger roared proudly, the peace process had delivered the 1998 Good Friday Agreement, and Irish Studies initiatives flourished on both sides of the Atlantic and around the world.

Disciplines and Conflicts

Searching through the mission statements of Irish Studies journals, associations, academic centres, and conferences, you would be hard-pressed to find one that does not include some aspiration to disciplinary inclusivity. In this respect, Irish Studies typifies the modern university. Radical sociology lecturer and neo-liberal vice chancellor will both pay obeisance to the goal of interdisciplinary research. Disciplinary restrictions, like protectionist economics or denominational differences, should be thrown off for open markets and ecumenism. However, for all the aspiration of boundary crossing, one has to acknowledge the remarkable intactness of the humanities disciplines, albeit sometimes within new institutional agglomerations, such as schools and centres. Regardless of the ambitions of the theorists of the 1970s and 1980s, neither Irish Studies nor cultural studies have ousted the traditional departments even, or especially, in Irish universities and in the more established universities in the United States and the UK. Typically, if you choose Irish Studies as an undergraduate, you will take courses across established disciplines, not through a devoted Irish Studies department. The traditional disciplines have stayed rooted and have to a large extent determined much of the focus of Irish Studies in history and literature. Indeed, one could argue that the rhetoric of interdisciplinarity is dependent upon the preservation of those old disciplinary structures: the interdisciplinary aspiration and the disciplinary rootedness locked in a reciprocal reinforcement.

Often the disciplinary crossing is peaceful and non-controversial. Irish literary studies have often drawn, uncontroversially, on history. The Irish situation always made it difficult for the ideal of formalist close reading, focused on text rather than context, to become dominant because politics was so blatant and hard to ignore in Irish letters, as Yeats himself was acutely aware. There is an august tradition of straightforward literary history in Irish Studies, and our period begins with two dominant examples, the final book of the leading historian F. S. L. Lyons, *Culture and Anarchy in Ireland, 1890–1930* (1979), and the Trinity College literary scholar Terence Brown's *Ireland: A Cultural and Social History, 1922–1979* (1981). A different sort of historicism began to emerge in English departments in the 1980s, however, influenced variously by French structuralist theory, Marxism, and postcolonialism. Declan Kiberd's *Inventing Ireland* (1995) was an instant classic. Abundant in aperçus and daring ideas, it argued for the postcolonial 'invention' of Ireland through its literature. More heavily theoretical postcolonial readings of Irish literature were provided by the California-based cultural theorist David Lloyd, beginning with *Anomolous States: Irish Writing and the Postcolonial Moment* (1993). Seamus Deane's *Strange Country: Modernity and Nationhood in Irish Writing since 1790* (1997), based on his 1995 Clarendon lectures in Oxford, also adopts a colonial model, surveying Irish literary and intellectual history to understand the genealogy of the Irish national tradition. It is this side of literary studies, exemplified by the Field Day movement, which I will discuss later, that mostly draws the ire of anti-nationalist historians and other commentators, who suspect its theoretical, postcolonial sheen might be old-style grievance politics dressed in flashy new garb or as the literary scholar Edna Longley found it, 'old whines in new bottles'.[5]

For the postcolonialists, on the other hand, the revisionists and antinationalists were naïve positivists, fetishising empiricism while theoretically ill-informed, blithe about their own biases and smug liberalism. The most well-known figure on the so-called revisionist side is the distinguished historian, Yeats biographer, and essayist R. F. Foster, who I have already mentioned. For Foster, the role of a healthy Irish Studies is to counter received myths, nationalist and loyalist, with objective, conscientious, detailed scholarship, open to nuance, complexity, variegation, and occluded histories. This often involved drawing attention to salutary connections between Britain and Ireland that the old nationalist story omitted. So, for example, scholarly recovery of the large numbers of Irish who fought on the British side in the Great War, under-acknowledged after the foundation of the Irish state, was a key achievement of revisionist historiography, undoubtedly impacting on wider Irish culture and policy. The success of this professionalised and detailed historiography could allow Foster to declare in the first issue of the *Irish Review* in 1986 that 'We Are All Revisionists Now'.[6] The ethos here was liberal, humanist, internationalist, and pluralist. The radical side of Irish Studies, however, such as that led by Seamus Deane, detected an unacknowledged establishment ideology lurking behind the 'pseudo-scientific orthodoxy' and self-styled liberalism of revisionism, one that is 'obviously tailored to match the prevailing political climate'.[7]

Both sides could treat the other with scorn: testy exchanges and waspish reviews were commonplace. As a graduate student in Irish Studies in Oxford in the mid-1990s, with the Troubles entering their final phase, I remember a feeling of urgency and import when we discussed Irish national identity, colonialism, or the history of Irish–British relations. It was hard not to be aware that it was all unfinished business, that the shootings and bombings that still filled the newspapers directly pertained to these issues. At the same time, the atmosphere could hardly be characterised as one of free and open inquiry: Irish Studies was divided into camps and cabals, bristling with agendas and assumptions. Whole institutions and departments were associated with revisionist or nationalist orientations, with accusations of exclusionary tactics on both sides.

It would be misleading, however, to think that the nationalist/revisionist debate was simply a case of disciplinary confrontation, with ranks of liberal and scholarly historians lined up against radical and theoretical literary critics. There has been internecine sparring within disciplines too. Edna Longley, a literary critic based at Queen's University Belfast, has been a proponent of evaluative criticism and literary close reading, sceptical about the rise of literary theory and a strong defender of the notion of poetic value. She has also been a fierce foe of the nationalist and postcolonial side of Irish literary studies, from within the literary field. Similarly, while it is probably true that most Irish historians could be classified as revisionist, there have also been prominent nationalist historians who have queried some of the procedures, assumptions, and conclusions of the revisionist project. In a much-debated essay, 'Nationalism and Historical Scholarship in Ireland' (1988–9), the Cambridge historian Brendan Bradshaw argues for a more affective mode of history, questioning the ethos of rigorous impartiality and the value-free empirical method avowed by the founding fathers of revisionist Irish historiography, T. W Moody (1907–84) and Robert Dudley Edwards (1909–88). Is it ever possible to be truly value free? And, when faced with calamity, famine, tragedy, and trauma, is it appropriate to be so? Bradshaw's essay queried the tonal register of mainstream Irish historiography – neutral and ostensibly objective, but often sliding into knowing irony, a leaching of emotional and moral response that is itself a sort of performance. It was a tone ill-fitted to what Bradshaw called the 'catastrophic dimension of Irish history'.[8]

If one finds splits between nationalists and revisionists within as well as between historians and literary critics, it is conversely true that both domains share assumptions and perspectives. Perhaps more than both would wish to acknowledge. Both see themselves, broadly, on the pluralist and progressive side of politics, in opposition to (real or imagined) reactionaries and conservatives, a role they often imagine each other as covertly occupying. Loosely speaking, the revisionist/historical side emerges from a liberal and enlightened politics, while the postcolonialist/literary side position themselves with a more radical tradition of critique. This difference should not obscure a number of shared positions: both pit themselves firmly against the myths of romantic nationalism; both decry and disown a mono-cultural, confessional Irish state. While social conservatism flexed political muscles in Ireland in the 1980s, there was an effective consensus among Irish intellectuals against it. Consensus, like happiness, tends to write white. Ironically, therefore, the social transformations of Ireland since 1980 received less attention because – in the academic sphere – they were less contested. If the 'national question' and issues of identity dominated intellectual discourse, it was not just because the Troubles pressed urgently on contemporary politics, though this was doubtlessly part of it. It was also that this area was the one where the two camps disagreed.

The disagreement sucked oxygen away from vital areas and a more expansive vision of Irish Studies. Perhaps if there had been more formidable social and economic conservative intellectuals to combat, Irish Studies might have spent more energy engaging with the social issues. As it was, the work of feminist critics and historians, and indeed social scientists, on issues such as poverty, sexual ethics, gender rights, migration, and rights for travellers tended to be marginalised. The preoccupation with identity and the national question also kept the main track of Irish Studies in history and literature, with disciplines such as music, art, dance, architecture, and theology playing marginal roles. There was certainly research in these areas. But they tended to stay in their disciplinary homes rather than be amalgamated into the institutional and intellectual nodes that academics call 'Irish Studies', or to be included as an addition or afterthought. One could also claim that Irish Studies, while it was theoretically alert to the legitimacy of colonialism, was not particularly effective in building productive bridges with sociology and the social sciences, which also drew on colonial paradigms. That side of Irish Studies flourished in spaces like the University of North London (under the directorship of the leading sociologist Mary Hickman), but the theoretical work of literary studies, while it often deployed the same theoretical lodestars, tended to engage and clash with history and politics more than with sociology. Journals like *The Irish Journal of Sociology* founded in 1991, developed on parallel rather than interactive lines with more mainstream Irish Studies.

The same might be said of Irish feminism. Irish feminist criticism has been a forceful intellectual and cultural presence in Irish universities but, arguably, was long overlooked by the official 'Irish Studies' institutions. Women's studies centres were established in University College Dublin and Trinity College in the late 1980s, as part of the international interest in this burgeoning field. Yet Margaret Kelleher could observe as late as 2003, that 'with the exception of some individual critics, Irish studies as a discipline remains singularly ill-informed of (and by) the debates and concerns that occupied Irish feminist criticism in the last decade'.[9] Yet Kelleher identifies the primary mode of the cluster of Irish feminist literary criticism in the late 1980s and early 1990s as 'critique', an unmasking of the rhetoric and ideology of womanhood, as advanced by American feminist critics such as Elaine Showalter. In that respect it chimed with the theoretical and political side of Irish Studies more generally. Both embraced what has come to be called, after Paul Ricoeur, the 'hermeneutics of suspicion', a sceptical and genealogically-minded approach that sought to debunk myths and expose ideologies and was especially favoured by leftist cultural theory. Again, it is the shared method and procedure that made the clashes between Irish feminists and postcolonial Irish studies all the more explosive when they occurred, as they did most prominently over the publication of the *Field Day Anthology* in 1991.

Field Day

The opening night of Brian Friel's *Translations* in Derry's Guildhall, on 23 September 1980, marked a watershed in Irish and cultural life, as seen elsewhere in this volume. This truth applies no less to academic Irish Studies, to which Field Day's energy and ethos made a signal contribution. The play itself was shot through with scholarship, both in its technique and its theme: its deployment of historical research and its debt to George Steiner's *After Babel* (1975), for instance, and its tribute to humane and classical learning, represented by the schoolmaster, Hugh. The Field Day theatre company set out to find imaginative and linguistic solutions to the political sclerosis of the Troubles, and the clichéd myths of identity that had fuelled them. It quickly grew into a larger intellectual project, not least through the drive of newly appointed director Seamus Deane, who organised the publication of pamphlets and articles by major Irish and international intellectuals and academics.[10] The pamphleteering side to Field Day, publishing and disseminating the most sophisticated and celebrated theorists in Ireland and the world, was an overt attempt to make intellectual work and scholarship politically effective, to 'contribute to the solution of the present crisis by producing analysis of the established opinions, myths and stereotypes which had become both a symptom and a cause of the current situation'.[11] The bridging of academic and political spheres in this way was not unprecedented in the Irish context. Special recognition should go to the journal *The Crane Bag* (1977–85), a somewhat idiosyncratic forum for cultural debate in the 1980s, that drew on modern theory, and to which we owe the mythical notion of the 'fifth province' (often erroneously ascribed to Field Day). Modern Ireland is made up of four provinces, but the Irish name for 'province' is *coicead*, meaning fifth. Where might this mysterious fifth province be and what might it represent? To Irish intellectuals in the late eighties, influenced by continental theory and writing against the social strife and identitarian logjam in Ireland, the concept afforded a useful metaphor for inclusion: 'The obvious impotence of the various political attempts to unite the four political and geographical provinces would seem to indicate another kind of solution, another kind of unity, one which would incorporate the "fifth" province.'[12]

Few would or could object to Field Day's ambition to challenge stereotypes and open up new ways of thinking about identity. Yet Field Day's insistence that Irish problems were inextricable from British imperialism, and its Northern emphasis more generally, disturbed those revisionist liberals keen to emphasise the cross-fertilisations of British-Irish history and to usurp nationalist myths and narratives. 'There were times in the 1980s', Colm Tóibín declared infamously in the 1990s, 'when it was hard not to feel that Field Day had become the literary wing of the IRA'.[13] The relevance of the colonial frame to Ireland was not one, however, that Field Day was prepared to forsake. In his 1990 Introduction to *Nationalism, Colonialism and Literature*, which collected the Field Day pamphlets by Terry Eagleton, Fredric Jameson, and Edward Said, Deane could not be more explicit:

> Field Day's analysis of the situation derives from the conviction that it is, above all, a colonial crisis. This is not a popular view in the political and academic establishment in Ireland. Historians in particular have been engaged for more than twenty years in what is referred to as a revision of Irish history, the chief aim of which was to demolish the nationalist mythology that had been in place for over fifty years, roughly from 1916 to 1966.[14]

That colonial frame, internationally influential in the humanities at the time, provided a powerful tool for cultural understanding of Ireland's situation. Later in the pamphlet, Deane also makes explicit another informing belief, also indebted to the direction of left-leaning international literary studies in the 1980s. He sets his face against cultural idealisation or any notion that there is an aesthetic realm separate or separable from politics and history, against 'the Arnoldian notion that the work of art that most successfully disengages itself from the fruits of its origin and production is, by virtue of that "disengagement," most fully and purely itself. It is "universal," the proper thing for art to be'.[15] It is significant that he makes this claim introducing three leaders in the academic detonation of literary studies as an autonomous discipline. Eagleton, Jameson, and Said had built their formidable reputations confounding the notion that literature or criticism could ever be an arena of apolitical evaluation or interpretation, an enterprise that in various ways had dominated literary studies before the theoretical turn in the 1970s, but was roundly routed thereafter. Literature, whatever its erstwhile claims to the numinous or sacred, should be unmasked and historicised. It is not then simply that literary studies has moved into history: it is rather that literary theory, of which Field Day is the Irish manifestation, has insisted on the radical historicity of texts and the radical textuality of history.

This context helps in part to explain the informing principle behind – and the subsequent vulnerability of – the much-anticipated *Field Day Anthology of Irish Writing*, which appeared in 1991 under Deane's general editorship. A mammoth collection in three volumes, the anthology covers a period of 1,500 years, totalling over 4,000 pages: it was the largest scholarly undertaking of its kind in Irish letters. That the title of the anthology adopts the word 'Writing' rather than 'Literature' is indicative of its ambition to shake off any old-style, *belle-lettristic* associations. 'Literature' might have seemed evocative of high culture. This was a period when English departments were wary of the ideological goblin secreted in that value-laded word. It recognises that hierarchies are created in particular circumstances and for contingent reasons. The anthology was not simply gathering together the 'best' writing in any quasi-Arnoldian sense. It aimed for the horizontal axis of range rather the vertical one of quality. It was an intrepid enterprise of scholarly recovery and translation and remains a treasure trove of previously unpublished and often neglected Irish writing.

Yet, ironically, disavowing a principle of aesthetic exclusivity, or a naturalised canon, rendered the anthology particularly vulnerable to accusations of bias. If all could be included, then why were some things excluded? Moreover, despite the avowed swerve from 'literature' and old-style canonicity, the anthology devotes whole sections to traditional literary figures such as Swift, Edgeworth, Yeats, and Joyce. Though the anthology is formally eclectic, with pamphlets, journalism, letters, and speeches, there is still a bias towards the traditional literary forms such as poetry and fiction in most sections. So however much it owns its status as a gathering of cultural and historical documents, it is still a recognisably *literary* anthology, wedded to the traditional canon and the accustomed consecrations of literary reputation. Yet, it is ill-equipped to defend this position. The anthology teetered between its avowed historicist, anti-hierarchical orientation and a literary critical institution that it was not quite ready to renounce. It was prone to attack precisely on the basis of the materialist and critical historicism that it had so firmly asserted.

Ostensibly the aim of this anthology was to articulate, in its manifold variety, an integrated national narrative. As Deane put it in his 'General Introduction': 'There *is* a story here, a metanarrative, which is, we believe, hospitable to all the micro-narratives that, from time to time, have achieved prominence as the official version of the true history, political and literary, of the island's past and present.'[16] So behind the attention to difference lies a conviction in the overall coherence of the idea of Ireland, a belief that would be flaunted by Field Day's detractors as evidence that there was an old-school nationalist agenda lurking behind the theoretical sophistication. Talk of a metanarrative also signalled an inclusivity that might seem impertinent or hubristic to those who found exclusions in the selected canon, most notoriously the under-representation of women's writing. The attacks from the revisionist historians and anti-nationalists who throughout the 1980s had disdained Field Day could be expected. Far more damaging was the outrage from feminist critics, sidelined from the main centres of Irish Studies and smarting from the political and social setbacks of the 1980s. To be under-represented in this self-styled 'metanarrative', especially by those who claimed a dissident and critical ethos like their own, was galling and came at a particularly livid and sensitive time in Irish cultural and social history. Socially conservative forces had won key referenda in the 1980s, securing constitutional prohibitions on divorce and abortion. At the same time, the election of the socially progressive Mary Robinson as the Irish President at the end of 1990 was a beacon of hope, and anticipated the changes that would come in the following decade. The Field Day anthology in this environment seemed out of kilter, wedded to a male, canonical, literary tradition despite its fine disavowals of hierarchies and selection.

Deane quickly acknowledged the force of the feminist critique, while remaining scornful of the revisionist one. A supplementary volume would be published to make good the omission. This turned into two volumes, under a team of women scholars and editors, most of whom, significantly, were historians. The result was 3,200 pages testifying to women's contribution to Irish affairs over 1,400 years. Volumes Four and Five, entitled *Irish Women's Writing and Traditions,* may have begun as a corrective and a supplement to the original volumes but in the end they turned into a bumper trawl of women's writings, 'both encyclopedic and kaleidoscopic'.[17] Though a print anthology, it reflects the omnivorous appetite of the emerging digital age with which it coincided.[18] It also indicates the editors' desire to expand not just the selection made by the original volumes but to explode the principles of selection themselves, which have kept women out so widely and for so long. These volumes are emancipatory and inclusive, capturing a swathe of writing of varying quality by and about Irish women – including journalism, pamphlets, oral traditions, and theology – across eras, themes, and topics. However, the size and the eclecticism of the resulting volumes, while affording scholars with an invaluable resource for future scholarship, also led some readers to challenge its ethos and criteria. '"Inclusiveness" here carries its own censoring agenda', concluded Aisling Foster in her *Guardian* review: 'inside this fat anthology is a thin one screaming to be let out.'[19] Should an anthology forsake the principles of selection? Some readers, especially time-poor general and non-academic ones, sometimes need nothing more than a gatekeeper, an expert who can select the most noteworthy work, however ideologically contaminated such selection might inevitably be. As the digital age revolutionises access to the written word, this need for discrimination and evaluation, on whatever basis, becomes all the more pressing.

After the Storm

The nationalist-revisionist debates of the 1980s and 1990s are far less livid now than they were during the Troubles. The outbreak of a fragile peace in Ireland is one reason for this, though the proliferation of so-called peace walls and the controversy over flags, emblems, and the status of the Irish language strongly suggests that the North is still riven by binary identity thinking. The options promised by the Good Friday Agreement – that the citizens of Northern Ireland could choose to be Irish or British or both – relied on the frictionless borders afforded by the European Union. At the time of writing, Brexit remains a clear and present danger to the new equilibrium. The rise of English nationalism, frustrating the goals of a modern, Europeanised, liberal Ireland, inverts a pervasive view that the problem with Ireland was that it was too tribal and atavistic. Deane's insistence that nationalism was not simply an Irish problem, but has always been deeply formed by its British counterpart, now seems prescient.[20]

The earlier culture war has also been eased by broader shifts in the humanities. So-called 'Theory' creates less scandal around departments of

English these days. It has, generally, been absorbed into wider practice or settled into a calm historicism, which has supported the work of recovering forgotten and overlooked narratives. Our understanding of terms like the Irish Revival and Irish modernism have been hugely expanded and enriched in the last generation as a result. Postcolonial theory, so dominant in earlier Irish Studies conferences and journals, seems to have receded as an overarching paradigm in which to understand the Irish situation. The anomalous condition of Ireland, hovering as it does between colony and coloniser, is widely acknowledged. Luke Gibbons's definition of Ireland – 'a first world country, but with a third world memory' – proved highly quotable for a time.[21] But the Celtic Tiger's excesses of the late 1990s and early 2000s perhaps made Irish self-comparison with the wretched of the earth unseemly.

Irish literary studies has followed international trends, with significant works in areas like disability studies, queer studies, and the burgeoning field of environmental humanities.[22] Some of these furrows promise to develop the relatively sparse conduits between literary studies and the social sciences in Irish Studies. All also force Irish Studies to think beyond its national grooves both geographically and conceptually. Questions of gender and sexuality can no longer tenably be regarded as an exotic offshoot of Irish Studies, or worse, scotomised altogether. That the performance and subversion of gender norms has always been central to the Irish story and its relation to the power of church and state is impossible to ignore. The institutional and religious sexual abuse that has come to light in recent public inquiries has greatly impacted Ireland's social mores and, along with other areas like Famine studies, has fed the rise of trauma and memory studies.[23] The various aspects of private and public memory, what is commemorated and why, what repressed and why, has been a site of much activity in recent years, particularly with the so-called 'Decade of Centenaries' that mark the foundation of the Irish state. Yet this decade, so far, has proved remarkably uncontroversial. The commemoration of the centenary of the 1916 Rising seemed to bring together nationalist and revisionist factions, with little of the friction that marked the old culture wars.

The changed atmosphere has taken much of the heat but also some of the life out of Irish Studies. The stakes are not always clear in the way they were when identity seemed literally lethal. Irish Studies is, generally, less internecine and embittered than it was thirty years ago. But it is also less animated by urgency, perhaps even, in the wider academic world, less 'special'. This has been exacerbated by the rise of the so-called 'transnational turn' that has moved attention away from nation states as discrete entities, towards more comparative and global perspectives. The best Irish Studies was never provincial, either in its focus or its method: Ireland has always been a node invariably caught up in international networks of movement and exchange, of people and ideas. But the academic interest has pushed this reality to the fore and provided a new and challenging context for Irish Studies to justify itself.

The shifting of focus away from Irish Studies due to the end of the Troubles and the transnational turn have occurred when the wider institutional and financial environment threatens humanities research more broadly. The introduction of tuition fees in the UK and general shifts in the prestige and cultural capital of traditional humanities has fed a wider sense of crisis. Add to this the upsurge in the academic precariat, with most new Irish Studies lecturers unable to find secure academic employment, a decrease in student enrolments in many areas, and an increase in sceptical policymakers and university administrators eager for relevance and economic benefit, and Irish Studies seems in difficult straits. The controversial and much-protested closure of the distinguished and long-standing Irish Studies Centre at St Mary's University Twickenham in late 2016 seemed to confirm the sense that Irish Studies was losing its traction in the UK. At the same time however, the British Association of Irish Studies remains vibrant, as does ACIS, IASIL (International Association for the Study of Irish Literatures), and the EFACIS (the European Federation of Associations and Centres for Irish Studies). Many of these organisations have bloomed because of the opportunities for international collaboration afforded by the Internet and digital technology. These possibilities are making new archives and resources available, as well as making small nodes in a global Irish studies network vastly more interconnected. It means that Irish Studies programmes outside the well-worn Anglophone world are springing up, rhizomatically, in China, Brazil, Japan, Hungary, and the Czech Republic.

The new networks and the digital platforms promise to transform Irish Studies, rendering it transnational not just in terms of where it takes place, but also in terms of how it conceives of Ireland and Irishness, and how these concepts might operate relationally and circulate globally. New technologies also afford opportunities for professional and coordinated engagement with the Irish diaspora around the world, an engagement in line with official government policy. Interest in diasporic Irishness chimes with the transnational concerns of much current work in the humanities and affords a fillip to the Irish Studies programmes scattered around the world, often in cities that are destinations of Irish migration, such as New York, Liverpool, and Melbourne. The study of the Irish abroad and Irish migration is certainly not new – and has been a steady part of multidisciplinary Irish Studies throughout the period under question. Academic literature exists on the Irish in Australia, in Canada, in Britain, and in the United States, and less frequently on the Irish diaspora and emigration experience as a whole.[24] But it has been more richly theorised in recent years, absorbing the advances of postcolonial and cosmopolitan theory, and deploying the possibilities of digital networks. It involves a massive broadening of the adjective 'Irish' in Irish Studies and a re-thinking of simplistic ideas of diaspora as alternately exile or opportunity, banishment from home or escape to liberation. How identities develop transnationally, the complex relation between source and host nation and what is the appropriate way to think about cultural encounter has been a key focus of thinking about diaspora in an era of dislocation and globalisation, both physical and cultural.

Porous borders have, certainly, always been salutary for Irish Studies and increased focus on the global Irish promises rich new resources and, potentially, a radically dilated subject matter. If we were to pick one word to characterise the development of Irish Studies since 1980, it could well be 'expansion'. It has, as an ethos, tended to prize boundary-crossing and inclusion of various sorts, be they the tearing down of disciplinary barriers, or the democratisation of subject matter. History has moved away from high politics and elite communities and towards the popular and the social. Literary Studies has sought to move beyond old-fashioned, exclusive canons and genres. The state has yielded to the diasporic nation. At the same time, however, Irish Studies needs to maintain a discursive and identifiable subject matter. The possibilities afforded by digital technology mean that Irish Studies has oceans of information and data to navigate. There are manifold possibilities afforded by these resources. Yet they do demand, at some stage, an assertion of vertical control over the horizontal expansion. It will be one of the purposes of Irish Studies going forward not only to accumulate, gather, and expand, but also to sift, select, and constrict. A human reading life is limited and, ultimately, the guardians of Irish Studies will need to be gatekeepers and arbiters, helping the wider public make decisions and choices about which texts are to be read, which voices heard.

Notes

1. For a highly influential account of how modern Irish writing became consecrated internationally, see Pascale Casanova, *The World Republic of Letters*,

trans. M. B. DeBevoise (Cambridge, MA: Harvard University Press, 2004), pp. 303–22.
2. Illustrative monographs include Emer Nolan, *James Joyce and Nationalism* (London: Routledge, 1996); Andrew Gibson, *Joyce's Revenge* (Oxford: Oxford University Press, 2002); John P. Harrington, *The Irish Beckett* (Syracuse, NY: Syracuse University Press, 1991); and Emilie Morin, *Samuel Beckett and the Problem of Irishness* (Basingstoke: Palgrave Macmillan, 2009).
3. Christina Hunt Mahony, 'Changing Transatlantic Contexts and Contours: Irish Studies in the United States', in Liam Harte and Yvonne Whelan, eds., *Ireland Beyond Boundaries: Mapping Irish Studies in the Twenty-First Century* (London: Pluto Press, 2007), pp. 17–27 (p. 18).
4. Shaun Richards, '"Our Revels Now Are Ended": Irish Studies in Britain – Origin and Aftermath', in *Ireland Beyond Boundaries*, pp. 48–57 (p. 50).
5. Edna Longley, 'More Martyrs to Abstraction', *Fortnight*, 206 (July/August 1984), pp. 18–20 (p. 18). Historians who have disputed the colonial model in Ireland include Stephen Howe, *Ireland and Empire: Colonial Legacies in Irish History and Culture* (Oxford: Oxford University Press, 2002); and Liam Kennedy, *Colonialism, Religion and Nationalism in Ireland* (Belfast: Institute of Irish Studies, 1996).
6. R.F. Foster, 'We Are All Revisionists Now', *The Irish Review*, 1 (1986), pp. 1–5.
7. Seamus Deane, 'Wherever Green is Red', in Máirín Ní Donnchadha and Theo Dorgan, eds., *Revising the Rising* (Derry, Northern Ireland: Field Day, 1991), pp. 93–105 (p. 93).
8. Brendan Bradshaw, 'Nationalism and Historical Scholarship in Modern Ireland', *Irish Historical Studies*, 26.104 (November 1989), pp. 329–51 (p. 340).
9. Margaret Kelleher, '*The Field Day Anthology* and Irish Women's Literary Studies', *The Irish Review*, 30 (2003), pp. 82–94 (p. 82).
10. See Marilynn J. Richtarik, *Acting Between the Lines: The Field Day Theatre Company and Irish Cultural Politics, 1980–84* (Oxford: Oxford University Press, 1995).
11. Seamus Deane et al., *Ireland's Field Day* (Notre Dame, IN: University of Notre Dame Press, 1986), p. vii.
12. Mark Patrick Hederman and Richard Kearney, 'Editorial I/Endodermis', *The Crane Bag*, 1.1 (Spring, 1977), pp. 3–5 (p. 4).
13. Colm Tóibín, '"On the Literary Wing", Review of Marilyn J. Richtarik, *Acting Between the Lines: The Field Day Theatre Company and Irish Cultural Politics 1980-1984*', in *The Times Literary Supplement*, 4804 (28 April 1995), p. 10.
14. Seamus Deane, 'Introduction', in Terry Eagleton, Fredric Jameson, Edward W. Said, eds., *Nationalism, Colonialism, Culture* (Minneapolis and London: University of Minnesota Press, 1990), pp. 3–19 (p. 6).
15. Ibid., p. 7.
16. Seamus Deane, 'A General Introduction', *The Field Day Anthology of Irish Literature*, 3 vols. (Derry, Northern Ireland: Field Day Publications, 1991), I, pp. xix–xxvi (p. xix).

17. 'Preface', *The Field Day Anthology of Irish Writing, Volumes 4 and 5: Irish Women's Writing and Traditions* (Cork, Ireland and New York: Cork University Press and New York University Press, in association with Field Day, 2002), IV, pp. xxxii–xlii (p. xxxii).
18. See Anne Jamieson on some of these parallels and also the pitfalls of the prospective digital version of all five volumes: '"Women's Literary History in Ireland": Digitizing *The Field Day Anthology of Irish Writing*', *Women's History Review*, 26.5 (2017), pp. 751–65.
19. Aisling Foster, 'Too much, but Still Not Enough', *The Guardian*, 4 January 2003: www.theguardian.com/books/2003/jan/04/featuresreviews.guardianreview2 [accessed 1 October 2018].
20. Deane, 'Introduction', *Nationalism, Colonialism, Culture*, pp. 7–8.
21. Luke Gibbons, 'Ireland and the Colonization of Theory', *Interventions*, 1.1 (1998), p. 27.
22. See Mark Mossman, *Disability, Representation and the Body in Irish Writing* (Basingstoke: Palgrave Macmillan, 2009); Patrick R. Mullen, *The Poor Bugger's Tool: Irish Modernism, Queer Labor and Postcolonial History* (Oxford: Oxford University Press, 2012); and Eoin Flannery, *Ireland and Ecocriticism: Literature, History and Environmental Justice* (New York: Routledge, 2015).
23. For a helpful bibliography, see Oona Frawley, 'Ireland and Memory Studies', *Oxford Bibliographies*, 11 January 2018: www.oxfordbibliographies.com/view/document/obo-9780199846719/obo-9780199846719-0137.xml [accessed 10 November 2018].
24. Patrick O'Sullivan's six volume, multidisciplinary edited work *The Irish World Wide* (Leicester: Leicester University Press, 1992–7) is an exception to this national focus; so too are such illustrative volumes as Donald Akenson, *The Irish Diaspora: A Primer* (Belfast: Institute of Irish Studies, 1993).

CHAPTER 18

Historical Transitions in Ireland on Screen

Barry Monahan

ANGUS
        We are sent
To give thee from our royal master thanks,
Only to herald thee into his sight,
Not pay thee.

ROSS
And, for an earnest of a greater honor,
He bade me, from him, call thee thane of Cawdor:
In which addition, hail, most worthy thane,
For it is thine.

BANQUO
        What, can the devil speak true?

MACBETH
The thane of Cawdor lives. Why do you dress me
In borrow'd robes?

Macbeth, I.3

These lines from Shakespeare's *Macbeth* represent the moment at which the eponymous tragic character hears of his promotion to the political position of 'Thane of Cawdor' by King Duncan. In an earlier scene, during an encounter with the three Witches, the mystical characters had already predicted the event. Banquo's first response, shocked by the realisation of the earlier prophesy, indicates his belief that the malign characters had a hand in its implementation. Macbeth, however, being more suspicious of the news, uses a metaphor of clothing – here implied as dress code pertaining to social and political status – to express his disbelief in the coincidence. The difference in their reactions is slight, but it manifestly places Banquo's credulity in the power of the supernatural beings against Macbeth's coming to terms with his own possible agency in his professional advancement and, consequently, the requirement for action to effect his progression. This double-sided approach to the theme of human self-determination haunts – literally – the whole narrative of the Bard's Scottish Play. On the one hand, if implacable external forces intervene in our fate, our free will is closed and we can do nothing to change circumstances. If, on the other hand, we have a role to play in our destiny, it may be that this is sometimes accomplished by dressing above our station or, put differently, by borrowing unfamiliar techniques or unowned technologies for our benefit.

Throughout the history of cinema in Ireland, the nation's size – both demographically and economically – and its marginal position in relation to the dominant Hollywood centre of production have had substantial determining roles. The unstable fluctuations of indigenous film production have been played out on a stage that has, in many respects, placed self-determination, national policymaking, and strategic practice by indigenous film-makers against influences of external market forces, dominant industrial modes, and international box office preferences. As a minor and marginal cinema, like many other national cinemas that lie outside the mainstream commercial circuit, Ireland has often needed to dress above its status by 'borrowing robes'. Across a number of categories, I hope to examine the different ways in which the smaller (Irish, outsider) player has experienced and navigated its position of inferiority and disadvantage through various forms of borrowing. In each case detailed here, notions of borrowing can be understood as forms of transition. This usefully (although perhaps counter-intuitively) frames the situation of Irish cinema as an empowered liminal mechanism; neither rigidly and inflexibly opposed to international developments in the medium, nor bound to them on a predetermined course that isolates the country within its own solitary market and cultural potential. Borrowing as a mode of transitional evolution thus becomes a form of possession without ownership, residency without tenure, and offers the possibility of use without permanent, fixed transformation.

Borrowing Machinery and Text: The Modern Nation in Transition (1921–1959)

The ratification of the Irish Free State Constitution Act in December 1922 marked the beginning of autonomous rule in Ireland by endorsing the Anglo-Irish Treaty of 1921. With this could occur the first sovereign legislative expressions of an earlier cultural nationalism that had provided the political and military momentum towards independence. The earliest government acts were a conservative manifestation of the political position of a rural, Gaelic, and Catholic middle class, whose reactionary ideology would overshadow the nascent state for several decades. The Censorship of Films, the Legislation on Divorce, and the Censorship of Publications Acts (1923, 1925, and 1929, respectively) indicate a discernible distrust of modernist influences on the country. However, they do not so clearly indicate the degree to which the ruling classes had become increasingly out of step with popular sentiment. The evidence of this disjunction may be usefully traced in reactions to external popular cultural forms, and specifically towards the cinema, the apparatus *par excellence* of transnational modernism. Kevin Rockett has indicated that the popular fascination with (predominantly) American cinema was something of which 'the middle class conservatives who took power in 1922 were only too well aware' as that form of entertainment 'was more attractive than the limited and often repressive offerings of the regenerated native Irish culture'.[1] He has pointed to a certain anxiety among authorities, noting that 'the success of the cultural nationalist project could be fatally undermined by [...] Hollywood "values," that is, consumerism as the new ideology of consumption in America.'[2]

I am invoking the benign term 'borrowing' here to indicate the state's cautious relationship with the medium, one enforced aggressively through its official censorship. Paradoxically, however, rather than seek to support cinematic self-representation and work to establish a production base for film-making in Ireland, the ruling parties eschewed this responsibility. This attitude of indifference lasted at least until the mid-1950s, when the government was involved in negotiations for the establishment of Ardmore Studios in Bray, County Wicklow.[3] Ian Jarvie makes the deficiency explicit when he places cinema at the core of any nation's modernisation and, from this perspective, Ireland's tentative relationship with the medium – borrowed but not taken into possession – is symptomatic of the ideological position that the state validated.[4] For cultural nationalist practitioners within the literary context, Declan Kiberd has noted Irish proponents' desire to break from its authors' colonial literary heritage, warning that to 'challenge English ideas is merely to treat symptoms; only by rejecting English forms could the mind be opened to the democratic muse'.[5] Similarly, the 'movies' were increasingly seen – between the world wars – as a decadent, corrupting, and modernising apparatus of an American culture and capitalist centre of production.

From the earliest stirrings of cultural nationalism, Irish literary modernism had established its position on the global English language stage with work by Joyce, Yeats, Beckett, O'Casey, and Shaw. Consequently, a considerable percentage of the on-screen representations of Ireland, the Irish, and the country's history was borrowed from written sources.[6] For reasons often motivated by commercial profit, where overseas production companies sought to buy into the popularity of Ireland's rich novelistic and dramatic heritage and recognition, the first half of the twentieth century saw a number of adaptations of work by Synge, O'Casey, Shaw, and other dramatists who were associated with the national theatre. Interest and financial motives also attracted prominent Hollywood and British directors such as John Ford, Orson Welles, Bryan Desmond Hurst, and Alfred Hitchcock. Perhaps out of step with the genre that became his signature mode, the latter was responsible for directing Ireland's first sound film adaptation, with his production of O'Casey's *Juno and the Paycock* in 1930.

From as early as 1935, with John Ford's screen version of Liam O'Flaherty's *The Informer*, through to Joseph Strick's *Ulysses* in 1967, the Irish literary canon has been borrowed in the provision of a diverse and cinematically praiseworthy contribution to representations of the nation's narratives. Possibly the best known of these was Ford's 1952 version of Irishman Maurice Walsh's short story 'The Quiet Man', an enduring classic which was followed by the American director's screen version of Frank O'Connor's 'The Majesty of the Law', the first part of a trilogy of short films released under the title *The Rising of the Moon* (or *Three Leaves of the Shamrock*, in the United States) in 1957. The heritage of Irish short stories provided a repository of material for feature length and shorter films: O'Connor's *My Oedipus Complex* – released as *Larry* in 1959 – was directed by Shelah Richards and Robert Dawson; Seán Ó Faoláin's 'The Woman Who Married Clark Gable' was given a screen interpretation in 1985 by Thaddeus O'Sullivan; and Joyce's 'The Dead' was directed by John Huston (his last film) in 1987.

These are representative examples of the rich heritage of literary short stories that amply held their aesthetic, tonal, and thematic wealth when converted to screen. More contemporary, internationally recognised Irish directors such as Neil Jordan and Jim Sheridan have occasionally turned to literary sources with considerable success and, to date, between them they have been responsible for the adaptation of Dublin-born artist Christy Brown's autobiography *My Left Foot* (1989), Sebastian Barry's *The Secret Scripture* (2016), as well as Patrick McCabe's *The Butcher Boy* (1997) and *Breakfast on Pluto* (2005). It is also telling, perhaps, that two Irish literary screen adaptations performed well at the 2016 Academy Awards, where Lenny Abrahamson's filmed version of Emma Donoghue's *Room*, and

John Carney's production of Colin Tóibín's *Brooklyn* (both released in 2015) were positively acknowledged. This international interest demonstrates some degree of recognition in the value of borrowing from the work of internationally acclaimed Irish novelists, and it suggests that the practice is likely to continue to be an important aspect in the work of Irish filmmakers.

Borrowing Historiography: Addressing Earlier Misrepresentations (1980–1987)

After six decades without any statutory support for film production in Ireland, several years of political lobbying by a group of national cinema enthusiasts finally paid off with the establishment of the Irish Film Board (*Bord Scannán na hÉireann*) in 1980. This collective of passionate cinephiles would later contribute a modest but important body of work in the first sustained movement of indigenous film production on the island. The cultural transitions and changes in political attitude that led to the drafting of the Film Board Bill, and thus initiated the establishment of the Board itself, were slight but significant. For the first time since the foundation of the state, cinema was deemed more worthy of support than it was to be constrained by censorship and regulation. Its merits as a valid form of cultural expression were still relegated by the political elite in favour of validating its market position as an industrial practice,[7] but this did not dampen the appetite for production among the new Irish film directors, who were soon to be known as the 'first wave'.

Working under a long shadow of flawed, non-indigenous representations of Ireland on screen, predominantly by British and American film companies, much of the thematic content of the work of directors such as Bob Quinn, Joe Comerford, Cathal Black, Thaddeus O'Sullivan, Pat Murphy, Margo Harkin, and Vivienne Dick developed as a constructed rebuttal to decades of overseas misrepresentations of Ireland's characters, stories, and history. As a contribution to Irish cinematic historiography, this movement was imbued with political criticism, social commentary, and a fervent desire to challenge both the earlier narratives of Ireland and the limits of the formal capabilities of the medium. Martin McLoone summarised an important characteristic of first-wave films, noting that 'when this recognisably indigenous body of films began to emerge in Ireland from the mid-1970s on, it demonstrated a critical engagement with the legacy of Irish cultural nationalism'.[8] He then listed what he identified as 'a coherent set of overlapping themes',[9] all of which imply a historiographical address to, or an attempt to engage with – rather than simply reject – previous portrayals of Irish life, society, and history on screen. This historiographical engagement is an obvious method of empowerment for indigenous film-makers as it firstly borrows, and then re-appropriates, the texts of one's own history, formerly written by an 'Other'. The first-wave film-makers were motivated by a need to correct biased – and politically inflected – misrepresentations of the country and its history. In counteracting earlier depictions, they were concerned with establishing an indigenous aesthetic and expression, what Rockett has identified as 'committed critical engagements with Irish culture and society'.[10] Pat Murphy's *Anne Devlin* (1984), which was produced with Film Board funding, engaged with historical narratives head on by re-centring the role of its eponymous character, Robert Emmet's housekeeper and a subversive activist who was linked to the United Irishmen. Others of the first-wave film-makers addressed the contemporary sociological consequences of various historical legacies: while Cathal Black's *Our Boys* (1981) examined the ideological impact of the Catholic Church in second level schooling, Neil Jordan's *Angel* (1982) and Pat Murphy's *Maeve* (1981) both presented narratives of personal and political identity in Northern Ireland. Another group of writer-directors was less directly engaged with stories of Ireland's history, but their formal innovation – on the levels of narrative structure, stylistic rendering, and cinematic coding – implicitly addressed more traditional (thus historically established) mainstream methods by which the country had been represented. The grainy images, chiaroscuro lighting, and *cinéma-vérité* aesthetics of films such as Cathal Black's *Pigs* (1984), Bob Quinn's *Budawanny*, and Joe Comerford's *Reefer and the Model* (both 1987) were stylistic predilections that sat well with the alternative, somewhat picaresque, and non-linear modes by which their plots unfolded. True to the best political practice of engaged marginal national film-makers, this 'accented iteration' (in Hamid Naficy's term) realised a vocation identified by John Hill, who notes that 'it is precisely because Hollywood increasingly speaks with a globalising voice that competing voices, rooted in local cultures, have become that much more important and necessary'.[11]

The internationally competing voices from Irish film-makers in this instance received their greatest statutory support with the establishment of the Film Board in 1980, but, regrettably, the operations of the same body were suspended in 1987 against a backdrop of economic depression and what the government claimed were unsustainable losses in the sector. The initial activity nonetheless had left some cause for optimism, as Rockett explains: the 'long, hard fight over many decades by Irish film activists to raise national consciousness in favour of an indigenous Irish cinema only began to achieve significant results in the 1980s'.[12] Notwithstanding the brevity of its first incarnation, the board facilitated the development of an identifiable indigenous cinematic culture, which, in spite of its relatively small number of productions, had a noteworthy impact on transforming the representations of Ireland on screen. Consequently, a small number of innovative film-makers working at a significant time of cultural transition radically challenged earlier mainstream 'received' versions of the filmed nation. They achieved this by borrowing the established narrative, thematic, and aesthetic spaces in which earlier misrepresentations had operated in ideologically limited ways, and they manoeuvred within these against conventionally established modes. The impact of their legacy was felt increasingly in the years following the suspension of the activities of the Film Board in 1987. By the time that the board was revived in 1993, at first under the chairmanship of activist Lelia Doolan, and subsequently with Rod Stoneman (former commissioning editor at Channel 4) as its chief executive, a dedicated body of rising young film students and enthusiasts had been trained and were ready to benefit from the limited funding newly available.

Borrowing Aesthetics: Market Transitions and Playing with Mainstream Genre (1993–2003)

There was a notable qualitative change in the body of films produced after 1993 compared with those of the first-wave school in the 1980s, marking another important phase of transition in Ireland's indigenous screen output. While Rockett accurately summarised the new films' reception and analysis by suggesting that 'many of them lack the critical or cultural engagement so evident in the films of their predecessors [and] lack any persuasive critical, cultural or political engagement with Irish society at all', there was much merit to the films produced with support from the relaunched board.[13] It would be fair to suggest that a motivating element in their demotion of contemporary sociological thematic concerns with locally focused 'critical, cultural or political engagement' was an expressed attempt to move away from the cinematic style and content of their first-wave progenitors.[14] The second-wave films shifted attention to a broader self-reflexive dialogue with cinematic form, and away from more explicit, outward-looking social commentary. Indeed, the context for the impetus behind the films produced during this transitional phase was well set historically, in mainstream qualities, codes, and conventions that the young Irish film-makers borrowed liberally for their own repurposing.

From the earliest years of the studio system following the development of sound cinema in the late 1920s, commercial imperatives and practical considerations ensured the establishment of a relationship between major production companies and given generic practices. It was normal to see the use of available studio resources – in everything from star and director contractual connections to sound stage facilities and artistic expertise – in the consolidation of output by the major companies around patterns of identifiable film genre production. MGM became known for lavish musicals and costume melodramas, Universal was recognised for its darker horrors, and Warner Brothers had an association with gangster films and lighter romances. This aesthetic practice continued with some consistency for decades – at least until the beginning of the decline of the studio system in the 1950s – and affirmed Hollywood as the dominant player in the creation of genre. The semantics and syntactics through which genre films worked became recognisable elements in categories of narrative, character, and aesthetics.[15] They were not merely established *a priori* as qualities which international audiences could identify, but were also important features in the contractual, financially underpinned orders of regulation into which spectators could buy, and through which their understanding of the cinematic text could function. Periodically, minor national cinemas – working through identifiable movements or with one-off productions – borrowed the language of genre and gave it an indigenous inflection with the use of local themes, stories, and characterisations. This was evident in the Irish context when, from the mid-1990s onwards, many second-wave directors explored ways of appropriating, addressing, or subverting the established codes of different genres.

Several of the second-wave Irish film-makers saw genre as a useful arena for the insertion of local sensibilities into existing international patterns and procedures of production. Films like *I Went Down* (Paddy Breathnach, 1997), *When Brendan Met Trudy* (Kieron J. Walsh, 2000), and *Boy Eats Girl* (Stephen Bradley, 2005) appropriated genre syntactics (of the crime, romantic comedy, and horror genres respectively) and played with parody and meta-cinematic conventions. This tendency demonstrated considerable sophistication, giving evidence of the fact that 'the making and use of genres rely on accumulated experience of films constructed within the parameters – the horizon of expectations – of the particular generic worlds in question'.[16] At the same time, it confirmed directors' confidence that audiences would understand their intertextual referencing of, and toying with, conventional cinematic modes and generic tropes. Affirmatively, as John Hill has noted, such tendencies on the contemporary Irish screen were 'rooted in the particularities of a specific culture, which "replies" to the "universalising" discourse of Hollywood's global cinema in the accent of the local and the regional'.[17] As other films such as the romantic comedy *About Adam* (Gerry Stembridge, 2001) and the horror *Dead Bodies* (Robert Quinn, 2003) attest, often the peculiarities of indigenous cultures, histories, localities, societies, and characters can be rendered more distinctively because of their amalgamation with, or insertion into, generic frameworks that are otherwise lacking in national specificity. Terry Byrne concluded a piece on the dialectical relationship between peripheral and mainstream cinemas with some optimism, noting that in the best cultural practice 'the films being made by indigenous Irish directors are part of a dialogue with the world as well as with their own people'.[18] By borrowing the vocabulary of genre films, a whole generation of Irish filmmakers found channels through which they could voice new ideas specifically relating to cinematic history, styles, and stories in ways that also articulated novel experiences of an Irish society in economic transition.

Borrowing Technology: A Nation's Projection through Global Channels (2000 Onwards)

The new millennium witnessed a continuation of the rise in the use and effectiveness of the World Wide Web as a platform for interpersonal and international connections and information exchange. Arguably, this has given renewed impetus to the application of theories of transnationalism to film studies that were first mobilised in the early 1990s. I would argue that there was, and still is, little that is edifying about these approaches, simply because the medium, from its birth over a century earlier, had *always* been an *inherently* transnational one. The epitome of a cultural expression that was eminently exportable, it was constantly global in its co-production practices, and universal in its themes, stories, and personnel. Rather, questions relating specifically to *national* cinemas have been re-invigorated to some extent because of the technological development of the Internet. Both national cinema studies and the international platform have invited renewed interest in the providence and destinations of films that are increasingly distributed and viewed on line. Of this period, Luisa Rivi has noted that it is 'fashionable to discuss Europe in postnational terms, with traditional boundaries being blurred and deemed to become unrecognisable', before convincingly concluding that it was 'precisely the persistence of the nation-state, with its form of political associations and communal belonging that will provide a unique opportunity to shape and sustain such a supranational enterprise'.[19] Stephen Brockmann has also argued that nations remain 'the primary players on the global stage',[20] and he sees no reason for any weakening of their sovereignty. He holds that 'the peoples and nations of the world are interacting with each other now more frequently, and more intensely, than ever before, but there is little evidence that for this reason the concept of the nation has become outdated'.[21]

A more significant development in the rise of the Internet as an information super-highway is that this has coincided with a significant increase in the numbers of film personnel – directors, writers, actors, and producers – involved in television work. Although American production and distribution networks formerly concentrated uniquely on distribution to cinema exhibition chains, they now place the television and multiplatform market firmly in their crosshairs. In fact, there has even been a discernible alteration in how the televisual narrative is defined, experienced, and consumed. This change has effected a cross-pollination as much as it has facilitated an amalgamation of the formal elements of both media. While this may promise a certain democratisation of the cinematic distribution (and, by consequence, of its production), there is little evidence that a minor national cinema will benefit in competitive struggles for a market share in any *significant* way. Nonetheless, individual cases from smaller nations might demonstrate affirmative developments with the concurrent rise in film artists working in television, and the use by distribution companies of internet platforms.

In the Irish context, the writer-director team Eugene O'Brien and Declan Wrecks produced a six-part television series, *Pure Mule*, which was supported by the state broadcaster Raidió Teilifís Éireann, in 2005. They subsequently worked on a filmed adaptation of O'Brien's stage play *Eden* (2008), and the following year they returned to the small screen with two concluding episodes of the earlier series, titled *Pure Mule: The Last Weekend*. Mark O'Halloran and Lenny Abrahamson also successfully worked in both media as a writer-director team. Having achieved considerable critical acclaim for their feature film debut *Adam & Paul* in 2004, they developed a four-part television series based partly on some of the characters, locations, and situations from the film. Under the ironic title, *Prosperity*, the series was set during the months leading up to the global economic recession, and it was produced by Element Pictures and aired by RTÉ in September 2007. Like *Pure Mule*, it displayed the benefits of exporting aesthetic and thematic questions from the large to the small screen. Typically, the faster-paced dialogue, editing, and scene shifting of television was replaced by a more moderate cinematic rhythm; multi-angle shots took the place of fixed, fourth-wall perspectives that were the hallmark of situation comedies and soap operas; and narratives unfolded with longer expositional sequences and less talking-head immediacy. What is notable about these narratives, as they were set during the final years of Ireland's economic boom, was their prescience and sense of fatalism – embedded in characterisation, stories, and aesthetics – of what was to come. *Adam & Paul* and *Prosperity* disregarded their on-screen contemporaries' images of an economically prosperous national and capital city, as well as the aesthetic qualities also identified with that cinema.[22] In this, they focused on characters who had been left behind during the surge in personal and exchequer wealth, spending, and borrowing, and instead presented a darker reality that had been displaced and forgotten by those for whom acquisition had been so normalised. The narrative and tonal qualities with which the O'Halloran and Abrahamson collaborations projected contemporary Dublin would become established and recurring markers in other visual narratives after the implosion of the global economy in 2008. Reckless institutional lending and irresponsible borrowing were at the core of the international economic crash and, while its impact is not easily quantifiable, the years that followed the initial collapse proved to be a period of exceptional difficulty for the film-makers of marginal smaller national industries.[23]

In August of 2008, Element Pictures produced *Little White Lie*, a made-for-television film that was co-written by Barry Murphy and Stuart Carolan. There may have been a degree of social commentary and critique of the posturing of newly well-heeled Irelanders as the tele-film told the tale of a young down-on-his-luck actor who tells a girl that he is a (one assumes more socially appealing) psychiatrist, in order to attract her. Stuart Carolan subsequently created *Love/Hate*, a favourably criticised and popular television drama series aired by the national broadcaster over five seasons, in twenty-eight episodes, from 2010 until 2014. As *Love/Hate* focused on the interpersonal stories of Dublin-based criminals, the series represented the rising affluence and conspicuous consumption of the drug lords in a way that was comparable with their 'legitimate' socially mobile counterparts in the banking and property sectors: Irish classes similarly spoiled and narcissistically hedonistic in their positions of newly acquired wealth. Another noteworthy example of this trans-media migration was the Irish Film Board and Vico Films' 2016 feature-length production, *The Young Offenders*. The success of the film secured a broadcast deal for writer and director Peter Foott for a six-part television series with the same title, based on the adventures of the two comically and criminally inclined protagonists and their community. Once again, the episodic narratives concentrated on the lives of two working-class characters and their comical exploits as the teenage pair sought personal and social acceptance in a newly configured Irish class system.

Amazon and Netflix have also provided platforms for the on-demand streaming of Irish feature productions, and the latter was responsible for acquiring (and therefore 'branding') the feature film *The Siege of Jadotville* from Parallel Films in 2016. The inventive approach to film production and distribution has been spearheaded by the co-founders of Element Pictures: Andrew Lowe and Ed Guiney. Not only has Element had remarkable success with both Irish and not-uniquely Irish projects – Lenny Abrahamson's *Room*, Yorgos Lanthimos' *The Lobster* (both 2015), and *A Date for Mad Mary*, directed by Darren Thornton in 2016, being recent examples – but the company has innovatively spread its creative forces through newly available platforms. Investing in both the hardware and software of exhibition, in 2012 Element acquired and opened a rejuvenated Lighthouse Cinema in Smithfield, Dublin, and also launched the online platform Volta for the on-demand streaming of Irish films. Notwithstanding differences in theme and topic, all of the stories produced by these new companies positioned their characters in situations of personal struggle and isolation, forcing degrees of introspection. Their circumstances required of them a renegotiation of their selfhood in marginal spaces, whether domestic, social or geographical. What is evident is that following more than a decade after the nation's self-congratulation at its economic prosperity, the wealth of the country has not been evenly shared and many in Irish society have been disadvantaged or marginalised as the rising tide left their boats stranded and forgotten.

Borrowing Authority: Gender Roles on the Irish Cinematic Landscape

Ireland's has been a minor cinema from its inception and, by virtue of its economic size, it most probably always will be. The theoretical aspirations behind transnational cinematic analysis might have been driven by a faith in new technological mechanisms to bolster disadvantaged players, but this was nothing new: cinema was always in its essence a modern apparatus of transnational disposition. It has always facilitated a crossing of borders with textual adaptations from other geographical places, fostered the international movement of actors and crews who emigrated and immigrated into different industries (with a universal concentric focus on Hollywood), displayed a universal appeal with mythical and fundamentally human stories and themes, and worked via a portability of product that saw thousands of reels of film exported around the globe on a daily basis. With themes, narratives, personnel, product, and distribution networks, everything about the new modern medium was fundamentally transnational from its inception.

The various 'borrowings' detailed above go some way to explain how a disadvantaged group – here the peripheral national cinema – can appropriate and address the dominant centre and its mechanisms. However, the robes of authority can also be acquired and taken into possession. The film stage in Ireland has been affected by the same gender imbalance as the international industry has been historically. This fact, however, may overshadow the important and sophisticated roles played by Irish women in the country's film story. The first-wave directors Margo Harkin and Pat Murphy, and the 'no wave' film-maker Vivienne Dick, were not only pioneers who carved out a cultural space for female artists working in the medium in Ireland, but from the 1970s – with Lelia Doolan – they were also key activists in the garnering of Irish governmental support for film. In 2000, Lance Pettitt could celebrate the rise in the number of film festivals in the country: 'the fact that the Cork (1956) and Dublin (1985) film festivals have been joined by festival venues in Derry (1987), the Film Fleadh in Galway (1988), Belfast (1990) and Limerick (1995) are signs that there is a healthy growth in film culture'.[24] At present, there are many reasons for optimism as the number of females occupying key positions on the boards of these festivals is significant. Grainne Humphreys is the director of the Dublin Film Festival, the chief executive officer of the Galway Film Fleadh is Miriam Allen, and Fiona Clark is the Festival Producer and chief executive officer of the Cork Film Festival. Funding boards are also populated with talented members, representing a move towards equality of gender: the Arts Council representative for Visual Culture is Fionnuala Sweeney, and the chief executive officer of Screen Producers Ireland is Elaine Geraghty. Kassandra O'Connell is the dynamic head of the Irish Film Archive at the Irish Film Institute, and Sunniva O'Flynn is the head curator at the same institution. As well as a healthy gender balance in its members, the Irish Film Board also currently has Annie Doona as its chair.

It is hoped that the support from these national institutions will continue to spur a rise in the number of female writers and directors working in Ireland. Among others, to date, Carmel Winters (*Snap* [2010], *Floats Like a Butterfly* [2018]), Emer Reynolds (*Here Was Cuba* [2013], *The Farthest* [2017]), Juanita Wilson (*As If I Am Not There* [2010], *Tomato Red* [2017]), Oonagh Kearney (*Wonder House* [2012], *Women's Christmas Night* [2016]), Rebecca Daly (*Mammal* [2016], *Good Favour* [2017]), and Liz Gill (*Gold in the Streets* [1997], *Goldfish Memory* [2003]), have all made important creative, intellectual, and cultural contributions to the Irish film canon. If a worrying deficit remains, it is in the uneven international recognition of our female actors who, for reasons that Ruth Barton and Ciara Barrett have cogently argued, do not seem to achieve the same level of celebrity status as their male counterparts.[25] We can only work towards redressing this market-driven imbalance as our industry platform continues to strengthen. Nonetheless, the overall situation bodes well for the future, and we may be cautiously optimistic about Ireland's cinematic prospects and our continuing – in spite of many historical stops and starts – to punch well above our weight on national and international screens. At periods of transition, there are evidently wonderful opportunities for prudent borrowing of the cinematic apparatus – techniques, technologies, historiographies, narratives, aesthetics, and conventions – and a careful and creative management of all of these elements will re-affirm Ireland's important contribution to the international art form.

As has ever been the case, our national film-makers, stars, and stories must produce work to the most exacting standards in order to capture the attention of large enough audiences to make an international impact. In the face of the powerful Hollywood-based industrial machine this will never be an easy task and, even with enabling ventures like co-productions with film-makers across the EU and from other jurisdictions, or art-house, festival, direct-to-TV, or on-line broadcast mechanisms in place, the battle for a space for cultural expression will be perpetual and will require increasingly inventive responses for the forging of an international space for ourselves.

Notes

1. Kevin Rockett, 'Aspects of the Los Angelisation of Ireland', *Irish Communications Review*, 1 (1991), pp. 18–23 (p. 18).
2. Rockett, 'Aspects of the Los Angelisation of Ireland', p. 19. Also see Kevin Rockett, *Irish Film Censorship: A Cultural Journey from Silent Cinema to Internet Pornography* (Dublin: Four Courts Press, 2004).

3. See Barry Monahan, *Ireland's Theatre on Film: Style, Stories and the National Stage on Screen* (Dublin: Irish Academic Press, 2009); and Kevin Rockett, Luke Gibbons and John Hill, eds., *Cinema and Ireland* (London: Routledge, 1988).
4. Ian Jarvie, 'National Cinema: A Theoretical Assessment', in Mette Hjort and Scott MacKenzie, eds., *Cinema and Nation* (London: Routledge, 2000), pp. 75–87 (p. 82).
5. Declan Kiberd, *Inventing Ireland: The Literature of the Modern Nation* (London: Vintage, 1996), p. 118.
6. For a detailed account, see Monahan, *Ireland's Theatre on Film*.
7. See Rockett, 'Postscript', in *Cinema and Ireland*, pp. 258–74.
8. Martin McLoone, 'National Cinema and Cultural Identity: Ireland and Europe', in John Hill, Martin McLoone, and Paul Hainsworth, eds., *Border Crossing: Film in Ireland, Britain and Europe* (Belfast and London: Institute of Irish Studies, Queens University Belfast and the British Film Institute, 1994), pp. 146–73 (p. 157).
9. Ibid.
10. Rockett, 'Culture, Industry and Irish Cinema', in *Border Crossing*, pp. 126–39 (p. 127).
11. See Hamid Naficy, *An Accented Cinema* (Princeton, NJ: Princeton University Press, 2001); Hill, 'Introduction', in *Border Crossing*, pp. 1–33 (p. 5).
12. Rockett, 'Culture, Industry and Irish Cinema', p. 126.
13. Ibid., p. 127.
14. See Barry Monahan, 'The Pedagogical Culture of Irish Film Production: A Short History', in Isabelle Le Corff and Estelle Epinoux, eds., *Cinemas of Ireland* (Newcastle upon Tyne: Cambridge Scholars Publishing, 2009), pp. 86–100.
15. See Rick Altman, 'A Semantic/Syntactic Approach to Film Genre', in Leo Braudy and Marshall Cohen, eds., *Film Theory and Criticism*, 5th edn (New York and Oxford: Oxford University Press, 1999), pp. 630–41.
16. Christine Gledhill, 'Genre and Nation', in Brian McIlroy, ed., *Genre and Cinema: Ireland and Transnationalism* (New York: Routledge, 2007), pp. 11–25 (p. 21).
17. Hill, 'Introduction', *Border Crossing*, p. 6.
18. Terry Byrne, *Power in the Eye: An Introduction to Contemporary Irish Film* (Lanham, MD and London: Scarecrow Press, 1997), p. 211.
19. Luisa Rivi, *European Cinema after 1989: Cultural Identity and Transnational Production* (Basingstoke: Palgrave Macmillan, 2007), p. 3.
20. Stephen Brockmann, *A Critical History of German Film* (New York: Camden House, 2010), p. 8.
21. Ibid.
22. See Martin McLoone, 'Cinema, City, and Imaginative Space: "Hip Hedonism" and Recent Irish Cinema', in *Genre and Cinema: Ireland and Transnationalism*, pp. 205–16.
23. For detailed commentaries on the sector before, during, and in the years following the crash, see Tony Tracy and Roddy Flynn, 'Irish Cinema – Year

in Review', *Estudios Irlandeses,* 1–12 (2005–16): www.estudiosirlandeses.org/ [accessed 30 March 2019].
24. Lance Pettitt, *Screening Ireland: Film and Television Representation* (Manchester: Manchester University Press, 2000), p. 43.
25. See Ciara Barrett, 'Black and White and Green All Over? Emergent Female Stardom in Contemporary Popular Cinema', in Barry Monahan, ed., *Ireland and Cinema: Culture and Contexts* (Basingstoke: Palgrave Macmillan, 2015), pp. 59–70; and Ruth Barton, *Acting Irish in Hollywood* (Dublin: Irish Academic Press, 2006).

CHAPTER 19

Irish Blockbusters and Literary Stars at the End of the Millennium

Stephen Watt

> It was a bright Saturday morning in Chicago [...]. My wife and I, enjoying a rare weekend together *sans* children, were in search of gifts for them [...]. Our trek ended on an upper level of Water Tower Place at the WTTW Store of Knowledge, a store that markets items associated with series and performances shown on public broadcasting stations (PBS). And there was his image on a large-screen television over our heads and on the pyramids of video cassettes that surrounded us. Just over the craned necks of viewers and almost syncopated to the strained breathing of two elderly women directly below the giant TV, the well-oiled chest of Michael Flatley heaved and rolled. 'He's Irish, you know,' one admirer misstated.[1]

I wrote this reminiscence in the late 1990s, though my identification of this precise moment may seem superfluous. 'Pyramids of video cassettes' scream 'late twentieth century', and the meteoric rise of Michael Flatley and *Riverdance* in the mid-1990s confirms this dating. Not since the 1850s and 1860s when various forms of Irish popular culture accompanied waves of immigrants to New York, Boston, and Philadelphia was America so immersed in all things Irish.[2] Across the street from Water Tower Place on Chicago's Michigan Avenue, a giant Borders Bookstore, now closed, had erected its own pyramids of Thomas Cahill's *How the Irish Saved Civilization* (1994) and Frank McCourt's *Angela's Ashes* (1996). And Borders' music section featured U2's *Achtung Baby* (1991) and *Zooropa* (1993), several albums by the Cranberries, and the soundtrack from *The Commitments*, Alan Parker's 1991 adaptation of Roddy Doyle's novel. On Broadway, the decade was initiated by two extraordinary Irish plays: Brian Friel's *Dancing at Lughnasa* (1990), which moved to New York in 1991 and won a Tony for Best Play, and Frank McGuinness's *Someone Who'll Watch Over Me* (1992), the recipient of numerous awards and nominations. American filmgoers found the

Troubles in Northern Ireland and their possible exportation to the States especially fascinating, and such thrillers as *Patriot Games* (1992), *Blown Away* (1994), and *The Devil's Own* (1997) catered to this interest. However undistinguished, *Patriot Games* garnered a box office of over $83 million domestically and $173 million worldwide.[3] Like *Riverdance* and *Angela's Ashes*, this adaptation of Tom Clancy's novel pitting Harrison Ford against Northern paramilitaries might qualify as a *blockbuster*. But, given their significant American influences and inflections, are *any* of these cultural sensations Irish blockbusters?

While commercial success constitutes the primary denotation of 'blockbuster', few definitions, no matter how expansive, can explain a performer's or text's intense popularity at a particular historical moment. The phenomenon of *Riverdance*, for instance, is attributable to a number of factors, not the least of which is Michael Flatley's (and his co-star Jean Butler's) appeal as a *star*, itself a slippery term as the culture of celebrity has been reified within the academy as a rich and variegated object of study. Emily Hodgson Anderson and Sharon Marcus note, respectively, that star-actors like Donegal-born Charles Macklin on London's eighteenth-century stage and Sarah Bernhardt at the *fin de siècle* helped refine distinctions between mere 'celebrity' and deserved 'fame' or stardom. And stars often do far more significant cultural work than forming the locus of mass adulation. In 1741, Macklin elevated Shakespeare's Shylock from an ethnic laughing stock to a figure of tragic dimension, in the process making himself and the restored text of *The Merchant of Venice* a 'hit'.[4] From before her first American tour in 1880 until her last in 1913–14, Bernhardt epitomised the myriad, even contradictory, qualities of the theatrical star: 'exemplary' in some roles in her embodiment of 'normative values' but, like Oscar Wilde, 'impudent' in others, at times even 'shameless'.[5] Stars, like blockbusters, can be complicated things. Yet, whether endorsing or subverting dominant ideologies, a star's 'doings and way of life arouse a considerable and sometimes even a maximum degree of interest'.[6] However 'elite' or 'privileged' such luminous figures might become, they typically do not 'excite envy or resentment', in part because – as Joseph Roach underscores in defining the 'It' factor – they 'succeed by the copresence' of such 'mutually exclusive attributes' as 'strength and vulnerability, innocence and experience, singularity and typicality'.[7] When one of these pairs of attributes begins to lapse, a star's fans at times resuscitate or even invent it.[8] Moreover, almost anyone can become a star – even the son of Irish immigrants like Flatley, born and raised on the South Side of Chicago.

Many 'blockbusters' possess a similar hybridity, popular not merely as a vehicle for a star-actor, dancer, or writer but, in some instances, notorious for their disruption of orthodoxy: the hybridity of *Riverdance* appeared not only in its two Irish-American leads, but also its modified step dancing. In 'Blockbusters and Banned Books', Louis Menand recalls the histories of writers like Henry Miller, D. H. Lawrence, and James Joyce, the publishers who supported them, and their novels' explicit – and, in their day, legally actionable – representations of the body and human sexuality. Barney Rosset and Grove Press's battle to publish Lawrence's *Lady Chatterley's Lover* in America, for example, culminated both in a 1959 legal decision and a perch for Lawrence on *The New York Times*' bestseller list some thirty years after its original 1928 publication; by the end of the decade, five paperback editions were on the market with some six million copies sold.[9] The case at the end of the twentieth century with Frank McCourt's *Angela's Ashes*, albeit in no way so legally momentous as those surrounding *Lady Chatterley* or *Ulysses*, was nonetheless controversial. By 2000, the memoir had sold some four million copies, appeared on *The New York Times*' bestseller list for over two years, been translated into twenty languages, and adapted for both the stage and screen. But not without ructions. McCourt's mother denounced a performance of the theatrical version of her son's memoir as a 'pack of lies', and in 2000 filmgoers in Limerick, where much of the narrative is set, objected to his representation of life in the city in which he grew up: 'Worse than the ordinary miserable childhood is the miserable Irish childhood, and worse yet is the miserable Irish Catholic childhood.'[10] And the misery the young McCourt endured, to the dismay of its citizens, firmly attached itself to Limerick.

McCourt was awarded the Pulitzer Prize for the book, confirming that at times blockbusters not only earn their creators vast sums of money, lead to fame, and provoke either controversy or titillation, but also obtain the markers of substantial literary or artistic merit. In addition to the recognition lavished on McCourt and *Angela's Ashes*, two of the decade's most critically acclaimed films were made by Irish directors: Neil Jordan's *The Crying Game* (1992) and Jim Sheridan's *In the Name of the Father* (1993), both of which enjoyed considerable, albeit not blockbuster-like, success at the box office. Made for slightly over £2 million, *The Crying Game* earned over $62 million in America and received numerous awards and nominations: a BAFTA award as best British film, Jordan's receipt of an Academy Award for Best Original Screenplay, and Oscar nominations for actors Stephen Rea and Jaye Davidson. *In the Name of the Father* enjoyed similar success both at the box office, earning over $65 million worldwide, and with critics, as its lead actors (Daniel Day-Lewis, Emma Thompson, and Pete Postlethwaite) were each nominated for Academy Awards and won several international awards as well.[11] Equally important, *The Crying Game* in particular has proved to be a fecund text for scholars working on such issues as gender and sexuality, ethnicity and postcolonialism, and their implication in the physical force tradition of militant Irish nationalism.[12]

In the last decade of the twentieth century, however, no Irish writer, performer, or text won greater critical recognition – or was a bigger star – than Seamus Heaney. For, some eight months after the opening of *Riverdance* at Dublin's Point Theatre in February 1995, the Nobel Prize Committee announced Heaney's selection as the laureate in literature, recognising in its October 5 announcement the 'lyrical beauty and ethical depth' of his writing, which 'exalt[s] everyday miracles and the living past'.[13] This international recognition elevated Heaney, already widely celebrated by both academic and more popular critics, to the level of literary star. Or, stated in another, much hipper way, he became what Paul Muldoon, comparing him to an earlier laureate, William Butler Yeats, proclaimed him to be when learning of his death in August 2013 – a rock star:

> Yeats [...] actually didn't have anything like the celebrity or, frankly, the ability to touch the people in the way that Seamus did [...]. It was almost like he was indistinguishable from the country. He was like a rock star who also happened to be a poet.[14]

Muldoon's observation is useful in several ways, not the least of which is that his juxtaposition of literary 'celebrity' with rock stardom creates an opportunity both to theorise the differences that obtain between this unlikely pairing and, perhaps surprisingly, to unpack their similarities. Rock stars benefit from a strategic promotional *production* – publicity campaigns, international tours, photo shoots, and all the stratagems professional management can contrive – while, other than readings or lectures to select audiences, interviews, and book signings to promote their work, literary (and academic) stars rely heavily on a considered and thoughtful *reception*. Here, more than fandom or teenybopper hysteria is involved. In this regard literary stardom resembles academic stardom, itself the object of concerted attention in the 1990s as scholars interrogated the fame of cultural theorists and eminent literary critics whose influence transformed the academy, largely by revising disciplines. But are the differences between icons from mass culture and those from the academy really so vast? David Shumway, for example, who would almost certainly disagree with any insinuation that literary stardom is *completely* dependent upon thoughtful consumption, compares the staid, 'undifferentiated' photographic images of such literary critical lions as F. O. Matthiessen and George Lyman Kittredge from the first half of the century with a more candid photograph of a dishevelled Harold Bloom and a 'glamour shot' of Jacques Derrida complete with 'chiaroscuro lighting', dramatic gesture, and careful scenic composition in order to confirm the incursion of movie star promotional techniques into academic iconography.[15] The images of the earlier scholars map neatly onto their 'limited fame' – indeed, their conventional 'head shots' with glimpses of dark suits, white shirts, and nondescript ties convey enervation, not excitement – while the photograph of Derrida rivals the same evocative images of James Joyce and especially Samuel Beckett, or rather his face, as realised by some of the twentieth century's most talented artists and photographers, including Gisèle Freund and John Haynes.[16] In addition, in a way that few academics enjoyed in mid-century, in the 1980s and 1990s articles on the so-called 'Yale Critics' – Bloom, Derrida, J. Hillis Miller, Geoffrey Hartman, and Paul de Man – circulated in *The New York Times Magazine* and elsewhere, as the academic humanities began to be recognised by the popular press and, in some cases, pilloried in such screeds as Roger Kimball's *Tenured Radicals: How Politics Has Corrupted Our Higher Education* (1990) and Dinesh D'Souza's *Illiberal Education: The Politics of Race and Sex on Campus* (1991). Academic and literary stars *are* stars, in part, because they penetrate the popular imaginary and, like Sarah Bernhardt playing a 'Fallen Woman', their stardom may be tinctured with notorious or subversive shades.

Literary stars – no matter how impressive their Ivy League salaries or honoraria to present lectures or readings off campus – shine in a vastly different economic galaxy than their counterparts in the world of popular music. Save for the most prolific and, for the most part, banal of authors of pulp fiction today, of page-turning romances or crime fiction, literary stardom, at least in terms of commercial gain, often affords writers a comfortable existence somewhere in between a multimillion-dollar mansion and a threadbare attic garret (although the extreme poverty and resultant difficulties of both rock and literary stars discovered far too late are well known). As Declan Kiberd notes in *The Irish Writer and the World* (2005), unlike European modernists the best-known writers associated with the Irish Revival 'did not proclaim the need for eternal antagonism between bohemian and bourgeois'.[17] He identifies Shaw in particular, who 'wrote mainly for money and earned lots', as providing the most compelling evidence for his thesis.[18] But, as Shaw impishly recalls in his autobiographical volume *Sixteen Self Sketches* (1949), 'nobody taught me to write my plays, which were denounced as no plays until they made so much money that the fashion changed, and I was hailed successor to Shakespear[e]'.[19] Sometimes, in other words, an exceptionally talented, critically applauded writer does not earn a lot of money; and, at other times, a writer who earns a lot of money, simply by virtue of this commercial success, is eventually recognised by critics as being another Shakespeare. Such writers, as Shaw implies and not unlike the Yale Critics or emergent rock musicians, change 'the fashion', the academic discipline, or the course of an art form: Beckett as Jimi Hendrix in the later 1960s revolutionising the playing of electric guitars, Shaw as Adele in our own century writing ballads with a new and energising force.

All of these and more implications reside in the terms 'blockbuster' and 'literary star', as the ascendance of both *Riverdance* and Seamus Heaney in the 1990s demonstrates.

The Attractions of a Blockbuster: *Riverdance*

Choreographed by Irish-American performers Jean Butler and Michael Flatley with music by Bill Whelan, it began on 30 April 1994, as a nearly seven-minute entertainment during an interval in the Eurovision song contest, a popular television programme produced that year in Dublin and seen by some 300 million viewers across Europe. By 1995 *Riverdance* had expanded into a ninety-minute show that introduced a new, more exciting form of Irish step dancing – which in its premiere featured, ever so briefly, Flatley's tapping, Hibernian-inflected 'moonwalk' modelled on Michael Jackson's famous dance move – as well as elements of flamenco and Russian folk dance. By 1996, as Natasha Casey describes, *Riverdance* had grown into a 'music and dance "extravaganza", proving enormously successful first in Ireland, where it played to sold-out crowds, then in London and around the world'.[20] Part of that world is, of course, America, where it opened in March at Radio City Music Hall, returning there in 1997 and 1998, and was also performed at the Kennedy Center and at arenas across the country. It was revived as *Riverdance – On Broadway* on 16 March 2000 at Broadway's Gershwin Theatre, where it ran for 17 months, closing in August 2001, and troupes have toured the show every year since its premiere. Long before the new millennium, however, Flatley had left, as Butler would by January of 1997. In 1996, he developed what would become a competing show entitled *Lord of the Dance* (later, *Michael Flatley's Lord of the Dance*), which on 27 June 1996, like its predecessor, opened at Dublin's Point Theatre. It similarly enjoyed enormous success, particularly in America, as a headline for a profile of Flatley in *The New York Times* in the spring of 1997 suggests: 'The Man behind the Duel between Irish Blockbusters'. By this time, some 2.5 million people around the world had bought tickets for *Riverdance* and over 600,000 had seen *Lord of the Dance*,[21] which Flatley took to the New York-New York casino on the Las Vegas Strip in July 1998. Four years later, by the time of its closing at New York-New York, the show had been performed some 1,560 times and attracted an audience of nearly 1.25 million people.[22] Flatley re-opened the show at the Venetian Hotel later that year and, in one of its several iterations over the years, gave a twentieth-anniversary performance at the Colosseum at Caesar's Palace on 17 March 2016. He also appeared at President Donald Trump's inauguration in January 2017.

The first performance of *Riverdance* in 1994 elicited an eruption of applause and a standing ovation that presaged the longevity the show would enjoy. As a brief entertainment to fill the short time of an interval, it was introduced as a 'full-bodied orchestral dance piece', yet it began slowly not with dance or movement, but rather with Katie McMahon's haunting soprano voice and those of the Celtic choral group, Anúna. Together, on a dark stage with shimmers of light and blue, they sang a melody of love and devotion, accented by a shot of water lightly rippling. A river of desire and emotion, in other words, flowed gently but without dancing or even much movement. To the soprano's opening lyric – 'Hear my cry | In my hungering search for you' – a chorus responded with its oath of love: 'I am living to nourish you, cherish you, | I am pulsing the blood in your veins.'[23] The mood is quiet and sensual, as the waters of a river course through the countryside bringing life and a commitment of devotion to it.

After another verse, the focus shifts quickly to a large green cloak under which Jean Butler, tall and elegant in a short black dress and silk stockings with her dark red hair flowing, appears, and the dance begins. Against a dark setting of black and blue, Butler dances alone to a spirited beat, leaping and stepping in expert time. Then, four drummers at stage left appear, pounding a new, lively rhythm and, opposite them in a bright green silk shirt and black trousers, Michael Flatley leaps into view, tapping to their beat. A path of light turns red on the floor and panels of an orange-red illuminate the background; a sun has arisen to meet the earth and water, providing heat and energy. For a brief period, Flatley engages in a rhythmic skirmish with the drummers, his tapping matching their increasingly elaborate syncopation. Then, he finds Butler on stage, and the pair dance together in a dazzling duet before being joined by six and, later, some two dozen other step dancers, all moving in unison to a lively flourish of music and a spectacular finish.

From this auspicious beginning, it was clear that both *Riverdance* and Flatley were destined for fame, his stardom hinted at both by his costuming – he was the only dancer on stage not attired in all black – and the bold lighting changes that underscored the energy he brought to the performance. His bright green shirt, matching the colour of the cloak from which his partner had emerged earlier, separated him from his cohort of step dancers, distinguishing him as a kind of icon of a bold, energetic Ireland and a star in the making. This shirt, modestly buttoned, would give way in *Lord of the Dance* to a white silk chemise that could be totally *unbuttoned* (and replicated in televised performances on PBS, as shoppers at Chicago's Store of Knowledge can attest). Then, both to advertise *Michael Flatley's Lord of the Dance* and to serve as the cover for an album featuring Ronan Hardiman's score for it (1996), a shirtless and toned Flatley appeared, legs spread in a kind of crouch with right bicep flexed and left arm extended straight upward as if saluting the heavens. By the fall of 2015 and the premiere of *Lord of the Dance: Dangerous Games*, however, a noticeable heavier, fifty-seven-year-old Flatley appeared fully clothed, wearing a long coat and appearing onstage only in the finale. Ticket buyers were informed that this eight-week limited run would be his last, as retirement loomed in the horizon, and thus his appearance in only one scene was hardly surprising.[24]

But twenty years earlier he was the focus of audiences' attention. And, as Natasha Casey outlines, Flatley and *Riverdance* offered audiences a sumptuous array of attractions. For one, Flatley and Butler's performance 'broke the traditional rules of Irish dancing' by combining the pair's 'modern ("sexy") approach with the rather worn, more traditional (never "sexy") dance form'.[25] The result, in the terms Joseph Roach cultivates in describing the 'It' factor, is the pair's 'effortless look of public intimacy'; their touches are never vulgar, but alluring in their disruption of the well-known, overtly stiff conventions of step dancing. Moreover, echoing Marvin Carlson's conception of the 'haunted' stage, their movements cause audiences familiar with such conventions to renegotiate their memories of prior dance performances, the result of which is an acute awareness that something new and exciting is happening.[26] Yet another attraction for those aware that Flatley and Butler were born in America concerns what Casey terms the former's portrayal of himself as 'the embodiment of the American Dream', a self-fashioning sustained by his recounting in interviews his struggles in a working-class neighbourhood of Chicago.[27] For middle-class spectators, then, Flatley's rise to prominence parallels the promise of upward mobility that defines the American dream. Such a promise prominently includes the equal rights of Black Americans, as in a later segment of *Riverdance* a Black gospel choir enters singing, 'when will our freedom come?'. The connection between the civil rights movement in 1960s America and the civil rights demonstrations of Catholics in Northern Ireland during the Troubles is well known, and popular blues-inflected music and films like *The Commitments* re-iterate this relationship. So does *Riverdance*.

For Casey, though, as significant as these attractions are, *Riverdance* most importantly provides viewers with fresh Irish-American identities. No leprechauns, no gun-toting terrorists in balaclavas, no reprise of John Wayne taming a 'wild Irish girl' like Maureen O'Hara in John Ford's *The Quiet Man* (1952), no amusing and inebriated Stage Irishman full of blarney and blather transplanted to a Boston pub – the Irishness and Irish-Americanness of *Riverdance* are vibrant and exciting. This vitality is clearly connected, as Casey notes, to a folk tradition,[28] and perhaps one not so terribly distant from the peasant tradition J. M. Synge, Lady Gregory, and others inaugurated in the Irish Literary Theatre at the beginning of the century. If this is true, then it also suggests that some blockbusters possess a signification that extends beyond the individual, one that speaks of a community – or nation – and to the very land the nation occupies. Such is also the case with Ireland's last Nobel laureate, Seamus Heaney.

Seamus Heaney – Rock Star?

> Fans make an affective investment in the objects of their taste and they construct, from those tastes, a consistent but necessarily temporary identity. [...] The fan's culture is the site of everyday enjoyment and pleasure, but also of an affective empowerment that provides strategies for survival and for a limited control over one's identity.
> – Lawrence Grossberg

'Stars' who otherwise have little in common – professional athletes, prominent actors, pop singers – share at least one commonality: fans. Unpacking the politics and postmodernity of mass culture, particularly rock music, Lawrence Grossberg unintentionally identifies elements relevant to an assessment of Seamus Heaney's stardom by citing the role that affect (or the 'affective'), identity, and the 'everyday' play in his celebrity.[29] Like Casey's privileging of Irishness and Irish-American identity in

Riverdance, fans of rock musicians and singers forge an identity, however temporary, inflected by their affective investments. In some instances, these transactions alter everyday reality as, say, in the case of later twentieth-century subcultures – hippies, punk rockers, Goths, and others – in which a fan's hair, dress, and even language, their *style*, are re-iterated daily.[30] Grossberg goes on to compare fans to both ideologues and fanatics, the former of whom have at least one thing in common with literary critics: 'Ideologues [. . .] make an affective investment based upon an exterior judgement of the quality of the specific text.'[31] To be sure, some literary and cultural critics might scrutinise artefacts for which they have little regard, but this is surely the exception, not the rule. More typically, critics engage texts they find rich, substantial, and important; and Seamus Heaney's work qualifies on all these counts. Moreover, uncanny parallels exist between critical discourse on fandom and the commendations cited above of Heaney's achievement. The Nobel Prize announcement lauded the presence of 'everyday miracles' in his poetry, and comparing Heaney and Yeats, Paul Muldoon lauded his ability to 'touch the people', almost as if he were 'indistinguishable from the country'.[32] Not surprisingly, this encomium echoes influential readings of Heaney's work, and may explain – at least in part – his status as a star.

Chief among these readers is the American literary critic Helen Vendler, whom Heaney once described as not only a 'dear' friend to him and his wife Marie, but also a 'mighty fortress' and advocate, someone with whom he enjoyed a relationship akin to those he had with fellow poets.[33] Heaney was also grateful for Vendler's advocacy of his work, a position that for some exceeded the boundaries of objective criticism and moved her project into the different domains of promoter – or even fan.[34] As her engagement with Heaney's poetry evolved, the tone of her work suggests this difference. In *The Music of What Happens: Poems, Poets, Critics* (1988), for example, Vendler positions Heaney in several different contexts, one of which is within the pantheon of great poets, modern and otherwise. That is to say, her chapter on Heaney precedes meditations on such twentieth-century writers as Stephen Spender, Donald Davie, Allen Ginsberg, and Sylvia Plath; and her exposition of Heaney's work begins with the much larger claim that he is 'as much the legitimate heir of Keats or Frost as of Kavanagh or Yeats, and the history of his consciousness is as germane to our lives as that of any other poet'.[35] In fact, such names as Walt Whitman, William Wordsworth, and Keats recur in the chapter, so that even though her attention to *Wintering Out* (1972) and *North* (1975) re-inscribes the Irish and specifically Ulster influences on Heaney's writing, the 'black river of himself', to borrow a metaphor from the 'The Grauballe Man', leads to the very delta of the Western tradition.[36]

Her emphasis ten years later in *Seamus Heaney* (1998) is somewhat different, as its opening paragraph begins with two historical facts: Heaney's receipt of the Nobel Prize and the impact of the Troubles in Northern Ireland on his writing, extraordinary conditions that 'forced' him into 'becoming a poet of public as well as private life'.[37] As an interpretive key, the latter point is the more important; indeed, Farrar, Straus and Giroux routinely evokes the former in the promotional notation 'Winner of the Nobel Prize in Literature' on the covers of such volumes as *Opened Ground: Selected Poems 1966–1996* (1998), *District and Circle* (2006), and the re-issued *Selected Poems 1966–1987* (2014). In *Seamus Heaney*, Vendler refines her claim about the Troubles and his public writing – and what she terms his capacious 'anonymity' – in chapters entitled 'Archaeologies: *North*' and 'Anthropologies: *Field Work*', alluding to two volumes published during some of the worst of the violence. The former topic, Heaney's archaeological excavation of the land itself, is foreshadowed by such early poems as 'Digging' from *Death of a Naturalist* (1966), and finds a magnificent reprise in 'The Grauballe Man', which delineates the features of a 1,500-year-old relic exhumed in Jutland. But the archaeologist, the principled digger, is also a social anthropologist – or ethnographer – reporting on the social turbulence of the 1970s. A bruising and disturbing poem, 'Punishment' from *North* documents a scapegoat ritual in which a 'tribal, intimate revenge' of head-shaving, tarring, and feathering (and worse) is exacted against 'betraying sisters', young women believed to be adulteresses or consorts of men on the other side of the impasse.[38] In 'Casualty' from *Field Work*, Heaney summarises the events of 'Bloody Sunday' in Derry in 1972 as he also recalls a fisherman he knew who was killed in the bombing of the pub in which they used to drink and talk. The man, '[a] dole-kept breadwinner | But a natural for work', was 'blown to bits | Out drinking in a curfew | Others obeyed'.[39] Here, he describes everyday conversation and fraternity in a public house, then reaches out to the community and the land itself in trying to 'puzzle' the riddle of senseless atrocity; at times, as Muldoon noted, he is 'indistinguishable' from the country itself, reeling from sorrow and shock.

In the introduction to *Seamus Heaney*, Vendler's tone subtly slips from the evaluative register of a literary historian (as in *The Music of What Happens*) to the more personal valence of an admirer. She recounts first hearing Heaney read his poetry in 1975 at the Yeats Summer School in Sligo and then reviewing *North* some months later; and she candidly admits she has 'been writing about him ever since'. How different is her 'startled and wholehearted response' to his work from the 'affective investment' a fan makes in a singer?[40] How different is what she describes as the 'power' of Heaney's 'extraordinary poetry' from that of music?[41] Does writing about an author 'ever since' hearing him almost twenty-five years earlier resemble the inflection of everyday life that Lawrence Grossberg theorises?

And then there is the almost impossible project of separating the man from his work – and the man from his community and country. As the poet's long-time friend Shaun O'Connell recalls in discussing 'Casualty' with him, Heaney emphasised the 'tense balance' that exists between 'we' and 'I', between 'tribal loyalty and individual expression'.[42] Recalling Joseph Roach's exfoliation of the contradictions that inhere in the 'It factor', O'Connell also underscores similar balances in Heaney himself: his friend Seamus was 'ever thoughtful and self-ironic' and 'never assumed the manner of great man';[43] he was 'assured yet humble, gracious but unwilling to be defined by the myths of "Famous Seamus" that others might impose upon him';[44] and '[p]layfulness and graciousness were Heaney's alternating currents'.[45] The result of such delicate, finely calibrated tensions and oppositions was as certain as it was transformative: Heaney's friendship and art 'changed' O'Connell's 'life'.[46] In this way, a literary star offers fans more than a 'temporary' identity, but something more enduring.

Unlike Helen Vendler or Shaun O'Connell, who each knew Seamus Heaney well, other than attending several of his public readings I had the good fortune of his company only twice. The first occasion was at the Synge Summer School in July 2006, shortly before he suffered a stroke, which convened that summer at Avondale House in Wicklow. I had given a morning lecture at the small auditorium that was once a peasant chapel on the estate and, sitting in the audience before the next event was to commence, I felt a tap on my shoulder. It was Heaney, asking if the seat next to me was taken. It wasn't, and we began a lively and all-too-short conversation about Synge and the nineteenth-century theatre he had inherited, parts of which were briefly reprised after his reading two nights later. He was, as O'Connell explains, gracious and in this instance even apologetic for not hearing my lecture. And, in April of 2010, he came to Indiana University to read and we had lunch together. When the conversation drifted towards his friend Brian Friel, I inquired about his health (Friel had suffered a stroke as well). Heaney, with a mischievous grin on his face, had just seen Friel, who reportedly quipped, 'different strokes for different folks'. When the laughter subsided, my mind immediately seized upon this refrain in the 1968 song 'Everyday People' by Sly and the Family Stone, an embarrassing connection I kept to myself. But perhaps there was no reason for my momentary discomfiture; after all, literary stars like Seamus Heaney are much like rock stars, and rock stars know popular music.

Notes

1. Stephen Watt, 'The Irish Invade America! Terrorism, Gender, and Assimilation', *New Hibernia Review/Iris Éireannach Nua*, 2.2 (1998), pp. 9–27 (p. 9).
2. In *Ireland and Irish America: Culture, Class and Transatlantic Migration* (Notre Dame, IN: Field Day Press, 2008), Kerby Miller speculates that some 1.9 million Irish immigrated to North America between 1845 and 1855 (p. 10). In *Ethnic Americans: A History of Immigration*, 5th edn (New York: Columbia University Press, 2009), Leonard Dinnerstein and David M. Reimers estimate that 2.2 million Irish entered the United States between 1840 and 1870 (p. 24).
3. Released in 1997, and starring Harrison Ford and Brad Pitt, *The Devil's Own* grossed almost $141 million worldwide; by contrast, *Blown Away*, after an impressive opening weekend, faded in popularity.
4. Emily Hodgson Anderson, 'Celebrity Shylock', *PMLA*, 126.4 (2011), pp. 935–49 (p. 941).
5. Sharon Marcus, 'Salomé!! Sarah Bernhardt, Oscar Wilde, and the Drama of Celebrity', *PMLA* 126.4 (2011), pp. 999–1021 (pp. 1010–11).
6. Richard Dyer, *Stars*, new edn (London: BFI Publishing, 1998), p. 7.
7. Joseph Roach, 'The Doubting Thomas Effect', *PMLA*, 126.4 (2011), pp. 1127–30 (p. 1128).
8. See, for example, my *'Something Dreadful and Grand': American Literature and the Irish-Jewish Unconscious* (Oxford: Oxford University Press, 2015). When a star actor like Henry Irving or Martin Harvey visited Dublin, fans would gather around his hotel hoping to meet him. Doing their part to accentuate the heroic and melancholy characters these actors often portrayed, newspapers reported (falsely) that Harvey was dying of consumption – or alcoholism – and that Irving's wife was secretly confined to a mental institution (pp. 108–9).
9. See Louis Menand, 'Banned Books and Blockbusters', *The New Yorker*, 12 December 2016, pp. 78–85.
10. Frank McCourt, *Angela's Ashes* (New York: Scribner, 1996), p. 11. See also Tara Mack, 'Anger Rises from *Angela's Ashes*', *Washington Post*, 20 January 2000, p. C1. The film version was released in 1999: www.washingtonpost.com/wp-srv/WPcap/2000-01/20/061r-012000-idx.html [accessed 26 August 2019].
11. Sheridan also received major awards for *My Left Foot* (1989) and *The Field* (1990).

12. See, for example, Kathleen Lyons, 'Transcultural Cinema: Reading Race and Ethnicity in Neil Jordan's *The Crying Game*', *South Atlantic Review*, 67.1 (2002), pp. 91–103; and Aisling B. Cormack, 'The Troubled Intersection of Political Violence and Gender in Neil Jordan's *The Crying Game* and *Breakfast on Pluto*', *Éire-Ireland*, 49.1–2 (2014), pp. 164–92.
13. See 'The Nobel Prize in Literature 1995': www.nobelprize.org/prizes/literature/1995/press-release/ [accessed 17 February 2019].
14. Paul Muldoon, as quoted in Margalit Fox, 'Seamus Heaney, Irish Poet of Soil and Strife, Dies at 74', *The New York Times*, 30 August 2013: www.nytimes.com/2013/08/31/arts/seamus-heaney-acclaimed-irish-poet-dies-at-74.html [accessed 17 February 2019].
15. David R. Shumway, 'The Star System in Literary Studies', *PMLA*, 112.1 (1997), pp. 85–100 (p. 90). For a further discussion of academic stardom, see the issue on 'academostars', *the minnesota review*, n.s. 52–4 (2000).
16. A stunning picture of Beckett, in shadows, smoking and looking downward appears in Gisèle Freund, *Gisèle Freund—Photographs* (1985). James Knowlson and photographer John Haynes published *Images of Beckett* in 2003, and the catalogue of Irish photographer John Minihan's 2006 exhibition *Beckett*, shown in London, New York, and several venues in Ireland, was published in 2007.
17. Declan Kiberd, *The Irish Writer and the World* (Cambridge: Cambridge University Press, 2005), p. 273.
18. Ibid.
19. Bernard Shaw, *Sixteen Self Sketches* (London: Constable, 1949), p. 70.
20. See Natasha Casey, '*Riverdance*: The Importance of Being Irish', *New Hibernia Review/Iris Éireannach Nua*, 6.4 (2002), pp. 9–25 (p. 10).
21. Valerie Gladstone, 'The Man Behind the Duel between Irish Blockbusters', *The New York Times*, 2 March 1997, p. B8: www.nytimes.com/1997/03/02/theater/the-man-behind-the-duel-between-irish-blockbusters.html [accessed 26 August 2019].
22. Casino Press Releases, 'Final Week for "Michael Flatley's Lord of the Dance" – Ends Successful Four Year Run at New York-New York July 28', July 2002: https://lvpress.lvol.com/casino-press-releases/42-new-york-new-york-hotel-and-casino-press-releases/355-final-week-for-michael-flatleys-lord-of-the-dance-ends-successful-four-year-run-at-new-york-new-york-july-28 [accessed 17 February 2019].
23. Bill Whelan, *Riverdance: Music from the Show* (Dublin: Celtic Heartbeat, 1995).
24. Brian Seibert, 'Review: Michael Flatley's New Show Has Unicorns, Rainbows, and Some Footwork, Too', *The New York Times*, 11 November 2015: www.nytimes.com/2015/11/12/arts/dance/michael-flatley-lord-of-the-dance-dangerous-games-review.html [accessed 17 February 2019].
25. Casey, '*Riverdance*: The Importance of Being Irish', p. 10.
26. Joseph Roach, *It* (Ann Arbor, MI: University of Michigan Press, 2007), pp. 3, 6. See also Marvin Carlson, *The Haunted Stage: The Theatre as Memory-Machine* (Ann Arbor, MI: University of Michigan Press, 2001).

27. Casey, '*Riverdance*: The Importance of Being Irish', pp. 10, 13.
28. Ibid., pp. 18–20.
29. Lawrence Grossberg, *Dancing in Spite of Myself: Essays on Popular Culture* (Durham, NC: Duke University Press, 1997), pp. 247–8.
30. See Dick Hebdige, *Subculture: The Meaning of Style* (London: Routledge, 1987 [1979]).
31. Grossberg, *Dancing in Spite of Myself*, p. 248.
32. See 'The Nobel Prize in Literature 1995'.
33. See Dennis O'Driscoll, *Stepping Stones: Interviews with Seamus Heaney* (New York: Farrar, Straus and Giroux, 2008), pp. 347–8.
34. In *Stepping Stones*, Heaney concedes that he is 'hugely in [Vendler's] debt because of her advocacy' (p. 347).
35. Helen Vendler, *The Music of What Happens: Poems, Poets, Critics* (Cambridge: Harvard University Press, 1988), p. 149.
36. Seamus Heaney, *North* (London: Faber and Faber, 1975), p. 28.
37. Helen Vendler, *Seamus Heaney* (Cambridge, MA: Harvard University Press, 1998), p. 1.
38. Heaney, *North*, p. 38.
39. Seamus Heaney, *Field Work* (London: Faber and Faber, 1979), pp. 21–2.
40. Vendler, *Seamus Heaney*, p. 3.
41. Ibid., p. 4.
42. Shaun O'Connell, 'Neither Here nor There: Remembering Seamus', *The Massachusetts Review*, 57.1 (2016), pp. 178–92 (p. 186).
43. Ibid., p. 182.
44. Ibid., p. 179.
45. Ibid., p. 188.
46. Ibid., p. 178.

CHAPTER 20

Contemporary Literature and Public Value

Margaret Kelleher

Working Artists

On 22 April 2017, the Saturday edition of the *Irish Independent* ran the following headline: 'Tóibín likens Arts Council to North Korea in row over Aosdána funding.'[1] The article detailed two documents central to this 'row': first, a recent review by the Arts Council of Ireland/An Chomhairle Ealaíon of the operations of its subsidiary organisation Aosdána, an association of artists; and second, a letter by Colm Tóibín, former council member, strongly opposing the review's proposed changes. Aosdána was founded in 1981 by the Arts Council with the stated purpose 'to honour artists whose work has made an outstanding contribution to the creative arts in Ireland, and to encourage and assist members in devoting their energies fully to their art'.[2] Membership, which is for life, is limited to 250 artists and is the result of nomination and election by those already within the association. In one of former Taoiseach Charles Haughey's more lauded legacies, a 'cnuas' or tax-free bursary is awarded to Aosdána members. Following a series of amendments, the annuity now stands at €17,180, paid for life but reviewed every five years, and paid only to those members whose annual earnings do not exceed one and half times the value of the cnuas. In 2017, some 145 of Aosdána's 250-person membership were eligible for the award.[3]

The Arts Council's review, as reported by the *Irish Independent* and also by the same day's *Irish Times*, proposed that it should have more direct involvement in Aosdána's operation and elections and also recommended a more stringent review of the allocation of the cnuas. A subtle, but telling, proposed change in the wording for cnuas eligibility signalled an emphasis on greater, or at least more visible, artistic productivity: from 'full-time practising artist' to 'working artists engaged in productive practice'. Tóibín's letter, not published in full but alluded to in some detail by both newspapers, took particular issue with this recommendation, as sounding 'oddly North Korean', and 'like a phrase that could have been used by Stalin about recalcitrant farmers in the Soviet Union'.[4] He excoriated the Council for considering measures whereby the cnuas would be suspended for artists temporarily incapacitated due to ill health or for those deemed 'unproductive'. And, to support his objections, he proffered a number of compelling instances from Irish literary history: W. B. Yeats, author in his last days of 'Cuchulain Comforted'; James Joyce, who could be viewed as having 'produced' nothing (other than working drafts) between 1922 and 1939; or John McGahern, who did not publish a novel between 1979 (*The Pornographer*) and 1990 (*Amongst Women*).[5]

Arguments regarding the funding of Aosdána, and of the Arts Council itself, are not new and this specific controversy disappeared quickly from the headlines. Yet behind the scenes the issues continue to reverberate in the context of broader questions regarding the funding, status, and value of the arts in Ireland.[6] 'Making the case' for our work in the arts and humanities can seem a tiresome and vexatious subject, yet a discourse regarding the public value of the arts gains steadily in importance and, with respect to contemporary Irish literature, has powerful but largely unquestioned tenets.[7] Most recently, the deployment of internationally successful authors and artists as cultural ambassadors brings with it a form of celebrity worthy of notice.[8] But these issues have a longer gestation: over the last four decades, government policy towards the arts has awkwardly combined a commitment to expanding arts participation and audience engagement with the support and nurturing of creative talent; or, to put this tension less benignly, a desire for visible, quantifiable 'output' versus the inevitably jagged creative trajectories of individuals. And, as this essay will explore, a fault line of growing significance lies between public support for the arts as a form of social cohesion and a championing of the artist, or artists' potential, as a disruptive force.

The Arts Council, 1980–2020

The Arts Council was established under the Arts Act of 1951 with the following key functions: to stimulate public interest in the arts; to promote the knowledge, appreciation, and practice of the arts; to assist in improving the standards of the arts; and to organise or assist in the organising of exhibitions (within or without the state) of works of art and artistic craftsmanship. A second clause ordained that 'the Council shall advise the Government or member of the Government on any matter (being a matter on which knowledge and experience of the arts has a bearing) on which their advice is requested'.⁹ However, in practice, the historical relationship between government and Council has often been uneasy, with unsuccessful efforts made by Charles Haughey and others to bring the Council's remit under the direct control of the Department of Finance, along with other challenges to its statutory autonomy. A further Act in 1973 sanctioned the appointment of a full-time director and expanded the scope of its operations. It permitted the Council to establish committees in 'any or all of the following' areas: painting, sculpture, and architecture; music; drama, literature, and the cinema.¹⁰ The year 1973 also marked the commencement of the directorship of Colm Ó Briain, whose eight-year post saw a period of crucial expansion in the Council's activities. Between 1972/3 and 1975, its annual state grant increased from £85,000 to £200,000; by 1983 it was just under £5 million.¹¹ In the intervening years, responsibility for the funding of the Abbey and Gate Theatres, Irish Theatre Company, and Dublin Theatre Festival had also transferred to the Arts Council.

According to the Arts Council's annual report for 1980, 'the year was marked by a new confidence in the arts', but early developments that year were less than promising.¹² In April an extensive survey of living and working conditions of artists in Dublin was published.¹³ Its findings were bleak and underlined the precariousness of artists' careers: 75% of creative artists (including writers, painters, and sculptors) and 50% of 'interpretative' artists (actors, dancers, musicians) had other occupations (mostly part-time teaching) in addition to their artistic work; 23% of creative artists were without earnings for at least a month a year; over 60% of all artists had no pension provision. Significant inequities were also evident: 50% of the total income earned by creative artists was held by the top 18% while half of the interpretative artists earned less than 20% of income in that sector. In that year, the majority of artists qualifying for income tax exemption earned under £1,000 a year.¹⁴ The survey proved to be an important spur for the establishment of Aosdána the following year, by Charles Haughey, then Taoiseach, and following the advice of his arts adviser, poet and journalist Anthony Cronin.¹⁵ Its name was proposed by Council member and archaeologist Máire de Paor (*aes dána* being 'the poets of the tribe' in ancient Ireland);¹⁶ in 2003, Cronin was elected as *saoi,* an honour bestowed for 'singular and sustained distinction in the creative arts' and held by other literary figures such as Seamus Heaney, Edna O'Brien, and, controversially, Francis Stuart.

The Arts Act of 2003 repositioned the Arts Council in relation to the government and strengthened the policymaking role of the government minister with responsibility for the arts; while interpreted by many as a dilution of the Council's status, the Act did include an explicit provision that the Council is independent of the Irish government in its funding decisions.[17] However, its own funds now derive in full from the government's Department of Culture, Heritage and the Gaeltacht and make the Council the state's single largest instrument of arts funding, representing just over 49% of the national cultural budget in 2018.

During the recession years, the Arts Council and its awardees experienced significant reductions in the state grant: in 2007 Arts Council funding was €83 million, by 2014 that had fallen to under €57 million. While increases have occurred in the years 2014–18, the Council's funding – €68.2 million in 2018 – has not yet returned to its 2007 level.[18] Despite state plaudits of culture's 'soft power' and international reputation, Irish funding for the arts also compares unfavourably with European neighbours: as the National Campaign for the Arts observed in November 2017, Ireland spent 0.2% of its Gross Domestic Product on cultural services that year, placing it in the bottom three EU countries for cultural spending.[19] The emergence of the new entity Creative Ireland (a governmental arts initiative first established for the commemorative year of 2016/1916 but relaunched in Spring 2017 as a five-year programme from 2017 to 2022) has also generated concerns as to a dilution of the Council's role and a redirection of arts funding under direct governmental authority.[20]

Other aspects of the condition of the arts in 1980 bear sobering comparison with today. In the spring of that year, *Sense of Ireland*, a large-scale festival of Irish arts and culture, was held in London, featuring over ninety events in theatre, music, literature, the visual arts, film, crafts, dance, photography, architecture, and archaeology.[21] While the events were large in reach and ambition (featuring Irish artists from North and South, and with the explicit objective of increasing 'understanding and friendship between the people of these islands'), a number of commentators urged caution. In an essay entitled 'The Artist in Ireland' and published in the imposing exhibition catalogue, Seamus Deane provided a withering analysis of the current relationship between the artist and a newly consumerist society:

> The intricate game of financial and commercial monopoly which has been proceeding over the last twenty years has created a climate in which art has itself become one of the commodities in which people deal. Reputations, first editions, paintings and sculptures, commissioned music, commissioned theatre are now all an integral part of the cultural scene. Arts Council subsidies and tax-free artists, an increasing academic industry in the history and tradition of Irish art have all combined to dispel the notion that exile is

any longer a necessity. A climate of liberal opinion has created an undiscriminating respect for the artist and his products.[22]

Deane's analysis of the consequences of such a climate of 'undiscriminating respect' for artistic production is similarly hard-hitting: 'The idea of alienation has almost entirely lost its heroic or subversive aspect. Instead, it has become popularised. The artist wears his isolation as the businessman wears his suit, regularly and expectedly. [. . .] Some artists have felt obliged to attempt to deal with the general crisis; some have felt equally to ignore it.'[23] And while events in Northern Ireland from the late 1960s onwards had 'at first' what Deane termed a 'tonic' effect on artistic production, the consequences in his view were fleeting.[24] 'The general public has responded well to any attempts to aestheticise contemporary politics and sullenly to attempt to politicise art. Such is the nature of consumerism', he concluded.[25] Reading these comments decades later, and in the wake of economic rise and spectacular fall, Deane's critique retains its bite; yet any requirement on the artist to 'deal with the general crisis' remains problematic, and a prescription much resisted by artists themselves.

Values and Valuing

The subject of the arts and public value has also preoccupied literary critics in recent years. Helen Small's 2013 book *The Value of the Humanities* begins: 'The humanities might ideally find justification simply in our doing them.'[26] The sentiment is an attractive one: might the best way to justify our practice as literary scholars and teachers, as readers and audiences of literature, as authors and cultural practitioners, be, simply put, to continue to 'do what we do'? To mount a defence against perceived threats – be they to the humanities, or to literary studies, or to the value of the aesthetic – risks giving greater coherence and visibility to such counter forces. On the other hand, public values, and the processes by which such values come to be accepted or resisted, deserve scrutiny, critique, and close reading, the very skills which we literary critics claim as our trademark. And while periods of past economic crisis in Ireland brought to the fore a discourse sharpened by urgent social needs, subsequent financial recovery – for some – can offer the opportunity either to advance a longer-term discussion of public cultural good or to re-inforce a quietist self-congratulation.

In her judicious and philosophically informed study, Small identifies five elemental arguments for the value of the humanities. The first is a justification of their distinctive disciplinary character, that humanities 'study the meaning-making practices of the culture, focusing on interpretation and evaluation with an indispensable element of subjectivity'.[27] The second – especially relevant to contemporary Irish discourse on the arts – is an assertion of social use, a defence that spiritedly engages with, rather than avoids, models of use-value: 'that the humanities are useful to society in ways that put pressure on how governments commonly understand use, especially the prioritization of economic usefulness and the means of measuring it'.[28] The third claim (and one with a strong literary pedigree) is 'that the humanities have a contribution to make to our individual and collective happiness', a case that extends back, as Small shows, to John Stuart Mill's defence of poetry as a 'means of educating the feelings'.[29] The fourth, and most overly political, argument, quickly summarised as 'Democracy Needs Us', is that 'the humanities, centrally concerned as they are with the cultural practices of reflection, argument, criticism and speculative testing of ideas, have a substantial contribution to make to the good working of democracy'.[30] And the fifth, differing from the 'consequentialist' character of the other four claims and all the more alluring for that reason, rests on intrinsic value: that 'the humanities matter for their own sake'.[31] Small's work is especially admirable in avoiding the defensive tone and simplifying vocabulary that can characterise other discussions of this topic. As Ronan McDonald has cogently observed, 'academics who might be inclined to question and probe beneath assumptions and ideologies – whose contribution to society might lie precisely in analying and theorizing the genealogy of our values – have instead found themselves ventriloquizing the idiom of marketing managers and administrators, a language that too often deploys a grammar and codification unable to express novel modes of the good'.[32] McDonald's 2015 collection, *The Values of Literary Studies: Critical Institutions, Scholarly Agendas*, is shaped by his own conviction that 'we find the values *of* literary studies, at least in part, by identifying and articulating the values *in* literary studies'.[33] One of the best examples of this comes in Derek Attridge's essay, in an eminently quotable formulation of what is distinctive about the literary experience: 'The value of literature as literature, then, lies not in any predictable effects but in the continuous exploration by writers of what lies outside the limits of the knowable world and in the repeated experience of alterity by readers.'[34] Attridge's ensuing delineation of why 'this matters' is, by contrast, more subdued in tone and modest in aspiration: 'These are valuable functions because a culture that is entirely enclosed within its familiar boundaries, operating with its familiar stereotypes and prejudices, is one that cannot fully foster the potential of its members.'[35]

This emphasis on valuation as a recurring process – the 'continuous exploration by writers' and 'the repeated experience of alterity by readers' – points to an awkward subject within any discussion of aesthetic value: namely, about the relationship between personal acts of 'valuing' or valuation and the emergence of established, shared values. Charles Altieri usefully delineates these terms in his essay 'The Phenomenology of Literary Valuation' (also in McDonald's collection), where he writes: 'I distinguish between valuings that refer to specific acts of focusing on what agents can bring to the world and values that result from repeated reflection on these events.'[36] 'Valuation', then, can be understood as an individual act of imaginative participation accompanied by self-reflection, by means of which significance is attributed to experience. The establishment of 'values' is a more complex process, which, by producing shared 'standards and expectations', has important social implications: in Altieri's words, 'repeated valuations shape investments in aspects of our experiences that become constitutive features of our personal and social identities'.[37] For the subject of literature and public value, this translates to the following question: how can, or should, the individual aesthetic experience – be it for the reader/audience or author/artist – be converted to arguments concerning social good?

Tradition and the Individual Talent

In *Making Great Art Work*, its overall strategy document for 2016–25, the Arts Council has prioritised two areas in particular: 'the artist' and 'public engagement'.[38] And in the last two decades it has introduced two high-profile initiatives to enhance the public status of the literary writer. The first is the Ireland Chair of Poetry, awarded for a three-year period, and funded by Queen's University Belfast, Trinity College Dublin, University College Dublin, the Arts Council of Northern Ireland, and the Arts Council. The Chair was established as an all-island response to the most illustrious of international poetic accolades: the award of the Nobel Prize in Literature to Seamus Heaney in 1995. Since its founding, the Chair has grown in stature and public ambition; in the words of the chairperson of the Board of Trustees, Bob Collins, 'it recognizes the poetic tradition on the island of Ireland and the value and vitality of the poetic community. And crucially, it proclaims the enduring importance of the prophetic voice of the poet and re-centres poetry in the public life of the people'.[39] Since its inception, the Chair has been held by John Montague, Nuala Ní Dhomhnaill, Paul Durcan, Michael Longley, Harry Clifton, Paula

Meehan, and, at the time of writing, Eiléan Ní Chuilleanáin, each of whom has delivered an annual lecture in addition to other teaching and outreach work. Additionally, an annual Chair of Poetry bursary is awarded to a 'poet of promise', along with an annual student prize.

The longer-term impact of this initiative is to be seen in the publication of the lectures as an elegant essay series, produced by University College Dublin Press and titled *The Poet's Chair*. This distinctive body of work redresses the scarcity of commentaries by poets in recent years (Boland's *Object Lessons* was published in 1995), and it also defies pilfering for pithy quotations on public value. Instead, the volumes illustrate each poet's individual preoccupations, with some recurring subjects, such as a strong insistence on the European dimensions of Irish writing, both as poetic source and as literary audience. Thus, Montague's subject is 'the poet and his community', including the challenges and rewards of poetic translation; Durcan discusses the influence of his contemporaries Anthony Cronin, Michael Hartnett, and Harry Clifton, whom he reads as 'Three European Poets'; and Clifton challenges some of the complacencies surrounding notions of the national in his transnational scrutiny of 'Ireland and its Elsewheres' of Britain, Europe, and the United States.

The essays by Longley, Ní Dhomhnaill, and Meehan maintain a more personal focus on the creative imagination, and yet the remarkable breadth of cultural references from which they draw (the classics and natural history by Longley, folklore archives by Ní Dhomhnaill, recent geological and genetical findings by Meehan) attests to the dynamic and diverse sources of their literary inspiration. 'To be a poet is to be alive to both precursors and contemporaries', Longley observes in 'A Jovial Hullaboo', and this and other essays bring vividly to life the significance of both predecessor and peer for his writing life.[40] Meehan's richly layered and generative meditations, on 'craft and inspiration', journey furthest into creative innerscapes. Thus the opening essay 'Imaginary Bonnets with Real Bees in Them' illuminates the 'magic power' of words, 'in terms of their auditory force on the physical body', and their 'shadow power too in the ghost life of the word, the etymology, the discrete history that each word carries with it, etymologies that if we could trace far enough back might be analogous to hearing the buzzing of the one-hundred million-year old bee in amber'.[41]

The second initiative, the Laureate for Irish Fiction, was introduced in 2015 in partnership with University College Dublin, New York University, and *The Irish Times*. The inaugural Laureate (2015–18) was Anne Enright, whose themes and priorities, announced on the commencement of her three-year post, included 'nurturing the short-story form at home' and publicising 'the translation of Irish work into other languages for publication abroad'.[42] These objectives have been well fulfilled through a series of public events across the country, entitled 'The Long Night of the Short Story', which celebrated the work of many writers of short fiction, and her ambassadorial work for Literature Ireland, the organisation charged with international promotion and translation of Irish writing. Her Laureate lectures, however, received the most media notice and their strong national and international impact is already evident, including 'Antigone in Galway', a deeply moving meditation on 'the dishonoured dead' of Mother and Baby Homes and Magdalen Laundries, and 'The Count: What the Figures Say about Being a Female Irish Writer Today', an incisive analysis of gender patterns in the contemporary reviewing of Irish literary culture.[43] The second Laureate for Irish Fiction is Sebastian Barry, appointed for the period 2018–21, and his designated topics include 'The Golden Age of Writers and Readers'. In choosing this, Barry has turned his attention, and the public eye, to the forces that shape literary reputations and that both enable and limit readers' encounters with culture. And strikingly, in his opening lecture on 'The Lives of the Saints' (a tribute to his 'secular avatars' and literary mentors, including Val Mulkerns, Leland Bardwell, Michael Hartnett, and Benedict Kiely), Barry paid warm tribute to the crucial role of the cnuas in his personal and professional life.[44]

Public Engagement with Literary Work

A national survey conducted by the Arts Council in 2018, entitled 'Attendance, Participation and Engagement with the Arts in Ireland', brings somewhat reassuring information on national reading practices, given the frequently expressed concerns regarding the effects of digital media on literacy and cultural engagement.[45] Of those surveyed (a total of 1,068 adults, aged 16 and over), 73% 'read for pleasure' in the preceding twelve months, including 43% who had read a 'work of fiction, novel, story or play', 22% 'non-fiction or factual reading relating to the arts [...] (not newspapers or magazine)', and 12% 'poetry'. Of those surveyed, 34% had visited a public library to read or borrow books in the previous twelve months, 15% had read an e-book using a Kindle or other digital reading device (24% among those aged under 24), 10% had listened to audio books, and 9% had listened to book readings on radio. These findings regarding the significance of digital media for cultural engagement are underlined by other sources: for example, according to the Reuters' Digital News Report for 2018, 45% of Irish people use the radio as their source for news, among the highest proportion in any of the countries surveyed, and 38% of Irish people had listened to at least one podcast in the last month (compared, for example, with 18% of people in the UK).[46]

Funding decisions over the last decade can be viewed on the Arts Council database, and historical decisions are recorded in its publicly available annual reports.[47] The list of strategic funding awards in the field of literature (English language) for 2018 makes for impressive reading, with the largest amounts allocated to resource centres such as Poetry Ireland (€333,000), Literature Ireland (€200,000), the Munster Literature Centre (€130,000), and the Irish Writers' Centre (€100,000). Strategic funding of €70,000–75,000 was awarded to three festivals (the International Literature Festival, Dublin; Cúirt International Festival, Galway; and the Writers' Week, Listowel) and to a number of publishers, including Little Island (€70,000), Tramp Press (€50,000), Lilliput Press (€71,000), and Salmon Poetry (€41,000). Publishing ventures such as *The Dublin Review* (€57,000) and *The Stinging Fly* (€83,000) also feature on this list. And in the area of Irish-language strategic funding, awards were made to the annual festival Imram (€65,000) and to the publishers Cló Iar-Chonnachta (€76,000) and Cois Life (€35,000); in July 2018, it was announced that Cois Life, established in 1995, would cease trading at the end of 2019, a large loss to the Irish publishing scene.

Literary festival activity in Ireland is especially vital at present, as can be seen from the Council's festival investment scheme, though such events are usually resourced by large amounts of volunteer labour. A total of 215 applications was received in 2018 alone and 155 small awards were made (many in the region of €5,000), including to the Ennis Book Club Festival (€20,000), the diplomatically titled Limerick Literary Festival in Honour of Kate O'Brien (€5,000), the Dromineer (Tipperary) Literary Festival (€8,000), and the Strokestown International Poetry Festival (€15,000). These initiatives, which occupy much of the space formerly occupied by literary summer schools, have also greatly extended their international coverage in recent years; in addition, the growth of events outside of the typical urban centres is also impressive. Similarly, a surge in publishing outlets is evident from other of the Council's funding schemes, including literary and arts journals such as *Banshee* (€30,000), Curlew Editions' publication of *Winter Papers* (€34,000), *gorse* (€20,000), the Fish annual anthology (€15,000), the Irish-language journal *Comhar* (€20,000), and the newly established *Well Review* (€20,000). The almost exclusive funding of print journals is worth noting; an allocation of €11,000 for a new poetry podcast to Rockfinch productions is one of the few indicators of support for new media platforms.[48]

In 2018, the Arts Council published a short but incisive *Literature Policy and Strategy* document, the first for this specific area in many years; in it, the Council rightly situates itself as a 'key player in the provision of a national infrastructure for literary culture in Ireland'.[49] Changes in commercial publishing that have seen the emergence of ever-larger international conglomerates, in contrast with the heroic dynamism of small indigenous operations such as Tramp Press and The Stinging Fly, have clearly sharpened the Council's determination to support smaller-scale operations at home. In the words of the strategy document, 'as the international, commercial publishing industry benefits a number of established Irish writers, Arts Council support is concentrated on indigenous, independent literary publishing houses and journals that platform new voices, experimental work and distinctive Irish writers'.[50] Consequently, the policy explicitly and promisingly states the Council's interest in bringing to the fore voices that are 'new, risky or experimental' and its determination to sustain 'diverse platforms – journals, pamphlets, new media', especially given commercial publishing's 'increasingly risk-averse nature'.[51] However, the full potential of such diverse platforms and new media is yet to appear in the Council's list of grantees. In addition, although the particular vulnerability of Irish-language literature and its publishers is well noted – 'this vulnerable sector faces a significant number of challenges, including audience development, readership, translation, partnerships, promotion and critical writing'[52] – specific measures, including a recognition of the richly bilingual practice of many young writers, are yet to be named.

The Gender of Value

Enright's final Laureate lecture, mentioned above, is a powerful indictment of sexist practices in Irish reviewing culture, supported by strong statistical evidence similar to that gathered by Vida, the American-produced online resource for women in the literary arts. The ongoing work by the organisation MEAS (Measuring Equality in the Arts Sector in Ireland) shows a worrying continuance of gender inequity within the Irish publishing scene: their careful analysis of poetry publishing from 2008 to 2017, for example, yields a figure of 743 published male authors of poetry and poetry-related publications and 441 female.[53] As their work also reveals, the most striking disparities during this period in relation to the gender of authors – substantially more male than female – exist within large poetry presses such as Dedalus, Gallery, and Salmon, who also receive the largest amount of state funding in their field.

The 'excellence' argument, infamously raised in the context of the Abbey Theatre's first schedule for 2016 and the consequent *Waking the Feminists* movement, was adroitly addressed by Enright in her 2017 lecture:

> The argument about excellence – that women's work just isn't good enough – is incredibly hurtful given that there is so much mediocre work by men around. Theatre is a high-stakes medium. Some of the Abbey plays I have seen over the years have been wonderful, and some truly excruciating. I would fall out of the theatre afterwards thinking there was no point in being high-minded: what we needed was more – or at least some – ghastly plays by women.[54]

However, the 'excellence' argument has a habit of reappearing. One notable instance occurred during the controversy regarding Gerald Dawe's *The Cambridge Companion to Irish Poets* (2017), and its dismaying inclusion of four female subjects from a total of thirty poets featured in the volume. In a reflection – more robust explanation than apology – on his volume published in *The Irish Times* in February 2018, Dawe explained that 'the invitation to prepare a Companion was clearly predicated on poetic value – excellence and influence', and he went on to defend his (especially disappointing) selection of contemporary poets with the following observation: 'the choice was made to close the historical circle at the turn of the millennium with those poets who had already established international recognition with the bulk of substantial work behind them, and literary reputations critically acknowledged as such with scholarship'.[55] Such comments make ever more necessary an in-depth analysis of how literary reputations are made, who confers 'international recognition', and whose scholarship is noticed and by whom.

Patterns of male affiliation and influence have long genealogies – the table of contents for Dawe's volume makes this strongly visible – and their disruption is not an easy task. One strategy is the continuing work of literary retrieval, as in the FIRED! Irish Women Poets and the Canon initiative[56] that developed in direct response to Dawes's *Cambridge Companion*, but securing a longer-term place in the canon or curriculum for such writers also requires a re-inspection of the governing literary aesthetic through which value is conferred. In the case of Irish poetry, an aesthetic that privileges distinctiveness and rupture has dominated (the high-profile staging of an attempt to slay the father being the means to paternal respect), so much so that a study of selected individual writers can still seem the means of understanding a whole field. Conversely, in the case of Irish theatre, a growing danger exists that women's work is equated with the collaborative, the company, the workshop – and that the option of a (funded) career as a dramatic author is disappearing rapidly.

Literature and the Nation, Beyond 2020

As part of the ever-more-urgent positioning of Ireland as a dynamic nation in the global sphere, culture and its 'soft power' have received more state attention. Buoyed by the success of its 2016 official commemorative programme, the government sanctioned an elaboration of this work to be run by Creative Ireland for the period 2017–22, in its words 'to facilitate an ecosystem of creativity'.[57] Clearly signalled here is a new level of ambition for the place of culture within a state programme, an 'all-of-government initiative' with a keen eye on international positioning: 'It is an initiative that can define us for generations to come. It can redefine our role as a small sovereign republic in a globalised world. It is an important statement to ourselves and to the world.'[58] And the national objectives of the programme are spelt out in some detail: 'During this year, 2016, as we commemorated the events that led to the foundation of our state, we rediscovered the power of cultural creativity to bring communities together, and to strengthen our sense of identity. [. . .] The best way to nurture the creative imagination is through active engagement with arts and culture. Promoting creativity provides us with a strategy for individual wellbeing, social cohesion and economic success.'[59]

Such enthusiastic use of the word 'rediscovery' might rankle with the many creative practitioners who protected and sustained cultural activities during periods of financial recession and brutal cutbacks in their funding. And the references to a strategy of 'individual wellbeing', 'social cohesion', and 'economic success' bring an instrumentalism that is, on first reading, admirably explicit but in the longer term concerning as to its implementation. Recent internal reviews of government spending and 'value for money' have included the strong recommendation to the Arts Council that it 'incorporate the need to maximise the socio-economic value of the arts' in its 'goals and objectives'.[60] To date the Council has shown an admirable resistance to a narrowly utilitarian agenda, pledging itself, in subtle phrasings, to 'actively championing the distinctive value and importance of the arts' and to being 'more visibly active in promoting the arts and in advocating their social value and economic benefit'.[61] The continuance of a rich 'ecosystem of creativity' beyond 2020, within Ireland as well as in its international reputation, will require an environment in which individual artists are nurtured and recognised, respected and remunerated.[62]

Notes

1. John Spain, 'Tóibín Likes Arts Council to North Korea in Row over Aosdána Funding', *Irish Independent,* 22 April 2017: www.independent.ie/irish-news/tibn-likens-arts-council-to-north-korea-in-row-over-aosdna-funding-35644221.html [accessed 5 February 2019].
2. See Aosdána: http://aosdana.artscouncil.ie [accessed 5 February 2019].
3. See Aosdána, 'Cnuas': http://aosdana.artscouncil.ie/Cnuas.aspx [accessed 5 February 2019].
4. Spain, 'Tóibín Likes Arts Council to North Korea in Row over Aosdána Funding'.
5. Mark Hilliard, 'Colm Tóibín Slates Proposal to Cut Grants for Non-Productive Artists', *The Irish Times,* 22 April 2017: www.irishtimes.com/news/ireland/irish-news/colm-tóibín-slates-plan-to-cut-grants-for-non-productive-artists-1.3057110 [accessed 5 February 2019].
6. For a wonderfully witty treatment of this subject, see Éilís Ní Dhuibhne, 'A Literary Lunch' and 'City of Literature', which portray the (gendered) operations of a funding group, before and after the Celtic Tiger, in her *Selected Stories* (Dublin: Dalkey Archive, 2017).
7. An important recent exception was the panel discussion 'Culture as a Bridge' at the Global Ireland 2025 seminar in Dublin Castle, 9 January 2019, which included strong contributions by Anne Enright and Fintan O'Toole. One of Enright's comments at the panel – 'writers do things for Ireland because they like Ireland but I wouldn't push it' – was widely tweeted.
8. See the government announcement on 7 January 2019: https://merrionstreet.ie/en/News-Room/Releases/Minister_Madigan_announces_five_new_Cultural_Ambassadors_for_Ireland.html [accessed 4 February 2019].
9. My discussion of the history of the Arts Council is greatly indebted to Brian Kennedy's report, *Dreams and Responsibilities: The State and the Arts in Independent Ireland,* commissioned by the Arts Council and first published in 1990. Kennedy's report had itself a contentious reception, including objections by Anthony Cronin that his role had not been sufficiently recognised. Many copies were shredded soon after its publication, but it was reprinted by the Council in 1998. It is available online at the Arts Council website: www.artscouncil.ie/uploadedFiles/DreamsandResponsibilities.pdf [accessed 31 March 2019]. For an account of the 1990s controversy surrounding Kennedy's report, see Paddy Woodworth, 'Global Vision', *The Irish Times,* 20 August 2012: www.irishtimes.com/culture/art-and-design/global-vision-1.540075 [accessed 5 February 2019].

10. See 'Arts Act, 1973': www.irishstatutebook.ie/eli/1973/act/33/enacted/en/html [accessed 5 February 2019]. Also see Kennedy, *Dreams and Responsibilities*, pp. 104–7.
11. However, as Kennedy notes, funding to the Arts Council was very small in scale in comparison with capital funding projects of the time: for example, between 1951 and 1984 the Arts Council received a total of £23 million, but in the mid-1980s the government spent £23 million on the restoration of the Royal Hospital Kilmainham (now IMMA); see Kennedy, *Dreams and Responsibilities*, p. 127.
12. Ibid., p. 118.
13. Ibid., p. 117.
14. In 1969, Charles Haughey, then Minister for Finance, first introduced a tax exemption on artistic earnings.
15. Aosdána was launched in 1981 as an 'affiliation of artists' whose 'work had made an outstanding contribution to the arts in Ireland'; see Kennedy, *Dreams and Responsibilities*, p. 118.
16. Ibid., p. 118.
17. See 'Arts Act, 2003': www.irishstatutebook.ie/eli/2003/act/24/enacted/en/html [accessed 5 February 2019].
18. See Arts Council of Ireland, 'Funding': www.artscouncil.ie/funding/ [accessed 5 February 2019].
19. See National Campaign for the Arts, 'Who We Are': http://ncfa.ie/about/ [accessed 5 February 2019].
20. An opinion piece by John McAuliffe, then deputy chair of the Arts Council, which was deeply critical of the government's 'reboot' of Creative Ireland, was published under the headline 'Heather Humpreys Taking Political Control of Arts Funding', *The Irish Times*, 25 October 2017: www.irishtimes.com/opinion/heather-humpreys-taking-political-control-of-arts-funding-1.3267250 [accessed 7 February 2019].
21. The catalogue of the exhibition is itself a striking publication and very interestingly discussed by Linda King, 'A Sense of Ireland: Reflecting and Refracting Modernity in Irish Culture', *Irish Studies Review*, 26.3 (2018), pp. 318–34.
22. Seamus Deane, 'The Artist in Ireland', in John Stephenson, ed., *A Sense of Ireland* (Dublin: privately printed, 1980), p. 35.
23. Ibid., pp. 35–6.
24. Ibid., p. 35.
25. Ibid., p. 36.
26. Helen Small, *The Value of the Humanities* (Oxford: Oxford University Press, 2013), p. 1.
27. Ibid., p. 4.
28. Ibid.
29. Ibid., pp. 5, 102.
30. Ibid., p. 6.
31. Ibid.

32. Ronan McDonald, 'Introduction', in Ronan McDonald, ed., *The Values of Literary Studies: Critical Institutions, Scholarly Agendas* (Cambridge: Cambridge University Press, 2015), pp. 1–12 (p. 2).
33. Individual essays reference a range of conceptual frameworks including feminism (Robin Truth Goodman), modernist criticism (James Chandler), psychoanalysis (Jean-Michel Rabaté), and world literature (Debjani Ganguly).
34. Derek Attridge, 'Literary Experience and the Value of Criticism', in McDonald, ed., *The Values of Literary Studies*, pp. 249–62 (p. 255).
35. Ibid.
36. Charles Altieri, 'The Phenomenology of Literary Valuation', in McDonald, ed., *The Values of Literary Studies*, pp. 44–58 (p. 46).
37. Ibid.
38. Arts Council of Ireland, *Arts Council Strategy (2016–2025)*: www.artscouncil.ie/arts-council-strategy/ [accessed 5 February 2019].
39. Bob Collins, 'Foreword', to Harry Clifton, ed., *Ireland and its Elsewheres* (Dublin: University College Dublin Press, 2015), pp. ix–x (p. ix).
40. Michael Longley, *One Wide Expanse* (Dublin: University College Dublin Press, 2015), p. 17.
41. Paula Meehan, *Imaginary Bonnets with Real Bees in Them* (Dublin: University College Dublin Press, 2016), p. 19.
42. See Arts Council of Ireland, 'Laureate for Irish Fiction 2015–2018': www.artscouncil.ie/Arts-in-Ireland/Literature/Laureate-for-Irish-Fiction-2015–2018 [accessed 5 February 2019]. Enright's first laureate lecture was published in the *London Review of Books*, 37.24 (17 December 2015); and her third as 'Diary', in the *London Review of Books*, 39.19 (21 September 2017).
43. I discuss Enright's 'Antigone in Galway' lecture in more detail in 'One Hundred Years a Nation – New Modes of Commemoration', in Paige Reynolds, ed., *The New Irish Studies* (Cambridge: Cambridge University Press, forthcoming).
44. See 'Sebastian Barry Salutes the Writers Who Inspired Him', *The Irish Times*, 10 September 2018: www.irishtimes.com/culture/books/sebastian-barry-salutes-the-writers-who-inspired-him-1.3624111 [accessed 5 February 2019].
45. See Arts Council of Ireland, *Attendance, Participation & Engagement with the Arts in Ireland 2018*: www.artscouncil.ie/uploadedFiles/wwwartscouncilie/Content/Arts_in_Ireland/Strategic_Development/Arts-Council-National-Survey-2018.pdf [accessed 4 February 2019].
46. See Nic Newman, et al., *Reuters Institute Digital News Report 2018*: www.digitalnewsreport.org/ [accessed 5 February 2019]. Warm thanks to Katherine McSharry for these references.
47. See Arts Council of Ireland, 'Who We Funded': www.artscouncil.ie/Who_we_funded/. All information on 2018 funding is taken from this source.
48. For an insightful analysis of Irish poetry publishing online (and its absence), see Ken Keating, 'Irish Poetry Publishing Online', *Éire-Ireland*, 52.1&2 (Spring/Summer 2017), pp. 321–36.

49. See Arts Council of Ireland, *Making Great Art Work: Literature Policy & Strategy 2018*: www.artscouncil.ie/Publications/All/Literature-Policy-and-Strategy-2018 [accessed 4 February 2019].
50. Ibid., p. 2.
51. Ibid., p. 4.
52. Ibid.
53. See Measuring Equality in the Arts Sector: Literature in Ireland: https://measorg.com/ [accessed 5 February 2019].
54. Enright, 'Diary', *London Review of Books*, 39.19 (21 September 2017), pp. 33–5.
55. Gerald Dawe, 'Selected Poets and Their Work "Alive and Present to the Reader"', *The Irish Times*, 24 February 2018: www.irishtimes.com/culture/books/selected-poets-and-their-work-alive-and-present-to-the-reader-1.3394727 [accessed 5 February 2019].
56. For more details on Fired!, see: https://awomanpoetspledge.com/ [accessed 5 February 2019].
57. This quotation comes from the programme overview document, *Clár Éire Ildánach, Creative Ireland Programme, 2017–2022*, p. 5: www.creativeireland.gov.ie/sites/default/files/media/file-uploads/2017-12/Creative Ireland Programme.pdf [accessed 5 February 2019].
58. *Clár Éire Ildánach, Creative Ireland Programme*, p. 6. The international dimensions of this programme have been re-inforced by the government's *Global Ireland 2025* initiative, a plan to 'double the scope and impact of Ireland's global footprint' between 2018 and 2025 and which self-describes as 'the most ambitious renewal and expansion of Ireland's international presence ever undertaken in terms of diplomacy, culture, business, overseas aid, tourism and trade.' See: www.ireland.ie/en/stories/global-ireland-irelands-global-footprint-2025 [accessed 5 February 2019].
59. Ibid., p. 5.
60. See Department of Public Expenditure and Reform, *Spending Review 2018: Implementation of the Value for Money and Policy Review of the Arts Council*: www.per.gov.ie/en/spending-review/ [accessed 4 February 2019].
61. Arts Council of Ireland, *Making Great Art Work: Leading the Development of the Arts in Ireland*, September 2015, pp. 38–9: www.artscouncil.ie/uploadedFiles/Making_Great_Art_Work.pdf [accessed 4 February 2019].
62. My thanks to Katherine McSharry, Sarah Bannan, and Emily Mark-Fitzgerald for the information they provided. The views expressed here are mine, written in an individual capacity.

Coda: The Irish Times, *Tramp Press, and the Future Present*

Paige Reynolds

For a scholar, or even an enthusiast, of Irish literature, one distressing transition characterising the contemporary era might be seen in the rapid ascension of digital culture. In our darkest fears, the ubiquity of newfangled devices projecting easily digestible prose, images, and sounds portends a world in which the book, or even reading itself, is rendered extinct. Yet heartening signs of the tenacity of print are evident in the flourishing of literary magazines such as *The Stinging Fly* or *Winter Papers*, or in the survival of 'brick and mortar' bookstores like Hodges Figgis in Dublin or Vibes and Scribes in Cork. Such examples confirm that Irish publishing has been quick to react to the perceived threat of new technologies, not least by strategically employing them to cultivate wider and more diverse reading audiences. Two influential Irish publishers, *The Irish Times* and Tramp Press, though vastly different in mission and scale, have successfully adapted to the digital age while maintaining a deep commitment to literature and readers.

Founded in 1859, *The Irish Times* is a daily newspaper based in Dublin with a history of providing news, opinion, and analysis to readers across the English-speaking world. As an Irish paper of reference, it does the customary work of a commercial newspaper by detailing events and attitudes at home and abroad through its reports, opinion pages, photographs, and advertisements. Though based in Dublin, this paper aims to represent the interests of all of Ireland, north and south of the border, and has increasingly turned its attention to global issues, as seen in its placement of international correspondents. With a readership of roughly 650,000, the *Times*, like most papers that have survived the digital age, offers its contents not only in print but also on the web. In seeming contrast, Tramp Press, established in 2014, is a small independent literary press. Founded and helmed by Lisa Coen and Sarah Davis-Goff, Tramp currently publishes three works of literary fiction a year, and from its early days has introduced readers to an impressive roster of critically acclaimed books, including Sara

Baume's *Spill Simmer Falter Wither* (2015), Mike McCormack's *Solar Bones* (2016), and Emilie Pine's memoir *Notes to Self* (2018). Also based in Dublin, Tramp Press appeals to a specialised audience of discerning readers, though it has global ambitions for its publications.

The Irish Times and Tramp Press are successfully navigating challenges that face publishing in our image-flooded, digital present. For these media outfits, as for most, market forces are a central concern. The *Times* is a large organisation beholden to advertisers and subscribers, while Tramp is a smaller business that obtained crucial seed funding from the Arts Council though it must also rely on sales to support its ventures. Both are attuned to their profit margins; to survive the rapidly changing media landscape, both must nimbly adjust to variable market forces and technologies. Each has therefore embraced the role that the Internet might play in its success. In 1994, the *Times* was the first newspaper in the UK and Ireland, and among the first thirty newspapers internationally, to establish a website. The *Times* has at moments struggled to adapt its long-established publishing practices to new media platforms, but Tramp – born in the digital age – has from the outset capitalised on digital technologies to control costs without compromising the quality of its publications or the working conditions of those whom it employs. It has also cannily used social media and internet marketing to build its brand. From its digital newsletter deposited in subscriber email boxes to the clever tweets scripted by its founders, Tramp successfully promotes its individual publications and keeps readers abreast of happenings that signal its growing stature in contemporary letters.

The mission, form, and contents of the texts published by these institutions help to illuminate aspects of their historical moment. *The Irish Times* has, across three centuries, reflected contemporary norms and expectations. Founded in the nineteenth century with a moderate nationalist Protestant bent, it is regarded today as a generally progressive newspaper, one with neoliberal sympathies. For those seeking a broad understanding of contemporary Ireland, alterations in the paper's form and content signal cultural shifts across the past four decades.[1] Amid the economic instability of the 1980s, the *Times* began to offer more financial advice columns. In the 1990s, as scandals rocked the financial, political, and religious foundations of Irish society, its reporting responded to the public demand for transparency. In 1992, the paper broke the story of Bishop Eamonn Casey's affair with Annie Murphy, as well as that of the X case – and thereby played a crucial role in undermining the protective silences that had long been granted the Catholic Church and Irish state. That same year, in its coverage of Charles Haughey's removal from office, the paper looked closely at the cult of personality surrounding the Taoiseach in a mode not entirely dissimilar from subsequent accounts offered by Colin Murphy's play *Haughey/Gregory* (2018) or RTÉ's series *Citizen Charlie* (2014).[2] In the late 1990s, expanded sections for science and real estate testified to Celtic Tiger priorities. And in the twenty-first century, amid changing patterns of emigration and immigration, and their effects on national self-understanding, the long-running column 'An Irishman's Diary' stands alongside revealing interviews with an array of immigrants to Ireland.[3]

Tramp Press, with its much shorter institutional history, offers through its publications a sense of Irish writers and readers in the twenty-first century. Founded in a moment of digital dominance and anxieties about the death of reading, Tramp is devoted to the print publication of new writing and recovered texts and draws its title from the unorthodox, and often heroic, vagabonds found throughout the drama of J. M. Synge. Its critical and commercial success attest not only to the business savvy of its founders, but also to the quality of Irish prose being produced in the early twenty-first century, a moment that the second Laureate for Irish Fiction, Sebastian Barry, has proclaimed 'an unexpected golden age of Irish prose writing'.[4] This 'golden age' results from factors ranging from the proliferation of creative writing programmes to venturesome literary periodicals that publish new voices, including *Banshee* and *The Dublin Review*. As a publisher, Tramp evinces a similar commitment to cultivating, mentoring, and publishing fresh talent: its editors fearlessly plough through a 'slush pile' of unsolicited manuscripts to identify and develop new work. Their assiduous vetting has already resulted in a body of award-winning literary fiction: their authors have taken home the International Dublin Literary Award, Irish Book Awards, and Rooney Prizes, among others.[5]

In our highly mediated culture, Tramp maintains a personal relationship with its individual authors from the early creative to the later promotional stages. In contrast to current practice at many publishing houses, which have reduced editorial staff or outsourced editorial labour due to financial constraints, Tramp prioritises the role of the literary editor. Coen and Davis-Goff are public figures whose editorial interventions are part of their brand. Through its editorial policies, Tramp has nudged forward its clearly articulated aesthetic and political values. As Coen and Davis-Goff announce to writers interested in submitting manuscripts, they welcome all 'exceptional' writing, but 'if you address us as "Dear Sirs", or list only male influences, we will decline to consider your work'.[6] Likewise, they seek to cultivate writers of colour and other under-represented voices in Irish literature. By insisting on equitable representation as a principle and seeking it in practice, Tramp Press endeavours to reflect the increasing diversity of twenty-first-century Ireland.

The mission statements of these institutions suggest that an overt admixture of tradition and innovation may be one quality that has helped both respond to the challenges presented to publishing in their times. The 'About Us' summation of Tramp Press offered on its website asserts, 'people who love books will always want excellent writing. We want to help them get their hands on it.'[7] This statement is, in many ways, at odds with our understanding of the contemporary moment: it is focused on books not screens, it values excellence rather than democratic access, it suggests an inherent and essential relationship with literature, and it advocates for the material, for getting 'hands' on the 'it' of a published text. In its statement, the *Times* declares a commitment to representing political, cultural, and economic transitions, even as it announces ideological principles that chime with long-standing Irish cultural norms, such as the 'promotion of a friendly society where the quality of life is enriched by the standards of its education, its art, its culture and its recreational facilities, and where the quality of spirit is instinct with Christian values, but free from all religious bias and discrimination'.[8] This resonates with what the sociologist Tom Inglis has labelled 'Catholic capitalism', the contradictory logics of religious self-denial and the embrace of consumerism in contemporary Ireland. In this instance, an international newspaper with an abiding commitment to neoliberalism can portray itself as seeking 'social justice' and 'peace and harmony', as well as profit.[9]

The juxtaposition of Tramp Press and *The Irish Times* brings to light another important commonality: both manifest a deep and specific commitment to publishing and promoting Irish contemporary literature. The *Times*, as Terence Brown notes, has long had a 'literary slant', with writers from Brian Friel to Rob Doyle serving as regular columnists.[10] According to Brown, coverage of Seamus Heaney's Nobel Prize win in 1995 by the paper's literary editors Brian Fallon (1977–88) and John Banville (1988–99), and by staff writers such as Eileen Battersby, 'brought a distinctive critical edge to the paper's coverage of literature in a decade when in the academy and in the media the concepts of postmodernity and literary theory were challenging the status of literature as a privileged discourse'.[11] The literary pages of *The Irish Times* reflect as well as modify national conversations about literature. The literary editor Caroline Walsh (1999–2011), for example, championed contemporary Irish fiction, women writers, and literature in translation. The current literary editor, Martin Doyle, has continued these initiatives, placing needed emphasis in particular on the recuperation of women writers, as evidenced in the online series 'In Praise Of', where contemporary writers and academics highlight the work of a chosen Irish woman writer. As Anne Enright noted in 2017, however, the *Times* like many publications has an evident gender bias in its literary reviews, with substantial attention more frequently awarded to work by men.[12] And there remains in the literary pages a pressing need to situate Irish writing in a larger global framework.

With its vast reach, *The Irish Times* nonetheless does contemporary Irish writing an enormous service. It prints excerpts from recent books, offers readers a weekly 'Saturday Poem', showcases winners of the Hennessy New Irish Writing awards for short fiction and poetry, and publishes the work of children and teenagers involved in Fighting Words, an organisation that provides free tutoring and mentoring in creative writing. This commitment to democratic access to contemporary Irish writing is abetted by '*The Irish Times* Book Club', which examines a selected book through articles, interviews, extracts, and a summative podcast. The texts selected for the Book Club are not safe choices. June Caldwell's *Room Little Darker* (2018), a sexually graphic and formally difficult collection of short stories, and Lisa Harding's *Harvesting* (2017), a novel focused on sex trafficking, have been recent selections. In making these choices, the paper pushes the bounds of public taste.

By regularly publishing reviews of scholarly tomes and features written by academics, the *Times* also takes seriously the value of academic analysis. In 2016, for example, the paper offered a series looking back on the 1981 hunger strikes in Northern Ireland, reviewing its own coverage of the events, as well as incorporating assessments from scholars of such topics as the material culture of the strikes, the gender politics of their representation, and the influence of the strikes on poetry from both sides of the border.[13] The productive synergy among the tasks of writer, critic, reporter, and scholar defines the careers of some of the paper's luminaries: the journalist Nuala O'Faolain penned the bestselling memoirs *Are You Somebody?* (1996) and *Almost There* (2003), and Fintan O'Toole, a former literary editor who contributes to the opinion, news, and culture pages, has been commissioned by Faber to write the official biography of Seamus Heaney.

If the changing nature of Irish culture over centuries has been registered in the form and content of *The Irish Times*, the carefully curated publications of Tramp Press tell us much about the tenor of twenty-first-century

Ireland. McCormack's *Solar Bones*, a novel written in one extended sentence, records the first-person musings of an engineer living in post-crash Ireland, and the collection *Dubliners 100*, edited by Thomas Morris, invited writers such as Evelyn Conlon and Eimear McBride to re-imagine stories from Joyce's collection a century after its publication, underscoring the Irish modernist's enduring influence on contemporary writing. Tramp also has an abiding commitment to representations of an increasingly global and diverse Ireland, albeit one filtered at present through the perspective of white writers and editors. Oona Frawley's novel *Flight* (2014), the first book Tramp published, chronicles the relationship between a Zimbabwean immigrant and her Irish employer during the boom; Belinda McKeon's edited collection *A Kind of Compass: Stories on Distance* (2015) gathered short fiction from Nigeria, Iran, Japan, and elsewhere; and *The Iron Age* (2017), by the Finnish-born cartoonist Arja Kajermo, recounts the coming-of-age of a young girl in Finland after the Second World War.

Thus far, Tramp has prioritised literary fiction. But it has ventured into memoir with the publication of Pine's *Notes to Self*, a deeply confessional book whose critical and commercial success in Ireland speaks to the desire to unmoor a national tradition of secret-keeping. And *A Brilliant Void: A Selection of Classic Irish Science Fiction* (2018), edited and introduced by Jack Fennell, insists on the literary merit of generic forms long dismissed as 'low brow'. In common with *The Irish Times*, and reflective of the twenty-first-century mania for commemoration, Tramp has committed to resurrecting and revising the Irish literary past. To date, its 'Recovered Voices' series has published titles such as Charlotte Riddell's *A Struggle for Fame* (1883, rpt. 2016), Maeve Kelly's *Orange Horses* (1990, rpt. 2017), and Dorothy Macardle's gothic classics, *The Uninvited* (1942, rpt. 2015) and *The Unforeseen* (1946, rpt. 2017); each edition includes a scholarly but accessible introduction that champions the book and explains the rationale for its publication. Even in its early days, Tramp promises to have an influence on Irish literature akin to that of its predecessors Hogarth and Grove Press on the avant-garde or Virago and Attic Press on women's writing. Their stated goal is to become an internationally renowned imprint, like Faber and Faber or Éditions Gallimard, whose prestigious backlist sells well enough to help support the cultivation of new work.

Just as *The Irish Times* encourages readers to post responses to its online articles, Tramp also invites direct engagement from readers. The social media posts affiliated with Tramp, written under the aegis of the brand as well as by the individual founders, are candid and often political: they might as readily promote a political concern like 'Repeal the Eighth' as the launch of a new book. A small company, Tramp is unafraid to court debate, as it did when Coen and Davis-Goff challenged the rules of the Man Booker Prize for Fiction, a prestigious award available to long-form fiction written in English.[14] Since 1980, an impressive roster of Irish and Northern Irish writers have been awarded the Booker: Roddy Doyle won for *Paddy Clarke Ha Ha Ha* (1993), John Banville for *The Book of Evidence* (1989) and *The Sea* (2005), Anne Enright for *The Gathering* (2007), and Anna Burns for *Milkman* (2018). But prior to 2018, the Booker was available only to work published in the UK. In opinion pieces, triggered by the ineligibility of McCormack's critically acclaimed *Solar Bones*, Davis-Goff argued that novels written in Ireland and published by an Irish imprint, such as Tramp, should be eligible for the Booker Prize.[15] Soon after, the Booker rules were changed by opening access to books published by Irish imprints. As a result, the international renown of the Booker is available to writers who publish in Ireland, and Irish publishers like Tramp can benefit from the profits triggered by a winning author. But there remains a caveat: the Booker requires that the publisher have an office in the UK, which rules out independent presses in Ireland without the means to do so. This instance reveals that, even as they flourish amid the book trade's rapidly changing landscape, Irish writers continue to face particular challenges in the global marketplace, ones that might impel Irish writers to publish elsewhere.

This is a moment of vibrant public advocacy in Ireland, one in which citizens have noisily protested and productively intervened to advance causes from gender equity in the theatre to same-sex marriage. As institutions, *The Irish Times* and Tramp Press have had a similarly positive influence on contemporary culture through their broad-minded promotion of contemporary Irish writing. This does not mean that these companies are faultless, nor does it suggest that their commitments will not, or should not, change going forward. But in this moment, as divergent as their organisational structures and objectives might seem, they nevertheless share a common mission in advocating literature, and particularly Irish literature, as an essential and durable cultural instrument – one that not only helps readers apprehend their contemporary moment, but also encourages them to think critically about the past and to imagine possible futures. Both manifest a 'future present' that understands literature and literary critical imagination as central to lived experience, and they provide the humanities, under duress in this historical moment, two institutions that are, in different but valuable ways, supporting writers and readers of Irish literature across the globe.

Notes

1. See Terence Brown, *The Irish Times: 150 Years of Influence* (London: Bloomsbury, 2015); and Mark O'Brien, *The Irish Times: A History* (Dublin: Four Courts Press, 2008); as well as Conor Brady, *Up with the Times* (Dublin: Gill and Macmillan, 2005), which documents his experience as *Times* editor from 1986 to 2002.
2. See also Anthony Roche, 'The Stuff of Tragedy? Representations of Irish Political Leaders in the "Haughey" Plays of Carr, Barry and Breen', in Scott Brewster and Michael Parker, eds., *Irish Literature since 1990: Diverse Voices* (Manchester: Manchester University Press, 2009), pp. 79–97.
3. The *Irish Times* reporter Sorcha Pollack excerpts some of these interviews in *New to the Parish: Stories of Love, War, and Adventure from Ireland's Immigrants* (Dublin: New Island Books, 2018).
4. See Sebastian Barry, 'We Are in an Unexpected Golden Age of Irish Prose Writing', *The Irish Times*, 8 February 2018: www.irishtimes.com/culture/books/sebastian-barry-we-are-in-an-unexpected-golden-age-of-irish-prose-writing-1.3384853 [accessed 17 February 2019].
5. See Paige Reynolds, '"Publish Little, and Publish Well": An Interview with the Founders of Tramp Press', *Éire-Ireland*, 52.1&2 (Spring/Summer 2017), pp. 372–90.
6. 'Submissions', *Tramp Press*: www.tramppress.com/submissions/ [accessed 17 February 2019].
7. 'About Us', *Tramp Press*: www.tramppress.com/about/ [accessed 17 February 2019].
8. 'About Us: The Irish Times Trust', *The Irish Times*: www.irishtimes.com/about-us/the-irish-times-trust [accessed 17 February 2019].
9. Tom Inglis, *Global Ireland: Same Difference* (London: Routledge, 2008), pp. 13–16.
10. Brown, *The Irish Times*, p. 381. *The Irish Times* is not alone in this endeavour; the *Irish Independent*, *The Guardian*, and *The New York Times* are among English-language newspapers consistently offering attentive coverage of contemporary Irish literature.
11. Ibid., pp. 381–2.
12. Anne Enright, 'Diary', *London Review of Books*, 39.18 (21 September 2017), pp. 33–5.
13. 'The Hunger Strikes', *The Irish Times*: www.irishtimes.com/culture/heritage/the-hunger-strikes [accessed 17 February 2019].
14. Sarah Davis-Goff and Lisa Coen, 'Irish Publishers Left on Shelf by Man Booker Prize', *The Irish Times*, 1 August 2016: www.irishtimes.com/opinion/irish-publishers-left-on-the-shelf-by-man-booker-prize-1.2741071; and Sarah Davis-

Goff, 'Why Are Irish Publishers Shut Out of the Man Booker Prize?', *The Guardian*, 14 September 2016: www.theguardian.com/books/booksblog/2016/sep/14/why-are-irish-publishers-shut-out-of-the-man-booker-prize. See also Lisa Coen and Sarah Davis-Goff, 'Why the Man Booker Rule Change Could Revolutionise Ireland's Literary Culture', *The Prospect,* 9 January 2018: www.prospectmagazine.co.uk/other/why-the-man-booker-rule-change-could-revolutionise-irelands-literary-culture [all accessed 17 February 2019].

15. McCormack's *Solar Bones* was nominated only after Tramp sold the rights to Canongate in Scotland, which also publishes Kevin Barry.

Index

Abbey Theatre, 32, 152, 153, 155, 156, 158, 162, 163, 164, 202, 247, 281, 282, 377, 386
abortion, 6, 105, 165, 193, 229, 230, 235, 239, 240, 295, 337
About Adam (Stembridge), 352
Abrahamson, Lenny, 347, 353, 354, 355
abuse, 106, 107, 187, 188, 281. *See also* Catholic Church abuse scandals; Industrial Schools
Academy Awards, 347, 362, 363
Achtung Baby (U2), 360
Adam & Paul (Abrahamson), 353, 354
Adams, A. P., 74
addiction, 32, 158
Adigun, Bisi, 187
Adorno, Theodor W., 47, 57
Aventures de Tintin, Les (Hergé), 318
Africa
  asylum seekers from, 105, 190
  slave trade in, 192
African Americans
  Irish diasporic experience in US and, 174
  Irish history in dialogue with history of, 14
  Irish works with pop music by, 86, 217
African characters in Irish works. *See* black characters in Irish works
African community, in Dublin, 14
After Babel (Steiner), 334
After Politics (Ghassan), 182
Ahern, Bertie, 278, 279, 281
Ahern, Cecilia, 97
aisling, 73, 132
'Aisling' (Muldoon), 73
Akinjobi, Olutoyin Pamela, 192
Akpoveta, Ebun Joseph, 183, 187, 188
Akutagawa, Ryūnosuke, 319
'Albert Chain, The' (McGuckian), 55
alcoholism, 32, 84, 163, 206
'Alerted' (Heaney), 117
Alexander, Neal, 140
Alias Grace (Atwood), 177
Alice Trilogy (Murphy), 202, 205

All That Fall (Beckett), 299
All the Beggars Riding (Caldwel), 145
Allen, Miriam, 356
Almost There (O'Faolain), 396
Altieri, Charles, 381
Altuna-García de Salazar, Asier, 188
Amazon, 258, 355
'Ambition' (Carson), 69
Amelia (Parkinson), 101
American Conference for Irish Studies (ACIS), 329
Amongst Women (McGahern), 214–16, 217, 233, 376
Amuigh Liom Féin (Ó Conaola), 34
Anderson, Emily Hodgson, 361
Angel (Jordan), 349
angel of history (Benjamin), 138, 146
Angela's Ashes (McCourt), 10, 233, 360, 361, 362
Anglo-Irish Treaty (1921), 345
Anne Devlin (Murphy), 349
Anomalous States (Lloyd), 331
ANU Productions, 86, 87, 163, 164, 282
Anúna (choral group), 366
Aosdána, 11, 38, 375, 377
Aran Islands, 9, 15, 130, 172
archives, 38, 87, 146, 340
Ardmore Studios, 346
Are You Somebody? (O'Faolain), 13, 396
Aristocrats (Friel), 202, 205
Ark, The: A Cultural Centre for Children, 96
Arlen House, 309
Arlington (Walsh), 86
Arnold, Mavis, 279
Artane Industrial School, 286
Artemis Fowl series (Colfer), 103
'Artist in Ireland, The' (Deane), 379
Arts Acts
  1951, 376
  1973, 377
  2003, 377
Arts Council England, 250

401

Arts Council of Ireland, 11, 27, 38, 98, 102, 309, 375, 376–9, 381, 383, 384, 388, 393
  Ireland Chair of Poetry and, 381–2
  Laureate for Irish Fiction and, 382–3
  Literature Policy and Strategy document from, 385
  Making Great Art Work strategy document for 2016–2025, 381
  National Writers' Workshop and, 27
  Visual Culture representative of, 356
Arts Council of Northern Ireland, 381
arts festivals, 12, 96, 378
As If I Am Not There (Wilson), 357
Asking for It (O'Neill), 107
'Asylum' (Carson), 69
'At a Potato Digging' (Heaney), 116
'At Ardboe Point' (Heaney), 116
'At Poll Salach. Easter Sunday, 1998' (Longley), 48
At Swim, Two Boys (O'Neill), 222
'At Toomebridge' (Heaney), 111
'Athair' (Ó Conghaile), 314
Atkinson, Coral, 177
Attic Press, 397
Attridge, Derek, 381
Atwood, Margaret, 177
audiobooks, 37, 320, 383
Australia, 14, 104, 177, 310, 341
autobiographical novels, 13, 67
autobiographies, 13, 175, 316, 347, 365
awards and prizes, 10, 28, 37, 38, 97, 107, 184, 197, 307, 314, 347, 360, 362, 363, 381, 394, 398
Away (Urquhart), 177
'Away From It All' (Heaney), 116
Azams, Osaro, 194

Baboró Arts Festival, 96
Bachelard, Gaston, 127
'Badagry' (Hart), 192
BAFTA awards, 10, 362
Bailegangaire (Murphy), 202, 203, 204, 205
Bakhtin, Mikhail, 318
Balcony of Europe (Higgin), 223
Banim, John and Michael, 212
Banshee (journal), 384, 394
Banville, John, 9, 97, 395
  Birchwood, 212
  Shroud, 223
  The Book of Evidence, 398
'Baoite' (Mac an Iomaire), 32
Barnes, Ben, 155, 158, 164
Barrett, Ciara, 357
Barry, Sean, 284
Barry, Sebastian, 13, 347, 383, 394
  Days Without End, 223

Barry, Kevin, 15
Barrytown Trilogy (Doyle), 216–17
Barton, Ruth, 357
Bashō, 127
Battersby, Eileen, 395
Baudelaire, Charles, 127
Bauman, Nicola, 250
Baume, Sara, 393
Beairtle (Ó Curraoin), 310
'Beannaithe' (Jenkinson), 32
Beat poets, 35
Beatha Dhónaill Dhuibh (Ó Súilleabháin), 33
Beatles/Stones analogy, for Friel and Murphy, 201, 204
Beauty Queen of Leenane, The (McDonagh), 314
Beckett, Samuel, 45, 53, 56, 93, 168, 203, 226, 318, 328, 347, 364, 365
  All That Fall, 299
  Embers, 92–3
  Krapp's Last Tape, 85
Behan, Brendan, 226
  Borstal Boy, 217
Belfast, 69, 127, 128, 140, 356
'Belfast' (Flynn), 127–8, 137
'Belfast' (MacNeice), 128
Belfast Agreement (1998), 65, 75, 222, 263, 264, 265, 268. *See also* Good Friday Agreement
Belfast Confetti (Carson), 50, 65, 69
Bell, The (magazine), 213, 215
Bend for Home, The (Healy), 233
Benjamin, Walter, 137, 146
Bennett, Claire-Louise, 9
Bennett, Ronan
  The Catastrophist, 223–4, 225
Berlant, Lauren, 249, 254
Bernhardt, Sarah, 361, 364
Between Here and There (Morrissey), 178
Bhean Feasa, An (Titley), 31
Big Guide to Irish Children's Books, The (Coghlan and Keenan), 99
Big House novel, 81, 212, 213, 223
Big House of Inver, The (Somerville and Ross), 212
Bildungsroman (coming-of-age novel), 219–22
  Deane's *Reading in the Dark* as, 221–2
  Good Friday Agreement and Celtic Tiger experiences in, 222
  Joyce's *Portrait of the Artist as a Young Man* and, 219
  McCabe's *The Butcher Boy* as, 220–1
Binchy, Chris, 182
Binchy, Maeve, 15, 313
Birchwood (Banville), 212
Birmingham University Centre for Cultural Studies, 329
black characters in Irish works, 105, 186, 187

Akpoveta's novel *Prison Without Walls*
    with, 188
  Dimbo's novel *She Was Foolish?* with, 187
  Doyle's short story 'I Understand' with, 185
  interracial romance theme with, 184
Black Robe (Moore), 223
Black, Cathal, 348, 349
'Blackberry-Picking' (Heaney), 116
Blanchot, Maurice, 275
Blaris Moor (McGuckian), 128
'Blockbusters and Banned Books' (Menand),
  362
Bloodaxe Books, 312
Bloody Sunday (1972), 68, 203, 370
Bloom, Harold, 364
Blown Away (film), 361
Blue Boy, The (Brokentalkers), 282
Blyton, Enid, 318
Boland, Eavan, 9, 111–18, 123
  A Woman Without a Country, 112
  'An Irish Childhood in England, 1951', 173
  'Colony', 113
  'Domestic Interior', 113
  Domestic Violence, 112, 123
  In a Time of Violence, 114
  'In Our Own Country', 112
  'Inscriptions', 114
  'Marriage', 113
  'Mise Éire', 112, 232
  New Collected Poems, 113
  Object Lessons, 382
  Outside History, 112
  'Outside History', 232
  'Suburban Woman', 113
  'That the Science of Cartography Is
    Limited', 114
  'The Emigrant Irish', 173
  The Lost Land, 112
  The War Horse, 113
  'Three Songs for a Legend', 113
  'Writing in a Time of Violence', 114
Bolaño, Roberto, 268
Bolger, Dermot, 309
  Internal Exiles, 170
  Ireland in Exile, 170, 171
  The Journey Home, 170, 233
book clubs, 106, 320, 384, 396
Book of Evidence, The (Banville), 398
Book of the Year Award, 37
Booker Prize, 398
bookstores, 37, 106, 192, 193, 392
Borstal Boy (Behan), 217
Boss, Owen, 86
Boston College Irish Studies programme, 328
'Bothán' (Ó Muirthile), 39

Boucicault, Dion, 93
Bourke, Angela, 29
Bowen, Elizabeth, 212, 226
Boy Eats Girl (Bradley), 351
Boy in the Striped Pyjamas, The (Boyne), 100
Boyne, John, 100
  The Heart's Invisible Furies, 240–1
Boys of Foley Street, The (ANU Productions), 87
Bradley, Stephen, 351
Bradshaw, Brendan, 332
Brannigan, John, 139
Breakfast on Pluto (Jordan), 268
Breakfast on Pluto (McCabe), 264–8, 347
*Breaking Ground, The Story of the London Irish
  Women's Centre* (documentary film), 175
Breaking the Wishbone (Parkinson), 105
Breathnach, Colm, 30
Breathnach, Paddy, 351
Brennan, Deirdre, 32, 309
Brennan, Maeve, 177
Brennan, Sarah Rees, 100
Brexit, 1, 5, 9, 136, 338
Brexit Shorts (*The Guardian* series), 147
Briathra, Béithe agus Banfhilí (Ní Fhrighil), 36
Bridges series of picture books, 105
Bright Wave, The/An Tonn Gheal (Bolger),
  309, 310
Brilliant Void, A (Fennell), 397
British Association of Irish Studies (BAIS),
  329, 340
Brockmann, Stephen, 353
Brodsky, Joseph, 116
Broken Harbor (French), 248, 249, 250, 251, 254–7
Brokentalkers, 90, 282
Brooklyn (Tóibín), 10, 176, 348
Brown, Christy, 347
Brown, Terence, 236, 330, 395
Bruton, John, 152
Buckley, Christine, 279
Budawanny (Quinn), 349
Buddenbrooks (Mann), 214
Burke Brogan, Patricia, 237, 283
Burns, Anna, 7, 398
'Burren Prayer' (Longley), 132–3
bursaries scheme, 38, 197, 375
Bushe, Paddy, 39
Butcher Boy, The (McCabe), 5, 220–1, 222,
  235, 347
Butler, Jean, 361, 365, 366, 367
By Night in Chile (Bolaño), 268
Byrne, Terry, 352

Cahill, Susan, 106, 174
Cahill, Thomas, 360
Caldwell, Lucy, 81, 145, 396

Calling Cards (Fallon and Mac Aodha), 309
Cambridge Companion to Irish Poets, The (Dawes), 386
Cambridge University, Irish Studies at, 329
Campbell, Siobhán, 147
Camus, Albert, 319
Canada
   Irish community in, 14, 15, 177, 341
Captain Lavender (McGuckian), 52–5
Captains and the Kings, The (Johnston), 212
Carleton, William, 212
Carlson, Marvin, 367
Carney, John, 348
Carolan, Stuart, 354
Carr, Marina, 7, 81
Carson, Ciaran, 48–51, 319
   'Ambition', 69
   'Asylum', 69
   Belfast Confetti, 50, 65, 69
   'Dresden', 70
   'Hamlet', 50
   Last Night's Fun, 70
   Opera Et Cetera, 49
   The Irish for No, 49, 65, 69, 70
   The New Estate, 48, 50
   'The New Estate', 48–9
Carson, Jan, 143
Carson, Liam, 38
Caruth, Cathy, 69
Casey, Eamonn, 33, 393
Casey, Maude, 172
Casey, Natasha, 365, 367, 368
Casserly, Maeve, 288
'Casualty' (Heaney), 370, 371
Catalan language, Irish translations from, 318, 319
Catastrophist, The (Bennett), 223–4, 225
Cathleen Ní Houlihan (mythic figure), 71
Catholic Church, 1, 32, 33, 228–9, 230, 231, 232, 233, 234, 235, 236, 238, 239, 240, 313, 393
   Doyle's *Paddy Clarke Ha Ha Ha* on, 236
   MacLaverty's novel *Midwinter Break* showing attitudes towards, 240
   McCourt's memoir *Angela's Ashes* on, 233
   McDonagh's Leenane Trilogy on, 235
   McGahern's work on, 233, 234
   Murphy's *The Sanctuary Lamp* on, 203
   O'Brien's work exploring, 299
Catholic Church abuse scandals, 5, 222, 228, 229, 237, 239, 279, 280, 281, 282, 283, 287, 288–9, 339
   Abbey Theatre response to, 281
   Industrial Memories project on, 283–4, 285, 286
   MacLaverty's novel *Lamb* on, 231
   Magdalen Laundries and, 5, 87, 237, 238, 283, 295, 301, 383
   McCabe's *The Butcher Boy* on, 235
   Mother and Baby Homes and, 5, 161, 295, 383
   Taoiseach Ahern's apology for, 278, 279, 281
Cavafy, C. P., 314
Cead Aighnis (Ní Dhomhnaill), 28, 311
'Céad Siolla Dheirdre' (Ní Ghríofa), 30
'Ceann Dubh Dílis' (Ó Searcaigh), 29, 33
Cei Cinci din Conamara (Ó Conghaile), 314
Celan, Paul, 311
celibacy, clerical, as theme, 32, 33, 313
Celibates (Standún), 313
Celtic Tiger, 1, 8, 9, 44, 58, 84, 96, 105, 129, 168, 174, 176, 217, 222, 247, 257, 263, 329, 394
Celtic Tiger, The: Ireland's Continuing Economic Miracle (Sweeney), 158
Celtic Woman, 10
censorship, 213, 346, 348
'Cessation 1994' (Heaney), 275
Chaila, Denise, 183, 194
Chair of Poetry, 381–2
Chanáil, An (Fitzpatrick), 104
Chekhov, Anton, 81, 205
Chekhov's First Play (Dead Centre), 90
'Cherishing the Irish Diaspora' (Robinson), 173
Cherry Orchard, The (Chekhov), 205
chick lit, 11, 251, 258
Chieftain's Daughter, The (McBratney), 100
child abuse, 32, 105, 281
   Bolger's novel *The Journey Home* on, 233
   Catholic Church scandals and. *See* Catholic Church abuse scandals
   Doyle's memoir *The God Squad* on, 232
   Fahey's memoir on, 232
   Flynn's memoir *Nothing to Say* on, 232
   Goldenbridge Industrial School and, 232, 279, 288, 289
   Healy's memoir *The Bend for Home* on, 233
   Industrial Schools and, 5, 161, 232, 278, 279, 280, 295
   Magdalen Laundries and, 5, 87, 237, 238, 283, 295, 301, 383
   Mother and Baby Homes and, 5, 161, 295, 383
childhood, 96, 97, 106
   Bildungsroman (coming-of-age novel) and, 219
   Donoghue's novels on, 296
   Doyle's *The God Squad* memoir of, 232
   Gregg's play *Perv* on sexual abuse in, 87–90
   McCourt's memoir *Angela's Ashes* as, 233, 362
Children of the Famine trilogy (Conlon-McKenna), 100
Children of the Poor Clares (Arnold and Laskey), 279
Children's Books in Ireland (magazine), 99

Children's Books Ireland awards, 97, 107
'Children's Children' (Carson), 143
Children's Laureate (Laureate na nÓg), 96
children's literature, 96–108, 318
Children's Literature Association of Ireland, 99
Children's Press, 98
Children's Referendum, 96
Chinese language, Irish translations from, 319
Chomhairle Ealaíon, An. *See* Arts Council of Ireland
Christian Brothers, 231, 283, 286
'Chugat' (Davitt), 35
'Church and Its Spire, The' (McGahern), 234
Cia Ludens company, 282
CICA (Commission of Investigation to Inquire into Child Abuse), 280. *See also* Ryan Report (2009)
cinema, 211, 344–57. *See also* documentary films; and specific films
  Irish Film Board establishment and, 348, 349
Cíocras (Standún), 33, 313
Cion Mná (Standún), 33, 313
Circling the Triangle (Cruikshank), 106
citizenship, 138, 195
Citizenship Referendum (2004), 14, 186, 188
civil partnerships, Northern Ireland, 6
civil rights movement, United States, 368
Clancy, Andrew, 92
Clancy, Tom, 361
Clark, Fiona, 356
class, 183, 185, 213. *See also* middle class; working-class communities
  McGahern's *Amongst Women* on, 233
  Murphy's plays investigating, 206
  Scott's novels on Traveller community and, 105
Cleary, Joe, 11, 68, 170, 211–26
Cléireach, An (Ó Scolaí), 31
Clifton, Harry, 381, 382
Cló Iar-Chonnacht (publishing house), 12, 37, 310, 312, 313, 315, 317, 320, 384
Cló Mhaigh Eo (publishing house), 37, 103, 104
Clóchomhar, An (publishing house), 37
ClubLeabhar.com (online book club), 320
Cnuas (annual stipend), 38, 375–6, 383
Coen, Lisa, 392, 394, 398
Cogaí (Ó Muirí), 34
Cohen, Leonard, 38
Cois Life (publishing house), 36, 37, 313, 320, 384
Coiscéim (publishing house), 37, 312, 318, 319
CoisCéim Dance Theatre, 163
Colfer, Eoin, 103
'Colleen Rue, The' (aisling), 73
Collins, Bob, 381

Colm Bán, An (Ó Muirthile), 35
Colm Ó Briain, 377
colonialism
  colonial charity model in advocacy and, 183
  Friel's play *Translations* on, 3, 67, 202
  Hart's poem 'Badagry' on, 192
  Irish poetry and legacies of, 47
  Jakpa's poem 'Harmattan' and, 191
  Muldoon's poem with Native American themes and, 75
'Colony' (Boland), 113
colour, writers of. *See* migrant writers of colour; writers of colour
Colours of Man, The (Ó Conghaile), 314
Colum, Padraic, 98
'Come to the Bower' (Heaney), 117
Comerford, Joe, 348, 349
Comhar (journal), 37, 38, 384
coming-of-age novel. *See* Bildungsroman
coming-out stories, 222, 314
Commission of Investigation to Inquire into Child Abuse (CICA), 280. *See also* Ryan Report (2009)
Commitments, The (Doyle), 216, 360, 368
community arts, and migrant communities, 196
Conaire Mór (Johnson), 29
Conlon, Evelyn, 397
  My Head Is Opening, 173
  Not the Same Sky, 177
  'Transition', 173
Conlon-McKenna, Marita
  Children of the Famine trilogy, 100
  No Goodbye, 105
Connemara, 9, 29, 37, 129, 130, 313
Connemara Five, The (Ó Conghaile), 314
Constellations (Gleeson), 13
'Contemporary Uses for a Belfast Box Room' (Carson), 143
contraception
  Catholic Church's view on the use of, 230
  legalisation of, 6, 228
Conversations on a Homecoming (Murphy), 206
Cooper, Melinda, 256
Corcadorca, 90
Cork Film Festival, 356
Corkery, Daniel, 122, 213
  Synge and Anglo-Irish Literature, 213
  Threshold of Quiet, 213
Cosgrove, Aedín, 92
Costello, Mary, 217
Coughlan, Claire, 257
Council of Europe, 316
Counter-Revivalist realism, 223
Country Girls trilogy, *The* (O'Brien), 170, 214, 220, 295

Country Girls, The (O'Brien), 96, 170, 214, 220, 296
Cowboys and Indians (O'Connor), 171
Cowen, Brian, 282
Cranberries, 360
Crane Bag, The (journal), 334
Crann faoi Bhláth, An/The Flowering Tree (Kiberd), 309, 310
Cré na Cille (Ó Cadhain), 307, 310, 315–18
Create, the National Development Agency for Collaborative Arts, 197
Creative Ireland, 378, 387
creative writing programmes, 394, 396
crime fiction, 11, 250, 257, 258. *See also* police procedural
Cripple of Inishmaan, The (McDonagh), 172
Criss-Cross Mo Chara (Mac Lochlainn), 309
Cronin, Anthony, 377, 382
Cronin, Michael, 311, 312, 315, 319
Crossan, Sarah, 106
Crouch, Tim, 153
Cruikshank, Margrit, 106
Crying Game, The (Jordan), 4, 362–3
Cuaifeach mo Londubh Buí (Mac Annaidh), 34
Cúigear Chonamara (Ó Conghaile), 314
Cullinan, Elizabeth, 177
Culture and Anarchy in Ireland, 1890–1930 (Lyons), 330
Culture Ireland, 11
Cumann na bhFoilsitheoirí, 37
cummings, e.e., 35, 36
Curlew Editions, 384
Czech language, translations into, 317, 318

D'Souza, Dinesh, 364
Dahl, Roald, 318
Daisy Chain War series (O'Neill), 100
Dalkey Archive Press, 317
Daly, Rebecca, 357
dance, 82, 362, 365, 366, 367
dance festivals, 282, 379
Dancers Dancing, The (Ní Dhuibhne), 106
Dancing at Lughnasa (Friel), 82–3, 202, 203, 205, 360
Danish language, translations into, 316, 318
Dark, The (McGahern), 96, 170, 214, 220
Darkest Corner series, Abbey Theatre, 281
Date for Mad Mary, A (Thornton), 355
Davie, Donald, 369
Davies, Howard, 163
Davis-Goff, Sarah, 392, 394, 395, 398
Davitt, Michael, 31
 'Chugat', 35
 'Deora do Mheiriceá', 35
 'Paranóia', 35

Selected Poems, Rogha Dánta, 309
Dawe, Gerald, 386
Dawson, Graham, 140
Dawson, Juno, 106
Dawson, Robert, 347
Days Without End (Barry), 223
de Fréine, Celia, 39, 309
de Man, Paul, 364
de Paor, Louis, 32, 36, 310, 312, 317
 'Disappearing Language', 312
 'Galway Kinnell sa Ghaillimh', 36
 Leabhar na hAthghabhála, Poems of Repossession, 312
de Paor, Máire, 377
de Paor, Pádraig, 36
de Valera, Eamon, 96, 154, 230
De Valera's Ireland, 221, 230, 274
de Waal, Kit, 175
'Dead, The' (Joyce), 347
Dead Bodies (Quinn), 352
Dead Centre, 90
Deane, Seamus, 73, 331, 334
 Reading in the Dark, 13, 65, 68, 221–2
 'The Artist in Ireland' (Deane), 379
Dear Daughter (television documentary), 279
'Death of a Field' (Meehan), 131–2
Death of a Naturalist (Heaney), 111, 370
Decade of Centenaries, 12, 152, 339
Dedalus Press, 197, 386
Deep (Scannell), 90
Deevy, Teresa, 93
Deirdre and Naoise legend, 30
'Deora do Mheiriceá' (Davitt), 35
Deportees, The (Doyle), 14, 185
DeptCon, 106
Derrida, Jacques, 364
Derry, 4, 68
 Bloody Sunday (1972) in, 68, 203, 370
 film festival in, 356
 journalist McKee's murder (2019) during riots in, 5
Derry Girls (television series), 4
Desmond, Barry, 236
Desmond, Gerald Fitzgerald, 3rd Earl of, 31
detective fiction, 11, 223, 251. *See also* crime fiction; police procedural
Devaney, Patrick, 105
Devil I Know, The (Kilroy), 9
Devil's Own, The (film), 361
Devlin, Anne, 73
 Ourselves Alone, 65, 70–1
Diabhlaíocht Dé (Ó Conghaile), 34
Dialann Bóthair (Ó Muirthile), 310

Diary of a Wimpy Kid, The (Kinny), 318
diaspora, 168, 169–74, 175, 176, 340
Díbirt Dé (Standún), 33
Dick, Vivienne, 348, 356
Dickinson, Emily, 274
'Digging' (Heaney), 116, 191, 192, 370
digital humanities, 6, 16, 285, 288
 Industrial Memories project and, 283
digital media, 84, 86, 383
 Echoes from the Past (digital walking tour), 288–9
 podcasts and, 384, 385, 396
Dillon, Eilís, 98
Dimbo, Ifedinma, 183, 187, 192
 She Was Foolish?, 187
dinnseanchas tradition, 9, 58
Direct Provision system, 14, 189, 190
 Okorie's 'This Hostel Life' set in, 189–90
Dirty Dust, The (Ó Cadhain), 315
disability studies, 339
'Disappearing Island, The' (Heaney), 116
'Disappearing Language' (de Paor), 312
distant reading, 285
District and Circle (Heaney), 178, 370
diversity
 access to resources and respect for difference in, 188
 increase since mid-1990s in, 13
 Irish novels addressing, 104
 picture books on, 105
 Poetry Ireland's strategy on, 197
 racialisation during Celtic Tiger period amidst increase in, 105
 slam poetry's emphasis on, 194
 Tramp Press and, 395
 white perspective and models of, 187
divorce
 amendment (1995) allowing, 6, 295
 legislation (1925) forbidding, 346
 public acceptance of Catholic views on, 230
 referendum (1986) securing prohibition of, 229, 337
 youth literature addressing, 105
Dochtúir Áthais, An (Mac Cóil), 34
documentary films, 87, 175, 279, 281. *See also specific films*
documentary theatre, 87
documentary-based literary narrative, *Echoes from the Past* app as, 289
'Domestic Interior' (Boland), 113
Domestic Violence (Boland), 112, 123
'Dónall Óg' (song), 29
Donlon, Paula, 235
Donoghue, Emma, 7, 10, 347

'Going Back', 171
 Hood, 171
Doolan, Lelia, 350, 356
Doona, Annie, 356
Dorcey, Mary, 7
Dougherty, Jane Elizabeth, 106
Douglass, Frederick, 176
Dowd, Siobhán, 106
Doyle, Malachy, 99
Doyle, Martin, 396
Doyle, Paddy, 232, 279
Doyle, Rob, 395
Doyle, Roddy, 97, 182, 187, 216
 'I Understand', 185
 Barrytown trilogy, 216–17
 Paddy Clarke Ha Ha Ha, 398
 Playboy of the Western World adaptation by, 187
 The Commitments, 216, 360, 368
 The Deportees, 14, 185
 The Snapper, 216, 234, 313
 The Van, 216
Dréachta Chrích Fódla (Ó Cíobháin), 30
Drennan, Mary, 279
'Dresden' (Carson), 70
'Drifting Off' (Heaney), 116
Driscoll, Beth, 250
Drucker, Johanna, 284
drug addiction, as theme, 32, 33, 158
drug dealing, as theme, 32, 86, 255, 354
Druid Theatre, Galway, 205
dual-language publishing, 307–12
Duanaire 1600–1900, An: Poems of the Dispossessed (Tuama and Kinsella), 308
Dublin, 37, 38, 59, 104, 123, 163, 194, 354, 377, 384
Dublin Archdiocese, child abuse in, 161, 229
Dublin Film Festival, 356
Dublin Fringe Festival, 12, 194
Dublin Review of Books, 12
Dublin Review, The, 12, 384, 394
Dublin Theatre Festival, 12, 163, 282, 377
Dublin trilogy (O'Casey), 152, 159, 217
Dubliners (Joyce), 213
Dubliners 100 (Morris), 397
Duck and Swan (Quinn), 105
'Duel Citizenship' (Chaila), 194
Dún na mBan Trí Thine (Ní Dhuibhne), 29
Dunbar, Robert, 108
Duraković, Ferida, 311
Durcan, Paul, 381
 'Making Love outside Áras an Uachtaráin', 230
 'Three European Poets', 382
Dutch language, translations into, 317, 318
Dylan, Bob, 35, 38

Eagleton, Terry, 335
early Irish literature, retellings and adaptations of, 29–30
Eason bookstore, 106
Easter Rising (1916), 5, 152–3, 154, 155, 339
  O'Casey's play *The Plough* on, 152
'Ebenezer's Memories' (O'Donnell), 143
ebooks, 250, 320, 383
Echoes from the Past (digital walking tour), 288–9
'Echtrae Chondlai' (Mac Aodha), 30
Eclipsed (Burke Brogan), 237, 283
economic crisis (2008), 2, 8, 121, 125, 159, 174, 193, 238, 247, 354. *See also* recession
Eden (O'Brien), 353
Edgeworth, Maria, 98, 328, 336
Éditions Gallimard, 397
EFACIS (European Federation of Associations and Centres for Irish Studies), 340
Ehin, Kristiina, 319
Eighth Amendment
  abortion banned under, 6, 235, 337
  referendum to repeal, 6, 193, 229, 230, 239
Éire-Ireland (journal), 329
Ejorh, Theophilus, 196
Electric Light (Heaney), 130–1
'Elegy for an Irish Speaker' (McGuckian), 52
Element Pictures, 353, 354, 355
Eliot, George, 214
Elizabeth I, Queen of England, 32
Elizabeth II, Queen of England, 152
Elle, Farah, 197
Elliot, Marianne, 329
Ellmann, Richard, 328
El-Tayeb, Fatima, 183
'Eliza' (Heaney), 116
Embers (Beckett), 92–3
Embers of Words (Ejorh), 196
'Emigrant Irish, The' (Boland), 173
emigration, 1, 15, 168, 169, 170, 172, 174, 175, 176, 178, 206
Empson, William, 51
End of Irish History?, The (Coulter and Coleman), 158
End or The Beginning of Love, The (McGahern), 170
Ennis Book Club Festival, 384
Enright, Anne, 174, 175, 217, 226, 252, 258, 382, 385, 386, 396
  cliché in novels of, 248, 249, 252–4
  The Forgotten Waltz, 9, 246–7, 248, 249, 250, 251, 258
  The Gathering, 5, 175, 295, 398
  The Green Road, 179, 217–18
  The Pleasure of Eliza Lynch, 178, 223
  The Wig My Father Wore, 175
  What Are You Like?, 175
environmental humanities, 339
Enyi-Amadi, Chiamaka, 183, 195, 196, 197
epics, 28, 29, 30
Estonian language, Irish translations from, 319
ethnic communities, 13, 14, 183, 188, 190, 193, 194, 197, 363
ethnographic realism, 212
étranger, L' (Camus), 319
Eureka Street (McLiam Wilson), 66, 76–77
European Federation of Associations and Centres for Irish Studies (EFACIS), 340
Eurovision Song Contest, 2, 365
Evans, Estyn, 328
'Eveline' (Joyce), 30
Evidence I Shall Give, The (Johnson), 282
excellence argument, about women's writing, 386
experimental modes, 28, 33–5, 183

Faber and Faber, 396, 397
Fadem, Maureen E. Ruprecht, 139
Fahey, Bernadette, 232
fairy tales, feminist retellings of, 107
Faith Healer (Friel), 204
Falci, Eric, 1–18, 111–18
Fallon, Brian, 395
family novel, 214, 216, 217, 219
Famine (Great Hunger, 1845–1849)
  Atkinson's *Not the Same Sky* on, 177
  Boland's *In a Time of Violence* on, 114
  children's literature on, 101
  Conlon-McKenna's *Children of the Famine* trilogy on, 100
  emigration and, 125, 177
  Friel's *Translations* on, 201, 202
  Murphy's *Famine* on, 201
  stories of emigration and, 168
  trauma and memory studies related to studies of, 339
  Urquhart's *Away* on, 177
Famine (Murphy), 201, 202
Famous Five, The (Blyton), 318
Fanning, Charles, 176
Fanon, Frantz, 183
fantasy fiction, 100
Farcry Productions, 282
Farrar, Straus and Giroux (publishing house), 370
Farrell, James T., 177
Farthest, The (Reynolds), 357
Fat Lad (Patterson), 66, 76

Fatima Mansions, Dublin, Walsh on demolition of, 59
Fear a Phléasc, An (Ó Conghaile), 34, 314
Fear an Tae (Ó Muirthile), 32
Fear Dána, An (Titley), 31
Fear Nach nDéanann Gáire, An (Ó Conghaile), 34, 314
Feasta (journal), 37
Feis (Ní Dhomhnaill), 28, 311
Felicia's Journey (Trevor), 173
FeliSpeaks, 194, 195–6
female genital mutilation (FGM), 195
feminism, 7, 13, 32, 101, 107, 195, 214, 229, 333
  feminist activism, 7, 13, 107, 196
  feminist criticism, 7, 300, 333–4
  feminist writers, 7, 113, 115, 195, 247, 300, 311, 315, 334
Fennell, Jack, 397
Ferns Report (2005), 6, 161, 229
Ferriter, Diarmaid, 13, 228–41
Fianna cycle, 31
Field Day, 3, 66, 331, 334–8
Field Day Anthology of Irish Writing, The, 7, 310, 334, 336
  Volumes Four and Five, *Irish Women's Writing and Traditions*, 7, 338
Field Day Theatre Company, 66, 205, 334
Field Work (Heaney), 370
fifth province, 3, 66, 335
Fifty Minute Mermaid, The (Ní Dhomhnaill), 311
Fighting Words (organisation), 396
Film Board, 348, 349, 350, 354, 356
film festivals, 356, 357, 378
film production, 345, 346, 348, 351
films, 4, 86, 351, 352, 355, 368. *See* cinema; documentary films; *and specific films*
Finnegans Wake (Joyce), 90
FIRED! Irish Women Poets and the Canon initiative, 387
First Verse, The (McCrea), 222
Fish Anthology series, 384
FitzGerald, Garret, 236
Fitzgerald, Gerald, 3rd Earl of Desmond, 31
Fitzpatrick, Marie-Louise, 102, 104
'Flags and Emblems' (Wheatley), 139
Flaherty, Robert, 172
Flanagan, Victoria, 104
Flatley, Michael, 360, 361, 365–7
Flight (Frawley), 14, 185–7, 397
Flight of the Earls (1607), 31
Floats Like a Butterfly (Winters), 357
Flower Master, The (McGuckian), 72
Flynn, Gerard Mannix
  James X, 282
  Nothing to Say, 232, 279
Flynn, Leontia, 122, 129
  'Belfast', 127–8, 137
  McGuckian's poems and, 51–2
Foley's Asia (Sheehan), 223
folk tradition, 29, 311, 368
folklore, 28–9, 50, 103
Fontenoy (Mac Cóil), 31
Foott, Peter, 355
'For Our Mothers' (Olusanya), 196
Foras na Gaeilge, 38
Ford, John, 347, 368
Forgotten (Kinevane), 90
Forgotten Waltz, The (Enright), 9, 246–7, 248, 249, 250, 251, 258
formalism, and Irish poetry, 44, 46, 56
Forsyte Saga, The (Galsworthy), 214
Foster, Aisling, 338
Foster, Roy, 237, 329, 331
Fouéré, Olwen, 90
Fowley-Doyle, Moira, 106
Fox series (McCaughrean), 100
Francis, Pope, 229
Frankfurt Book Fair, 99
Frawley, Oona, 14, 182, 187, 397
  Flight, 185–7
Freedom of the City, The (Friel), 203
French language, 35, 318
French, Tana, 249
  Broken Harbor, 248, 249, 250, 251, 254–7
Freund, Gisèle, 364
Fried Plantain Collective, 194
Friel, Brian, 67, 201–6, 371, 395
  Aristocrats, 202, 205
  Dancing at Lughnasa, 82–3, 202, 203, 205, 360
  Faith Healer, 204
  Field Day Theatre Company and, 205
  Give Me Your Answer, Do!, 203, 205
  Making History, 205
  Molly Sweeney, 205
  Performances, 205
  Philadelphia, Here I Come!, 202, 206
  The Freedom of the City, 203
  The Gentle Island, 203
  The Home Place, 205
  The Mundy Scheme, 203
  'Theatre of Hope and Despair', 203
  Translations, 3, 65, 201–2, 334
  Wonderful Tennessee, 203
Friel, Maeve, 102
'From the Canton of Expectation' (Heaney), 116
'From the Frontier of Writing' (Heaney), 116
'From the Land of the Unspoken' (Heaney), 116
'From the Republic of Conscience' (Heaney), 116
Frost, Robert, 369

Fuíoll Feá, An – Rogha Dánta/Wood Cuttings – New and Selected Poems (Ó Muirthile), 310
Fulton, John, 236
Futa Fata (publishing house), 103
Future of England Study, 139

Gaelchultúr, 320
Gaiety Theatre, Dublin, 161, 162, 163
Gallery Press, 12, 309, 386
Galsworthy, John, 214
Galway Film Fleadh, 356
'Galway Kinnell sa Ghaillimh' (de Paor), 36
Galway literary festival, 384
García Marquez, Gabriel, 214
Gargantua (Rabelais), 319
Garvin, Tom, 228, 236
Gate Theatre, Dublin, 153, 163, 377
Gathering, The (Enright), 5, 175, 295, 398
'Gathering Mushrooms' (Muldoon), 73
'Gathering Thoughts' (Okorie), 188
gay community. *See also* homosexuality; lesbian community; LGBTQ+ community; queer community
  Boyne's novel *The Heart's Invisible Furies* set in, 240–1
  coming-out narratives in, 222, 314
  Conghaile's novel set in, 33
  election of first openly gay Taoiseach from, 2
  Enright's novel about relationships in, 218
  first Irish youth novel set in, 105
  Friel's play set in, 203
  marriage equality referendum campaign with individual stories from, 240
gay marriage. *See* same-sex marriage
gay writer. *See also* LGBTQ+ writers
Gearrscéalta ár Linne (Ó Conchubhair), 34
gender, 30, 155, 339, 385, 386
  gender equity, 6, 153, 398
  gender roles, 187, 355–7
Generation (McGrath), 179
genre fiction
  growing importance and visibility of, 11
  publishing and growth of, 250
  women writers and market for, 257–8
genre films, 351–2
Gentle Island, The (Friel), 203
George, Terry, 4
Geraghty, Elaine, 356
German language, translations into, 317, 319
German theatre, 163
Ghost Estate (Wall), 121
'Ghost Estate' (Wall), 125
ghost estates, 125
'Ghost Estates' (Woods), 125

Ghost-Haunted Land (Long), 140
Gibbons, Luke, 339
Gigli Concert, The (Murphy), 204, 205
Gill, Liz, 357
Gillis, Alan
  'Progress', 137, 140
Giltspur trilogy (MacRaois), 100
Ginsberg, Allen, 369
Girbés, J. C., 318
Girl is a Half-Formed Thing, A (McBride), 90, 106, 222, 295, 299
Girls in Their Married Bliss (O'Brien), 214
Give Me Your Answer, Do! (Friel), 203, 205
'Gleann Maoiliúra' (Jenkinson), 32
Gleeson, Sinéad, 13
Glover, Ann ('Goody'), 31
God Squad, The (Doyle), 232, 279
'Going Back' (Donoghue), 171
Gold in the Streets (Gill), 357
Golden Notebook, The (Lessing), 297
Goldenbridge Girls' Industrial School, Dublin, 232, 279, 288, 289
Goldfish Memory (Gill), 357
Goldsmith Press, 309
'Gone' (Heaney), 116
Good Favour (Daly), 357
Good Friday Agreement (1998), 1, 2, 4, 136, 158, 329, 338. *See also* Belfast Agreement
Good Soldier Švejk and His Fortunes in the World War, The (Hašek), 318
Gordon, Mary, 177
gorse (journal), 12, 384
'Gort na gCnámh' (Ó Searcaigh), 33
Gothic fiction, 28, 100, 146, 211, 220, 397
Gough, Julian, 178, 247
graphic novels, 37, 104
'Grauballe Man, The' (Heaney), 370
Graveyard Clay (Mac Con Iomaire and Robinson), 315, 316
Great Hunger (Great Famine). *See* Famine
Greek mythology, 30, 173
Green Road, The (Enright), 179, 217–18
Gregg, Stacey
  Perve, 87–90
  Shibboleth, 147
  'Your Ma's a Hard Brexit', 147
Gregory, August, Lady, 30, 93, 368
Grehan, Meg, 105
Griffin, Sarah Maria, 106
Groarke, Vona
  'House-bound', 123, 124
  Other People's Houses, 123–4
Grossberg, Lawrence, 368, 369, 371
Grove Press, 362, 397
Guantánamo (Falkoff), 319

Guardian, The, 9, 158, 338
 'Brexit Shorts', 147
Guildhall, Derry/Londonderry, 3, 65, 66, 334
Guiney, Ed, 355
Gúm, An, 103, 307, 315
Guthanna Binne Síoraí, 32
Guy Domville (James), 225

Haefs, Gabriel, 317
Hage, Ghassan, 182, 191
haiku form, 35, 128
'Hailstones' (Heaney), 116
Haley, Alex, 214
Hamilton, Hugo, 13
Hamlet (Shakespeare), 50, 91
'Hamlet' (Carson), 50
Hamnet (Moukarzel and Kidd), 90–2
Hanging Gardens, The (McGuinness), 81
Hanna, Adam, 9, 72, 121–33
Harding, Lisa, 396
Harkin, Margo, 348, 356
Harlequin imprint, 250, 258
'Harmattan' (Jakpa), 191–2
Harris, Michael, 269
Harry Potter (Rowling), 318
Hart, Dagogo, 183, 192
Harte, Liam, 175
Hartman, Geoffrey, 364
Hartnett, Michael, 39, 382
Harvesting (Harding), 396
Hašek, Jaroslav, 318
Haughey, Charles, 375, 377, 394
Haughey/Gregory (Murphy), 394
Haughton, Chris, 103
Havel, Vaclav, 275
Haw Lantern, The (Heaney), 115–18
Haynes, John, 364
Healy, Dermot, 232
Heaney, Seamus, 226, 377
 'Alerted', 117
 'At a Potato Digging', 116
 'At Ardboe Point', 116
 'At Toomebridge', 111
 'Away From It All', 116
 'Blackberry-Picking', 116
 Boland's work focusing on the past contrasted with, 111–18
 'Casualty', 370, 371
 'Cessation 1994', 275
 'Come to the Bower', 117
 Death of a Naturalist, 111, 370
 'Digging', 116, 191, 192, 370
 District and Circle, 178, 370
 'Drifting Off', 116
 Electric Light, 130–1
 'Eliza', 116
 Field Work, 370
 'From the Canton of Expectation', 116
 'From the Frontier of Writing', 116
 'From the Land of the Unspoken', 116
 'From the Republic of Conscience', 116
 global recognition of Irish literature and, 9
 'Gone', 116
 'Hailstones', 116
 hope of recovery and, 264, 275–6
 impact of property development and, 121, 130–1
 'In Gallarus Oratory', 116
 'In Small Townlands', 116
 'In the Beech', 116
 'In the Chestnut Tree', 116
 literary stardom of, 363, 368–72
 'Mycenae Lookout', 111
 Nobel Prize for Literature for, 9, 363, 369, 370, 381, 395
 North, 67, 177, 369, 370
 'On the Road', 116
 Opened Ground, Selected Poems 1966–1996, 370
 'Parable Island', 116
 proposed biography of, 396
 'Punishment', 67, 370
 reaction to IRA's cessation of military operations by, 263–4
 'Remembering Malibu', 116
 'Requiem for the Croppies', 111
 Seeing Things, 115
 Selected Poems 1966–1987, 370
 Station Island, 111, 115
 'Station Island', 113
 Stepping Stones, 131
 Sweeney Astray, 111
 'The Disappearing Island', 116
 'The Grauballe Man', 370
 The Haw Lantern, 115–18
 'The Irish Poet and Britain', 178
 'The Mud Vision', 116, 117
 'The Spoonbait', 117
 translations of, 319
 'Twice Shy', 116
 'Unwinding', 116
 'Westering', 116
 'Whatever You Say Say Nothing', 117
 Wintering Out, 177, 369
Heart's Invisible Furies, The (Boyne), 240–1
Heather Blazing, The (Tóibín), 234
Heidemann, Birte, 139
Henn, T.R., 328

Hennessy, Claire, 107
  Like Other Girls, 105
Hennessy Literary Awards, 314, 396
Here Was Cuba (Reynolds), 357
Hergé, 318
Herrin, Jeremy, 163
Heussaff, Anna, 39
Hickman, Mary, 333
Higgin, Aidan
  Balcony of Europe, 223
  Langrishe, Go Down, 212
Higgins, F. E., 100
Hijmans, Alex, 39, 317
Hill, John, 349, 352
hip-hop, 194
Hiring Fair, The, trilogy (O'Hara), 101
Hirsch, Edward, 28
Hirsch, Marianne, 289
historical fiction, 7, 13, 14, 30, 129, 212, 223, 248
  children's literature and, 99, 100–2
  examples of, 30–1, 177, 179
  historical sources and, 30–1
Hitchcock, Alfred, 347
Hobbit, The (Tolkien), 318
Hoffman, Tyler, 194
Hogarth Press, 397
Holmes, Sean, 155, 161, 162, 163
Home Place, The (Friel), 205
homelessness, 105, 158, 163
Homer, 319
homoerotic poetry, 29, 33, 314
homosexuality. *See also entries beginning with* gay, lesbian, LGBTQ+, *or* queer
  as previously taboo subject, 32
  contemporary Irish novel's exploration of, 32
  decriminalisation of, Northern Ireland (1982), 6
  decriminalisation of, Republic of Ireland (1993), 6, 33, 105, 295
  novels for teenagers representing, 105
  Ó Conghaile's exploration of, 314
  Searcaigh's poetry celebrating, 313
  significant changes in cultural attitudes towards, 105
Honest Ulsterman (periodical), 12
Hood (Donoghue), 171
Hood, Kim, 107
Horgan, Joe, 175
Horrid Henry (Simon), 318
Hounds of the Morrigan, The (O'Shea), 100
House, The (Murphy), 202, 205
House of Splendid Isolation (O'Brien), 269
'House-bound' (Groarke), 123, 124
How the Irish Saved Civilization (Cahill), 360
Howard, Aideen, 281

Howie the Rookie (O'Rowe), 90
Hudson Letter, The (Mahon), 178
Hughes, Declan, 201, 202
Hughes, Langston, 36
Humphreys, Grainne, 356
Hunger (McQueen), 4
hunger strike (1981), 4, 65, 73, 396
'Hurry Up Hot-Foot' (Adams), 74
Hurst, Bryan Desmond, 347
Huston, John, 347
Hynes, Garry, 155, 156, 157, 158, 159, 162, 164

I dTír Mhilis na mBeo (Ó Ceallacháin), 34
I dTír Strainséartha (Mac Cóil), 31
I Went Down (Breathnach), 351
I, Malvolio (Crouch), 153
I, Peaseblossom (Crouch), 153
'I Understand' (Doyle), 185
'I Will Not Be Shamed' (Enyi-Amadi), 195
Ideal Husband, An (Wilde), 225
Illiberal Education (D'Souza), 364
Imleabhair Thaighde series, 37
immersive theatre, 81, 86, 90, 163, 165
Immigrant Council of Ireland, 196
Imram (literary festival), 38, 384
In a Time of Violence (Boland), 114
'In Belfast' (Morrissey), 137
In Bruges (McDonagh), 172
'In Gallarus Oratory' (Heaney), 116
'In Our Own Country' (Boland), 112
'In Small Townlands' (Heaney), 116
'In the Beech' (Heaney), 116
'In the Chestnut Tree' (Heaney), 116
In the Forest (O'Brien), 222
In the Name of the Father (Sheridan), 362
in vitro fertilisation (IVF), 32, 230
incest, 32, 33
Industrial Memories project, 283–4, 285, 286, 288
Industrial Schools, 5, 161, 278, 279, 280, 295
  Doyle's memoir *The God Squad* on, 232
  Flynn's memoir *Nothing to Say* on, 232
  Healy's memoir *The Bend for Home* on, 233
Informer, The (O'Flaherty), 347
Inglis, Tom, 395
Inis, The: Children's Books Ireland Magazine, 99
Innes, C.L., 71
Innti (journal), 27, 35
Innti poets, 11, 35, 36
'Inscriptions' (Boland), 114
Institute of Irish Studies, Queen's University Belfast, 328
interculturalism, 184–7
Internal Exiles (Bolger), 170
International, The (Patterson), 140

Inventing Ireland (Kiberd), 330
Iqbal, Muhammad, 319
IRA, 65, 66, 67, 217, 335
　Heaney's reaction to cessation of military operations by, 263–4
Ireland: A Cultural and Social History (Brown), 330
'Ireland and its Elsewheres' (Clifton), 382
Ireland Chair of Poetry, 381–2
Ireland in Exile,(Bolger), 170, 171
'Ireland Inspires' (video), 152
Irish American Cultural Institute, 329
'Irish Childhood in England, 1951, An' (Boland), 173
Irish Film Archive, 356
Irish Film Board, 348, 349, 350, 354, 356
Irish Film Institute, 356
Irish for No, The (Carson), 49, 65, 69, 70
Irish Independent, 156, 257, 375
Irish Journal of Sociology, The, 333
Irish Language Book of the Year Award, 38
Irish Legends for the Very Young (Sharkey), 99
Irish music. *See* traditional Irish music
'Irish Poet and Britain, The' (Heaney), 178
Irish Research Council, 283
Irish Review, 331
Irish Society for the Study of Children's Literature, 99
Irish Studies, 15, 320, 327–41
　American universities with programmes in, 328, 330
　British universities with programmes in, 328, 329, 330, 340
　Field Day and, 334–8
　international institutions and, 328, 339, 340
　Irish feminist criticism and, 333
Irish Times, The, 12, 152, 153, 158, 160, 247, 375, 382, 386, 392–3, 395
　analysis of hunger strike (1981) by, 396
　Book Club of, 396
　commitment to publishing and promoting contemporary Irish literature by, 395, 396, 398
　digital age and, 392, 393
　reviews in, 35, 396
　website of, 393
Irish Voice in America, The (Fanning's), 176
Irish Women's Writing and Traditions (*The Field Day Anthology of Irish Writing*, Volumes Four and Five), 7, 338
Irish Writer and the World, The (Kiberd), 364
Irish Writers' Centre, 384
Irish-American identities, and *Riverdance*, 368

Irish-American performers, in *Riverdance*, 360, 362, 365
Irish-American writing, 176, 177
Irish-language literature, 11, 27–39, 193, 313–14, 315, 328, 370, 375–88, 392, 398
'Irishman's Diary, An' column, *The Irish Times*, 394
Iron Age, The (Kajermo), 397

Jackson, Michael, 365
Jakpa, Oritsegbemi Emmanuel, 14, 183
　'Harmattan', 191–2
James X (Flynn), 282
James, Henry, 224–6
Jameson, Fredric, 335
Japan, 178, 319
Jarvie, Ian, 346
Jeffares, Norman, 328
Jeffers, Oliver, 104
Jenkinson, Biddy, 32, 310
　'Beannaithe', 32
　'Gleann Maoiliúra', 32
　Táinrith, 29
John Paul II, Pope, 228–9
Johnson, Diarmuid
　Conaire Mór, 29
　Tuatha Dé Danann, 29, 38
Johnson, Richard, 282
Johnston, Jennifer, 7, 212
Jones, Marie, 15
Jordan, Neil
　Angel, 349
　Breakfast on Pluto, 268
　literary sources used by, 347
　The Crying Game, 4, 362–3
Jordan, Wayne, 162
journals, literary. *See* literary magazines and journals
Journey Home, The (Bolger), 170, 233
'Jovial Hullaboo, A' (Longley), 382
Joyce, James, 154, 168, 213, 219, 222, 226, 318, 328, 336, 347, 362, 364, 376
　'Eveline', 30
　'The Dead', 347
　A Portrait of the Artist as a Young Man, 96, 168, 213, 219, 299
　Dubliners, 213
　Finnegans Wake, 90
　Ulysses, 362
Joyce, Trevor, 45, 56
Judith trilogy (Scott), 105
Juno and the Paycock (O'Casey), 163, 347
Justice for the Undocumented (group), 196

Kajermo, Arja, 397
Kavanagh, Patrick, 213, 226, 369

Keane, Molly, 212
Kearney, Oonagh, 357
Kearney, Seán, 314
Keats, John, 369
Keefe, Joan, 316
Keegan, Claire, 217
Keenan, Celia, 101, 103
Kelleher, Margaret, 11, 247, 334, 375–88
Kelly, John, 329
Kelly, Maeve, 397
Kenner, Hugh, 328
Kennon, Patricia, 11, 96–108
Kenny, Enda, 301, 302
Kenny, Pat, 153
Kerry Babies, 87, 106, 173
Kerwick, Lavinia, 173
Kesici, Özgecan, 183
Key, The/An Eochair (Ó Cadhain), 317
Kiberd, Declan, 231, 266, 318, 346
  Inventing Ireland, 330
  The Irish Writer and the World, 364
Kidd, Ben, 90
Kidnapped (Stevenson), 318
Kilroy, Claire, 9
Kimball, Roger, 364
Kind of Compass, A (McKeon), 397
Kindle digital reading device, 383
Kinevane, Pat, 90
King, Jason, 182, 185
Kinnell, Galway, 36
  'Saint Francis and the Sow', 36
Kinney, Jeff, 318
Kinsella, Thomas, 308, 319
Kirkland, Richard, 139
Kirkus Review, 219
Kittredge, George Lyman, 364
Ko Un, 319
Krapp's Last Tape (Beckett), 85

La disparition (Perec), 34
Lady Chatterley's Lover (Lawrence), 362
'Lady Lazarus' (Plath), 53
Lady Na Master & the Synaptic Room (Olusanya), 195
Lake, The (Moore), 213
Lally the Scut (Spallen), 147
Lamb (MacLaverty), 231
Landy, Derek, 100
Lane, Tom, 288
Langlois, Christopher, 13, 263–76
Langrishe, Go Down (Higgin), 212
Lannigan, Liam, 187
Lanthimos, Yorgos, 355
'Laoi Chumainn' (Ó Searcaigh), 33

Larry (Richards and Dawson), 347
Laskey, Heather, 279
Last Night's Fun (Carson), 70
'Last of the Mohicans' O'Connor, 171
Last September, The (Bowen), 212
Laundry (ANU Productions), 87, 238, 282
Laureate for Irish Fiction, 382–3
Laureate na nÓg (Children's Laureate), 96
Lavin, Mary, 213
Lawrence, D. H., 362
Le bateau ivre (Rimbaud), 36
Leabhar Breac (publishing house), 29, 37, 312, 319
Leabhar na hAthghabhála: Poems of Repossession (de Paor), 312
Leavetaking, The (McGahern), 170
Leavy, Susan, 283, 287
Lefebvre, Henri, 126
Lehmann, Edyta, 30
Lehner, Stefanie, 4, 136–48
Lenihan, Brian, 169
Lennon, Tom, 105
Lentin, Louis, 279
Lentin, Ronit, 183
lesbian community, 33, 105, 222. *See also* gay community; homosexuality; LGBTQ+communities; queer community
Lesser Bohemians, The (McBride), 295, 299
Lessing, Doris, 297
Letterfrack Industrial School, Connemara, 232
Levine, Caroline, 254
Lewis, C. S., 318
LGBTQ+ communities, 7, 86. *See also* gay community; homosexuality; lesbian community; queer community
LGBTQ+ writers, 7, 193. *See also* gay writer; queer writer
Lie of the Land, The (O'Toole), 169
Light of Amsterdam, The (Park), 145
Light of Evening, The (O'Brien), 176
Light, Alison, 250
Lighthouse Cinema, 355
Like Other Girls (Hennessy), 105
Lilliput Press, 12, 384
Limerick, 356, 362
Limerick Literary Festival, 384
Lingard, Joan, 98
Lingo (spoken word festival), 194
Lion, the Witch and the Wardrobe, The (Lewis), 318
Lippy (Dead Centre), 90
literary festivals, 12, 38, 328, 378, 384
literary magazines and journals, 37, 213, 215, 392, 394. *See also specific titles*

Arts Council's funding of, 384, 385
children's literature in, 99
Irish Studies and, 329, 330, 333
postcolonial theory in, 339
writers of colour in, 193, 197
Literature and Culture in Northern Ireland since 1965 (Kirkland), 139
Literature Ireland (organisation), 315, 383, 384
Literature of Northern Ireland: Spectral Borderlands, The (Fadem), 140
Literature of the Irish in Britain, The (Harte), 175
Literature Policy and Strategy (Arts Council), 385
Litir, An (Mac Cóil), 31
Little Gem (Murphy), 90
Little Island (publishing house), 102, 384
Little Mermaid fairy tale, 107
Little Red Chairs, The (O'Brien), 264, 268–76
Little White Lie (Murphy and Stuart Carolan), 354
Liverpool, University of, Institute of Irish Studies, 329
Lloyd, David, 11, 44–61, 67, 331
Lobster, The (Lanthimos), 355
Logue, Antonia, 13
London, 65, 170, 175
London Irish Fictions (Murray), 175
Lonely Girl, The (O'Brien), 214, 297
Lonergan, Patrick, 11, 83, 158, 201–6
Lonesome West, The (McDonagh), 81, 314
Long Night of the Short Story, The (public events series), 383
Long, Declan, 140
Longley, Edna, 136, 331, 332
Longley, Michael, 9, 121, 133, 381
'A Jovial Hullaboo'. 382
'At Poll Salach. Easter Sunday, 1998', 48
'Burren Prayer', 132–3
Ireland Chair of Poetry and essay and, 382
The Weather in Japan, 132
Lord of the Dance (theatrical show), 365, 367
Lordan, Dave, 193
Lost Land, The (Boland), 112
Lost Lives project, 140
Lost O'Casey, The (ANU Productions), 163
Love Apple, The (Atkinson), 177
Love Bean, The (Parkinson), 104
Love Leabhar Gaeilge initiative, 37
love songs, 29, 252
Love/Hate (Carolan), 354
Lovers (Standún), 313
Lovett, Ann, 5, 87, 106, 173, 231–2
Lowe, Andrew, 355
Lowe, Louise, 86
'Luck' (Kinnell), 36
Luck of Ginger Coffey, The (Moore), 177

Lukács, Georg, 212
Lynch, P. J., 104
Lynch, Patricia, 98
Lyons, F.S.L., 330
Lyotard, Jean-François, 128

Maas, Sarah J., 106
Mac a' Bhaird, Proinsias, 38
Mac an Iomaire, Darach, 32
Mac Anna, Tomás, 156, 164
Mac Annaidh, Séamus
  Cuaifeach mo Londubh Buí, 34
  Mo Dhá Mhic, 34
  Rubble na Mickies, 34
Mac Aodha, Aifric
  'Echtrae Chondlai', 30
  'Scéal Syrinx', 30
Mac Cóil, Liam
  An Dochtúir Áthais, 34
  An Litir, 31
  Fontenoy, 31
  I dTír Strainseartha, 31
Mac Con Iomaire, Liam, 315, 317
Mac Conghail, Fiach, 153, 160
Mac Éinrí, Piaras, 174
Mac Giolla Léith, Caoimhín, 27
Mac Laughlin, Jim, 169
Mac Lochlainn, Gearóid, 39, 309
Mac Mathúna, Seán, 27
Mac Síomóin, Tomás, 35, 309, 319
Macardle, Dorothy, 397
Macbeth (Shakespeare), 344
Macklin, Charles, 361
MacLaverty, Bernard
  Lamb, 231
  Midwinter Break, 240
MacNeice, Louis, 127
  'Belfast', 128
MacRaois, Cormac, 99, 100
Madden, Deirdre, 146, 217
Madhavan, Cauvery, 187
Maeve (Murphy), 349
magazines, literary. *See* literary magazines and journals
Magdalen Laundries, 5, 87, 237, 238, 283, 295, 301, 383
Magdalene Sisters, The (Mullan), 5, 87, 237, 300
magic realism, 29, 34, 143
Mahon, Derek, 178
Mahony, Christina Hunt, 328
'Majesty of the Law, The' (O'Connor), 347
Making Great Art Work (Arts Council or Ireland), 381
Making History (Friel), 205

'Making Love outside Áras an Uachtaráin' (Duncan), 230
Mammal (Daly), 357
Man Booker Prize for Fiction, 398
Man of Aran (Flaherty), 172
Mandelstam, Osip, 53, 116
Mann, Thomas, 214
Marcus, Sharon, 361
Margellos World Republic of Letters series, 315, 317
Mark and the Void, The (Murray), 9
Mark Keane, 283, 285, 286
Markus, Radvan, 317, 318
marriage
  abuse in, 187, 188
  marriage equality referendum, 240
  mixed marriage, 143
  public acceptance of Catholic views on, 230
  same-sex. *See also* same-sex marriage
  taboo of having a child outside of marriage, 33, 230, 234, 241
'Marriage' (Boland), 113
Marriage Equality Act (2015), 6, 105, 165, 230, 240, 295
Martín-Ruiz, Sara, 193
Marxism, 330
Marxist tradition, 60
mass media, 81, 82, 93, 279. *See also* media
Master, The (Tóibín), 224–6
Matthiessen, F. O., 364
May, Theresa, 138
McAleese Report (2013), 237
McBratney, Sam, 100
McBride, Eimear, 7, 295, 397
  A Girl Is a Half-Formed Thing, 90, 106, 222, 295, 299
  O'Brien's work contrasted with, 295–302
  The Lesser Bohemians, 295, 299
McCabe, Eugene, 146
McCabe, Patrick, 147, 264, 268
  Breakfast on Pluto, 264–8, 347
  The Butcher Boy, 5, 220–1, 222, 235, 347
McCafferty, Nell, 229
McCafferty, Owen, 143
McCann, Colum, 176
  This Side of Brightness, 14, 176
  Transatlantic, 14, 176
McCarthy, Niall, 235
McCaughrean, Tom, 100
McCormack, Mike, 393, 397, 398
  Solar Bones, 121, 126–7, 131
McCourt, Frank
  Angela's Ashes, 10, 233, 360, 361, 362
McCrea, Barry, 222

McCrory, Moy
  'Prize Giving', 172
  The Water's Edge, 172
McDermott, Alice, 177
McDonagh, Martin, 86
  Cripple of Inishmaan, 172
  In Bruges, 172
  The Beauty Queen of Leenane, 314
  The Lonesome West, 81, 314
  Three Billboards Outside Ebbing, Missouri, 172
McDonald, Ronan, 15, 327–41, 380
McGahern, John, 9, 376
  Amongst Women, 214–16, 217, 233, 376
  Doyle's fiction compared with, 216
  family novels influenced by, 217
  Irish realism and, 213
  That They May Face the Rising Sun, 216, 234
  'The Church and Its Spire', 234
  The Dark, 96, 170, 214, 220
  The End or The Beginning of Love, 170
  The Leavetaking, 170
  The Pornographer, 376
McGill, Bernie, 143
McGrath, Paula, 179
McGuckian, Medbh, 51–2, 59, 66, 71–3, 122, 311
  Blaris Moor, 128
  Captain Lavender, 52–5
  'Elegy for an Irish Speaker', 52
  'The Albert Chain', 55
  The Flower Master, 72
  'The Sofa', 72–3
  'The Soil-Map', 72
  'Who Is Your City?', 128
McGuinness, Frank, 7, 360
  The Hanging Gardens, 81
McGurl, Mark, 258
McIvor, Charlotte, 182
McKee, Lyra, 5
McKeon, Belinda, 217, 397
McLaren, Graham, 164
McLoone, Martin, 348
McMahon, Katie, 366
McNamee, Eoin, 142
McPherson, Conor
  The Weir, 83–4, 91
McQueen, Steve, 4
McSorley, Edward, 177
McWeeney, Myles, 257
McWilliams, David, 123, 124, 160
McWilliams, Ellen, 14, 168–79
Me, Mollser (White), 153
#MeToo movement, 13

Meade, L. T., 98
MEAS (Measuring Equality in the Arts Sector in Ireland), 385
media, 4, 38, 81–93, 97, 104, 107, 152, 173, 183, 193, 279, 281, 288, 383, 393. *See also* cinema; digital media; multimedia; newspapers; radio; social media; television; video
media technologies, 84–86, 92, 93
Meehan, Paula, 5, 6, 121, 382
  'Death of a Field', 131–2
  Dublin suburbs depicted by, 123
  'The Statue of the Virgin at Granard Speaks', 231
Meeting the British (Muldoon), 178
Melody for Nora (O'Sullivan), 101
memoir, 13, 222, 232, 279, 281
  Bildungsroman (coming-of-age novel) and, 219
  Doyle's *The God Squad*, 232
  McCourt's *Angela's Ashes*, 233, 362
  O'Brien's *Mother Ireland*, 170
  O'Faolain's work in, 396
  Pine's *Notes to Self*, 397
Memory Stones, The (O'Riordan), 175
Men of Arlington (documentary film), 175
Menand, Louis, 362
Mendes, Sam, 162
mental health issues, as theme, 32, 107
Merchant of Venice, The (Shakespeare), 361
Metro Eireann, 185, 188
Mhac an tSaoi, Máire, 7, 30, 32, 36, 308
  English translations of, 315
  Paróiste Míorúilteach, An/The Miraculous Parish, 315
  Scéal Ghearóid Iarla, 31
Michael Flatley's Lord of the Dance (theatrical show), 365, 367
middle class, 213, 249–52
middlebrow fiction, 250, 252, 254
Middlemarch (Eliot), 214
Midwinter Break (MacLaverty), 240
migrant communities, 105, 182, 183
migrant justice campaigns, 196
migrant writers of colour, 182, 183, 187–91, 192, 193, 194, 196, 197
  performance and spoken word and, 192, 193
migrants, 183, 184
  Akpoveta's novel *Prison Without Walls* on, 188
  Dimbo's novel *She Was Foolish?* on, 187
  Doyle's short story 'I Understand' on, 185
  Frawley's novel *Flight* on, 185–7
  Okorie's short story 'This Hostel Life' on, 189–90
  Okorie's short story 'Under the Awning' on, 189–90

migration, 1, 168, 182, 184, 341. *See also* emigration; immigration.
  1980s and 1990s period in, 169–74
  Frawley's novel *Flight* in exploration of, 185–7
  white Irish writers' dominance in treatment of, 184, 187
Milkman (Burns), 398
Mill for Grinding Old People Young, The (Patterson), 129–30
Miller, Henry, 362
Miller, J. Hillis, 364
Miłosz, Czesław, 116
minority communities. *See also* ethnic communities
  gender-based violence in, 188
  state-led integration strategies and interculturalist rhetoric and, 197
minority writers, 193, 194, 197. *See also* migrant writers of colour
'Mise Éire' (Boland), 112, 232
Mishra, Nita, 192
Mitchell, George, 176
Mo Chathair Ghríobháin agus Scéalta Eile (Ó Conaola), 34
Mo Dhá Mhicí (Mac Annaidh), 34
Molly Sweeney (Friel), 205
Monahan, Barry, 10, 344–57
monologue, 90, 91, 92, 204
Monshengwo, Kensika, 183
Montague, John, 381, 382
Moody, T. W., 332
Moore, Brian
  Black Robe, 223
  The Luck of Ginger Coffey, 177
Moore, George, 213, 219, 226
  The Lake, 213
Moran, James, 11, 152–65
'More a Man Has the More a Man Wants, The' (Muldoon), 74–5
Moreo, Elena, 183
Moretti, Franco, 285
Morning After Optimism, The (Murphy), 205
Morris, Thomas, 397
Morrissey, Sinéad, 7, 178
  'In Belfast', 137
  'Tourism', 138
Morrissy, Mary, 13
Moth Magazine, The, 12
Mother and Baby Homes, abuse of children in, 5, 161, 295, 383
Mother Ireland (O'Brien), 170
Moukarzel, Bush, 90
Moynihan, Sinéad, 174

Mtowa, Anesu Khanya, 194
'Mud Vision, The' (Heaney), 116
Muldoon, Paul, 65, 73–5, 113, 178, 311, 363, 369
  'Aisling', 73
  'Gathering Mushrooms', 73
  Meeting the British, 178
  Native American themes used by, 74–5
  New Weather, 178
  Quoof, 73, 74
  'The More a Man Has the More a Man Wants', 74–5
  Winnebago Trickster cycle and, 74
Mulhall, Anne, 14, 182–97
Mullan, Peter, 5, 237, 300
Mullen, Michael, 100
multicultural Ireland, 182–4, 185, 187
  increase in number of people migrating to Ireland in 1990s and, 182
  migrant writers of colour and questioning of, 187
  white Irish writers and, 182, 184
multiculturalism, and children's literature, 104, 105
multimedia, 81, 86, 87, 93, 104, 193, 282
Munch-Petersen, Ole, 316
Mundy Scheme, The (Friel), 203
Munster Literature Centre, 384
Munster, Ní Mhóráin's work on, 39
Murphy Report (2009), 229
Murphy, Annie, 393
Murphy, Barry, 354
Murphy, Colin, 240, 394
Murphy, Elaine, 90
Murphy, Pat, 348, 349, 356
Murphy, Tom, 201–6
  A Whistle in the Dark, 202, 206
  Alice Trilogy, 202, 205
  Bailegangaire, 202, 203, 204, 205
  Conversations on a Homecoming, 206
  Famine, 201, 202
  The Gigli Concert, 204, 205
  The House, 202, 205
  The Morning After Optimism, 205
  The Sanctuary Lamp, 202, 203, 205
  The Wake, 203, 205
Murray, Neil, 164
Murray, Paul, 9
Murray, Tony, 175
music, 38, 163
  ANU Productions' use of, 87
  Dead Centre's *Hamnet* with, 91
  Doyle's *The Commitments* and, 217, 368
  Enright's *The Forgotten Waltz* and, 252
  Friel's use of, 82, 83, 204, 205
  Murphy's use of, 204, 205
  Riverdance's non-traditional use of dance and, 367
  Riverdance's use of songs and, 366, 368
  traditional. See traditional Irish music
  Walsh's *The Walworth Farce* and, 85, 86
Music of What Happens (Vendler), 369, 370
My Head Is Opening (Conlon), 173
My Language, My Words project (Immigrant Council of Ireland), 196
My Left Foot (Brown), 347
My Oedipus Complex (O'Connor), 347
'Mycenae Lookout' (Heaney), 111
mystery fiction. See crime fiction; police procedural
myths, 18, 28, 29, 30, 71, 74, 99, 103, 104, 130, 173, 176, 231, 232, 241, 313, 335, 371

Na Buachaillí Bána (Ó Searcaigh), 313
Naficy, Hamid, 349
Nanny's Night Out (O'Casey), 163
National Campaign for the Arts, 378
National Theatre Scotland, 164
National Theatre, London, 156, 163, 164
National Writers' Workshop, 27
Nationalism, Colonialism and Literature (Deane), 335
'Nationalism and Historical Scholarship in Ireland' (Bradshaw), 332
Native Americans, Muldoon's poetry on, 74–5, 178
Nedeljković, Vukašin, 190, 197
Needlework (Sullivan), 107
Negra, Diane, 251
Ness, Patrick, 106
Netflix, 355
Netherland (O'Neill), 179, 223
Neville, Stuart, 142
New Collected Poems (Boland), 113
New Communities Partnership, 196
New Estate, The (Carson), 48, 50
'New Estate, The' (Ciaran), 48–9
New Oxford Book of Irish Verse, The (Kinsella), 308
New Weather (Muldoon), 178
New York, 176, 341, 360, 365
New York Times, The, 258, 362, 364, 366
New York University, Irish Studies at, 328, 382
New Yorker, The, 9, 177, 315
New Zealand, novels on Irish in, 177
newspapers, 37, 67, 173. See also *Irish Times*; media
NGOs, 196. See also specific organisations
Ní Anluain, Éilis, 39
Ní Annracháin, Máire, 36

Ní Bheildiúin, Ceaití, 38
Ní Chinnéide, Dairena, 38
Ní Chléirchín, Caitríona, 31, 32
Ní Chuilleanáin, Eiléan, 7, 311, 382
Ní Dhomhnaill, Nuala, 28–9, 32, 36, 309, 311, 381, 382
  Cead Aighnis, 28, 311
  Feis, 28, 311
  Selected Poems: Rogha Dánta, 309
  The Fifty Minute Mermaid, 311
Ní Dhuibhne, Éilís, 247
  Dún na mBan Trí Thine, 29
  The Dancers Dancing, 106
Ní Fhrighil, Ríóna, 11, 37, 307–21
Ní Ghearbhuigh, Ailbhe, 11, 27–39, 310
Ní Ghlinn, Áine, 32
Ní Ghríofa, Doireann, 30
Ní Houlihan, Cathleen (mythic figure), 71
Ní Mhóráin, Bríd, 38
Ní Thuathail, Róis, 32
Niazi, Munir, 319
Nic Dhiarmada, Bríona, 27, 28, 31, 36, 39
  Téacs Baineann, Téacs Mná, 36
Nic Eoin, Máirín, 34
Nielsen Bookscan, 106
Nigerian characters, in Irish works, 185, 187, 188
Nigerian writers, in Ireland, 187, 192
Night Stages, The (Urquhart), 177
'Nineteen and Sixteen' (Shortt), 153–4
'No Angel' (McGil), 143
No Escape (Rafferty), 281–2, 283
No Goodbye (Conlon-McKenna), 105
No Peace for Amelia (Parkinson), 101
Nobel Prize for Literature, 9, 363, 369, 370, 381, 395
non-governmental organisations (NGOs), 196.
  See also specific organisations
Normal People (Rooney), 296, 300
Norris, David, 152
North (Heaney), 67, 177, 369, 370
North London, University of, Irish Studies at, 333
Northern Irish literature, 136–48
Norwegian language, translations into, 316, 318
Not the Same Sky (Conlon), 177
Notes to Self (Pine), 393, 397
Nothing Tastes as Good (Hennessy), 107
Nothing to Say (Flynn), 232, 279
Notre Dame, University of, Irish Studies at, 329
Number 5 (Patterson), 141

Obert, Julia C., 4, 65–77
Object Lessons (Boland), 382
Ó Béarra, Feargal, 29, 319
O'Brien, Edna, 7, 169, 170, 214, 377
  A Pagan Place, 299
  A Scandalous Woman, 300
  Girls in Their Married Bliss, 214
  House of Splendid Isolation, 269
  In the Forest, 222
  McBride's work contrasted with, 295–302
  Mother Ireland, 170
  The Country Girls, 96, 170, 214, 220, 296
  The Country Girls trilogy, 170, 214, 220, 295
  The Light of Evening, 176
  The Little Red Chairs, 264, 268–76
  The Lonely Girl, 214, 297
O'Brien, Eugene, 353
O'Brien, Flann, 222, 226
O'Brien, Kate, 213
O'Brien Press, 98, 102, 105, 315
Ó Broin, Fiach Mac Aoidh, Lord of Ranelagh, 32
Ó Cadhain, Máirtín, 27, 35, 226, 307, 308
  Cré na Cille, 307, 310, 315–18
  The Dirty Dust, 315
  The Key/An Eochair, 317
  The Road to Brightcity, 308
  translating *Cré na Cille* and, 315–18
O'Casey, Sean, 153, 155, 158, 160, 162, 163, 347
  Abbey Theatre productions of *The Plough* from 1991 to 2016 and, 153, 155–63, 164
  Dublin Trilogy, 152, 159, 217
  global English language stage and, 347
  Juno and the Paycock, 163, 347
  reviews of *The Plough* at, 153
  Shortt's parodic poem on *The Plough* and, 153–4
  The Silver Tassie, 159, 162
Ó Ceallacháin, Colm, 34
Ó Cíobháin, Pádraig, 30
Ó Conaola, Dara, 34
Ó Conchubhair, Brian, 32, 34
Ó Conghaile, Mícheál, 28, 29, 33, 37, 222, 313, 314
  An Fear a Phléasc, 34, 314
  An Fear Nach nDéanann Gáire, 34, 314
  Cei Cinci din Conamara, 314
  Cúigear Chonamara, 314
  Diabhlaíocht Dé, 34
  Sna Fir, 33, 314
  The Colours of Man, 314
  The Connemara Five, 314
O'Connell, Kassandra, 356
O'Connell, Shaun, 371
O'Connor, Frank, 213, 347
O'Connor, Joseph, 13, 169
  Cowboys and Indians, 171
  'Last of the Mohicans', 171
  Star of the Sea, 176
  True Believers, 171

Ó Curraoin, Seán, 310
Ó Dálaigh, Muireadhach Albanach, 31
Ó Direáin, Máirtín, 309
Ó Doibhlin, Breandán, 308
O'Donnell, Mary, 182
O'Donnell, Peadar, 226
O'Donnell, Roisín, 143
O'Donnell, Vincent, 104
O'Donoghue, Bernard, 313, 329
O'Driscoll, Dennis, 131
Ó Dúill, Gréagóir, 39
Odyssey (Homer), 319
Oeser, Hans-Christian, 319
O'Faolain, Julia, 300, 301
O'Faolain, Nuala
   Almost There, 396
   Are You Somebody?, 13, 396
Ó Faoláin, Seán, 213, 347
Ó Faoláin, Simon, 38
O'Flaherty, Liam, 347
Ó Floinn, Tomás, 310
O'Flynn, Sunniva, 356
Ó Gallchoir, Cliona, 105
Ó Guairim, Josie, 38
O'Guilin, Peadar, 100
O'Halloran, Mark, 353, 354
O'Hara, Elizabeth, 101
Oireachtas na Samhna Literary Awards, 38, 307, 314
O'Kelly, Donal, 14
Okorie, Melatu Uche, 183, 187, 192, 197
   'Gathering Thoughts', 188
   This Hostel Life, 14, 188
   'This Hostel Life', 189–90
   'Under the Awning', 190–1
Old Vic Theatre, London, 162
O'Leary, Philip, 320
Oliveira, Abby, 194
Olusanya, Felicia, 183, 194, 195–6
   'For Our Mothers', 196
   Lady Na Master & the Synaptic Room, 195
Ó Muirí, Daithí, 34
Ó Muirthile, Liam, 35
   An Colm Bán, 35
   An Fuíoll Feá – Rogha Dánta/Wood Cuttings – New and Selected Poems, 310
   'Bothán', 39
   Dialann Bóthair, 310
   Fear an Tae, 32
   knowledge of French language and culture of, 35
   Tine Chnámh, 32
One Hundred Years of Solitude (García Marquez), 214
online resources, 38, 193, 320, 355, 385, 392, 393

Only Ever Yours (O'Neill), 107
'On the Road' (Heaney), 116
Ó Neachtain, Joe Steve, 38
O'Neill, Catherine, Countess of Tyrone, 31
O'Neill, Hugh, 205
O'Neill, Jamie, 7, 222
O'Neill, Joan, 100
O'Neill, Joseph, 179, 223
O'Neill, Louise, 106, 107
O'Neill, Rory, 7
Opened Ground (Heaney), 370
Opera Et Cetera (Carson), 49
Optic Verve (Walsh), 57–9, 60–1
Oral History Archive, Stormont House Agreement, 146
Orange Horses (Kelly), 397
Ó Rathaille, Aogán, 31, 132
Ordnance Survey of Ireland, 3, 66
O'Reilly, Sean, 142
Orientalism (Said), 15
Ó Ríordáin, Seán, 35, 308
O'Riordan, Kate, 175
O'Rowe, Mark, 86
   Howie the Rookie, 90
   O'Casey's *Juno and the Paycock* version of, 163
orphanages. *See* Industrial Schools
Osborne, John, 298
O'Scanlon, Patricia, 313
Oscar awards, 10, 362
Ó Scolaí, Darach, 319
   An Cléireach, 31
   Táin Bó Cuailgne, 29
Ó Searcaigh, Cathal, 28, 309, 313–14
   'Ceann Dubh Dílis', 29, 33
   'Gort na gCnámh', 33
   'Laoi Chumainn', 33
   Na Buachaillí Bána, 313
   Out in the Open, 313
O'Shea, Pat, 100
Ó Siadhail, Pádraig, 29, 36, 39
Ó Snodaigh, Pádraig, 37
Ostermeier, Thomas, 163
O'Sullivan, Mark, 101, 105
O'Sullivan, Thaddeus, 347, 348
Ó Súilleabháin, Séamus Barra, 33
Other People's Houses (Groarke), 123–4
Other Rooms (ANU Productions), 87
O'Toole, Fintan, 96, 148, 169, 174, 247, 396
   The Lie of the Land: Irish Identities, 169
Ó Tuairisc, Eoghan, 308
Ó Tuairisg, Lochlainn, 317
Ó Tuama, Seán, 308, 310
Our Boys (Black), 349
Ourselves Alone (Devlin), 65, 70–1
Out in the Open (Ó Searcaigh), 313

Out of the Flames (O'Donnell), 104
Outside History (Boland), 112
'Outside History' (Boland), 232
Over the Water (Casey), 172
Oxford Book of Irish Verse (MacDonagh and Robinson), 308
Oxford University, Irish Studies at, 329

Paddy Clarke Ha Ha Ha (Doyle), 398
Paddy Indian (Madhavan), 187
Pagan Place, A (O'Brien), 299
Pan Pan Theatre, 92–3
Panti Bliss, 7
'Parable Island' (Heaney), 116
Parallel Films, 355
'Paranóia' (Davitt), 35
Park, David, 145
  Swallowing the Sun, 142
  The Light of Amsterdam, 145
  The Truth Commissioner, 144
  Travelling in a Strange Land, 145
Parkinson, Siobhán
  Amelia, 101
  Breaking the Wishbone, 105
  first Laureate na nÓg appointment of, 96
  No Peace for Amelia, 101
  The Love Bean, 104
Parmar, Sandeep, 191
Paróiste Míorúilteach, An/The Miraculous Parish (Mhac an tSaoi), 315
Partition (1921), 56, 63, 138
Parts, The (Ridgway), 222
Patrick, Saint, 104
Patriot Games (Clancy), 361
Patriot Games (film), 361
Patterson, Glenn, 66, 75–6, 122, 140
  Fat Lad, 66, 76
  Number 5, 141
  That Which Was, 141
  The International, 140
  The Mill for Grinding Old People Young, 129–30
  The Third Party, 143
  thriller genre and, 142
Paulin, Tom, 329
Pearse, Patrick, 154, 156, 157, 159, 162
peasant play, 81
Pelevin, Viktor, 319
Perec, George, 34
performance poetry, 193, 194
Performances (Friel), 205
Perve (Gregg), 87–90
Peters, J. D., 289
Petit Prince, Le (Saint-Exupéry), 318
Pettitt, Lance, 356

'Phenomenology of Literary Valuation, The' (Altieri), 381
Philadelphia, Here I Come! (Friel), 202, 206
picture books, 103, 104, 105, 318
Pigs (Black), 349
Pine, Emilie, 6, 278–89, 393, 397
place name poetry (*dinnseanchas* tradition), 9, 58
Plain Jane (Hood), 107
Plath, Sylvia, 369
  'Lady Lazarus', 53
Playboy of the Western World, The (Synge, adapted by Doyle and Adigun), 187
Pleasure of Eliza Lynch, The (Enright), 178, 223
Pleasures of Gaelic Poetry, The (Mac Réamoinn), 308
Plough and the Stars, The (O'Casey), 152, 153–4, 155, 158, 160, 162, 163
  Abbey Theatre productions from 1991 to 2016 of, 153, 155–63, 164
podcasts, 384, 385, 396
Poems from Guantánamo (Falkoff), 319
Poet's Chair, The (essay collection), 382
poetry. *See also* Irish poetry
Poetry Book Society, 312
Poetry Ireland, 184, 197, 384
Poetry Ireland Review, 12, 197
police procedural, 250, 251, 256, 257
  cliché in, 248, 252, 255
  French's *Broken Harbor* as, 249, 250, 251, 252
  middle-class readers and, 250, 251
Poolbeg Press, 99, 313
Poor Clare nuns, 279
Pornographer, The (McGahern), 376
Portia Coughlan (Carr), 81
Portráidí online archive, 38
Portrait of the Artist as a Young Man, A (Joyce), 96, 168, 213, 219, 299
Post Irish Book Awards, An, 37, 107, 394
Post-Agreement Northern Irish Literature (Heideman), 139
postcolonial theory
  decline in influence of, 339
  readings of Irish literature and, 330, 331
Postmodern Condition, The (Lyotard), 128
pregnancy
  Catholic attitudes towards, 234, 241
  in vitro fertilisation (IVF) and, 32, 230
  novels on migrant issues and, 186, 188
  poem on 'fallen women' and, 231
  public awareness of Lovett case and, 231–2
  taboo of having a child outside of marriage, 33, 230, 234, 241
  teen pregnancy, youth literature addressing, 105, 106

pregnancy (cont.)
    unplanned pregnancy, novels on, 105, 173, 234
    women sharing stories about, 231
presses. *See* publishers
priests
    Bishop Casey's affair with Annie Murphy, 33, 393
    celibacy of, as theme, 32, 33, 313
    women as, 32, 230
Prime Time Investigates (television programme), 279
'Prize Giving' (McCrory), 172
Production of Space, The (Lefebvre), 126
'Progress' (Gillis), 137, 140
Prose, Francine, 258
Prosperity (television series), 353, 354
Provisional IRA, 67, 263
publishers and publishing, 10, 12, 37, 39, 97, 98, 99, 103, 192, 193, 196, 197, 250, 251, 257, 279, 295, 312, 314, 318, 320, 362, 384, 385, 392, 393, 394, 398. *See also specific publishers*
    dual-language, 307–12
    global context and trends and, 319–21, 385
    Irish children's literature and, 98, 99, 100, 101, 103
    young adult books in Irish and, 102, 106
Publishers' Association, The, 37
publishing houses, 29, 37, 98, 102, 103, 104, 308, 309, 310, 312, 313, 315, 318, 370, 385, 394, 398. *See also specific publishing houses*
Punchdrunk, 164
'Punishment' (Heaney), 67, 370
Pure Mule (television series), 353

Queen's University Belfast
    Ireland Chair of Poetry and, 381
    Irish Studies at, 328
queer community. *See also* gay community; homosexuality; lesbian community; LGBTQ+community
    novels for teenagers with characters from, 105
queer literature in Irish language, 313–14
queer studies, 339
queer writer. *See also* gay writer; LGBTQ+ writers
    Ó Conghaile's work as, 33
Quiet Man, The (Ford), 347
'Quiet Man, The' (Walsh), 347
Quietly (McCafferty), 143
Quinn, Bob, 348, 349
Quinn, Gavin, 92
Quinn, John, 105
Quinn, Justin, 178
Quinn, Robert, 352
Quoof (Muldoon), 73, 74

Rabelais, François, 319
race, 14, 105, 183
racial diversity
    increase since mid-1990s in, 13
    Irish novels addressing, 104
    racialisation during Celtic Tiger period amidst increase in, 105
racialisation
    emergence of during Celtic Tiger period, 105
    of migrancy, 183
Radin, Paul, 74
radio, 231, 279, 383, 384
    Friel's *Dancing at Lughnasa*'s use of, 82–3
    McPherson's *The Weir* and, 83
radio play, Beckett's *Embers* as, 92–3
Radway, Janice, 250
Raftery, Mary, 287
    No Escape, 281–2, 283
    States of Fear television documentary series, 279, 281, 300
Raidió na Gaeltachta, 11
Raidió Teilifís Éireann, 353
Rakish Paddy Blues (Mac Lochlainn), 309
Ramazani, Jahan, 74
Ranelagh, Fiach Mac Aoidh Ó Broin, Lord of, 32
rape
    abortion prohibition and, 235
    Catholic abuse scandals and, 161, 237
    girls' young adult literature on, 107
    Irish novels with theme of, 269, 271, 299, 300
    Irish poetry with theme of, 33
Raven (poet), 194
Raven Arts Press, 309
Rea, Stephen, 163
reading, 103, 284–7, 289, 383, 392
Reading in the Dark (Deane), 13, 65, 68, 221–2
Real Charlotte, The (Somerville and Ross), 212
realism, 5, 65, 211
realist novel, 27, 211–26, 250
Reapy, E. M., 177
recession, 8, 246, 249. *See also* economic crisis (2008)
Red Dirt (Reapy), 177
Reddy, Maureen, 185
Redress Act (2002), 280
Redress Board, 280
Redress State (Thorpe), 282
Reefer and the Model (Comerford), 349
Reid, Meta Mayne, 98
Rekdal, Jan Erik, 316
religion, 32, 183, 228, 236. *See also* Catholic Church
    Dowd's novel on teenage pregnancy and, 106
    Doyle's *Paddy Clarke Ha Ha Ha* on, 236

Enyi-Amadi's poem on female genital mutilation and, 195
McGahern's *Amongst Women* on, 233
Murphy's plays investigating, 206
O'Brien's work exploring, 299
Ryan's *The Spinning Heart* on lack of, in people's lives, 238
'Remembering Malibu' (Heaney), 116
reparative remembering, 140
'Requiem for the Croppies' (Heaney), 111
Residential Institutions Redress Board, 280
Reuters' Digital News Report, 384
revisionist historians, 157, 224, 331, 332, 335, 337
Reynolds, Emer, 357
Reynolds, Paige, 1–18, 81–93, 392–9
Richard III (Shakespeare), 163
Richards, Shaun, 329
Richards, Shelah, 347
Ricoeur, Paul, 288, 334
Riddell, Charlotte, 397
Ridgway, Keith, 7, 182, 222
Rimbaud, Arthur, 36
Rising of the Moon, The (Ford), 347
Riverdance (theatrical show), 10, 360, 361, 365–8
riverrun (Fouéré), 90
Rivi, Luisa, 353
Roach, Joseph, 361, 367, 371
Road to Brightcity, The (Ó Cadhain), 308
Robinson, Mary, 6, 99, 173
Robinson, Tim, 9, 121, 129
 Graveyard Clay, 315
Rockett, Kevin, 346, 349, 350
Rockfinch Productions, 385
Rogha an Fhile (Ó Tuairisc), 308
Roman Catholic Church. *See* Catholic Church
romance, 184, 187, 188, 224, 250, 351, 352
 cliché in, 248, 252–4
 commodification of middle-class women's desire in, 251
 Doyle's short story 'I Understand' as, 185
 Enright's *The Forgotten Waltz* as, 249, 250, 252, 254
 origin of genre, 250
Room (Abrahamson), 347, 355
Room (Donoghue), 10, 347, 355
Room Little Darker (Caldwell), 396
Rooney, Sally, 10, 296, 300
Roots (Haley), 214
Rosenstock, Gabriel, 35, 310, 319
Rosminian order, 283, 286
Ross, Martin, 212
Rosset, Barney, 362
Rossiter, Ann, 173
Rowling, J. K., 318
RTÉ, 11, 155, 279, 353, 394

Dear Daughter documentary on, 279
States of Fear documentary series on, 279, 281, 300
Ruane, Medb, 235
Rubberbandits, 154–5
Rubberbandits Guide to 1916, The (television programme), 154–5
Rubble na Mickies (Mac Annaidh), 34
Rubin, Joan Shelley, 250
Rudden, Dave, 100
Rushe, Desmond, 156
Russian language, Irish translations from, 319
Ryan Report (2009), 6, 161, 229, 280, 281, 282, 284–7, 289
 Echoes from the Past (digital walking tour), 288–9
 Industrial Memories project using digested version of, 283–4, 285, 286
Ryan, Annie, 90
Ryan, Donal, 9, 126, 182, 217
 The Spinning Heart, 121, 124, 238

Said, Edward, 15, 335
Saint-Exupéry, Antoine de, 318
'Saint Francis and the Sow' (Kinnell), 36
Sáirséal agus Dill (publisher), 307, 308, 315, 320
Salmon Poetry (publishing house), 12, 384, 386
same-sex marriage
 legalisation (2015) of, Republic of Ireland, 6, 105, 165, 230, 240, 295
 Northern Ireland and, 6
 public advocacy for, 398
Sanctuary Lamp, The (Murphy), 202, 203, 205
Sarma, Ursula Rani, 14
satire
 Catholic Church scandals and, 230
 Doyle's *Paddy Clarke Ha Ha Ha* as, 236
 Friel's *The Mundy Scheme* as, 203
Scandalous Woman, A (O'Brien), 300
Scannell, Raymond, 14
'Scaradh na gCompánach' (Ní Chléirchín), 31, 32
Scáthach (Breathnach), 30
Scéal Ghearóid Iarla (Mhac an tSaoi), 31
'Scéal Syrinx' (Mac Aodha), 30
Sclabhaí, An (Ó Raghallaigh), 104
Scotland
 Brexit discussions and nationalists in, 138, 148
 long tradition of cross-currents between Ireland and, 148
 national theatre of, 164
 Norther Ireland and Scottish identity, 148
 receptivity to Europeanness in, 136
 women poets who have migrated from, 184
Scott, Michael
 Judith trilogy, 105

Scott, Michael (cont.)
  Secrets of the Immortal Nicholas Flame
    series, 100
Scott, Sir Walter, 75
Scully, Maurice, 47, 56, 57
  Things That Happen, 57
Sealy, Douglas, 309
Seamus Heaney (Vendler), 370
Secret Scripture, The (Barry), 347
Secrets of the Immortal Nicholas Flame series
    (Scott), 100
secularism, 236
  creative work exploring implications of
    increase in, 235
  impact on religious institutions of, 236
  increasing pervasiveness of, 228, 230
  Pope John Paul II on need to resist, 228
  referendum to appeal Eighth Amendment
    and, 239, 240
Seeing Things (Heaney), 115
Selected Poems 1966–1987 (Heaney), 370
Selected Poems: Rogha Dánta (Ní
    Dhomhnaill), 309
Selected Poems: Rogha Dánta, 1968–1984
    (Davitt), 309
Selected Poem: Tacar Dánta (Ó Direáin), 309
self-publishing, 193, 250
Sense of Ireland (festival), 378
Serpell, Namwali, 248, 252
Sewell, Frank, 33
Sex in a Cold Climate (documentary), 87
sexual abuse
  Catholic Church scandals and. *See also*
    Catholic Church abuse scandals; Industrial
    Schools
  childhood. *See* Catholic Church abuse
    scandals; childhood sexual abuse
  family novel on, 217
  McGahern's *Amongst Women* on, 233
sexual themes in writing, 32, 33, 313
  Gregg's play *Perv* and, 87–90
  Ó Searcaigh's poetry and, 33
sexual violence, 274, 296, 299, 301, 302
Shakespeare, Hamnet, 91
Shakespeare, William, 90–2, 153
  Hamlet, 50, 91
  Macbeth, 344
  Richard III, 163
  Shaw and, 365
  The Merchant of Venice, 361
shame, novels exploring, 195, 231, 234, 299, 300,
    302, 361
Shan, Darren, 100
Sharkey, Niamh, 99, 103
Shaw, George Bernard, 93, 347, 365

She Was Foolish? (Dimbo), 187
Sheehan, Ronan, 223
Sheridan, Jim, 347, 362
Sheridan, Richard Brinsley, 93
Shibboleth (Gregg), 147
Shortt, Pat, 153–4
Showalter, Elaine, 334
Shroud (Banville), 223
Shumway, David, 363
Shunt, 164
Siege of Jadotville, The (film), 355
Silhouette Books, 251
Silver Tassie, The (O'Casey), 159, 162
Simon, Francesca, 318
Sin Eaters, The (ANU Productions), 87
Singer, Isaac Bashevis, 35
Sinn Féin, 65
Sisters of Charity, 283
Sisters of Mercy, 283, 286
site-specific theatre performances, 81, 86, 90, 163,
    164, 165, 228, 237, 288
Sixteen Self Sketches (Shaw), 365
Skein Press, 188, 197
slam poetry, 36, 194
Slane Girl story, 107
Slipping Letters Beneath the Sea (Horgan), 175
Small, Helen, 379–380
Sna Fir (Ó Conghaile), 33, 222, 314
Snap (Winters), 357
Snapper, The (Doyle), 216, 234, 313
Snáthaid Mhór, An (publishing house), 103
social class. *See* class
social media, 13, 37, 107, 393, 397
'Sofa, The' (McGukian), 72–3
'Soil-Map, The' (McGukian), 72
Solar Bones (McCormack), 121, 126–7, 131, 393,
    397, 398
Some Mother's Son (George), 4
Someone Who'll Watch Over Me
    (McGuinness), 360
Somers-Willett, Susan B. A., 194
Somerville, Edith, 212
songs
  ANU Productions' use of, 87
  Enright's *The Forgotten Waltz* and,
    252
  Gregg's play with sexual material from lyrics
    of, 88
  Irish translations of American songs, 38
  Muldoon's poetry and borrowing from, 73
  Ní Dhomhnaill's poetry and, 29, 311
  Ó Searcaigh's poems and, 29
  poets' use of, 28–9
  repetition of, in traditional Irish music, 70
  Riverdance's use of, 366

Space Between, The (Grehan), 105
Spallen, Abbie, 147
Spanish language, Irish translations from, 319
Speckled People, The (Hamilton), 13
Spender, Stephen, 369
Spill Simmer Falter Wither (Baume), 393
Spinning Heart, The (Ryan), 121, 124, 238
spoken word poetry, 194, 195
  independent development of, 193
  marginalised identities and, 194
  migrant rights articulated in, 196
  migrant writers of colour and, 193, 194
  writers of colour and, 192
'Spoonbait, The' (Heaney), 117
Sruth Teangacha/Stream of Tongues (Mac Lochlainn), 309
St Mary's University Twickenham, Irish Studies Centre, 329, 340
St Joseph's Industrial School, Letterfrack, Connemara, 232
St Michael's Industrial School, Cappoquin, Waterford, 232
St Vincent's Girls' Industrial School, Goldenbridge, Dublin, 232, 279, 288, 289
Standún, Pádraig, 313
  A Woman's Love, 313
  An tAinmhí, 313
  Celibates, 313
  Cíocras, 33, 313
  Cion Mná, 33, 313
  Díbirt Dé, 33
  Lovers, 313
  Stigmata, 313
  Súil le Breith, 33, 313
Star of the Sea (O'Connor), 176
'State Acknowledges the Right to Life of the Unborn, The' (Donlon), 235
States of Fear (television documentary series), 279, 281, 300
Station Island (Heaney), 111, 115
'Station Island' (Heaney), 113
'Statue of the Virgin at Granard Speaks, The' (Meehan), 5, 231
Steiner, George, 334
Stembridge, Gerry, 352
step dancing, 362, 365, 367
Stepping Stones (Heaney), 131
Stevenson, Robert Louis, 318
Stigmata (Standún), 313
Stinging Fly Press, The, 385
Stinging Fly, The (periodical), 12, 193, 197, 384, 392
stipend (cnuas) for writers, 38, 375–6, 383
Stoneman, Rod, 350
Stones/Beatles analogy, for Friel and Murphy, 201, 204
Stormont House Agreement, 146
Story of Lucy Gault, The (Trevor), 212
Story of the Night, The (Tóibín), 223
storytelling, 29, 142, 145, 146, 301
  Carson's use of, 70
  Friel's work and, 204
  graphic novels and, 104
  McPherson's *The Weir* and, 83
  Murphy's work and, 204
  O'Brien's work and, 300
  Thompson's stories for young people and, 100
  Troubles literature and, 66, 69
Strange Country (Deane), 331
Strick, Joseph, 347
Strokestown International Poetry Festival, 384
Strong, Eithne, 32
Struggle for Fame, A (Riddell), 397
Stuart, Francis, 226, 377
'Suburban Woman' (Boland), 113
Súil le Breith (Standún), 33, 313
Sullivan, Deirdre, 106, 107
Surface Break, The (O'Neill), 107
surrealism, 34, 143, 144
Swallowing the Sun (Park), 142
Sweeney Astray (Heaney), 111
Sweeney, Fionnuala, 356
Swift Pure Cry, A (Dowd), 106
Swift, Jonathan, 98, 336
Swing of Things, The (O'Reilly), 142
syllabic poetry, 31
Synge and Anglo-Irish Literature (Corkery), 122, 213
Synge, J. M., 30, 93, 347, 368, 371, 394
  Aran Islands and, 15
  The Playboy of the Western World, 187

taboo-breaking literature, 28, 32–3
Taibhdhearc, An, 32
Táin Bó Cuailgne (Ó Scolaí), 29
Táin Bó Cuailnge (epic), 29, 319
tAinmhí, An (Standún), 313
Táinrith (Jenkinson), 29
Tales from Old Ireland (Doyle), 99
Tangleweed and Brine (Sullivan), 107
Téacs agus Comhthéacs (Ní Annracháin and Nic Dhiarmada), 36
Téacs Baineann, Téacs Mná (Nic Dhiarmada), 36
technology. *See* digital media; media technologies; multimedia
teenagers, literature for. *See* young adult literature
television, 85, 86, 87, 154, 173, 211, 353–5
Tenured Radicals (Kimball), 364

Terfous, Sasha, 194
Testament of Mary, The (Tóibín), 90
TG4, 11, 317
'That the Science of Cartography Is Limited' (Boland), 114
That They May Face the Rising Sun (McGahern), 216, 234
That Which Was (Patterson), 141
Thatcher, Margaret, 65
The Best Are Leaving, The (*Wills*), 175
'Theatre of Hope and Despair' (Friel), 203
THEATREclub, 90, 163
   We Don't Know What's Buried Here, 5
These Rooms (ANU Productions and CoisCéim Dance Theatre), 163
Things That Happen (Scully), 57
Third Party, The (Patterson'), 143
'This Country That Is Yours' (Mishra), 192
This Hostel Life (Okorie), 14, 188
'This Hostel Life' (Okorie), 189–90
This Side of Brightness (McCann), 14, 176
THISISPOPBABY, 90
Thompson, Kate, 100
Thornton, Clara Rose, 194
Thornton, Darren, 355
Thornton, Liam, 189
Thorpe, Dominic
   Redress State, 282
Three Billboards Outside Ebbing, Missouri (McDonagh), 172
'Three European Poets' (Durcan), 382
Three Leaves of the Shamrock (Ford), 347
Three Sisters (Chekhov), 81
'Three Songs for a Legend' (Boland), 113
Threshold of Quiet (Corkery), 213
Time Present Time Past (Madden), 146
Tine Chnámh (Ó Muirthile), 32
Tionscnamh Filíochta Nuala Ní Dhomhnaill (de Paor), 36
Titley, Alan, 315, 316
   An Bhean Feasa, 31
   An Fear Dána, 31
   Mac Abbaudh's novel described by, 34
'To Those Who Have Inherited a Country' (Horgan), 174
Tobin, Maurice, 284
Tóibín, Colm, 182, 217
   Aosdána funding and writer stipend issues and, 375–6
   Brooklyn, 10, 176, 348
   LGBTQ+ communities and, 7, 226
   The Heather Blazing, 234
   The Master, 224–6
   The Story of the Night, 223
   The Testament of Mary, 90

Tolkien, J. R. R., 318
Tomato Red (Wilson), 357
Tony awards, 10, 360
'Tourism' (Morrissey), 138
tourism industry, 10, 11, 12, 96, 99, 138, 159, 171
Townsend, Sarah, 11, 246–58
Tracy, Dale, 184
traditional Irish music
   Carson's work and, 69, 70
   Flatley and *Riverdance* and, 367
   Friel's *Lughnasa* and, 82, 83, 205
   Muldoon's poetry and, 73
   Murphy's *The Wake* and, 205
   Ó Conghaile's use of folk-song tradition from, 28
   Ó Searcaigh's use of love songs from, 28
   O'Casey's *The Plough* and, 158
   Riverdance's step dancing with, 362, 365, 367
   Thompson's stories for young people and, 100
   Troubles literature and, 66
Tramp Press, 12, 384, 385, 393, 394, 396, 397
   commitment to publishing and promoting contemporary Irish literature by, 392, 394, 395, 398
   digital age and, 392, 393
   founding and background of, 394
   market forces and, 393
   mission statement of, 395
Transatlantic (McCann), 14, 176
'Transition' (Conlon), 173
Translations (Friel), 3, 65, 201–2, 334
translations into Irish language, 36, 38, 102, 318–19
translations of Irish-language literature, 307–21
translators
   Arts Council's funding for, 309
   Irish writers as, 38, 308, 311, 314
transnationalism
   cinema and, 352, 355
   historical novels and, 30, 179
   Irish Studies and, 327, 340
Trapped (Akpoveta), 188
Traveller communities, 14, 105, 333
Travelling in a Strange Land (Park), 145
Trén bhFearann Breac (Nic Eoin), 37
Trevor, William
   Felicia's Journey, 173
   The Story of Lucy Gault, 212
Tribal Scars (Devaney), 105
Trick to Time, The (de Waal), 175
trilingual poetry anthologies, 319
Trinity College Dublin
   Ireland Chair of Poetry and, 381
   Irish Studies at, 328
   women's studies centre at, 333

Trócaire/Poetry Ireland annual poetry competition, 184
Tromdhámh, An (Ó Béarra), 29, 319
Troubles literature, 65–77
  Carson's poetry and, 68–70
  Deane's *Reading in the Dark* and, 221–2
  Devlin's play *Ourselves Alone* and, 70–1
  Friel's play *Translations* and, 201–2
  McGuckian's poetry and, 71–3
  McLiam Wilson's *Eureka Street* and, 76–7
  Muldoon's poetry and, 73–5
  Patterson's work and, 75–6
Troubles, the, 1, 4, 65–67, 163, 206, 214, 217, 223, 264, 334, 361, 368, 370
True Believers (O'Connor), 171
Truth Commissioner, The (Park), 144
Tuath Dé Danann (epic), 319
Tuatha Dé Danann (Johnson), 29, 38
Twelve, The (Neville), 142
21 Dán/21 Poemes/21 Poemas (Mac Síomóin), 319
'Twice Shy' (Heaney), 116
Two Days in Aragon (Keane), 212
Tyrone, Catherine O'Neill, Countess of, 31

U2, 10, 360
Uí Mhaicín, Máire, 38
Ultras, The (McNamee), 142
Ulysses (Joyce), 362
Ulysses (Strick), 347
'Under the Awning' (Okorie), 190–1
UNESCO, 316
Unforeseen, The (Macardle), 397
Uninvited, The (Macardle), 397
United Nations Convention on the Rights of the Child, 96
University College Dublin, 382
  Industrial Memories project at, 283
  Ireland Chair of Poetry and, 381
  Irish Studies at, 328
  women's studies centre at, 333
University College Dublin Press, 382
University College Cork, 27
University College Galway, 27
University of Liverpool, Institute of Irish Studies, 329
University of North London, Irish Studies at, 333
University of Notre Dame, Irish Studies at, 329
'Unwinding' (Heaney), 116
Urquhart, Jane, 177

Value of the Humanities, The (Small), 379–80
Values of Literary Studies, The (McDonald), 381
Van, The (Doyle), 216
Vendler, Helen, 369, 370, 371

Vico Films, 354
Vida, 385
video. *See also* multimedia
  Catholic Church abuse scandals on, 282
  Dead Centre's *Hamnet* with, 91, 92
  migrant writers of colour using, 193
video-poem, 195
violence
  Carson's poetry on the Troubles and, 69
  Donoghue's novels on, 296
  Kenny's essay on more compassionate Ireland and, 301
  McBride's *A Girl Is a Half-Formed Thing* on, 299, 302
  McGahern's *Amongst Women* on, 233
  McGuckian's poetry on the Troubles and, 71
  O'Brien's *A Pagan Place* on, 299
  O'Brien's *The Little Red Chairs* on, 274
  spoken word performances on women's lives and, 195
Virago (publisher), 397
Volta, 355

Waddell, Martin, 104
Wake Forest University Press, 12
Wake, The (Murphy), 203, 205
Waking the Feminists movement, 386
Wales, National Theatre of, 164
Walker Éireann imprint, 104
Wall, William
  Ghost Estate, 121
  'Ghost Estate', 125
Wallace, Clare, 86
Walsh, Caroline, 395
Walsh, Catherine, 56, 57
  demolition of Dublin's working-class Fatima Mansions as topic of, 59
  Optic Verve, 57–9, 60–1
Walsh, Enda, 86
  Arlington, 86
  The Walworth Farce, 84–6
Walsh, Kieron J., 351
Walsh, Maurice, 347
Waltons, The (television series), 85
Walworth Farce, The (Walsh), 84–6
War Horse, The (Boland), 113
Water Horse, The (Ní Dhomhnaill), 311
Water's Edge, The (McCrory), 172
Watt, Stephen, 10, 360–72
'We Are All Revisionists Now' (Foster), 331
We Don't Know What's Buried Here (THEATREclub), 5
Weather in Japan, The (Longley), 132
web. *See* online resources
Weir, The (McPherson), 83–4, 91

Welch, Robert, 28
Well Review, 384
Welles, Orson, 347
Welsh, Robert, 318
West, Ollie, 91
'Westering' (Heaney), 116
'What About Us', 195
What Are You Like? (Enright), 175
Wheatley, David, 139
Whelan, Bill, 10, 365
Whelan, Gerald, 100
'What About Us' (Olusanya), 195
'Whatever You Say Say Nothing' (Heaney), 117
When Brendan Met Trudy (Walsh), 351
When Love Comes to Town (Lennon), 105
'Where am I from?' (Mtowa), 194
Whistle in the Dark, A (Murphy), 202, 206
White Lies (O'Sullivan), 105
White, Ali, 153
whiteness, 182, 183, 184, 187, 191, 194, 328
Whitman, Walt, 369
'Who Is Your City?' (McGuckian), 128
'Why Islanders Don't Kiss Hello' (Campbel), 148
Wig My Father Wore, The (Enright), 175
Wilde, Oscar, 225, 226, 328
  Bildungsroman and, 219, 222
Wilkinson, Sheena, 106
Wills, Clair, 7, 52, 295–302
  The Best Are Leaving, 175
Wilson, Juanita, 357
Wilson, Robert McLiam
  Eureka Street, 66, 76–7
Winnebago Trickster Cycle, 74
Winter Papers (journal), 384, 392
Wintering Out (Heaney), 177, 369
Winters, Carmel, 357
Wolfhound Press, 99
'Woman Who Married Clark Gable, The' (Faoláin), 347
Woman Without a Country, A (Boland), 112
Woman's Love, A (Standún), 313
Women Writers in the New Ireland (WWINI), 192
Women's Christmas Night (Kearney), 357
women's lives
  abortion controversy and, 235
  children's literature on, 101
  Devlin's play *Ourselves Alone* on the Troubles and, 70–1
  emigrant life in Britain and, 172, 175
  fallen women theme and, 231, 237, 364
  legitimization of female experience in literature and, 32
  Lovett case of schoolgirl's death in childbirth and, 5, 87, 106, 173, 231–2
  Magdalen Laundries scandal and, 5, 87, 237, 238, 283, 295, 301, 383
  myth of Irish chasteness and purity and, 231, 232, 241, 313
  novels dealing with political topics in, 223
  romance genre and, 250, 251
  spoken word performances on, 195
  taboo of having a child outside of marriage, 33, 230, 234, 241
  the Troubles and, 65
women's studies centres, 333
Wonder House (Kearney), 357
Wonderful Tennessee (Friel), 203
Woods, Joseph, 125
Word Up Collective, 194
Wordsworth, William, 369
working-class communities
  political novels dealing with, 223
  Rubberbandits viewpoint based in, 155
working-class community
  Bildungsromane set in, 222
  Devlin's *Ourselves Alone* and, 70
  education and advancement narrative in, 221
  Flatley's recounting struggles in, 368
  Foott's *The Young Offenders* set in, 355
  national borders and, 182
  O'Hara's trilogy on nineteenth-century Irish working women in, 101
  site-specific, immersive performances on neglected experiences of, 86
  social transformations by writers from, 193
  Walsh's poem on Dublin demotion of Fatima Mansions in, 59
Wrecks, Declan, 353
writers of colour. *See also* migrant writers of colour
'Writing in a Time of Violence' (Boland), 114
Writing of the Disaster, The (Blanchot), 275
WWINI (Women Writers in the New Ireland) Network, 192

YA Book Club, 106
YA literature. *See* young adult literature
Yale Critics, 364
Yale University Press, 315
Ye, Zhang, 319

Yeats, W. B., 30, 154, 168, 226, 328, 330, 336, 347, 363, 369, 376
Yellow Nib, The (periodical), 12
You May Talk Now (Drennan), 279
young adult literature, 97, 105–8
　age of readers of, 106
　bookstore YA category first introduced in, 106
　difficult and taboo subjects addressed in, 105, 107
　diversity in, 104
　first Irish novel for adolescents in, 106
　graphic novels and, 104
　Irish girls portrayed in, 106–8
　publishing crossover appeal of, 106
　range of authors in, 106
　translations into Irish of, 318
　women writers in, 106
Young Offenders, The (Foott), 354
Young, Paperless and Powerful (campaign), 196
'Your Ma's a Hard Brexit' (Gregg), 147
youth literature. *See* children's literature; young adult literature

Zooropa (U2), 360